YEARBOOK OF INTERNATIONAL HUMANITARIAN LAW

YEARBOOK OF INTERNATIONAL HUMANITARIAN LAW

VOLUME 2
1999

T·M·C·ASSER PRESS

Published by T.M.C.ASSER PRESS,
P.O. Box 16163, 2500 BD The Hague, The Netherlands

Cover photograph courtesy of Corinne Dufka/Human Rights Watch

ISBN 90-6704-119-X
ISSN 1389-1359

**T.M.C. Asser Instituut - Institute for Private and Public International Law,
International Commercial Arbitration and European Law**
Institute Address: R.J. Schimmelpennincklaan 20-22, The Hague, The Netherlands; Mailing Address:
P.O. Box 30461, 2500 GL The Hague, The Netherlands; Tel.: +31(0)703420300; Fax: +31(0)-
703420359; Internet: www.asser.nl.
Over thirty years, the T.M.C. Asser Institute has developed into a leading scientific research institute
in the field of international law. It covers private international law, public international law, including
international humanitarian law, the law of the European Union, the law of international commercial
arbitration and increasingly, also, international economic law and the law of international commerce.
Conducting scientific research, either fundamental or applied, in the aforementioned domains, is the
main activity of the Institute. In addition, the Institute organizes congresses and postgraduate courses,
undertakes contract-research and operates its own publishing house.
Because of its inter-university background, the Institute often cooperates with Dutch law faculties
as well as with various national and foreign institutions. The Institute organizes *Asser College Europe*,
a project in cooperation with East and Central European countries whereby research and educational
projects are organized and implemented.

CORRESPONDENTS

The Yearbook of International Humanitarian Law *extends its sincere thanks and appreciation to its correspondents, without whose assistance the compilation of this volume would not have been possible:*

AFRICA
Professor Larbi Chaht Abdelkader, *Algeria*
Professor Ahmed Abou El Wafa, *Egypt*
Mr Michael Ibanga, *Nigeria*
Dr B.O. Okere, *Nigeria*
Professor Amechi Uchegbu, *Nigeria*
Professor Michael G. Cowling, *South Africa*
Professor John Dugard, *South Africa*

ASIA-PACIFIC
Professor Tim McCormack, *Australia/New Zealand/Pacific Islands*
Mr M. Amir-Ul Islam, *Bangladesh*
Professor Zhang Yong, *China*
Professor V.S. Mani, *India*
Ms Sarah Khan, *India*
Mr Fadillah Agus, *Indonesia*
Professor Hideyuki Kasutani, *Japan*
Professor Akira Mayama, *Japan*
Dr Surya P. Subedi, *Nepal*
Professor Alberto T. Muyot, *the Philippines*
Mr Vincent Pepito F. Yambao, Jr., *the Philippines*
Mr Jayantha W. Atukorala, *Sri Lanka*

EUROPE
Dr Thomas Desch, *Austria*
Mag. Peter Kustor, *Austria*
Professor Marc Cogen, *Belgium*
Professor Eric David, *Belgium*
Professor Ivo Josipović, *Croatia*
Professor Maja Seršić, *Croatia*
Mr Jan Hladik, *Czech Republic*
Mr Tanel Kerikmäe, *Estonia*
Professor Lauri Hannikainen, *Finland*
Mr Juhani Parkkari, *Finland*
Professor Paul Tavernier, *France*
Professor Miodrag Starcević, *Federal Republic of Yugoslavia*
Mr Sascha Rolf Lüder, *Germany*
Mr Gregor Schotten, *Germany*
Mr Jann K. Kleffner, *Germany*
Dr Maria Gavouneli, *Greece*
Professor Péter Kovács, *Hungary*

Professor Colm Campbell, *Ireland*
Mr Ray Murphy, *Ireland*
Professor Sergio Marchisio, *Italy*
Dr Fabio Raspadori, *Italy*
Dr Mario Carta, *Italy*
Ms Liana Pecorano, *Italy*
Professor Mr Nico Keijzer, *the Netherlands*
Ms Elies van Sliedregt, *the Netherlands*
Professor Dr Jerzy Menkes, *Poland*
Professor Igor Blishchenko, *Russian Federation*
Mr Jose Doria, *Russian Federation*
Professor Antoni Pigrau i Solé, *Spain*
Mr Frederik Danelius, *Sweden*
Dr Alain Dennis Henchoz, *Switzerland*
Ms Anne-Marie LaRosa, *Switzerland*
Mr Paul Berman, *United Kingdom*
Professor Françoise Hampson, *United Kingdom*

MIDDLE EAST
Professor Djamchid Momtaz, *Iran*
Mr Mehrdad Rezaeian, *Iran*
Professor Eyal Benvenisti, *Israel*
Professor Ruth Lapidoth, *Israel*
Mr Mustafa Mari, *Occupied Territories*

NORTH AMERICA
Professor René Provost, *Canada*
Professor William A. Schabas, *Canada*
Lt. Col. (ret.) Burrus M. Carnahan, *USA*
Cmmdr. Ronald Neubauer, *USA*

CENTRAL AND SOUTH AMERICA
Professor José Alejandro Consigli, *Argentina*
Mr Gabriel Valladares, *Argentina*
Professor Hernán Salinas Burgos, *Chile*
Mr R.A. Prieto Sanjuán, *Colombia*
Professor Alfonso Velázquez, *Paraguay*
Colonel Enrique Hernández, *Uruguay*

TABLE OF CONTENTS

CORRESPONDENTS' REPORTS

Tim McCormack; Thomas Desch; Peter Kustor; Laurence Weerts; Anne
Weyembergh; Jann K. Kleffner; William A. Schabas; Hernán Salinas Burgos;
R.A. Prieto Sanjuán; Maja Seršić; Jan Hladik; Tanel Kerikmäe; Paul Tavernier;
Sascha Rolf Lüder; Gregor Schotten; Maria Gavouneli; Péter Kovács; Sarah
Khan; Mehrdad Rezaeian; Ray Murphy; Colm Campbell; Liana Pecorano; Mario
Carta; Fabio Raspadori; Hideyuki Kasutani; Elies van Sliedregt; Mustafa Mari;
Alfonso Velázquez; Alberto Muyot; Vincent Pepito F. Yambao; Igor
Blishchenko; Jose Doria; John Dugard; Antonio Pigrau i Solé; A.D. Henchoz;
Anne-Marie LaRosa; Burrus M. Carnahan and Ronald D. Neubauer

DOCUMENTATION

DOCUMENTS   437

BIBLIOGRAPHY

TABLE OF CASES   609

INDEX   615

ABBREVIATIONS

ABl	Amtsblatt
AC	Appeal Cases
AD	Annual Digest of Public International Law Cases
AFDI	Annuaire français de droit international
Afr. JI & CL	African Journal of International & Comparative Law
AJIL	American Journal of International Law
All ER	All England Law Reports
Amer. Univ. ILJ	American University International Law Journal
AP	Associated Press
APL(s)	Anti-personnel landmine(s)
Arizona JI &CL	Arizona Journal of International and Comparative Law
ASEAN	Association of South East Asian Nations
ATCA	Alien Tort Claims Act (USA)
Austr. Rev. Int. & Eur. L	Austrian Revue of International and European Law
BGBl	Bundesgesetzblatt (Austria)
B.O.	Boletín Oficial de la República Argentina
Boston Univ. ILJ	Boston University International Law Journal
BYIL	British Yearbook of International Law
Calif. Western ILJ	California Western International Law Journal
Can. JL & Jur.	Canadian Journal of Law and Jurisprudence
Case Western Reserve JIL	Case Western Reserve Journal of International Law
CHR	(United Nations) Centre for Human Rights
CICR	Comité International de la Croix Rouge
CIS	Commonwealth of Independent States
CLJ	Criminal Law Journal
CLR	Commonwealth Law Reports
CMAC	Court Martial Appeal Court
Cmnd.	Command Papers
Colorado JI Environ. L & Pol.	Colorado Journal of International Environmental Law and Policy
Colum. HRLR	Columbia Human Rights Law Review
Columbia JTL	Columbia Journal of Transnational Law
Cr. App. R	Criminal Appeals Reports
Crim. LR	Criminal Law Review
CTBT	Comprehensive Test Ban Treaty
CTS	Commonwealth Treaty Series
CWC	Chemical Weapons Convention
Dalhousie LJ	Dalhousie Law Journal
Denver JIL & Pol.	Denver Journal of International Law and Policy
DoD	Department of Defense (USA)
ECHR	European Convention on Human Rights
EHRR	European Human Rights Reports
EJIL	European Journal of International Law

Eur. Comm. HR	European Commission of Human Rights
Eur. Ct. HR	European Court of Human Rights
Eur. J. Crime, Crim. L & Crim. Jus	European Journal of Crime, Criminal Law and Criminal Justice
F Supp.	Federal Supplement
Fed. Rep.	Federal Reporter
FCJ	Federal Court of Justice (Canada)
Fordham ILJ	Fordham International Law Journal
FRY	Federal Republic of Yugoslavia
GA	(United Nations) General Assembly
GA Res.	(United Nations) General Assembly Resolutions
GAOR	(United Nations) General Assembly Official Records
GC	Geneva Conventions
Georgetown Int. Environ. LR	Georgetown International Environmental Law Review
GrCC	Greek Criminal Code
GU	Gazzetta Ufficiale (Italian Official Gazette)
HCJ	High Court of Justice
HRLJ	Human Rights Law Journal
HRQ	Human Rights Quarterly
I/A Comm. H.R.	Inter-American Commission of Human Rights
I/A Court H.R	Inter-American Court of Human Rights
ICA	International Council on Archives
ICBL	International Campaign to Ban Landmines
ICBS	International Committee of the Blue Shield
ICC	International Criminal Court
ICCPR	International Covenant on Civil and Political Rights
ICJ	International Court of Justice
ICJ Rep.	International Court of Justice Reports
ICLQ	International and Comparative Law Quarterly
ICOM	International Council of Museums
ICOMOS	International Council on Monuments and Sites
ICRC	International Committee of the Red Cross
ICTR	International Criminal Tribunal for Rwanda
ICTY	International Criminal Tribunal for the Former Yugoslavia
IHL	International Humanitarian Law
ILC Yearbook	Yearbook of the International Law Commission
ILM	International Legal Materials
ILR	International Law Reports
ILSA JI & CL	ILSA Journal of International and Comparative Law
IMT	International Military Tribunal
Indian JIL	Indian Journal of International Law
IRA	Irish Republican Army
IRRC	International Review of the Red Cross
Israel YB HR	Israel Yearbook on Human Rights
Israel LR	Israel Law Review
JIL & Prac.	Journal International Law and Practice
JPI	Judicial Police Inspectors

LAS	League of Arab States
Leiden JIL	Leiden Journal of International Law
LNTS	League of Nations Treaty Series
LOAC	Law of Armed Conflict
Loy. LA Il & CLJ	Loyola Los Angeles International and Comparative Law Journal
Loyola I & CLJ	Loyola International and Comparative Law Journal
MCC	Military Criminal Code
Mich. JIL	Michigan Journal of International Law
MLR	Modern Law Review
Moscow JIL	Moscow Journal of International Law
MPYBUNL	Max Planck Yearbook United Nations Law
MPYIL	Max Planck Yearbook of International Law
NATO	North Atlantic Treaty Organisation
NCOs	Non-Commissioned Officers
NGO	Non-Governmental Organisation
NILR	Netherlands International Law Review
NLR	Naval Law Review
Nordic JIL	Nordic Journal of International Law
NPC	New Penal Code
NQHR	Netherlands Quarterly of Human Rights
NY Univ. JIL & Pol.	New York University Journal of International Law and Politics
NYIL	Netherlands Yearbook of International Law
ÖAD	Österreichische Außenpolitische Dokumentation (Austria)
OAS	Organisation of American States
OIOS	(UN) Office of Internal Oversight Services
ONU	Organisation Nations Unies
ONUC	United Nations Force in the Congo
OPCW	Organisation for the Prohibition of Chemical Weapons
OTP	Office of the Prosecutor (of the ICTR and/or ICTY)
PMG	Peace Monitoring Group
POW	Prisoner of War
QB	Queen's Bench
RDI	Rivista di diritto internazionale
RDPC	Revue de droit pénal et de criminologie
RGDIP	Revue générale de droit international public
RICR	Revue International de la Croix Rouge
RSCDPC	Revue de science criminelle et de droit pénal comparé
SC	(United Nations) Security Council
SCR	Supreme Court Reports
SFRY	Socialist Federal Republic of Yugoslavia
SG	(United Nations) Secretary-General
SIPRI	Stockholm International Peace Research Institute
SZIER/RSDIE	Schweizerische Zeitschrift für internationales und europäisches Recht / Revue Suisse de droit international et de droit européen
Texas L Rev	Texas Law Review
Tilburg For. LR	Tilburg Foreign Law Review

Transn. L & Contemp. Probs.	Transnational Law and Contemporary Problems
TRC Report	(South African) Truth and Reconciliation Commission Report
UN Doc.	United Nations Documents Series
UNAMIR	United Nations Assistance Mission for Rwanda
UNCHR	United Nations Commission on Human Rights
UNDP	United Nations Development Program
UNEF	United Nations Emergency Force (in the Sinai)
UNESCO	United Nations Educational, Scientific and Cultural Organisation
UNFICYP	United Nations Force in Cyprus
UNHCR	United Nations High Commission for Refugees
UNHFOR	United Nations Human Rights Field Office in Rwanda
UNICEF	United Nations (International) Children's (Emergency) Fund
UNIDIR	United Nations Institute for Disarmament Research
UNIFIL	United Nations Interim Force in Lebanon
UNIIMOG	United Nations Iran/Iraq Military Observer Group
UNIKOM	United Nations Iraq/Kuwait Observer Mission
UNITAF	United Nations Task Force (in Somalia)
UNOMSIL	United Nations Observer Mission in Sierra Leone
UNOSOM	United Nations Operation in Somalia
UNPF	United Nations Peacekeeping Force
UNPROFOR	United Nations Protection Force (in Bosnia and Herzegovina)
UNSC	United Nations Security Council
UNTAC	United Nations Transitional Authority in Cambodia
UNTS	United Nations Treaty Series
UNWCC	United Nations War Crimes Commission
Virginia JIL	Virgina Journal of International Law
WCR	War Crimes Reports
WHO	World Health Organisation
WLR	Weekly Law Reports
Yale JIL	Yale Journal of International Law
YIHL	Yearbook of International Humanitarian Law
Zör	Zeischrift für öffentliches Recht (Austrian Journal of Public and International Law)
ZaöRV	Zeitschrift für ausländisches öffentliches Recht und Völkerrecht

ARTICLES

THE UNDERTAKING TO RESPECT AND ENSURE RESPECT IN ALL CIRCUMSTANCES: FROM TINY SEED TO RIPENING FRUIT[1]

Frits Kalshoven[2]

1.   PREPARING THE GROUND

The four Geneva Conventions of 1949 for the protection of war victims open with an unusual provision: it is the undertaking of the contracting states 'to respect and to ensure respect for [the Conventions] in all circumstances'.[3] Why reaffirm that contracting states are bound to 'respect' their treaty obligations? Does 'all circumstances' add anything special to this fundamental rule of the law of treaties? And what about 'ensure respect': should that not be regarded as implicit in 'respect', in the sense of a positive counterpart to the negative duty not to violate the terms of the Conventions?

I readily admit that common Article 1 was not the first provision of the Conventions to capture my attention: there was, after all, so much to discover in these impressive structures that Article 1 could easily be passed over as an innocuous sort of opening phrase. Two things have changed this. One was the insistence of the International Committee of the Red Cross (ICRC) that a State Party to the Conventions is not only itself bound to comply with its obligations under

---

1. © F. Kalshoven, 1999.

2. Professor emeritus of international humanitarian law, University of Leiden; President, International Fact-Finding Commission; member of the Board of Recommendation, *Yearbook of International Humanitarian Law*. The author wishes to thank Jean Pictet and René-Jean Wilhelm, lawyers with the International Committee of the Red Cross through World War II and for many years thereafter, for their information, advice and encouragement. He also thanks Ms. Catherine Brown, of the US Department of State, for having involved him in the case of Jesus del Carmen Medina and for her support. And he dedicates this study, which originated as a book-project but transmuted into the present article, to the memory of Claude Pilloud, idealistic realist for long years in the service of the International Committee of the Red Cross, who may have been guilty of 'creative interpretation' but doubtless was morally right.

3. Geneva Convention I for the Amelioration of the Condition of the Wounded and Sick of Armed Forces in the Field, 1949, 75 *UNTS* (1950) 31 (A. Roberts and R. Guelff, *Documents on the Laws of War* 2nd edn. (Oxford, Clarendon Press 1989) p. 169; Geneva Convention II for the Amelioration of the Condition of Wounded, Sick and Shipwrecked Members of the Armed Forces at Sea, 1949, 75 *UNTS* (1950) 85 (Roberts and Guelff, p. 193); Geneva Convention III Relative to the Treatment of Prisoners of War, 1949, 75 *UNTS* (1950) 135 (Roberts and Guelff, p. 215); and Geneva Convention IV Relative to the Protection of Civilian Persons in Time of War, 1949, 75 *UNTS* (1950) 287 (Roberts and Guelff, p. 271).

these instruments but is under a legal obligation to make sure that other States Parties do likewise. The more this thesis of the ICRC was forced upon us, the less likely it seemed to me that this could indeed be an international legal obligation upon contracting states.

The other factor was an American case that was brought to my attention.[4] A Salvadoran woman, Ms Jesus del Carmen Medina, had fled her war-torn country in November 1980 and 'entered the United States without inspection by a US Immigration Officer.' In 1984, brought before an Immigration Court in Texas, she applied for asylum. It was also argued on her behalf, in the alternative, that the US was precluded from deporting her to El Salvador, as that would mean exposing her to violations of Article 3 common to the Geneva Conventions and thus, by virtue of common Article 1, involved the responsibility of the United States to ensure respect for the Fourth or Civilians Convention, and notably for common Article 3.[5]

The judge found that the Fourth Convention gave him jurisdiction to grant to a respondent relief in deportation proceedings over and above any relief available under the provisions of the Immigration and Nationality Act, as implemented by regulation. He also, surprisingly, held that Ms Medina, 'a Salvadoran citizen who [was] not taking an active part in the hostilities, [was] a protected person under the minimum provisions set forth in Article 3'. Even more surprisingly, he concluded from the evidence she had submitted that she had not met her burden of proof in showing that El Salvador was currently violating Article 3. He therefore denied her Request for Withholding of Deportation but granted her the privilege of voluntary departure. He moreover certified his decision to the Board of Immigration Appeals, in view of his findings regarding 'unusually complex and novel questions of law'.

---

4. The quotations concerning the case (which has not been published) are from documents in the author's possession. It appeared in the first instance before the Executive Office for Immigration Review, Harlingen, Texas, upon an Order to Show Cause, filed by the Immigration and Naturalization Service, on 29 March 1984, in reference to the respondent. The Immigration Judge rendered his decision on 25 July 1985 (Case No. A26 949 415: In the Matter of Jesus del Carmen Medina, in Deportation Proceedings), ordering moreover that it be certified to the Board of Immigration Appeals because this case involves unusually complex and novel questions of law. The Board handed down its Decision on 7 October 1988 (Case No. A26 949 415 – Harlingen, In re. Jesus del Carmen Medina, in Deportation Proceedings: Certification).

5. Common Article 3 provides in relevant part that in the event of an internal armed conflict, 'each Party to the conflict shall be bound to apply, as a minimum, the following provisions: (1) Persons taking no active part in the hostilities, including members of armed forces who have laid down their arms and those placed *hors de combat* by sickness, wounds, detention, or any other cause, shall in all circumstances be treated humanely, without any adverse distinction founded on race, colour, religion or faith, sex, birth or wealth, or any other similar criteria. To this end, the following acts are and shall remain prohibited at any time and in any place whatsoever with respect to the above-mentioned persons: (a) violence to life and person, in particular murder of all kinds, mutilation, cruel treatment and torture; (b) taking of hostages; (c) outrages upon personal dignity, in particular humiliating and degrading treatment; (d) the passing of sentences and the carrying out of executions without previous judgment pronounced by a regularly constituted court, affording all the judicial guarantees which are recognized as indispensable by civilized peoples.' (etc.)

On appeal, these 'unusually complex and novel questions of law' were amply debated, with *amicus curiae* briefs from the American Civil Liberties Union, the Lawyers' Committee for Human Rights, and (in a different vein) the Department of State. In its decision of October 1988, the Board concluded: that Article 3 stood apart in the Conventions; that the notion of 'protected person' in the Fourth or Civilians Convention obtained only in international armed conflicts; that it was unclear 'what obligations, if any, Article 1 was intended to impose with respect to violations of the Convention by other States'; and that, in any event, Article 1 was not self-executing. Also rejecting the further argument that customary international law prohibits states from forcibly repatriating 'war refugees', i.e., persons who flee an area of armed conflict without being refugees under the 1951 Convention and the 1967 Protocol Relating to the Status of Refugees,[6] the Board reversed the judge's finding 'that the Fourth Convention provides a potential basis for relief from deportation within the jurisdiction of the immigration judge,' and affirmed his decision to deny Ms Medina's requests for asylum and withholding of deportation, yet granted her the privilege of voluntary departure.[7]

While the ICRC statements had made me wonder, the case of Ms Medina convinced me that common Article 1 and the 'unusually complex and novel questions of law' it could give rise to might well deserve further investigation; a task I decided to undertake. The present paper contains the fruits of these labours. It deals, at length, with the drafting history of common Article 1 (section 2), the interpretation the ICRC placed upon it in its Commentary to the Conventions of 1949 (section 3), and subsequent developments from the Teheran Human Rights

---

6. Convention Relating to the Status of Refugees, 1951, 189 *UNTS* (1951) 137; Protocol Relating to the Status of Refugees, 1967, 606 *UNTS* (1967) 267.

7. According to available information, Ms Medina was never deported, having become a beneficiary of a new US policy granting 'temporary protected status' to persons who had fled a war zone.

The Geneva Conventions are referred to in another case which was decided in September 1988 by the US Court of Appeals, Fourth Circuit. The case concerned a Salvadoran draft evader, who petitioned for review of a final order of deportation, issued by the Board of Immigration Appeals in December 1987, denying his motion to reopen deportation proceedings to allow a hearing on his request for political asylum in the US. Holding that petitioner had made out a *prima facie* case, and that he merited political asylum on the basis of his sincere refusal to participate in acts of atrocity committed by the Salvadoran Armed Forces and the likelihood that he would be punished for his refusal to serve with those forces, the Court 'reversed and remanded' the Board's decision. The petitioner had also claimed that he should not be forced to return to a country which was regularly violating the Geneva Conventions. The Court mentions this claim in a footnote, stating that it was unclear whether it could be maintained. It specifies that El Salvador was a party to the Conventions as well as to Additional Protocol II of 1977, the United States only to the Conventions. Since the latter 'protect those individuals who are endangered by international armed conflicts, while Protocol II protects potential victims of non-international conflicts', petitioner's request amounted to a demand 'that we apply the norms of the Conventions which the United States have signed to a situation to which they do not explicitly extend'. This was a remarkable statement, given that the Court had earlier quoted extensively from common Article 3. The claim played no part in the decision to reverse and remand. *M.A. A26851062* v. *US Immigration and Naturalization Service,* 29 September 1988. 858 *F*.2d 210 (4th Cir. 1988).

Conference of 1968 to the adoption in 1977 of Protocol I Additional to the 1949 Geneva Conventions and the ICRC Commentary thereto (section 4). A final section (5) gives a brief impression of other uses or interpretations of the Article, by an interested party like the Palestinians, by an independent actor like the International Court of Justice, and by academics, including myself.

2.   UNCERTAIN INCEPTION: THE DRAFTING HISTORY OF COMMON ARTICLE 1

The purpose of this section is to find an answer to these questions: What is the origin of the phrase 'to ensure respect' in Article 1 common to the 1949 Geneva Conventions? Who wrote it? What did its author or authors hope to achieve? And what about those who negotiated and ultimately adopted the Conventions: what was their understanding of the phrase?

2.1   An insignificant seed: Article 25(1) of the 1929 Sick and Wounded Convention

Our search for the origin of the phrase may conveniently start one phase earlier, with the previous major revision and development of the law as embodied in the Geneva Conventions.[8] The occasion was the Diplomatic Conference of 1929, and it resulted in the adoption of two Conventions, signed at Geneva on 27 July 1929.[9] One, 'for the Amelioration of the Condition of the Sick and Wounded in Armies in the Field', replaced the earlier Conventions on the same subject.[10] The other, 'relative to the Treatment of Prisoners of War', was the first convention devoted exclusively to that subject; it was stated to be 'complementary to' the chapter on prisoners of war in the Regulations annexed to the Hague Convention on Land Warfare of 1899, revised in 1907.[11] Each Convention contains an article (Articles 25 and 82, respectively) which reads as follows:

---

8. For an *exposé* that goes back further into history, the reader is referred to the comments on common Article 1 in the Commentary to the Conventions, published under the general editorship of Jean S. Pictet; see *infra* section 3.

9. D. Schindler and J. Toman, *The Laws of Armed Conflicts, A Collection of Conventions, Resolutions and Other Documents*, 3rd edn. (Dordrecht, Martinus Nijhoff 1988) pp. 325, 339.

10. Art. 34. The earlier Conventions were the Geneva Convention for the Amelioration of the Condition of the Wounded in Armies in the Field of 22 August 1864 (the original Convention at the root of the entire structure of Geneva law) and the Geneva Convention for the Amelioration of the Condition of the Wounded and Sick in Armies in the Field of 6 July 1906. For texts of the earlier Conventions, see Schindler and Toman, op. cit. n. 9, at pp. 279, 301. Also available online at the ICRC's IHL treaty database: http://www.icrc.org.

11. Chapter 2 of the Regulations. For the text of the 1899 and 1907 versions of the Hague Convention and Regulations, see Schindler and Toman, op. cit. n. 9, at p. 63.

The provisions of the present Convention shall be respected by the High Contracting Parties in all circumstances.

If, in time of war, a belligerent is not a party to the Convention, its provisions shall, nevertheless, be binding as between all the belligerents who are parties thereto.

The statement in the first paragraph that contracting states shall respect the provisions of the Convention may look like a perfect example of a truism: there is, after all, no need for a treaty expressly to reaffirm that *pacta sunt servanda*. Yet, the records of the Conference show that the drafters had no such empty gesture in mind. As we shall see, paragraph 1 is the more or less accidental and, in effect, largely meaningless by-product of a heated debate about an entirely different issue of some importance, viz., the application of the Conventions in a war between belligerents not all of whom are parties to these instruments.

On the latter subject, earlier law of war treaties often contained a clause which not only confined their binding force to the contracting states (and specifically to the 'case of war between two or more of them') but excluded their binding effect 'from the time when, in a war between Contracting Powers, a non-Contracting Power joins one of the belligerents' (as the clause reads in the 1899 Hague Convention on Land Warfare).[12] In the Sick and Wounded Convention of 1906 this notorious, so-called *si omnes* clause provides that its 'provisions shall cease to be obligatory if one of the belligerent Powers should not be a signatory to the Convention'.[13]

In the draft Conventions it submitted to the Conference of 1929, the ICRC had included in the chapters on application and execution a provision designed to overcome the potentially drastic effects of the *si omnes* clause.[14] Thus, Article 24 of the draft Sick and Wounded Convention (Article 25 in the definitive version) provided that, apart from the limitation to contracting states in the event of a war between two or more of them, a contracting state would only be freed from its obligations under the Convention if it had to fight the army of a non-contracting belligerent, and then only in relation to that belligerent.[15]

---

12. Art. 2 of the Convention, Schindler and Toman, op. cit. n. 9, at p. 71. The version of 1907 contains a simpler text, to the effect that the provisions of the Convention and Regulations 'do not apply except between Contracting Powers, and then only if all the belligerents are parties to the Convention'.

13. Art. 24 of the 1906 Convention. It should be noted that the original Geneva Convention for the Amelioration of the Condition of the Wounded in Armies in the Field, of 1864, had not contained any provision on the issue of its applicability.

14. In practice, contracting states to the various conventions containing a *si omnes* clause had not given it effect in the course of the First World War.

15. *Actes de la Conférence diplomatique de Genève de 1929.* See, *inter alia*, the records of the 14th session of the First Commission, 16 July 1929, pp. 321-322, where the ICRC proposal is read out: *Les dispositions de la présente Convention ne sont obligatoires que pour les Puissances contractantes en cas de guerre entre deux ou plusieurs d'entre elles.*
Elles ne cessent de l'être qu'au cas où l'un de ces Etats se trouve avoir à combattre les forces armées d'un ou autre Etat qui ne serait pas partie à cette Convention et à l'égard de cet Etat seulement.

While the debate in the First Commission (which dealt with the Sick and Wounded Convention) showed broad support for the idea of abolishing the *si omnes* clause, the ICRC text was considered insufficiently clear. A British amendment received a warmer welcome. Phrased positively, it provided that contracting states are obliged to respect the provisions of the Convention in all circumstances, except when a belligerent Party is not a party to the Convention: in that event, its provisions would not apply between that Party and its adversaries but would still have to be respected between the belligerents who were parties to the Convention.[16]

The structure of the British proposal was clear: Respect was due in all 'circumstances' except one, viz., participation in the war by a non-contracting belligerent. This would be the sole 'circumstance' that could justify non-application of the Convention, and then only between a contracting state and its non-party enemy. The crux of the provision obviously lay in the latter restriction: it was that part of the provision which effectively did away with the *si omnes* principle.

After some discussion, the First Commission left to a drafting committee the task of giving draft Article 24 its final shape. This because the Second Commission (which dealt with the draft for a Prisoners of War Convention) was seized of the same issue, and it was realized that an identical solution had to be provided for both Conventions.

From the Drafting Committee (on which both Commissions were represented) the definitive version of Article 25 (and Article 82 of the Prisoners of War Convention) emerged in the shape of two sentences, as quoted above. The sentences were moreover fashioned as two paragraphs, with one paragraph providing for 'respect in all circumstances' and the other for the exception concerning the non-party belligerent.

Even in the absence of a record of the work of the Drafting Committee, it is not too difficult to guess what may have been its motives in giving the Article this final shape. For one thing, it is shorter and simpler than the British text. For another, the first sentence of the British text, taken by itself, could still be read as a reaffirmation of the *si omnes* principle, and it was precisely this principle the Conference had sought to abolish once and for all. In both respects, the final version is an improvement over the British proposal (and, for that matter, over the original ICRC text).

With all this, the Drafting Committee had remained well within its mandate, since its rephrasing had not modified the meaning of the text read as a whole. Of interest for our purposes is its decision to distribute the text over two paragraphs. This was merely in conformity with the style maintained throughout the Convention and irrelevant as far as substance goes. Yet the optical effect was that the sentence in

---

16. Ibid., p. 322: *Les dispositions de la présente Convention doivent être respectées par les Hautes Parties Contractantes en toutes circonstances, sauf le cas où une Puissance belligérante ne serait pas partie à cette dernière. En ce cas, les dispositions de la Convention ne seront pas applicables entre ce belligérant et ses adversaires, mais devront néanmoins être respectées dans les rapports entre les belligérants parties à la Convention.*

the first paragraph came to stand out as a thing apart and, hence, could also be believed to have a distinct meaning of its own.

This view is actually taken in the Commentary to the Sick and Wounded Convention, which the ICRC published in 1930. The author, Paul Des Gouttes, a Swiss lawyer and member of the Committee, had acted as Secretary-General of the Conference. Discussing Article 25 (as the other Articles) paragraph by paragraph, he states that with the first paragraph the duty of contracting parties had been underscored to implement (the relevant provisions of) the Convention in all circumstances, i.e., both in time of peace and war. He adds that emphasis had been laid on the character of 'general obligation' of the Convention.[17]

Read thus, the words 'all circumstances' served to put beyond doubt that, apart from the obvious duty of contracting states to implement in time of war the rules in the Convention specifically written for that occasion, other rules would have to be implemented even in time of peace. The paragraph might thus be regarded as a formal rebuttal of the (not completely hypothetical) argument that the Convention, as a treaty on a topic of the law of war, can only become applicable with the outbreak of war.[18]

Des Gouttes' interpretation was not just an invention of his own. As the records show, its origin lies in a brief exchange of views that occurred in the First Commission. Referring to the original ICRC draft for Article 24, the Chinese delegate said he failed to understand why it appeared effectively to limit the binding force of the Convention to a situation of war: there were, after all, quite a few provisions in the Convention (such as rules about the use of the red cross or red crescent, legislative and other measures for the instruction of armed forces and the punishment of violations, etc.) which had to be implemented in time of peace. The British delegate then pointed out that the amendment he had proposed, in contrast with the ICRC text but without in any way modifying the substance of the draft Article, actually covered the point raised by his Chinese colleague. For, he said, the phrase stating that contracting states must respect the provisions of the Convention in all circumstances could be read as including time of peace.[19] This splendid example of an occasional argument may well have served to make the British amendment even more palatable to his co-delegates.

The argument, although advanced at a time when the draft text was still in the shape of a single sentence, provides sufficient support for Des Gouttes' subsequent reading of the first paragraph of Article 25 in its final incarnation, as confirming the duty of contracting parties to implement relevant provisions of the Convention

---

17. *La Convention de Genève du 27 juillet 1929, Commentaire par Paul Des Gouttes* (1930), p. 186: *On a voulu signaler ici que la Convention doit s'appliquer en toutes circonstances – ce que ne disait pas celle de 1906 – en temps de paix comme en temps de guerre, quant aux dispositions qui se trouvent appliquables dans l'un comme dans l'autre cas. On a insisté sur son caractère d'obligation générale.*

18. It should be noted that this argument does not find support in any language in the Convention, which in fact is completely silent on its scope *ratione temporis*.

19. *Supra* n. 15, pp. 329-330: remark by Mr Chi Hung Hsiao (China), reply by Mr Warner (UK), comment by the Chairman of the Commission.

both in time of peace and war. Yet, to distill from the recorded drafting history of the Article, including the brief and quite incidental exchange between the Chinese and British delegates on one specific point, the much broader conclusion that there had been in the Conference an insistence on a (vague and undefined) character of 'general obligation' of the Convention as a whole, may be reading rather more into it than it can bear.

Taking into account this drafting history of Article 25, I feel justified in qualifying paragraph 1 as an insignificant by-product of the debate about the abolition of the *si omnes* clause. Strikingly, when the end result of the work of the First Commission on the Sick and Wounded Convention was introduced to the plenary Conference, the rapporteur spoke at length about the way the issue of *si omnes* had been resolved, but he did not so much as refer to the first paragraph.[20]

Before leaving 1929, I should mention an entirely different point raised in Des Gouttes' commentary: Could 'in all circumstances' perhaps have been intended to cover situations of civil war as well? No, he says, for a number of reasons. For one thing, the issue had never arisen in the debate. For another, such a completely different result would have required a radical adaptation of the Convention's provisions. And, last but not least, the hypothesis was effectively excluded by the provision in the second paragraph of Article 25, that 'if, in time of war, a belligerent is not a party to the Convention, its provisions shall, nevertheless, be binding as between all the belligerents who are parties thereto'. States, Des Gouttes adds for good measure, were not prepared to accept to be bound except on the international plane.[21]

The point of interest here is that Des Gouttes so obviously wanted to raise the issue of civil war. The inclusion of this paragraph in the commentary published by the ICRC goes to confirm its long-standing interest in the issue, an interest that already in 1921 had resulted in the adoption of a resolution by the Xth International Conference of the Red Cross on the right to relief of 'all victims of civil wars and social and revolutionary disturbances'.[22] When the time came for yet another revision of the Geneva Conventions, i.e., after the Second World War (and, perhaps even more significant in the present context, after the Spanish Civil War), the concern about the implications of 'civil war' and the need to introduce into the international law of war accepted humanitarian standards for such internal situations had come to figure even higher on the agenda of the Committee.

---

20. Ibid., pp. 621-622. The rapporteur of the Second Commission had less to say about the identical Article 82 in the Prisoners of War Convention (pp. 636-637). Obviously, the argument about the significance of that Article is the same as about Article 25 of the Sick and Wounded Convention.

21. Ibid. The author continued: '*Mais il serait hautement souhaitable que les partis dressés l'un contre l'autre dans une guerre civile se souvinssent des dispositions humaines de la Convention afin de les observer entre eux.*' See also *infra* subsection 3.14.

22. For an excerpt of the resolution (No. XIV) see International Committee of the Red Cross, International Federation of Red Cross and Red Crescent Societies, *Handbook of the Red Cross and Red Crescent Movement,* 13th edn., (Geneva, ICRC 1994) [hereinafter, *Handbook*], p. 784.

2.2   Sprouting: preparations for the Diplomatic Conference of 1949

A series of meetings preceded the Diplomatic Conference which considered and finally adopted the four Conventions of 1949.[23] Draft texts submitted by the ICRC were examined, successively, by a preliminary conference of Red Cross societies (Geneva, 26 July-3 August 1946), a conference of government experts (Geneva, 14-26 April 1947), and the XVIIth International Conference of the Red Cross (Stockholm, August 1948). In the present section I report what little I have been able to find, both in the published records of these events and in the archives of the ICRC, about the history behind the phrase 'to ensure respect' and the ideas that may have moved its authors.

I note straightaway that the phrase does not emerge in any written text until just before the Stockholm Conference. This may be due to the fact that, at the time of the meetings of 1946 and 1947, the ICRC itself was still thinking along the traditional lines set out in 1929. An internal note in the ICRC archives, written by Claude Pilloud, the ICRC staff lawyer specifically charged at the time with the development of the general provisions of the Conventions, bears me out on this point. Dated 11 April 1947, a few days before the conference of government experts, the note contains a proposal for a common Article 2 that simply copies the provision about 'respect in all circumstances' in the two Conventions of 1929.[24] Evidently, the only changes contemplated at that stage were that the phrase would figure in all four Conventions and would be given a more prominent place.

A first indication of a different mood is found in an internal note dated August 1947, with Pilloud's reactions to views expressed by the government experts on the question of how to bring civil war within the scope of the rules or principles of the Geneva Conventions.[25]

As noted above, this issue had not been on the agenda of the Conference of 1929. The subsequent active involvement of the ICRC in internal armed conflicts, notably in the Spanish Civil War, had resulted in the adoption by the XVIth International Conference of the Red Cross (London, 1938) of a resolution expressing the need to obtain the application of humanitarian principles in such conflicts.[26] In 1946, the

---

23. First or Sick and Wounded Convention; Second or Maritime Warfare Convention; Third or Prisoners of War Convention; Fourth or Civilians Convention. While Conventions I-III were revisions of earlier Conventions of 1906 and 1929, the Convention on the protection of civilians was entirely new. For full references, see *supra* n. 3.

24. Article II: '*Les dispositions de la présente Convention doivent être respectées en toute circonstance.*' The note, dated 11 April 1947, is found in a dossier entitled '*Notices ayant servi à la Revision des Conventions remises au classement telles-quelles en Sept. '47 par Cl. Pilloud.*'

25. Note dated 18 August 1947 by Cl. Pilloud, Head of the Legal Division: '*Documentation à l'intention des participants à la séance du 25 août 1947 à 14h.30.*'

26. The Conference requested the ICRC and national societies 'to endeavour to obtain':
a) the application of the humanitarian principles which were formulated in the Geneva Conventions of 1929 and the Xth Hague Convention of 1907, especially as regards the treatment of the wounded, the sick, and prisoners of war, and the safety of medical personnel and medical stores;
b) humane treatment for all political prisoners, their exchange and, so far as possible, their release;
c) respect of the life and liberty of non-combatants;

debate had been resumed on the basis of a proposal, submitted by the ICRC to the preliminary conference of Red Cross societies, which cautiously invited parties to a civil war to declare that, subject to reciprocity, they would apply the principles of the Conventions. That conference had adopted a more audacious stance: it had substituted 'armed conflict within a State' for 'civil war', deleted the restriction to 'principles', and replaced the reservation of reciprocity with the option for a party to the conflict to state its refusal to apply the Conventions.

The 1947 conference of government experts, in turn, steered a middle course: it reinstated 'civil war' but added 'in the metropolitan or colonial territory of a State'; returned to the principles of the Conventions; and instead of either reciprocal declarations or an express opt-out possibility, opted for reciprocity in actual application.[27]

Taking up this matter of reciprocity, Pilloud emphasizes the need to get rid of the principle of reciprocity as a determinant for the application of the Conventions in civil war. He suggests that this might perhaps be achieved by a provision to the effect that governments, by signing the Conventions, engage not just themselves as governments but the totality of the population they represent. The effect would be that in the event of civil war, all parts of the population could be regarded as *ipso facto* bound by the Conventions. Such a provision, he adds, would be analogous to the phrase in the Preamble to the Charter of the United Nations: 'We the peoples of the United Nations ...'.[28]

---

d) facilities for the transmission of news of a personal nature and for the reunion of families;
e) effective measures for the protection of children, ... (etc.)
For text of Res. XIV, see *Handbook,* op. cit. n. 22, p. 642.

27. A great deal has been written about the drafting history of common Article 3. I may refer the reader to the survey by Rosemary Abi-Saab in her book *Droit humanitaire et conflits internes: Origines et évolution de la réglementation internationale* (Paris, Pedone 1986); on the various preparatory meetings, pp. 43-47.

As regards reciprocity, it is of interest to compare the above discussion with the situation of 1929. In that year, the rule that in the event of an international armed conflict the Conventions would 'be binding as between all the belligerents who are parties thereto' but not in the relations between those parties and a non-party belligerent, had been introduced as a device to get rid of the earlier *si omnes* clause in law of war treaties and, thus, as a step forward.

28. Note by Pilloud dated 18 August 1947, *supra* n. 25, p. 4.

La formule adoptée par les experts au sujet de la guerre civile ne semble pas donner satisfaction, car elle implique le principe de la réciprocité que la Division juridique voudrait, dans toute la mesure du possible, éliminer. C'est pourquoi la Division juridique désirerait mettre sur pied une disposition qui prévoit que les Gouvernements, en signant la Convention, s'engagent non seulement en tant que Gouvernements, mais engagent aussi l'ensemble de la population dont ils sont les représentants. On pourrait alors en déduire que toutes parties de la population d'un Etat qui entreprend une action en guerre civile est liée ipso facto par la Convention.

Ce serait en somme une formule analogue à celle de la Charte des Nations unies qui commence par les mots 'Nous les peuples des Nations unies ...'

En tout état de cause, la Division juridique préférerait une formule analogue à celle qui avait été prévue par la Conférence préliminaire des Croix-Rouges de l'an dernier disant que la Convention sera appliquée par les parties au conflit aussi longtemps que l'une d'elles n'aura pas déclaré publiquement qu'elle ne peut pas s'y soumettre.

Pilloud's suggestion had no immediate effect: the addressees of the note, a meeting of ICRC dignitaries, simply did not enter into his argument.[29] Indeed, a subsequent proposal for the redrafting of the Sick and Wounded Convention, contained in an internal note of 23 October 1947, once again returned to the text of 1929 about 'respect in all circumstances'; this even to the point of keeping it in its old place (as Article 28).[30]

In spite of this lack of response, I regard Pilloud's suggestion as of singular importance, foreshadowing as it does the introduction of the phrase 'to ensure respect' in the future Article 1 of the Conventions of 1949. His idea comprised three elements. The first, the engagement of governments, is synonymous to an undertaking on their part to 'respect' the law. The second, the engagement of all parts of the population, is tantamount to an undertaking to 'ensure' that the population too will respect the law, in particular – as he specifies – with regard to civil war. And the suggested analogy to the famous phrase 'We the peoples' in the Preamble to the United Nations Charter was obviously meant to lend extra force to the latter undertaking.[31]

Then, suddenly and without further warning, our long-expected phrase turns up in the draft texts for revised or new Conventions the ICRC submitted in May 1948 to the Stockholm Conference.[32] The identical opening article in each Convention provides that:[33]

The contracting Parties undertake, in the name of their peoples, to respect and to ensure respect for the Conventions in all circumstances.

The ICRC comments to the proposed Article[34] distinguish three elements: (1) the undertaking of contracting Parties to respect the Conventions in all circumstances; (2) a similar undertaking to ensure such respect, once again in all circumstances;

29. Report on meeting of representatives of the Bureau and the Legal Division of the ICRC, 25-27 August 1947; the meeting adopted for internal armed conflict a draft Article 1(3), phrased as follows: '*En cas de conflit armé à l'intérieur d'un Etat et de ses dépendances, les dispositions de la Convention seront également appliquées par les parties au conflit.*'

30. Note of Jean S. Pictet to the members of the Bureau and the Juridical Commission of the ICRC. The only novelty in the note was a suggestion to add an Article 1 providing that *the wounded and sick* shall be respected and protected 'in all circumstances'.

31. Pilloud appears to have used the phrase in a sense diametrically opposite to its meaning in that preamble, which is formulated (though probably not seriously intended) as an endeavour of the peoples to bind their governments.

32. *Projet de Conventions revisées ou nouvelles protégeant les victimes de la guerre.* The ICRC archives do not contain any internal document explaining this sudden appearance. Most regrettable is the absence of Pilloud's private papers concerning this period; it is assumed that he disposed of them. In the recollection of René-Jean Wilhelm, at the time Pilloud's colleague in the legal office, the preparation of the common articles was entirely left to Frédéric Siordet, adviser to the ICRC, and Pilloud; letter to the author dated 19 August 1992.

33. Ibid., p. 4: Art. 1. In the original French: '*Les Hautes Parties contractantes s'engagent, au nom de leur peuple, à respecter et à faire respecter la présente Convention en toutes circonstances.*'

34. Ibid., p. 5.

and (3) a solemn declaration of governments that they accept these undertakings in the name of their people. For our purposes, the comments to the second and third elements are of interest.

As for the second element, the ICRC explains that for the system of protection envisaged in the Conventions to become effective, contracting parties must not only apply it themselves but they must also do whatever they can to ensure that the humanitarian principles underlying the Conventions are universally applied.[35]

With respect to the third element, the ICRC reiterates the wish, expressed earlier by Pilloud, to see 'the peoples' associated with the respect due to these principles and with the execution of the obligations that result therefrom, adding that this may facilitate the application of the Conventions in times of civil war.[36]

My question about the historical meaning of the phrase 'to ensure respect' thus leads to this further question: what did the authors mean by 'universally' as used in the comment to the second element; and how did it relate to the notion of the 'peoples' as used in the third?

Especially in light of subsequent developments, one might be tempted to interpret the term as 'worldwide', implying that each contracting party undertakes to ensure respect by all other contracting parties. Yet, in its historical context, this seems an utterly implausible interpretation. For one thing, for a concept belonging to the realm of international relations to figure without explanation between two elements relating to the domestic level would be very strange indeed. Even more significantly, there is simply nothing to suggest that the authors of the proposed text, with Claude Pilloud as the key figure among them, were thinking along those lines. Rather, as may be evident from the foregoing, their concern at the time was implementation at the domestic level, and notably implementation of the main principles in the event of civil war (or, as it was increasingly indicated, non-international armed conflict). I am indeed convinced that the authors used 'universally' here in the sense of 'by all concerned' or 'the whole population' – a notion which they hoped would encompass 'all parties' to such a conflict.

Viewed thus, the undertaking to ensure 'universal' application takes its place as an indispensable step preceding and introducing the idea of associating the population with the respect due the principles. This element seems to have

---

35. *'Le CICR juge nécessaire de faire ressortir que le système de protection prévu par la présente Convention exige, pour être efficace, que les Hautes Parties contractantes ne se bornent pas à appliquer elles-mêmes la Convention, mais qu'elles fassent également tout ce qui est en leur pouvoir pour que les principes humanitaires qui sont à la base de cette Convention soient universellement appliqués.'*

36. *'. . . le CICR a eu l'intention d'associer les peuples eux-mêmes au respect des principes qui sont à la base de la présente Convention et à l'exécution des obligations qui en découlent. Le texte aura, en outre, l'avantage de faciliter l'application de la Convention, notamment en temps de guerre civile.'*

It seems somewhat surprising that, in contrast with Pilloud's note, the commentary links the reference to civil war to the third element with its remark about the 'peoples', rather than to the preceding paragraph about ensuring respect. In comparison, the later product cannot be said to have brought greater clarity to the matter at issue.

comprised two closely connected concerns. One, of a general order, was the effect the successive rounds of codification were having on the development of humanitarian law. With every new round, the Conventions became more complex and detailed. This might be necessary to make them acceptable to the governments who were negotiating the texts in time of peace; at the same time, their increasingly complicated and technical character risked making people involved in war lose sight of the essential ideas of respect and protection underlying the rules. For the ICRC, and certainly for someone like its lawyer, Jean Pictet, this could indicate the need to compensate for the complexity of the Conventions by disseminating their main principles to the general public.

The other, more specific concern was the need to find agreement on humanitarian principles governing internal armed conflict. As Pilloud had emphasized in his note of August 1947, for such rules to be acceptable to governments they must be applicable to all sides to the conflict. Even more than in an armed conflict between states, this presupposes a widespread awareness of what the principles are about. While the idea of associating the whole population with the respect due to the principles covered this concern, it also represented an attempt, in line with Pilloud's thinking, to get around the requirement of reciprocity.

The proposal for Article 1, therefore, was part and parcel of the ICRC's incessant efforts to weave into the fabric of the Geneva Conventions a recognition that basic precepts of humanitarian law must be respected in internal armed conflict. As noted above, one attempted line was to introduce into the body of the Conventions a specific provision to that effect. If this attempt were to bear fruit, a rule eliminating the requirement of reciprocity, as now suggested for Article 1, would act as an important complement to the new provision. If (as could not be excluded at the time) the attempt were to founder, the rule of Article 1 would stand out as the sole device to cope with the problems of non-international armed conflict.

Unfortunately (though not exceptionally), the records of the Stockholm Conference shed little further light on the issue. In the plenary sessions, not a word was said about Article 1; this in accordance with the President's policy to avoid plenary discussions about specific articles. The Legal Commission, for its part, dealt with and voted on Article 1.[37] In the course of the brief discussion, Professor Frede Castberg, speaking for Norway, welcomed the suggestion of the ICRC that certain provisions of the Conventions would be binding on individual members of the population, especially in the event of 'civil war'; but, he added, this idea could be expressed with greater clarity.[38] Rather than making an attempt to provide such additional clarity, Mr Starr, of the American Red Cross, thereupon simply proposed the deletion of the phrase 'in the name of their people'; a suggestion that did not

---

37. Stenographic record of the Legal Commission, pp. 33-36: 4th session, 27 August 1948.

38. Professor Castberg's statement, rendered in French, reads in part: *'Je ne présente pas d'autre formule, mais je tiens à préciser que nous marquons notre accord quant à l'intention que les dispositions seront obligatoires pour les individus,* surtout en cas de guerre civile.' (my emphasis)

elicit any comment and, when put to the vote, was accepted by 17 votes against five, with four abstentions.[39]

Neither in these two interventions nor at any other stage of the Stockholm Conference was there the merest reference to the phrase 'to ensure respect' as proposed by the ICRC, let alone to its comments on the proposal. In the end, the plenary Conference, without much discussion, approved the texts of four draft Conventions, for referral to the Diplomatic Conference planned for 1949. In these texts, draft Article 1, as the ICRC proposal, minus the phrase deleted as a result of the American amendment, read as follows:[40]

> The High Contracting Parties undertake to respect, and to ensure respect, for the present Convention in all circumstances.

It is noteworthy that, in the process, the clause about the non-party belligerent – which dealt with the *si omnes* issue and thus had constituted the essence of the Article in the Conventions of 1929 – had become disengaged from the 'respect' provision. Figuring in the draft Conventions as paragraph 3 of Article 2, on 'application of the Conventions', it read: 'If one of the Powers in conflict is not party to the present Convention, the Powers who are party thereto shall notwithstanding be bound by it in their mutual relations.' And the matter of application in time of peace, which the British delegate had so cleverly explained as covered by the phrase 'all circumstances', likewise was taken care of elsewhere, in the opening words of Article 2, paragraph 1: 'In addition to the stipulations which shall be implemented in peacetime, ...'

Precious little had therefore remained of the original motives behind Articles 25 and 82 to lend substance to the new draft Article 1. For its authors, its main *raison d'être* now appeared to lie in getting populations involved in the process of creating and maintaining respect for the principles embodied in the Conventions, thus binding them to such respect even in time of civil war or non-international armed conflict. All this in marked contrast to 1929, when neither civil wars nor, obviously, direct involvement of populations had been on the delegates' minds.

Before leaving the Stockholm Conference, two further points should be noted. First, for all its lack of attention to Article 1, the Conference had spent a good deal of energy on the substantive aspects of the issue of civil war, or internal armed

---

39. While Mr Starr offered no argument for this act of surgery, it may simply have stemmed from fear of something new that had not figured in earlier texts. The record only mentions the fact that he spoke on behalf of the sub-commission that examined the draft Prisoners of War Convention. Of this body, no records have been found. Mr Starr, charged with international affairs in the American Red Cross, subsequently took part in the Diplomatic Conference of 1949 as a member of the American delegation.

40. Draft Conventions 'as approved by the XVIIth International Red Cross Conference' and submitted to the Diplomatic Conference of 1949. Final Record of the Diplomatic Conference of 1949 (hereinafter Final Record), Vol. I, pp. 47, 61, 73, 113.

conflict. The outcome of its deliberations was the addition of a fourth paragraph to draft Article 2. The paragraph read as follows:[41]

> In all cases of armed conflict not of an international character which may occur in the territory of one or more of the High Contracting Parties, each of the adversaries shall be bound to implement the provisions of the present Convention. The Convention shall be applicable in these circumstances, whatever the legal status of the Parties to the conflict and without prejudice thereto.

The other point concerns the matter of a preamble. On a French initiative, the Conference had approved a draft preamble for the new Civilians Convention. It defined the undertaking of contracting states, 'conscious of their obligation to come to an agreement in order to protect civilian populations from the horrors of war, ... to respect the principles of human rights which constitute the safeguard of civilisation'; and it provided the following catalogue of rules which the Parties would have to apply in particular, 'at any time and in all places':[42]

(1) Individuals shall be protected against any violence to their life and limb.

(2) The taking of hostages is prohibited.

(3) Executions may be carried out only if prior judgment has been passed by a regularly constituted court, furnished with the judicial safeguards that civilized peoples recognize to be indispensable.

(4) Torture of any kind is strictly prohibited.

Both in the introductory evocation of the reasons for a Civilians Convention and in the ensuing catalogue of human rights, the source of inspiration for this text is evident: it was the Second World War with its occupations in Europe and elsewhere which had finally made governments realize that the few rules on occupation in The Hague Regulations of 1907[43] were no longer adequate to cope with such situations.[44] The Civilians Convention was therefore felt to be of such momentous importance as to deserve a somewhat monumental preamble of its own.

---

41. Ibid.

42. Final Record, Vol. I, p. 113. A final paragraph specified that: 'These rules, which constitute the basis of universal human law, shall be respected without prejudice to the special stipulations provided for in the present Convention in favour of protected persons'.

As I was told by René-Jean Wilhelm, who was already with the ICRC at the time of the Stockholm Conference, one of the French delegates, Mr Albert Lamarle, at the time of the Second World War had been involved with the resistance in France. That experience and his ensuing interest in human rights may well have prompted his proposing a text which clearly reflected the ideas on human rights that were being developed at the time.

43. Regulations Respecting the Laws and Customs of War on Land, Section III: Military Authority over the Territory of the Hostile State. The Regulations are an annex to the Convention (IV) Respecting the Laws and Customs of War on Land, signed at The Hague on 18 October 1907. For text, see Schindler and Toman, op. cit. n. 9, p. 69.

44. Attempts undertaken by the ICRC before the War to make governments accept more adequate rules for such situations reaped no result.

Inspired by this example, the ICRC after the Conference wrote its own draft for a preamble, destined this time for all four Conventions. Following a first paragraph with a highly abstract statement about the nature of 'respect for the personality and dignity of human beings' as a 'universal principle ... binding even in the absence of any contractual undertaking', a second paragraph describes in the following terms the ensuing basic precepts of humanitarian law:

> Such a principle demands that, in time of war, all those not actively engaged in the hostilities and all those placed *hors de combat* by reason of sickness, wounds, capture, or any other circumstance, shall be given due respect and have protection from the effects of war, and that those among them who are in suffering shall be succoured and tended without distinction of race, nationality, religion, belief, political opinion or any other quality.

The third paragraph demands the contracting states to solemnly affirm their will to conform to that principle; to express their intention to implement it as elaborated in each of the Conventions and, surprisingly, to undertake to respect, and to ensure respect for, the Conventions in all circumstances.[45]

Both draft preambles were equally interesting. The Stockholm draft was couched in human rights terms, a type of language that, although at the time not particularly fashionable in red cross circles, was rapidly gaining respectability elsewhere; witness the adoption by the UN General Assembly, on 10 December 1948, of the Universal Declaration of Human Rights. The ICRC draft, for its part, reverted to more traditional Geneva phraseology. Reflecting the concern mentioned earlier about the increasing complexity of the Conventions and the resultant enhanced difficulty of ensuring their implementation in time of war, it could serve as a vehicle to spread the message of the fundamentals underlying these complex and overly detailed Conventions.

Another point of interest is that both texts define the situation they were written for as 'war'. Taking into account that the Stockholm Conference had approved a draft Article 2 on application of the Conventions that explicitly distinguished situations of international and non-international armed conflict, the draft preambles clearly used 'war' in a non-technical sense covering either situation. As far as the ICRC draft is concerned, this implies that the incorporation in the third paragraph of the text of draft Article 1 did not necessarily point to a change in its intentions with regard to that text.

---

45. Text in a note dated February 1949 and entitled *Remarks and Proposals submitted by the International Committee of the Red Cross – Documents for the consideration of Governments invited by the Swiss Federal Council to attend the Diplomatic Conference of Geneva (April 21, 1949)*. I have not been able to obtain a copy of the note in English. The first two paragraphs are reprinted in the Commentary to each Convention (e.g., Commentary I, p. 21). In the (original) French version, the third paragraph, different for each Convention, reads as follows (p. 8):
Les Hautes Parties contractantes affirment solennellement leur volonté de se conformer à ce principe. Elles entendent en régler l'application aux ... par la présente Convention, et s'engagent à respecter et à faire respecter celle-ci en toutes circonstances.

One is tempted to ask whether a preambular 'undertaking to respect and to ensure respect in all circumstances' would have the same legal effect as it could have in the opening Article of the Conventions. For the ICRC, this question apparently did not arise: its comment to the proposed text in the 'Remarks and Proposals' does not mention the issue. It does make another interesting point, though: the ICRC actually would have preferred to see its draft for a preamble included as the opening Article of each Convention. And, once again to our considerable surprise, it suggests that it could then be indicated as 'Preamble' in the margin.[46]

With all this, the stage was set for the Diplomatic Conference that the Swiss Federal Department was convening for August 1949. It would have before it the texts of the four draft Conventions approved by the Stockholm Conference, expedited by the ICRC in November 1948 to the governments invited to participate in the Conference. In March 1949, the ICRC also transmitted to these selfsame governments its note with 'Remarks and Proposals'.[47]

2.3   Checked growth: The Diplomatic Conference of Geneva of 1949

Delegates of 59 states participated in the Diplomatic Conference, held at Geneva from 21 April to 12 August 1949. Prominent among the non-governmental experts at the Conference were the representatives of the ICRC: notably, Jean S. Pictet, Director-Delegate of the ICRC; Frédéric Siordet, legal adviser to the ICRC; Claude Pilloud, Head of the Legal Division; and René Jean Wilhelm, member of that Division.[48]

The Conference had been set up, as usual, with a Bureau and a Drafting Committee. To deal with the substance of the four draft Conventions, the Rules of Procedure provided for three committees of the whole: Committee I for the 'sick and wounded' as well as 'maritime warfare', Committee II for 'prisoners of war' and Committee III for the 'protection of civilians'; and, to coordinate their work, a Coordination Committee.[49] The plenary Conference established at an early stage a Joint Committee to deal with the numerous common Articles. This was a joint meeting of the three Committees and, hence, like these Committees, a committee of the whole.[50] The Joint Committee, in its turn, soon decided to set up a 12-

---

46. Ibid.

47. Ibid. Regrettably, the 'Remarks and Proposals' are not included in the Final Record: neither in Vol. I as an annex to the Stockholm draft Conventions, nor in Vol. III, with the amendments submitted during the Conference.

48. The official title of the Conference was 'Diplomatic Conference convened by the Swiss Federal Council for the Establishment of International Conventions for the Protection of War Victims and Held at Geneva from 21 April to 12 August 1949.' For the list of delegates, experts and observers, see Final Record, Vol. I, pp. 158 et seq.

49. Final Record, Vol. I, pp. 181, at 185: Rules 15-17.

50. Final Record, Vol. IIA, pp. 21-24: 4th plenary meeting, 25 April 1949: Procedure for the Discussion of the Articles Common to all four Conventions. The Joint Committee met under the chairmanship of Professor Maurice Bourquin (Belgium), Chairman of Committee II.

member Special Committee, at the outset mandated especially to discuss the delicate problems posed by draft Article 2(4), in other words, the issue of non-international armed conflict.[51] Its terms of reference were subsequently extended to cover all 'other intricate questions which might be submitted for its consideration by the Joint Committee.'[52]

Draft common Article 1 logically fell within the province of the Joint Committee,[53] and equally logically, it was the first of the common provisions to come up for consideration. This was quickly postponed, however, when the Chairman suggested that 'it was probable that the Committee would have to discuss it in connection with the Preamble'.[54]

The 'probable connection with the Preamble' obviously referred to the two draft preambles discussed in the previous section. The opening paragraph of the Stockholm draft spoke of an 'undertaking to respect'. On simple grounds of linguistic and legal coherence, a discussion of this phrase would have to take account of the identical wording in Article 11, if only to find out whether the phrase 'to undertake' in a preamble has the same legal implications as when it is used in the body of a treaty. And the ICRC draft not only repeated in its closing sentence the exact words of draft Article 1; it actually indicated that the ICRC regarded it as an integral part of each Convention and hoped that it might become their opening Article 1.[55]

While the link between draft Article 1 and the draft preambles was thus abundantly clear, another point was less so. Since the Stockholm draft was intended for the Civilians Convention only and the ICRC draft was not completely identical for all four Conventions, it could be asked whether the Joint Committee really was the proper organ of the Conference to deal with the preamble. It did not take the Bureau long to conclude otherwise and to decide 'that the best course would be

---

51. Final Record, Vol. IIB, p. 16: 3rd meeting of the Joint Committee, 29 April 1949.

52. Ibid., p. 26: 7th meeting of the Joint Committee, 17 May 1949.

53. Final Record, Vol. IIA, p. 620: statement of the Chairman in opening the 2nd meeting of Committee III: 'It was proposed to submit the Preamble to the Joint Committee for consideration, and several members of Committee III had suggested the advisability of awaiting the results of the discussion by the Joint Committee before embarking on any discussion in Committee III.' In a similar vein: Mr Abercrombie (UK) at the 4th meeting of Committee I, 28 April 1949; Final Record, Vol. IIA, p. 51.

54. Final Record, Vol. IIB, p. 9: meeting of 26 April 1949. As the Chairman said: 'Up to the present only in one Convention is proposed a Preamble, namely in the Convention for the Protection of Civilians. But it had been suggested – and the suggestion had met with considerable approval – that all the Conventions should have a Preamble. But Preambles, like the prefaces of books, although placed at the beginning of the Conventions, were written after them.'

55. Both Pictet and Wilhelm confirmed this preference more than once in the course of the proceedings. See, e.g., Final Record, Vol. IIA, pp. 112-114 (Pictet, speaking under the item Consideration of Preambles for the Sick and Wounded and Maritime Warfare Conventions, 'said that the I.C.R.C. had really intended that the text suggested in "Remarks and Proposals" should form the first Article of the Conventions rather than a Preamble to them'); ibid., p. 322 (Wilhelm, speaking to the subject of a preamble to the Prisoners of War Convention, concluded that 'The I.C.R.C. suggested that the Preamble should figure as Article 1, because experience had shown that Conventions were very often reproduced without their preambles.')

to instruct Committees I, II and III each to consider separately the Preamble to the Convention for which it was responsible'.[56] This removed the obstacle for consideration of Article 1 by the Joint Committee, and the Chairman informed the Committee accordingly.[57]

Pilloud, the only person to take the floor after this announcement, said that draft Article 1 was along the lines of Article 25(1) of the Sick and Wounded Convention of 1929 and Article 82 of the Prisoners of War Convention of 1929. He also mentioned, without comment, that the Stockholm Conference had deleted from the original ICRC draft the words 'in the name of their peoples'.[58] In this remarkably short, uninspired and uninformative 'introduction' (if one could call it that) the only point of note is that Pilloud did not so much as hint at a potential extra-domestic effect of the proposed text. Be this as it may, the Joint Committee, having heard his statement, referred draft Article 1 without discussion to the Special Committee.

In the Special Committee, few delegates took part in the consideration of the draft Article.[59] The first speaker, Mr Maresca (Italy), voiced his feeling that the terms 'undertake to ensure respect' lacked clarity and that, '[a]ccording to the manner in which they were construed, they were either redundant, or introduced a new concept into international law.' This was an astute observation: to his lawyer's eye there certainly must have been something strange about the proposed text. Unfortunately, as far as the records show, he did not elaborate the point, and neither was it taken up by other delegates. The next two speakers, Professor Castberg (Norway) and Mr Yingling (USA) confined themselves to explaining that (in Castberg's words) 'the object of this Article was to ensure respect of the Conventions by the population as a whole'.[60]

Pilloud thereupon referred to the proposed draft Article 1 which the ICRC had submitted to the Stockholm Conference. On that occasion, he said, it had 'emphasized that the Contracting Parties should not confine themselves to applying the Conventions themselves, but should do all in their power to see that the basic humanitarian principles of the Conventions were universally applied'. Here the term 'universally' turned up again, and once again without explanation of its meaning,

---

56. Final Record, Vol. IIA, p. 33: 6th Plen. Meeting, 30 May 1949, statement of the President.
57. Final Record, Vol. IIB, p. 26: 7th meeting, 17 May 1949.
58. Ibid.
59. Final Record, Vol. IIB, p. 53: 9th meeting, 25 May 1949.
60. Mr Yingling added that 'Article 1 did not imply the obligation to enact penal sanctions'. This remark may have been inspired by the difficult discussions with the Soviet bloc about penal sanctions for war crimes.
It is of interest to note that at a different time and place and in respect of a different convention, the identical words were interpreted in the opposite sense. In a case involving Art. 1(1) of the American Convention of Human Rights, the Inter-American Court of Human Rights interpreted the obligation of the states parties to 'ensure' the free and full exercise of the rights recognized by the Convention to every person subject to its jurisdiction, as implying their duty to 'prevent, investigate and punish any violation' of those rights. I/A Court H.R., *Velásquez Rodríguez* case, Judgment of 29 July 1988, Series C No. 4, para. 166.

but also, more importantly, without the speaker taking issue with the explanation of the object of the Article as offered earlier by the government representatives.

Conversely, and equally significantly, the latter delegates do not appear to have perceived in Pilloud's words a contradiction of their own statements: his words did not draw any comments, whether in retort from the delegates who had preceded him or from the only delegate to speak after him, Mr Lamarle (France).[61]

After this remarkably short discussion, the Special Committee on 25 May 1949 adopted Article 1 without modification.[62] This also concluded the official consideration of the Article by the Diplomatic Conference. The Joint Committee and subsequently the Plenary Assembly adopted it without any further debate.[63]

Apart from its official consideration, Article 1 was mentioned twice in the debate about draft Article 2(4): the provision on internal armed conflict. The first occasion occurred when the Special Committee discussed the problem of how to bind a rebel party to humanitarian rules accepted by the government as treaty law, i.e., the issue which more than anything else had prompted Pilloud to prepare draft Article 1. In the course of the debate, Professor de Geouffre de la Pradelle, delegate of Monaco, advanced the argument that the rebels could be regarded as already bound by the Conventions, for these two reasons:

> First, because the humanitarian provisions of the Geneva Conventions are of a super-contractual character; and also, and more particularly, because the Contracting Parties undertake not only to respect them, but to ensure respect for them, *an article providing for their dissemination among the population through instruction.* Therefore, the rebels are a part of the population in revolt of the Contracting State.[64]

The only person to react to this remarkable explanation was Professor Paul Carry, a member of the ICRC. Far from taking issue with his French colleague, he 'stated that the International Committee of the Red Cross would welcome the reinsertion of the words "in the name of their peoples" which the Stockholm Conference had deleted from Article 1'.[65]

The other occasion arose in connection with the reference in a draft text (as in the final Article 3) to 'each Party to the conflict', implying that both the governmental and rebel sides are equally regarded as parties. Speaking to this point,

---

61. This delegate (whom we met earlier in the context of the Stockholm Conference; *supra* n. 42) in effect 'considered that the term "to ensure respect" had the same purpose as the expression "in the name of their peoples", which had been deleted without a modification'.

62. Final Record, Vol. IIB, p. 53: 9th meeting, 25 May 1949.

63. Upon the report of the Special Committee (1st report, Final Record, Vol. IIB, p. 107), the Joint Committee in its 8th meeting unanimously adopted 'the new Article 1, reproducing the text of Stockholm' (29 June 1949, ibid., p. 27). Since the Article had passed the Joint Committee without discussion, its report to the Plenary Assembly does not provide any comment on the Article (ibid., p. 128). The 18th Plenary meeting on 28 July 1949 adopted common Articles 1 and 2 at a stroke (ibid., p. 325).

64. Final Record, Vol. IIB, p. 79: 24th meeting, 15 June 1949; my italics.

65. Ibid.

Mr Lamarle 'indicated that the expression "each Party to the conflict ..." had been introduced as a result of the comment made in the course of the debates, that *in accordance with Article 1, the Contracting State undertook to ensure respect for the Convention by its nationals*' (etc.).[66] As on the earlier occasion, here again the link between Article 1 and the issue of civil war was manifest. I note with some regret that no other delegate took up the argument, whether in support or dissent.[67]

2.4   The rise and fall of the draft preambles

Even with the adoption of Article 1, there always loomed the ICRC draft for a preamble, which it would prefer to see included as the opening Article. Whether this would indeed end up as the new Article 1 depended on the deliberations in the various Committees on the matter of the preamble. Both for this reason and because of the intrinsic affinity between Article 1 and the Stockholm and ICRC draft preambles, I insert here an overview of the discussions that decided the fate of these draft texts, beginning with the Stockholm draft for a preamble to the Civilians Convention.

Committee III, charged with the consideration of the draft Civilians Convention, took up the Stockholm draft. After a first round of discussions it referred the matter to a working party.[68] This eventually produced a longish text in two parts, the preamble proper and a set of 'Preliminary Provisions'. The text represents a fascinating cocktail of the ideas underlying the Stockholm draft and the ICRC proposal, mixed with ideas derived from the Universal Declaration of Human Rights.[69] Since the cocktail had failed to find unanimous agreement in the Working

---

66. Ibid., p. 84: 28th meeting, 24 June 1949; my italics.

67. It is of interest to note that when the Special Committee began its work, one of the proposals on draft Art. 2(4), submitted by France, suggested 'to restrict the application of the provisions of the Convention, within the scope of the fourth paragraph to Article 2, to the case when the adverse party possessed an organized military force, an authority responsible for its acts acting within a determinate territory and *having the means of respecting and ensuring respect for* the Convention'. (my italics). Ibid., p. 121: 7th Report of the Special Committee, 16 July 1949.

68. Final Record, Vol. IIA, pp. 691-694: 23rd meeting, 25 May 1949; pp. 694-697: 24th meeting, 27 May 1949.

69. Final Record, Vol. III, p. 98: Annex 191; the full text reads as follows:
The High Contracting Parties confirm their unanimous resolution to make every attempt and to do all that lies in their power to protect present and future generations from the scourge of war. They feel, however, that it is indispensable in cases where, notwithstanding their wishes and endeavours, a conflict might arise, to take all measures which may contribute to the prevention of a recurrence of the atrocities committed during recent world wars and to the protection of civilian populations from the tragic consequences of the conflict.
Their desire is inspired by the eternal principles of law, which are the foundation and the safeguard of civilization.
The High Contracting Parties solemnly condemn the acts of barbarism which have revolted the conscience of mankind, and intend to prevent their recurrence. To this effect, they desire to ensure the respect of human personality and dignity by putting beyond reach of attack those rights and liberties which are the essence of its existence. Whatever their nationality, race, sex, political opinion, philosophy or religion, human beings shall have every guarantee of protection for their

Party, the rapporteur introduced the text in Committee III, adding that it was merely a basis for discussion.

In the ensuing discussion it was soon apparent that opinions in the Committee varied widely, both on the proposed text and on the question of whether a preamble was needed at all. The end came with the adoption, by 27 votes to 17, of a Canadian proposal to omit the Preamble altogether, including the Preliminary Provisions. This left the Chairman no choice but to conclude that there would be no Preamble to the Civilians Convention and no further discussion on the subject.[70]

A striking aspect of this discussion in Committee III is that no one spoke on behalf of the ICRC, whether to offer comments on the Stockholm draft or to introduce his own proposal for a preamble to this as to the other Conventions.

Its own draft preamble came up for discussion, successively, in Committees I and II. Its experts explained its purpose: It was to place right at the beginning of the Conventions, in forceful terms and elaborated into basic rules, the guiding principle underlying these instruments and inspiring all their provisions, viz., that of respect for the human person. The text would bring this principle within easy reach of the general public. The experts also underscored the preference of the ICRC to see its text included as Article 1 in the Conventions, if only because experience showed that treaties were often reproduced without their preambles.[71]

Both Committees at an early stage referred the matter to a working party. At the suggestion of Jean Pictet, Committee I first took a vote on the question of principle whether a preambular general statement of principles should be inserted at the beginning of the two Conventions, subjected to its consideration. With 12 votes

---

physical integrity and their spiritual independence. Those who suffer, the wounded, sick, infirm, as well as prisoners or internees, must receive aid and proper care. All are entitled to protection and assistance.

Preliminary Provisions

The following acts shall be prohibited and shall remain prohibited at any time or in any place whatsoever:

(a) human beings shall not be subjected to attempts against their life or injury to their physical integrity. The following shall be considered grave crimes: murder, torture, mutilation, including scientific experiments, as well as any other means for the extermination of the civilian population;

(b) the taking of hostages;

(c) deportations, either individual or collective;

(d) attacks against the dignity of persons, in particular humiliating or degrading treatment or discriminatory treatment based upon differences of race, colour, religion, beliefs, sex, birth or social status;

(e) the pronouncement of sentences and penal sanctions carried out without preliminary trial by a regularly constituted tribunal giving all the necessary legal guarantees recognized by civilized nations as indispensable;

(f) collective penalties as well as any measures of intimidation or terrorism; the destruction of any real and personal property belonging to private individuals or to the State, as well as to social and co-operative organizations when this is not rendered absolutely necessary by military operations.

70. Final Record, Vol. IIA, pp. 777-782: 45th meeting, 9 July 1949.

71. *Supra* n. 55. Pictet defined 'the great fundamental principle underlying the Geneva Conventions' as 'respect for those who suffered, and for those who, being disarmed, were no longer friends or foes, but simply defenceless beings'.

in favour and 7 against, the answer was positive.[72] In Committee II, no such preliminary vote was taken.[73]

The Working Party of Committee I produced a text in three paragraphs.[74] The middle one, expounding in well-chosen terms the principle of 'respect for the personality and dignity of the human being', had met with general approval.[75] It was preceded by a paragraph which, following a suggestion by the Holy See (but over the opposition of the Eastern block) stated that the principle, as proclaimed by religions, was of divine origin.[76] The third paragraph, which originally contained no more than a solemn affirmation that the contracting parties would 'adhere to this principle', had been enriched with an amendment introduced by Ukraine on behalf of the socialist delegates and adding 'that breaches of this principle shall be prohibited and severely punished'. (At the time, this idea of a general duty to deal effectively with war crimes was less than popular in the Western world.)

Obviously, opinions again differed widely among the delegates, not so much on the core of the proposed text as on the ideologically determined fringes. A heated debate[77] was followed by a series of votes, first, on whether to omit the preamble altogether. Since this implied overriding the Committee's earlier decision of principle that there would be some sort of a preambular text, a two-thirds majority was required. With 22 against 13 and 3 abstentions, the vote fell short of that

---

72. Final Record, Vol. IIA, pp. 112-114: 24th meeting, 31 May 1949.

73. Ibid., p. 323: 20th meeting, 16 June 1949; Committee II referred the proposal to its Drafting Committee No. 2.

74. Ibid., p. 164: 34th meeting of Committee I, 30 June 1949: report of the Working Party.

75. The text read as follows: 'This principle commands the alleviation of sufferings occasioned by war and requires that all those who are not directly engaged in the hostilities as combatants and all those who, because of sickness, wounds, capture or any other circumstances, have been withdrawn from hostilities, shall be duly respected and protected and that those among them who are suffering shall be aided and cared for regardless of race, nationality, religion, political opinion or other circumstance.'

76. It read: 'Respect for the personality and dignity of the human being is a universal principle which is binding even without contractual undertakings. Religions proclaim its divine origin and all people consider it a fundamental of civilization.'

77. Final Record, Vol. IIA, pp. 165-168: 35th meeting, 1 July 1949. In the course of the debate, Pictet once again explained the position and concerns of the ICRC. Its object 'had been to place at the beginning of the Conventions, so that it would be easily and clearly grasped by [the] general public, the guiding principle underlying the Conventions and inspiring all their provisions, namely that of respect for the human person. It was a corollary of that respect that those who were not taking part in hostilities and those who had been placed *hors de combat*, should be protected, whether friends or foes, without any distinction based on nationality, race, religion or political opinion. That principle was the corner stone of the whole institution of the Red Cross and the Geneva Conventions. It was thanks to it that the Red Cross had become universal and had been able to accomplish its work. (...) The International Committee of the Red Cross, therefore, ventured to recommend that the Preamble to be adopted should be an element of union, emboding [sic] at least the one principle on which all could agree – that of respect for suffering humanity. The purpose of the Conference was to agree upon the provisions in the humanitarian conventions, and not upon the philosophical or metaphysical motives which inspired them and which might be different for different nations. He hoped that if the proposal to omit the Preamble was adopted, it would at least be possible to retain the basic principles set out in the second paragraph.'

requirement. Further votes followed: one, to defeat the Ukrainian amendment, and another to accept a Canadian one to the text of the second paragraph.[78] Then, by a final vote of 25 to 7, with 3 abstentions, Committee I adopted the Preamble to the Sick and Wounded and Maritime Warfare Conventions.

The debate in Committee II on the report of its Working Party[79] brought to light the same differences of opinion as had surfaced in Committee I. Again after animated debate,[80] two votes were taken: one, on the text of a preamble; and, after it was adopted (by 20 votes to 17, with one abstention) a second one on whether this text should be the Preamble to the Convention . The latter vote produced the reverse result: the proposal was rejected by 20 votes to 9, with 2 abstentions.[81] This meant that there would be no preamble to the Prisoners of War Convention.

The net result of the discussions in the three Committees was that Committee I was the only one to have adopted preambles for the two Conventions it was considering, whereas the other Committees had ultimately but quite unambiguously rejected the proposed texts. To mend this incongruous situation, the Coordination Committee recommended that Committee I reconsider its decision.[82] This was rapidly done, and with a vote of 13 to 1 and 5 abstentions, Committee I finally bowed its head to the will of the majority.[83] With this vote, the possibility had also finally disappeared for a substantive text, adopted by way of preamble, to be transformed into the opening article of the Conventions.

One last reference to the question of a preamble remains to be noted here. Speaking in the penultimate Plenary Meeting, Mgr. Paul Bertoli, representative of the Holy See, explained the reasons why his delegation had wished to see reflected in the preamble the notion of the 'divine origin of all rights which protect human liberty and dignity': 'to lay in that manner the foundation stone of the edifice we have tried so laboriously to build is a constructive act'.[84]

The point that stands out is the width of the gap separating Mgr. Bertoli's view on the function of the preamble from that of the ICRC experts: in their case,

---

78. Col. Crawford (Canada) suggested an amendment to the second paragraph, to replace 'requires that all those' by 'requires that members of the armed forces'. The amendment was adopted by 18 votes to 2, with 8 abstentions.

79. Final Record, Vol. IIA, p. 366: 27th meeting, 7 July 1949. The report of Drafting Committee No. 2 showed that it had taken the text adopted by Committee I as the basis for its discussion. An USSR amendment aimed to remove the reference to religion and to include an express statement about the will to punish; a Swiss amendment amounted to an almost literal reproduction of the text adopted by Committee I.

80. Ibid., pp. 393-394: 31th meeting, 12 July 1949; pp. 395-398: 32nd meeting, 15 July 1949.

81. Ibid., pp. 397-398. The final vote reflects the feeling in Committee II that a preamble should be unanimously adopted or rejected. On the question of the utility of a debate with such an uncertain outcome, Mr Stroehlin (Switzerland) had noted that '[e]ven if it was decided not to have a preamble, it would be useful, from the point of view of the future, to have the views expressed on that subject recorded in the Final Record of the Conference.' Ibid., p. 393.

82. Final Record, Vol. IIB, p. 145: meeting of 18 July 1949, proposal of Thailand.

83. Final Record, Vol. IIA, pp. 181-182: 39th meeting, 18 July 1949, i.e., the same day as the recommendation by the Coordination Committee.

84. Final Record, Vol. IIB, p. 522: 36th Plenary Meeting, 11 August 1949.

primarily a highly desirable tool for the widest possible dissemination of basic precepts of humanitarian law; for him (and, it should be conceded, more in line with the general idea of a preamble): the expression of a higher philosophical principle underlying that body of law. Should the ICRC have submitted its proposal from the outset as a draft for a common article of the four Conventions, it might have avoided the confusion of ideas that destroyed its project. It also, in retrospect, might have preferred to have put this substantive text in the place of the so much vaguer 'respect and ensure respect' provision of Article 1.

2.5   A measly little sprig: conclusions about the negotiations

What does it all add up to? The most obvious comment is how conspicuously little time and energy the Diplomatic Conference of 1949 spent on draft Article 1.

One important factor was its character as originally designed by the ICRC. Among its efforts to solve the riddles of civil war, draft Article 1 stood for the procedural line, aiming to expand the binding effect of a government's acceptance of the Conventions to the entire population and with that, as it believed, to a future insurgent party.[85] At the Conference, this approach soon became overshadowed by the strenuous efforts, both in the Joint Committee and the Special Committee, to find agreement on substantive norms for 'civil war', whether in the shape of preambular language or as a distinct treaty provision. With the delegates' attention focused first and foremost on those aspects of the problem, their interest for draft Article 1 was reduced to a minimum. Yet the fact remains that in that context, two delegates did refer to Article 1; not, to be sure, when the draft Article was officially up for consideration, but in subsequent discussions, precisely about the issue of civil war.

Another point is that as far as bare text is concerned, draft Article 1 did not offer all that much. As we saw, the Stockholm Conference had left it virtually deprived of its original 1929 meaning, and in 1949, except for the factor of civil war, precious little in the shape of substantive ideas was adduced to fill the gap. Indeed, a far more interesting project – and one that caught much more attention both from government delegates and the experts of the ICRC – was its proposal for a preamble, or, to be more precise, for an opening article presented as a preamble.

---

85. After the Conference, Frédéric Siordet published an article entitled 'Les Conventions de Genève et la guerre civile' (*Revue internationale de la Croix-Rouge* (1950) pp. 104-122, 187-212). While his main focus is on the drafting history of Art. 3, he also discusses the difficulty involved in holding rebels bound to respect rules of international law they never adhered to, and and the efforts made by the ICRC to overcome this difficulty. In that context he mentions the proposal for Art. 1: 'Les Hautes Parties Contractantes s'engagent, *au nom de leur peuple*, à respecter et faire respecter la présente Convention en toute circonstance.' (pp. 120-121 (his italics)). He fails to mention that the Stockholm Conference had deleted the 'name of the people'). Further on, he reiterates how the ICRC first believed that to bind a rebel party to an international convention might be impossible; and then points to the words in Art. 3: 'Chacune des Parties au conflit sera tenue ...,' a phrase which as he notes caused very little discussion, the only concern of governments being to prevent the rebel party acquiring a legal status.

To sum up: The drafting history of Article 1 at the Diplomatic Conference, taken by itself, reads as a surprisingly meagre story. Government representatives simply stated as a plain fact that, by accepting Article 1, a contracting state 'undertook to ensure respect for the Convention by its nationals.' No one ever challenged this position, the experts of the ICRC not excluded. Pilloud, while repeating (without elaborating the point) that the text was designed to achieve 'universal' respect for humanitarian principles, did not suggest that this meant anything other than respect by the whole population. Indeed, when the only other ICRC delegate to contribute to the debate, Professor Carry, expressed the wish to see the words 'in the name of their peoples' reinserted in draft Article 1, this could be understood as an implicit acceptance of the correctness of this reading.

Despite my thorough investigations, I have not found in the records of the Diplomatic Conference even the slightest awareness on the part of government delegates that one might ever wish to read into the phrase 'to ensure respect' any undertaking of a contracting state other than an obligation to ensure respect for the Conventions by its people 'in all circumstances'.

Both according to the original intention of the ICRC and in the expressed view of the two delegates who spoke to the point, that obligation would be especially relevant for the event of internal armed conflict. Ironically, that situation had eventually become covered by common Article 3, the text of which resulted in major part from the Stockholm and ICRC drafts for a preamble.

The upshot of it all is that the decidedly modest content of the provisions on 'respect' in the two Conventions of 1929 had been substituted with a different but not much more important content of the new Article 1 common to the four Conventions of 1949. The 'insignificant seed' had truly sprouted into a 'measly little sprig'!

3.   HEAD GARDENER AT WORK – THE ICRC COMMENTARIES TO THE CONVENTIONS OF 1949

The story of the 'subsequent developments' begins with the activities initiated by the ICRC in its role as guardian or, in our botanical setting, 'head gardener' of the Conventions. Soon after the Diplomatic Conference of 1949 had closed its doors, it decided to undertake an article-by-article Commentary to the four Conventions. It entrusted the actual writing to 'the members of its staff who, from the end of the last world conflict – and even before – had worked on the revision of the Conventions, and were closely associated with the discussions of the Diplomatic Conference of 1949 and the meetings of experts which preceded it.'[86] Under the general editorship of Jean S. Pictet, successive volumes (in French) were published in 1952 (Convention I), 1956 (Convention IV), 1958 (Convention III) and 1960

---

86. Commentary, Foreword, para. 2.

(Convention II). English translations followed in 1952 (Convention I), 1958 (Convention IV) and 1960 (Conventions II and III).

Given the many important innovations the new Conventions had brought to the body of Geneva law, the publication of the Commentaries was bound to be of great practical value to all those who would have to work with these instruments. Not that the Commentaries were intended to provide an official, authentic interpretation of the texts. Forestalling any possible misunderstandings on this score, the ICRC notes in the Foreword to each volume that:[87]

> Although published by the International Committee, the Commentary is the personal work of its authors. The Committee, moreover, whenever called upon for an opinion on a provision of an international Convention, always takes care to emphasise that only the participant States are qualified, through consultation between themselves, to give an official and, as it were, authentic interpretation of an intergovernmental treaty.

3.1   The 1952 commentary to Convention I

The ICRC entrusted the task of writing the comments on Article 1 to its legal adviser, Frédéric Siordet. Although no records have been found that corroborate the point, I do not doubt that he was assisted in this work by Claude Pilloud, the staff lawyer who had been most closely connected with the drafting of the Article.

The general set-up of the comments is identical in all four volumes: splitting the Article in three fragments, the authors first tackle 'respect', then 'ensure respect', then 'all circumstances'. Since their comments differ in detail in the successive volumes of the Commentary, we will have a close look, first, at these three parts of the text published in 1952.

3.1.1   *'to respect'*

Starting out with a bit of history, the authors quote Article 25 of the 1929 Wounded and Sick Convention: 'The provisions of this Convention shall be respected by the High Contracting Parties in all circumstances.' Embellishing an already rather fanciful remark by their predecessor, Paul des Gouttes,[88] they assert that the idea behind this text was 'to give a more formal character to the mutual undertaking by insisting on its character as a general obligation'. While the 'character as a general obligation' had been invented by the author of the Commentary to the 1929 Convention, the 'more formal character' added another festoon to this piece of decoration.

---

87. Ibid.

88. Text at note 17; after stating that the drafters of Art. 25 had wished to emphasize that the Convention applied both in war and peace, Des Gouttes added the comment that: '*On a insisté sur son caractère d'obligation générale.*'

Jumping from 1925 to 1949, the authors assert that both the prominent position and the actual wording of Article 1 have the effect of strengthening the existing undertaking to respect. And they continue:[89]

> By undertaking at the very outset to respect the clauses of the Convention, the Contracting Parties draw attention to the special character of that instrument. It is not an engagement concluded on the basis of reciprocity, binding each party to the contract only in so far as the other party observes its obligations. It is rather a series of unilateral engagements solemnly contracted before the world as represented by the other Contracting Parties. Each State contracts obligations *vis-à-vis* itself and at the same time *vis-à-vis* the others. The motive of the Convention is such a lofty one, so universally recognised as an imperative call of civilisation, that one feels the need for its assertion, as much because of the respect one has for it oneself as because of the respect for it which one expects from one's opponent, and perhaps even more for the former reason than for the latter.

What 'measly little sprig'?; we are here at the heart of civilisation! But what, one wonders, are the authors doing here: writing a legal comment on the terms of Article 1, or attempting to delight us with a brilliant picture of a better world? Writing almost half a century later and only too painfully aware of the many instances of total disregard for the 1949 Conventions and for the rest of humanitarian law that have occurred since, I cannot but feel that their assessment of an existing 'universal recognition as an imperative call of civilisation' was much too optimistic. The long experience of the ICRC with belligerent behaviour might have led them to exactly the opposite conclusion: that contracting states, though only too well aware of their obligation under international law to respect the letter of any treaty they are party to, had perceived a particular need to reaffirm this obligation in the new Geneva Conventions, precisely because the provisions of such instruments are so regrettably prone to being coldly disregarded in the turmoil of war.

For all its abundant rhetoric, the quoted text contains two propositions of material significance. One concerns the non-reciprocal character of the Conventions: the other, evidently regarded as a sequel to the first, is the description of its character in terms that evoke the notion of obligations *erga omnes*. While one may be prepared to agree with these propositions and in particular with the first one, the point is that neither proposition can be derived in law or logic from the mere undertaking of contracting states to 'respect' the Conventions: divorced from its qualifying words ('in all circumstances') this term cannot sustain the claim that there is a principle of non-reciprocity underlying the Conventions.

In sum, the first part of the commentary, rather than being directed specifically at the 'undertaking to respect' as a treaty provision to be interpreted as such, instead provides us with a glimpse of the 'lofty' views of the authors on the Convention as a whole.

---

89. Commentary I, p. 25.

3.1.2   *'to ensure respect'*

The authors begin their discussion of the undertaking 'to ensure respect' by noting that '[t]he wording may seem redundant'. The reason they give for this perceived redundancy, as well as the arguments they offer by way of explanation of the phrase, once again deserve to be quoted in full:[90]

> When a State contracts an engagement, the engagement extends *eo ipso* to all those over whom it has authority, as well as to the representatives of its authority; and it is under an obligation to issue the necessary orders. The use of the words 'and to ensure respect' was, however, deliberate: they were intended to emphasise and strengthen the responsibility of the Contracting Parties. It would not, for example, be enough for a State to give orders or directives to a few civilian or military authorities, leaving it to them to arrange as they pleased for the details of their execution. It is for the State to supervise their execution. Furthermore, if it is to keep its solemn engagements, the State must of necessity prepare in advance, that is to say in peacetime, the legal, material or other means of loyal enforcement of the Convention as and when the occasion arises. It follows, therefore, that in the event of a Power failing to fulfil its obligations, the other Contracting Parties (neutral, allied or enemy) may, and should, endeavour to bring it back to an attitude of respect for the Convention.

Yet another striking line of argument! For one thing, the assertion that an engagement contracted by a State 'extends *eo ipso* to all those over whom it has authority' overlooks two well-known problems of international law. Not in every domestic legal order does a treaty, once accepted, belong to the law of the land. Even where that is the case, another question is whether and to what extent the treaty is accorded self-executing effect – and the answer to that question varies from country to country. The Geneva Conventions are not above these legal niceties. And, one may ask, over whom do the authors think a state has 'authority'?

Then, with the focus shifting from authority to responsibility, we are informed that the phrase 'to ensure respect' was deliberately chosen 'to emphasise and strengthen the responsibility of the Contracting Parties'. Small matter that the records show nothing of the kind: this is just one more indication that the authors were a long way from providing a faithful comment on the Article as it had emerged from the Conference.

More important is how and to what effect the phrase is supposed to perform the trick of 'emphasising and strengthening' the responsibility of contracting states under international law. The relevant rules of that body of law define in some detail the scope and limits of state responsibility for internationally wrongful acts, including violations of treaty obligations. A provision in a treaty emphasizing this fact would be as innocuous as it is redundant. And an undertaking 'to ensure

---

90. Ibid., pp. 18-19; footnote omitted.

respect' is much too vague and imprecise to augment states' existing international responsibility.

But then, the authors may not have been using the word 'responsibility' in this technical sense but, rather, as a common term denoting the duty of states to live up to their treaty obligations. This would be in line with the examples they offer of down-to-earth practical measures aimed at rendering the Convention more effective, viz., supervision of execution as well as peacetime preparation for a correct implementation in time of war. It would also be in line with the overall impression of the text under consideration as a description of the character of the Convention rather than a comment on the specific text of Article 1.

3.1.3   *'It follows, therefore'*

The closing sentence of the authors' comment on 'to ensure respect' begins with the words, 'It follows, therefore'. This confronts us with a riddle: It follows, from what? Not, for sure, from the advice in the last but one sentence to prepare in peacetime for the case of armed conflict: the reference to 'other Contracting Parties (neutral, allied or enemy)' presupposes that the Power failing in the fulfilment of its obligations is a state at war. A glance at the original French text suffices to show that this is a false problem, however. In that version, the phrase opens with 'Ainsi encore', that is, more correctly, 'Likewise'. When we substitute this as the opening word in the English text, it is evident that the authors did not intend a direct link as of cause and effect between the two sentences.

What remains is the striking contrast between the earlier part of the paragraph and the closing sentence: out of the blue, the latter confronts us with actors not parties to an armed conflict but which yet are expected to display a certain conduct in relation to the conflict. The last sentence thus turns into something of an appendix to the paragraph. Now, the appendix in the human body seems to have no significant function: should we assume that the sentence likewise was nothing but an ineffective appendix from its inception? Since the authors cannot have wished to produce such a meagre result, they must have had a better motive. This makes us wonder: Where did they find inspiration for their statement, and what did they expect to achieve?

That the drafting history of Article 1 cannot have been the authors' source of inspiration is obvious: more than anyone else they must have been aware how weak was the basis in the records for an attempt to interpret any part of the Article as a binding treaty provision. This makes it plausible that they did not bother about past history and found their inspiration in their own minds.

Are we to believe that the authors wished to suggest that the 'undertaking to ensure respect' had the effect of adding to a contracting state's right ('may') to 'endeavour to bring [another State] back to an attitude of respect' for the Conventions, a legally binding obligation actually to do so? The clause has often been interpreted in that sense, first and foremost by the ICRC.

I cannot accept that the authors wanted to make such a drastic suggestion. More likely, they simply saw an opportunity to introduce at this stage the idea that states not involved in an armed conflict might wish to assume an active role, as an additional means for the promotion of respect for the Conventions over and above the formally accepted but not overly effective mechanisms of enforcement provided in these instruments.[91] Their reasoning may have gone along these lines: Respect of multilateral treaties is a common interest of the contracting states. Yet usually they are not too keen to make a fuss over breaches that do not affect them in their direct, legally protected interests. A *demarche* not based on such a direct interest even risks being denounced as intervention in the internal affairs of the alleged actor state. But surely, the mere risk of an unpleasant reaction need not prevent a state from doing what it considers right, i.e., telling a treaty partner that its behaviour militates against the common interest of the other partners, and inviting it to mend its ways. This applies *a fortiori* in the case of treaties like the 1949 Conventions, with their perceived *erga omnes* character and with an 'object and purpose' that clearly goes to the essence of humanity.

While this explains 'may', by 'should' the authors plausibly hoped to incite States Parties to overcome their habitual queasiness and assume a more 'activist' stance in relation to events beyond their borders that put the continued respect of the 1949 Conventions in jeopardy. It is unlikely, however, that they expected to bring about – as it were, single-handedly – a firm legal obligation (an 'undertaking') of contracting states to 'ensure' that one of their brethren, suspected of violating the Conventions, would mend its ways and henceforth 'respect' these instruments. Such an obligation did not exist before the Diplomatic Conference and could not be deduced in any manner from the deliberations at the Conference. Nor is the term 'should' particularly suited to express such an obligation. And after all, as stated explicitly in the Foreword to the Commentaries, authoritative interpretation of the Conventions is a function left to the contracting states themselves.

3.1.4   *'in all circumstances'*

As noted above, the authors did not include the phrase 'in all circumstances' in their discussion of 'respect' and 'ensure respect'. Tackling it next as a separate notion, they cited the comment by their predecessor, Paul Des Gouttes, that while the identical words in the 1929 Convention had not been meant to imply civil war,

---

91. In support of the contention in the text, I refer to a letter Mr René-Jean Wilhelm wrote to me on 19 August 1992. Mentioning that neither Mr Siordet nor Mr Pilloud (who within the ICRC had been responsible for the general provisions) was a specialist in international law, he writes:
'Il me semble que si de vrais 'publicistes' avaient participé à la rédaction du projet d'article 1, ils n'auraient sans doute pas fait figurer dans le même membre de phrase une obligation (I) disons classique, à savoir l'obligation d'un Etat partie de prendre tant les mesures législatives, administratives, etc. internes qu'implique pour cet Etat, en vertu du droit international général, le fait de devenir et d'être partie à une Convention [...], et une obligation (II) d'une toute autre nature, une obligation qui est alors un "novum", à savoir de faire en sorte que les autres Etats parties respectent les Conventions, obligation qui serait aussi celle d'Etats non impliqués dans le conflit.'
He goes on to suggest that interpretation II was devised only after the 1949 Conference, in the course of the writing of the Commentary. This is precisely my contention too.

application of its humanitarian provisions by the parties to such a war would be 'eminently desirable'. Such voluntary application had occurred in some measure, e.g., in the Spanish Civil War. Contracting states had now gone much further: under common Article 3, they 'undertook in advance, in the event of a non-international armed conflict, to respect, if not the Convention, at least the regulations contained in that Article'. This 'revolution in international law' justified the conclusion that, as in 1929, 'in all circumstances' does not relate to internal armed conflict. Instead, and barring the provisions applicable in peacetime, the words meant that:

> ... as soon as one of the conditions of application for which Article 2 provides is present, no Power bound by the Convention can offer any valid pretext, legal or other, for not respecting the Convention in all its parts. The words 'in all circumstances' mean in short that the application of the Convention does not depend on the character of the conflict. Whether a war is 'just' or 'unjust,' whether it is a war of aggression or of resistance to aggression, the protection and care due to the wounded and sick are in no way affected.

With that, the authors surely had succeeded in finding an original meaning for the phrase, which actually reflected a topical issue. According to one school of thought, the United Nations Charter, with its ban on aggression, precluded an aggressor from claiming the protections offered by international humanitarian law. The opposite view was that even though the ban might have such an effect in some areas of international law, it could not set aside the principle of the equality of belligerents as an absolutely essential prerequisite of international humanitarian law. The debate was not purely academic either. It had a place in the Cold War, with the then-Soviet side being the main proponents of the former position, and their Western opponents of the latter.[92]

In this debate, the authors, as true Red Cross adepts, could only be expected to side with the opponents of the 'ban' argument. The suggestion, implicit in the quoted paragraph, that their view actually was deduced from the phrase 'in all circumstances' and hence reflected a consensus at the Conference, was without any basis in the drafting history of Article 1, though. The episode also shows that they had apparently decided to abandon the ideas they had earlier advocated in preparing for the Diplomatic Conference of 1949, and to forget the (rare) comments the words 'in all circumstances' had actually drawn in the course of the Conference.

Rounding off their comments on common Article 1, the authors state that:

---

92. In later years, the argument against the equality of belligerents would be used by or on behalf of those involved in wars of national liberation. Their contention that the colonial Powers were aggressors and therefore the peoples fighting for self-determination were entitled to disregard any constraints of humanitarian law, met the same counter-argument that this went against the very core of humanity as the basis of that body of law.

In view of the preceding considerations and of the fact that the provisions for the repression of violations have been considerably strengthened, it is evident that Article 1 is no mere stylistic clause, but is deliberately invested with imperative force, and must be obeyed to the letter.

3.1.5   *evaluation*

After all my comments on their comments, it will come as no surprise that I cannot share their enthusiasm for the 'preceding considerations'. In effect, and in marked distinction to the bulk of the Commentary, their comments on Article 1 do not represent a serious attempt to interpret its wording 'to the letter' and with due respect for its drafting history. The comments do provide an, at times rhetorical, *exposé* of the authors' views on the character and 'imperative force' of the Convention as a whole. These views are interesting enough to have deserved their place in the literature on the Convention. They cannot however support the (slightly exaggerated) statement that Article 1 'is deliberately vested with imperative force, and must be obeyed to the letter': that force is inherent in its character as a binding treaty provision but applies solely to its meaning as such, not to interpretations placed upon it without support in history or logic.

In this regard, I note with regret that the procedure the authors chose, of breaking up Article 1 into three bits, left 'all circumstances' dangling in the air, disconnected from 'respect' and 'ensure respect'. In particular, the failure to discuss 'respect in all circumstances' as an undivided whole may have made the authors lose sight of the significance that may be attributed to that expression. In view of the many rules in the Conventions that must be complied with 'in all circumstances' they might have concluded what to me is obvious: that the 'ordinary meaning' of 'respect in all circumstances' is respect under each and every factual condition, whether favourable or adverse: 'for better or for worse'. Put differently, 'respect in all circumstances' means respect where the fortunes of war make compliance especially difficult or where an enemy no longer appears to respect the rules; i.e., 'respect' in the face of arguments of necessity or negative reciprocity.

The outstanding feature of the authors' comments on common Article 1 remains their valuable suggestion concerning the active role third states 'may, and should' play in the promotion of respect for the Conventions. Unfortunately, the manner in which they put forward this idea, as an appendix to a paragraph on other matters, was not conducive to a better understanding, either of the Article or of their comments, and has provided grounds for the erroneous assertion that third states would be legally bound to do so.

3.2   The subsequent Commentaries to the 1949 Conventions

In the 1956 Commentary to the Fourth Convention, the comment on Article 1, although somewhat shorter, has retained its structure and much of its language.[93] The comment on the phrase 'to ensure respect' is completed with a new sentence following after the statement that contracting states 'may, and should, endeavour to bring [a belligerent failing in its obligations] back to an attitude of respect for the Convention'. The added sentence reads as follows:

> The proper working of the system of protection provided by the Convention demands in fact that the Contracting Parties should not be content merely to apply its provisions themselves, but should do everything in their power to ensure that the humanitarian principles underlying the Conventions are applied universally.

This phrase sets forth with even greater clarity the authors' stance on the role of contracting states in promoting respect for the Convention (this time the Fourth). It does not, however, bring out any presumed, previously hidden intention of the authors to introduce a firm legal obligation of this order.

In the paragraph on 'in all circumstances', the non-applicability to 'civil war' is restated in remarkably blunt terms: 'The words "in all circumstances" (...) do not, of course, cover the case of civil war, as the rules to be followed in such conflicts are laid down by the Convention itself, in Article 3.' Forgotten are the days of the Diplomatic Conference, when the opposite was just as strongly suggested as a matter of course.

Then, the statement that whenever one of the conditions of application of the Convention is met, no contracting state can offer any valid pretext 'for not respecting the Convention in its entirety', now is followed by a sentence opening with: 'The words in question also mean' (replacing the earlier 'mean in short'). This suggests that the argument about the irrelevance of assertions concerning the character of the conflict, 'just' or 'unjust' war, or 'aggression' should be regarded as independent of the no-valid-pretext statement. The point is not elucidated, though.

The 1958 Commentary to the Third Convention again offers some changes.[94] In the comment on the phrase 'to ensure respect', the original sentence about the role of third states ('It follows, therefore, ...') has been replaced by:

> This applies to the respect of each individual State for the Convention, but that is not all: in the event of a Power failing to fulfil its obligations, each of the other Contracting Parties (neutral, allied or enemy) should endeavour to bring it back to an attitude of respect for the Convention.

---

93. Commentary IV (English version published in 1958), pp. 15-17.
94. Commentary III (English version published in 1960), pp. 17-18.

Thus, the confusing phrase, 'It follows, therefore', has disappeared, only to be substituted with the hardly clearer 'that is not all': the authors must have been convinced that there was some mysterious link between the two statements. The verb 'may' that preceded 'should' has vanished as well, without being replaced by another term. The reason for this omission is unclear, and so is its effect.

Then, the comment on the phrase 'in all circumstances' is reduced to its bare essentials:

> The words 'in all circumstances' refer to all situations in which the Convention has to be applied and these are defined in Article 2. It is clear, therefore, that the application of the convention does not depend on whether the conflict is just or unjust. Whether or not it is a war of aggression, prisoners of war belonging to either party are entitled to the protection afforded by the Convention.

Strikingly, the notion of 'civil war' is no longer mentioned at all. The no-valid-pretext argument has disappeared too, and, with that, any questions about its relation to the argument concerning just or unjust wars or war of aggression.

The fourth and last Commentary to be published, to the Second Convention, appeared one year later, in 1959. Surprisingly, and without explanation, the comments on Article 1 largely revert to the second, 1956, version, abandoning the modifications introduced in 1958.[95] In the comment on 'to ensure respect' the clause 'may, and should' is reinstated, and while the part on 'in all circumstances' is still silent on 'civil war', the no-valid-pretext argument is back again, with the paragraph on aggression (etc.) following 'also'.

3.3   Conclusions

The paragraphs written by way of comment on Article 1 make interesting reading, though not for the purpose of gaining an insight into the legal significance of Article 1. Their most striking feature is that they are so conspicuously out of line with the comments on the other articles of the Conventions. While the latter comments generally inform the reader about the drafting history of each article, and suggest interpretations in the light thereof as well as of their actual wording, the comments on Article 1 do nothing of the sort. They hardly ever refer to its negotiating history, and the various bits and pieces of its actual text are used as little more than a pretext for a discourse on the character of the Conventions as a whole, as perceived by the authors. Quite peculiar in this respect is the manner in which the clauses 'to respect' and 'to ensure respect' are treated completely separately from the phrase 'in all circumstances', thus making us lose sight of the historical and, indeed, intrinsic link between the phrases.

Other intriguing aspects concern the radical departure from earlier views on the relevance of Article 1 for internal armed conflict, and the suggestion that the phrase

---

95. Commentary II (English version published in 1960), pp. 24-26.

'in all circumstances' was designed to forestall arguments about the non-applicability of the Conventions in an unjust war or a war of aggression. As noted above, the latter suggestion did not reflect international consensus at the time. We will moreover see later that the international community subsequently distanced itself from both of these viewpoints.

Our comparison of the comments on Article 1 in the successive Commentaries showed up several variations in the detail of their language. For the most part, the changes plausibly were occasioned by considerations of economy, in conformity with a general trend to reduce in the later Commentaries, the space allotted to the common articles. I have found no indication that any of the omissions or amendments represented a real change of opinion.

I may repeat my conviction that the authors never meant to suggest that contracting states not party to an armed conflict are under an affirmative international legal obligation to 'ensure' that belligerent parties respect the Conventions. And once again, even had they wished to do so, their suggestion could not have carried that effect.

Finally, I doubt that even at the time of writing the Commentary, the authors entertained such high expectations about the Conventions as their comments suggest: their long acquaintance with the actuality of armed conflict must have given them some scepticism on this score.[96] Perhaps, therefore, we should understand, and appreciate, their show of optimism about the intrinsic force of Article 1 as an attempt to exorcise the evil spirits constantly threatening the respect for humanitarian standards.

4.   THE GARDENING CONTINUES: FROM THE TEHERAN CONFERENCE TO THE ICRC COMMENTARY ON THE PROTOCOLS OF 1977

When it comes to evil spirits, there were two phenomena in the post-1949 period that could qualify as especially threatening to fundamental notions of humanitarian law. One was the build-up of nuclear armaments; the other, the so-called wars of national liberation waged in a succession of territories under colonial domination. In either case, the fate of the civilian population was at stake: theoretically (and fortunately only so, after the overwhelming impact of Hiroshima and Nagasaki) in the case of nuclear weapons, on account of the counter-city strategy as a method of deterrence; very much in a practical sense in the liberation wars, by the widespread recourse to guerrilla tactics in populated areas. A related cause of concern in the latter wars was the situation of captured guerrilla fighters: should these 'irregular' fighters be regarded, or at least treated, as prisoners of war, or could they be dealt with as criminals and terrorists?

---

96. When I got to know Claude Pilloud in the early 1970s, he was as firmly dedicated as ever to the cause of humanitarian law. At the same time, he was only too well aware of the tremendous difficulties attending its enforcement.

In the Red Cross world, indiscriminate (nuclear or guerrilla) warfare and the risks it poses to the civilian population provoked a long series of resolutions speaking out against such forms of warfare. One of these, Resolution XXVIII of the XXth International Red Cross Conference (Vienna, 1965), stands out as a milestone in the development of international humanitarian law. Considering 'that indiscriminate warfare constitutes a danger to the civilian population and the future of civilization', the Resolution 'solemnly declares' four principles for the protection of the civilian population, to be heeded by 'all Governments and other authorities responsible for action in armed conflicts'. The fourth and last 'principle' is 'that the general principles of the Law of War apply to nuclear and similar weapons'. While the latter statement of principle was of interest with a view to the possibility of nuclear 'mega-war', the phrase referring to 'all Governments and other authorities responsible for action in armed conflicts' was of more immediate practical effect in that it implied the application of the principles for the protection of civilians against the hazards of war in all armed conflicts, be they international or internal, conventional or guerrilla.[97]

The other side of the matter, the fate of captured guerrilla fighters, led to a characteristically pragmatic reaction of the ICRC. Focussing on the protection of such detainees, it sought access to all places of detention, reported its findings to the responsible governments and authorities, and, as appropriate, suggested improvements in their treatment.[98] At the same time, not wishing to get entangled in the political aspects of the wars of national liberation, it refrained from taking a public stand on the controversial issue of recognition of the guerrilla fighters as combatants entitled to prisoner of war status as provided in the Third Convention of 1949.

Precisely such claims were formulated with increasing insistence in other quarters, notably in the Third World. While the stance of these countries was first and foremost political, there could be no doubt that, even with the recent Geneva Conventions of 1949, the existing treaty law of armed conflict was inadequate to cope with this as with the many other problems arising out of the modern forms of warfare. It was equally clear that the force of political developments in the 1950s and 1960s made the need to take up these problems all that more urgent.

4.1   A self-appointed assistant gardener: Sean MacBride

In the wake of the International Red Cross Conference of 1965, another push in the same direction came from the International Conference on Human Rights, held in 1968 in Teheran. Just before it closed its doors, it adopted a resolution on 'human rights in armed conflicts' calling for renewed efforts to improve the applicable law. Since the resolution contains language of some relevance to the idea of Article 1 as a useful device for the promotion of compliance with the rules of international

---

97. Schindler and Toman, op. cit n. 9, p. 259; *Handbook*, op. cit. n. 22, at p. 773.

98. Michel Veuthey, *Guérilla et droit humanitaire* (Geneva, Institut Henry-Dunant 1976) pp. 245 et seq.

humanitarian law, it deserves to be dealt with here. For its drafting history, I have relied to a large extent on a study by Keith Suter on international law aspects of guerrilla warfare.[99] His study clearly shows the all-important role played in this process by the rightly famous Irish human rights lawyer and activist, Sean MacBride.

In the 1960s, Sean MacBride had assumed the function of Secretary-General of the International Commission of Jurists, a Geneva-based non-governmental human rights organization with ramifications all over the world. His function gave MacBride a leading role in the organization of the Teheran Conference. In the course of the work he became convinced that the Conference could provide a much desired opportunity to take up outstanding issues of humanitarian law, or, in his terminology, 'human rights in armed conflict', notably the need to protect civilian populations against the vagaries of modern warfare. This despite the fact that matters of humanitarian law strictly speaking did not belong to the realm of human rights and, with that, of the International Commission of Jurists: at the time, the difference, nay, the distance between the two disciplines was felt strongly in many quarters. Fortunately, the close contacts between ICRC functionaries such as Claude Pilloud and a man like Sean MacBride (not by any means an 'authorized gardener' of the Geneva Conventions) did not noticeably suffer from such, in retrospect, rather academic considerations.

From 1965 MacBride tested out his ideas on various occasions. Of particular relevance to the matter of common Article 1 was the address he gave in 1967 at a distinguished international gathering.[100] His subject was 'The Strengthening of International Machinery for the Protection of Human Rights', and he opened his address with a list of what he regarded as the main types of human rights violations. His list included, first and foremost, 'massive but temporary wholesale violations of human rights in international armed conflicts'; and secondly, such violations in internal conflicts. In that context he raised this question:

> Has the time not come, when it would be desirable, that whenever an internal conflict or disturbance arises in any part of the world the Secretary-General of the UN, or some other UN authority, should specifically and unequivocally bring to the notice of the belligerents the provisions of the 'law of nations' as elaborated by the Hague and Geneva Conventions as well as the provisions of the Universal Declaration of Human Rights? In cases where the belligerents are receiving active support from outside states, these states should also be requested to use their best endeavour to ensure the proper application of these minimal humanitarian rules. They should be reminded that by Article 1 of the Geneva Conventions they have bound themselves not only to respect the conventions themselves but to ensure their respect in all

---

99. K.D. Suter, *An International Law of Guerrilla Warfare* (New York, St. Martin's press 1984). Chapter 2, 'Creating the issue: the 1968 United Nations Human Rights Conference and Non Governmental Organizations,' provides detailed information about Sean Mac Bride's authorship of the resolution.

100. The Nobel symposium on 'International Protection of Human Rights', Oslo, September 1967; Suter, ibid., pp. 26, 27.

circumstances. If a procedure of this nature were adopted it would minimize some of the brutality which is so prevalent in internal conflicts; it would be essential that this machinery should operate automatically wherever an internal conflict is anticipated.

Note that with respect to internal armed conflict, MacBride identified as the applicable 'law of nations', besides the complete 1949 Geneva Conventions, the Hague Convention of 1899/1907 on the law of land warfare and, indeed, the Universal Declaration of Human Rights. In the next breath he even adds 'that the spirit and terms [of this Declaration], which appears to be gaining authoritative recognition as a code binding on all nations under international law, would clearly support the principles discussed above'. And all this at a time when common Article 3 was the only humanitarian law provision formally applicable to internal armed conflicts and states more often than not treated these as their internal affairs regardless! Speaking as he did, MacBride showed himself to be much more of a human rights activist than a conventional lawyer.

Equally worthy of note is how, with a view to the promotion of respect for humanitarian law in internal armed conflict, MacBride attributes roles to the United Nations as well as to states actively supporting a party to the conflict. With respect to that specific category of states, he refers to Article 1 of the Geneva Conventions, by which they 'have bound themselves ... to ensure [respect for the Conventions] in all circumstances'. Of interest is his suggestion that a reminder of the content and purport of Article 1 might induce these 'actively supporting' states to 'use their best endeavour to ensure the proper application' of the 'minimal' [sic!] humanitarian rules embodied in the above-mentioned instruments. The restriction to states in an active supporting mode, which does not follow from the text of Article 1, may have stemmed from the realistic consideration that those states might be more likely than others to assume such a role. Another point of note is MacBride's total disregard for the assertion in the ICRC Commentary that Article 1 lacked effect in situations of internal armed conflict.

An NGO Human Rights Conference, held in Geneva in January 1968 with MacBride in the chair, provided one more testing ground for his ideas. The Conference concluded, *inter alia,* that 'Governments and the United Nations, together, must ensure that [the Geneva Conventions] are known to all and respected in all circumstances'.[101] This was a very vague formulation, and the reference to 'Governments' even suggested a lack of awareness that with the Conventions of 1949, respect of common Article 3 had become an obligation (whether of law or fact) for all the parties to an internal conflict, and not for the incumbent government alone. However, while the quoted text is open to such criticisms, the event may have provided the requisite backing and encouragement for Sean MacBride to introduce his ideas at the Teheran Conference.

---

101. Suter, op. cit. n. 99, pp. 27-28.

4.2   The Teheran Conference on Human Rights, 1968

The Human Rights Conference opened in Teheran on 22 April 1968, and in the weeks that followed it worked its way through a long series of draft resolutions on numerous aspects of human rights in the world. Late in the proceedings, on 5 May, a first draft for a resolution on 'human rights in armed conflicts' was officially distributed.[102] With some amendments[103] it was then introduced on 9 May, at the 13th and last session of the Second Committee – really in the nick of time.[104] Speaking for the sponsors (and, we may assume, for Sean MacBride as the *auctor intellectualis* behind the draft resolution), Mr Shahabuddin (India) pointed out that:

> The purpose was to draw the attention of the international community to the inadequate implementation of the existing humanitarian international conventions and rules in armed conflicts and to study the need for additional conventions in that field or for revising existing conventions, so as to ensure the better protection of civilians, prisoners and combatants in all armed conflicts and the prohibition and limitation of the use of certain methods and means of warfare.

With regard to the need to modernize the code of warfare embodied in the Hague Conventions, if only in the light of the development of chemical and other weapons of mass destruction, Mr Shahabuddin correctly pointed to the absurd situation that 'the most recent codification' of that body of law dated from 1907. As he reminded his audience: 'The Hague Conventions of 1899 and 1907 had, indeed, envisaged the drawing up of "a more complete code of the laws of war," but that code had not yet seen the light of day.'[105]

With respect to the problems of contemporary, non-conventional warfare, he felt that the increasing exposure of civilian populations to 'the dangers and consequences of hostilities' led to a need for 'up-to-date and comprehensive international safeguards'. Improved safeguards were equally necessary for 'other victims of armed conflicts', and notably 'freedom-fighters', who were subjected to 'torture and execution ... at the hands of colonial and racist regimes', whereas in the eyes of the sponsors of the draft resolution they 'should be treated as prisoners-of-war or political prisoners'.

---

102. A/CONF.32/C.2/L.45.

103. A/CONF.32/C.2/L.45/Rev.1; sponsors: Czechoslovakia, India, Jamaica, Uganda, United Arab Republic.

104. A/CONF.32/C.2/SR.13.

105. The phrase, 'a more complete code of the laws of war', is found at the outset of the so-called Martens clause, a preambular paragraph in the 1907 Convention which reads as follows: 'Until a more complete code of the laws of war has been issued, the high contracting Parties deem it expedient to declare that, in cases not included in the Regulations adopted by them, the inhabitants and the belligerents remain under the protection and the rule of the principles of the law of nations, as they result from the usages established among civilized peoples, from the laws of humanity, and the dictates of the public conscience.'

To effectuate this ambitious agenda, the sponsors proposed a complex procedure, with the General Assembly being 'requested to invite the Secretary-General to set up a committee of experts to study the problem in consultation with the International Committee of the Red Cross'. Member States should be reminded of 'the existing conventions and rules of international law on the subject in question and they should be urged to respect them'. And to round it all off, 'the United Nations, which represented the collective conscience of mankind, should seek a solution of the problem' – surely a remarkable expression of confidence in that body?

With some amendments (to meet concerns of the Swiss delegate relative to the independent position of the ICRC) but without further debate on the merits, the Committee adopted the draft resolution by 53 votes to none, with one abstention. Three days later, on 12 May, the 25th plenary session of the Conference without any discussion adopted Resolution XXIII, by 67 votes to none, with two abstentions.[106]

Mr Shahabuddin, it may be noted, had not had much to say about common Article 1 and its possible implications for a state not involved in an armed conflict, even one actively supporting a party to the conflict. The one and only phrase in his introduction that may be read as linked to that issue was his suggestion that states should be reminded of the existing rules of humanitarian law and 'should be urged to respect them'. In contrast, Resolution XXIII contains a preambular paragraph which has a direct bearing on our question. In this (ninth) paragraph the Conference notes that:

> States parties to the Red Cross Geneva Conventions sometimes fail to appreciate their responsibility to take steps to ensure the respect of these humanitarian rules in all circumstances by other States, even if they are not themselves directly involved in an armed conflict.

I do not know who drafted this paragraph; the records of the Conference shed no light on this issue, and Keith Suter is silent on the subject. I can only comment that, like the earlier utterances of Sean MacBride, this text is far from suggesting that States Parties to the 1949 Conventions are under a firm legal obligation to ensure respect for their provisions by other states. 'Fail to appreciate', 'responsibility' instead of duty, 'take steps': these are all very cautious formulations. Even so, the text does provide a useful reminder that states not directly involved in an armed conflict are nonetheless entitled to 'take steps to ensure' that their colleagues respect the rules they voluntarily accepted as law.

---

106. Res. XXIII on 'Human Rights in Armed Conflicts'; A/CONF.32/41, Final Act p.18.

4.3   **Impact of Resolution XXIII**

Without any doubt, Sean MacBride has been completely serious in his attempts to enhance the role of third states in promoting belligerent parties' respect of humanitarian law. Yet neither he himself in his various utterances on the subject, nor Resolution XXIII of the Teheran Conference, expressed that idea in terms of a legal obligation. Obviously, neither he nor those other persons who took part in the drafting of the resolution, sought to formulate a rule of law. Their aim was, rather, to win support for the political idea of third-party promotion of human rights in a setting of armed conflict.

The Teheran Conference was an event organised by the United Nations and with state representatives as the main actors. It thus provided the first occasion for states to elucidate their views on the right interpretation of common Article 1, notably of the clause 'to ensure respect in all circumstances'. The conclusion must be that they did not: they accepted without debate a text that was so weak as to be almost meaningless. But then, at the time, the matter of 'human rights in armed conflicts' was a human rights subject only in name, and the participants at the Conference may not all have been aware of the various possible interpretations of Article 1. Most of them, in other words, were unqualified as 'gardeners' of the Geneva Conventions, and their apparent failure to give attention to a matter that did not really fall within their field of expertise cannot be held against them.

The fact remains that the Teheran Conference did include in the preamble to resolution XXIII, a paragraph reminding 'States parties to the Red Cross Geneva Conventions' of their occasional failure to appreciate their responsibility to 'take steps to ensure the respect of these humanitarian rules in all circumstances by other States'. With a bit of good will, this paragraph may be said to reflect the ICRC commentators' views on the role of third states, which 'may and should' take such steps in the event of serious violations of humanitarian law by warring parties.

Although of limited significance for our understanding of common Article 1, Resolution XXIII has been remarkably successful in its substantive demands. On 19 December 1968, the UN General Assembly adopted Resolution 2444 (XXIII) inviting the Secretary-General, 'in consultation with' the ICRC and 'other appropriate international organizations', to study 'steps which could be taken to secure the better application' of humanitarian law in all armed conflicts, as well as the need for additional legal instruments 'to ensure the better protection of civilians, prisoners and combatants in all armed conflicts and the prohibition and limitation of the use of certain methods and means of warfare.' Within ten years, a diplomatic conference adopted the two 1977 Protocols Additional to the 1949 Geneva Conventions on the protection of war victims;[107] and soon thereafter, in

---

107. Protocol I Relating to the Protection of Victims of International Armed Conflicts, 1125 *UNTS* (1979) 3 (Roberts and Guelff, op. cit. n. 3, p. 387); Protocol II Relating to the Protection of Victims of Non-International Armed Conflicts, 1125 *UNTS* (1979) 609 (Roberts and Guelff, op. cit. n. 3, p. 447).

1980, a UN conference adopted a convention that set limits to the use of certain conventional weapons.[108]

While the substantive *desiderata* of the Teheran resolution thus were rapidly fulfilled, the same was not true for the procedural element it contained. In effect, General Assembly Resolution 2444 (XXIII) did not reiterate the complaint in the preamble of the Teheran resolution about states' failure to appreciate their responsibility to react to other states' encroachments of humanitarian law. At best, the invitation to the Secretary-General to study steps conducive to a more faithful implementation of existing humanitarian rules could be considered as including, or at any rate as not excluding, a possible constructive role in this sphere for states not themselves directly involved in an armed conflict.

4.4   A short story: The Additional Protocols of 1977

The next opportunity for states to shed light in a collective setting on what they regarded as the right interpretation of common Article 1 came with the Diplomatic Conference on the Reaffirmation and Development of International Humanitarian Law, which met at Geneva in four yearly sessions from 1974 to 1977.[109] Would they grasp it this time?

Draft Additional Protocol I, as prepared by the ICRC,[110] did not contain a provision repeating the language of common Article 1 of 1949.[111] Instead, draft Article 1 specified that the Protocol would be supplementary to the Geneva

---

108. Convention on Prohibitions or Restrictions on the Use of Certain Conventional Weapons Which May be Deemed to be Excessively Injurious or to Have Indiscriminate Effects, with annexed Protocols on Non-Detectable Fragments (Protocol I), Prohibitions or Restrictions on the Use of Mines, Booby-Traps and Other Devices (Protocol II) and Prohibitions or Restrictions on the Use of Incendiary Weapons (Protocol III), adopted 10 October 1980; 1342 *UNTS* (1980) 137 (Roberts and Guelff, op. cit. n. 3, p. 471).

109. Its Official Records (hereinafter: Records), in 16 volumes, were published by the Swiss Federal Political Department in 1978. More readily accessible sources to the same material are Howard S. Levie, *Protection of War Victims: Protocol I to the 1949 Geneva Conventions*, Vols. I-IV (Dobbs Ferry, NY, Oceana Publ. 1979-1981) with Supplement (Dobbs Ferry NY, Oceana Publ. 1985); and, by the same author, *The Law of Non-International Armed Conflict, Protocol II to the 1949 Geneva Conventions* (Dordrecht, Nijhoff 1987).

110. Records, Vol. I Part III, pp. 3 et seq.

111. Explaining this omission, Antoine Martin said that most of the experts the ICRC had consulted had seen no need to reaffirm the general principles common to the Geneva Conventions, or common Article 1 in particular. Meeting of Committee I, 15 March 1974 (CDDH/SR.6), para. 28. On the preparatory phase and in particular the two sessions of the Conference of Government Experts (1971, 1972), see F. Kalshoven, 'Reaffirmation and development of international humanitarian law applicable in armed conflicts: the Conference of Government Experts, 24 May-12 June 1971', 2 *NYIL* (1971) pp. 68-90, and F. Kalshoven, 'Reaffirmation and development of international humanitarian law applicable in armed conflicts: the Conference of Government Experts (second session), 3 May-2 June 1972', 3 *NYIL* (1972) pp. 18-61. On the first session of the Diplomatic Conference, see F. Kalshoven, 'Reaffirmation and development of international humanitarian law applicable in armed conflicts: the first session of the diplomatic conference, Geneva, 20 February-29 March 1974', 5 *NYIL* (1974) pp. 3-34.

Conventions, and defined its scope of application by means of a reference to Article 2 common to the Conventions of 1949.[112] This simple way out of the question of scope was not to the liking of numerous delegations, notably from the Third World and the Soviet bloc, who wanted to extend the scope with wars of national liberation, as properly belonging in the category of international armed conflicts. Several amendments to add to draft Article 1 language to that effect were tabled in March 1974, at the very outset of the discussions in Committee I on the common articles.[113]

Another amendment, submitted at the same time by a handful of delegations, proposed to substitute draft Article 1 with a text in three paragraphs, the first of which reiterated the text of common Article 1 of 1949. The second, like the ICRC draft, defined the scope of the Protocol by referring to Article 2 of 1949, and the third contained a modernised version of the Martens clause.[114]

In the course of the ensuing long, difficult and occasionally bitter debate about the character of wars of national liberation, colonialism, humanitarian law, *ius in bello* versus *ius ad bellum*, some few representatives found occasion to sneak in a word in favour of the proposal to reiterate the text of common Article 1 in the opening Article of the Protocol, but without commenting on its meaning.[115]

Two other delegates actually offered comments on the merits of the proposal. Speaking for the United Kingdom (a co-sponsor of the amendment), Colonel G.I.A.D. Draper drew attention to the words 'undertake to respect and to ensure respect for' and 'in all circumstances', which 'in view of their importance, ... had been taken bodily from Article 1 common to all four Conventions'.[116] He did not elaborate on the importance of the quoted words. The other delegate, Ambassador

---

112. 'The present Protocol, which supplements the Geneva Conventions of August 12, 1949, for the Protection of War Victims, shall apply in the situations referred to in Article 2 common to these Conventions.'

113. One, CDDH/I/5, sponsored by Algeria, Czechoslovakia, the German Democratic Republic, Hungary, Poland, the Soviet Union and Tanzania, proposed to include 'armed conflicts where peoples fight against colonial and alien domination and against racist regimes' among the international armed conflicts. The other, CDDH/I/11, sponsored by Algeria, Australia, Cameroon, Egypt, Ivory Coast, Kuwait, Libya, Nigeria, Norway, Pakistan, Sudan, Syria, Democratic Yemen, Yugoslavia and Zaire, sought the same result with respect to 'armed struggles waged by peoples in the exercise of their right of self-determination, as enshrined in the Charter of the United Nations and defined by the Declaration on Principles of International Law concerning Friendly Relations and Co-operation among States in accordance with the Charter of the United Nations'. Variations on the same theme were subsequently presented in rapid succession by various groups of delegations, ultimately resulting in a merger of the two main ideas.

114. CDDH/I/12 and Corr.1 and Add.1, 8 March 1974, sponsors: Argentina, Austria, Belgium, the Federal Republic of Germany, Italy, the Netherlands, Pakistan, and the United Kingdom.

115. Meeting of Committee I, 11 March 1974 (CDDH/I/SR.3), para. 11: Mr De Breucker (Belgium): 'Paragraph 1 of amendment CDDH/I/12 and Add.1 had been taken from the Geneva Conventions'; para. 31: Mr Cristescu (Romania) 'considered that paragraph 1 of proposed amendment CDDH/I/12 and Add.1 was acceptable (...)'. Meeting of Committee I, 15 March 1974 (CDDH/I/SR.6), para. 24: Mr Obradović 'appreciated the value of paragraphs 1 and 3 of amendment CDDH/I/12 and Add.1 and Corr 1' (...).

116. Meeting of Committee I, 12 March 1974 (CDDH/I/SR.4), para. 26.

B. Akporode Clark of Nigeria, stated that Article 1 'broke new ground in 1949 by introducing the idea of unilateral obligation not subject to reciprocity: from that point of view, paragraph 1 [of the proposed amendment], which reaffirmed already recognized principles, was acceptable.'[117]

Ambassador Clark has remained the only participant at the Diplomatic Conference of 1974-1977 to actually give an interpretation of common Article 1 of 1949 and, with that, of the phrase 'respect and ensure respect in all circumstances' which ultimately found its place in Protocol I as the opening paragraph of Article 1, on 'general principles and scope of application'. Note that he made no mention of the suggestion that Article 1 might (also) imply a role for third states not involved in an armed conflict. I also note, with pleasure, that he interpreted Article 1 as reflecting the non-reciprocal character of the obligations arising out of the Conventions; and, with some regret, that he believed this to have come about in 1949, whereas this interpretation of 'respect in all circumstances' had been given already in 1929 (and been largely forgotten by 1949).

Two things stand out from the above account of the drafting history of Article 1, paragraph 1, of Protocol I. One, the Diplomatic Conference incontestably reaffirmed by its vote the terms of Article 1 of 1949, now also incorporated in the Protocol. Two, the Conference equally plainly failed utterly in fulfilling the expectation that it might shed light on the interpretation of these terms. Specifically, there was not a single reference to the suggested implications for third states; and the only real comment on the meaning of the text reverted to an interpretation of 'respect in all circumstances' that dated back to 1929 rather than 1949. There is, in sum, almost nothing in the drafting history of Article 1, paragraph 1, that could be relied upon one way or another in explaining the meaning of its text.

Another element of the drafting history of Protocol I has a bearing on an entirely different matter. As related earlier, the authors of the comments on common Article 1 contended that the phrase 'in all circumstances' made the application of the Conventions independent of the character of the conflict: 'Whether a war is 'just' or 'unjust', whether it is a war of aggression or of resistance to aggression, the protection and care due to [the persons protected under the Conventions] are in no way affected.'[118] In plain contrast with this contention, the debate at the Diplomatic Conference about the scope of application of Protocol I and, indeed, of the 1949 Conventions, largely turned precisely on these notions of 'just' or 'unjust' war, aggression or resistance, mainly in relation to wars of national liberation (and the war in Vietnam in particular). And while many delegates did support the thesis that even in such wars, the rules of humanitarian law must be applied by all sides regardless of the cause of the war, many others held the opposite view, maintaining that a people fighting for its liberation from colonial oppression could not be bound to respect rules that would hamper it in the conduct of its just war.

---

117. Ibid., para. 35.
118. Text quoted in section 3.1.4, *supra*.

In the end, it proved necessary to include in the Preamble to Protocol I a paragraph which excludes any argument that the Protocol or the 1949 Conventions 'can be construed as legitimizing or authorizing any act of aggression or any other use of force inconsistent with the Charter of the United Nations'; and another which reaffirms, the other way round, that their provisions 'must be fully applied in all circumstances to all persons protected by these instruments, without any adverse distinction based on the nature or origin of the armed conflict or on the causes espoused by or attributed to the Parties to the conflict'. The need to include this language effectively defeats the argument that common Article 1 once and for all had settled these issues.

One last point: while the text of common Article 1 of 1949 was incorporated, and thereby reaffirmed, in Protocol I on international armed conflicts, no such thing happened with Protocol II on internal armed conflicts. It is far from me to suggest that, as a consequence, the principle of 'respect and ensuring respect in all circumstances' does not apply in the situations of armed conflict that fall within the terms of that Protocol. Yet, the fact stands out that the delegates who negotiated Protocol II shied away from incorporating the principle in this first humanitarian law treaty written exclusively for situations of internal armed conflict. Their silence finally does away with the initial expectation of Pilloud and consorts, that the undertaking to 'ensure respect in all circumstances' would prove an important instrument in promoting the cause of humanitarian law in situations of internal armed conflict by binding the insurgents to its terms – an expectation the authors of the comments on Article 1 of 1949 had given up earlier.

The silence also stands in marked contrast to Resolution XXIII of the Teheran Conference, with its preambular reminder of states' 'responsibility to take steps to ensure the respect of [the Geneva Conventions] in all circumstances by other States (…)'. Fortunately, many states not directly involved in internal conflicts feel no qualms about gently prodding the parties to respect the precepts of humanitarian law, in spite of the stern warning in Article 3 of Protocol II against any attempt at 'intervening, directly or indirectly, for any reason whatever, in the armed conflict or in the internal or external affairs of the High Contracting Party in the territory of which that conflict occurs'.

In sum, although the Diplomatic Conference of 1974-1977 adopted Article 1, paragraph 1, of Protocol I and in so doing technically may be said to have 'reaffirmed' the text of common Article 1, it did so only in the context of international armed conflicts and even then in such a nonchalant fashion that the participating states cannot seriously be said to have contributed to the strength and healthy development of the 'measly little sprig' of 1949.

4.5   The ICRC Commentary on the Protocols of 1977

It took the ICRC nearly a decade to produce its Commentary on the Protocols of 1977: the original French version appeared in 1986, the English translation in 1987. Alexandre Hay, its then President, spoke in his Foreword with satisfaction of 'the completion of a long task which is of particular importance to the ICRC'.[119] The outcome of this 'long task' was certainly impressive: a volume of over 1,500 closely printed pages: not much less than the total number of pages of the Commentaries on the four Conventions of 1949. Yet these Conventions together counted 429 articles (plus annexes), as compared to the 130 articles (plus annexes) of the Protocols.

How did the ICRC see its role, and that of its staff members who wrote the comments? Did it believe, as on the earlier occasion, that '[a]lthough published by the International Committee, the Commentary is the personal work of its authors' and 'only the participant States are qualified, through consultation between themselves, to give an official and, as it were, authentic interpretation' of the Conventions?[120] As if in response to this question, the Foreword states that the ICRC 'allowed the authors their academic freedom, considering the Commentary above all as a scholarly work, and not as a work to disseminate the views of the ICRC'.[121] Academic freedom, scholarly work, no dissemination of ICRC views: it sounds almost too good to be true.

In actual fact, the authors were staff members; every bit of text was discussed in a reading committee of staff members; a second version was examined by a small editing staff (again, staff members), and 'then discussed with the author so that the substance – and to some extent, the form – could be harmonized with the other texts so as to ensure the greatest possible uniformity of the work'. It was then for the author 'to draft a third version of the text, which is in principle that contained in the work'.[122] After such a thorough treatment, the final text could be expected to be uniform in form as well as substance, i.e., doctrine. So much for academic freedom, one is inclined to say.

Official interpretation left to states, no dissemination of ICRC views? The first point is not mentioned at all, the second largely contradicted by the explanation in the Foreword that the ICRC had decided to publish the Commentary 'because it is conscious of its role as a guardian of international humanitarian law and is convinced of the importance of this work for those entrusted with implementing the Protocols or ensuring that they are widely disseminated, particularly among government and academic circles, and in Red Cross and Red Crescent circles'. An Editors' note adds that the Commentary is based, beside the work of the Diplomatic Conference, on 'other preparatory work'.[123] Much of that was of its own making, though on the basis of consultations with government and other experts.[124] And as regards the influence of the non-ICRC experts, the General

---

119. Commentary on the Additional Protocols of 8 June 1977 to the Geneva Conventions of 12 August 1949, English version, p. xiii.

120. Text at n. 87 *supra*.

121. *Supra* n. 119.

122. Editors' note, p. xxvi.

123. Ibid., p. xxv.

124. Apart from the Conference of Government Experts, referred to *supra* in n. 111, there had also been various private meetings and discussions with Red Cross experts.

Introduction signed by Jean Pictet (who had taken over from Claude Pilloud after his untimely death in November 1984) informs us that the draft Protocols the ICRC had drawn up for submission to the Diplomatic Conference:[125]

> ... took into account most of the views given by those consulted, though they did not follow them entirely, as the ICRC could not agree with them on all points. In some cases proposals put forward were contradictory, and it was necessary to make a choice. In other cases, when the requirements of the Red Cross so dictated, the ICRC had to take the initiative itself and assume full responsibility. In elaborating the basic texts, the ICRC endeavoured to remain true to the spirit in which it had always sought guarantees for the benefit of victims of conflicts, ever since 1864, as required by humanitarian considerations, but also, in order to be realistic, taking into account military and political constraints.

This description of the final phase in the 'preparatory work' amounts to a surprisingly frank admission of bias in favour of the 'requirements of the Red Cross' and 'humanitarian considerations'. In 'elaborating the basic texts' the ICRC evidently never pictured itself in the role of a rapporteur on the work of the expert meetings – a function which would have required a faithful reflection of all the various shades of opinion voiced by the experts. Not having been asked to act as such, and at a stage of the proceedings where governments still had the final word, it chose to weigh the outcomes of the meetings in the light of its own responsibility as guardian of humanitarian law. In the circumstances, the resultant humanitarian bias could certainly be regarded as justifiable tactics. As the quoted paragraph shows, even after the Conference the authors of the Commentary felt no shade of remorse at this earlier stance: the text breathes satisfaction at a job well done – so much so that one would not be surprised to find that a similar bias in favour of 'humanitarian considerations' governed the process of writing, rewriting, editing and publishing the Commentary as well.

It is not the place here to examine the four corners of the Commentary to find out to what extent this has in fact been the case. For my purposes, a close look at the text of the comments on Article 1, paragraph 4, of Protocol I may suffice.

The authors begin by reiterating the point made by Antoine Martin in the course of the Conference, that the ICRC had not repeated Article 1 in its draft Protocol. In their explanation: 'As the Protocol is subject to the general provisions and principles of the Conventions, by virtue of the fact that it is an instrument additional to the Conventions, this general principle would have applied for the Protocol even if it had not been stated in so many words.'[126] Drawing the consequence from this statement, they add that '[t]he Commentary on Article 1 of the Conventions continues to apply fully, and the reader is referred to it. We will merely reiterate the essential points below, adding a few new elements.'[127]

---

125. *Supra*, n. 119, p. xxxi.
126. Ibid., p. 34: para. 36.
127. Ibid., p. 35: para. 37.

In view of what we found earlier in our reading of the four versions of the Commentary on the Conventions, the interesting question is: which version shall we be referred to: the first one published, because it was the most extensive? Or a later one, because it suited present purposes better?[128] And, of course, what new elements have been added?

Not new is the division of the work into sections: as in the earlier Commentary on the Conventions, the comments are divided over the undertaking to respect, the phrase 'to ensure respect', and the concluding words 'in all circumstances'. Stating that the undertaking to respect merely confirms the rule *pacta sunt servanda*, the authors conclude that 'the import of this paragraph does not lie in the first part'. They add that the term 'undertake', 'which appears only occasionally in the Protocol', is 'a more solemn turn of phrase' than 'shall'[129] thus providing us with an unequivocal confirmation of their view of the text as containing an internationally binding obligation.

The comment on the phrase 'to ensure respect' reiterates that, at first sight, this too might seem to be superfluous. For,[130]

the duty to respect implies that of ensuring respect by civilian and military authorities, the members of the armed forces, and in general, by the civilian population as a whole. This means not only that preparatory measures must be taken to permit the implementation of the Protocol, but also that such implementation should be supervised. In this respect, the phrase 'to ensure respect' essentially anticipates the measures for execution and supervision laid down in Article 80 (*Measures for execution*).

However, there is more to it: 'the phrase "to ensure respect" should also be considered to reflect another aspect, which is described in the Commentary on the Conventions as follows: ...' – and the quotation that follows[131] refers the reader, not to the first-published version but to the third. Why to that one? In effect, it is

---

128. Interestingly, the footnote after the referral to the earlier Commentary does not refer to one or other of its versions but to the paper by Luigi Condorelli and Laurence Boisson de Chazournes, '*Quelques remarques à propos de l'obligation de 'respecter et faire respecter' le droit international humanitaire 'en toutes circumstances*', in C. Swinarski., ed., *Etudes et essais sur le droit international humanitaire et sur les principes de la Croix-Rouge, en l'honneur de Jean Pictet* (Geneva, ICRC, The Hague, Martinus Nijhoff Publishers 1984) pp. 17-35; see also *infra* text at n. 150.

129. Op. cit n. 119, paras. 39, 40.

130. Ibid., p. 41. Article 80 prescribes 'all necessary measures for the execution of [the] obligations under the Conventions and this Protocol', and enjoins 'The High Contracting Parties and the Parties to the conflict' to 'give orders and instructions to ensure observance of the Conventions and this Protocol, and [to] supervise their execution'.

131. 'In the event of a Power failing to fulfil its obligations, each of the other Contracting Parties, (neutral, allied or enemy) should endeavour to bring it back to an attitude of respect for the Convention. The proper working of the system of protection provided by the Convention demands in fact that the States which are parties to it should not be content merely to apply its provisions themselves, but should do everything in their power to ensure that it is respected universally.' Ibid., para. 42.

the only one which does not read 'may and should' but merely 'should', thereby laying extra emphasis on the latter term as the crucial verb defining the role of third states in the promotion of respect for humanitarian law by their colleagues involved in an armed conflict.[132]

Of course, 'should' is not the same as 'shall': it may be a mere admonition, or a weak sort of obligation. As the Commentary explains, the ICRC regards it in the first place as a ground to prod states to take an active part in the promotion of humanitarian law.[133] In the next paragraph, it goes one step further, however, making its intentions clearer:[134]

> Finally, and most importantly, the Diplomatic Conference fully understood and wished to impose this duty on each Party to the Conventions, and therefore reaffirmed it in the Protocol as a general principle, adding in particular to the already existing implementation measures those of Article 7 (*Meetings*) and 89 (*Co-operation*).

It may be evident from the earlier discussion of the work of the Diplomatic Conference that the (incontestable) reiteration and (merely technical) reaffirmation of the text of common Article 1 in Protocol I cannot seriously be claimed to express anything like a full understanding and wish of that Conference with respect to the text they were simply repeating verbatim. There was, moreover, no-one at the Conference who ever ventured to suggest that the text contains a 'duty' for states to do what the ICRC wishes them to do.

The Commentary adds with apparent regret that '[neither] the Diplomatic Conferences which drafted the Conventions and the Protocol, nor these instruments, defined very closely the measures which the Parties to these treaties should take to execute the obligation to "ensure respect" by the other Parties'. other than by means of the examples of Articles 7 and 89.[135] I would have been greatly surprised had this been otherwise, given that no-one at the Conferences of 1949 or 1977 ever discussed the text of the Article in terms even remotely resembling

---

132. See also *supra* section 3.2.

133. Commentary, p. 36, para. 43: 'This interpretation was not contested and it is on this interpretation that the ICRC has taken a number of steps, confidentially or publicly, individually or generally, to encourage States, even those not Party to a conflict, to use their influence or offer their cooperation to ensure respect for humanitarian law. Leaving aside any bilateral or multilateral measures taken by States, which rarely become known, it should be pointed out that the organized international community has frequently and emphatically manifested its concern that humanitarian law should be respected.'

134. Ibid., paras. 44, 45. Arts. 7 and 89, referred to in the quoted text, read as follows: 'Art. 7 – The depositary of this Protocol shall convene a meeting of the High Contracting Parties, at the request of one or more of the said Parties and upon the approval of the majority of the said Parties, to consider general problems concerning the application of the Conventions and of the Protocol.
Art. 89 – In situations of serious violations of the Conventions or of this Protocol, the High Contracting Parties undertake to act, jointly or individually, in co-operation with the United Nations and in conformity with the United Nations Charter.'

135. Commentary, pp. 36-37, para. 46.

the ICRC's interpretation, let alone that they qualified it as an obligation, as the ICRC now openly does, finally letting the cat out of the bag.

Of interest is how the Commentary then goes on to indicate limitations to the actions states may legitimately take to promote respect for humanitarian law by parties to an armed conflict. Since these limitations would apply irrespective of whether the actions are in execution of an obligation or on the basis of a right, they deserve to be quoted here. They are:[136]

> ... those imposed by general international law, particularly the prohibition on the use of force. Even if the United Nations were to take coercive measures involving the use of armed force in order to ensure respect for humanitarian law, the limitation would be that of the very respect due to this law in all circumstances. It suffices to say that whenever such measures are necessary, each Party to humanitarian law instruments should examine the wide range of diplomatic or legal measures which can be taken to ensure respect for that law.

The limitations suggested here on individual or collective activities for the promotion of humanitarian law are very sound advice indeed. One might wish to see an organ like the Security Council heeding it, as the text goes, 'in all circumstances'.

The phrase 'in all circumstances', is next in line for comment.[137] In broad terms, it 'prohibits all Parties from invoking any reason not to respect the Protocol as a whole, whether the reason is of a legal or other nature'. Specifically, questions of 'just' or 'unjust' wars, aggression or self-defence, should not affect the application of the Protocol: 'this type of discrimination is explicitly prohibited by the fifth paragraph of the Preamble'. In a similar vein, 'Any idea of reciprocity should also be discarded, viz., a Party should be prevented from claiming to be exempt from the obligation to respect a particular provision, or the Protocol as a whole, because an adversary had not respected this provision or the Protocol as a whole.'[138] The ICRC commentators make good here what their predecessors in their comments on the 1949 Conventions had neglected to say.

With negative reciprocity thus excluded, 'this does not apply to the type of reciprocity which could be termed "positive", by which the Parties mutually encourage each other to go beyond what is laid down by humanitarian law'. A most ambitious reading, this, of the notion of positive reciprocity: one normally would be satisfied, and regard it as an instance of positive reciprocity, if one party decides

---

136. Ibid.

137. Ibid., p. 37-38, paras. 49-51.

138. The final paragraph of the comments on Art. 1 elaborates the point: 'The prohibition against invoking reciprocity in order to shirk the obligations of humanitarian law is absolute. This applies irrespective of the violation allegedly committed by the adversary. It does not allow the suspension of the application of the law either in part or as a whole, even if this is aimed at obtaining reparations from the adversary or a return to a respect of the law from him. This was confirmed quite unambiguously in Article 60 of the Vienna Convention on the Law of Treaties, which lays down under what conditions a material breach of a treaty can permit its suspension or termination; that article specifically exempts treaties of a humanitarian character.'

to (continue to) respect the law because its adversary is doing the same. But of course, going beyond mere obligation would be even more positive.

Reverting to a more modest mode, the comment recognises that 'the concept of reciprocity on which the conclusion of any treaty is based also applies to the Conventions and the Protocol: they apply between the Parties which have consented to be bound by them'.

4.6   Evaluation

Beginning at the end, the ICRC comments on Article 1, paragraph 1, of Protocol I may be fairly positively assessed, if only because they no longer exude the exuberance that characterized the comments on common Article 1 of 1949. Yet some degree of 'bias in favour of humanitarian considerations' is evident. There is the selective referral to the Commentary on the Third Convention, speaking only of 'should' (legal obligation?) where the earlier and later Commentaries all had 'may and should' (legal permission plus moral exhortation). There is the unexplained shift from 'should' to 'duty', to 'obligation'. And there is the vain attempt to make us believe that the Diplomatic Conference 'fully understood and wished to impose this duty on each Party to the Conventions', whereas the records show that the Conference was hardly aware of the fact that they were reaffirming common Article 1 at all (with everybody's attention going to the hot issue of wars of national liberation).

Much more clearly than in the earlier Commentaries, the authors of the Commentary on the Protocols declare themselves in favour of the thesis that a state's undertaking 'to ensure respect' obliges it to take action against other states that do not fully respect the rules of humanitarian law; and obliges it as a matter of international law, not just as a moral duty. They fail to convince me, though: there is nothing in the published records of the Conference that supports their contention.

Having said that, there are other aspects to the comments which I regard as quite positive: notably, the way the authors handle the matter of reciprocity, and their admonishment about limitations on legitimate actions aiming to promote respect for humanitarian law but involving recourse to force. This last bit in particular should be on the desks of all decision-makers considering such activities, to avoid the effect of human disaster resulting from ill-considered humanitarian action.

This section dealt not only with the ICRC Commentary on the Protocols of 1977: it started out with the Conference of Teheran, and it referred in passing to the Diplomatic Conference of 1974-1977. What about the role of states in clarifying the issue of the true significance of Article 1? Here we can be exceptionally brief: if there was such a role, they have very cleverly hidden it. The very few words government representatives spent on the issue were either too vague or too noncommittal to permit any conclusion, other than that they were thinking of other things at the time. Never did they utter a word in support of the contention that they accepted as a legal obligation, a 'duty' to ensure respect by their colleagues.

5.   HARVESTING – CONCLUDING REMARKS

After the above in-depth discussion of the genesis and fate of common Article 1 up to the late seventies, it is now time to turn briefly to the past two decades, and first, to the dictum of the International Court of Justice in the *Nicaragua* case concerning violations of humanitarian law committed by the *contras* in their protracted armed struggle against the Sandinista Government and the question of responsibility of the United States for those acts.[139]

One problem facing the Court was that the United States in accepting its jurisdiction,had excluded 'disputes arising under a multilateral treaty, unless (1) all parties to the treaty affected by the decision are also parties to the case before the Court, or (2) the United States specially agrees to jurisdiction'.[140] Since the United States had shown no inclination to 'specially agree' to the Court's jurisdiction in this case, the Court saw itself forced to base its argumentation exclusively on customary international law, including such rules of treaty law as it believed it could regard as a reflection of customary law.

Among the latter rules the Court found common Articles 3 and 1 of the Geneva Conventions. It held that the rules defined in Article 3, apart from being applicable in internal armed conflicts, 'also constitute a minimum yardstick' for international armed conflicts, as well as being 'rules which, in the Court's opinion, reflect what the Court in 1949 called "elementary considerations of humanity"'[141] – so that it '[found] them applicable to the present dispute, and [was] thus not required to decide what role the United States multilateral treaty reservation might otherwise play in regard to the treaties in question.' Turning next to Article 1, it stated that:[142]

> ... there is an obligation on the United States, in the terms of Article 1 of the Geneva Conventions, to 'respect' the Conventions and even 'to ensure respect' for them 'in all circumstances,' since such an obligation does not derive only from the Conventions themselves, but from the general principles of humanitarian law to which the Conventions merely give specific expression.

From this it concluded that the United States was under 'an obligation not to encourage persons or groups engaged in the conflict in Nicaragua to act in violation of the provisions of Article 3 common to the four 1949 Geneva Conventions ...' (etc.).[143]

Given the US reservation, the Court could not derive this 'obligation not to encourage' from Article 1 as a treaty provision; nor did it say that States Parties

---

139. *Military and Paramilitary Activities in and against Nicaragua (Nicaragua* v. *United States of America)*, Merits, Judgment, *ICJ Rep.* (1986) p. 14.

140. Ibid., as quoted in the Judgment, para. 42; p. 31.

141. Ibid., para. 218, p. 114. The Court referred to its Judgment in *Corfu Channel*, Merits, *ICJ Rep.* (1949) p. 2.

142. *Supra* n. 139 para. 220.

143. Ibid.

to the Conventions are under an obligation to ensure that other states respect their rules of humanitarian law. Yet there is a tendency to read this into its dictum; to my mind, without justification: there is a considerable distance between the negative duty to refrain from encouraging people on your side to disregard the law, and a positive duty to induce people on the other side of the fence to respect the law.

Did the Court perceive in common Article 1 the expression of an existing rule of customary law? The quoted text speaks, rather, of 'the general principles of humanitarian law to which the Conventions merely give specific expression'. One wonders, was the Court referring here to (a special branch of) the 'general principles of law recognized by civilized nations', mentioned in Article 38(c) of its Statute as one of the sources of law it must apply? Textually, this is not at all implausible; after all, virtually all states, and therefore certainly all those that may be regarded as civilized, are parties to the Conventions and thus may be assumed to 'recognize' any 'general principles of humanitarian law' underlying the 'obligation' of Article 1. Yet the Court failed to specify which 'general principles of humanitarian law' might be involved here. In the absence of such elucidation, for instance, in the shape of a catalogue of the relevant principles, its sweeping statement amounts to nothing more than the assertion that Article 1, along with the other provisions of the Geneva Conventions, reflects customary law.

That this assertion is not free from doubt was emphasized already by Judges Roberto Ago and Sir Robert Jennings in their Separate resp. Dissention Opinions. Ago expressed his reluctance 'to be persuaded that any broad identity of content exists between the Geneva Conventions and certain "fundamental general principles of humanitarian law", which, according to the Court, were pre-existent in customary law'.[144] In an equally skeptical vein, Jennings referred to his 'very serious doubts whether [the] conventions could be regarded as embodying customary law'.[145]

The *Nicaragua* Judgment is a typical instance of the Court wanting to see customary law and therefore finding it, without adducing any proof for its finding. Even so, it did not find much: the 'obligation' not to encourage persons or groups engaged in an armed conflict in a neighbouring state to act in violation of the provisions of common Article 3 amounts to little more than a confirmation of the

---

144. Pp. 181, at 184. Ago entertained 'serious reservations with regard to the seeming facility with which the Court – while expressly denying that all the customary rules are identical in content to the rules in the treaties (para. 175) – has nevertheless concluded in respect of certain key matters that there is a virtual identity of content as between customary international law and the law enshrined in certain major multilateral treaties concluded on a universal or regional plane. [Thus, he was] most reluctant to be persuaded that any broad identity of content exists between the Geneva Conventions and certain 'fundamental general principles of humanitarian law', which, according to the Court, were pre-existent in customary law, to which the Conventions "merely give expression" (para. 220) or of which they are at most "in some respects a development" (para. 218).'

145. Pp. 528, at 537. Jennings continued: 'Even the Court's view that the [rules of] common Article 3, laying down a "minimum yardstick" (para. 218) for armed conflicts of a non-international character, are applicable as "elementary considerations of humanity", is not a matter free from difficulty.'

well-established principle of non-intervention – a principle particularly dear to the hearts of Latin Americans, especially in their relations with their big brother in the North. The Court, in other words, did not even get close to affirming the thesis that Article 1 lays upon the states parties to the Geneva Conventions an obligation of what might be termed 'humanitarian intervention'.[146]

The Palestinians and their supporters are international actors who fervently adhere to that thesis. Their argument: by virtue of common Article 1, all states, and particularly those with close relations with Israel, are under an obligation to ensure that Israel respects all the rules of the Fourth Convention relative to military occupation. In support of their contention, they rely squarely on the ICRC Commentaries to the Conventions. Their interest was and is, of course, to see that Israel remains under constant international pressure to relinquish the territory it keeps occupied. Given that interest, they may be forgiven for accepting the ICRC stance as gospel truth.[147]

Of greater, indeed academic, interest are the views developed by Luigi Condorelli and Laurence Boisson de Chazournes in 1984 in their contribution to the volume of studies and essays in honour of Jean Pictet.[148] They too interpreted the comment on common Article 1 in the ICRC Commentaries as the expression of a legal obligation. Regarding it as diplomatically confirmed by the adoption of Resolution XXIII of the 1968 Teheran Conference and again with the vote for Article 1(1) of Protocol I in 1977, they added that, unfortunately, there was no consistent practice of states in applying the Article, and the ICRC frequently appeared reticent in expressly asking for state action on the basis of Article 1.[149] Even so, they saw a solid basis for the conclusion that there exists 'a principle of general international law that obliges all States to "ensure respect" for humanitarian law'.[150] Note that

---

146. An openly critical analysis of the Court's reasoning on the matter of responsibility of the United States for the acts of the *contras* is found in the Judgement of 15 July 1999 of the Appeals Chamber of the International Criminal Tribunal for the Former Yugoslavia, in the *Tadić* case, Part IV, paras. 99-145. Case No. IT-94-1-A, 15 July 1999.

147. In a discussion I had several years ago with representatives of the Palestinian human rights organization, Al Haq, they showed great surprise at my criticism of the ICRC position, and were not really prepared to take it seriously.

148. *Supra* n. 128.

149. Ibid., pp. 26-29.

150. Ibid., p. 29 (my translation). The full text of the paragraph reads as follows: '*On peut conclure que l'impossibilité de rassembler un nombre élevé d'éléments constitutifs de la pratique internationale ne doit pas être mal évaluée. Les quelques éléments fort suggestifs qu'on vient de mettre en lumière, joints à l'absence de contestations concernant la légitimité (et non pas le bien-fondé) des démarches prises par des Etats tiers à un conflit auprès des Parties à celui-ci en vue du respect du droit humanitaire, constituent une base suffisante en l'espèce pour affirmer l'existence d'un principe de droit international général comportant l'obligation pour tous les Etats de 'faire respecter' le droit humanitaire.*

Ce qui a été soutenu précédemment (...) à propos de l'obligation de "respecter" doit alors, à la lumière de ces remarques, être réitéré mutatis mutandis pour ce qui est de l'obligation de "faire respecte". Le principe de droit international général imposant une telle obligation influence de façon marquée le jeu des normes auxquelles elle se réfère. Cette obligation pèse, en effet, sur tous les Etats pour ce qui est du respect du droit humanitaire coutumier par tout autre Etat. Concernant le respect

the authors used this phraseology well before the Court had rendered its Judgment in the *Nicaragua* case; did the Court perhaps borrow the phrase from them?

The authors went on to explain that since each state owes respect of humanitarian law to all other states, every state had a legal interest to require that its colleagues meet their humanitarian obligations; as set forth in the Judgment of the International Court of Justice in the *Barcelona Traction* case, these are obligations *erga omnes*.[151] But beyond this legal interest and, therefore, right of each state, it was also its duty to act in order to obtain due respect of humanitarian law. The authors noted the paucity in the Conventions and Protocol I of means for the implementation of what they indicated as a 'right-duty' ('*droit-devoir*'); reason why they themselves supplied an interesting catalogue of possible ways for states to meet their 'right-duty' under common Article 1. And they concluded that by virtue of Article 1, the humanitarian obligations of states possess specific characteristics that profoundly influence their functioning; characteristics that stem from the categorical nature of these obligations and the interest the international community as a whole has in their respect.[152]

Theodor Meron, writing after the *Nicaragua* Judgment, is reticent about the customary law character of common Article 1.[153] He sees no evidence that 'when the Geneva Conventions were adopted (...) the negotiating states believed that they were codifying an existing principle of law'. Moreover, the occasional subsequent practice of states in appealing to other states to respect the Conventions 'may merely indicate that [they] are complying with their treaty obligation "to ensure respect" for the Conventions' and therefore may provide 'little support for the customary law nature of the norms implicated'.[154]

Then also, 'the reach of the duty "to ensure respect" is not entirely clear'. Meron regards 'the Court's opinion that the United States may not encourage persons or groups engaged in the Nicaraguan conflict to act in violation of common Article

---

des normes humanitaires de caractère strictement conventionnel, l'obligation en question pèse sur l'ensemble des Etats Parties à la convention à l'égard de tout Etat Partie lui aussi à la même convention.

151. Ibid., p. 29. In the words of the authors: '*Par le jeu de l'article 1 (...) l'obligation de respecter le droit humanitaire général rend donc chaque Etat débiteur du respect de ce droit à l'égard de tous les autres. Ceci implique bien évidemment que tout Etat a un intérêt juridique, indépendemmant de sa participation à un conflit déterminé, à exiger que les autres Etats s'acquittent de leurs obligations humanitaires. Autrement dit, ces obligations semblent appartenir à la catégorie des obligations erga omnes auxquelles se réfère en des termes généraux le célèbre obiter dictum de l'arrêt de la Cour internationale de justice concernant* l'affaire de la Barcelona Traction.'

152. Ibid., p. 32: 'L'article *1 des* Conventions de Genève de 1949 *et du* Protocole additionnel I de 1977 *confère aux obligations humanitaires des caractéristiques spécifiques qui en influencent profondément le fonctionnement. Ces caractéristiques trouvent leur source dans la nature particulière qu'imprime aux normes de droit humanitaire le principe grâce auquel les obligations qui en découlent sont inconditionnelles et leur respect intéresse la communauté internationale dans son ensemble.'*

153. *Human Rights and Humanitarian Norms as Customary Law* (Oxford, Clarendon Press 1989).

154. Pp. 28, 30, referring to the Judgment of the ICJ in the *North Sea Continental Shelf Cases, ICJ Rep.* (1969) at p. 43.

3 [as] indisputably correct': this negative duty rests on the 'principles of good faith and of *pacta sunt servanda*'. But apart from that, there is a positive duty:[155]

> ... the fundamental obligation implies that each state must exert efforts to ensure that no violations of the applicable provisions of humanitarian law (i.e.'to respect') are committed, at the very least by third parties controlled by that state.

With the closing part of this sentence, Meron brings the matter back to the *Nicaragua* case and the question of whether the United States 'controlled' the *contras*: not, according to the Court, to the extent necessary to hold the United States responsible for the violations allegedly committed by the *contras*; yet, plausibly, enough to hold that the United States should have exerted efforts to ensure that they did not commit such violations.

It is interesting to juxtapose Meron's views with those of an American judicial body, the Board of Immigration Appeals.[156] Referring to an earlier paper in which Meron had already expressed the same view,[157] the Board begs to differ: 'the negotiating history of Article 1 suggests that the words "to ensure respect" were intended primarily to obligate States to ensure respect of the Convention by its own civilian and military authorities'. Moreover, 'it is doubtful whether Article 1 was intended to impose an affirmative duty on States of the nature argued by the respondent with regard to possible violations of Article 3 by other States, particularly those not under their control'.[158]

So, whereas for Meron the 'affirmative duty' applies 'at the very least' in respect of third parties under a state's control (and therefore, perhaps, also beyond that limit), the Board doubts whether there is such a duty at all, and if so, certainly not with regard to parties not under a state's control. Computing the two opinions, the conclusion may be that the 'affirmative duty' may or may not exist, and if so, only with respect to parties under a state's control.

This brings me to the views I collected over the past years from various personalities involved with matters of international law. First, several legal advisers, when asked whether they regarded common Article 1 as imposing an obligation upon their governments to ensure respect of the Conventions by other states, all answered in the negative. They did however believe that their governments, as parties to the Geneva Conventions, were definitely entitled to appeal to parties to armed conflicts to respect the applicable humanitarian law.

I then asked the same question of Dr Yves Sandoz, top lawyer of the ICRC. Affirming that there was such a legal obligation, he defined its content as the

---

155. Ibid., pp. 30-31.

156. The reference is to the Decision of the Board in the *Medina* case, *supra* n. 4.

157. 'The Geneva Conventions as Customary Law,' in 81 *AJIL* (1987) pp. 348, at 354-355.

158. The Board refers here to the ICRC Commentary on the Fourth Convention, which happens to be the only one of the four Commentaries to state bluntly that '[t]he words 'in all circumstances' which appear in [this Article] do not, of course, cover the case of civil war, as the rules to be followed in such conflicts are laid down by the Convention itself, in Article 3.' See *supra* section 3.2.

'obligation for governments to consider seriously whether there is something they might do in respect of the situation' (not his literal words, but a fair rendering of what he said). An 'obligation to consider' is not a particularly taxing one, to say the least.

I finally discussed the question with Dr Cornelio Sommaruga, President of the ICRC. When I explained my view that no matter what common Article 1 does, it cannot be said to impose upon states a legal obligation to act against other states that fail in their respect of the Conventions, he agreed. He added: 'No legal obligation but a moral one – and that is even more important.'

That opinion I wholeheartedly share. With Dr Sommaruga, I believe that when it comes to reading into Article 1 any effect beyond the sphere of the state's internal affairs, it lies in adding to the state's *right* as a Party to the Conventions to make other states respect their terms, *a moral incentive* or 'obligation' to do so. This duty is not confined to considering ('seriously') whether the state – i.e., the political decision-makers – might undertake something [action] in respect of a situation of apparent disregard of humanitarian law somewhere in the world. It implies that in weighing the admittedly many factors involved in the process of decision making, the moral duty to 'ensure respect' for international humanitarian law carries particular weight: the graver the 'situation of apparent disregard', the heavier the weight of this factor. And this not for political but for 'humanitarian' reasons: the body of international humanitarian law is too precious for the states of this world to suffer its neglect or wilful disregard.

Agreeing with Dr Sommaruga, I also posthumously agree with Frédéric Siordet and Claude Pilloud. True, their statement about the 'other Contracting Parties (neutral, allied or enemy)' who, in the event of a belligerent Power failing in its duty to respect the Conventions, 'may, and should, endeavour to bring it back to an attitude of respect' for the law was written in such a way that their successors at the ICRC could construe it as the expression of an international legal obligation. I am however convinced that what they were urging was a stringent moral duty for all states parties to protect the vulnerable body of humanitarian law the states had themselves erected. I add that in contrast to what they had apparently come to believe, this moral duty obtains as much in respect of internal armed conflicts as of international ones.

The point remains that the primary legal obligation arising from common Article 1 is for States Parties to impose respect for the applicable rules of international humanitarian law, 'in all circumstances', on their armed forces, including armed groups under their control, and on their populations: for the implementation of this obligation they can be held legally responsible. No such legal liability attaches to their moral duty to endeavour to ensure respect by their peers. Since it is their right to do this under the law of treaties, they cannot be reproached for doing so either. But a failure to speak out, to appeal, to urge – in the last resort: to act, by way of humanitarian intervention – can be held against them as a shortcoming in the moral order that underlies the Geneva Conventions and, indeed, the whole of international humanitarian law.

To conclude: If the international community is looking for a suitable 'new millennium pledge', the United Nations might consider the adoption of a solemn, moral 'undertaking to respect and to ensure respect for international humanitarian law in all circumstances'. A combined General Assembly and Security Council resolution carrying this message would represent an unexpectedly valuable fruit of the insignificant seed planted fifty years ago in 1949.

THE SECOND PROTOCOL TO THE 1954 HAGUE CONVENTION FOR THE PROTECTION OF CULTURAL PROPERTY IN THE EVENT OF ARMED CONFLICT[1]

Thomas Desch[2]

1. REASONS FOR AND PROCESS LEADING TO THE SECOND PROTOCOL

1.1 Introduction

On 26 March 1999, the Diplomatic Conference on the Second Protocol to the 1954 Hague Convention for the Protection of Cultural Property in the Event of Armed Conflict (hereinafter, 1954 Convention[3]), held in The Hague from 15 to 26 March 1999, adopted a Second Protocol to that Convention.[4] The reasons leading to the elaboration and adoption of the Second Protocol to the 1954 Hague Convention for the Protection of Cultural Property in the Event of Armed Conflict (hereinafter, Second Protocol) are manifold.

Firstly, armed conflicts that have taken place since the entry into force of the 1954 Convention, such as in Cambodia, the Middle East or the former Yugoslavia, have revealed its deficiencies. In particular, the Convention lacked full application, as most of the armed conflicts have been of a non-international character; furthermore, it lacked proper implementation, as the system of execution of the Convention, which is based on a functioning Protecting Power- and Commissioner General-system, proved to be unworkable in practice; and, finally, it lacked adequate provisions to cope with the extensive and systematic destruction of cultural

---

1. © T. Desch, 1999.

2. Thomas Desch is Head of the Independent Section on International Law in the Federal Ministry of Defence of the Republic of Austria. He was a member of the Austrian delegation to the Diplomatic Conference on the Second Protocol and Chairman of the Working Group on Chapter 2 established by the Conference. The author is grateful to Gregor Schusterschitz of the Austrian Ministry for Foreign Affairs for his valuable suggestions and comments on the final version of this article. The views expressed in this article are those of the author alone and do not commit the Austrian government.

3. 249 *UNTS* (1954) 240; the Convention and its (First) Protocol entered into force on 7 August 1956.

4. See UNESCO Doc. HC/1999/7 as amended by the Plenary of the Diplomatic Conference on 26 March 1999 and as afterwards corrected in close cooperation with the Chairman of the Drafting Committee, text published in 38 *ILM* (1999) pp. 769 et seq.

property during armed conflict, as it contains no mandatory criminal sanctions regime.[5] In particular, the armed conflicts in Croatia and in Bosnia and Herzegovina – where the destruction of cultural property was part of the policy of so-called 'ethnic cleansing' – led to international efforts to revise the 1954 Convention with the goal of improving the protection of cultural property in the event of armed conflict.

The development of international law since the entry into force of the 1954 Convention was another reason for its revision. This included the adoption in 1977 of two Protocols additional to the Geneva Conventions of 1949,[6] the creation in 1993 and 1994 of *ad hoc* international criminal tribunals for the prosecution of persons responsible for serious violations of international humanitarian law committed in the former Yugoslavia[7] and in Rwanda,[8] and the adoption in 1998 of the Statute of the International Criminal Court (ICC).[9] Although these developments were not the main reason for creating a new Protocol, they turned out to be instrumental during the negotiations where these (and other) recent treaty norms were frequently referred to while shaping the new instrument.[10]

Finally, the traditional approach of diplomats and international lawyers to solving problems by creating new law also turned out to be determinative for the review process of the 1954 Convention.

1.2   The review process of the 1954 Convention

The review process of the 1954 Convention commenced in the early-1990s, when the Secretariat of UNESCO – amongst other measures aimed at improving the functioning of the 1954 Convention – invited a consultant to prepare a study analyzing the implementation of the 1954 Convention and proposing steps for improving its relevance to contemporary conditions.[11] The study, published in 1993,

---

5. See E. Clement, 'Some Recent Practical Experience in the Implementation of the 1954 Hague Convention', 3 *International Journal of Cultural Property* (1994) pp. 11 et seq. with further references; T. Desch, 'The Convention for the Protection of Cultural Property in the Event of Armed Conflict and its Revision', 11 *Humanitäres Völkerrecht* (1998) pp. 103 et seq.; J. Hladik, 'The Review Process of the 1954 Hague Convention for the Protection of Cultural Property in the Event of Armed Conflict and its Impact on International Humanitarian Law', 1 *YIHL* (1998) pp. 313 et seq.

6. Protocol Additional to the Geneva Conventions of 12 August 1949 and Relating to the Protection of Victims of International Armed Conflicts (hereinafter, Protocol I), and Protocol Additional to the Geneva Conventions of 12 August 1949 and Relating to the Protection of Victims of Non-International Armed Conflicts (hereinafter, Protocol II), 1125 *UNTS* (1977) 3.

7. See UN SC Res. 808 (1993) and 827 (1993).

8. See UN SC Res. 955 (1994).

9. See UN Doc. A/CONF.183/9, 17 July 1998.

10. See also the fourth paragraph of the Preamble of the Second Protocol.

11. These measures include the publication by UNESCO in 1994 (in French) and in 1996 (in English, together with Dartmouth Publishing Company Limited) of a commentary on the 1954 Convention, written by J. Toman, and the organization in 1995, 1996 and 1997 of regional seminars in cooperation with the ICRC on the protection of cultural property in the event of armed conflict.

attested the 1954 Convention, including its Regulations for the Execution of the Convention and its (first) Protocol (concerning the protection of cultural property exported from occupied territory), to be 'still entirely valid and realistic' and to 'remain fully applicable and relevant to present circumstances', and identified the problem as being essentially 'one of the failure in the application . . . rather than of inherent defects in the international instruments themselves'.[12] The study therefore considered measures for achieving greater recognition, acceptance and application of the Convention to be of utmost priority, and contained appropriate recommendations to the States Parties to the 1954 Convention, to UNESCO, to the United Nations, to states not parties to the Convention as well as to non-governmental organizations.[13] Whereas the focus of the study's conclusions and recommendations was on various practical measures, such as changes in national legislation, preventive measures in peacetime and dissemination of the provisions of the 1954 Convention to military personnel, it also proposed possible amendments of the Convention such as, *inter alia*, to reconsider the definition of cultural property, which was identified as 'rather out-of-date and very imprecise'; to establish 'some appropriate, relatively simple and quick' dispute settlement procedure; to abandon the 'military necessity' exemption; to enlarge the definition of cultural property under special protection to also cover the most important museums, libraries or archive repositories; and to reject the concept of the protection of natural sites within the Convention.[14]

Most of the study's recommendations and proposals, however, were not followed during the review process. The first major deviation from the study's recommendations took place when, following the publication of the study, a group of selected experts, including legal experts and experts in the military field, was formed by the Secretariat of UNESCO, to examine the 1954 Convention in the light of the study. The group held three meetings (in July 1993 in The Hague, in February 1994 in Lauswolt, also in the Netherlands, and, finally, in November/December1994 in Paris). At the second meeting, a small drafting group formulated some written proposals concerning changes to the text of the Convention, the so-called 'Lauswolt-Document'.[15] Already at this juncture it became clear that the review process would focus on creating a new legal instrument instead of considering practical measures to improve the implementation of the existing ones.

On 13 November 1995, the Director General of UNESCO convened a Meeting of the States Parties to the 1954 Convention, only the second since the first such meeting in 1962. It was attended by the representatives of 69 States Parties to the 1954 Convention and by several observers. The meeting adopted a resolution stres-

---

12. P. Boylan, *Review of the Convention for the Protection of Cultural Property in the Event of Armed Conflict (The Hague Convention of 1954)*, (Paris, UNESCO 1993) 1993 p. 7.

13. Ibid., pp. 7-18.

14. Ibid., pp. 16-18.

15. See UNESCO Doc. CLT/95/CONF/009/2.

sing, *inter alia*, the importance of holding a meeting of governmental experts, which would consider all proposals on the improvement of the Convention.[16]

Upon the invitation by UNESCO, this meeting of governmental experts took place from 24-27 March 1997 in Paris. Participation was restricted to 20 States Parties (!), which were selected by the Executive Board from the respective regional groups within UNESCO. The States Parties not selected, among them Austria, could only participate as observers. At this meeting, various proposals to improve the protection of cultural property in armed conflicts were for the first time discussed at the level of governmental experts. Among the items dealt with were the concept of ('imperative' or 'unavoidable') military necessity; measures to safeguard cultural property; the improvement of the special protection regime; the treatment of serious violations of the Convention; the responsibility of states as well as individual criminal responsibility for offences against the Convention; the mutual assistance of states in criminal matters; the application of the 1954 Convention in non-international armed conflicts; and the creation of new institutions to improve the application of and respect for the Convention. The results of this meeting of governmental experts were incorporated in the so-called 'revised Lauswolt-Document'.[17]

The revised Lauswolt-Document, however, still contained some grave deficiencies which made its content fall partly behind the normative standards already achieved in the 1954 Convention. The new formulations of the draft text, for example those concerning state responsibility or individual criminal responsibility, proved to be completely inadequate in light of the norms already existing under customary international law. One of the reasons for these deficiencies lay in the fact that only a few delegations included lawyers, in particular experts in the field of international humanitarian law. The delegations were mainly composed of diplomats and cultural experts. Although the armed forces bear the main responsibility for applying and respecting the core provisions of the 1954 Convention, only five delegations – all of them observer delegations – included a representative of the respective Ministry of Defence. Furthermore, it could be observed that the internal communication of states between the different branches of government concerned with questions of the revision of the Hague Convention (in particular diplomats, cultural experts, international law experts, and military experts) in many cases functioned badly or did not take place at all.

The revised Lauswolt-Document was forwarded, together with a commentary by the UNESCO Secretariat in the form of an information document,[18] to the Third Meeting of the States Parties to the 1954 Convention, which took place in Paris at the invitation of UNESCO on 13 November 1997. This meeting, in which 65 States Parties took part and six states not party to the 1954 Convention participated as observers, allowed comment on the progress achieved up to that point in the

---

16. See the final report of the Second Meeting of the High Contracting Parties to the 1954 Convention, UNESCO Doc. CLT-95/CONF.009/5, Paris, November 1995.

17. See the final report of this meeting of governmental experts, UNESCO Doc. CLT-96/CONF.603/5, Paris, 30 April 1997.

18. UNESCO Doc. CLT-97/CONF.208/2, Paris, October 1997.

review process and on probable future action. The meeting discussed, *inter alia,* the advantage of retaining the concept of military necessity; the creation of individual criminal responsibility for crimes against cultural property; the desirability of revising the special protection regime; and some institutional issues with regard to improving the implementation of the 1954 Convention. It turned out, however, that the opinions on the desirable content of these substantial issues, as well as on the underlying concepts of international law, differed considerably. Austria, among other delegations, therefore pointed out that the present draft provisions were not yet sufficiently final for adoption at a Diplomatic Conference – which was announced to be hosted by the Netherlands in March 1999 – and that a further meeting of governmental experts was required.[19]

Upon request by the Chairman of the Third Meeting of States Parties to the 1954 Convention,[20] Austria agreed to organize a meeting of governmental experts in Vienna in Spring 1998, which this time would be open to participation by all interested states, including non-States Parties, as well as representatives of international governmental and non-governmental organizations. Furthermore, states were encouraged to include in their preparation for the meeting as well as in their delegations representatives of all branches of government dealing with the protection of cultural property in armed conflict.

Representatives of 75 states, among them 14 observer delegations from non-States Parties, as well as representatives of four international governmental and non-governmental organizations, participated in the meeting of governmental experts from 11-13 May 1998 in Vienna.[21] For the first time in the review process, as many as 14 delegations included international humanitarian law or military experts.

The meeting dealt with the following five issues that were identified as the core issues of the ongoing review process: The form of the new instrument, the concept of military necessity, the special protection regime, questions of jurisdiction and responsibility for violations of the 1954 Convention, and institutional matters. With regard to the form of the new instrument, most of the delegations shared the assessment that an optional protocol additional to the 1954 Convention would be the best solution for the form of the new instrument, and that it was not obligatory to follow the procedure outlined in Article 39 of the 1954 Convention. On military necessity, a majority of delegations was in favour of retaining the concept, which should, however, in no way be seen as military convenience but appear in the text as explicitly and clearly as possible, as a barrier against the destruction of cultural property. Since the special protection regime provided for in the 1954 Convention was considered unsatisfactory, a number of delegations pointed out that an efficient special protection regime inevitably demands a solid institutional basis and has to

---

19. See the final report of the Third Meeting of the High Contracting Parties to the 1954 Convention, UNESCO Doc. CLT-97/CONF.208/3, Paris, November 1997.

20. The meeting was chaired by Adriaan Bos, Legal Advisor of the Dutch Ministry for Foreign Affairs.

21. This meeting was chaired by Franz Cede, Legal Advisor of the Austrian Ministry for Foreign Affairs.

be complemented by respective measures at the national level, which should be a prerequisite for entering a site in the list of specially protected property under the new regime. On jurisdiction and responsibility for violations of the 1954 Convention, consensus prevailed that states should be obliged to prosecute grave breaches committed against cultural property in the event of armed conflict. With regard to institutional matters, the majority of delegations expressed support for a permanent intergovernmental Committee instead of a non-permanent Bureau of States Parties, which should be composed of no more than 12 members on the basis of equitable geographic distribution.

The results of the Vienna expert meeting[22] were merged into a comprehensive working document drafted in treaty language,[23] which was elaborated by UNESCO jointly with the government of the Netherlands and sent to states, the ICRC and selected international organizations for their comments. On the basis of these comments, UNESCO and the government of the Netherlands prepared the final draft, which served as a basis for negotiations at the Diplomatic Conference held in The Hague in March 1999.

Besides the Vienna meeting, close cooperation between the member states of the European Union – which prepared themselves in several coordination meetings for the Diplomatic Conference – had been instrumental to the conference's outcome. The papers elaborated and discussed in that context served as a basis for working papers and amendment proposals during the Diplomatic Conference and decisively contributed to the final text of the Second Protocol.

1.3   The Diplomatic Conference on the Second Protocol

Ninety-three states, members of UNESCO or the UN, among them 74 out of 95 States Parties to the 1954 Convention[24] and 19 non-States Parties,[25] were represented at the Diplomatic Conference. In addition, observer delegations from

---

22. See the report submitted by the Director General to the Executive Board of UNESCO on the results of the Vienna expert meeting, UNESCO Doc. 155 EX/51, 17 August 1998.

23. Preliminary Draft Second Protocol to the 1954 Hague Convention, UNESCO Doc. HC/1999/1, October 1998.

24. Namely, Albania, Argentina, Armenia, Australia, Austria, Azerbaijan, Belarus, Belgium, Bosnia and Herzegovina, Bulgaria, Cambodia, Cameroon, Canada, Colombia, Côte d'Ivoire, Croatia, Cuba, Cyprus, Czech Republic, the Democratic Republic of the Congo, Egypt, Estonia, Finland, France, Georgia, Germany, Ghana, Greece, Guatemala, Holy See, Hungary, India, Indonesia, Islamic Republic of Iran, Israel, Italy, Jordan, Kuwait, Lebanon, Libyan Arab Jamahiriya, Luxembourg, Mali, Malaysia, Mongolia, Morocco, Netherlands, Niger, Nigeria, Norway, Oman, Pakistan, Panama, Peru, Poland, Qatar, Romania, Russian Federation, Saudi Arabia, Senegal, Slovakia, Slovenia, Spain, Sudan, Sweden, Switzerland, Syrian Arab Republic, Tajikistan, Thailand, the former Yugoslav Republic of Macedonia, Tunisia, Turkey, Ukraine, Uzbekistan and Yemen.

25. Namely, Algeria, Botswana, Chile, China, Denmark, Ethiopia, Ireland, Japan, Philippines, Portugal, Republic of Korea, South Africa, Suriname, Tonga, Turkmenistan, United Kingdom, United States of America, Uruguay and Vietnam.

Palestine, the ICRC and from the International Committee of the Blue Shield[26] took part in the Conference.[27] The Conference elected Adriaan Bos, the Netherlands, as President. The representatives of Argentina, Senegal, the Syrian Arab Republic and Thailand were elected Vice-Presidents. The Conference also elected a Rapporteur (Hungary), and established as subsidiary bodies a Credentials Committee (chaired by Germany) and a Drafting Committee (chaired by Switzerland).[28]

The basic working documents used by the Conference were the 'Draft Second Protocol to the Hague Convention for the Protection of Cultural Property in the Event of Armed Conflict',[29] a reference document to this draft,[30] and a synoptic report[31] of comments by states and the ICRC on the Preliminary Draft Second Protocol. The work of the Conference took place in the Plenary as well as in Working Groups which were established on the following issues: Scope of application (Chapters 1 and 5), general protection of cultural property (Chapter 2), enhanced special protection of cultural property (Chapter 3), jurisdiction and responsibility (Chapter 4), and, institutional matters (Chapter 6). Finally, the compromise text developed in the Working Groups was referred to the Plenary for acceptance. On 26 March 1999, the Conference adopted by consensus the Second Protocol to the Hague Convention of 1954 for the Protection of Cultural Property in the Event of Armed Conflict.[32]

1.4   The form of the new instrument

Following the results of the Vienna expert meeting, a majority of delegations represented at the Diplomatic Conference expressed their preference for an optional Protocol additional to the 1954 Convention. They shared the assessment that the Convention enjoyed a high reputation and wide acceptance in the international community and that states willing to accede to it should not be precluded from doing so. States Parties to the 1954 Convention should be enabled to agree on an improved protection regime *inter se* without changing the text of the 1954 Convention.

Since international law provides for the possibility of agreements to modify a multilateral treaty between *certain* of the parties only,[33] most delegations considered

---

26. An international non-governmental organization speaking on behalf of its constituent bodies: the International Council on Archives, the International Council of Museums, the International Council on Monuments and Sites, and the International Federation of Library Associations and Institutions.

27. See the Final Act of the Diplomatic Conference, paras. 1-5.

28. Ibid., paras. 6-9.

29. UNESCO Doc. HC/1999/1/rev.1, February 1999.

30. UNESCO Doc. HC/1999/INF/1 and HC/1999/INF.1/Add. 1.

31. UNESCO Doc. HC/1999/4 and Add.

32. See the Final Act of the Diplomatic Conference, paras. 11-13.

33. Cf., Art. 41 of the Vienna Convention on the Law of Treaties of 1969, and, as a practical example which has been frequently referred to in that context, the 1977 Protocols to the Geneva Conventions of 1949.

it not obligatory to follow the procedure outlined in Article 39 of the 1954 Convention.[34] In the opinion of these delegations, Article 39 only applies to changes to the text of the Convention itself as between *all* its Parties.[35] After intense discussions, the Diplomatic Conference decided to leave the rights and obligations of states which are only parties to the Convention intact and to draw up a supplementary Protocol to the 1954 Convention affecting only the rights and obligations between the parties to that instrument.[36]

2.   THE CONTENT OF THE SECOND PROTOCOL

2.1   **Scope of application**

Corresponding to the 1954 Convention, the Second Protocol applies in situations where the law of international armed conflicts applies, i.e., in the event of a declared war or any other international armed conflict, even if the state of war is not recognized by one or more of the parties to the conflict, or in all cases of partial or total occupation of the territory of a State Party, even if the occupation meets with no armed resistance.[37] Like the 1954 Convention, the Second Protocol contains provisions which also apply in time of peace.[38]

Unlike the 1954 Convention, however, which stipulates that the parties to an armed conflict not of an international character are bound to apply, 'as a minimum, the provisions of the present Convention which relate to respect for cultural property', and 'shall endeavour to bring into force, by means of special agreements, all or part of the other provisions' of the Convention,[39] the Second Protocol

---

34. Only a few states, in particular France and Israel, claimed that the Conference was bound by Article 39, in particular its paragraph 5, and had therefore to take its decisions unanimously. Due to the ensuing dispute over the applicable decision-taking procedures, the Conference did not succeed in formally adopting its rules of procedure. The Draft Rules of Procedure – Doc. HC/1999/3 of February 1999, however, which provided that the Conference should use its best endeavours to ensure that the work is accomplished by general agreement and that, in case all feasible efforts to reach general agreement have failed and a matter is put to the vote, decisions on all matters of substance shall be taken by a two-thirds majority of the States Parties to the 1954 Convention present and voting – were nevertheless provisionally used until the end of the Conference.

35. See Art. 39(5) of the 1954 Convention together with the title of Art. 39 and with its para. 7.

36. See the second, the third and the fourth paras. of the Preamble, and, in particular, Arts. 2, 4 to 7, 9, 16(2), and 21 of the Second Protocol; cf., also the clarification provided by the Working Group on Chapters 1 and 5 that the word 'supplements' in Art. 2 signifies that the Protocol does not affect the rights and obligations of States Parties to the Convention, see the Final Act of the Diplomatic Conference, para. 11.

37. See Art. 3(1) (in the following, references to Articles without indication of the treaty are meant to refer to the Second Protocol).

38. The following Articles of the Second Protocol contain provisions which also apply in times of peace: Arts. 5, 10, 11, 14 to 21, 23 to 33, 37 and most of the final clauses, i.e., Arts. 39 to 47 with the exception of Art. 44.

39. See Art. 19(1) and (2) of the 1954 Convention.

purports to apply as such and as a whole to situations of non-international armed conflicts.[40]

Like other treaties of international humanitarian law, the Second Protocol does not define the term 'armed conflict'.[41] Article 22(2) merely stipulates that situations of internal disturbances and tensions, such as riots, isolated and sporadic acts of violence and other acts of a similar nature do not come within the scope of application of the Second Protocol.[42] The term 'armed conflict' must therefore be interpreted in the light of the meaning it has acquired under customary international law, which explicitly continues to govern questions not regulated by the provisions of the Second Protocol.[43]

Analogous with other treaties of modern international humanitarian law, the Second Protocol explicitly stipulates that, even in situations where one of the parties to an armed conflict is not bound by this Protocol, the Parties to this Protocol shall remain bound by it in their mutual relations. They shall furthermore be bound by this Protocol in relation to a state party to the conflict which is not bound by it, if the latter accepts the provisions of this Protocol and so long as it applies to them.[44]

2.2   General provisions regarding protection

Building on the same definition of 'cultural property' as contained in the 1954 Convention,[45] Chapter 2 of the Second Protocol, which supplements the respective provisions of Chapter I of the 1954 Convention, focuses on four major issues: The safeguarding of cultural property in times of peace (Art. 5), the waiver of the obligation to respect cultural property on the basis of imperative military necessity (Art. 6), precautionary measures during armed conflict (Arts. 7 and 8), and the protection of cultural property in occupied territory (Art. 9).

Article 5 of the Second Protocol provides examples of preparatory measures to be taken in time of peace for the safeguarding of cultural property against the foreseeable effects of an armed conflict pursuant to Article 3 of the 1954 Con-

---

40. See Art. 3(1) in combination with Art. 22(1). For further details see 2.5 *infra.*

41. The term does not appear under the definitions contained in Art. 2 nor is it defined in Arts. 3 or 22.

42. Cf., Art. 1(2) of Protocol II.

43. See the fifth paragraph of the Preamble of the Second Protocol. The term 'armed conflict' has recently been defined by the International Criminal Tribunal for the Former Yugoslavia as a situation of 'resort to armed force between States or protracted armed violence between governmental authorities and organized armed groups or between such groups within a State', in *The Prosecutor* v. *Duško Tadić*, Decision on the Defence Motion for Interlocutory Appeal on Jurisdiction, Case No. IT-94-1-AR72, 2 October 1995, 35 *ILM* (1996) pp. 32 at 54, para. 70. For comment, see C. Greenwood, 'International Humanitarian Law and the Tadić case', 7 *EJIL* (1996) p. 265.

44. See Art. 3(2).

45. See Art. 1(b) which refers to Art. 1 of the 1954 Convention. This provides another example of a deviation from the UNESCO study's recommendations, which suggested to revise the definition of cultural property, see P. Boylan, op. cit. n. 12, at p. 16.

vention. Such measures shall include, as appropriate, the preparation of inventories, the planning of emergency measures for protection against fire or structural collapse, the preparation for the removal of movable cultural property or the provision for adequate *in situ* protection of such property, and the designation of competent authorities responsible for the safeguarding of cultural property.[46]

The most difficult issue under Chapter 2, and probably the most controversial one during the whole review process, was the waiver of the obligation to respect cultural property on the basis of imperative military necessity pursuant to Article 4(2) of the 1954 Convention.[47] The concept of military necessity has a long tradition in international humanitarian law, being included in many treaties.[48] It is generally understood to limit the freedom of action of the belligerents, and can only be invoked as a ground for waiving otherwise strict obligations where the law explicitly so provides.[49] In order to emphasize the exceptional character of this concept, it is often further qualified by a narrowing formula such as the ones used in Article 4(2) or in Article 11(2) of the 1954 Convention.[50] The Convention, however, does not define what constitutes 'imperative' or 'unavoidable' military necessity,[51] which makes it difficult for each State Party to interpret these terms.[52]

---

46. States Parties may also call upon UNESCO for technical assistance in that regard, see Art. 33.

47. According to this provision, the obligation to respect cultural property, i.e., the obligation to refrain from any use of the property and its immediate surroundings for purposes which are likely to expose it to destruction or damage in the event of armed conflict and to refrain from any act of hostility directed against such property, may be waived 'only in cases where military necessity imperatively requires such a waiver'.

48. See for example, Art. 23(g) of the Regulations Respecting the Laws and Customs of War on Land 1907 ('unless...imperatively demanded by the necessities of war'); Arts. 12 ('as far as military considerations permit') and 42 ('in so far as military considerations permit') of the First Geneva Convention 1949; Art. 23 of the Third Geneva Convention 1949 ('whenever military considerations permit'); Arts. 18 ('in so far as military considerations permit'), 49 ('unless...imperative military reasons so demand'), 83 ('whenever military considerations permit') and 143 ('except for reasons of imperative military necessity') of the Fourth Geneva Convention 1949; or Art. 54 ('where required by imperative military necessity'), 62 ('except in case of imperative military necessity') and 71 ('only in case of imperative military necessity') of Protocol I.

49. The primacy of '*Kriegsraison*' over '*Kriegsmanier*' was rejected by the Nuremberg Tribunal, see, *inter alia*, J. Toman, *The Protection of Cultural Property in the Event of Armed Conflict* (Paris, UNESCO/Aldershot, Dartmouth Publishing (1996) pp. 73 et seq. with further references; see also B. Carnahan, 'Lincoln, Lieber and the Laws of War: The Origins and Limits of the Principle of Military Necessity', 92 *AJIL* (1998) pp. 213 et seq.

50. See for example, Art. 23(g) of the Regulations Respecting the Laws and Customs of War on Land 1907, Arts. 49 and 143 of the Fourth Geneva Convention 1949, or Arts. 54, 62 and 71 of Protocol I.

51. On the negotiating history as well as some guidance with regard to the interpretation of these terms, see Toman, op. cit n. 49, at pp. 67-82 and 144-147.

52. Austria, for example, in its guidelines for the protection of cultural property issued by the Federal Ministry of Defence on 12 February 1993, has interpreted this provision as requiring a higher level of proof than normal military considerations; only in cases where there are no alternatives for fulfilling the mission and where the tactical cohesion of forces from the level of battalion upwards cannot be preserved or is seriously in danger of disruption, thereby depriving the superior level of command of its freedom of action, may the Austrian military commander from the level of battalion upwards avail itself of this waiver.

With the entry into force of the 1977 Protocol I additional to the Geneva Conventions of 1949,[53] the interpretation of the 1954 Convention became even more difficult. Article 52 of Protocol I introduced the notion of 'military objectives' into the law of armed conflict, whereby objects which, by their nature, location, purpose or use make an effective contribution to military action and whose total or partial destruction, capture or neutralisation, in the circumstances ruling at the time, offers a definite military advantage, may be regarded as a legitimate military target and thus be attacked.[54] On the basis of that concept, Protocol I strictly prohibits either the commission of any acts of hostility directed against cultural property, or the use of such property in support of the military effort.[55]

In contrast to the 1954 Convention, where both the attacking and the defending sides could avail themselves of the waiver on the basis of imperative military necessity, the defending side under Protocol I was in a worse position in comparison with the attacking side, since it could not avail itself of any exception to the obligation not to use cultural property in support of military action. The attacking side, however, was privileged by Protocol I in comparison with the 1954 Convention insofar as it could legitimately attack cultural property which has become a military objective in the sense of Article 52(2) of Protocol I without any further proof that military necessity imperatively required it to do so.[56] This discrepancy between Protocol I and the 1954 Convention was obviously recognized during the negotiations on Protocol I but was not satisfactorily resolved: Protocol I merely states that its prohibitions with regard to the protection of cultural property shall be 'without prejudice to the provisions of' the 1954 Convention.[57]

In the first phase of the review process of the 1954 Convention, it seemed as if the concept of imperative military necessity would be abandoned altogether.[58] However, this would have lowered the standard of protection of cultural property in the event of armed conflict, especially for that party to the conflict which exceptionally needed to use cultural property in support of military action, and have led to the primacy of the protection of objects over that of human lives – a

---

53. Protocol I entered into force on 7 December 1978.

54. See Art. 52 (2) of Protocol I.

55. See Art. 53(a) and (b) of Protocol I.

56. Precisely the words 'only' and 'imperatively' ensure the protection of cultural property from damage or destruction even if the cultural property concerned or its surroundings are used for military purposes, see the preparatory works for Art. 4 of the 1954 Convention, reproduced in Toman, op. cit. n. 49, at p. 70.

57. See Art. 53 of Protocol I. This provision, however, led to different standards of protection of cultural property in armed conflict, depending on whether all the parties to the armed conflict were parties to both the 1954 Convention and to Protocol I or not, see Y. Sandoz, et al., eds., *Commentary on the Additional Protocols of 1977 to the Geneva Conventions of 1949* (Geneva, ICRC/The Hague, Nijhoff 1987) para. 2046.

58. While the UNESCO study published in 1993 recommended the deletion of the concept altogether, see Boylan, op. cit. n. 12, at p. 17, the 'revised Lauswolt-Document' formulated the obligation to respect cultural property in the way Protocol I did, i.e., no reference to a waiver on the basis of imperative military necessity was made.

hierarchy that could not reasonably be upheld.[59] In the second phase of the review process, beginning with the Second Meeting of the States Parties to the 1954 Convention in November 1995, a growing number of states defended the value of the concept of military necessity. Finally, at the Vienna Expert Meeting in May 1998, a majority of states was in favour of retaining the concept while at the same time further clarifying its content.

Article 6 of the Second Protocol is the result of extensive discussions held at the Diplomatic Conference, in particular in the Working Group on Chapter 2. It combines two initially opposite approaches, namely, the suggestion to keep the waiver clause of Article 4(2) of the 1954 Convention and to make it more specific, and the proposal to abandon the waiver and to replace it by the concept of 'military objectives' as contained in Article 52 of Protocol I. Intensive negotiations finally led to a merger of the two approaches and in particular to a solution of the highly debated question of when and how cultural property could become a military objective and how to best reflect the 'imperative' character of the circumstances under which the waiver might be invoked.

According to Article 6, which corroborates and supplements Article 4 of the 1954 Convention, a waiver on the basis of imperative military necessity pursuant to Article 4(2) of the Convention may only be invoked to direct an act of hostility against cultural property when and for as long as that cultural property has, by its function, been made into a military objective, and there is no feasible alternative available to obtain a similar military advantage to that offered by directing an act of hostility against that objective.[60] Furthermore, Article 6 also specifies the circumstances under which a waiver on the basis of imperative military necessity may be invoked to use cultural property for purposes which are likely to expose it to destruction or damage in the event of armed conflict.[61] Finally, Article 6 adds two further restraints to the invocation of the waiver pursuant to Article 4(2) of

---

59. For critical remarks on this particular aspect of the review process of the 1954 Convention, see Desch, loc. cit. n. 5, at pp. 103 et seq., and, by the same author, 'Revision of the 1954 Hague Convention for the Protection of Cultural Property in the Event of Armed Conflict - wherefore?', Lecture given on the occasion of the General Assembly of the Austrian Society for the Protection of Cultural Property on 22 October 1998 in Vienna, *Writings of the Austrian Society for the Protection of Cultural Property No. 5*, Vienna 1999.

60. See Art. 6(1)(a)(i) and (ii). The wording of sub-para. 1(a)(i) is the result of a compromise between two conflicting views: Some delegations, in particular Egypt and other Arab states, were only ready to accept that cultural property could by its use become a military objective, whereas they rejected the idea that cultural property could become a legitimate military target by its mere nature, location or purpose. Other delegations, however, in particular the United States and other NATO States, were afraid of setting a dangerous precedent by modifying the definition of 'military objectives' by adapting it to a particular category of objects, and were of the opinion that cultural property could also by its location or purpose become a legitimate military target even if it was not used by the adversary at the moment of the attack. The compromise solution was to explicitly refer to the definition of 'military objectives' used in Art. 52 of Protocol I in Art. 1(f) of the Second Protocol, while at the same time making it clear in Art. 6 that cultural property could only become a military objective if 'by its function' it has 'been made into' such an objective.

61. See Art. 6(b).

the 1954 Convention, by requiring a certain level of command at which the decision should be taken, and by introducing an obligation whenever circumstances permit to give an effective advance warning before cultural property is attacked.[62]

Article 7, titled 'Precautions in attack', and Article 8, titled 'Precautions against the effects of hostilities', introduce the main contents of the respective provisions of Protocol I on the distinction between civilian objects and military objectives into the protection regime of the 1954 Convention.[63]

Article 9 deals with the protection of cultural property in occupied territory. It supplements Articles 4 and 5 of the 1954 Convention, and partly replaces the (First) Protocol to the 1954 Convention.[64] Article 9 applies between States Parties to the Second Protocol only and only in relation to territory which has been occupied by another State Party. It obliges the Occupying Power to prohibit and prevent any illicit[65] export, other removal or transfer of ownership of cultural property, any archaeological excavation, save where this is strictly required to safeguard, record or preserve cultural property, or, any alteration to, or change of use of, cultural property which is intended to conceal or destroy cultural, historical or scientific evidence.[66] Finally, Article 9 stipulates that any archaeological excavation of, alteration to, or change of use of, cultural property in occupied territory shall, unless circumstances do not permit, be carried out in close cooperation with the competent national authorities of the occupied territory.[67] The wording of Article 9 pursues the aim of ensuring the highest possible standard of protection for cultural property in occupied territory while, at the same time, not losing sight of the practicability of these provisions, in particular in situations of long-term occupation.

2.3   Enhanced protection

Since the 'special protection' regime under the 1954 Convention had turned out to be more or less ineffective in practice, and to be, paradoxically, legally less protective than the regular protection regime,[68] the Diplomatic Conference decided to establish a new (and third) category of cultural property, under 'enhanced

---

62. See Art. 6(c) and (d).

63. Cf., Arts. 57 and 58 of Protocol I.

64. Cf., Art. I(1) of the (First) Protocol to the 1954 Convention and Art. 9(1)(a) of the Second Protocol.

65. The term 'illicit' is defined as meaning 'under compulsion or otherwise in violation of the applicable rules of the domestic law of the occupied territory or of international law', see Art. 1(g); the main element of this definition is taken from Art. 11 of the 1970 UNESCO Convention on the Means of Prohibiting and Preventing the Illicit Import, Export and Transfer of Ownership of Cultural Property.

66. See Art. 9(1).

67. See Art. 9(2) which, in that respect, even goes further than the respective Principle 32 of the UNESCO Recommendation on International Principles Applicable to Archaeological Excavations, adopted by the General Conference at its ninth session, New Delhi, 5 December 1956.

68. For further details see Desch, loc. cit n. 5, pp. 103 et seq., at 106.

protection'.[69] Due to the supplementary character of the Second Protocol, the application of the provisions of Chapter 3 is without prejudice to the application of the provisions of Chapter I of the 1954 Convention and of Chapter 2 of the Second Protocol, as well as to the application of the provisions of Chapter II of the 1954 Convention save that, as between states bound by the provisions of the Second Protocol, where cultural property has been granted both special protection and enhanced protection, only the provisions of enhanced protection shall apply.[70]

In order to be eligible for enhanced protection, cultural property must fulfill the following conditions: It must be cultural heritage of the greatest importance for humanity,[71] be protected by adequate domestic legal and administrative measures recognising its exceptional cultural and historic value and ensuring the highest level of protection, and it must not be used for military purposes or to shield military sites and a declaration must have been made by the Party which has control over the cultural property confirming that it will not be so used.[72] While the first and the third condition are indispensable, the second (adequate domestic measures) is not. In exceptional cases, where a State Party requesting inclusion of cultural property in the list of cultural property under enhanced protection cannot fulfil the criteria of Article 10(b), enhanced protection may nevertheless be granted, provided that the requesting state submits a request for international assistance under Article 32 of the Second Protocol.[73]

The granting of enhanced protection is dependent upon a request by the state which has either jurisdiction or control over the cultural property concerned.[74] Thus not only the state on the territory of which a certain cultural property is located may request the granting of enhanced protection but also, for example, the State Party occupying the territory concerned. The Second Protocol encourages states to make such requests by requiring states to submit to the Committee for the Protection of Cultural Property in the Event of Armed Conflict[75] a list of cultural property for which they intend to request the granting of enhanced protection, and by empowering the Committee, acting on its own or upon a respective recommendation by other States Parties, by the International Committee of the Blue

---

69. According to Art. 1(e), 'enhanced protection' means the system of enhanced protection established by Arts. 10 and 11.

70. See Art. 4(b).

71. The term 'greatest' was deemed necessary to distinguish that property from cultural property of 'great' (regular protection) and of 'very great' (special protection) importance. The term 'humanity' as opposed to 'all peoples' underlines the common interest in safeguarding important cultural heritage.

72. See Art. 10 in combination with Art. 11(7).

73. See Art. 11(8).

74. See Art. 11(2) and (9). Due to the importance to humankind of the property concerned, it was felt necessary to allow for as many states as possible to make such a request. The granting of enhanced protection is, however, dependent upon a declaration by the State Party which has control over the cultural property, confirming that it will not use the property concerned for military purposes or to shield military sites, see Arts. 10(c) and 11(7) and (9).

75. This Committee is established by Art. 24; see 2.6 *infra*. One of its functions is to grant, suspend or cancel enhanced protection for cultural property, see Art. 27(1)(b).

Shield, or by other non-governmental organisations with relevant expertise, to invite a particular State Party to make such a request.[76] Furthermore, neither the request for inclusion of cultural property situated in a territory, sovereignty or jurisdiction over which is claimed by more than one state, nor its inclusion, shall in any way prejudice the rights of the parties to the dispute over the territory.[77]

Upon receipt of a request, the Committee shall inform all States Parties of the request, which may, within 60 days, submit representations concerning the conditions mentioned in Article 10 for placing the cultural property concerned under enhanced protection.[78] In case it receives representations, the Committee shall provide the requesting party with a reasonable opportunity to respond before taking the decision, which shall in such case be taken by a qualified majority.[79] In deciding upon a request, the Committee is encouraged to ask the advice of governmental and non-governmental organisations, as well as of individual experts.

Enhanced protection shall be granted to cultural property by the Committee from the moment of its entry in the International List of Cultural Property under Enhanced Protection.[80] The Director General of UNESCO shall, without delay, send to the Secretary General of the United Nations and to all States Parties to the Second Protocol notification of any decision of the Committee to include cultural property on the List.[81]

Enhanced protection may be withdrawn where cultural property no longer meets any one of the criteria mentioned in Article 10. In such a case, the Committee may, after having afforded an opportunity to the States Parties to the Second Protocol to make their views known, either temporarily suspend the enhanced protection status or definitely cancel that status by removing that cultural property from the List.[82] The Director General of UNESCO shall, without delay, send to the Secretary General of the United Nations and to all States Parties to the Second Protocol notification of any decision of the Committee to suspend or cancel the enhanced protection.[83]

Besides the regular procedure for granting enhanced protection, the Second Protocol also provides for an emergency procedure in case of armed conflict.[84] Upon the outbreak of hostilities, a party[85] to the conflict may request, on an

---

76. See Art. 11(1) to (3).

77. See Art. 11(4).

78. See Art. 11(5).

79. In deviation from the regular decision-taking procedure pursuant to Art. 26, which requires a majority of the members of the Committee present and a majority of two-thirds of its members voting, Art. 11(5) requires a majority of four-fifths of its members present and voting.

80. See Art. 11(10) in combination with Art. 1(h). According to Art. 27(1)(b), this List shall be established by the Committee.

81. See Art. 11(11).

82. See Art. 14(1) and (4).

83. See Art. 14(3).

84. See Art. 11(9).

85. As the term 'Party' with a capital 'P' is defined in Art. 1(a) as meaning a State Party to the Second Protocol, the right to make a request under the emergency procedure does not extend to non-state Parties to a non-international armed conflict which occurs on the territory of a State Party;

emergency basis, enhanced protection of cultural property under its jurisdiction or control by communicating this request to the Committee. The Committee shall transmit this request immediately to all Parties to the conflict. Representations from the Parties concerned will be considered by the Committee on an expedited basis. Pending the outcome of the regular procedure for the granting of enhanced protection, the Committee may grant provisional enhanced protection, provided that the conditions of Article 10(a) and (c) are met. The decision to grant provisional enhanced protection shall be taken as soon as possible and by a qualified majority,[86] with the proviso that States Parties which are Members of the Committee shall not participate in the voting on any decisions relating to cultural property affected by an armed conflict to which they are parties.[87]

The protection afforded to cultural property under enhanced protection differs from the level of protection of cultural property under regular protection pursuant to Chapter 2 of the Second Protocol and to Chapter I of the 1954 Convention, as well as from the standard of protection provided for cultural property under special protection pursuant to Chapter II of the 1954 Convention mainly in three ways. Firstly, there is no possibility of a waiver of the obligation of the parties to an armed conflict to ensure the 'immunity'[88] of cultural property under enhanced protection by refraining from making such property the object of attack or from any use of the property or its immediate surroundings in support of military action.[89] If cultural property under enhanced protection is used in support of military action it loses its enhanced protection either by suspension or cancellation of the enhanced protection status by the Committee in accordance with Article 14,[90] or, automatically, by, and for as long as, having become, by its use, a military objective.[91]

Secondly, even if the cultural property concerned has, by its use, become a military objective and thereby lost its enhanced protection status, it may only be the object of attack if the attack is the only feasible means of terminating such use of the property, if all feasible precautions are taken in the choice of means and

---

on the applicability of the Second Protocol to non-international armed conflicts see 2.5 *infra*.

86. Art. 11(9) requires a majority of four-fifths of its members present and voting.

87. See Art. 26(3).

88. The term 'immunity' in Art. 12 has been taken from Art. 9 of the 1954 Convention, where it is misleading as well, since it is normally used in international law to describe situations where a state is barred from exercising its jurisdiction with regard to particular persons or objects.

89. See Art. 12 of the Second Protocol which applies to military operations in the event of armed conflict only. Both the terms 'object of attack' and 'military action' are narrower than the respective terms 'acts of hostility' and 'military effort' or 'military purpose', which are (partly) used in Arts. 4 and 9 of the 1954 Convention and in Art. 53 of Protocol I.

90. See Art. 13(1)(a) in combination with Art. 14(2) of the Second Protocol. See also Art. 14(1) according to which the use for military purposes or to shield military sites in contravention of Art. 10(c), which also applies in peacetime, may also lead to a suspension or cancellation of the enhanced protection status.

91. See Art. 13(1)(b). In contrast to cultural property under regular protection (see 2.2 *supra*), cultural property under enhanced protection can only become a military objective by its use. This different wording was deliberately chosen in order to mark the different level of protection and to keep that provision in line with Art. 10(c).

methods of attack, with a view to terminating such use and avoiding, or in any event minimising, damage to the cultural property, and if, unless circumstances do not permit, due to requirements of immediate self-defence, the attack is ordered at the highest operational level of command,[92] effective advance warning is issued to the opposing forces requiring the termination of the use, and reasonable time is given to the opposing forces to redress the situation.[93]

Thirdly, making cultural property under enhanced protection the object of attack, or using cultural property under enhanced protection or its immediate surroundings in support of military action, constitutes, if committed intentionally and in violation of the Convention or the Second Protocol, a serious violation of the Protocol which entails individual criminal responsibility.[94]

While putting considerable effort into drafting Chapter 3 on enhanced protection, the Diplomatic Conference did not, however, decide on the marking of such property under such protection. The question whether a distinctive emblem should be created, or whether the emblem established by Article 16 of the 1954 Convention should be used for the marking of cultural property under enhanced protection, will finally have to be decided by the Committee.[95]

2.4   Criminal responsibility and jurisdiction

As mentioned earlier,[96] the weak enforcement mechanism of the 1954 Convention was considered to be one of its main deficiencies. Regarding a more effective enforcement mechanism, two approaches emerged during the preparations for the Diplomatic Conference: One group of states[97] favoured provisions similar to those used in Protocol I,[98] whereas other delegations wanted the Second Protocol to link up with recent developments in international law, in particular international criminal law.[99] At the Diplomatic Conference, the second approach prevailed. Chapter 4 of the Second Protocol supplements the 1954 Convention, in particular its Article 28 on sanctions, by establishing three categories of violations of the 1954 Convention or the Second Protocol: Serious violations of the Second Protocol which entail criminal responsibility and the perpetrators of which must either be tried or

---

92. Earlier proposals required that the decision should be taken at the highest national level of command. This requirement, however, was considered to be unworkable in practice, since, in armed conflicts involving multinational forces, attacks are ordered at multinational or allied command level only.

93. See Art. 13(2).

94. See Art. 15(1)(a) and (b) in combination with para. 2 (see 2.4 *infra*).

95. See Art. 27 on the functions of the Committee, in particular sub-paras. (a) and (c).

96. See 1.1 *supra*.

97. In particular, France, Switzerland, the United Kingdom and the United States.

98. See in particular, Art. 85 of Protocol I.

99. Such as, for example, the International Convention for the Suppression of Terrorist Bombings, adopted by the UN General Assembly on 15 December 1997, text published in 37 *ILM* (1998) pp. 251 et seq.

extradited,[100] other serious violations which entail criminal responsibility,[101] and, other violations of the Convention or the Protocol.[102]

The first category comprises the following acts when committed intentionally and in violation of the 1954 Convention or the Second Protocol: Making cultural property under enhanced protection the object of attack, using cultural property under enhanced protection or its immediate surroundings in support of military action, and extensive destruction or appropriation of cultural property protected under the Convention and the Second Protocol.[103]

The second category contains the following acts when committed intentionally and in violation of the 1954 Convention or the Second Protocol: Making cultural property protected under the Convention and the Second Protocol the object of attack, and theft, pillage or misappropriation of, or acts of vandalism directed against, cultural property protected under the Convention.[104]

The third category includes the following acts when committed intentionally: Any use of cultural property in violation of the 1954 Convention or the Second Protocol, and any illicit export, other removal or transfer of ownership of cultural property from occupied territory in violation of the 1954 Convention or the Second Protocol.[105]

Serious violations of the 1954 Convention or the Second Protocol shall entail criminal responsibility under domestic law. States Parties to the Second Protocol are obliged to adopt such measures as may be necessary to establish as criminal offences under their domestic law the offences under both the above-mentioned first and second category of violations and to make them punishable by appropriate penalties.[106] This does not preclude the incurring of individual criminal responsibility under international law, such as, for example, under the Rome Statute of the International Criminal Court.[107]

As the definitions of offences contained in Article 15(1) lack some precision, in particular in relation to the scope of application of the Second Protocol,[108] it will be the task of the States Parties to make them sufficiently strict when establishing these offences as criminal offences under their domestic law in order to comply

---

100. See Arts. 15(2) and 17(1).

101. See Art. 15(2).

102. See Art. 21.

103. See Art. 15(1)(a) to (c).

104. See Art. 15(1)(d) and (e).

105. See Art. 21(a) and (b).

106. See Art. 15(2), which further indicates that not only the perpetrator of the act shall be held criminally responsible but also those who contribute to the commission of the act, *inter alia*, by participating as an accomplice or by organizing or directing others to commit the act.

107. See Art. 16(2)(a) of the Second Protocol and, for example, Art. 5(1)(c) and 8(2)(b)(ix) of the Rome Statute of the International Criminal Court, adopted by the United Nations Diplomatic Conference of Plenipotentiaries on the Establishment of an International Criminal Court on 17 July 1998, UN Doc. A/CONF.183/9.

108. It is questionable whether the offences defined in Art. 15(1) are also intended to apply in situations of armed conflict not of an international character, see 2.1 *supra* as well as 2.5 *infra*.

with the general principles of criminal law, in particular the principle *nullum crimen sine lege*.[109]

States Parties to the Second Protocol are obliged to take the necessary legislative measures to establish their jurisdiction over (both categories of) serious violations of the Second Protocol, when either such an offence is committed in the territory of that state or the alleged offender is a national of that state.[110] This does not, however, preclude the right of States Parties to the Second Protocol to exercise their jurisdiction under national and international law that may be applicable.[111]

In case of serious violations under the above-mentioned first category, however, States Parties to the Second Protocol are obliged to establish their jurisdiction over such offences, including when neither the offence has been committed in their territory nor the alleged offender is their national but when the alleged offender is present in their territory.[112] Furthermore, they have the obligation to either try or extradite the alleged offender.[113] For the purposes of extradition, such offences shall be deemed to be included as extraditable offences in any extradition treaty existing between any of the States Parties before the entry into force of the Second Protocol, and shall be included in every extradition treaty to be subsequently concluded between them.[114] In the absence of an extradition treaty between them, States Parties may as well consider the Second Protocol as the legal basis for extradition in respect of such offences.[115] States Parties which do not make extradition conditional on the existence of a treaty shall recognise these offences as extraditable offences between them, subject to the conditions provided by the law of the requested State Party.[116] Furthermore, if necessary, such offences shall be treated, for the purposes of extradition between States Parties to the Second Protocol, as if they had been committed not only in the place in which they occurred but also in the territory of the Parties that have established jurisdiction in accordance with Article 16(1).[117] Finally, for the purpose of extradition, such

---

109. See Art. 15(2), second sentence. Besides the principle *nullum crimen sine lege*, these principles include the punishability of the attempt to commit such crimes, or the responsibility of superiors for offences committed by their subordinates, see, *inter alia*, Arts. 22, 25 and 28 of the Rome Statute of the International Criminal Court, adopted by the United Nations Diplomatic Conference of Plenipotentiaries on the Establishment of an International Criminal Court on 17 July 1998, UN Doc. A/CONF.183/9.

110. See Art. 16(1)(a) and (b).

111. See Art. 16(2)(a).

112. See Art. 16(1)(c). Though the wording of this provision does not contain the further qualification 'and it does not extradite that person' (cf., for example, Art. 6(4) of the International Convention for the Suppression of Terrorist Bombings), it was the clear understanding of the Diplomatic Conference that jurisdiction has only to be established when the state concerned does not extradite the alleged offender to another state having established jurisdiction according to Art. 16(1) (a) and (b).

113. See Art. 17(1). Compare also Arts. 49 of the First, 50 of the Second, 129 of the Third and 146 of the Fourth Geneva Convention of 1949.

114. See Art. 18(1).

115. See Art. 18(2).

116. See Art. 18(3).

117. See Art. 18(4).

offences shall not be regarded as political offences or as offences connected with political offences or as offences inspired by political motives.[118]

However, members of the armed forces and nationals of a state which is not Party to the Second Protocol, or has otherwise accepted its provisions[119] (except for those nationals serving in the armed forces of a state which is a Party to this Protocol), do not incur individual criminal responsibility by virtue of this Protocol, nor does this Protocol impose an obligation to establish jurisdiction over such persons or to extradite them.[120]

In connection with investigations or criminal or extradition proceedings brought in respect of (both categories of) serious violations of the Second Protocol, States Parties shall afford one another the greatest measure of assistance, subject, however, to existing international treaties or arrangements between them or, otherwise, to their domestic law.[121] For the purpose of mutual legal assistance, such offences shall not be regarded as political offences or as offences connected with political offences or as offences inspired by political motives.[122]

The third category of 'other violations' of the 1954 Convention or the Second Protocol does not (necessarily) entail criminal responsibility. The Second Protocol neither obliges States Parties to establish their jurisdiction over such violations, nor to either try or extradite the alleged offender. It merely obliges States Parties to adopt such legislative, administrative or disciplinary measures as may be necessary to suppress such violations.[123]

2.5   Protection of cultural property in armed conflict not of an international character

Chapter 5 of the Second Protocol extends the scope of application of the Second Protocol to non-international armed conflicts.[124] Unlike the respective provisions of the 1954 Convention, as well as of other international humanitarian law treaties which follow the traditional two-tier approach to the problem of regulating the

---

118. See Art. 20(1). Under the Second Protocol, a request for extradition may only be refused on the grounds listed in Art. 20(2).

119. Cf., Art. 3(2).

120. See Art. 16(2)(b).

121. See Art. 19. In an interpretative statement, the Chairman of the Working Group on Chapter 4 declared that '[n]othing in this Protocol, including Art. 19, in any way limits the State's ability to legislate, criminalize or otherwise deal with any substantive offences including conduct addressed in this Protocol. Nothing in Art. 19(2)(b) should be interpreted as in any way affecting the application of Art. 19(1)(a)'; see the Final Act of the Diplomatic Conference, para. 11.

122. See Art. 20(1). Under the Second Protocol, a request for mutual legal assistance based on serious violations of the Second Protocol may only be refused on the grounds listed in Art. 20(2).

123. See Art. 21 of the Second Protocol, as well as, similarly, Art. 28 of the 1954 Convention. Cf., also the respective provisions of the Geneva Conventions of 1949, such as Art. 146(3) of the Fourth Geneva Convention.

124. See Art. 22; regarding the scope of application of the Second Protocol, see also 2.1 *supra*.

behaviour of the parties to a non-international armed conflict,[125] Article 22 of the Second Protocol purports that the Second Protocol applies as a whole and without any further agreement of the parties to non-international armed conflicts.[126]

The attempt, however, to declare basically all the provisions of an international law treaty to be binding also upon actors who are neither subjects of international law nor parties to that treaty, ignores some of the most basic and still existing concepts of international law. Unless having been treated as insurgents and accepted by other states as belligerents, non-state actors in a non-international armed conflict are not, by the mere fact of rebellion or insurgency, subjects of international law.[127] Although customary international law has developed rules to govern non-international armed conflicts, covering also the protection of cultural property, only a number of rules and principles governing international armed conflicts have gradually been extended to apply to non-international armed conflicts, and this extension has not taken place in the form of a full and mechanical transplant of those rules to internal conflicts.[128] State practice has shown that, beyond a set of minimum rules reflecting 'elementary considerations of humanity'[129] applicable under customary international law to any armed conflict, the rules of international humanitarian law governing international armed conflicts, and in particular those enshrined in treaty law, need either the commitment in the form of an agreement or at least the unilateral commitment by non-state Parties to a non-international armed conflict to become binding upon them.[130] This practice corresponds with the general principle of international law, according to which a treaty does not create either obligations or rights for a third party without its consent.[131]

Beyond that, even the drafters of Article 22 felt the need to explicitly curtail its progressive character by adding some very traditional safeguard clauses emphasizing state sovereignty and the international rights of a state flowing therefrom.[132] Chapter 5 of the Second Protocol must therefore be interpreted in a more restrictive way than the wording of Article 22(1) would imply, in a sense that only those provisions of the Second Protocol shall apply in the event of an armed conflict not of an international character which can legally (from a formal

---

125. Cf., Art. 19 of the 1954 Convention, common Art. 3 of the Geneva Conventions of 1949, or Art. 16 of Protocol II, which require the parties to a non-international armed conflict to apply those provisions which must be regarded as a minimum standard under customary international law, and beyond that encourage them to endeavour to bring into force, by means of special agreements, all or part of the other treaty provisions.

126. See Art. 22(1).

127. See, *inter alia*, M.N. Shaw, *International Law*, 4th edn. (New York, Cambridge University Press 1997) pp. 798-800, with further references.

128. *Tadić*, Decision on Jurisdiction, *supra* n. 43 paras. 126 and 127.

129. Cf., the Judgment of the International Court of Justice in the *Nicaragua* case, Merits, *ICJ Rep.* (1986) pp. 14 et seq. (para. 218).

130. Cf., the State practice referred to in *Tadić*, Decision on Jurisdiction, *supra* n. 43 at paras. 102-107.

131. See Art. 34 of the Vienna Convention on the Law of Treaties 1969, 8 *ILM* (1969) p. 679.

132. See Art. 22(3) to (6).

as well as from a material point of view) and factually be applied by the parties, including the non-state Parties, to the conflict.[133]

2.6   Institutional issues

Chapter 6 of the Second Protocol establishes an institutional framework providing the States Parties with a means of being more closely involved in the protection of cultural property in the event of armed conflict.[134] This institutional framework includes the Meeting of the States Parties, the Committee for the Protection of Cultural Property in the Event of Armed Conflict, and the Fund for the Protection of Cultural Property in the Event of Armed Conflict.

The Meeting of the States Parties shall be convened at the same time as the General Conference of UNESCO, i.e., every two years, and in coordination with the Meeting of the States Parties to the 1954 Convention, if such a meeting has been called by the Director General of UNESCO.[135] At the request of at least one-fifth of the States Parties, an Extraordinary Meeting of the States Parties shall be convened by the Director General of UNESCO.[136] The Meeting of the States Parties shall elect the members of the Committee, endorse the guidelines developed by the Committee for the implementation of the Second Protocol, provide guidelines for, and supervise the use of the Fund by the Committee, consider the reports submitted by the Committee on the implementation of the Protocol, and discuss any problem related to the application of the Protocol, and make recommendations, as appropriate.[137]

The Committee for the Protection of Cultural Property in the Event of Armed Conflict shall be composed of representatives of twelve States Parties which shall be elected by the Meeting of the States Parties for four years and shall be eligible for immediate reelection only once.[138] In determining membership of the Committee, States Parties shall seek to ensure an equitable representation of the different regions and cultures of the world, and shall endeavour to ensure that the Committee as a whole contains adequate expertise in the fields of cultural heritage, defence or international law.[139] The Committee shall meet once a year in ordinary session, and in extraordinary sessions whenever it deems necessary, in order to develop guidelines for the implementation of the Protocol; to grant, suspend or cancel enhanced protection for cultural property and to establish, maintain and promote the List of cultural property under enhanced protection; to promote the identification of cultural property under enhanced protection; to monitor and supervise the

---

133. Cf., for example, most of the provisions of Chapters 4, 6 and 8 of the Second Protocol, which can be applied by States Parties only.
134. Compare also the third para. of the Preamble of the Second Protocol.
135. See Art. 23(1).
136. See Art. 23(4).
137. See Art. 23(3).
138. See Arts. 24(1) and 25(1).
139. See Art. 24(3) and (4).

implementation of the Protocol; to consider and comment on reports of the Parties; to seek clarifications as required and prepare its own report on the implementation of the Protocol for the Meeting of the States Parties; to receive and consider requests for international assistance; to determine the use of the Fund; and to perform any other function which may be assigned to it by the Meeting of the Parties.[140] When performing its functions, the Committee shall cooperate with the Director General of UNESCO as well as with relevant international and national governmental and non-governmental organizations, and may invite representatives of such organizations as well as of the ICRC to its meetings in an advisory capacity.[141] The Committee will be assisted by the Secretariat of UNESCO, which shall prepare the Committee's documentation and the agenda for its meetings and shall have the responsibility for the implementation of its decisions.[142]

The Fund for the Protection of Cultural Property in the Event of Armed Conflict shall constitute a trust fund, in conformity with the financial regulations of UNESCO, and shall serve to provide financial or other assistance in support of preparatory or other measures to be taken in peacetime, and to provide financial or other assistance in relation to emergency, provisional or other measures to be taken in order to protect cultural property during periods of armed conflict or of immediate recovery after the end of hostilities.[143] The resources of the Fund shall consist of voluntary contributions made by the States Parties; contributions, gifts or bequests made by other states, UNESCO or other organizations of the United Nations system, other intergovernmental or non-governmental organizations, and public or private bodies or individuals; any interest accruing on the Fund; funds raised by collections and receipts from events organized for the benefit of the Fund; and all other resources authorized by the guidelines applicable to the Fund.[144] Disbursements from the Fund shall be used only for such purposes as the Committee shall decide.[145]

2.7   Dissemination of information and international assistance

Chapter 7 of the Second Protocol contains a variety of provisions some of which do not fit together.[146] Due to time constraints at the Diplomatic Conference, Chapter 7, for which no working group was established, was not thoroughly discussed. It therefore contains provisions that were either simply copied from the 1954

---

140. See Arts. 24(2) and 27(1).
141. See Art. 27(2) and (3).
142. See Art. 28.
143. See Art. 29(1) and (2).
144. See Art. 29(4).
145. See Art. 29(3).
146. Cf., in contrast thereto, Chapter VII of the 1954 Convention where practically all the issues dealt with under Chapters 7 and 8 of the Second Protocol are addressed in a single chapter on the execution of the Convention.

Convention[147] and from other Conventions, or appear to be hastily drafted and negotiated.

Article 30 mainly deals with dissemination of the content of the Second Protocol among the population and, in particular, the military or civilian authorities of the States Parties, using mostly language of Article 25 of the 1954 Convention and adding some details.[148] The last part of Article 30, however, appears to be systematically misplaced as it contains an obligation for States Parties to communicate to one another the laws and administrative provisions which they may adopt to ensure the application of the Protocol, a provision which would have been better placed in Chapter 8 on the execution of the Protocol.[149]

Article 31, titled 'international cooperation', stipulates that in situations of serious violations of this Protocol, the Parties undertake 'to act', jointly through the Committee, or individually, in cooperation with UNESCO and the United Nations and in conformity with the Charter of the United Nations. Apart from the fact that it is not clear what this obligation exactly requires them to do,[150] it is not clear either whether the term 'serious violations of this Protocol' is to be understood as referring to Article 15 of the Second Protocol or whether it has a different meaning. Article 15, besides its ambiguous title, however, only deals with individual criminal responsibility for acts in violation of the 1954 Convention or the Second Protocol, and obliges states to take specific measures under their domestic law.[151] Article 31, on the contrary, the text of which has obviously been copied from Article 89 of Protocol I, addresses issues of state responsibility for violations of the Second Protocol[152] and obliges states 'to act' under international law. The term 'situations of serious violations of this Protocol' must therefore be interpreted as referring to situations where violations of the Second Protocol attributable to a State Party occur, which are of a serious character.[153] Although Article 15 may serve as a guideline for what the drafters of the Second Protocol considered to be violations

---

147. See for example, Art. 33(1) and (3).

148. See Art. 30(1), (2) and (3) sub-paras. (a) to (c).

149. See Art. 30(3)(d).

150. Cf., ICRC Commentary on Art. 89 of Additional Protocol I of 1977, where the prescribed action is – with a reference to Art. 56 of the UN Charter – summarized as 'acting for the protection of man, also in time of armed conflict', and where 'issuing of an appeal to respect humanitarian law', 'setting up enquiries on compliance' and 'coercive actions which include the use of armed force' are mentioned as examples of UN actions to which Art. 89 refers, *Commentary*, op. cit n. 57, paras. 3595-3597.

151. The *chapeau* of Art. 15(1) clearly indicates that it merely defines offences committed by individuals, see also 2.4 *supra*.

152. Cf., also Art. 38 which provides that no provision in the Second Protocol relating to individual criminal responsibility shall affect the responsibility of states under international law, including the duty to provide reparation.

153. It is interesting to note that during the 1977 Conference the meaning of the words 'in situations of serious violations of the Conventions or of this Protocol' was not elucidated, and that both in Committee and in the plenary Conference several delegations regretted that this provision was not considered and discussed in greater detail, see *Commentary*, op. cit. n. 57, at paras. 3587-3588.

of such a character, States Parties are free to also consider other violations of the Second Protocol as serious in the sense of Article 31, such as, for example, the systematic and widespread use of cultural property in violation of the 1954 Convention or the Second Protocol, the illicit removal of cultural property from occupied territory, in particular when committed as a part of a plan or policy, or the (continuous) violation by a State Party of its obligation to either try or extradite the alleged offender of a serious violation of the Second Protocol.

The remaining provisions of Chapter 7 are devoted to the issue of international assistance. Article 32 authorizes States Parties to request from the Committee international assistance for cultural property under enhanced protection as well as assistance with respect to the preparation, development or implementation of adequate domestic laws, administrative provisions and measures for the protection of such property.[154] This right to request assistance applies in peacetime as well as in times of armed conflict. Article 32 further invites parties to an armed conflict which are not Parties to the Second Protocol but which accept and apply (some of) the provisions to request appropriate international assistance from the Committee.[155] While the latter shall adopt rules for the submission of requests for international assistance and shall define the forms the international assistance may take, States Parties to the Second Protocol are encouraged to give technical assistance of all kinds, through the Committee, to those states or other parties to the conflict which request it.[156]

Article 33, finally, deals with peacetime assistance for States Parties in organizing the protection of their cultural property, such as preparatory action to safeguard cultural property, preventive and organizational measures for emergency situations and compilation of national inventories of cultural property. Each State Party to the Second Protocol may call upon UNESCO for technical assistance in this regard or in connection with any other problem arising out of the application of the Second Protocol. UNESCO, which is also authorized to make, on its own initiative, proposals on these matters to the States Parties, shall accord such assistance within the limits fixed by its programme and by its resources.[157] Within as well as outside the framework of UNESCO, States Parties are 'encouraged' to provide technical assistance at bilateral or multilateral level.[158]

2.8   Execution of the Protocol

Due to time constraints at the Diplomatic Conference, Chapter 8 – for which, like for Chapter 7, no working group was established – was not thoroughly discussed.

---

154. See Art. 32(1).
155. See Art. 32(2).
156. See Art. 32(3) and (4); see also the Resolution annexed to the Final Act of the Diplomatic Conference.
157. See Art. 33(1) and (3).
158. See Art. 33(2).

It therefore contains provisions that were either simply copied from the 1954 Convention[159] or appear to be hastily drafted and negotiated.

The main flaw of Chapter 8 lies in the fact that it builds on the system of Protecting Powers, which has in practice already under the 1954 Convention turned out to be ineffective.[160] While Articles 34 and 35 copy the respective provisions of the 1954 Convention,[161] Article 36 provides a procedure of conciliation in the absence of Protecting Powers: In an armed conflict where no Protecting Powers are appointed, the Director General of UNESCO may lend its good offices or act by any other form of conciliation or mediation, with a view to settling the disagreement.[162] In addition to that right of initiative of the Director General of UNESCO, the Chairman of the Committee for the protection of cultural property in the event of armed conflict may, at the invitation of one State Party or of the Director General of UNESCO, propose to the Parties to the conflict a meeting of their representatives, and in particular of the authorities responsible for the protection of cultural property, if considered appropriate, on the territory of a state not party to the conflict.[163]

It is not clear from the wording of this provision whether it applies in case of disagreement about the appointment[164] of delegates of Protecting Powers only, or whether it provides a general dispute settlement procedure for any disagreement among States Parties on the application or interpretation of the Second Protocol. As the Final Clauses of the Second Protocol do not contain a provision on the settlement of disputes, it seems as if Article 36 was intended to serve as a general dispute settlement clause. Its wording, however, limits its applicability to situations of armed conflict.

Article 37 which resembles the respective provision of the 1954 Convention,[165] obliges States Parties to translate the Second Protocol into their official languages and to communicate these official translations to the Director General of UNESCO. Furthermore, States Parties shall submit to the Committee for the protection of cultural property in the event of armed conflict, every four years, a report on the implementation of the Protocol, which will be considered and commented on by the Committee and merged into the Committee's own report to be prepared for the Meeting of States Parties.[166]

Article 38 contains a general reference to the responsibility of states under international law, including the duty to provide reparation, which shall not be affected by the provisions of the Second Protocol relating to individual criminal responsibility. While in the beginning of the review process of the 1954 Convention

---

159. See for example, Arts. 34, 35 and 37.
160. See, *inter alia*, Desch, loc. cit. n. 5, at pp. 103 et seq., at 107, with further references.
161. See Arts. 21 and 22 of the 1954 Convention.
162. See Art. 36(1).
163. See Art. 36(2).
164. Cf., Art. 3 of the Regulations for the Execution of the 1954 Convention.
165. See Art. 26 of the 1954 Convention.
166. See Art. 27(1)(d).

considerable emphasis was put on the issue of state responsibility, and the revised Lauswolt-Document contained several draft provisions on that issue, states represented at the Diplomatic Conference finally decided not to repeat wording that had already been drafted by other fora,[167] and to merely refer to the applicability of those rules of general international law.

2.9   Final clauses

The Second Protocol was negotiated in English and in French, the working languages of UNESCO, and finally drawn up also in Arabic, Chinese, Russian and Spanish, the other four official languages of UNESCO, all six texts being equally authentic. [168]

The Second Protocol shall be open for signature by States Parties to the 1954 Convention only, and shall be subject to ratification, acceptance or approval by those which have signed the Protocol, or, from 1 January 2000, to accession by the other States Parties to the 1954 Convention.[169]

The Second Protocol will enter into force three months after 20 instruments of ratification, acceptance, approval or accession have been deposited with the Director General of UNESCO, who is assigned depository tasks.[170] Thereafter, it shall enter into force, for each state, three months after the deposit of its instrument of ratification, acceptance, approval or accession.[171] For situations of armed conflict, the Second Protocol provides for an expedited entry into force for (as well as a delayed taking effect of a denunciation by) a party to an armed conflict.[172]

The Second Protocol does not contain a clause on reservations. Thus, the rules of general international law on reservations to multilateral treaties apply.[173]

---

167. See in particular the text of the draft articles on state responsibility provisionally adopted by the International Law Commission, Report of the International Law Commission on the Work of its 48th Session, *Official Records of the General Assembly, Fifty-first Session, Supplement No. 10* (A/51/10) pp. 125 et seq.

168. The official versions of the text of the Second Protocol in Arabic, Chinese, Russian and Spanish were provided by UNESCO after the end of the Conference and authenticated before the day of signature on 17 May 1999, see the Final Act of the Diplomatic Conference, paras. 12 - 14. Compare the 1954 Convention which was drawn up in English, French, Russian and Spanish, the four texts being equally 'authoritative', and has been translated into the other official languages of UNESCO's General Conference according to Art. 29 of the Convention.

169. See Arts. 40 to 42. At the official signing ceremony, held at The Hague on 17 May 1999, the following 27 states out of 95 States Parties to the 1954 Convention signed the Second Protocol: Albania, Austria, Belgium, Cambodia, Côte d'Ivoire, Croatia, Estonia, Finland, the Former Yugoslav Republic of Macedonia, Germany, Ghana, Greece, Holy See, Hungary, Indonesia, Italy, Luxembourg, Madagascar, the Netherlands, Nigeria, Pakistan, Qatar, Spain, Sweden, Switzerland, Syrian Arab Republic, and Yemen.

170. See Arts. 41(2), 42(2), 44, 45(2), 46 and 47.

171. See Art. 43.

172. See Arts. 44 and 45(3).

173. See in particular, Art. 19 et seq. of the Vienna Convention on the Law of Treaties of 1969.

3.   CONCLUSIONS

The Second Protocol to the 1954 Convention of 26 March 1999 represents a major step forward in the protection of cultural property under international humanitarian law. It supplements the 1954 Convention and, in particular, defines the circumstances under which a waiver on the basis of 'imperative military necessity' pursuant to Article 4(2) of the 1954 Convention may be invoked, thereby combining the concept of 'military necessity' with the principle of distinction between civilian objects and military objectives as defined in Protocol I of 1977. It provides for a new system of 'enhanced protection' for cultural property of the greatest importance for humanity, obliges States Parties to establish individual criminal responsibility under their domestic law for serious offences against cultural property, further expands the protection of cultural property in situations of non-international armed conflicts, and establishes an institutional framework which allows States Parties to be more closely involved in the protection of cultural property in the event of armed conflict.

THE PINOCHET CASES IN THE UNITED KINGDOM[1]

Colin Warbrick,[2] Elena Martin Salgado[3] and Nicholas Goodwin[4]

1.   INTRODUCTION[5]

The activities of the regime of General, then President, Pinochet[6] after his military coup in Chile in September 1973 are politically, legally and, one might almost say, popularly, one of the landmarks in the development of the international regime of human rights.[7] Pinochet, then Commander of the Armed Forces, led a coup against President Allende, which resulted in a Military Junta seizing power on 11 September 1973. Pinochet became President of Chile in 1974[8] and remained in that position until 11 March 1990, when democracy was restored. He continued on as Commander of the Armed Forces until March 1998, when he was made Senator for Life.

The legal significance of the reaction to events following the coup lies in the response of the United Nations to the excesses of the Pinochet government. The condemnation of Chile by the General Assembly for its policy of gross violations

---

1. © C. Warbrick, E.M. Salgado and N. Goodwin 1999.

2. Professor, Law Department, Durham University / Durham European Law Institute.

3. Research Assistant, Durham European Law Institute, Durham University.

4. Research Assistant, Durham European Law Institute, Durham University.

5. The three judgements so far given by the House of Lords are: *R* v. *Bow Street Metropolitan Magistrate*, ex parte *Pinochet Ugarte* (Amnesty International and others intervening) [1998] 4 *All ER* 897 [hereinafter referred to as *P1*]; *R* v. *Metropolitan Magistrate*, ex parte *Pinochet Ugarte* (No. 2) 1 *All ER* 577 [hereinafter *P2*]; and *R* v. *Metropolitan Stipendiary Magistrate and others*, ex parte *Pinochet Ugarte* (Amnesty International and others intervening) (No. 3) 2 *All ER* 97 [hereinafter *P3*]. References to 'the law of the United Kingdom' are to United Kingdom law as a whole, especially from an external perspective. References to 'English law' are to that part of United Kingdom law applicable to the *Pinochet* proceedings. All of the judgements issued in the *Pinochet* case are available online at http://www.derechos.rg/nizkor/chile/juicio/eng.html.

6. At various stages, Pinochet has been General Pinochet, President Pinochet and Senator Pinochet. He will be referred to simply as 'Pinochet' in this article.

7. P. Constable and A. Valenzuela, *A Nation of Enemies: Chile under Pinochet* (New York, Norton 1993).

8. The date of his Presidency was not resolved by the House of Lords. In *P3*, Lord Browne-Wilkinson said Pinochet became President 'at some stage'. Decree Law No. 527, 26 June 1974 described the President of the Junta as the 'Supreme Chief of the Nation' and Decree Law No. 806 said that the President of the Junta will be 'President of the Republic'. As it turned out, nothing depended upon when Pinochet became President.

of human rights was the first occasion on which the Assembly had taken this step without invoking either a threat to the peace or a consideration of self-determination.[9] It was a foundational step in the establishment of the competence of the United Nations over allegations of gross and flagrant violations of human rights in particular states. Politically, inside and outside the United Nations, states which had hitherto been very cautious about the investigation and condemnation of a state's internal policies spoke out against the events in Chile. Although without quite the same degree of ostracism, Chile joined South Africa as a pariah state. Like South Africa, Chile was not a completely closed society. A great deal became known about what was going on in Chile's jails; indeed Chile cooperated with the United Nations in an investigation of its human rights record that revealed the scale of the violations.[10] As Lord Browne-Wilkinson remarked in *Pinochet3*: 'There is no real dispute that during the period of the Senator Pinochet regime appalling acts of barbarism were committed in Chile ...'[11] If the regime denied the worst allegations against it, it did not wholly resile from justifying an internal security policy of great ferocity, alleged to be necessary to deal with an externally-supported opposition that wished only ill to President Pinochet's project of restoring both order and economic health to Chile.[12] When his formal time as President rather unexpectedly came to an end, Pinochet seemed to get clean away with responsibility for the policies which had been so widely condemned by arranging for constitutional and legal impediments to any proceedings in Chile which might have led to his accountability for what had gone on.[13] His foresight in taking such precautions was confirmed when Chile's Truth Commission documented the evidence that Pinochet's regime had indulged in institutional policies of torture and disappearance during much of its time in office.[14]

If ex-President, now Senator, Pinochet had nothing to fear at home, he seemed equally confident of protection abroad, at least in some states. He made several visits to Britain and, although there would have been hostility had these become publicly known, he faced no legal proceedings, even though there was a substantial group of Chilean expatriates in the United Kingdom – some driven there by Pinochet's policies, others the relatives of his victims – and there were non-governmental organisations in London ambitious to commence proceedings against

---

9. GA Res. 3448.

10. Report of United Nations *Ad Hoc* Working Group on Chile (1975-1978), E/CN.4/1266 (1978).

11. *P3*, p. 101h.

12. Pinochet issued a statement to the British media after his arrest in which he justified the coup: http://news.bbc.co.uk/hi/english/newsdi_209000/209742.stm.

13. On the amnesty law, see J. Mera, 'Chile: Truth and Justice under the Democratic Government', in N. Roth-Arriaza, ed., *Impunity and Human Rights in International Law and Practice* (New York, OUP 1995) pp. 171 at 180-183.

14. National Commission on Truth and Reconciliation (Rettig Report). English text published by Notre Dame University Press, 1993. The Report, which details several thousand cases of torture and disappearances involving thousands of victims, was part of the evidence on which Judge Garzón, the Spanish investigating magistrate, based his inquiries.

those they accused of serious human rights abuses, Pinochet included. It must, therefore, have come as a considerable shock to Pinochet to have been served with a provisional warrant for his arrest while he attended a London clinic on 16 October 1998. The warrant, obtained by the Metropolitan [London] Police, followed the issue of an international arrest warrant in Spain, shortly thereafter to be supplemented by another, alleging, *inter alia,* Pinochet's involvement in crimes of torture and hostage-taking. The action in Spain was part of intensive investigations into the conduct of Pinochet's government conducted by Judge-Magistrate Baltasar Garzón. Some of the allegations concerned actions directed against Spanish nationals, others were said to have had effects in Spain, some even to have involved conduct in Spain by Chilean officials.[15] It is necessary to cut quite a long story short. Judge Garzón's inquiries into events concerning Pinochet had been ongoing for some time before he issued the warrant seeking Pinochet's arrest in England.[16] His activities were challenged by the Spanish Prosecutor on the question of Spain's jurisdiction over the events. That jurisdiction was confirmed by the Audienca Nacional.[17] When Judge Garzón presented his request for Pinochet's extradition to the Spanish government, it forwarded the request to the British authorities in the normal way.

Extradition between the United Kingdom and Spain is governed by the European Convention on Extradition.[18] Pinochet, meanwhile, was challenging the legality in England of all the measures issued and taken against him. His case came to the Divisional Court on 28 October 1998, which held that Pinochet enjoyed immunity from criminal process (which included the extradition proceedings). However, on the basis of the extradition request from Spain and following an appeal by the Crown Prosecution Service,[19] it sent to the House of Lords the single question of:

'the proper interpretation and scope of the immunity enjoyed by a former head of state from arrest and extradition proceedings in the United Kingdom in respect of acts committed while he was head of state'.[20]

---

15. The details of the charges are in the judgment of Lord Slynn in *P1*, pp. 900j-901f. See also the indictment against Pinochet, reprinted in part in this volume at p. 515.

16. For a list of the orders, claims and decisions concerning Pinochet, see Correspondents' Reports at pp. 411-412 of this volume.

17. In two identical decisions: Audiencia Nacional, Sala de lo penal, Pleno Rollo de Apelación 84/98, Sumario 19/97, Juzgado Central de Instrucción N° Cinco, Madrid, 4 de noviembre de 1998 and Audiencia Nacional, Sala de lo penal, Pleno Rollo de Apelación 173/98, Sumario 1/98, Juzgado Central de Instrucción N° Seis, Madrid, 5 de noviembre de 1998. An unofficial English translation of the decision is reprinted at p. 505 of this volume. Professor Antonio Pigrau i Solé's commentary on the decision is in Correspondents' Reports at pp. 412 et seq. of this volume.

18. European Convention on Extradition 1957, *ETS* No. 24.

19. The Crown Prosecution Service (CPS) conducts extradition proceedings in the English courts on behalf of a requesting state. The decision of the Divisional Court had not yet been reported. It is available online at http://www.derechos.org/nizkor/chile/juicio/eng.html.

20. *P1*, p. 902c.

While the appeal was heard, Pinochet was released on conditional bail. Amnesty International was granted leave to intervene in the proceedings in the House of Lords.

2.   THE FIRST PINOCHET JUDGMENT IN THE HOUSE OF LORDS (*PINOCHET1*)

2.1   **The majority decision**

A majority (3-2)[21] in the first decision of the House of Lords of 25 November 1998, held that Pinochet had no immunity from criminal process in the United Kingdom with respect to the extradition requests referring to alleged acts of torture and hostage-taking, which were, the House of Lords implicitly accepted, extradition crimes for the purposes of Pinochet's return to Spain. This was so – although the conduct on which Spain's request was based was alleged to have taken place in Chile (i.e., outside Spain) – since the United Kingdom had claimed extraterritorial jurisdiction over these offences.[22]

Although not in identical terms, the two judges in the majority, Lords Nicholls and Steyn, decided that there was no immunity for acts which were outside the official functions of a head of state (and therefore also of an ex-head of state). As a matter of English law, the question is governed by section 20 of the State Immunity Act 1978 which assimilates the position of a head of state to that of a head of mission accredited to the United Kingdom (and of an ex-head of state to an ex-head of mission), subject to the 'necessary modifications' to take into account the head of state's functions. The cross-reference eventually takes one to Article 39(2) of the Vienna Convention on Diplomatic Relations[23] and brings into effect the distinction to be drawn between the immunity of an individual because of his status (immunity *ratione personae*) and his immunity with respect to the character of a particular act or omission (immunity *ratione materiae*).[24] By reason of his office, the diplomat enjoys immunity *ratione personae* from the criminal process of the receiving state: he may not be arrested, interrogated, tried or detained at all, regardless of the charges against him made by the local authorities or whether they relate to the business of his mission or concern transactions committed in his private life. As an ex-head of mission, his immunity depends upon the classification of the transactions with respect to which immunity is claimed. If they were 'acts performed by [him] in the exercise of his functions as a member of the mission ...', his immunity (now *ratione materiae*), as the Convention puts it, 'shall continue

---

21. The judges in the majority were Lords Nicholls and Steyn, with whom Lord Hoffmann concurred. The dissenting judges were Lords Slynn and Lloyd.

22. S.134 Criminal Justice Act 1988, see *infra* section 4.1.

23. 500 *UNTS* (1961) 95.

24. Y. Dinstein, 'Diplomatic Immunity from Jurisdiction *Ratione Materiae*', 15 *ICLQ* (1966) p. 76.

to subsist'. The combination of the State Immunity Act and the Vienna Convention meant that the question to be resolved by the House of Lords was what it understood by: '... acts performed by [an ex-head of state] in the exercise of his functions as a [head of state] ...', for only with respect to such acts would immunity continue to subsist.

Lord Nicholls said that an ex-head of state enjoyed a continuing personal immunity only with respect to those acts performed in the exercise of functions which international law recognised as functions of a head of state.[25] He went on, '... it hardly needs saying that torture of his own subjects, or of aliens, would not be regarded by international law as a function of a head of state ... Similarly, the taking of hostages ... has been outlawed by the international community as an offence.'[26]

There is a suspicion that Lord Nicholls did not discern the distinction between the substantive criminal responsibility of a head of state in international law and his immunity from process in a domestic court with respect to that liability, for he relied very much on the Nuremberg Charter and the judgment of the Tribunal for his conclusion.[27] He reached the same result, that there was no immunity, in answer to the claim that there was a 'residual' immunity for all ex-state officials for their official acts. Lord Nicholls said that the Torture[28] and Hostages Conventions[29] envisaged extraterritorial prosecution of some officials in terms which made no exception for ex-heads of state, and that there were no grounds for excluding them.[30]

Lord Steyn endorsed the view that international law, as it had developed from Nuremberg until 1973, the date of Pinochet's coup, excluded the conclusion that 'international crimes' – he listed genocide, torture, hostage-taking and crimes against humanity in war or peace – were acts which could be performed in the exercise of the functions of a head of state: 'The normative principles of international law do not require that such high crimes should be classified as acts performed in the exercise of the functions of a head of state.'[31]

Lord Steyn's references to the principles of international law were even sparser than those of Lord Nicholls but more enlightening, nonetheless, than the judgement of Lord Hoffmann, who said only that he agreed with Lords Nicholls and Steyn.

It is not surprising that the terms of the majority judgment were welcomed by human rights groups, because they appeared to hold that the particular charges here were examples, perhaps rather clear ones, of a more general proposition that internationally criminal violations of human rights would not fall within the functions

---

25. *P1*, p. 939h.

26. *P1*, p. 939j.

27. *P1*, p. 940b-f.

28. Convention against Torture and Other Cruel, Inhuman or Degrading Treatment or Punishment 1984, 1465 *UNTS* (1984) 85.

29. International Convention against the Taking of Hostages 1979, 1316 *UNTS* (1979) 205.

30. *P1*, p. 941c-f.

31. *P1*, p. 945j.

of a public official and that immunity *ratione materiae* could never be claimed in proceedings concerning them. Whether this conclusion would have been persuasive to other courts called upon to decide the same issue in other jurisdictions is, however, doubtful, given the scantiness of the reasoning in support of the majority position.

2.2   Lord Slynn's dissenting judgment

If any real enlightenment is to be gained from *Pinochet1*, it comes from the judgment of Lord Slynn, quite the most accomplished of the several judgements delivered in the two substantive decisions of the House of Lords. Lord Slynn agreed that the matter of immunity was governed by section 20 of the State Immunity Act. The continuing immunity enjoyed by an ex-head of state on departure from office was confined to the exercise of his functions as head of state.[32] Lord Slynn would not accept that international law defined in general the functions of a head of state, rather that international law recognised those functions attributed to him by his national law. Nor was he prepared to concede that international law excluded from the national catalogue of powers those the exercise of which constituted crimes against international law. The head of state's functions could include acts that are criminal and no line could be drawn 'between acts whose criminality and moral obliquity is more or less great'.[33] Following a review of the literature and the functions of state immunity, of which he regarded the immunity of the head of state as being a part, Lord Slynn concluded that customary law provided a continuing immunity *ratione materiae* for ex-heads of state.[34] He then considered whether there had been any developments in international law which reduced this protection. While he acknowledged that states had been moving towards withdrawal of immunity in proceedings before international tribunals, he described some of the statements to which the House of Lords had been referred, and which asserted even more substantial inroads into immunity in domestic proceedings 'as aspirations, as embryonic'.[35] This sceptical approach to the processes of international law was the right one (as the problems encountered by the judges in *Pinochet3* showed when they unsuccessfully sought agreement on more ambitious statements about the content of international law) and it informed the remainder of Lord Slynn's judgment. He said:

> 'It does not seem to me that it has been shown that there is any state practice or general consensus, let alone a widely supported convention, that all crimes against international law should be justiciable in national courts on the basis of universality of jurisdiction. Nor is there any *ius cogens* in respect of breaches of international law

---

32. *P1*, p. 908a.
33. *P1*, p. 908f.
34. *P1*, p. 911c.
35. *P1*, p. 913d.

which require that a claim of a state or head of state immunity, itself a well-established principle of international law, should be overridden.'[36]

and later:

'There is no universality of jurisdiction of crimes against international law: there is no universal rule that all crimes are outside immunity *ratione materiae*.'[37]

He noted that there had been doubts about the exact reach of crimes against humanity and that many of the developments referring to international law had been slow or incomplete. He looked for a clear treaty rule that defined the crime, provided for national jurisdiction and which established, 'that having been a head of state is no defence and that *expressly or impliedly* the immunity is not to apply so as to bar proceedings against him.'[38]

When he came to examine the treaties called in aid by the Crown Prosecution Service, he found no clear statement of the conditions he had adumbrated. As for the Torture Convention, he refused to accept that the 'public officials' whose conduct constituted the offence of torture as therein defined included heads of state[39] and he found nothing in the Hostages Convention to indicate a contrary intention there either. Here, one can wonder if Lord Slynn's conclusion on the Torture Convention at least can stand with his position quoted immediately above that the immunity may be limited 'expressly or impliedly'. His grounds for distinguishing heads of state from other public officials were not convincing. He did so by referring to the several international instruments which have established international tribunals and which make it clear that official status is no bar to international criminal responsibility in terms which invariably list 'head of state' in addition to 'public official' among the categories of persons so responsible.[40] This might go to show that the Torture Convention did not intend to establish the responsibility of heads of state for torture but it does not determine whether immunity in national proceedings had been withdrawn or not, for, as Lord Slynn said earlier, the international practice was relevant only to responsibility before international tribunals and not immunity before national ones.[41]

This last step, that the Torture Convention could not be read in any other way than to exclude the immunity of public officials, was the one ultimately taken by a majority in the House of Lords in *Pinochet3*, aided, it has to be noted, by the concession of the Chilean government that Pinochet was a 'public official' for the purposes of the Torture Convention.

---

36. *P1*, p. 913d-e.
37. *P1*, p. 914d.
38. *P1*, p. 915d, emphasis added.
39. *P1*, p. 917f.
40. *P1*, p. 917b-e.
41. *P1*, p. 913b.

Whatever one thinks of the last stage of Lord Slynn's judgment, its overall thrust deserves respect. Establishing that conduct is criminal in customary international law is beset by the uncertainties of the customary law process. This is a matter of particular concern if recourse is to be had to national courts, whose principles of legality might not be satisfied by the vagueness of the products of customary international law. Indeed, even for international tribunals, the basic instruments establishing them have invariably given attention to the detailed elaboration of the crimes within their jurisdictions (even though it is also claimed that they are crimes against customary international law), suggesting that the states in their external relations recognise the same limitations of customary international law that their judges might be expected to notice domestically. Not that international tribunals always feel constrained by these standards. One of the most stringent criticisms of the Nuremberg Tribunal was that it applied vague and *ex-post facto* law,[42] and the Appeals Chamber in *Tadić* had little difficulty in discerning the criminalisation by customary international law of conduct in non-international armed conflicts.[43] Lord Slynn's circumspection not only had regard to the particular law-making processes of the international legal system but reflected the differences between it and the character of national legal orders, where, surely, the step taken by Judge Cassese in *Tadić* would have been much more difficult and some aspects of the Nuremberg process impossible.[44]

3.   THE SECOND PINOCHET JUDGMENT IN THE HOUSE OF LORDS
       (*PINOCHET2*)

Immediately after the judgment in *Pinochet1* had been delivered, there were whispers against Lord Hoffmann, alleging that, by reason of his wife's involvement as an administrative worker for Amnesty International, he could be charged with bias or the appearance of bias which would vitiate the judgement. Nonetheless, at first, proceedings took their expected course. The Home Secretary issued his authority to proceed with the extradition, a considered decision, which took into account those factors, such as Pinochet's age and health which might have been raised in any attempt to challenge his decision.[45] Pinochet, still on bail, made a brief appearance before the extradition magistrate but by then the clamour against Lord Hoffmann was gaining ground, now based on his involvement as a trustee of a fund which supported some (unrelated) activities of Amnesty International. Eventually,

---

42. For consideration of these arguments, see J. Stone, *Legal Controls of International Conflict* (London, Stevens 1959) pp. 357-363.

43. *The Prosecutor* v. *Duško Tadić,* Decision on the Defence Motion for Interlocutory Appeal on Jurisdiction, Case No. IT-94-1-AR72, 105 *ILR* 419, paras. 128-137.

44. Lord Lloyd dissented also, holding that there was an immunity for an ex-head of state under customary international law, *P1*, p. 930g, and under the State Immunity Act, *P1*, p. 933d.

45. HC Debs, Vol. 322 WA 213-217, 9 Dec 1998. The challenge duly arrived but was overtaken by the new authority to proceed issued after *Pinochet3*, see *infra*, section 6.

and quite without precedent, a new bench of the House of Lords was convened to consider whether the allegations against Lord Hoffmann's impartiality, real or perceived, vitiated the judgement in *Pinochet1*. In a judgement of some interest in English administrative law but which need not detain us here, the House of Lords, on 15 January 1999, did indeed find such fault and vacated the original judgment in *Pinochet1*. The judgement is thus without effect in English law, but such persuasiveness that it possesses remains available to other courts inside and outside the United Kingdom.

A new bench of seven judges, itself unusual though not unprecedented, was convened to hear the case anew. There were certain changes from the original proceedings, quite apart from the much greater time for counsel on both sides to prepare their arguments. Chile was admitted to intervene as a party, it having become clear that what was at issue was the claim to state immunity of Chile, rather than some personal claim of Pinochet. The government of Chile had been asserting from the very beginning of the saga its priority to decide whether criminal proceedings should be brought against Pinochet and denying that there were insuperable legal obstacles arising from the Amnesty Law[46] which would prevent a criminal trial in Chile.[47] Chile did not ask for Pinochet's extradition. Even more significant as it turned out, the Crown Prosecution Service had presented on behalf of the government of Spain an extended list of charges to form the basis of the extradition request.[48] Some of these related to the period before the coup in Chile and, of course, before Pinochet could have been head of state. Therefore, there could be little question of immunity applying to these allegations and it was necessary for Pinochet's lawyers to challenge their status as extradition crimes if they were to avoid proceedings with respect to them continuing.

4.   THE THIRD PINOCHET JUDGMENT IN THE HOUSE OF LORDS
       (*PINOCHET3*)[49]

There are two difficulties in giving a coherent account of the third Pinochet decision. One of the issues, the question of the extradition crimes, is wholly a point of English law and turns upon a matter – the territoriality of the criminal law – which is unfamiliar to lawyers from most other legal systems. On the other point,

---

46. Decree Law 2.191, introduced by the military government in 1978, provides an amnesty law preventing prosecution of individuals implicated in certain criminal acts committed between September 1973 and March 1978.

47. See for instance, statement of Foreign Minister Insulza after his failed attempt to persuade the British and Spanish governments to release Pinochet, 2 December 1998, http://cnn.com/WORLD/europe/9812/02/pinochet.01/.

48. The various charges in the provisional warrants and the extradition request, translated into corresponding English offences for the purpose of establishing extradition crimes, are set out in Lord Hope's judgment, *P3*, pp. 132j-135j.

49. Rendered on 24 March 1999. The judges in the majority were Lords Browne-Wilkinson, Hope, Hutton, Saville, Millett and Phillips. Lord Goff dissented.

state immunity, while six of the judges in the House of Lords were agreed upon the outcome in *Pinochet3*, it is a taxing search to find a reason for their decision to which a majority of them was committed. The treatment of many aspects of international law is confused, sometimes to the point of incomprehensibility.

4.1   Extradition crimes and double criminality

The complication which arose here – how did the notion of double criminality affect the determination of whether the allegations against Pinochet were extradition crimes?, which could be an issue for any domestic legal system – was exaggerated by two factors. One was the peculiar common law notion of the territoriality of crime; the other is the incoherent development of extradition law in the United Kingdom.

The common law first of all. At common law, the locus of conduct constituting a crime is not simply a matter of jurisdiction but of substantive criminality; where conduct takes place is an element of its criminality. As far as England is concerned, the basic principle is that only conduct which takes place in England is criminal.[50] Parliament may and frequently has extended this narrow reach of liability, the example relevant here being section 134 of the Criminal Justice Act 1988, which makes torture, as there defined, a crime wherever and by whomsoever committed.

Double criminality is a feature of extradition law in general, though its details differ from system to system: the conduct which constitutes the offence in the requesting state has also to constitute an offence under the law of the requested state.[51] Common law states have to add a rider: 'would have to constitute an offence in the law of the requested state if it had taken place there'. Where the conduct is wholly territorial no great problems arise. Where some or all of the conduct takes place outside the territory of the requesting state, they do.[52] Section 2 of the Extradition Act 1989 includes the following on extradition crime:

(1) In this Act, except in Schedule 1, 'extradition crime' means -

...

    (b) an extra-territorial offence against the law of a foreign state... which satisfies -
      (i) the condition specified in subsection (2) below

...

(2) The condition mentioned in subsection (1)(b)(i) above is that in corresponding circumstances equivalent conduct would constitute an extra-territorial offence against the law of the United Kingdom...

---

50. (English) Law Commission Report No. 91, 'Territorial and Extraterritorial Extent of the Criminal Law' (1978). 'England' for this purpose is 'England and Wales'. The law in Northern Ireland is the same. For Scotland, see P. Ferguson, 'Jurisdiction and Criminal Law in Scotland and England', *Juridical Review* (1987) p. 179.

51. C. van den Wyngaert, 'Double Criminality as a Requirement to Jurisdiction', in N. Jareborg, ed., *Double Criminality* (Uppsala, Iustus Forlag 1989) p. 43.

52. G. Mullan, 'The Concept of Double Criminality in the Context of Extraterritorial Crimes', 1 *Criminal Law Review* (1997) p. 17.

Spain was requesting Pinochet's extradition, in the main, for offences constituted by conduct which took place wholly outside Spain. Section 2(2) would be satisfied only if English law regarded such extraterritorial conduct as constituting a crime under English law 'in corresponding circumstances'. It did not, for instance, for genocide (a request for Pinochet's extradition on which had been removed by the Home Secretary when issuing his authority to proceed), which is a wholly territorial offence in English law,[53] but it did for torture because of section 134 of the Criminal Justice Act. It should be emphasised that it was necessary to rely on this provision for the purposes of double criminality. It was true that what Pinochet was alleged to have done in Chile would have constituted offences in England – grievous bodily harm etc. – but as these were not extraterritorial offences, his conduct in Chile with respect to a request from Spain would not have satisfied the double criminality test.

In the Divisional Court, Lord Bingham had given a literal interpretation of section 2(2), saying that what was required was that the conduct would constitute an offence under English law at the time of the extradition request, which, of course, extraterritorial torture did at the time of the request for Pinochet's extradition. The matter was not considered by the House of Lords in *Pinochet1*.

However, in *Pinochet3*, for the reasons explained, it was an issue: his lawyers could not rely on immunity alone. The language of the Extradition Act might have appeared to be clear enough, but it was a consolidating as well as a reforming Act. United Kingdom extradition law had had different arrangements for extradition with foreign states under the Extradition Act 1870 and with states of the Commonwealth (and colonies) under the Fugitive Offenders Act 1967.[54] Though the bulk of United Kingdom extradition practice now conforms with European states under the European Convention on Extradition – to give effect to which was a substantial objective of the 1989 Act – some of the old arrangements with foreign and Commonwealth states continue in force and provision is made for them in the 1989 Extradition Act. The language of the Extradition Act for cases outside Part III could bear a retrospective interpretation,[55] and the language of the Extradition Act 1870 (which is preserved by Schedule 1) refers to the putative criminality of conduct in England for the purposes of double criminality 'at the time and date of the alleged crime', thus introducing an element of retroactively into the test in addition to the location of the conduct constituting it.[56] It was the position of all the Law Lords that section 2 should not be read in such a way as to remove this condition from extraditions under the old arrangements, rather that all extraditions should be subject to the old understanding.[57] In Pinochet's case, this meant that his conduct was to

---

53. Genocide Act 1969, s. 1.

54. There is yet another scheme, for the return of fugitives to Ireland, the Backing of Warrants (Republic of Ireland) Act 1965.

55. Lord Browne-Wilkinson, *P3*, p. 106b-f.

56. See further, Lord Browne-Wilkinson, *P3*, pp. 104d-107d.

57. Lord Millett would have avoided the effect of the retrospectivity rule because he regarded torture as a crime by English law throughout the relevant period by reason of its criminality in customary international law, *P3*, p. 178b-d.

be assessed in light of English law at the time his conduct took place. Until 29 September 1988, when section 134 of the Criminal Justice Act came into force, his conduct in Chile would not have constituted an offence in England, the double criminality test would not have been satisfied and he could not have been extradited to Spain to face charges based on conduct before that date. Lord Hope's conclusion was that only one charge of torture and one charge of conspiracy to torture survived this analysis. In addition, the double criminality test was satisfied for a single charge of conspiracy to murder in Spain because English law regards conspiracy abroad to commit an offence in England as an offence within its jurisdiction, so that the facts which constituted the offence in Spain (instigation of an offence) would putatively have constituted an offence in England too.[58]

It would, perhaps, be going too far to say that Lord Browne-Wilkinson's decision on the retrospectivity point was wrong but it was plainly unfortunate and might have been avoided. Section 2(1) says clearly: 'In this Act, except in Schedule 1, 'extradition crime means'...', (though this would not dispose of his arguments about Commonwealth extraditions). Furthermore, there is recent authority which distinguished between 'extradition crime' for section 2 and 'extradition crime' for Schedule 1, though on a different point.[59] It is hard to see what public policy was served by Lord Browne-Wilkinson's interpretation: the fugitive's conduct was an offence by the law of the trial court at the time it was committed so there is no substantive retrospectivity deficiency in that law. The conduct would have been an offence if committed in England at the time of the extradition, so extradition would not be inimical to any English public interest. Moreover, if his line were followed, there would be obstacles to the effective operation of any treaty regime of which extradition formed a part if the United Kingdom was not among the earliest parties to the scheme. Lord Browne-Wilkinson's judgement means that in the absence of specific words in the implementing legislation, United Kingdom courts will not be able to cooperate with other parties with respect to conduct taking place within their jurisdiction before the United Kingdom had enacted its implementing legislation.

Lord Hope found that the conduct upon which the allegations of hostage-taking were founded would not constitute the crime of hostage-taking in English law, regardless of any considerations of time and place, for they averred that the purpose of detaining the hostages was to influence their conduct, not that of others, as the offence required.[60]

4.2   The immunity question

At the beginning of the final judgment in the interminable Tin Council litigation of 1989, Lord Templeman isolated the issue on which the whole case turned. It was,

---

58. Lord Hope, *P3*, pp. 138d-141g.
59. *R* v. *Home Secretary*, ex parte *Gilmore* [1998] 1 *All ER* 264.
60. *P3*, pp. 137a-138d.

he said, 'a short question of the construction of the plain words of a statutory instrument';[61] this after months of argument in many courts about the international law of international organisations and its justiciability in the English court. And in *Pinochet3*, almost the same thing might have been said: it was a matter of statutory interpretation (though arguably not entirely so) even after days of argument about some of the most contested points of international law. The Law Lords did reach an identifiable majority position on the state immunity point in domestic law (though they relied as well on the words of the Torture Convention). They also agreed on some points of international law which it was not necessary for them to decide.[62] On the other hand, it is hard to find any degree of common understanding on a point of international law that might have been relevant to their decision.

The statutory provision which had to be interpreted and on which everything turned was section 134(1) of the Criminal Justice Act:

A public official or person acting in official capacity, whatever his nationality, commits the offence of torture if in the United Kingdom or elsewhere he intentionally inflicts severe pain or suffering on another in the performance or purported performance of his official duties.

The provision creates an offence subject to extraterritorial, universal jurisdiction. An essential element of the offence is that the torture be committed by a public official. It was accepted by Chile that Pinochet had been a public official at the time of the alleged offences.[63] If he were immune from prosecution or extradition, then so would be every other public official defendant accused of or wanted for torture, and the extraterritorial innovation of the Criminal Justice Act would have been without practical effect.[64] To interpret the section in any other way would have contradicted one of the basic principles of statutory interpretation: that Parliament should not be presumed to have legislated otiosely. However, unambiguity of legislation is a conclusion to be reached at the end of the arguments rather than the premise from which the argument starts. It is seldom the case that a judge will say: 'The words are clear and admit of only one meaning. I need to hear no argument on the matter.' As we have already seen about the meaning of 'extradition crime', the understanding of a word may depend upon the context in which it is read; the single sentence or the whole statute. However, the admissible 'context' may be even wider than the word's immediate documentary surroundings, embracing all the extra-statutory aids to interpretation that the English court deems appropriate to the task of discerning the intention of Parliament as expressed in the language of

---

61. *Maclaine Watson & Co Ltd* v. *Department of Trade and Industry* [1989] 3 *All ER* 523, 526g.

62. See *infra*. p. 108.

63. See *infra*. n. 107.

64. Lord Goff, *P3*, p. 127d, suggested that extraterritorial jurisdiction would be available where there is a waiver by the state of which the defendant was a public official but the remoteness of the case serves to make the opposite point.

a statute. These supplementary means are particularly extensive where matters of international law are relevant. There are two applicable principles of statutory interpretation which come into play, one much stronger than the other. Where, from the text of the Act or otherwise, there is evidence that Parliament intended to give effect to a treaty obligation of the United Kingdom, the language of the statute will be given the meaning of the treaty, where that is at all possible.[65] Furthermore, the meaning of the treaty is to be determined according to the rules of interpretation of international law, including such supplementary means as it would allow, such as preparatory work.[66] The strength of this presumption is based on the reasonable proposition that compliance with the terms of the treaty was Parliament's intention, it being the case that legislation is always necessary to give domestic legal effect to the United Kingdom's treaty obligations. The weaker presumption is that Parliament is presumed not to intend to legislate contrary to the international obligations of the United Kingdom at large. Clear words of a statute to the contrary would prevail and other presumptions might take priority.[67]

Matters of international law would have become relevant to the interpretation of section 134 if its language were, even only plausibly, ambiguous. In fact, they entered the interpretative process from a different direction because the House of Lords did not start from section 134. Instead, the dynamics of the procedure affected the way the question was decided. Immunity questions are preliminary matters for, if the person claiming immunity succeeds, then the court has no jurisdiction to proceed to any question covered by the immunity. Accordingly, the judgements started with the claims to immunity raised by Pinochet and the government of Chile. The House of Lords was back again with section 20 of the State Immunity Act 1978, the provision considered already. All the judges who addressed the point found difficulties in making the 'necessary modifications' to use the law of diplomatic immunity as the basis for the immunity of heads of state. The State Immunity Act had been amended during its passage so that a provision which would have restricted the immunity of a head of state to acts done in the United Kingdom was taken out.[68] Although there is no explanation in the Parliamentary record for this change, it is well-known that the government was concerned about the position of President Amin of Uganda, who had threatened from time to time to visit this country, and powers were given in section 20(3) to enable entry to be denied to him. The absence of any specific limitation in the legislation encouraged the judges to a wide understanding of the 'functions' of a head of state; they were to be defined by his national law and were limited neither by the locus of the place where they were exercised nor by reference to the external or diplomatic role of the head of state. What is more, the mere fact that the acts of the head of state were criminal, by his own law or by the law of the state in which he was asserting his immunity, was not enough to defeat the immunity; if

---

65. *The Eschersheim* [1976] 1 *All ER* 920, 924, per Lord Diplock.
66. *Fothergill* v. *Monarch Airlines* [1981] *AC* 251.
67. *Alcom* v. *Republic of Colombia* [1984] 2 *All ER* 6.
68. HL Debs., Vol. 538, col. 1, 18 March 1978.

anything, it is a reason for confirming it.[69] For some of the judges, section 20 of the State Immunity Act gave effect to the immunities of a head of state under customary international law. Others, additionally or as an alternative, sought to discover what the customary law was. Relying mainly on Sir Arthur Watts's Hague Lectures,[70] they found that customary law likewise provided a wide immunity for a widely drawn range of official functions. So, if the acts of torture and murder alleged against Pinochet were official acts, then, other things being equal, he was entitled to immunity *ratione materiae* in the extradition proceedings. That is what Lord Lloyd had decided in *Pinochet1* and what Lord Goff said in *Pinochet3*. Indeed, it was what all the judges conceded in *Pinochet3* with respect to the charge of conspiracy to murder.

Other things being equal and, even if international law provided a ground upon which the claim to immunity could be defeated, could an English court give effect to it, given the language of the State Immunity Act? Limiting the protection provided by the State Immunity Act required justification but it could be found in one of the presumptions of statutory interpretation referred to above, that the language of the statute was to be read in the light of the United Kingdom's international obligations, including those arising under customary international law. In *Alcom*, Lord Diplock had used this approach to find an immunity from execution of a civil judgment (required by customary international law), where the Court of Appeal in the same case had not been able to discover such protection on the face of the statute.[71] The various formulations tried by the Crown Prosecution Service and Amnesty International to establish limits on the law of ex-head of state immunity boiled down to two arguments: one, that by international law, it could not be an official function of a head of state to commit an international crime (possibly, an international crime which violated a rule of *ius cogens*); the other, that, though this kind of conduct remained within the function of a head of state, international law had provided that there would be no immunity with respect to it.

Sir Arthur Watts's lectures had referred to one limitation on the protection of a head of state:

> For international conduct which is so serious to be tainted with criminality to be regarded as attributable only to the impersonal State and not to the individuals who ordered or perpetrated it is both unrealistic and offensive to common notions of justice. The idea that individuals who commit international crimes are *internationally* accountable for them has now become accepted as a part of international law.[72]

There are thus limitations about what this proposition entails, in particular, it has no necessary implications for proceedings before a domestic court. The provision

---

69. For example, Lord Browne-Wilkinson, *P3*, p. 113e.

70. Sir Arthur Watts, 'Legal Position in International Law of Heads of State, Heads of Governments and Foreign Ministers', 274 *Hague Receuil* (1994) p. 11.

71. *Supra* n. 67.

72. *Supra* n. 70, p. 82, emphasis in original.

in the London Charter was necessary to establish that there could be individual responsibility for international crimes,[73] that is to say, a matter of substantive law. Once that was established, it followed that there could be no immunity before the Tribunal for those who claimed their acts were acts of the German state. This was confirmed in the Nuremberg Principles and has found reflection in the Statutes of the *ad hoc* tribunals[74] and the Statute of the International Criminal Court.[75] However, Lord Goff, dissenting, was persuaded that these provisions on responsibility derived their authority from international agreement or from the competence of the Security Council and had no determinative consequences for immunity before national courts,[76] while others used them to show the content of the international criminality could be applied to heads of state.[77] Of itself, this could not resolve the domestic immunity question, which thus was whether there was any other international law basis for deciding for non-immunity. The judgements in *Pinochet3* are exceedingly unhelpful in answering it, and there does not appear to be a proposition of general customary law which commands the support of a majority of the judges.

The judgment in *Pinochet3* has been variously classed as a skillful exercise in judicial appreciation[78] and as a conspiracy to hide a majority opinion at odds with *Pinochet1*, which could not bring itself to reach a conclusion which would produce a reaction of incomprehension in public opinion as to how such a difference was possible.[79] The inability of the majority to fashion a single judgement based on an agreed reasoning appears, in part at least, to have been due to a failure to appreciate the nature of international law and some of its most controversial concepts. In this respect, the judgements are in marked contrast to that of Lord Slynn in *Pinochet1*. Where the judges address the sources of international law expressly, their grasp is unconvincing.[80] Mostly, though, they make only indirect acknowledgement of the nature of the law-making process, particularly as it applies to the fundamental propositions to which the judgements refer.

The lack of rigour was most pronounced regarding *ius cogens*. Lord Millett appeared to regard *ius cogens* and *erga omnes* as synonyms.[81] Lord Browne-Wilkinson and Lord Hope referred to '*ius cogens*' offences[82] ('such high crimes

---

73. London Charter of the International Military Tribunal, Art. 7, *UKTS* No. 27 (1946).

74. Statute of the International Criminal Tribunal for the Former Yugoslavia, Art. 7(2), annexed to Security Council Resolution 827; Statute of the International Criminal Tribunal for Rwanda, Art. 6(2), annexed to Security Council Resolution 955.

75. Rome Statute of the International Criminal Court, Art. 27, which, uniquely has separate provisions governing responsibility, Art. 27(1), and non-immunity, Art. 27(2).

76. *P3*, pp. 119j-120d.

77. Lord Hutton, *P3*, pp. 161b-163b.

78. Lady Fox, 'The Pinochet Case No. 3', 48 *ICLQ* (1999) p. 687.

79. *The Economist* (7 March 1999) p. 34.

80. For instance, Lord Phillips, *P3*, pp. 182j-185c, including judicial decisions and 'the writing of authors' as sources on a par with custom and confusing the general principles of law recognised by civilised nations with the general principles of international law.

81. *P3*, p. 177c.

82. *P3*, p. 109b (Browne-Wilkinson).

as have achieved the status of *ius cogens*'[83]) – a concept unknown to international law. Lord Browne-Wilkinson's position was that 'offences *ius cogens* may be punished by any state',[84] while Lord Millett added the qualification that crimes against international law required not only conduct in violation of a rule *ius cogens* but that the conduct must be 'so serious and of such a scale that [it] can justly be regarded as an attack on the international legal order'.[85] Because it is a claim for a hierarchically superior rule, the assertion that a rule is a rule of *ius cogens* is a powerful tool but there is a shortage of practice about the identity of these rules and the consequences of their violation. That the prohibition of torture was a rule of *ius cogens* did not have determinative effect, for, as we shall see, the proposition on which a majority were agreed found an exception only with respect to immunity *ratione materiae*. If *ius cogens* were part of the explanation for this, surely immunity *ratione personae* would have yielded as well.

If *ius cogens* was not a satisfactory way to resolve the matter, the judges turned to international crimes. It is useful here to introduce a non-technical distinction between crimes by international law and crimes against international law. By the first is meant crimes created by states in domestic law as a result of an international obligation, usually by treaty, to make defined conduct criminal. The various anti-terrorism treaties are prominent examples. The conduct required to be made criminal may be (but need not be) also criminal in international law: genocide and grave breaches of the Geneva Conventions are examples. Criminality against international law arises under customary law, though individual crimes may be codified for various purposes, and it does not necessarily follow that states have an obligation to make the conduct which constitutes them criminal in their domestic laws.[86] If conduct is criminal only in international law, persons accused of it may be tried only in international courts (subject to a *caveat* to follow immediately), so practice which establishes the non-immunity (in reality, responsibility) of heads of state before these tribunals has no necessary implication for domestic trials. A possible exception is where a national legal system receives customary international law directly into its legal order and is prepared to regard the existence of an international crime as a crime also in national law. Was it, then, possible to show that there was an international crime of torture? A majority of the House of Lords said that it was but the explanations of the content and source of the crime were quite different. Lord Browne-Wilkinson said that torture on a large scale was a

---

83. *P3*, p. 147f (Hope).

84. *Supra* n. 82.

85. *P3*, p. 177d. Lord Millett relied on the decision of the ICTY in *Prosecutor* v. *Anto Furundžija*, Judgement ICTY IT-95-17/1-T, paras. 153-157 for the *ius cogens* quality of the prohibition of torture and on *A-G for Israel* v. *Eichmann* 36 *ILR* 5 for the necessity of scale to establish criminality.

86. The conclusion of the ICTY Appellate Chamber in *Tadić* that some conduct occurring in non-international armed conflict was criminal in international law did not, of itself, create an obligation on States to criminalise such conduct in their domestic law, *Prosecutor* v. *Tadić, supra* n. 43.

crime in international law because it would constitute a crime against humanity.[87] Lord Hope agreed on the need for widespread torture as an element of international criminality but he made no reference to crimes against humanity.[88] Both these conclusions must have been, though their authors do not say so, based on customary international law. Lord Millett agreed that torture was a crime in customary international law and he, too, imposed a requirement of systematic torture.[89] Lord Hutton agreed but he would have held that even a single act of torture constituted a crime against international law.[90] While there is here a conclusion supported by a majority that large-scale torture is a crime against international law, it was of no relevance to the determination of the case because only Lord Millett was willing to find that torture was also a crime in English law, by reason of the rule in the *Trendtex* case[91] that customary law was part of the law of England. Some of the judges said that the Torture Convention did not create the crime of torture but simply provided a mechanism for the better pursuit of its practitioners[92] but, for those who took the view that torture as an international crime needed an element of scale, the Convention must have extended the boundary of criminality to single acts, if only in the laws of the states parties.

On the other hand, while states may not be obliged to make conduct constituting international crimes by international customary law criminal in their domestic law, they may be entitled to do so. Clearly, they would not be prohibited from doing so if they could establish one of the well-recognised bases for exercising prescriptive jurisdiction over the conduct, for instance that it took place in their territory or was committed by one of their nationals. The crucial question is whether a state may criminalise conduct on a universal basis, so that it may claim, as against any other interested state – say the territorial state or the state of nationality of the defendant – the right to bring criminal proceedings against a person on no grounds other than his presence in its territory. Chile's argument that its claim to jurisdiction as the territorial state took priority over that of any other party was expressly rejected by Lord Hutton.[93]

None of the judgements accepted as an unqualified proposition that crimes against international law admit of the exercise of universal jurisdiction. Two judges thought that there was universal jurisdiction by international law, i.e., the power of states to exercise jurisdiction for 'certain offences', but what were they? Lord Browne-Wilkinson talked about offences *ius cogens* and required as well large scale violations,[94] similarly Lord Millett – *ius cogens* and an attack on the international legal order[95] – but Lord Phillips thought that it was still 'an open question' whether

---

87. *P3*, p. 108d.
88. *P3*, p. 151c.
89. *Supra* n. 81.
90. *P3*, p. 166j.
91. *Trendtex Trading Corp Ltd* v. *Central Bank of Nigeria* [1977] 1 *All ER* 881.
92. Lord Browne-Wilkinson, *P3*, p. 109g; Lord Hutton, pp. 163h-164j.
93. *P3*, p. 166a.
94. *P3*, p. 109b.
95. *P3*, p. 177d.

international law 'recognises' universal jurisdiction for crimes against international law.[96] Even if this line of inquiry had reached the opposite conclusion, the matter would not have certainly been determined against Pinochet for, even where there was universal jurisdiction, it did not follow, in the opinion of any of the judges, that immunity would not be just as applicable as it would be in ordinary criminal proceedings.[97] This was an acknowledgement of the process of transformation which is at work when the national legislator enacts the statute criminalising domestically the conduct which constitutes the crime at the international level. It is a different crime, subject to a whole regime for deciding criminal responsibility and the attribution of punishment of each national legal order. Certainly, where crimes by customary international law are concerned, there are reasons of legal certainty, alluded to by Lord Slynn in *Pinochet1*, for requiring the act of transformation rather than allowing national judges to ascribe criminal responsibility on the basis of what will all too likely be an incomplete investigation into an incomplete legal rule.

At this stage, the judges in *Pinochet3* had reached, by much inferior routes, the final position of Lord Slynn in *Pinochet1*. However, an overwhelming majority of them were prepared to take the extra step which Lord Slynn was not and to rely on the Torture Convention to decide the issue before them. Here, there was a measure of agreement among an identifiable majority of the House of Lords. There was broad agreement about what the Convention did and did not do:

(a) it did not create the crime of torture in international law but required that parties make the crime of torture as defined in the Convention an offence in their national laws;

(b) it created a mechanism for the more effective punishment of those responsible for torture by placing an obligation on parties to submit for prosecution the cases against those alleged to have committed torture or to extradite those against whom it chose not to proceed;

(c) it allowed, although it did not require, a state party to make the crime of torture one of universal jurisdiction;[98]

(d) although it did not have a provision limiting or removing the immunity of state officials, the Convention could not be read sensibly as allowing it to continue.

The final element was put in forthright terms by Lord Saville:

'So far as the States that are parties to the Convention are concerned, I cannot see how, so far as torture is concerned, this immunity can exist consistently with the terms of that Convention. Each State party has agreed that the other States parties can exercise jurisdiction over alleged official torturers found within their territories, by

---

96. *P3*, p. 188j.

97. Lord Browne-Wilkinson, *P3*, p. 114f-g; by implication, Lord Hope, p. 150f; Lord Phillips, pp. 189j-190a.

98. Lord Browne-Wilkinson, *P3*, pp. 108d-111b. Apart from Lord Goff, the other judges agreed with his analysis.

extraditing them or referring them to their own appropriate authorities for prosecution; and thus to my mind can hardly simultaneously claim an immunity from extradition or prosecution that is necessarily based on the official nature of the alleged torture...[99] To my mind, these terms [of the Convention] demonstrate that the states who have become parties have clearly and unambiguously agreed that official torture should now be dealt with in a way which would otherwise amount to an interference in their sovereignty.'[100]

Similarly, Lord Millett:

'The definition of torture, both in the Convention and *section 134* (emphasis added), is in my opinion entirely inconsistent with the existence of a plea of immunity *ratione materiae* ... The official or governmental nature of the act, which forms the basis of the immunity, is an essential ingredient of the offence. No rational system of criminal justice can allow an immunity which is co-extensive with the offence.'[101]

And Lord Phillips:

'The only conduct covered by this Convention is conduct which would be subject to immunity *ratione materiae*, if such immunity were applicable. The Convention is thus incompatible with the applicability of immunity *ratione materiae*.'[102]

Lord Hutton said:

'I consider that the clear intent of the provisions is that an official of one state who has committed torture should be prosecuted if he is present in another state.'[103]

He made it clear that this finding applied to single acts of torture, as well as torture on a large scale. However, unlike the other judges who relied on the Torture Convention, Lord Hutton took a different view of its effect:

'My conclusion ... is based on the view that the commission of acts of torture is not a function of a head of state ...'[104]

Although this might seem to undermine Lord Hutton's support for the three opinions just referred to, since his conclusion is restricted to torture as defined in the Convention, nothing seems to turn on his explanation of why the Convention reads as it does. As with the other judges, it was the text of the Convention which determined the issue. Lord Browne-Wilkinson's position was similar. He provided

---

99. *P3*, p. 169f-g.
100. *P3*, p. 170c.
101. *P3*, pp. 178j-179a.
102. *P3*, p. 190h-j.
103. *P3*, p. 165c.
104. *P3*, p. 166e.

a detailed explanation why, '... the notion of continued immunity for ex-heads of state is inconsistent with the provisions of the Torture Convention', but, like Lord Hutton, he gave as the reason for why the Convention was drafted as it was 'that the implementation of torture as defined by the Convention cannot be said to be a state function'[105] and, again like Lord Hutton, he regarded the entry into force of the Convention as the vital element in establishing this as a matter of international law.

So we find that a majority of the House of Lords agreed that there is no immunity *ratione materiae* for acts of torture as defined in the Convention from a reading of the words of the Convention. These judges were undoubtedly helped to this decision by the concession of the government of Chile and by Pinochet that he was (or rather, had been) a public official within the terms of the Convention when he had been head of state.[106] Since the words of section 134 of the Criminal Justice Act 1988 are the same, the same conclusion might well have been reached on a reading of the statute.[107]

It followed that there was no immunity under international law for Pinochet after 30 September 1988 (when Chile became a party to the Torture Convention[108]) against other states parties. Pinochet could not have been prosecuted for extraterritorial torture in the United Kingdom until the Criminal Justice Act came into force on 29 September 1988 and, arguably, the denial of his immunity in domestic proceedings would have been good against Chile only when the United Kingdom became a party to the Convention on 8 December 1988[109] and accepted the same obligations as Chile. Since Spain was a party to the Convention from 21 October 1997, no separate issue of Pinochet's immunity between Spain and Chile arose.

The supporting judgment of Lord Hope is more difficult to fathom. For him, the entry into force of the Torture Convention for Chile was the crucial step in limiting the application of Pinochet's claim to immunity *ratione materiae* but, he went on, only 'in the event of allegations of systematic or widespread torture...'.[110] Widespread torture was a crime by customary international law and was contrary to an *ius cogens* norm. Given his earlier decimation of the offences for which Pinochet might be extradited, it is difficult to see how Lord Hope's exception applied in this case, save that he regarded the remaining charge of conspiracy to torture as covering the later elements of a long campaign of torture. It would follow from his reasoning that immunity *ratione materiae* would not be available for an isolated act of official torture, but that was the only other offence that Lord Hope's

105. *P3*, p. 115c.

106. Referred to by Lord Browne-Wilkinson, *P3*, p. 110g, indicating that he thought that the concession was correctly made.

107. See the quotation from Lord Millett, *supra* n. 101.

108. Though the actual date should have been 30 October 1998 the date the Convention was in force for Chile, Torture Convention, Art. 19.

109. Again, strictly, 8 January 1989, when the Convention was in force for the United Kingdom.

110. *P3*, p. 152c.

analysis of the extradition offence had left standing against Pinochet. His explanation for his conclusion was that:

> 'We are dealing here with the remnants of an allegation that [Pinochet] is guilty of what would now, without doubt, be regarded by customary international law as an international crime.'[111]

Finally, there is Lord Goff's dissenting judgment. He agreed that the Torture Convention was at the core of the immunity question but he proceeded from the absence of a specific provision in it which limited immunity to hold that state immunity was intended to survive, in the absence of proof that it was excluded by an implied term. His search for an implied term was much influenced by considerations of waiver of immunity. He was dubious about the whole endeavour, expecting an express term for a matter which he deemed of such importance. He conceded that implied terms could be relied upon only 'in the most obvious cases' and, for a variety of policy reasons, he was not prepared to allow that Article 1 of the Torture Convention was 'an obvious case'.[112] As to whether the argument based on the express words of Article 1 of the Convention avoided the need for such an inquiry, he was scathing. It had not been raised in *Pinochet1*, he said, and had emerged only in the course of argument in *Pinochet3*:

> 'It is surprising that an important argument of this character, if valid, should have been overlooked by fourteen counsel (including three distinguished Professors of International Law) ...'[113]

The Professors of International Law can defend themselves but Lord Goff hardly seemed to be fair to Lord Nicholls who used closely the same analysis in *Pinochet1*. He was there referring to the Hostages Convention as well as the Torture Convention when he said:

> 'It is not consistent with the existence of these crimes that former officials, however senior, should be immune from prosecution outside their own jurisdictions. The two international conventions made it clear that these crimes were to be punishable by courts of individual states.'[114]

Lord Goff alone would have sustained the plea of state immunity for all the charges in the extradition warrant which remained alive. On the other hand, the judges were agreed that there would have been immunity *ratione personae* for a serving head of state (and any other state official entitled to such immunity) for official torture,

---

111. *P3*, p. 151h.
112. *P3*, pp. 120c-130h.
113. *P3*, p. 123f.
114. *P1*, p. 941e.

even on a large scale,[115] and further that there was immunity *ratione materiae* in this case for conspiracy to murder.[116] These inconsistencies are bound to raise disquiet, which cannot entirely be dispelled on the first point by arguing that it was not necessary for the court to decide it, for everyone agreed that Pinochet no longer enjoyed a personal immunity. From the point of view of English law, there is a strong case for saying that, if the majority was right about the interpretation of the Torture Convention and, therefore, of section 134 of the Criminal Justice Act, the same priority of the torture provision should be given over a claim of immunity *ratione personae* – the domestic law basis of personal diplomatic immunity being either common law (incorporating customary international law) or a prior statute to the Criminal Justice Act, the Diplomatic Privileges Act 1964; either should yield to the plain words of section 134. However, this would be a radical conclusion which should wait its proper time for determination. The continuing immunity with respect to conspiracy to murder underlines the importance of the language of the Criminal Justice Act (or the Torture Convention) for the majority decision and points to the moral of the case for the future and for other states.

5.   CONCLUSION

The judgment in *Pinochet3* is binding only for English law. Its wider impact depends upon its persuasiveness. The limits of its persuasiveness stem from the inconclusive treatment of the issues of international law raised by the parties. The excursions into *ius cogens* and international criminal law did not bring back any clear or agreed analysis and those uncertainties will adversely affect the impact elsewhere of the judgement. It would be unfair to put the whole responsibility for this on the judges. Their task was made harder by the lack of real development of the international legal system in the practice of states, a deficiency which academic writing and political aspiration tries to hide by reference to such matters as a hierarchy of legal rules. The outcome in *Pinochet3* is a fine example of the concern expressed by Professor Weil in his famous article 'Towards Normative Relativity in International Law?', that the attempt to admit these new forms of legal ordering into the international legal system other than through the ordinary law-making processes would lead to the diminution of the orthodox, if modest, achievements of international law.[117]

Nonetheless, if the courts of other states endorse Lord Hope's view that international treaties ought to be interpreted in a uniform way, then the courts of other parties to the Torture Convention ought to give the interpretation accorded to it by the House of Lords very serious consideration before departing from its conclusion. The question of immunity *ratione materiae* for proceedings under the

---

115. The most remarkable support for this came from Lord Hope, *P3*, p. 149e, who described the immunity of serving heads of state as *ius cogens*.

116. Lord Browne-Wilkinson, *P3*, p. 115e.

117. 77 *AJIL* (1983) pp. 413, 441.

Torture Convention or national legislation which implements it or for associated extradition proceedings should go the same way. The non-immunity in criminal matters extends to all state officials, though here *Pinochet3* may simply be confirming international (and indeed British) practice.[118] Certainly, some of the claims about the potential effects of *Pinochet3* – that it renders Margaret Thatcher susceptible to criminal proceedings in foreign courts for events in the Falklands campaign or Edward Heath for Bloody Sunday – are exaggerated: either they were susceptible before *Pinochet3* or they are not now.

Does the narrow ratio have any purchase beyond the Torture Convention? It did for Lord Nicholls, who would have applied the same reasoning to the Hostages Convention. The language there is not express and he relied on the background of its negotiation.[119] A similar inquiry into other anti-terrorism treaties would not necessarily yield the same conclusion. The Hijacking Treaty[120] was directed at the acts of 'private' terrorists and it was part of the argument of the United States and the United Kingdom in the *Lockerbie* case that the Montreal Convention on Attacks against Aircraft was not relevant to this case of state terrorism.[121] Overriding a plea of immunity *ratione materiae* in such cases must be based on other grounds than the applicability of a provision which leaves no scope for immunity. *Pinochet3* is of no help in telling us what these might be, so fractured are the reasons given by the judges and so defective their international legal method.

What it does do is emphasise the need for the effective implementation by domestic legislation of developments in international criminal law if states wish to take advantage of the possibility of trial in their own national courts for international purposes. It is not only Lord Millett's point that national courts can only do what they may do but that, in the criminal sphere, judges are particularly likely to be conscious of considerations of legality – about non-retrospectivity, about the precision of the standards, about immunity – regarding which international law has not, until recently, taken sufficient care. While the words of the Criminal Justice Act might be enough to explain why an English court took the decision it did, the international legitimacy of the decision in this case depended on the Torture Convention. *Pinochet3* says that if the requisite steps of implementation are taken, if words are used of sufficient clarity, there is no reason why national courts may not hear proceedings against even the most mighty of violators of international criminal law who come within their jurisdiction, so long as the extraterritorial reach of the national legislation is based on a ground binding on the other state, of which

---

118. English courts have exercised jurisdiction over the criminal acts of foreign officials in England, e.g., *R* v. *Lambeth Justices*, ex parte *Yusufu*, *Criminal Law Review* (1985) p. 510, and a Scottish court is currently doing so in the *Lockerbie* case (though probably this is a case of waiver).

119. *P1*, p. 938c-e.

120. Hague Convention for the Suppression of Unlawful Seizure of Aircraft 1970, 860 *UNTS* (1971) 105.

121. *Questions of Interpretation and Application of the 1971 Montreal Convention arising from the Aerial Incident at Lockerbie* (*Libyan Arab Jamahiriya* v. *United Kingdom*) (*Preliminary Objections*) *ICJ Rep.* (1998) 13, para. 24.

the clear words of an international convention binding on both states is the best evidence.

There are no other international treaties like the Torture Convention which admit of no ambiguity of their meaning. Most crimes against international law may, as a matter of their definition, be committed by officials or private persons alike – genocide, war crimes, crimes against humanity – however much more likely it is, in fact, that they will be committed by those with official power. The same is true for crimes by customary international law. At first sight, this might suggest that *Pinochet3* will be a judgement of quite limited effect, even if it was more persuasive than it actually is. New treaties are unlikely and unilateral legislative initiatives would encounter other problems. The development of the various international criminal tribunals might seem a more fruitful way forward. In fact, the two strands are coming together. States which wish to ratify the Statute of the International Criminal Court must consider what steps they should take to be able to take advantage of the principle of complementarity in the Statute, i.e., that the international jurisdiction is to be exercised only in those cases where an appropriate national jurisdiction cannot or will not proceed with the case.[122] In order to have that option, states will have to have offences in their domestic law which correspond with those within the jurisdiction of the Court. A wide jurisdictional base, even if not universality, will also be required. States, then, are actively contemplating legislation to create extraterritorial crimes of genocide, crimes against humanity and crimes in internal armed conflict. What *Pinochet3* suggests is that they should use the opportunity to make it plain, one way or the other, whether immunity, *ratione materiae* or *ratione personae*, applies to prosecution of these offences or to extradition proceedings in respect of them. But *Pinochet3* does not decide that the step of removing immunity will necessarily be internationally legitimate at the level of substantive jurisdiction. The Torture Convention was sufficient to establish a jurisdictional base in English and Spanish law which could be asserted against Chile but there was no further confirmation of an extraterritorial basis for the exercise of national jurisdiction over international crimes in general by a majority in *Pinochet3*. Lord Millett's assertion that such a ground could be found in the incorporation of customary international law had no other support.

This limitation in *Pinochet3* might be dismissed as being a point unnecessary for decision, though to do so further reduces the significance of the judgment. Other courts would have to have recourse to developments elsewhere, perhaps the judgment in *Re Pinochet*[123] of the Court of First Instance in Brussels, where the

---

122. Statute of the International Criminal Court, Arts. 1 (jurisdiction of the ICC 'shall be complementary to national criminal jurisdictions'), 17(1)(a) and (b) cases inadmissible unless state with jurisdiction unwilling or unable to investigate or prosecute.

123. I am grateful to Dr. Andrew Oppenheimer for a translation of the judgement which will shortly appear in the *International Law Reports*. The Judgment is also reproduced in an unofficial English translation at p. 475 of this volume, and is analysed in Correspondents' Reports at p. 335 of this volume. See also *Furundžija, supra* n. 85, para. 156 making the same arguments (except the question of domestic immunity). For details of other recent cases asserting universal jurisdiction, REDRESS, *Universal Jurisdiction in Europe* (London, REDRESS Trust 1999).

Court was prepared to accept the maximum argument put by the Crown Prosecution Service in *Pinochet1* and *3* that Pinochet's alleged crimes constituted crimes against humanity, that there was a rule of customary law (even a rule of *ius cogens*) allowing national jurisdiction on a universal basis over crimes against humanity and the investigation and prosecution of all people – viz., no immunity. The decision has been criticised.[124] Since then a law has been introduced in Belgium which provides for universal jurisdiction over the offences within the Court's jurisdiction and an express exclusion of immunity.[125] It is a further example of a national legal system being happier with its own legal base, rather than relying on the doctrines of international law.

6.   POSTSCRIPT

All the judges in *Pinochet3* suggested that the Home Secretary should reconsider the authority to proceed which he had issued after *Pinochet1* in the light of the much-reduced list of extradition crimes which they had approved. On 15 April 1999, the Home Secretary issued a new authority to proceed on the two charges of torture and conspiracy to torture.[126] The remaining charges were serious; if the UK did not authorise extradition, the authorities would have had to consider prosecution to comply with the obligation under the Torture Convention; and any reservations relating to Pinochet's age and health were, doubtless, rather easier to allay since, at the same time, the trial of Andrzej Sawoniuk for war crimes in Belarus during the Second World War was coming to an end. Sawoniuk was 79 and was convicted.[127] In the light of the judgment in *Pinochet3*, Judge Garzón forwarded to the British government a series of extra charges to be considered in the extradition proceedings, falling essentially into two classes: those concerning events after 8 December 1988 and those alleging a continuing offence, unresolved disappearances being sources of claims of torture against the disappeared or their relatives.[128] Quite apart from whether the extradition court will hold them admissible in England, at the time of writing, the authority of Judge Garzón was being challenged in Spain on the ground that these new cases constitute a new request for extradition and require the participation of the executive in their presentation to the British government.[129]

In the ordinary course of events, the extradition hearing would now have returned to the magistrate's court. Instead, on 30 April 1999, Pinochet's lawyers

---

124. J. Verhoven, *Journaux des Tribunaux* (1999) p. 311.

125. Loi du 10 février 1999 relative à la répression des violations graves du droit international humanitaire. Published in *Moniteur belge* (23 March 1999). Unofficial English translation reprinted at p. 539 of this volume.

126. HC Debs Vol. 329, col. 311, 15 April 1999.

127. For a discussion of this case, see Bryan and Rowe at p. 307 of this volume.

128. See *Kurt* v. *Turkey*, ECtHRs (1998) 15/1997/799/1002, paras. 130-134.

129. *El Pais* (6,7 May 1999).

sought judicial review of the Home Secretary's second authority to proceed, thus further delaying the start of the extradition proceedings.[130] The extradition proceedings themselves may take many months and hold the possibility of further appeals to the House of Lords. If the House of Lords decides that Pinochet may be extradited to Spain, even that would not be the end of the matter. The decision to order the extradition would be a decision for the Secretary of State of the day, a decision itself expressly subject to further judicial review,[131] with yet another trip to the House of Lords in prospect. If all this were not enough, provided the proceedings run for long enough, the Human Rights Act 1998 will have been brought into force, allowing both sides to put to the English court arguments based on the European Convention on Human Rights, with the important consequence that Pinochet could be further detained in England until these contentions were disposed of, something which there would be no power to order while such questions were being canvassed before the European Court in Strasbourg. In the meantime, he is remanded on conditional bail while the proceedings continue.

---

130. Leave was refused on 26 May 1999.
131. Extradition Act 1989, s. 12.

THE JURISDICTION OF THE INTERNATIONAL CRIMINAL COURT[1]

Shabtai Rosenne[2]

1.   INTRODUCTION

This article will review the jurisdiction of the new International Criminal Court (ICC) under the Rome Statute of 17 July 1998.[3] Jurisdiction will be examined

---

1. © S. Rosenne, 1999.

2. Member of the Institute of International Law; Honorary member of the American Society of International Law; Honorary president of the Israel Branch of the International Law Association.

3. UN Doc. A/CONF.183.9. The certified true copy of that 'authentic' text was circulated by the Secretary-General in note C.N.560.1998.TREATIES-2 (Depositary Notification), 15 October 1998. However, that text contains many inaccuracies and discrepancies between one or other of the language versions. At the first session of the Preparatory Commission (PrepCom) the Under-Secretary-General, Legal Counsel (Corell) announced that a correction process had been commenced with circular note C.N.502.1998.TREATIES-3 (Depositary Notification), 25 September 1998, that further errors had come to light, and that an official version of the Statute, including the corrections, would be issued during the July session of PrepCom. Press Release L/2912, 26 February 1999, p. 5. A second set of corrections was circulated in C.N.357.1999. TREATIES-14 (Depositary Notification), 18 May 1999. On 17 August 1999, after the end of the second session of the PrepCom, the Secretariat issued new texts incorporating the corrections noted in the two depositary notices, under symbol PCNICC/1999/INF/3. That is for the information of the PrepCom, and it has been taken into account in this article. In C.N.537.1999. TREATIES-16 (Depositary Notification), 1 July 1999, the Secretary-General issued some further proposed corrections to the English, French, Russian and Spanish authentic texts. It is not clear on what basis the Secretariat was acting in this matter, or how and when a fully correct authentic text in all six languages will be available. By virtue of Art. 79 of the Vienna Convention on the Law of Treaties, 1969 (1155 *UNTS* 331), the correction of agreed errors in the authentic text of a treaty is a matter for the signatory states and the contracting states, together with the depositary. For the view of the United States on this aspect, see the Note of 5 November 1998 from the Permanent Mission of the United States to the Secretary-General, reproduced in 93 *AJIL* 484 (1999). There is no provision regarding the correction of errors that are not agreed, but principle would suggest that all the states that participated in the adoption of the text ought to be involved. Vienna Convention, Art. 9. The position of states that have ratified the Statute on the basis of the original authentic text is not clear. The Note of 15 October states that certified true copies are established specifically for the purpose of enabling the Governments concerned to complete the internal procedures of ratification, acceptance, approval or accession. There is no known instance of the correction of an entire convention in all six authentic texts. For the correction of the entire Chinese text of the Genocide Convention, cf., GA Res. 691 (VII), 21 November 1952. And see my *Developments in the Law of Treaties 1945-1986* at p. 436 (Cambridge, Cambridge University Press 1989). In addition, virtually none of the documentation

ratione personae and *ratione materiae*, including in each case its scope *ratione temporis*, concentrating on two separate aspects of jurisdiction as they appear in the Statute. These are jurisdiction to bring charges against an alleged offender and to bring that person to trial, and as a corollary, jurisdiction to detain or arrest an accused or suspected person. Given that it is early in the history of the Rome Statute, some consideration of other issues raised by the Statute is also necessary.

As a general proposition, the Decision on the Defence Motion for Interlocutory Appeal on Jurisdiction of the Appeals Chamber of the International Criminal Tribunal for the Former Yugoslavia (ICTY) in the *Tadić* case gives a useful working description of what 'jurisdiction' means in the context of an international criminal tribunal:

> '[J]urisdiction is not merely an ambit or sphere (better described in this case as "competence"); it is basically – as is visible from the Latin origin of the word itself, *jurisdiction* – a legal power, hence necessarily a legitimate power, "to state the law" *(dire le droit)* within this ambit, in an authoritative and final manner.
>
> (. . .)
>
> A narrow conception of jurisdiction may, perhaps, be warranted in a national context but not in international law. International law, because it lacks a centralized structure, does not provide for an integrated judicial system operating an orderly division of labour among a number of tribunals, where certain aspects or components of jurisdiction as a power could be centralized or vested in one of them but not the others. In international law, every tribunal is a self-contained system (unless otherwise provided).'[4]

In substance and *mutatis mutandis*, this definition is very close to the general explanation of jurisdiction in the practice of the International Court of Justice.

2.   THE ROME STATUTE AS AN INTERNATIONAL TREATY

Recalling first that the Rome Statute is an international treaty, as such it comes within the scope of the Vienna Convention on the Law of Treaties of 23 May 1969.[5] It is also the constituent instrument of an international organization of a special type:

---

of the Rome Conference and the Report of the Committee of the Whole on which the final decisions were made, is available, not even on the website that the UN has created for the International Criminal Court. This seriously hampers all attempts to understand the Rome Statute. On the PrepCom, see text to n. 15 *infra*.

For an account by participants of the Rome Conference, see R.S. Lee, ed., *The International Criminal Court: The Making of the Rome Statute-Issues, Negotiations, Results* (The Hague, Kluwer Law International 1999). Lee was the Executive Secretary of the Rome Conference.

4. *Prosecutor* v. *Duško Tadić* (Jurisdiction), Case No. IT-94-I-AR72, Decision of 2 October 1995; *ICTY Judicial Reports*, 1994-1995 (I) 343, 365 (paras. 10-11); 105 *ILR* at 457.

5. See n. 3 *supra*.

an autonomous judicial organization.[6] As an international treaty coming within the scope of the Vienna Convention, its interpretation is governed by Articles 31 to 33 of that instrument. The rules on treaties and third states (Arts. 34 to 38) are relevant to the position of states not parties to the ICC Statute. As the Statute is the constituent instrument of an international organization, Article 5 of the Vienna Convention is also germane.[7] However, as an international treaty of a particular type, the Statute gives rise to specific problems of interpretation.[8] The significance of this is that, while no doubt relevant interpretations of their Statutes by the ICTY and the International Criminal Tribunal for Rwanda (ICTR) may help in interpreting and applying the Rome Statute, and despite the fact that the Appeals Chamber of the ICTY has shown an inclination to find guidance in the Vienna Convention,[9] those two Statutes are not embodied in treaties that come within the scope of the Vienna Convention but in resolutions of the Security Council, subject to different canons of interpretation.[10] The Security Council, adopting a report of the Secretary-General, established the ICTY with a fairly wide material jurisdiction limited geographically and *ratione temporis*.[11] It also established the ICTR for the sole purpose of prosecuting persons responsible for genocide and other serious violations of international humanitarian law and related matters in Rwanda during a fixed period of time.[12]

The Rome Conference created three bodies with competence to interpret the Statute. They are the PrepCom already mentioned (n. 3 above); the Assembly of

---

6. The relationship agreement between the United Nations and the International Tribunal for the Law of the Sea, adopted by the General Assembly of the United Nations in Res. 52/251, 8 September 1998, uses that expression. That was the first relationship agreement between the United Nations and an international judicial organ created by a treaty drawn up under the auspices of the United Nations. We may presume that any relationship agreement to be concluded between the UN and the International Criminal Court will use a similar expression.

7. Art. 5 reads: 'The present Convention applies to any treaty which is the constituent instrument of an international organization, without prejudice to any relevant rules of the organization.'

8. *Legality of the Use by a State of Nuclear Weapons in Armed Conflict* advisory opinion, *ICJ Rep.* (1996)(I) pp. 66 at 75 (para. 19).

9. Cf., the joint separate opinion of Judges McDonald and Vohrah in *Prosecutor v. Erdemović*, Judgment, 7 October 1997, in the Appeals Chamber of the ICTY, Case No. IT-96-22-A; 111 *ILR* 315.

10. Cf., M. Wood, 'The Interpretation of Security Council Resolutions', 2 *Max Planck Yearbook of United Nations Law* (1998) p. 73. Nevertheless, the view is sometimes expressed that the Statutes of these Tribunals are nonetheless established by treaty – the Charter of the United Nations. J.A. Carrillo-Salcedo, 'The Inherent Powers of the International Tribunal for the Former Yugoslavia to issue "Subpoena duces tecum" to a Sovereign State', *Mélanges en honneur de Nicolas Valticos: Droit et justice* (1999) pp. 269, 278.

11. See SC Res. 808 (1993) and 827 (1993), of 22 February and 25 May 1993 respectively. The Statute of this Tribunal is annexed to the report of the Secretary-General submitted in accordance with Res. 808, *Official Records of the Security Council,* 48th year, Supplement for April, May, June 1993 (Doc. S/25704 and Add.1) at 117. This Statute is reproduced in the Tribunal's *Basic Documents* at p. 1, 2nd edn. (1998), which also reproduces the Secretary-General's report at p. 161.

12. The Statute is annexed to SC Res. 955 (1994), 8 November 1994.

States Parties established and institutionalized by Article 112 of the Statute;[13] and the Court itself, established by Article 1 and composed of the organs as set out in Article 34. In addition, Article 119 envisages a possible role for the International Court of Justice in settling disputes between States Parties relating to the interpretation or application of the Statute.[14] The PrepCom, composed of all the states that have signed the Final Act whether or not they are parties to the Statute, is a transitory body that will cease to exist with the conclusion of the first session of the Assembly of States Parties.[15] That Assembly will come into being with the entry into force of the Statute, that is, by virtue of Article 126(1), on the first day of the month after the 60th day following the date of deposit with the Secretary-General of the United Nations of the 60th instrument of ratification, acceptance, approval or accession. It consists of all the states that have expressed their consent to be bound by the Rome Statute and for which the Statute is in force. States that have signed the Statute or the Final Act may be observers.

The Court will come into existence after the first election of judges. The Assembly will decide that date on the recommendation of the PrepCom. The Court comprises, with the 18 judges, also the Office of the Prosecutor and the Registrar. The Prosecutor is to be elected by the Assembly (Art. 42(4)) and the Registrar by the judges (Art. 43(4)). Except for the PrepCom, which at the time of writing had held its first two sessions,[16] the other institutions will come into existence at an unknown date in the future.

---

13. The Assembly of States Parties is probably to be regarded as a 'treaty body' as that concept is developing in United Nations practice. Cf., *Establishment of the Court and relationship with the United Nations, List of main issues*. Background paper by the Codification Division, Doc. A/AC.249/1998/L.10 (mimeo., 20 December 1998). The Office of Legal Affairs of the UN Secretariat has consistently taken the view that a treaty body established by a treaty concluded under UN auspices is an organ of the UN. See opinions of 15 September 1969 on the privileges and immunities of the members of the Committee on the Elimination of Racial Discrimination, and of 17 August 1976 on the question of whether that Committee is a subsidiary organ of the UN. That Committee is composed of individuals, but it would seem that there is no difference of principle if the treaty organ is composed of the representatives of states.

14. One might hope that the Assembly of States Parties will be authorized under the Charter to request advisory opinions of the International Court. For reasons stated in the previous note, there is no reason why it should not be considered an organ of the United Nations within the meaning of Art. 96(2) of the Charter.

15. There will thus be a short overlap when both the PrepCom and the Assembly of States Parties will be in existence. That overlap will terminate with the conclusion of the first session of the Assembly.

16. Particulars of the first session of the PrepCom of 1999 are given in Press Release L/2912, 26 February 1999. See also *Proceedings of the Preparatory Commission at its first session (16-26 February 1999)*, Doc. PCNICC/1999/L.3/Rev.1 (2 March 1999). Proceedings of the second session of the PrepCom are given in Press Release L/2933, 13 August 1999; and *Proceedings of the Preparatory Commission at its Second Session (26 July-August 1999)* Doc. PCNICC/1999/L.4. Documents of the 1999 sessions of the Preparatory Commission are available online at http://www.un.org/law/icc/prepcomm/docs.htm. For an account of the first two sessions of the PrepCom, see K. Dörmann at p. 283 of this volume.

Consequently, the PrepCom is the currently existing entity qualified to interpret the Statute. However, its interpretations will not be binding for the Court once it has come into existence. For both the Court and the Assembly, the PrepCom makes recommendations. The position of the Court here (and of the Assembly) is similar to that of the International Tribunal for the Law of the Sea and the Meeting of States Parties under the United Nations Convention on the Law of the Sea. Both the Tribunal and the Meeting of States Parties have seen themselves as free to follow or not any relevant recommendations of the Preparatory Commission.[17]

It follows from the Statute being an international treaty that the date of its entry into force for a given state is directly relevant to the Tribunal's jurisdiction, both *ratione personae* and *ratione materiae*. For the first 60 states required to bring the Statute into force, that date is determined according to Article 126(1) of the Statute. Article 126(2) applies to states that become parties after the Statute's entry into force. For them, it enters into force on the first day of the month after the 60th day following the deposit of the appropriate instrument with the Secretary-General of the United Nations. By Article 12 of the Statute, that date can also be relevant in relation to the place where the alleged crime was committed. That would refer to the scope of the jurisdiction *ratione temporis*.

3.   THE STRUCTURE OF THE STATUTE

The general structure of the Statute requires notice.[18] As is customary, the Statute commences with a preamble, setting out the general objectives and purpose of the Rome Conference in adopting the instrument. The preamble is important for the interpretation of the instrument, following Article 31(2) of the Vienna Convention. However, its tenth paragraph is a substantive provision, which is picked up in the body of the Statute. It enunciates the principle of complementarity, a central feature of the Statute described more fully in section 4 below ('Emphasizing that the International Criminal Court established under this Statute shall be [Fr. *est*] complementary to national criminal jurisdictions.') Complementarity was a major political question throughout the negotiation of the Rome Statute. The tenth paragraph of the preamble is given substantive content both through the English

---

17. See on this S. Rosenne, 'International Tribunal for the Law of the Sea: 1996–97 Survey', 12 *The International Journal of Marine and Coastal Law* (1998) p. 487.

18. The final structure of the Rome Statute differs from the original proposal of the International Law Commission. That was structured as follows: Part 1 (Arts. 1 to 4), the establishment of the Court; Part 2 (Arts. 5 to 19), Composition and administration of the Court; Part 3 (Arts. 20 to 24), Jurisdiction of the Court; Part 4 (Arts. 25 to 31), Investigation and prosecution; Part 5 (Arts. 32 to 47), the Trial; Part 6 (Arts. 48 to 50), Appeal and review; Part 7 (Arts. 51 to 57), International co-operation and judicial assistance; Part 8 (Arts. 58 to 60), Enforcement; Annex, Crimes pursuant to [designated] treaties. That proposal did not contain final clauses. However, Appendix I discussed possible clauses of a treaty to accompany the draft statute. Vol. II/2 *ILC Yearbook* (1994) p. 20.

word 'shall', a word of obligation in legal drafting,[19] and explicitly in Article 1 on the establishment of the Court and in Article 17, on issues of admissibility. The expression 'national criminal jurisdictions' presumably extends to any form of national jurisdiction that is competent to try and punish an offender for the particular act(s) for which he or she could be indicted before the International Criminal Court, including, for this purpose, military courts acting under a national code of military justice.

The topic of Part 1 (Arts. 1 to 4) is the establishment of the Court. By Article 1, the Court is established as a permanent institution with power to exercise its jurisdiction over persons for the most serious crimes of international concern, as referred to in the Statute, 'and shall be complementary to national criminal jurisdictions'. This general functional jurisdiction is universal in scope. The limitation of the Court's jurisdiction to 'the most serious crimes of international concern, as referred to in the Statute' is an immediate source of ambiguity. It raises the question whether the general definitions contained in the Statute are sufficient as an indication of the most serious crimes of international concern, or whether some expression of international concern, either general or specific, is to be required for every individual prosecution. This question does not arise for ICTY or ICTR, as the Security Council has already given a general directive to those two bodies.

Part 2 (Arts. 5 to 21) deals with jurisdiction, admissibility and the applicable law. Article 5 is the principal provision setting out the crimes within the Court's jurisdiction *ratione materiae*. It lists four crimes – genocide, crimes against humanity, war crimes and the crime of aggression. Articles 6, 7 and 8 follow that bare statement, enumerating the particulars of genocide, crimes against humanity and war crimes 'for the purpose of this Statute'. This aspect is examined in section 5 below.

There is no explanation of the crime of aggression or of its elements as a matter of individual criminal responsibility. By the Final Act of the Conference,[20] the PrepCom is to prepare proposals for a provision on aggression, including the definition; the Elements of Crimes, including aggression; and the conditions under which the Court shall exercise its jurisdiction with regard to this crime. The PrepCom is to submit its proposals to the Assembly of States Parties at a Review Conference 'with a view to arriving at an acceptable provision on the crime of aggression for inclusion in this Statute'.[21] This means that the Statute anticipates

---

19. Cf., the explanation given by Sir Humphrey Waldock, special rapporteur on the law of treaties, at the 872nd meeting of the International Law Commission. Vol. I *ILC Yearbook* (1966) at p. 199.

20. Annex I, Resolution F, para. 7. For the Final Act, see Doc. A/CONF.138/10, 17 July 1998, available online at http://www.un.org/law/icc/index.htm.

21. Having regard to Art. 5(2) (see section 6 below), no further consideration will be given here to the crime of aggression, beyond noting that the reference is to individual responsibility for the crime, not the responsibility of the state as such. This follows from Art. 25(1). The crime of aggression for the purposes of this Statute is connected with the relationship to be established between the Court and the Security Council. Art. 2 provides that '[t]he Court shall be brought into relationship with the United Nations through an agreement to be approved by the Assembly

its own amendment some time after its entry into force. This is an unusual provision, and it might cause difficulties if the definition of aggression to be adopted raises constitutional problems for any of the States Parties at the time.[22]

Article 11 has the title 'jurisdiction *ratione temporis*'. The Court has jurisdiction 'only with respect to crimes committed after the entry into force of this Statute'. By paragraph 2, the Court may exercise jurisdiction over a state which becomes a party to the Statute after its entry into force only with respect to crimes committed after the entry into force of the Statute for that state, unless the state previously made a declaration by which it has – although not a party to the Statute – accepted the jurisdiction with respect to the crime in question. Time is certainly an element of jurisdiction, but it usually relates to the scope of the jurisdiction *ratione personae* or *ratione temporis*. It follows that the Court may not exercise jurisdiction in respect of a crime where the relevant state was not a party to the Statute at the relevant date and has not taken other steps to accept the exercise of jurisdiction with respect to that crime.

Part 3 (Arts. 22 to 33) sets out the general principles of criminal law (meaning *international criminal law*). For present purposes, it is sufficient to note Article 25(1) on individual criminal responsibility, which gives the Court jurisdiction 'over natural persons'. This excludes juridical persons from the scope of the Court's jurisdiction but not the individuals composing the juridical person. This provision is misplaced. It deals directly with the Court's jurisdiction *ratione personae*, and is not a principle of criminal law as such. The Nuremberg Tribunal had jurisdiction over entities that were not individuals. By Article 26, the Court has no jurisdiction over any person who was under the age of 18 at the time of the alleged commission of the crime. Presumably this refers to the Gregorian calendar. In the form in which it is presented, this limitation on the Court's jurisdiction could lead to difficulties where there is a series of multiple crimes which commenced when the accused was under the age of 18 years. This is an important example of what can be regarded as somewhat hasty drafting, inappropriate for a criminal statute.

Part 4 (Arts. 34 to 52) treats of the composition and administration of the Court. By Article 34 the Court is composed of the following organs: the Presidency (Art. 38), an Appeals Chamber, a Trial Chamber (of which there may be more than one), and a Pre-Trial Chamber (Art. 39), the Office of the Prosecutor (Art. 42), and the Registry (Art. 43). The inclusion of the Office of the Prosecutor as part of the Court is a questionable feature of the Statute. Experience shows that it can produce

---

of States Parties to this Statute and thereafter concluded by the President of the Court on its behalf.' One of the functions of the PrepCom is to prepare a draft of this relationship agreement. The Secretary-General is to convene the first Review Conference seven years after the Statute's entry into force.

22. Constitutional difficulties have already been raised. See for example the decision of the French Conseil constitutionnel of 22 January 1999, No. 98-408 DC, to the effect that ratification of the Rome Statute will require revision of the French Constitution. http://www.conseil-constitutionnel.fr/decision/98/98408/index.htm. An unofficial English translation of this decision is reprinted at p. 493 of this volume. For commentary, see P. Tavernier at pp. 360-362.

intolerable tension between an approach to the settlement of disputes based on *Fiat justitia, et pereat mundus* and one based on the ideal of *Seek peace and pursue it* (Psalm 34:15) between justice at all costs, and consideration of the political and diplomatic consequences of a particular prosecution at a particular time. It is presumably copied from Article 11 of the Statute of the ICTY. But the analogy is false. The ICTY was established by the Security Council for a specific purpose, and the Prosecutor is one of the instruments for achieving that purpose. The independence of the ICTY prosecutor is thus relative, and the Security Council has power to control it.

The subject of Part 5 (Arts. 53 to 61) is investigation and prosecution. The trial comes within the scope of Part 6 (Arts. 62 to 76). Trials *in absentia* are excluded. Article 63(1) requires that the accused be present during the trial. Part 7 (Arts. 77 to 80) addresses penalties. The normal maximum penalty is imprisonment for 30 years but a term of life imprisonment may be imposed when justified by the extreme gravity of the crime and the individual circumstances of the convicted person (Art. 77). Appeal and revision of the sentence are governed by Part 8 (Arts. 81 to 85). International co-operation and judicial assistance are the matter of Part 9 (Arts. 86 to 102). This relates to the duties of States Parties, but by Article 87(5) the Court may invite any state not a party to the Statute to provide assistance under Part 9 based on an *ad hoc* arrangement, an agreement, or on any other basis. That paragraph goes on to empower the Court to inform the Assembly of States Parties or, where necessary the Security Council, of failure by a non-party state to co-operate with requests made pursuant to the agreements reached. This provision represents a marked extension of the scope of operation of an international treaty, which for non-parties is *res inter alios acta*. It is therefore a potential source of difficulties. The enforcement of the Court's judgments and related matters are the substance of Part 10 (Arts. 103 to 111). Part 11, consisting of Article 112 only, establishes the Assembly of States Parties, which is the competent political organ for the non-judicial aspects of the Court's affairs. It corresponds to the General Assembly of the United Nations regarding the non-judicial aspects of the affairs of the International Court of Justice, and the Meeting of States Parties for the International Tribunal for the Law of the Sea. It elects the judges and the prosecutor. Amendments to the Statute are to be adopted either by the Assembly or by a Review Conference. Part 12 (Arts. 113 to 117) addresses the financing of the Court. The final clauses (Arts. 119 to 128) form Part 13.

4.   THE JURISDICTIONAL FUNCTION OF BEING A PARTY TO THE STATUTE

The consequences of a state becoming a party to the Statute are both institutional and jurisdictional. The institutional functions concern the state's rights and duties in relation to the Court as an international organ, and in relation to the other parties to the Statute. They are not the concern here. The jurisdictional consequences affect the jurisdiction of the Court *vis-à-vis* that state in relation to other states, whether or not parties to the Statute, and as regards that state's nationals. It also affects the obligations of that state both to the Court and to the other States Parties.

The first element is jurisdiction *ratione personae*. As stated, this is limited to natural persons over the age of 18 years, and its scope is subject to Article 11 *ratione temporis*. Beyond this, the Statute does not deal directly with jurisdiction *ratione personae* as a separate matter. It concentrates on obligations of the states concerned in relation to a particular crime and the person suspected as its perpetrator. Thus, Article 12, entitled 'Preconditions to the exercise of jurisdiction', sets out a series of provisions that add up to a statement of the Court's jurisdiction *ratione personae*. By paragraph 1, a state which becomes a party to the Statute 'thereby' accepts the Court's jurisdiction with respect to the crimes referred to in Article 5.[23] That has to be read with Article 13, on the exercise of jurisdiction. The Court may exercise its jurisdiction if (*a*) a situation in which one or more of such crimes appears to have been committed is referred to the Prosecutor by a State Party in accordance with Article 14; (*b*) a situation in which one or more of such crimes appears to have been committed is referred to the Prosecutor by the Security Council acting under Chapter VII of the Charter; or (*c*) the Prosecutor has initiated an investigation in respect of such a crime in accordance with Article 15(1), which authorizes the Prosecutor to initiate investigations *proprio motu* on the basis of information on crimes within the Court's jurisdiction.

To return to Article 12, under paragraph 2, the Court may exercise jurisdiction in the case of Article 13(*a*) or (*c*) if one or more of the following states are parties to the Statute or have accepted the Court's jurisdiction: (*a*) the state on the territory of which the conduct in question occurred or, if the crime was committed on board a vessel or aircraft, the state of registration of that vessel or aircraft; (*b*) the state of nationality of the person accused of the crime. Here the scope of the jurisdiction *ratione temporis* is limited by the date on which the state concerned became a party to the Statute. Article 12(2)(*b*) is the only provision in the Statute to mention the nationality of the person accused of a crime. Paragraph 2(*a*) opens the possibility of nationals of states that are not parties to the Statute and which therefore have not accepted the Court's jurisdiction becoming the subject of investigation at least, and possibly of prosecution and trial, for alleged crimes if the conduct occurred on the territory of a State Party. In the case of nationals of states that are not party to the Statute, jurisdiction *ratione personae* depends on the *locus in quo*. If that *locus* was territory of a State Party, jurisdiction *ratione personae* exists regardless

---

23. It is to be noted that this automatic assumption of jurisdiction through the act of becoming a party to the Statute is an extension of what has been the practice as regards the International Court of Justice. There, the act of becoming a party to the Statute implies acceptance of the Court's jurisdiction to render advisory opinions and its so-called incidental jurisdiction, but not its jurisdiction over the merits of a contentious case. This extension is justified in the case of the constituent instrument of a permanent international criminal court. It would be self-defeating were the consent of a state to be required for the Court to have jurisdiction in a particular case.

of the nationality of the person accused, subject to the limitation *ratione temporis*. There is a temporal question here: must the territory be the territory of a State Party at the time of the commission of the offence?

This provision seems to raise another question which the Statute does not answer clearly. The provisions on complementarity, discussed below, mean that an individual suspected of criminal activities under his or her national law may be tried by the national jurisdictions. Those jurisdictions will apply the régime of the national law. The definitions of the crimes in Articles 6, 7 and 8 – definitions that are specifically limited 'for the purpose of this Statute' – differ in some respects (some of them minor, it is true) from the basic definitions in the international treaties from which they were taken. One consequence of this could be that an individual suspect may come within the scope of two different régimes, the national and that of the Statute. No doubt the *ne bis in idem* provision of Article 20 is intended to protect an accused person from that. But the differences introduced in the definitions of the crimes in Articles 6, 7 and 8 may leave an opening in which Article 20 will not provide protection. The question whether in all cases the accused should be a national of a State Party was considered by the International Law Commission when drafting its proposal for the court, and rejected.[24] This rejection may not be consistent with the general principle of complementarity which is supposed to lie at the core of the Rome Statute.

A decision to prosecute brings into operation Part 9. By Article 87(5), the Court may invite any state not a party to the Statute to provide assistance under this part 'on the basis of an ad hoc arrangement, an agreement with such State or any other appropriate basis'. No sanction is specifically written into the Statute in the event that a non-party declines any such invitation, but Article 112(2)(f), on the Assembly of States Parties, requires the Assembly 'to consider, pursuant to Article 87, paragraphs 5 and 7, any question relating to non-co-operation'. This is another far-reaching departure from the basic rule of the law of treaties that a treaty does not create either obligations or rights for a third state without its consent.

By Article 89, the Court may transmit a request for the arrest and surrender[25] of a person to any state on the territory of which that person may be found and shall request[26] the co-operation of that state in the arrest and surrender of such a person. States Parties are obliged to comply with such requests in accordance with their national law and Part 9. By Article 34 of the Vienna Convention on the Law

---

24. See the Commission's report in n. 18 *supra*, at p. 42.

25. Art. 102 defines 'surrender', for the purposes of Part 9, as the 'delivering up of a person by a State to the Court, pursuant to this Statute'. It distinguishes 'surrender' from 'extradition' which it defines as meaning the delivering up of a person by one state to another as provided by treaty, convention or national legislation. It is not clear what the word 'convention' (Fr. *convention*) means in this context. Either it is a tautology, or it means custom, but given the French text the tautology is probably the correct meaning here. Cf., on this the report of the International Law Commission on the law of treaties, Commentary on Art. 2 of its draft articles of 1966, para. (4), Vol. II *ILC Yearbook* (1966) at p. 188.

26. The original French text read here *peut solliciter*. This has been corrected to *sollicite* in the revised text, thus bringing it into line with the English version.

of Treaties, no such obligation can be imposed on a state that is not a party to the Statute. Here there may be a difference between cases which the Prosecutor has investigated following a decision by the Security Council acting under Chapter VII of the Charter and other cases. Security Council decisions of that kind may impose obligations on all states members of the United Nations. Those obligations follow directly from the Charter; moreover, by virtue of Article 103 of the Charter, they may have priority over all other treaty obligations. This can lead to an extension of the Court's jurisdiction *ratione personae.*

In either event, arrest of a person not a national of the arresting state, whether for 'surrender' or for 'extradition', and certainly for any proceedings before the arresting state's courts, can bring into operation the rules of diplomatic and consular protection and, if the state of the nationality of the arrested person is a party to the relevant instruments, the Vienna Conventions of 1961 and 1963 on Diplomatic and Consular Relations, and their Optional Protocols, respectively, conferring jurisdiction on the International Court of Justice.[27]

5.   COMPLEMENTARITY

An overriding element of the Statute and of the Court's jurisdiction is the principle of complementarity. This means that the Court is a complement to national criminal judicial systems which therefore have the primary responsibility for trying a case which may come within the Court's jurisdiction. This is a major difference between the Rome Statute and the Statutes of the ICTY and ICTR. Both those Statutes are based on the priority of their jurisdiction over that of national courts, and that gives rise to the procedure for requesting a national court to defer to the International Tribunals.[28]

The tenth paragraph of the preamble and Article 1 on the establishment of the Court (see section 2 above) announce the principle of complementarity in categoric terms. Articles 17 (Issues of admissibility) and 18 (Preliminary rulings regarding admissibility [*Décision préliminaire sur la recevabilité*]) are the principal sources of the detailed rules for the application of the principle of complementarity, together with Article 19 (Challenges to the jurisdiction of the Court or the admissibility of a case) as the machinery of its application. The principle can therefore have a direct impact on the new Court's jurisdiction, in any sense of the word 'jurisdiction'.

---

27. For those Conventions and Optional Protocols, see 500 *UNTS* 95 and 223; and 596 ibid. 261 and 487. Three cases have come before the International Court on the basis of those Optional Protocols: the *United States Diplomatic Staff in Tehran* case (*USA* v. *Iran*) (1980); the *Vienna Convention on Consular Relations* (Breard) (Provisional Measures) (*Paraguay* v. *USA*) case, *ICJ Rep.* (1998) p. 248 (discontinued at p. 426), and the *LaGrand* (Provisional Measures) (*Germany* v. *USA*) case, ibid. 1999, 9 (pending). The last two relate to criminal prosecutions of the applicant states' nationals.

28. ICTY Statute, Art. 9(2); ICTR Statute, Art. 8(2). For an example of a deferral order, see ICTY Trial Chamber decision of 8 November 1994 in *Prosecutor* v. *Tadić, ICTY, Judicial Reports,* 1994–1995 (I) 3. This was the ICTY's first decision.

Article 17 indicates where 'the Court', that is whatever organ of the Court is competent in the circumstances, shall determine that a case is inadmissible. This is an obligation on the 'Court'. In the context, it is the anchor for the concept of complementarity in this Statute. Article 17 requires the Court to determine that a case is inadmissible where (*a*) the case is being investigated or prosecuted by a state which has jurisdiction over it, unless that state is unwilling or unable genuinely to carry out that investigation or prosecution; (*b*) the case has been investigated by a state which has jurisdiction over it and the state has decided not to prosecute the person concerned, unless the decision resulted from the unwillingness or inability of the state genuinely to prosecute; (*c*) the person concerned has already been tried for conduct which is the subject of the complaint – the *ne bis in idem* principle set out more fully in Article 20; (*d*) the case is not of sufficient gravity to justify further action by the Court (this is not directly a matter of complementarity, but reflects the general approach of the Statute, that the Court's jurisdiction is limited to the most serious crimes of international concern). Given the reference in Article 17 to the preamble and Article 1, its provisions relate equally to jurisdiction and to admissibility.

This provision is certainly obscure, and is a potential source of major conflict with any state itself seeking to exercise jurisdiction and to oust the jurisdiction of the Rome Court. The language used in the provisions is loose and prone to subjective interpretation. This is the kind of provision for which it would be advisable to seek the interpretation of the International Court of Justice; a good reason for enabling the Assembly of States Parties to request advisory opinions.

Article 17 goes on to tackle unwillingness. By paragraph 2, in order to determine unwillingness in a particular case, the Court shall consider, having regard to the principles of due process recognized by international law, whether one or more of the following exist, as applicable: (*a*) the proceedings were or are being undertaken or the national decision was made for the purpose of shielding the person concerned from criminal responsibility for crimes within the jurisdiction of the Court referred to in Article 5; (*b*) there has been an unjustified delay in the proceedings which in the circumstances is inconsistent with an intent to bring the person concerned to justice; (*c*) the proceedings were not or are not being conducted independently or impartially, and they were or are being conducted in a manner which, in the circumstances, is inconsistent with an intent to bring the person concerned to justice. Paragraph 3 deals with the situation of a total or partial collapse of the national judicial system: 'In order to determine inability in a particular case, the Court shall consider whether, due to a total or substantial collapse or unavailability of its national judicial system, the state is unable to obtain the accused or the necessary evidence and testimony or otherwise unable to carry out its proceedings'. Article 17 uses the word 'State' without any qualification. It is not therefore limited to States Parties. It may not even be limited to independent states, especially if there is a disturbed and unclear situation resulting from the disintegration of a state.

It is by no means clear how the 'Court', whichever organ, can determine these things. They are characterized by subjectivities not easily given to judicial identification. For example, what are the 'principles of due process recognized by international law'? Where are they to be found? Article 10 of the Universal Declaration of Human Rights lays down that everyone is entitled in full equality to a fair and public hearing by an independent and impartial tribunal, in the determination of his rights and obligations and of any criminal charge against him.[29] This is amplified at length in Article 14 of the International Covenant on Civil and Political Rights, adopted by the General Assembly in Resolution 2200 A (XXI), 16 December 1966, which is binding on the parties to it.[30] There are fundamental differences between the Anglo-American common law approaches to 'due process' and that of the civil law. How can the 'Court' reconcile them without further directives in the form of binding rules adopted by the States Parties?

Article 18 refers principally to the duties of the prosecutor and an investigation. When the prosecutor has determined that in a situation under Article 13(*a*) or (*c*) there would be a reasonable basis to commence an investigation or has initiated an investigation, he or she is to notify 'all States Parties and those States which, taking into account the information available, would normally exercise jurisdiction over the crimes concerned'. The state notified, whether a party or not, may request the prosecutor to defer to its investigation of those persons unless the Pre-Trial Chamber, on the application of the prosecutor, decides to authorize the investigation. In that last circumstance, the state concerned or the prosecutor may appeal the Chamber's ruling to the Appeals Chamber, according to Article 82 of the Statute. A state which has challenged a ruling of the Pre-Trial Chamber under Article 18 may also challenge the admissibility of a case under Article 19 on the grounds of additional significant facts or significant change of circumstances. There is here an opening for major conflicts between a non-party state and the 'Court' over deferral.

The effect of Articles 17 and 18 is felt throughout the Statute. Article 19(1) requires the Court to satisfy itself that it has jurisdiction in any case brought before it.[31] It may of its own motion determine the admissibility of a case in accordance with Article 17. Paragraph 2 indicates who may challenge the jurisdiction or the admissibility: the accused or impugned individual, a state which has jurisdiction over

---

29. GA Res. 217 A (III), 10 December 1948.

30. 999 *UNTS* 171, 1059 *UNTS* 451, 1131 *UNTS* 396. The Secretary-General's report on the basis of which the Security Council adopted the Statute of the ICTY makes specific reference to the Convention in para. 101 and elsewhere in dealing with the trial itself. For a discussion of the meaning of 'fair trial' in the context of the ICTY, see the Judgment of 15 July 1999 of the Appeals Chamber in *Prosecutor* v. *Duško Tadić*, Case No. IT-94-1-A, paras. 29-56.

31. The expression that the Court must 'satisfy itself' that it has jurisdiction in any case brought before it requires a positive finding by the competent Chamber that it has jurisdiction in the case. The 1994 draft of the International Law Commission contained, in Art. 24, a provision along those lines. The Commentary explained that the article 'is intended to spell out the duty of the court (and of each of its organs, as appropriate) to satisfy itself that it has jurisdiction in a given case'. Vol. II/2 *ILC Yearbook* (1994) at p. 45. The same phrase 'satisfy itself' appears in Art. 53 of the Statute of the International Court of Justice, and has been interpreted in that sense. Cf., S. Rosenne, *The Law and Practice of the International Court 1920-1996*, III, 1401 (1997). No similar provision appears in the Statutes of the *ad hoc* Tribunals.

a case or a state from which acceptance of jurisdiction is required under Article 12. On the other hand, the state of which the accused is a national is *per se* not given this right. Paragraph 8 permits the prosecutor, pending a ruling by the Court, to seek authority from the Court to pursue necessary investigative steps of the kind to which Article 18(6) refers. Article 19(10) allows the prosecutor to submit a request for review of a decision that a case is inadmissible under Article 17 on the basis of new facts which negate the basis on which the case had previously been found inadmissible under Article 17. By paragraph 11, if the prosecutor, having considered the matters to which Article 17 refers, defers an investigation, he or she may nevertheless request the relevant state to make information on the proceedings available to the prosecutor. Under Article 53, on the initiation of an investigation, one of the prosecutor's duties in the initial phase is to consider whether the case is or would be admissible under Article 17. If the prosecutor decides that the case is inadmissible, he or she is to inform the Pre-Trial Chamber, the state making the referral or the Security Council of the conclusion and the reasons for it. Again there is no mention of the state of nationality of the suspected person.

By Article 57(2)(a), on the functions and powers of the Pre-Trial Chamber, the Chamber's orders and rulings (*décisions*) issued under Article 18 require the concurrence of the majority of its judges. Article 82 permits either party to appeal a decision with respect to jurisdiction or admissibility, in accordance with the Rules of Procedure and Evidence. These Rules do not exist yet.[32] They may come to have some effect on the general question of jurisdiction and admissibility. Article 90, on competing requests for the surrender of a person, distinguishes between the obligations of a State Party and those of another state. Where the requesting state is a party, the requested state is obliged to give priority to a request from the Court if the Court has, pursuant to Articles 18 and 19, made a determination that the case in respect of which the surrender is sought is admissible and that determination takes into account the investigation or prosecution conducted by the requesting state in respect of its request for extradition. Having regard for the general law of treaties, a requested state that is not a party cannot be obliged to conform to that disposition. By paragraph 4, if the requesting state is not a party, the requested state, if it is not under an international obligation to extradite the person to the requesting state, shall give priority to the request for surrender from the Court if the Court has determined that the case is admissible. Here again, if the requested state is not a party, it is difficult to see how it can be obliged to surrender the person concerned to the Court.[33]

---

32. See Art. 51 on the Rules of Procedure and Evidence. Art. 83 governs proceedings on appeal. Further at n. 47 *infra*.

33. Another problem will arise if the requested state is not a party. Art. 88 requires States Parties to ensure that there are procedures available under their national law for all forms of co-operation which are specified under Part 9. There is no such obligation for non-parties. States that are not parties to the Statute are unlikely to have national provisions for the surrender of persons to the Court, as distinct from their national provisions for extradition in the usual sense

Article 99 deals with the execution of requests for different forms of co-operation with the Court. By paragraph 4:[34]

Without prejudice to other articles in this Part, where it is necessary for the successful execution of a request which can be executed without any compulsory measures, including specifically the interview of or taking evidence from a person on a voluntary basis, including doing so without the presence of the authorities of the requested State Party if it is essential for the request to be executed, and the examination without modification of a public site or other public place, the Prosecutor may execute such request directly on the territory of a State as follows:	Sans préjudice des autres articles du présent chapitre, lorsque cela est nécessaire pour exécuter efficacement une demande à laquelle il peut être donné suite sans recourir à des mesures de contrainte, notamment lorsqu'il s'agit d'entendre ou de faire déposer une personne agissant de son plein gré, y compris hors de la présence des autorités de l'État requis quand cela est déterminant pour la bonne exécution de la demande, ou lorsqu'il s'agit d'inspecter un site public ou un autre lieu public sans le modifier, le Procureur peut réaliser l'objet de la demande directement sur le territoire de l'État, selon les modalités suivantes:
(*a*) When the State Party requested is a State on the territory of which the crime is alleged to have been committed, and there has been a determination of admissibility pursuant to article 18 or 19, the Prosecutor may directly execute such request following all possible consultations with the requested State Party[.]	(*a*) Lorsque l'État requis est l'État sur le territoire duquel il est allégué que le crime a été commis et qu'il y a eu une décision sur la recevabilité comme prévu aux articles 18 ou 19, le Procureur peut exécuter directement la demande, après avoir mené avec l'État requis des consultations aussi étendues que possible[.]

---

of the word. For definitions of 'surrender' and 'extradition' for the purposes of the Statute, see n. 25 *supra*.

34. The complicated structure of this provision requires the text to be given here in English and French.

6.   JURISDICTION *RATIONE MATERIAE*

As indicated, the principal source of jurisdiction *ratione materiae* is Article 5.[35]

Articles 6, 7 and 8 successively enumerate actions and behaviour which, for the purpose of this Statute, would constitute 'genocide', 'crimes against humanity', and 'war crimes'. Articles 5 to 8 give effect to the principle *nullum crimen sine lege*. The Statute adopts different techniques in spelling out the particulars of the different criminal activities.

The first technique, employed for genocide in Article 6 and for crimes against humanity in Article 7, is for the Statute to set out its own definition of the crime. The definition of genocide in Article 6 follows Article II of the Genocide Convention of 1948[36] but the Statute makes no cross-reference to that Convention. Article III of the Genocide Convention goes on to make conspiracy, incitement, attempt and complicity in relation to genocide also punishable under the Convention. The Statute, however, treats these ancillary crimes differently. Article 25 (in Part 3), on individual criminal responsibility, brings in criminal liability for those aspects of criminal behaviour. Paragraph 2(*e*) deals specifically with incitement to commit genocide, but the other ancillary aspects of the core crime are swallowed in the more general provisions of that article.[37] Article 4 of the ICTY Statute and Article 2 of the ICTR Statute follow more closely than the Rome Statute the structure of the Genocide Convention, by including as punishable under the rubric of genocide the ancillary offences of conspiracy to commit, incitement to commit, attempt to commit and complicity in genocide alongside genocide itself.[38] Although those two

---

35. Art. 5 (Crimes within the jurisdiction of the Court) reads:
1. The jurisdiction of the Court shall be limited to the most serious crimes of concern to the international community as a whole. The Court has jurisdiction in accordance with this Statute with respect to the following crimes: (a) The crime of genocide; (b) Crimes against humanity; (c) War crimes; (d) The crime of aggression.
2. The Court shall exercise jurisdiction over the crime of aggression once a provision is adopted in accordance with Articles 121 and 123 defining the crime and setting out the conditions under which the Court shall exercise jurisdiction with respect to this crime. Such a provision shall be consistent with the relevant provisions of the Charter of the United Nations.

36. 78 *UNTS* 277.

37. It should be noted that the ICJ placed together in a single sentence Arts. II and III of the Genocide Convention. Application of the Genocide Convention (Preliminary Objections) (*Bosnia and Herzegovina* v. *Yugoslavia*) case. *ICJ Rep.* (1996) (II) p. 595 at p. 615 (para. 31). The handling of genocide in the Rome Statute blurs the particular heinousness not only of the crime of genocide, but also of its ancillary crimes. They should be in a category of their own.

38. In the preparatory work for the Rome Conference, much thought was devoted to the question of the placement of the 'ancillary' crimes set out in Art. III of the Genocide Convention. See *Report of the Ad Hoc Committee on the Establishment of an International Criminal Court*, United Nations, General Assembly, *Official Records*, 50th session, Supplement 22 (A/50/22) paras. 59 to 62; *Report of the Preparatory Committee on the Establishment of an International Criminal Court*, ibid. 51st session, Supplement 22 (A/51/22), Vol. I, paras. 58 to 64 and Vol. II at p. 57; *Report of the Preparatory Committee*, Doc. A/CONF.183/2/Add.1. The question whether to include Art. III of the Convention in the definition of the crime of genocide in the Statute was related to the question of whether to include in the appropriate general part of

Statutes do not mention the Genocide Convention, the ICTR, in the two judgments it has already given, refers to the Convention and to the standard literature about it.[39]

Article 7 gives the meaning of crimes against humanity. The enumerated acts must have been committed 'as part of a widespread or systematic attack directed against any civilian population, with knowledge of the attack'. This is a wider, but probably more accurate exposition of what is really involved in this crime. That introductory phrase introduces a specific element of *mens rea*, something that may only have been implicit in the previous Statutes, and may be difficult to establish in the case of individuals. The Trial Chamber of the ICTY has given an important interpretation of the word 'any':

> The inclusion of the word 'any' makes it clear that crimes against humanity can be committed against civilians of the same nationality as the perpetrator or those who are stateless, as well as those of a different nationality.[40]

The function of this crime is to bring within the scope of international criminal law acts committed by a government against its own citizens. That was its purpose in the Nuremberg Tribunal. There, however, owing to a mistake or carelessness in the drafting of the London Agreement for the Prosecution and Punishment of the Major War Criminals of the European Axis of 8 August 1945,[41] the crime became limited *ratione temporis* to acts of that nature committed during the Second World War.

Article 7 is the first treaty text to state what are crimes against humanity. To some extent, it follows the definition contained in Article 5 of the ICTY Statute and Article 3 of the ICTR Statute, which were strongly influenced by the Draft Code of Crimes against the Peace and Security of Mankind of the International Law Commission.[42] Article 7 also includes acts such as enslavement, torture, and the

---

the Statute provisions on 'ancillary crimes' related to the 'core crimes'. The Rome Conference decided on the latter solution.

39. These cases are *Prosecutor* v. *Akayesu*, Judgment of 2 September 1998, Case No. ICTR-96-4-T (http://www.un.org/ictr/english/judgments/akayesu.html) (the accused pleaded not-guilty) and *Prosecutor* v. *Kambanda*, Judgment of 4 September 1998, Case No. ICTR-97-23-S-S (http://www.un.org/ictr/english/judgments/kambanda.html) (the accused pleaded guilty). These cases are excerpted in 37 *ILM* (1998) p. 1319 and p. 1411, respectively. On the *Akayesu* case, see 93 *AJIL* (1999) p. 195.

40. *Prosecutor* v. *Tadić* (1997), Case No. IT-94-1-T, 112 *ILR* 1, p. 21, para. 635.

41. 82 *UNTS* 279.

42. The Draft Code, which has been under consideration virtually throughout the existence of the International Law Commission, was finally adopted in 1996. Report of the International Law Commission on the work of its 48th session, 6 May-26 July 1996, ch. II. GAOR, 51st session, Supplement 10 (A/51/10). The General Assembly has not yet decided on the final disposition of this Draft Code. Different tribunals, including the ICTY, are showing an inclination to rely on it when dealing with crimes against humanity. Likewise the House of Lords in its judgment of 24 March 1999 in the *Pinochet* case (*R.* v. *Bartle and the Commissioner of Police for the Metropolis and others* (Ex parte *Pinochet*), *Weekly LR* (1999) 827.

crime of apartheid, all criminalized by international law elsewhere.[43] All three Statutes (Rome Statute, Art. 7(1)(*k*)) contain a wide *ejusdem generis* residual provision for other inhumane acts of similar character. Here too, none of the Statutes contains a cross-reference to any other treaty.

The Statute adopts a different approach for war crimes in Article 8. Unlike the other crimes, war crimes are well known in international law, and alongside relevant treaty definitions there is a large quantity of national and international jurisprudence about these crimes. There is a question how far the Rome Conference has gone in interfering with all those precedents. Article 8, paragraph 1 introduces a major limitation on the Court's jurisdiction: 'The Court shall have jurisdiction in respect of war crimes in particular when committed as part of a plan or policy or as part of a large-scale commission of such crimes.' This affects the issue of *mens rea*. The Statute goes far beyond the designation of 'grave breaches' in the Geneva Conventions of 1949 and the Additional Protocols of 1977.[44] After a general provision in paragraph 2(*a*) covering grave breaches of the Geneva Conventions, namely specific acts against protected persons or property under the relevant Convention, it goes on to deal separately with the laws and customs applicable in international armed conflict (Art. 8(2)(*b*)) and armed conflict not of an international character (paras. 2(*c*) to (*e*)). This enumeration contains several far-reaching innovations in comparison with the Geneva Conventions, and this, in the context of the complementary character of the jurisdiction of the Rome Court, may seriously complicate its subject-matter jurisdiction and be a cause of conflict. The enumeration excludes situations of internal disturbances and tensions – doubtless also a fecund source of controversy should occasion arise. There is no clear reason why there should be this major difference in the jurisdiction of the national courts and that of the international court on so fundamental an issue as the trial and punishment of persons charged with war crimes. The Rome Conference probably exceeded its mandate in making those changes. One result of this is, as stated, major obscurity over the régime to which any individual is subject at a given moment, and the possibility of major discrepancies between the national jurisdiction which has initial priority, and the international jurisdiction.

The ICC Statute refers to the Geneva Conventions but not to any other instruments.[45] While the Statutes of the *ad hoc* Tribunals also allude to these Conventions, they do so in an different way, reflecting the different functions of the Tribunals and the ICC. Article 8(2)(*a*) of the Rome Statute includes as war

---

43. A curious omission from the jurisdiction of the International Criminal Court is 'piracy', once regarded as the international crime *par excellence*. Cf., Art. 105 of the UN Convention on the Law of the Sea of 1992.

44. 75 *UNTS* 5 (Final Act), 31, 85, 135, 287; 1125 ibid. 3. This is noted by Th. Meron, *War Crimes Law Comes of Age* (Oxford, Oxford University Press 1998) p. 307. For a detailed account of the sources and relevant case law regarding the war crimes set out in Art. 8, prepared by the ICRC, see Doc. PCNICC/1999/WGEC/INF.2 and Add.1, 2.

45. In many countries the Conventions, duly ratified, may be part of the law of the land. Cross-referencing to other treaties can be a source of difficulty in the application of one or other of the two instruments, in cases where a state is party to only one of them.

crimes grave breaches of the Geneva Conventions, namely 'any of the following acts against persons or property protected under the provisions of the relevant Geneva Convention'. With some changes of order and of wording, this list follows closely a working paper submitted to the December 1997 session of the Preparatory Committee for the International Criminal Court by the International Committee of the Red Cross.[46] Article 8(2)(*b*) continues with a list of 26 other serious violations of the laws and customs applicable in international armed conflicts, 'within the established framework of international law'. Space does not permit the necessary detailed examination of these lists of war crimes and their comparison with the corresponding provisions of other relevant international treaties, including the Additional Protocols of 1977. However, the Rome Conference did introduce formulations of its own for some of these crimes, without full consideration, in the Committee of the Whole or in the Drafting Committee (or both) as required by the Rules of Procedure of the Conference.[47]

Another provision which may impact on the material jurisdiction of the Court and offset requirements of *mens rea*, appears in paragraph 3: 'Nothing in paragraph 2(*c*) and (*e*) shall affect the responsibility of a Government to maintain or re-establish law and order in the State or to defend the unity and territorial integrity of the State, by all legitimate means.'

Article 8(2)(*c*), (*d*), (*e*) and (*f*) deal with armed conflict not of an international character. Here there is a distinction between 'serious violations of article 3 common to the four Geneva Conventions of 1949' as set out in subparagraph (*c*), and 'other serious violations of the laws and customs applicable in armed conflicts not of an international character, within the established framework of international law', the object of subparagraph (*e*). With what is probably a marked increase in the scope of international humanitarian law in such cases, subparagraph (*f*) specifically applies to 'armed conflicts that take place in the territory of a State when there is protracted armed conflict between governmental authorities and organized armed groups or between such groups'. But what 'protracted armed conflict between governmental authorities and organized armed groups or between such groups' means, and whether it is really something for a court of law to pronounce upon, is another matter.

By Article 124, as a transitional provision, a state on becoming a party to the Statute may declare that, for a period of seven years after the entry into force of the Statute for that state, it does not accept the Court's jurisdiction with respect to the 'category of crimes' referred to in Article 8 when a crime is alleged to have been committed by its nationals or on its territory. This is the only provision in the Statute to accept that the national state of the accused may have a say in whether

---

46. This document does not appear among the relevant series of numbered documents. The reports of the Preparatory Committee present the different proposals without attribution of authorship. The text was furnished to me by the International Committee of the Red Cross.

47. For the Rules of Procedure see Doc. A/CONF.183/6, 23 June 1998. The significance and intent of the phrase 'within the established framework of international law' [*dans le cadre établi du droit international*] in this context is far from clear.

the Rome Court is to exercise jurisdiction over one of its nationals, and then only if that state is a party to the Statute.

A third technique for defining jurisdiction *ratione materiae* has been to leave the matter open and charge other bodies with filling the gap. The treatment of the crime of aggression affords one example of this (see n. 21 above). Terrorism and drug trafficking are other examples. Annex I, resolution E, of the Final Act recognizes that 'terrorist acts, by whomever and wherever perpetrated and whatever their forms, methods or motives, are serious crimes of concern to the international community'. It also recognizes that the 'international trafficking of illicit drugs is a very serious crime, sometimes destabilizing the political and social and economic order in States'. However, there was no agreement in the Rome Conference on a generally acceptable definition of those crimes. The Conference accordingly decided that a Review Conference pursuant to Article 123 of the Statute should 'consider the crimes of terrorism and drug trafficking with a view to arriving at an acceptable definition and their inclusion in the list of crimes within the jurisdiction of the Court'.[48] This is another example of anticipatory amendment of the Statute, raising the same problems as have been mentioned earlier.

In addition, all the crimes, and hence the jurisdiction of the Court, are affected by what are called 'Elements of Crimes'.[49] Here there is a major discrepancy between Article 9 and Article 21, certainly due to the unsatisfactory organization of the Rome Conference. Article 9 states that the Elements of Crimes shall assist the Court [*Les éléments des crimes aident la Cour*] in the interpretation of Articles 6, 7 and 8. Article 21 on the applicable law (but not the French text as it now stands) states that the Court shall apply in the first place this Statute, Elements of Crimes and its Rules of Procedure and Evidence. It is quite clear from the proceedings of the PrepCom that the Elements of Crimes will come to have a major impact on the Court's jurisdiction, but what that will be cannot be said at this stage.[50]

---

48. The Secretary-General is required by Art. 123 to convene the Review Conference seven years after the Statute's entry into force 'to consider any amendments to this Statute. Such review may include, but is not limited to, the list of crimes contained in article 5'. The failure of the Rome Conference to agree on a definition of drug trafficking as a crime within the jurisdiction of the Court is ironic. It was GA Res. 44/39, 4 December 1989, dealing with drug trafficking, that initiated the renewed consideration by the International Law Commission of the topic of the International Criminal Court. That resolution is even recited in para. 3 of the Final Act.

49. The PrepCom is to prepare the Elements of Crimes, together with the Rules of Evidence and Procedure, by 30 June 2000. They shall enter into force on adoption by a two-thirds majority of the members of the Assembly of States Parties. This language, which follows Art. 108 of the Charter of the United Nations, means a two-thirds majority of all the States Parties, whether or not present and voting at the meeting when the vote is taken. On the Elements of Crimes, see the 1996 Report of the Preparatory Committee on the Establishment of the International Criminal Court, vol. I, para. 56, *GAOR*, 51st session, Supplement 22 (A/51/22).

50. See Doc. PCNICC/1999/L.3/Rev.1, 2 March 1999, Annex III. At the very least they will affect the element of *mens rea* required for each individual crime.

7.   JURISDICTION TO ARREST

Different foundations apply to jurisdiction to detain and arrest. That derives from actions of the prosecutor. Article 13 lays down the general rule for the initiation of a criminal process in the Court. The Court may exercise its jurisdiction in three different situations: (a) where a referral to the prosecutor is made by a State Party in accordance with Article 14; (b) where the referral is made by the Security Council acting under Chapter VII of the UN Charter; and (c) where the prosecutor has initiated an investigation under Article 15 acting *proprio motu*. By Article 14, a State Party [*Tout État Partie*] may refer to the prosecutor a situation in which one or more crimes within the jurisdiction of the Court appear to have been committed, requesting the prosecutor to investigate the situation for the purpose of determining whether one or more specific persons should be charged with the commission of such crimes. Article 15 gives the prosecutor wide powers of investigation, being empowered to seek additional information from states, organs of the United Nations, intergovernmental or non-governmental organizations, or other 'reliable' sources, and may receive written or oral testimony. That is the preliminary phase.

If the prosecutor concludes that there is a reasonable basis to proceed with an investigation, the next step is to refer the matter to the Pre-Trial Chamber. The main functions of the Pre-Trial Chamber are set out in Article 57. By Article 58, the Pre-Trial Chamber issues the warrant of arrest or summons to appear, and by Article 58(5), on the basis of a warrant of arrest the Court may request the provisional arrest or the arrest and surrender of the person under Part 9 of the Statute. This is nevertheless subject to Articles 17 and 18, on preliminary issues of admissibility.

It is here that there is a difference between the States Parties and other states. By Article 86, States Parties are obliged to co-operate fully with the Court in its investigation and prosecution of crimes within the Court's jurisdiction. By Article 88, they are obliged to ensure that there are procedures available under their national law for all forms of co-operation specified under Part 9. By Article 89, the Court may transmit a request for the arrest and surrender of a person 'to any State on the territory of which that person may be found'. States Parties are obliged to comply with such requests 'in accordance with the provisions of this Part [9] and the procedure under their national law'. Under the general law of treaties, states that are not parties to the Statute are under no obligation in this respect, unless they have committed themselves *aliunde* according to Article 87(5).

This leads to provisional arrest, the subject of Article 92. In urgent cases, 'the Court may request the provisional arrest of the person sought', pending presentation of the formal request for surrender and the supporting documents. States Parties are obliged to comply with any request of this nature. No such obligation can arise for a state that is not a party.

8.   PROVISIONAL CONCLUSIONS ON JURISDICTION

The Rome Statute is incomplete so long as the Elements of Crimes and the Rules of Procedure and Evidence have not been adopted. That is likely to be a lengthy process: moreover, they cannot be adopted until the Statute is already in force, and the Assembly of States Parties is in existence. With that reservation, several provisional conclusions regarding the Court's jurisdiction under the Statute as it now stands can be made.

In the first place, the Court will only have jurisdiction over natural persons over the age of 18 years. That jurisdiction *ratione personae* has no necessary connection with the person's nationality. The scope of that jurisdiction *ratione temporis* depends on the relationship between the date or place of the conduct alleged to be criminal and the entry into force of the Statute.[51] Only acts committed after the entry into force of the Statute are justiciable by this Court (giving effect to the principle *nullum crimen sine lege*). Subject to that, jurisdiction *ratione personae* exists with regard to the perpetrator of any act classified by the Statute as a serious crime of international concern, coming within the scope of Article 5 of the Statute. Here the emphasis is on the perpetrator of the act.

Ratione materiae, and subject to the principle of complementarity, the impugned act must come within the scope of Article 5, together with the particularization of criminal conduct set out in Articles 6, 7 and 8. The required *mens rea* is indicated in the introductory words or the introductory paragraph of each of Articles 5, 6, 7 and 8.

The Court must establish that the case is not inadmissible, a negative proposition. Put in positive terms, the Court – in this respect it is the Pre-Trial Chamber – has to establish, by a majority (and subject to appeal), that the case is admissible. Here the Rules of Procedure and Evidence will play a major role for what in effect may well become a preliminary mini-trial, presumably without the presence of the suspected person in contradiction to the general rule against trials *in absentia*.

Given the language of the relevant provisions, this means in effect that at present the jurisdiction of the International Criminal Court is limited to the most serious crimes of international concern committed during armed conflict whether international or not or, in the case of crimes against humanity, 'systematic attack'. It does not extend beyond that.

Having regard to the requirements for admissibility in most instances, probably the most important feature of the Rome Statute is the possibility it opens for the Security Council acting under Chapter VII of the Charter to initiate international

---

51. The 'entry into force' of a multilateral treaty is a complicated matter. There is a distinction between its entry into force generally, and its entry into force for a particular state. See on this the resolution on the intertemporal problem in public international law adopted by the Institute of International Law at its Wiesbaden session in 1975. 56 *Annuaire de l'Institut de Droit international*, (1975) p. 536; reproduced in Institut de Droit international, *Tableau des Résolutions adoptées (1957–1991)* (1992) at p. 110. Further in S. Rosenne, *Developments in the Law of Treaties 1945–1986* (Cambridge, Cambridge University Press 1989) p. 76.

criminal proceedings by referring a case to the prosecutor (Art. 13(b)). The possibility even exists that the Security Council acting under Chapter VII of the Charter could decide to bring the Statute into force and use it if it considered it necessary for the exercise of its functions under Chapter VII. The standing Court will take the place of *ad hoc* Tribunals, which are always a source of political and intellectual difficulty. When the Security Council acting under Chapter VII initiates proceedings before the International Criminal Court, for all members of the United Nations differences between the obligations of States Parties to the Statute and other states lose their significance, since Article 25 of the Charter will be the governing provision. The two *ad hoc* criminal tribunals established by the Security Council under Chapter VII during the 1990s have not exhausted the types of situation in which serious crimes of international concern have been alleged.

JURISDICTION AND COOPERATION IN THE STATUTE OF THE INTERNATIONAL CRIMINAL COURT: PRINCIPLES AND COMPROMISES[1]

Hans-Peter Kaul[2] and Claus Kreß[3, 4]

1.   INTRODUCTION

At the Rome Conference on the adoption of the Statute of the International Criminal Court (hereinafter, the Statute and the ICC), the negotiators faced basically three types of problems. First, a considerable number of primarily technical difficulties stemmed from the differences between national systems of criminal law. This type of problem was characteristic for the discussions on general principles of criminal law (Part 3 of the Statute), criminal procedure (Parts 5, 6 and 8) and enforcement (Part 10). Second, a more limited number of disputed questions resulted from deeply-rooted differences in legal culture. This was true for the most important controversies on penalties (Part 7), in particular for the hotly debated death penalty, and for some specific points relating to the general principles of criminal law, in particular, the treatment of voluntary intoxication. Third, delegations were forced to break the impasse with regard to a set of unresolved key issues of a highly political nature. This article deals with two sets of issues belonging to the latter category: jurisdiction and cooperation.

The respective places of jurisdiction and cooperation within the Statute, i.e., Articles 5, 12 and 13 (in Part 2) and Articles 86 to 102 (all of Part 9),[5] tend to conceal the intimate interrelation between them. On a little closer look, though, the links between jurisdiction and cooperation become obvious. Functionally, the implementation of any set of jurisdictional rules defining the Court's sphere of

---

1. © H. Kaul and C. Kreß, 1999.

2. Head of the Public International Law Section of Germany's Foreign Office, Berlin; Deputy Head of Germany's Delegation to the Rome Conference on the Establishment of an International Criminal Court; Head of Germany's Delegation to the Preparatory Commission for the International Criminal Court.

3. Dr. jur. (Cologne), LL.M. (Cantab.), Deputy Head of the Public International Law Section of Germany's Ministry of Justice, Berlin; Member of Germany's Delegation to the Rome Conference on the Establishment of an International Criminal Court and to the Preparatory Commission for the International Court.

4. The views expressed in this article do not necessarily represent those of the German government.

5. In the following text, Articles without further reference are those of the Rome Statute.

activity depends on a complementary cooperation regime. Systematically, the key elements of the jurisdictional regime constitute starting points in framing the cooperation regime.[6] This is true, firstly, for the limits of the Court's jurisdiction: the choice between a regime of automatic jurisdiction, on the one hand, and a consent or an opt in/opt out system of jurisdiction, on the other hand, has direct repercussions in the area of cooperation.[7] It is important, secondly, for the very basic question of *Kompetenz-Kompetenz*. It is a cornerstone of the ICC's jurisdictional regime that it is up to the Court to rule authoritatively on the issue of jurisdiction. It follows immediately from this that a refusal to cooperate with the Court could not be based on the requested state's assessment that the Court has no jurisdiction in a given case.[8]

Beyond their functional and systematical interplay, jurisdiction and cooperation are also linked at the level of fundamental legal principles. Above all, jurisdiction and cooperation are obviously the decisive factors for the effectiveness of the future Court. Furthermore, they are the most important elements for an overall determination of the legal nature of the Rome treaty. One has to turn to these two areas to answer the question to what extent the Statute possesses an integral character instead of merely comprising a set of purely synallagmatical legal relationships. Similarly, analysis of the two regimes in question offers guidance to what degree the Statute is directly individual-related instead of constituting a purely interstate instrument. In short, in light of the rules on jurisdiction and cooperation, a judgment can safely be made as to what degree the Statute corresponds with one of the most important statements of the Appeals Chamber of the International Criminal Tribunal for the Former Yugoslavia (ICTY) in its seminal *Tadić* Decision (Jurisdiction) of 2 October 1995 (*Tadić* Jurisdiction Decision). According to this eloquent statement,[9] in the development of international law: 'a State-sovereignty-oriented approach has been gradually supplanted by a human-being-oriented approach.'[10]

This contribution will first deal with jurisdiction and cooperation in turn (Parts 2 and 3, respectively). In each case, the principles at stake will be discussed briefly.

---

6. For the need to bear that in mind in interpreting Part 9 of the Statute see C. Kreß, K. Prost, A. Schlunck and P. Wilkitzki, in O. Triffterer, ed., *Commentary on the ICC Statute* (Baden-Baden, Nomos Verlagsgesellschaft 1999) Preliminary Remarks on Part 9, marginal n. 2.

7. To illustrate this point: The option for a ground for refusal to surrender a person to the Court contained in Art. 87(3) option 2(a) of the Draft Statute (UN Doc. A/Conf.183/2/Add. 1, p. 159) was explicable solely on the basis of a jurisdiction regime based on specific state consent. This option for a ground for refusal to surrender remained pending during the Rome conference, with virtually no discussion being devoted to it, until the final decisions on jurisdiction were made.

8. At a late stage of the negotiations of what finally became Art. 89(2) of the Statute, an effort was made by some delegations to introduce the right to a final say of State Parties on the issue of jurisdiction through the back door of cooperation.

9. ICTY Case No. IT-94-1-AR72, 2 October 1995, reprinted in 16 *HRLJ* (1995) p. 458 (para. 97).

10. Cf., the challenging study of Ph. Allott, 'The Concept of International Law', 10 *EJIL* (1999) pp. 31 et seq., concluding with 'The New Paradigm' (p. 50) that shows some ressemblance with the statement of the ICTY.

The analysis then focuses on the course of the negotiations and the elements of the final compromises. On the basis of that, the article proceeds in Part 4 to an appraisal of the negotiations' outcome.

2.   JURISDICTION

Looking back to Rome, jurisdiction appears to have been the most important, politically the most difficult and therefore the most contentious question of the negotiations as a whole, in short: the 'question of questions' of the entire project. The United States was not the only one emphasizing 'that the issue of jurisdiction had to be resolved satisfactorily or else the entire treaty and the integrity of the Court would be imperiled'.[11] Given this fact, it is not exceedingly surprising that 'it is on this issue that the differences proved irreconcilable and consensus eventually broke down, leading to a vote at the end of the conference'.[12]

2.1   **Principles: universality versus state sovereignty**

A state which becomes a Party to the Statute thereby accepts the jurisdiction of the Court with respect to genocide, crimes against humanity and war crimes (hereafter, the international core crimes[13]), and no particular state – be it a State Party or a non-State Party – must give its specific consent to the exercise of this jurisdiction in a given case. This, in essence, is the regime that follows from an approach based on the principle of universal jurisdiction over the international core crimes. The universality approach starts from the assumption that, under current international law, all states may[14] exercise universal jurisdiction over the above-listed core crimes of international law. And it then adds to this assumption the very simple idea that states must be entitled to do collectively what they have the power to do individually. On the level of principles, the universality approach has to be contrasted with various approaches based on a more or less restrictively conceived principle of state sovereignty. Moderate variants of this approach may be called the nationality and/or the territoriality approaches. Hereafter, the jurisdiction of the Court is dependent on the consent of the national state of the suspect and/or the state on whose territory the crime has been committed. A fully fledged state sovereignty approach goes beyond the criteria of territoriality and nationality in requiring the consent of every state which is in any way directly concerned with or interested in the crime (the points of attachment can be the custody of the

---

11. D. Scheffer, 'The United States and the International Criminal Court', 93 *AJIL* (1999) p. 17.

12. Ph. Kirsch and J.T. Holmes, 'The Rome Conference on an International Criminal Court: The Negotiating Process', 93 *AJIL* (1999) p. 4.

13. Aggression, being the fourth international core crime, is not dealt with in this article.

14. The universality approach does not entail the wider-reaching assertion that all states have a duty to prosecute international core crimes.

suspect, the nationality of the victim or an extradition request). At the level of principles, the question as to whether the consent is expressed by way of ratification (system of automatic jurisdiction) or in a more specific form (system of [specific] consent) is of secondary importance. It is obvious, though, that the more specific the consent of a (or more) state(s) must be, the more emphasis is placed on the sovereignty of this (these) State(s). The alternative between automatic and (specific) consent-based jurisdiction is thus not only of a technical character but has substantive consequences.

Basically, two legal[15] criticisms have been addressed to the universality approach.[16] First, it is argued that the universality approach is not in line with the current status of general international law. Not all the crimes within the Court's jurisdiction are, according to this view, covered by universal jurisdiction so that one has to rely upon the other qualifications for international criminal jurisdiction, in particular, territoriality and nationality (hereafter, customary law argument). Second, it is held that giving the Court jurisdiction over a crime committed in the territory of a non-State Party or over suspected nationals of a non-State Party conflicts irreconcilably with the fundamental principle of treaty law that only states that are party to a treaty are bound by its terms (hereafter, treaty law argument). It must be stressed that the treaty law argument goes far beyond a mere criticism of the universality approach. Put to its extreme, the treaty law argument is to invalidate any treaty-based system of jurisdiction over international core crimes whose operation is independent of the consent of a non-State Party which, too, has a (non-exclusive) title of international criminal jurisdiction in the given case.[17]

It is submitted that the customary law argument fails the test of close scrutiny. Given the general consensus about the customary nature of universal jurisdiction over genocide[18] – the 'crime of crimes', in the words of the International Criminal Tribunal for Rwanda (ICTR)[19] – it is no longer necessary to say anything in this respect.

The applicability of the principle of universal jurisdiction under customary international law to those war crimes committed in an international armed conflict which are covered by Article 8(2)(a) and (b) (hereafter, war crimes) cannot seriously be questioned either. Concerning the crimes listed in Article 8(2)(a), i.e., the grave breaches of the Geneva Conventions of 12 August 1949, the respective

---

15. At this point, the article does not aim at an analysis of the political motivations underlying these criticisms.

16. Both points are made by Scheffer, loc. cit. n. 11, at p. 18.

17. For criticisms of the treaty law argument see also G. Hafner, K. Boon, A. Rübesame and J. Huston, 'A Response to the American View as Presented by Ruth Wedgwood', 10 *EJIL* (1999) pp. 116 et seq.; A. Cassese 'The Statute of the International Criminal Court: Some Preliminary Reflections', 10 *EJIL* (1999) pp. 159 et seq.

18. Cf., Art. 6 of the Statute; for a detailed demonstration of the applicability of the principle of universal jurisdiction under customary international law over genocide see A. Zimmermann, 'The Creation of a Permanent International Criminal Court', 2 *MPYIL* (1998) pp. 206 et seq.

19. Judgment of 4 September 1998 in *Prosecutor* v. *Kambanda*, ICTR 97-23-S, para. 16.

treaty provisions[20] – whose customary character was recently reaffirmed by the International Court of Justice (hereafter, ICJ) in the *Nuclear Weapons Opinion*[21] – explicitly provide for universal jurisdiction.[22] With respect to the war crimes contained in Article 8(2)(b), the customary validity of the universal jurisdiction principle has recently been shown by Andreas Zimmermann,[23] and it suffices to briefly summarize the points convincingly made by this author. He refers to a long-standing state practice to punish war crimes regardless of specific points of attachment to the respective *forum* (a practice which, in fact, predates the Geneva Conventions of 1949 (hereafter, GC). This practice, which in itself suffices to establish the customary status of the universality principle, was reaffirmed in the process of elaborating the First Additional Protocol of 1977 to the GC and by the now universal acceptance of some other pertinent international instruments.

Given the considerable disparity of the pertinent conventions prior to Rome, the legal situation may be seen as somewhat less straightforward with respect to crimes against humanity[24] than with respect to war crimes. A closer look, though, reveals that the customary principle of universal jurisdiction equally applies to crimes against humanity. This position can be based on state (judicial and legislative) practice, as has recently been shown by Kenneth C. Randall[25] and Andreas Zimmermann.[26] Beyond that, the position is justified as a matter of principle. Together with genocide, crimes against humanity are most directly covered by the ICJ's *dictum* in *Barcelona Traction*[27] on the *erga omnes* character of certain international rules, and the principle of universal jurisdiction must be understood as the legal vehicle by which states, acting on behalf of the international community, can react to any violation of such a rule. Finally, the customary validity of universal jurisdiction over crimes against humanity gains support from the evolving jurisprudence of the ICTY. In its sentencing practice, this Tribunal has had the opportunity to directly compare war crimes and crimes against humanity. In its Sentencing Judgment of 14 July 1997 in *Prosecutor* v. *Tadić*, the Trial Chamber made a statement which is very much in point:

---

20. Art. 49 of the First Geneva Convention, Art. 50 of the Second Geneva Convention, Art. 129 of the Third Geneva Convention and Art. 146 of the Fourth Geneva Convention.

21. Cf., esp. para. 79 of the Advisory Opinion of 8 July 1996, 35 *ILM* (1996) p. 827.

22. These provisions even enshrine an unqualified duty for States Parties *aut dedere aut judicare*.

23. Zimmermann, loc. cit. n. 18, at p. 212.

24. Cf., Art. 7 Statute.

25. K.C. Randall, 'Universal Jurisdiction under International Law', 66 *Texas Law Review* (1988) pp. 800 et seq.

26. Zimmermann, loc. cit., n. 18, at p. 211.

27. *ICJ Rep.* (1970) para. 33. In *Barcelona Traction* the Court only dealt with basic 'rights of the human person' and correspondingly with *erga omnes* obligations of states. The concept of a international core crime implies the idea of 'basic duties of the human person' and correspondingly *erga omnes* obligations of individuals. For a similar view cf., Randall, loc. cit. n. 25, at p. 830.

A prohibited act committed as part of a crime against humanity ... is, all else being equal, a more serious offence than an ordinary war crime. This follows from the requirement that crimes against humanity be committed on a widespread or systematic scale, the quantity of the crimes having a qualitative impact on the nature of the offence which is seen as a crime against more than just the victims themselves but against humanity as a whole.[28]

Taking this into account, it would seem very odd indeed to reject the customary validity of universal jurisdiction over crimes against humanity in the light of the undeniable applicability of the same principle to war crimes.

There remain war crimes committed in an internal armed conflict, which are listed in Article 8(2)(c) and (e) and which, for the sake of analytical clarity, are called *civil* war crimes in this study.[29] It is with respect to this category of crimes alone that the customary applicability of the universal jurisdiction principle was open to argument before the Rome conference started. On balance, the preferable view of current customary law is to affirm the extension of the universal jurisdiction principle to civil war crimes and to acknowledge a basically coherent jurisdictional regime under customary international law for all core crimes of the Statute. It is true that the Appeals Chamber of the ICTY rejected the extension of the grave breaches regime of the GC to civil war crimes in the *Tadić* Decision.[30] But this statement cannot be construed as to render this issue moot. Firstly, the majority of the Appeals Chamber recognized a trend under recent customary law to extend the grave breaches regime to civil war crimes, and Judge Abi-Saab in his dissent on this point[31] went so far as to acknowledge such an extension by way of subsequent practice to the GC. Secondly and decisively, the customary principle of universal jurisdiction may well govern civil war crimes independently from a grave breaches regime, as is the case with respect to the war crimes in Article 8(2)(b).[32] Starting from this premise, the *Tadić* Decision even lends strong support to an extension of universal jurisdiction to civil war crimes, as it is the key message of this decision that the customary law regarding civil war crimes has undergone a long process of assimilation to that of war crimes.[33] The *Tadić* Decision is not

---

28. Para. 73 of the judgment. This view has been endorsed by another Trial Chamber on 11 November 1999 (para. 28 of the judgment; with references to the corresponding jurisprudence of the ICTR in n. 47 Judge Robinson diss. Sub 1. of the sep. opinion) following the judgment of the Appeals Chamber of 15 July 1999.

29. On this point of terminology see C. Kreß, 'Der Jugoslawien-Strafgerichtshof im Grenzbereich zwischen internationalem bewaffneten Konflikt und Bürgerkrieg', in H. Fischer and S.R. Lüder, eds., *Völkerrechtliche Verbrechen vor dem Jugoslawien-Tribunal, nationalen Gerichten und dem Internationalen Gerichtshof* (Berlin, Berlin Verlag 1999) p. 36.

30. *Supra* n. 9, at pp. 454 et seq. (paras. 80 et seq.).

31. Ibid., at p. 470 (sub IV.)

32. Cf., *supra* in the text following n. 23.

33. For a detailed analysis of this crucial element of the *Tadić* Decision see C. Kreß, 'Friedenssicherungs- und Konfliktsvölkerrecht auf der Schwelle zur Postmoderne. Das Urteil des Internationalen Straftribunals für das ehemalige jugoslawien (Appeals Chamber) im Fall Tadić', *Europäische Grundrechte Zeitschrift* (1996) pp. 645 et seq.

the only piece of practice pointing in this direction. In the *Nicaragua* Judgment (Merits) of 27 June 1986,[34] the ICJ couched the rationale behind common Article 3 of the GC in the terms 'elementary considerations of humanity'. On this basis, one may assume that the ICJ would consider the duties incumbent on individuals under common Article 3 of the GC as possessing a character *erga omnes*. As to the civil war crimes which go beyond the realm of common Article 3 of the GC, states such as Belgium and Switzerland have recently exercised universal jurisdiction without having met with any protest.[35] After the conclusion of the Rome conference, the Statute itself may be seen as a powerful element of state practice supporting the extension of universal jurisdiction to civil war crimes. Reference can be made to preambular paragraph six which recalls 'the duty of every State to exercise its criminal jurisdiction over those responsible for international crimes'. This phrase may well be seen as an affirmation of the customary application of the universal jurisdiction principle to all international core crimes of the Statute including civil war crimes under Article 8(2)(c) and (e).[36] As a matter of principle, too, the extension of universal jurisdiction to civil war crimes is well justified. One may, of course, argue that the most relevant circumstantial factors of a single civil war crime (place of the crime, nationality of criminal and victim) – unlike the case of a war crime – usually relate only to one jurisdiction, and that a transnational spillover effect is not typical here, as an overall context of massive delinquency is – other than in the cases of genocide and crimes against humanity – no constituent element of the crime in question. But these points do not exhaustively deal with the rationales underlying universal jurisdiction under current international law.[37] One criterion which is usually referred to to explain universal jurisdiction is the particularly grave nature of the crime demanding the solidarity of the international community in its repressive efforts. In this respect, the most recent international reactions clearly reveal the fact that civil war crimes may provoke the same kind of international concern as war crimes. Another possible explanation of the universal jurisdiction principle points to what may be called an inherent skepticism in the willingness and/or ability of the state most directly concerned to genuinely prosecute the relevant international core crimes.[38] This explanation, again, appears to apply to civil war crimes as it does to the other international core crimes, as experience shows

---

34. *ICJ Rep.* (1986) p. 114 (para. 218).

35. For references see Zimmermann, loc. cit. n. 18, at p. 213 (fn. 163).

36. L. Condorelli, 'La Cour pénale internationale: un pas de géant (pourvu qu'il soit accompli ...)', 103 *RGDIP* (1999) p. 19; for a contrary view see T.N. Slade and R. Clark, 'Preamble and Final Clauses', in R.S. Lee, ed., *The International Criminal Court. The Making of the Rome Statute* (The Hague, Kluwer Law International 1999) p. 427, who call this preambular paragraph 'delightfully ambiguous'.

37. For an interesting analysis of the evolution of the rationales of universal jursidiction see Randall, loc. cit. n. 25, at pp. 803 et seq.

38. For a recent elaboration of this thesis see R. Merkel, 'Universale Jurisdiktion bei völkerrechtlichen Verbrechen', in K. Lüderssen, ed., *Aufgeklärte Kriminalpolitik oder Kampf gegen das Böse. Band III: Makrodelinquenz* (Baden-Baden, Nomos Verlagsgesellschaft 1998) pp. 261 et seq.

that for a number of reasons civil war states tend to be reluctant to genuinely prosecute the crimes committed during the conflict.

On the basis of the customary validity of universal jurisdiction over the international core crimes, the treaty law argument is flawed for at least two reasons.[39] Firstly, this argument artificially separates the Statute's jurisdictional regime from relevant customary international law. The treaty argument erroneously implies that a treaty-based regime of universal jurisdiction for international core crimes creates new rights *vis-à-vis* third states. In reality, though, such a regime does no more than to set up a new mechanism to (collectively) exercise already existing rights.[40] The second and equally fundamental flaw of the treaty law argument consists of reducing the issue of jurisdiction over international core crimes to a set of bilateral interstate legal relationships. Hereby it ignores the important, if not central, position of the individual in the realm of international criminal law. According to its very concept, an international core crime implies the violation of an international legal duty of an individual *vis-à-vis* the international community as such.[41] In short, the Statute deals with the collective reaction of its States Parties to the breach by an individual of his obligation *erga omnes*.[42] As a matter of principle, the jurisdiction regime of a treaty which sets up an international judicial body to judge international core crimes can thus not be construed as if it concerned only interstate relationships. On the contrary, the individual criminal must, for the very specific and limited purpose of international criminal law, be seen rather as an independent subject[43] of international law than as an extension of his national or territorial state. Consequently, the jurisdiction of the Court over nationals of non-States Parties to the extent implied in the universality approach should not be seen as imposing an obligation on a non-State Party (or infringing upon a right of such a state), but rather as responding to (existing) obligations of the individual under international law.

---

39. As convincingly demonstrated by the authors cited *supra* n. 17, the treaty law argument can also be refuted on the basis of a much more narrow jurisdictional concept.

40. This marks an important difference between core crimes of international law and the so-called treaty-based crimes which, for good reasons, have not found their way in the Statute. For a detailed analysis of the treaty law argument in the context of the treaty-based crimes see Randall, loc. cit. n. 25, pp. 821 et seq.

41. For an extended analysis see Ch. Bassiouni, 'Réprimer les crimes internationaux: *jus cogens* et *obligatio erga omnes*', in Comité International de la Croix Rouge, ed., *Répression nationale des violations du droit international humanitaire, Rapport de la réunion d'experts à Genève, 23-25 septembre 1997*, p. 29; cf., also J.-A. Carrillo-Salcedo, 'La Cour pénale internationale: l'humanité trouve une place dans le droit international', 103 *RGDIP* (1999) pp. 23 et seq.

42. See *supra* n. 27.

43. S. Sur, 'Vers une Cour internationale pénale: la Convention de Rome entre les ONG et le Conseil de sécurité', 103 *RGDIP* (1999) p. 35, holds that the Statute defines the individual as an object rather than as a subject of law because individuals cannot directly trigger the Court's jurisdiction. This is a matter of perspective. Sur chooses the perspective of procedural law. The qualification as 'independent subject of international law' in the above text refers to the individual's position under substantive international criminal law.

Having hereby reached the conclusion that the criticisms addressed to the universality approach do not find a solid basis in international law, the additional question remains whether the universality approach is a sound one as a matter of international legal policy. In other words, is it a wise approach for states to jointly go as far collectively as each of them is in a position to go individually?

The answer to this question of international legal policy quite obviously must be in the affirmative if emphasis is placed on international solidarity as the rationale for universal jurisdiction over international core crimes:[44] there can be no doubt that the joint exercise of universal jurisdiction by an international criminal court is the most direct expression of international solidarity in the fight against the most egregious crimes.[45] At this juncture, it is worth recalling that Article 6 of the Genocide Convention of 9 December 1948 provided for the possibility of establishing an international criminal court without at the same time acknowledging the power of every State Party to prosecute genocide internally based on universal jurisdiction.[46] Article 6 of the Genocide Convention is thus worded in a way as if States Parties were prepared to implement the idea of solidarity only on the international level. Against this background, it is difficult to understand why Ruth Wedgwood finds it less easy to accept that states exercise their jurisdiction over the nationals of third states collectively (i.e., in the form of an international body) than unilaterally.[47]

It is submitted that the universal approach is preferable as matter of international legal policy even if one starts from the assumption that it is the primary responsibility of (the) states (directly concerned) to prosecute an international core crime at the national level,[48] an assumption which would be consistent with an alternative rationale of the universal jurisdiction principle (mistrust in the most directly concerned state's willingness to prosecute). Should such a primary responsibility of (certain) states (most directly concerned) exist as a matter of principle (subsidiarity of international action) and/or of practicability (most directly connected internal *forum* as the criminal *forum conveniens*) – a difficult question which does not need to be pursued further for the limited purpose of this study – this primary responsibility by no means runs counter to the universality approach. This is because the universal approach implies neither exclusive jurisdiction nor

---

44. Cf., D. Oehler, *Internationales Strafrecht*, 2nd edn. (Köln, Carl Heymanns Verlag 1983) p. 543 (fn. 902).

45. Cf., the conclusion of Oehler, ibid.: 'Obviously an international criminal court [...] could best express the idea of solidarity of States' (translation by the authors).

46. Instead Art. 6 of the Genocide Convention appears to restrict the internal criminal jurisdiction to prosecute genocide to the territorial state.

47. We refer to the following passage in the article by R. Wedgwood, 'The International Criminal Court: An American View', 10 *EJIL* (1999) p. 99: 'A broad criminal jurisdiction has certainly been exercised by the United States in the prosecution of extraterritorial conduct [...]. But there is arguably a difference between exercising jurisdiction as part of a national criminal justice authority, and turning a defendant over to an international body in which his own state has chosen not to participate.'

48. For such a view see Sur, loc. cit. n. 43, pp. 32 et seq.

priority of jurisdiction of an international criminal court.[49] Thus, primary responsibility of states to prosecute internally, properly understood, does not affect the scope of jurisdiction of the international criminal court but must rather be reflected in the acceptance of priority of internal prosecution of States Parties, within a system of complementarity between national and international criminal jurisdictions.

In conclusion, the universality approach is clearly the preferable one as a matter both of international law and international legal policy.

2.2   Compromise: territoriality or nationality instead of universality

2.2.1   *The options at the beginning of the Rome Conference[50]*

The options which were on the negotiation table in the first phase of the Rome conference were basically as follows:[51] A jurisdictional regime based on the universality approach pure and simple was proposed by Germany.[52] The essence of this proposal was not to limit the ICC's jurisdiction by the requirement of the consent of a particular state, be it the territorial state, the state of the nationality of the suspect or any other state. The Court's jurisdiction would simply mirror the universal jurisdiction of its States Parties. The German proposal was supported by a number of other states, by the vast majority of Non-Governmental Organisations (hereafter, NGOs)[53] and last but not least by the International Committee of the Red Cross (hereafter, ICRC).[54]

---

49. M.E. Corrao, 'Jurisdiction of the International Criminal Court and State Consent', in F. Lattanzi, ed., *The International Criminal Court. Comments on the Draft Statute* (Naples, Editoriale Scientifica 1998) p. 92.

50. For an instructive overview about the course of the discussion up to the Rome Conference see E. Wilmshurst, 'Jurisdiction of the Court', in Lee, op. cit. n. 36, at pp. 127 et seq.

51. In summarizing the different options, the hypothesis of the ICC's jurisdiction being triggered by the Security Council is excluded. Many options reserved a special treatment for this hypothesis. For a more detailed description of these proposals mentioned *infra* in the text see Sh.A. Williams, in Triffterer, op. cit. n. 6., marginal n. 5 et seq.

52. See A/AC.249/1998/DP. 2, 23 March 1998 (the crime of aggression was not dealt with in this discussion paper). The first detailed proposal in this direction was submitted by Germany in February 1996.

53. See most recently   Amnesty International's paper 'Universal Jurisdiction' (May 1999; IOR 53/01/99). Most recently, Sur, loc. cit. n. 43, at pp. 35 et seq., has heavily criticised the active role which the NGOs played in the whole process of elaborating the Statute. It is difficult to understand Sur's anger. The support which virtually all NGOs lent to the proposal based on the universality approach is a good example of the fact that overall the NGOs' activities cannot be reduced to a narrow perspective of particular interests. The NGOs' preference for the universality approach was clearly a principled one, as has been shown *supra* sub II. 1., and gives certainly less reason to question the underlying 'political' motivation than the attitude taken by some states; for a positive judgment about the input of the NGOs in the process of negotiating the Statute see A. Bos, 'The International Criminal Court: a perspective', in Lee, op. cit. n. 36 at p. 470.

54. See the information conveyed by New Zealand, A/CONF.183/INF/9, 13 July 1998.

The proposal which came closest to the German one was introduced by the Republic of Korea at an early stage of the Rome conference.[55] South Korea narrowed the German approach by requiring the consent (expressed by way of ratification) of either the territorial state, the state of nationality of the suspect, the state of nationality of the victim or the custodial state. In practice, this model would have yielded basically the same results as the German proposal, as the sufficiency of the custodial state's consent under the South Korean model constitutes a practical requisite of the exercise of the Court's jurisdiction pursuant to the German approach.

A proposal which does reflect a qualified territoriality approach was made by the United Kingdom at the concluding round of negotiations of the Preparatory Committee in March/April 1998.[56] This proposal narrowed the ICC's jurisdiction by requiring the consent (expressed by way of ratification) of the territorial and the custodial state. At an early stage of the Rome conference the United Kingdom moved to a pure territorial approach by requiring only the consent of the territorial state.[57]

The options summarized so far can all be seen as variants of a system of automatic jurisdiction, as a state that ratifies the Statute thereby automatically accepts the ICC's jurisdiction. The remaining options all require a specific form of state consent to the ICC's jurisdiction, i.e., a consent beyond ratification. This is true, first, for the options representing the idea of an opt-in/opt-out regime initially developed by the International Law Commission (hereafter, ILC) in its Draft Statute.[58] The idea of an opt-in/opt-out regime is modelled on the jurisdictional regime of the ICJ,[59] which reveals its great deference to state sovereignty.[60] Such a regime, in essence, amounts to an *à la carte* approach: states would be in a position to submit to (or detract from) the ICC's jurisdiction through special declarations for certain categories of crimes or even individual crimes and/or for certain periods of time. An opt-in/opt-out-regime, in its different variants, was supported by a sizeable minority of 27 states in the first phase of the Rome conference.

Finally, a proposal which took the principle of statal consent almost to its logical extreme (which was therefore called 'state consent regime') was at the heart of the Draft Statute submitted by France to the Preparatory Committee in August 1996.[61] This proposal would have made the jurisdiction in every individual case

---

55. A/CONF. 183/C. 1/L. 6, 18 June 1998.

56. A/AC.249/WG.3/DP.1.

57. Williams, loc. cit. n. 51.

58. See Art. 22 of the ILC Statute; A/51/22, Supplement 22a, p. 73.

59. Cf., Art. 36 of the ICJ Statute.

60. In the light of the principles at stake in the particular context of international core crimes, principles which – as elaborated *supra* in the text sub II. 1 – differ markedly from those applicable in the purely interstate context of the ICJ jurisdiction, one can only subscribe to J. Dugard's statement that an opt-in/opt-out-regime is 'unduly deferential to state sovereignty' ('Obstacles in the Way of an International Criminal Court', 56 *CLJ* (1997) p. 336).

61. See Art. 34 of the French Draft Statute, A/AC. 249/L. 3, 6 August 1996.

dependent on the specific consent of all states directly concerned (i.e., the territorial state, the states of nationality of the suspect and the victim and, if applicable, the state applying for extradition and the custodial state). In its pure form, this proposal was not of great relevance in Rome. The contrary is true for the variant advocated by the United States, pursuant to which the state of nationality of the suspect would have the possibility to accept or reject a particular procedure.[62]

2.2.2   *The negotiations in Rome*[63]

The negotiation method pursued by Philipp Kirsch,[64] the Canadian ambassador and charismatic chairman of the conference's Committee of the Whole, was as follows: After numerous bilateral and group consultations, Mr Kirsch and the Conference Bureau successively presented various discussion papers to the participants in the course of the second half of the conference. The papers of 6[65] and 10 July[66] 1998 contained different options on the unresolved key questions of the Statute, particularly jurisdiction.[67] These options in turn were based on the various proposals and options of the Draft Statute. The second step involved holding comprehensive orientation debates on each of the discussion papers, in which each state taking the floor was invited to present its national views on precise questions formulated by the Conference Bureau. This procedure, largely 'accepted' by the conference, clearly had various aims: to focus the debate, to speed up the necessary opinion-building process among the delegates, to sound out the majority views and to eliminate proposals which were supported by only a few states. The ultimate goal was to achieve an appropriate empirical basis for the Conference Bureau to make a package proposal which had a good chance of being accepted. The procedure proved effective.

As expected, it soon became apparent that the possibility, already envisaged by the ILC, for the Security Council to refer particular 'situations' to the Court pursuant to Chapter VII of the UN Charter, continued to be practically undisputed. Only very few states, such as Mexico, and in particular India,[68] did not want to

---

62. For the 'authentic' description of the United States' proposal see Scheffer, loc. cit. n. 11, at p. 19.

63. This part of the study partly draws upon H.-P. Kaul, 'Special note: the Struggle for the International Court's Jurisdiction', 6 *European Journal of Crime, Criminal Law and Criminal Justice* (1998) pp. 364 et seq; cf., also H.-P. Kaul, 'Der Internationale Strafgerichtshof: Das Ringen um seine Zuständigkeit und Reichweite', in Fischer and Lüder, op. cit. n. 29, at pp. 177 et seq.

64. In the meantime Ph. Kirsch has given two accounts of the Rome negotiations; cf., the contributions, loc. cit. n. 12 (together with J. T. Holmes) and in Lee, op. cit. n. 36, at pp. 451 et seq.

65. A/CONF/C. 1/L. 53.

66. A/CONF. 183/C. 1/L. 59.

67. For a summary of these papers see M. Bergsmo, 'The Jurisdictional Regime of the International Criminal Court', 6 *European Journal of Crime, Criminal Law and Criminal Justice* (1998) p. 32.

68. For India's proposal see A/CONF. 183/C. 1/L. 79, L. 95.

allow the Security Council to have any role in connection with the Court's activities. The fact of this quasi-unanimity made it clear at an early stage that the power of the Security Council to activate the future ICC would become an important part of the jurisdictional regime.

Next, the German proposal was eliminated. The United States in particular had spoken very pointedly against this proposal. However, it was not so much US resistance as the lack of adequate support from other participants which led to its demise. Approximately 25 states explicitly supported Germany's proposal. In the orientation debate of 9 July 1998, no less than 23 states voiced their regret or surprise that this was not contained in the option paper of 6 July 1998. By contrast, the South Korean proposal was gaining an increasing number of supporters. This became abundantly clear at the orientation debates of 9 and 13 July 1998. In fact, these debates acted as a kind of opinion poll on the discussion papers of 6 and 10 July 1998. In view of the high level of support for the South Korean proposal (85 percent on 13 July 1998[69]), it was clear that in both discussion papers it would be the first option on jurisdiction. Given its overwhelming support, it is of particular interest to see how the final compromise which narrowed the ICC's jurisdiction considerably came about. With this we reach the dramatic endgame of the conference.

As so often in critical phases of the UN decision-making process, the well-established coordination mechanisms among the permanent members of the Security Council (hereafter, P-5) came into play.[70] Of these it was France in particular which, since the beginning of the conference, was looking for a way to exempt war crimes and crimes against humanity from compulsory jurisdiction. The United States, too, wanted to narrow the South Korean proposal to safely shield its nationals from the Court's jurisdiction over crimes against humanity and war crimes. On 15 July 1998, the P-5 apparently met to agree, in the usual way, on a 'compromise package' that was in keeping with their interests. The result was a temporary joint approach of the P-5 who, on 16 July 1998, informally presented to the Conference Bureau and selected states a restrictive package containing, firstly, the requirement for the territorial state's ratification of the Statute (in line with the British proposal), secondly, an opt-out possibility for war crimes and crimes against humanity for ten years, including the possibility to extend the period by simple majority (reflecting the French line), and, thirdly, the possibility for non-States Parties to prevent the ICC from exercising jurisdiction by a statement that the crime was committed on an 'official mission' (this being a restrictive US proposal which the United States also officially tabled on 16 July 1998).[71]

---

69. The NGO Coalition for an International Criminal Court made the process of consultations transparent by publishing its own, very carefully-produced evaluation reports.

70. In the words of Scheffer, loc. cit. n. 11, at p. 19: 'During the final week of the Rome Conference, the delegations of the Governments of the five permanent members of the Security Council [...] met intensively to arrive at a compromise package that could be presented to the conference.'

71. A/CONF. 183/C. 1/L. 90; cf., Scheffer, loc. cit. n. 11 at p. 20.

Later during the day, the United Kingdom, seconded by France, introduced a slightly revised version of the above package in an EU coordination meeting. The main change in this informal paper was that the opt-out possibility for war crimes and crimes against humanity could no longer be extended by a simple majority but that opt-out could be 'prolonged by the normal amendment procedures'. While the United Kingdom did not present this paper as a P-5 proposal or as a proposal of its own, it became clear that both the United Kingdom and France regarded the paper as a basis for compromise.

In this situation, Germany reacted by presenting an informal counter-proposal on the afternoon of 16 July 1998. It regarded the membership of either the custodial state or the state of the victim's nationality as also sufficient for the ICC to have jurisdiction. The 'French' opt-out clause was reframed as a 'confidence-building period'. It was limited to a three-year period, without possibility of extension, and restricted to war crimes. This counter-proposal of Germany was supported by a majority of the EU States and also by other like-minded states. It played a key role in the Conference Bureau, headed by Mr Kirsch, offering its final compromise proposal[72] which contained, firstly, automatic jurisdiction for all core crimes, secondly, the ratification of the territorial state or the state of nationality of the suspect as the prerequisite for the exercise of jurisdiction in a given case, and thirdly, a transitional period (only) for war crimes which enables States Parties to exclude jurisdiction over their nationals for seven years.

When the final package was presented in the Committee of the Whole on 17 July 1998, the United States requested a vote on the following amendment:

> With respect to States not party to the Statute the Court shall have jurisdiction over acts committed in the territory of a State not party, or committed by officials or agents of a State not party in the course of official duties and acknowledged by the State as such, only if the State has accepted jurisdiction in accordance with this article.

This amendment was defeated by a no-action motion, adopted by 113 in favour to 17 against with 25 abstentions. Hereby the last hurdle in the way to adoption of the Statute was scaled. The result of the decisive vote in the Plenary – a vote again requested by the United States – is well known: 120 in favour to 7 against with 21 abstentions.

2.2.3   *The key elements of the jurisdictional regime*

It seems appropriate at this point to summarize the compromise on jurisdiction. In a simplified form, the jurisdictional regime of the ICC consists of four elements:

---

72. A/CONF. 183/C. 1/L. 76/Add. 2; Scheffer, loc. cit. n. 11, at p. 20, portrays this package – it is respectfully submitted, not quite accurately – as the product of a 'mysterious, closed-door and exclusionary process of revision by a small number of delegates, mostly from the like-minded group'.

— The precondition for the 'normal' complementary jurisdiction of the Court to apply is that either the territorial state or the state of nationality of the suspect is a party to the Statute (Art. 12(2)).

— The transitional rule in Article 124 gives States Parties, by way of exception to the ordinary rule, the possibility to exclude the prosecution of war crimes committed on their territory or by its nationals for seven years following their accession to the Statute. Such a 'partial withdrawal' from the Statute can only be repeated under very narrowly defined circumstances since the transitional provision is linked to the strict conditions for amendments to the Statute.

— In the case of non-States Parties on whose territory or by whose nationals core crimes have been committed, the jurisdiction of the Court may also be based on their acceptance ad hoc expressed by a special declaration (Art. 12(3)).

— Notwithstanding the above-mentioned hypotheses, the Court has jurisdiction when the Security Council, acting under Chapter VII of the UN Charter, refers a country situation to it in which core crimes are presumed to have been committed on a large scale (Art. 13(b)). In such a case, it does not matter whether the state concerned is a party to the Statute or not.

Overall, the 'normal' regime is one of automatic jurisdiction based on an alternative application of the criteria of territoriality and nationality instead of universality. This normal regime is qualified by the possibility to transitionally opt-out of the jurisdiction based on the criteria of territoriality and nationality. Other than this normal regime, the jurisdiction triggered by the Security Council can be said to be universal in nature.

3.   COOPERATION

The ICC is not explicitly endowed with enforcement power nor can such a power be regarded as inherent in its functions.[73] At the same time, suspected persons and indispensable evidence are usually located in territories under the sovereign authority of states. This means that if these states could refuse to cooperate, the Court must 'turn out to be utterly impotent'.[74] For this simple reason the issue of cooperation goes to the heart of an effective Court; a fundamental point which unfortunately is constantly being confirmed by the experience of the ICTY.[75] On the other hand,

---

73. The negative answer of the Appeals Chamber of the ICTY, in its Judgment of 29 October 1997 on the Request of the Republic of Croatia for Review of the Decision of Trial Chamber II of 18 July 1997 in *Prosecutor* v. *Tihomir Blaškić*, para. 25, to the question whether an enforcement power can be seen as an inherent function is rightly related to any international judicial body.

74. A. Cassese, 'Reflections on International Criminal Justice', 61 *MLR* (1998) pp. 9 et seq.

75. On several occasions, the President of this Tribunal reported to the Security Council a failure to comply with the obligation to cooperate as contained in Art. 29 of the Tribunal's Statute (for references see the judgment of the Appeals Chamber of 29 October 1997 (*supra* n. 73) n. 47. Cf., also the Fourth Annual Report of the Tribunal in UN/Doc. S/1997/729, para. 183.

it is Part 9 of the Statute where statal obligations are most directly at stake. The cooperation regime thus touches most directly upon the principle of state sovereignty. These points alone explain why 'Part 9 of the statute represents hard-fought battles'.[76]

3.1   Principles: vertical versus horizontal cooperation

On the level of principles, a so-called horizontal approach conflicts with a vertical approach to cooperation.[77] The horizontal approach aims at transposing the traditional interstate law of extradition and mutual assistance to the context of international criminal justice. The relevant interstate law emphasizes state sovereignty and, correspondingly, attributes decisive weight to the interests of the requested state if they are at variance with the execution of the request.[78] The vertical approach departs from traditional interstate concepts of cooperation in that it attaches greater weight to the community interest in an international criminal prosecution than in conflicting interests of the requested state. According to the vertical approach, the relationship between States Parties and the Court is not one between two subjects placed on the same footing and essentially independent of one another. The relationship is instead qualified as a vertical one: the Court's complementary jurisdiction being seen as a kind of extension of national jurisdictions. The vertical approach is often referred to as aiming at the setting up of a regime *sui generis* of cooperation.[79]

It is submitted that the horizontal approach is fundamentally inappropriate in the context of an international judicial body responsible for judging international core crimes. The relationship between an international criminal court for the prosecution of the core crimes of international law and states cannot be equated to the interstate level. This is true not only in the context of an international criminal jurisdiction triggered by the Security Council under Chapter VII of the UN Charter (case of the two *ad hoc* Tribunals and Article 13(b) but also for a 'normal jurisdiction' (case of Article 12(2)). In the latter hypothesis, the relationship between the international criminal court and States Parties cannot simply be portrayed as one of subordination of one to the other. Within the complementarity system of the Statute, the

---

For a case of failure to cooperate with the International Criminal Tribunal for Rwanda see G. Sluiter, 'To Cooperate or not to Cooperate? The Case of the Failed Transfer of Ntakirutimana to the Rwanda Tribunal', 11 *LJIL* (1998) p. 383.

76. Scheffer, loc. cit. n. 11, at p. 15; similarly the coordinator of the debates on Part 9, Ph. Mochochoko (in Lee, op. cit. n. 36, at p. 317) speaks of 'a hard fought political compromise on complex issues'.

77. Cassese, loc. cit. n. 17, speaks of a conflict between the 'interstate' and the 'supra-state' model.

78. See the UN Model Treaties on Extradition and Mutual Assistance in Criminal Matters, UN Doc. A/CONF. 144/28/Rev. 1, pp. 64 and 75.

79. In its Judgement of 29 October 1997 (*supra* n. 73) the Appeals Chamber of the International Criminal Tribunal for the former Yugoslavia stated in para. 47 with regard to its Statute: 'Clearly, a 'vertical' relationship was thus established.'

relationship is particularly difficult to describe. One important aspect is the priority which is given to the prosecution at the level of States Parties. This aspect is not the crucial one with respect to cooperation, though. The cooperation regime only comes into play if the case is admissible before the Court, which means that prosecution at the level of a State Party does not (genuinely) take place. If the Court then takes the case at the international level this – at least from a functional perspective – does not constitute a judicial activity distinct from the one which could have been undertaken at the national level but as an effort to accomplish the same goal. This is one important message conveyed by the use of the term 'complementary international jurisdiction', and in this sense it is indeed accurate to see the Court's jurisdiction as the functional extension of the one of the States Parties or, in other words, to qualify the relationship between national and international jurisdiction as a vertical one.

In addition, the horizontal approach is not in line with the very nature of the prosecution of international core crimes. The latter activity cannot be reduced to the pursuit of the national interest of one (or more) states directly concerned by a crime, as is the case in normal mutual legal assistance. Rather, the prosecution of an international core crime – and here we return to the principles elaborated *supra* (Part 2.1) – serves a community goal so that a state which prosecutes an international core crime can well be seen – again in a functional sense – as the (temporary) agent of the international community as a whole.

The vertical approach has been criticised as unrealistic.[80] During and after the negotiations it was repeatedly argued that the whole cooperation regime should be framed with a requested state in mind which is generally willing to assist the Court. It would be pointless – so the reasoning went – to try to put strict legal constraints on a potentially unwilling state, constraints which could not be enforced anyway. Accordingly, the rules on cooperation should leave sufficient room to take the legitimate national interests – some of them allegedly being of a constitutional nature – of such a state into account. That meant qualifying the obligation to cooperate with the Court by broad references to the national law of the requested state and reducing the possibility of on-site investigations of the Court to virtually zero.

To a limited extent, the criticism directed at the vertical approach rests on a misunderstanding. The vertical approach readily acknowledges that the requested state would use its national procedures to execute requests for cooperation. In other words, the vertical approach does not ignore the central place of national procedures – which would, indeed, appear to be unrealistic – it just aims at ensuring that those procedures are being used to give effect to the Court's requests.

Apart from that, the arguments put forward to portray the vertical approach as unrealistic are not convincing. This is so even if the premise is accepted that the cooperation regime should be construed with a generally 'Court-friendly' state in mind. With respect to such a state, too, the cooperation regime must be such that it guarantees efficient cooperation in day-to-day practice. Recent experience with

---

80. For a brief summary of this criticism see Scheffer, loc. cit. n. 11, at p. 15.

the failure to surrender Ntakirutimana to the ICTR[81] clearly reveals that, even with respect to a truly 'court-friendly' state, cooperation can fail due to the fact that judges or other officials identify legal obstacles that they find impossible to surmount. This may well include obstacles of a constitutional nature. The vertical approach therefore quite realistically favors cooperation rules which lead to the elimination of such obstacles. As the reference to 'constitutional problems' was so often made in Rome in support of 'horizontal solutions', it seems worthwhile to explain this last point in somewhat greater detail by focussing on what was probably the most prominent example: the surrender of nationals to the Court. Many states, including a significant number of like-minded states, have in their constitutions a prohibition on the extradition of nationals.[82] At first glance, at least, such a prohibition constitutes an obstacle of a constitutional nature to effective cooperation with the Court. It seems a little bit too easy, though, to demand that a 'realistic' cooperation regime 'take' this constitutional obstacle 'into account' as it is no less realistic to note that to exclude nationals categorically from the obligation to surrender would run directly counter to the idea of a workable ICC. The very basic lesson to be drawn from this one example is that the innovative project to set up an international criminal judicial body may entail a reconsideration of national constitutional concepts which evolved at a time when the idea of an international criminal court was not yet on the agenda of constitutional decision-makers. Such a reconsideration may well lead to the disappearance of an apparent constitutional obstacle. Again, the issue of extradition of nationals is a good example as it is by no means established that a constitutional prohibition on extraditing nationals is applicable to the surrender of nationals to the Court.[83] Whether this is the case or not will largely depend on the methods of constitutional interpretation used in the respective national framework, a question which shall not be pursued here. The important point is the need to reconsider some very specific constitutional concepts, be it by way of teleological or evolutive interpretation of the *constitutio lata* or be it by way of decision *de constitutione ferenda*.

The final comment on the issue of realism in the area of cooperation briefly relates to the idea that the rules should be drafted with the 'Court-friendly' rather than with the 'unwilling' state in mind. This idea is somewhat puzzling in the light of the Statute's complementarity regime. The operation of the latter regime makes

---

81. See Sluiter, loc. cit. n. 75.

82. Cf., on this issue the excellent study by M. Plachta, '(Non-)Extradition of Nationals: A Never-ending Story?', 13 *Emory International Law Review* (1999) pp. 77 et seq. and C. Rinio, 'Die Auslieferung eigener Staatsangehöriger: Historische Entwicklung und neuere Tendenzen', 108 *Zeitschrift für die gesamte Strafrechtswissenschaft* (1996) pp. 356 et seq.

83. For the ongoing debate about the scope of Article 16(2) of Germany's constitution cf., B. Schöbener and W. Bausback, 'Verfassungs- und völkerrechtliche Grenzen der Überstellung mutmaßlicher Kriegsverbrecher an den Jugoslawien-Strafgerichtshof', *Die Öffentliche Verwaltung* (1996) pp. 621 et seq., *contra* K. Schmalenbach, 'Die Auslieferung mutmaßlicher deutscher Kriegsverbrecher an das Jugoslawientribunal in Den Haag', 36 *Archiv des Völkerrechts* (1998) pp. 285 et seq. It is likely that Germany will amend Art. 16(2). To some, including the present authors, this will be no more than a constitutional clarification.

it a very real option that the Court has to send requests for cooperation to states which it has determined to be unwilling to prosecute the concrete case. Certainly, unwillingness to prosecute does not automatically equate with unwillingness to cooperate but it is only realistic to assume that it may. Giving a *carte blanche* to the state which is reluctant to cooperate based on the argument that the Court lacks enforcement power is an odd approach to international treaty-making, where the lack of enforcement power is the rule and not the exception.

In conclusion, the vertical approach to state cooperation with the Court is the approriate one as a matter of principle and cannot convincingly be criticised for want of realism.

3.2   Compromises[84]

3.2.1   *The situation at the opening of the Rome Conference*

This basic controversy between the vertical and horizontal approaches is clearly reflected in the different terminological and substantive options in the Draft Statute's version of Part 9.[85] As a matter of terminology, the options 'extradition'/'surrender'/ 'transfer' run throughout the text. And with respect to the crucial question of substance, i.e., the degree of rigidity of the obligations to cooperate, a list of grounds for refusal sharply contrasts with the option to exclude any such ground. Broadly speaking, the great majority of the like-minded states supported solutions based on the vertical approach. Among the members of this group, the most active participants in the debate were Argentina, Australia, Austria, Belgium, Denmark, Finland, Germany, Italy, Malawi, the Netherlands, New Zealand, Norway, Portugal, Sweden, Switzerland and the United Kingdom. Special mention should be made of the particularly significant input by Canada, whose positions were brilliantly presented by Kimberly Prost. The most active adherents to the horizontal approach were a number of Arab States, China, India, Israel, Japan, Mexico and the United States. France made important individual contributions to the debates, which were, by and large, closer to the vertical line of reasoning.

Against this background, the negotiations on Part 9 posed a serious challenge for the chairman of the working group on cooperation, Phakiso Mochochoko (Lesotho).[86] He faced this challenge with great skill and a remarkable degree of patience and thus helped decisively in finalizing an unbracketed text just before the conference came to a close. Mochochoko chose the following route to bridge the wide gap that existed at the opening of the conference: He divided the informal consultations in three sub-groups. The first one, coordinated by Béatrice le Fraper

---

84. The following text partly draws upon C. Kreß, 'Penalties, Enforcement and International Cooperation in the Statute of the International Criminal Court', 6 *European Journal of Crime, Criminal Law and Criminal Justice* (1998) pp. 442 et seq.

85. UN Doc. A/CONF. 183/2/Add. 1, pp. 156 et seq.

86. Mochochoko gives his account of the negotiation process in Lee, op. cit. n. 36, pp. 305 et seq.

du Hellen (France), dealt with a number of rather technical questions of form and procedure and with the more delicate issue of a failure to cooperate. The second sub-group, coordinated by Mr Mochochoko himself, was charged essentially with the question as to whether grounds for refusal to cooperate should be recognized or not. A third sub-group, cooordinated by Trevor Chimimba (Malawi), tackled the vexed issue of on-site investigations. As a general negotiation line, Mr Mochochoko suggested to resolve the more technical points first and to turn subsequently to the more delicate issues of substance.

3.2.2   *The negotiations at Rome*

The following observations are limited to the three key issues of the cooperation regime: grounds for refusal to cooperate, on-site investigations, and consequences of a failure to cooperate.[87]

3.2.2.1   Ground for refusal

Reading Article 87(3), Option 2, and Article 90(2), Option 2 of the Draft Statute one finds, in short, the following candidates for grounds for refusal:

With respect to both surrender and other forms of cooperation:
— Non-acceptance of the Court's jurisdiction by the requested state;
— Conflict with national proceedings in the requested state;
— Evidentiary requirements in the requested state;
— Conflict with other international obligations of the requested state.

Specifically with respect to surrender:
— No surrender of nationals.

Specifically with respect to forms of cooperation other than surrender:
— Conflicting national law, *ordre public* or essential interests of the requested state.

Looking back on how the negotiations in Rome evolved, it appears as if these possible grounds of refusal fell within three distinct categories. The two candidates 'Non-acceptance of the Court's jurisdiction' and 'Parallel national proceedings against the same person for the same conduct' did not pose genuine cooperation problems but were rather reminders of the need for consistency between Part 9 and Part 2. 'Conflicting international obligations' was an issue that, at an early stage of the discussions, was consensually identified as a difficult subject requiring specific and carefully drafted solutions. The remaining part of the above list was the area where the differences of positions were most difficult to reconcile.

---

87. For a comprehensive commentary on the cooperation regime see C. Kreß et al., in Triffterer, op. cit. n. 6, Arts. 86 to 102.

3.2.2.1.1 Consistency with Part 2

The easiest point was 'non-acceptance of the Court's jurisdiction'. It was deferred to the very end of the debates to await the outcome of the discussions on jurisdiction. Once it was decided to create a system of automatic jurisdiction, the problem of 'non-acceptance of the Court's jurisdiction' became obsolete. Interestingly it was China which, at the very end of the informal consultations, proposed to eliminate this candidate from the list of grounds for refusals; which met with no dissent.

More complicated was the discussion on parallel national proceedings for the same conduct. A number of delegations doubted the need for a provision altogether. Reference was made to the system of complementarity and the principle of *ne bis in idem* as embodied in Part 2. Other speakers wished the inclusion in Part 9 of specific cross-references to Part 2. Such a cross-reference was acceptable to everybody provided that the cornerstone of complementarity under Part 2, i.e., the competence of the ICC to authoritatively rule on the issue, remained untouched.[88] The solution which was finally agreed upon is in line with this last point: its basic element is the possibility of the requested state to postpone the execution of the request as long as an admissibility ruling of the ICC is pending.[89]

3.2.2.1.2 Conflicting international obligations

Essentially two types of conflicts were identified: the case of a competing request for extradition and the case of conflicting immunities.

Competing requests

To deal adequately with competing requests turned out to be particularly difficult, not so much because of disagreement in principle but rather due to the complexity of the issue. The solution was found after a number of intensive deliberations, informally coordinated by Lionel Yee (Singapore), within a small group of delegates representing all different approaches to cooperation: Article 90 (relating to surrender) covers a number of scenarios which result from the combination of the following hypotheses: The competing request comes from a State Party/non-State Party; the Court has already/has not yet determined the admissibility of the case; the competing request concerns the same set of facts/different facts; specifically in case of a competing request from a non-State Party, an additional question is whether the requested state is under an obligation to extradite *vis-à-vis* the non-State Party or not. Article 90 goes through the relevant scenarios paragraph by paragraph, hereby offering a differentiated set of solutions. To mention just the two most difficult and important scenarios: In case there is a competing request for the same set of facts coming from a non-State Party to which the requested state is, in principle, under an international obligation to extradite and given that the ad-

---

88. The effort to touch upon this cornerstone has been referred to *supra* n. 8.

89. For a detailed analysis see the comments by Kreß, Prost and Prost and Schlunck on Art. 89 para. 2 and Art. 95, respectively, in Triffterer, op. cit. n. 6.

missibility of the case has already been determined by the Court, it is up to the state facing the two requests to make a choice (Art. 90(6)). In doing so, the requested state shall consider well known criteria, such as the respective dates of the requests and the interests at stake. It is of great importance to note that the requested state may well – according to the particular circumstances – give priority to the non-State Party's request.[90] A more limited degree of discretion is conceded to the requested state where the Court's request to have a person surrendered competes with a request for extradition – be it from a State Party, be it from a non-State Party – based on different facts. In this scenario, a decision to give priority to the request of the Court should be the rule as special consideration shall be given to the relative nature and gravity of the conduct in question (Art. 90(7)(b)). The system enshrined in Article 90 also applies to competing requests for other forms of cooperation (distinct from surrender) if it is impossible to meet both requests, e.g., by postponing or attaching conditions to one or the other request (Art. 93(9)(a)).

Immunities and other legal conflicts

The issue of conflicting immunities was rather reluctantly addressed by some delegations, which were of the view that developments in general international law had substantively reduced, if not eliminated, immunities with respect to the prosecution of an international core crime by an international criminal court, and thus the practical relevance of this conflict was negligible. However, on the insistence of some delegations and without there being time for a sufficiently thorough discussion, a provision on conflicting immunities was included, and hereto was added another provision referring to Status of Forces Agreements (without explicitly spelling this out). It is important to construe both provisions in a reasonable manner to avoid results that go beyond the actual intentions of the drafters and, more importantly, the purpose of the Statute. Article 98(1) covers immunities of a third state. The reference to 'third State' is not altogether clear as, on the basis of a grammatical interpretation, 'third State' may mean 'a State other than the requested State' or – narrower – 'a non-State Party'. It is submitted that the better case can be made for the first interpretation.[91] If an immunity exists under international law, the Court must first obtain the cooperation of the third state for the waiver of the immunity. It must be stressed that the existence of an immunity under general international law must be established by the Court before Article 98(1) comes into play.[92] Article 98(1) can by no means be construed as to revive

---

90. Cf., the critical observations by Cassese, loc. cit. n. 17, at p. 166.

91. First of all it must be noted that Part 9 refers to a non-State Party by using the words 'a State not party to the Statute' (cf., e.g., Art. 87(5)) instead of 'third State', and second, the drafters of this provision intended to take account of the fact that the inviolability of a diplomatic premise (the issue which was at the heart of the debate on the whole of Art. 98(1)) may be an obstacle to execute a request both *vis-à-vis* a State Party or a non-State Party. It is true, though, that such a meaning of 'third State' marks a departure from Art. 2(1)(h) of the Vienna Convention on the Law of Treaties.

92. Prost and Schlunck, in Triffterer, op. cit. n. 6, Art. 98, marginal n. 1.

immunities that international law no longer accepts.[93] In addition, Article 98(1) has to be read in conjunction with Article 86 which contains the important[94] general obligation to 'cooperate fully' with the Court. A strong case can be made that, due to this overarching obligation to cooperate, States Parties are under a duty to waive any immunity which continues to exist under international law in order to allow the execution of a request by the Court.

Article 98(2) technically operates in the same way as paragraph 1. And again, a reasonable interpretation is called for. The idea behind the provision was to solve legal conflicts which might arise because of Status of Forces Agreements which are already in place. On the contrary, Article 98(2) was not designed to create an incentive for (future) States Parties to conclude Status of Forces Agreements which amount to an obstacle to the execution of requests for cooperation issued by the Court. It is unfortunate that, due to a lack of time this point – to which we shall return later[95] – is not spelled out with sufficient clarity.

3.2.2.1.3 The hard points
Evidentiary requirements
This issue was one of the very few where the opinions split along the lines of the respective national legal traditions. Special evidentiary requirements exist in a number of common law countries such as Canada and the USA, and the delegations of those countries pointed to insurmountable constitutional obstacles to a waiver of these requirements even in the context of the ICC. An autonomous evidentiary regime – much more in line with the vertical approach, and favoured mainly by European civil law countries such as Austria, France, Finland, Germany and the

---

93. Cf., B. Broomhall, 'The International Criminal Court: A Checklist for National Implementation', in M. Cherif Bassiouni, ed., *ICC Ratification and National Implementing Legislation*, (Association International de Droit Pénal, éres 1999) pp. 113, at 137. There was simply no time for the Working Group on Cooperation to adequately discuss (and then possibly reach consensus) whether and, if so, to what extent immunities still exist under international law in case of the prosecution of an international core crime. When the case arises, the international judges may well hold that immunities of (former and serving) Heads of State or Government and of diplomats do not bar the Court from exercising its jurisdiction over a person coming within one of these categories. In other words, the Court may well take the exclusion of immunities (the term immunity being understood as to include immunity from arrest (inviolability)) in Art. 27 to accurately reflect the current state of customary international law (cf., A. Watts, 'The Legal Position in International Law of Heads of States, Heads of Governments and Foreign Ministers', 247 *Recueil des Cours de l'Académie de Droit International* (1994) p. 84). Such a view would not be inconsistent with the judgment of 24 March 1999 of the House of Lords in the *Pinochet* case (2 *All ER* 97) because of their Lordships' reaffirmation of an absolute immunity of serving Heads of State and serving diplomats is confined to national proceedings (a point which is explicitly made by Lord Brown-Wilkinson (ibid., 114), Lord Goff (ibid., 120-121), Lord Hope (ibid., 147 by reference to Lord Slynn's opinion in the judgement of 25 November 1998 (4 *All ER* 914)) and Lord Phillips (ibid., 189).

94. On the legal significance of this principle see Kreß, in Triffterer, op. cit. n. 6, Art. 86, marginal n. 10.

95. *Infra* n. 174.

Netherlands – could therefore not be achieved. The dilemma faced by the negotiators was the necessity, on the one hand, of meeting the said constitutional concerns and, on the other hand, of not creating a serious loophole which could be abused to circumvent the obligation to surrender. The following compromise package finally met with general consensus: No ground for refusal has been included in the Statute. However, according to Article 91(2), the request for surrender[96] shall contain not only sufficient information about the identity and the probable location of the person concerned and a copy of the arrest warrant but also such documents, statements or information as may be necessary to meet the requirements of the surrender process in the requested state. The latter requirements should not be more burdensome than those applicable to requests for extradition pursuant to treaties or arrangements between the requested state and other states. If possible, the requirements should be less burdensome, taking into account – the following wording is worth emphazising – the distinct nature of the Court. Finally, a State Party shall advise the Court upon request of the specific (evidentiary) requirements of its national law (Art. 91(4)).[97]

Parallel national proceedings for a different crime
This was one area where the vertical and horizontal approaches clashed strongly and directly. The United States in particular rejected – again advancing constitutional reasons – any solution which would have given unambiguous priority to the ICC. The compromise formulas in Article 89(4) (surrender) and Article 94 (other forms of cooperation) reveal what one may call 'constructive ambiguity': the requested state may not refuse the execution of the request but the execution may be postponed for a period of time as agreed upon with the Court.

National law, ordre public, essential national interests
Whether to accept conflicting national law, considerations relating to the *ordre public* and/or essential national interests as a ground for refusal to cooperate was a truly pivotal question which was answered only a few days before the end of the conference. The adherents to the horizontal approach, headed by the United States, firmly rejected an obligation to cooperate which was not qualified by a reference to national law. The supporters of vertical cooperation made it clear for their part that at least too broad a reference of that kind was not acceptable. After a significant number of compromise proposals proved incapable of securing general consensus, a small package deal was finally struck. The elements of this package are as follows: Firstly, States Parties shall cooperate 'under the procedures of their national law' (Arts. 89(1) and 93(1)). This reference to national procedures has to be read together with the duty under Article 88 to 'ensure that there are procedures available under their [the States Parties'] national law for all the forms of cooperation which are specified under this Part'. The obligation to surrender

---

96. Cf., the similar requirements in the context of requests for forms of cooperation other than surrender in Art. 96 of the Statute.

97. Cf. Art. 96(3) on requests for forms of cooperation other than surrender.

persons to the Court is not subject to substantive national law. With respect to the other types of assistance as specified in Article 93(1) a to k, the requested state may only invoke a conflicting 'existing fundamental legal principle of general application' (Art. 93(3)). Such a 'fundamental' principle will – in general – be constitutional in character[98] and its 'general application' precludes a kind of 'ICC-blockade-statute'. If such a conflicting legal principle exists, consultations shall be held aiming at a modified form of cooperation. The inclusion of this very specific threshold of substantive national law made it possible for the United States to agree to delete the reference to a ground for refusal based on the national *ordre public* or essential national interests. This agreement, however, was subject to a special treatment being given to 'national security information'. This issue was neuralgic for some states (France and the United States in particular) in the light of the nature of the crimes which were candidates for inclusion in the Statute (aggression and war crimes were of course of particular concern). At an early stage of the conference it was decided to deal with this question in Part 6 (The trial) and here it was the subject of very lengthy and controversial debates. The pertinent provision is contained in Article 72 to which Article 93(4) refers. Article 72[99] sets out a detailed scheme of consultations and specific measures, much in line with the criteria elaborated by the ICTY in the *Blaškić* Subpoena Decision[100] whenever a state considers its national security interests prejudiced by a disclosure of information to the Court. Where it comes to the point that a solution by cooperative means fails because the state does not act 'in accordance with its obligations under this Statute',[101] the Court can do no more, though, than to determine that fact and to refer the matter to the Assembly of States Parties (Art. 72 (7)(a)(ii)).[102]

Surrender of nationals

The issue of the surrender of nationals, too, remained unresolved until the very end of the negotiations.[103] Even among adherents of the vertical approach, reference was made to constitutional prohibitions to extradite nationals.[104] Two main arguments were advanced to help countries favouring the ground of refusal in question to step down from their position. Firstly, it was pointed out that based,

---

98. Cf., the – deliberately – broader reference to 'the law of the requested State' in the catch-all clause for not specified forms of cooperation (e.g., interception of communication) in Art. 93(11).

99. For an excellent analysis of this Article and the story behind it cf., Piragoff, in Lee, op. cit. n. 36, pp. 270 et seq.

100. *Supra* n. 73.

101. An explicit reference to *mala fide* cooperation was not acceptable to some delegations.

102. The alternative route to empower the Court to order or to request disclosure in such a case was part of a proposal of the United Kingdom which was supported by many delegations but remained unacceptable to some key states, particularly the United States and France.

103. In the eyes of the coordinator, this candidate for a ground for refusal was 'by far the most difficult' one; Mochochoko, in Lee, op. cit. n. 36, at p. 311.

104. These states mostly belonged to the civil law family (broadly understood to include Latin American and the Scandinavian legal systems) and to the Arab group. Amongst the common law countries, only Israel invoked the same kind of problem.

on the principle of complementarity, each State Party would be in a position to genuinely prosecute its nationals should the need arise instead of surrendering them to the Court. Secondly, it was stressed that the surrender of a national to the ICC by a State Party had to be carefully distinguished from interstate extradition, not just terminologically but also in substance. Whatever the reasons for not extraditing nationals to a foreign state might be, they would carry much less weight – so the argument went – in the context of surrender to the Court. Literally at the last minute of the deliberations of the working group on cooperation these arguments prevailed: The Statute does not give States Parties a ground for refusal with respect to their nationals, and the compromise proposal tabled by Denmark, Norway, Sweden and Switzerland at a fairly late hour to allow the surrender of nationals to be made conditional on the return of the convicted person for the service of the sentence was finally withdrawn.[105] As some delegations had indicated that an explicit distinction between surrender of a person (to the Court) and extradition of a person (to another state) in the Statute could facilitate their joining in the consensus, the two respective definitions have been included in Article 102.

3.2.2.2   On-site investigations

Article 99(4), which deals with on-site investigations, constitutes one of the most controversial provisions of the Statute. At least twenty hours of thorny negotiations were spent on this issue in the Committee of the Whole, in the Working Group and in different informal settings. An initial difficulty was to find the right place for a regime of on-site investigations. Some argued that the whole problem of prosecutorial measures on a State Party's territory was better situated in Part 5 (Investigation and prosecution) than in Part 9. Others feared that dealing with the issue in Part 5 could prejudice the omission of a requirement of the territorial state's prior consent. This was, of course, very much a question of perspective. In order not to waste time – the most precious commodity in Rome – with a debate about the best placement, the following division of work was made. Special treatment was given to a type of situation that is occasionally referred to in public international legal literature as the failed state scenario. This scenario is dealt with in Article 57(3)(d)[106] in Part 5. In such cases of breakdown of state authority there no longer exists – so the formal argument for excluding this scenario from Part 9 went – an addressee for a request on the territory concerned. Beyond this, *sedes materiae* of the statutory regime of on-site investigations has finally become Article 99(4). The

---

105. See Mochochoko, in Lee, op. cit. n. 36, at pp. 311 et seq.

106. It reads: 'In addition to its other functions under the Statute, the Pre-Trial Chamber may:

... authorize the Prosecutor to take specific investigative steps within the territory of a State Party without having secured the cooperation of that State under Part 9 if, whenever possible having regard to the views of the State concerned, the Pre-Trial Chamber has determined in that case that the State is clearly unable to execute a request for cooperation due to the unavailability of any authority or any component of its judicial system competent to execute the request for cooperation under Part 9.'

crucial issue throughout the negotiations was the one of prior territorial state consent, and again delegations were divided according to the respective degree of emphasis placed upon the value of state sovereignty. In a first step, consensus emerged on excluding any kind of compulsory measures. As to the rest, the United States, at a late stage of the informal consultations, proposed to distinguish between the state where the crime is alleged to have been committed and other states. This proposal was, although very reluctantly, accepted by the adherents of the vertical approach. The remaining difficulty was to find wording for investigations on the territories of the latter category of states. The complete compromise package contains the following: the requirement of prior state consent clearly does not exist with respect to the state where the crime is alleged to have been committed (Art. 99(4)(a)). Here, the Prosecutor may, if necessary, interview witnesses without the presence of the authorities of the requested state, or may take other non-compulsory measures (this time with the presence of state authorities). The legal situation becomes somewhat more ambiguous with respect to States Parties other than the territorial state. The formula chosen in Article 99(4)(b) is that the Prosecutor may take the measures in question 'subject to any reasonable conditions or concerns raised by that State Party'. These words, again, can be said to be constructively ambiguous. It is probably not wholly inaccurate to say that what is meant falls short of a consent requirement but goes beyond mere consultation. The immense difficulty in reaching consensus on this compromise became once more apparent when, on the occasion of its first presentation, it fell short of securing consensus in the Working Group. Only a second try at the last minute proved successful.[107]

3.2.2.3 Failure to cooperate

No explicit solution was found as to the consequences of a failure to cooperate with the Court. Article 87(7) is limited to empowering the Court to 'make a statement to this effect and to refer the matter to the Assembly of States Parties or, where the Security Council referred the matter to the Court, to the Security Council'. And Article 112(2)(f) does not say more than that the Assembly of States Parties may consider any question relating to non-cooperation. Thus, reference to the customary international law on state responsibility is necessary to spell out the consequences of non-cooperation.[108] The *Blaškić subpoena* decision of the ICTY[109] offers some guidance in this respect.[110]

---

107. For more details on these long hours of tension and suspense see Mochochoko, in Lee, op. cit. n. 36, at p. 316.

108. Correctly in this sense Cassese, loc. cit. n. 17, at p. 166.

109. *Supra* n. 73.

110. For an analysis of the interplay of the Statute and general international law see Kreß and Prost, in Triffterer, op. cit. n. 6, Art. 87 marginal n. 35 et seq.

3.2.3   *The key elements of the cooperation regime*

They can be summarized as follows:

— The Statute's cooperation regime does not include the traditional interstate grounds for refusal to cooperate. Part 9 rather makes use of more sophisticated instruments of conflict resolution, such as postponement and consultation clauses. With respect to forms of cooperation other than surrender, however, some of these clauses ('national security information','fundamental legal principle of general application of the requested state') come close to a ground for refusal.

— As a general rule, requests for cooperation will be executed by the authorities of the requested state in accordance with the procedures under its national law.

— The Prosecutor has been given a limited power to conduct on-site investigations on the territory of States Parties without first securing the consent of the requested state.

— The consequences of a failure to cooperate are largely governed by general international law.

4.   APPRAISAL – A GERMAN VIEW ON JURISDICTION AND COOPERATION

A comparison between what has been established[111] as the preferable approaches as a matter of principle, i.e., the universality approach to jurisdiction and the vertical approach to cooperation, with the outcome of the negotiations at Rome,[112] clearly demonstrates a significant gap between 'the ideal' and 'the real'. Certainly the 'sudden death' of the South Korean proposal on jurisdiction in the course of the final days of the conference constitutes the single most deplorable deviation from sound principles. In practice, the replacement of the South Korean proposal on jurisdiction by a jurisdictional regime based on the criteria of territoriality and nationality means that the ICC will not be able to exercise its 'normal' jurisdiction over genocide or crimes against humanity committed by a terroristic government on 'its' territory unless the state represented by this governement has ratified the Statute. This situation marks a painful weakness[113] of the jurisdictional regime and

---

111. Sub. 2.1. and 3.1.

112. Sub. 2.3.3 and 3.2.3.

113. Cf., the severe criticism by Condorelli, loc. cit. n. 36, at p. 16 et seq.: '*Ce système n'est pas seulement très critiquable et insatisfaisant en soi, vu qu'il n'ouvre même pas la compétence de la Cour au cas que ledit futur Pol Pot (ou Pinochet!) serait capturé à l'étranger, sur le territoire d'un autre Etat partie au Statut ou reconnaissant la compétence de la C.P.I. Il risque aussi, me semble-t-il, d'aboutir à des conséquences singulièrement perverses. En effet, tous les Etats dont les équipes dirigeantes, pour se maintenir au pouvoir, n'excluent pas d'avoir recours aux violations des droits de l'homme et du droit humanitaire contre les oppositions internes, auront doublement intérêt à ne pas devenir parties au Statut: en premier lieu, afin que la Cour ne puisse être saisie contre leurs hauts responsables par un autre Etat ou par le Procureur; en deuxième lieu, pour retarder autant que possible la mise en place de la Cour, c'est-à-dire le*

shows to what extent this regime falls short of universality. No less regrettable in substance is the opt-out clause in Article 124. Its practical impact is, however, fortunately reduced because of its most probably limited duration. For the time of its applicability, Article 124 offers to States Parties a possibility to shield their nationals from the Court's jurisdiction, a possibility which is not extended to non-States Parties. For the reasons explained *supra*,[114] this situation is not illegal and in particular it is not contrary to basic principles of treaty law but it is clearly unsatisfactory as a matter of legal policy.[115]

The cooperation regime, too, suffers from a considerable number of imperfections. Even though grounds for refusal to cooperate *strictu senso* have not been included in Part 9, the heavy weight attributed to national security information may amount to much the same in practice and may, if broadly applied,[116] have far-reaching and very unfortunate repercussions on the ICC's efficiency. In addition, some of the compromises[117] which had to be struck to meet the (partly constitutional) concerns of a number of delegations lend themselves to abusive interpretation. It will be of crucial importance that states, and finally the ICC itself, interpret these compromises in the light of the overarching principle of 'full cooperation' as enshrined in Article 86.[118] Finally, the possibility for the Prosecutor to conduct on-site investigations, though at least included as such, is regrettably limited in scope. It may be too harsh a criticism to call Part 9 a 'weak state co-operation regime'[119] but the cooperation regime is certainly not as strong as sound principles suggest.

As one cannot avoid the conclusion that Parts 2 and 9 of the Statute do not fully live up to the fact that in the development of international law 'a State-sovereignty-oriented approach has been gradually supplanted by a human-being-oriented approach',[120] the question arises why the compromise packages on jurisdiction and cooperation were finally acceptable to Germany, which firmly and consistently supported the universality approach to jurisdiction and the vertical approach to

---

moment à partir duquel le Conseil de sécurité disposera effectivement de la possibilité de mettre en branle la procédure de son propre chef.'; Wedgwood, loc. cit. n. 47, concludes at p. 101: 'Thus, the final text gives undue shelter to the very civil war conflicts that were the moral impetus for the negotiation of a Rome treaty'; cf., also the criticism by Cassese, loc. cit. n. 17, p. 161.

114. Sub. 2.1.

115. Correct Hafner et al, loc. cit. n. 17, at p. 119.

116. For a reference to the dangerous potential of this 'safeguard clause' with regard to French practices see Sur, loc. cit. n. 43, p. 42.

117. Cf., in particular the reference to 'fundamental principles of general application' in Art. 93(3) and the ill-defined postponement clauses in Art. 89(4) and Art. 94 (*supra* 3.2.2.1.3).

118. *Supra* n. 94.

119. Bergsmo, loc. cit. n. 67, at p. 37; Cassese, loc. cit. n. 17, at p. 164, holds that Part 9 represents 'a largely state-oriented approach'; compare the more positive assessment by Mochochoko, in Lee, op. cit. n. 36, at p. 317; Swart, Sluiter, von Hebel, Lammers and Schukking, eds., *Reflections on the International Criminal Court, Essays in Honour of Adriaan Bos* (The Hague, T.M.C. Asser Press 1999) pp. 124 et seq.; Kreß, loc. cit. n. 84, at p. 459.

120. Cf., *supra* n. 9.

cooperation. The answer is twofold. First one may emphasize the fact that the regimes of jurisdiction and cooperation are both 'Janus-headed' in that the ICC can analytically be decomposed into two Courts with two swords: the rather weak 'normal' Court, with a cumbersome and short jurisdiction/cooperation sword, and the rather powerful Court as 'judicial ally' of the Security Council, with a sharp jurisdiction/cooperation sword with a long outreach. In short, Article 13(b) recognizes the power of the Security Council under Chapter VII of the UN Charter to 'transform' the ICC's jurisdiction into a universal one, and nothing prevents the Security Council, while acting under this Chapter, from strengthening the cooperation regime by way of a specific resolution to this extent.

But even apart from the hypothesis of Security Council triggered judicial activity of the ICC, the acceptance of the final compromise, on balance, appears justified. The regimes of jurisdiction and cooperation both constitute very significant advances. Suffice it to compare the ICC's system of automatic jurisdiction with the much more modest regime proposed by the ILC in 1994, and to point out to what remarkable extent the ICC's cooperation regime departs from the horizontal approach as illustrated in the UN Model Treaties on Extradition and Mutual Legal Assistance in Criminal Matters.[121] In addition, there is the prospect that the weakness of the jurisdiction regime will be consumed by an increasing number of ratifications and that the obligation of all states under customary international law not only to respect but also to ensure the respect of international humanitarian law[122] adds a useful complement to the cooperation regime.[123] Finally, crucially important as they are, jurisdiction and cooperation are only two parts of the entire picture of the Rome Statute, which includes such remarkable achievements as the confirmation of an extensive list of civil war crimes, the definition of crimes against humanity punishable in war and peace, the elaboration of a general part of international criminal law and last but not least the establishment of an international criminal procedure which does not represent only one legal family.[124]

While it is clear that under all circumstances the integrity of the Rome Statute must and will be fully safeguarded, the burning question remains how to deal with the continuing dissatisfaction of the United States with some elements of it, in particular the reach of the jurisdictional regime. The main difficulty the United States faces with the jurisdictional regime clearly emerges from two important recent

---

121. *Supra* n. 78.

122. On the implications of this customary obligation as embodied in common Art. 1 of the Geneva Conventions see L. Condorelli and L. Boisson de Chazournes, in C. Swinarski, ed., *Etudes et essais sur le droit international humanitaire et sur les principes de la Croix-Rouge en l'honneur de Jean Pictet* (Geneva, CICR/The Hague, Martinus Nijhoff 1984) pp. 26 et seq. For a confirmation of this view in light of recent practice see L. Condorelli, in L. Condorelli, ed., *Les Nations Unies et le droit international humanitaire* (Paris, Pedone 1996) pp. 450, 461; for a more skeptical view see, C. Greenwood, 'International Humanitarian Law and United Nations Military Operations', 1 *YIHL* (1998) pp. 9 et seq., and F. Kalshoven at pp. 3 et seq. of this volume.

123. On the possible interplay between the statutory cooperation regime and customary international law see Kreß and Prost, in Triffterer, op. cit. n. 6, Art. 87, marginal n. 20.

124. Cf., Cassese, loc. cit. n. 17, at p. 146.

publications (David Scheffer's 'The United States and the International Criminal Court'[125] and Ruth Wedgwood's 'The International Criminal Court: An American View'[126]): the possibility of US nationals, soldiers in particular, being brought before the Court even if the United States is not a party to the Statute. The underlying political concern is the eventuality of efforts to misuse the Court for a campaign against a controversial US military action abroad.[127]

It is not difficult to understand the United States' concern; the actual difficulty resides in the fact that the United States continues to entertain doubts that its concern is not fully met by the Statute. As stated above,[128] the appropriate place to deal with the concern in question is the system of complementarity between national and international jurisdiction.[129] Article 19(2)(c) gives every national state of the suspect – be it a State Party or not – a right to challenge the jurisdiction of the ICC on the ground that it is genuinely investigating the case. If the Court establishes a genuine investigation by the national state, it must rule the case inadmissible. 'Thus, it would seem that the complementarity nature of the ICC effectively places beyond the reach of the Court all States (including non-States Parties) which investigate and prosecute relevant offences diligently and in good faith.'[130] Scheffer has made the point 'that complementarity is not a complete answer, to the extent that it involves compelling states (particularly those not yet party to the treaty) to investigate the legality of humanitarian interventions or peacekeeping operations that they already regard as valid actions to enforce international law.[131] This argument is not altogether clear. Under the Statute as it stands, the Court can – for want of a definition of aggression – not investigate the legality of a military action as such. It can only investigate possible war crimes (or crimes against humanity) committed in the course of such an action. Such an investigation would be entirely distinct from an investigation of the legality of the military action as such.[132] So there is no way the Court can compel a (non)-State Party to 'investigate the legality of humanitarian interventions or peacekeeping operations' if that state wants to successfully challenge the admissibility of the case. David Scheffer's argument, therefore, makes sense only with regard to a possible future version of the Statute which includes a definition of the crime of aggression.

---

125. *Supra* n. 11.

126. *Supra* n. 47.

127. Scheffer, loc. cit. n. 11, at p. 19; Wedgwood, loc. cit. n. 47, at p. 101.

128. *Supra* section II. 1. text following n. 49.

129. See generally J.T. Holmes, 'The Principle of Complementarity', in Lee op. cit. n. 36, pp. 41 et seq.

130. Bergsmo, loc. cit. n. 67, at p. 35

131. Loc. cit. n. 11, at p. 19.

132. Wedgwood, loc. cit. n. 47, at p. 102, asserts that 'a realist understands that the scrutiny of methods is often far more searching in an unpopular conflict'. If that is to suggest that the Court could be influenced in its judgment over questions of *ius in bello* by his (implicit) position on the issues of the *ius ad bellum* we respectfully disagree. There is no reason, even for a realist, to expect that the judges of the ICC would ignore a legal distinction so fundamental in international law as the one between between the *ius in bello* and the *ius ad bellum*.

Even then the concern behind the argument could be fully met by a reasonable definition of the crime of aggression which is limited to the truly uncontroversial cases. Germany has repeatedly made proposals along this line.[133]

Even though it is our firm view that the Statute fully addresses the basic political concern of the United States, it is of interest to conclude this study with a brief look at 'possible solutions to third party jurisdiction' alluded to by Ruth Wedgwood.[134] The first option, as initially presented by Theodor Meron,[135] is to give a non-State Party the right to extract acts committed by its nationals from the Court's jurisdiction by assuming responsibility for them 'as official acts'. It is obvious that this option almost mirrors the US proposal to amend the final package which was rejected by the overwhelming majority of the Rome Conference.[136] The earliest possible time to come back to this amendment proposal would therefore seem to be the first review conference. A second option relates to Article 98(2). The suggestion is to issue a 'binding interpretative statement in the Preparatory Commission' that both new and existing 'status of forces agreements' will be respected under Article 98(2). This proposal confirms the thesis underlying this study that jurisdiction and cooperation are intimately interlinked. This necessarily means that almost identical practical results can be reached by using either set of rules. Therefore, the crucial question is whether the suggested 'interpretation' of Article 98(2) does not lead to the same kind of watertight protection of soldiers of a non-State Party as the 'official acts-option'. If the answer to this were in the affirmative, it would be very hard indeed to concede by way of an interpretative statement that a State Party acted in conformity with its obligation to 'fully cooperate' with the Court in concluding new Statuts of Forces Agreement to this effect. The last option refers to Article 12(3). If the term 'crime in question' is understood to mean 'a specific incident', a non-State Party can face a kind of 'asymmetric liability': it may find one or more of its nationals exposed to the Court's jurisdiction following an *ad hoc* consent by, say, a non-State Party on whose territory the specific incident is alleged to have taken place and, at the same time, it would not be open to that state to charge (a) national(s) of the territorial non-State Party (possibly the opponent) with the same category of conduct in the same armed conflict. Ruth Wedgwood suggests to work on an interpretative statement of the words 'the crime in question' in Article 12(3) which is broad enough to guarantee what one may call 'symmetric liability'. As a matter of jurisdictional principles as elaborated above,[137] 'symmetric liability' is certainly not called for. As a matter of law, the concept of reciprocal state obligations which underlies the idea of 'symmetric liability' is not applicable in the concept of the prosecution of international core crimes committed by individuals. This legal

---

133. See the recent compilation of proposals on the crime of Aggression in UN Doc. A/PCNICC/1999/INF/2, 2 August 1999.

134. Wedgwood, loc. cit. n. 47, at pp. 102 et seq.

135. 'The Court We Want', *Washington Post* (13 October 1998).

136. *Supra* section 2.2 *in fine*.

137. *Supra* section 2.1.

prosecution of international core crimes committed by individuals. This legal assessment does not exclude, though, the realization that a non-State Party may feel politically uncomfortable with the eventuality of 'asymmetric liability'.[138]

In general, more and more will certainly realize that the regimes of jurisdiction and cooperation as contained in the Statute are not strong enough. In addition, they will note, that the complementarity regime of the Statute puts too much emphasis on the priority of the national criminal justice systems. This latter fact *per se* prohibits a further strengthening of the Statute's complementarity regime.

There is hope that over time the United States will increasingly recognize that its concerns are already fully met by a great number of 'safeguards' which have been included in the Statute as it stands. It would, no doubt, be in the interest of the International Criminal Court and most welcome to all supporters of this new institution if the United States could make its peace with the Statute to which it has contributed so much.

---

138. On this point see Hafner et al, loc. cit. n. 17, at p. 120.

WAR CRIMES IN NON-INTERNATIONAL ARMED CONFLICTS UNDER THE STATUTE OF THE INTERNATIONAL CRIMINAL COURT[1]

Djamchid Momtaz[2]

1.   INTRODUCTION

International humanitarian law applicable in non-international armed conflicts has long been characterized by the absence of universal competence to suppress serious violations of its provisions. This failure has been due to the reluctance of states – which are naturally prone to consider any limitation of their exclusive competence in this field as a threat to their sovereignty – to criminalize such acts under international law.

The first attempt at remedying such a situation was seen in the Draft Statute of an International Criminal Court (ICC), which was prepared by the International Law Commission (ILC) in 1994,[3] and inspired by the draft articles of the Code of Crimes against the Peace and International Security of Mankind, provisionally adopted by the ILC in 1991 at first reading.[4] Under the Draft Statute of the ICC, serious violations of the laws and customs applicable in armed conflicts would be under the jurisdiction of the Court.[5] The ILC had in mind exceptionally serious war crimes, such as those described in the pertinent article of the draft code referred to by the Commission, constituting an extremely grave violation of the principles and laws of international law applicable in armed conflicts.[6] In the commentary on

---

1. © D. Momtaz, 1999.

2. Professor of International Law at the University of Teheran; Associate member of the Institut de droit international; member of the Board of Editors, *Yearbook of International Humanitarian law*. The author acknowledges the assistance of Ms Avril McDonald, Managing Editor of the *Yearbook of International Humanitarian Law*, who made a number of helpful suggestions.

3. A/49/355, 1 September 1994.

4. Report of the International Law Commission on the Work of its 46th Session. General Assembly Official Records, Supplement Nr. 10. Doc. A/46/10 (1991).

5. Report of the International Law Commission on the Work of its 46th session. UN GAOR 45th Session. Supplement Nr. 10. Doc. A/49/10 (1994). For commentary, see J. Crawford, 'The ILC Adopts a Statute for an International Criminal Court', 89 *AJIL* (1995) pp. 404-416.

6. See Art. 22 para. 2; Rapport de la Commission du droit international sur les travaux de sa 43ème session. AG Doc. off. 46ème session. Supplément Nr. 10 Doc. A/46/10 (1991) p. 293. Examples of what would be considered as an exceptionally serious war crime are given in the ILC commentary on Art. 22: wilful killing; torture; biological experiments; taking of hostages;

this article, the ILC took care to specify that the expression 'armed conflict' covered the non-international armed conflicts that are the focus of common Article 3 of the Geneva Conventions of 12 August 1949,[7] as well as international armed conflicts.

This first step was of very limited scope. In fact, according to the ILC, in order to be criminalized, the laws and customs of war had to find their origin in general customary international law.[8] The provisions of Protocol II additional to the Geneva Conventions, entirely dedicated to non-international armed conflicts and generally not considered as the expression of a well-established custom, were thus excluded. An exception was made for the provisions of its Article 4 entitled *fundamental guarantees,* which develop those present in common Article 3 of the Geneva Conventions, which have been described as 'basic general principles of humanitarian law' by the International Court of Justice.[9]

Over the past several years, the law applicable in non-international armed conflict has undergone a rapid development.[10] This fact, along with the work of the Preparatory Commission for the Rome Conference, was a point of reference for states in favor of the extension of the competence of the Court to serious violations of international humanitarian law applicable in non-international armed conflicts.[11] They were encouraged in their efforts by the International Committee of the Red Cross (ICRC)[12] and by non-governmental organizations. This is how the negotiation text presented at the Diplomatic Conference and based on the work of the Preparatory Committee came to encompass, albeit in a different form, all of the provisions of Protocol II, serious violations of which were qualified as war crimes under the jurisdiction of the Court.[13]

At the Conference of Plenipotentiaries held in Rome from 15 June to 17 July 1998, the tendency towards including those crimes grew, due in part to the participation of those states which have suffered the human catastrophes wreaked

---

injustifiable delay in the repatriation of prisoners of war at the end of active hostilities; compelling a protected person to serve in the forces of a hostile Power; and ordering the displacement of the civilian population.

7. Ibid., p. 295.

8. Rapport de la Commission du droit international sur les travaux de sa 46ème session, AG Doc. off. 49ème session, Supplément Nr. 10 Doc. A/49/10 (1994) p. 80.

9. *Military and Paramilitary Activities in and against Nicaragua* (*Nicaragua* v. *US*) Merits (1986) *ICJ Rep.* para. 218 (Judgment of 27 June).

10. See L. Condorelli, 'La Cour pénale internationale: un pas de géant (pourvu qu'il soit accompli)', 103 *Revue Générale de droit international public* (1999) p. 13.

11. Known by the name of the 'like-minded group' were some 50 developing states and medium-size powers. See P. Kirsch and J.T. Holmes, 'The Rome Conference on an International Criminal Court: the Negotiating Process', 93 *AJIL* (1999) p. 4.

12. See, for example, the ICRC's working paper for the Preparatory Commission for the Establishment of an International Criminal Court, 14 February 1997, pp. 24-33.

13. Report of the Inter-Sessional Meeting from 19 to 30 January 1998 in Zutphen, the Netherlands. A/AC.249/L.13, 4 February (1998) pp. 21-32.

by internal armed conflicts.[14] A small minority of influential states, struggling against internal strife with the propensity to degenerate into armed conflicts, nevertheless maintained their opposition to the extension of the competence of the Court to war crimes committed during non-international armed conflicts.[15] In taking account of this reluctance and in order to facilitate a consensus, the Conference had to resort to compromise. Thus, only those violations of international humanitarian law in non-international armed conflicts which are generally accepted as criminal under international law have been criminalized by the Statute of the International Criminal Court. Those that continue to give rise to controversy and disagreement regarding their qualification under international law have not been included.

2.   THE EXTENSION OF THE RULES OF INTERNATIONAL HUMANITARIAN LAW TO NON-INTERNATIONAL ARMED CONFLICTS AND THEIR CRIMINALIZATION UNDER CUSTOMARY INTERNATIONAL LAW

The extension of the applicability of international humanitarian law to non-international armed conflicts has throughout the preparatory work and during the Conference of Rome been a prerequisite for the criminalization of violations under the Statute. This explains why the elaboration of the list of war crimes committed during these conflicts which should be under the jurisdiction of the Court sparked debate around the identification of the rules of international humanitarian law whose application has been extended by customary international law to non-international armed conflicts and those of them which have been criminalized.

The question of identification of the international humanitarian law rules applicable to non-international armed conflicts was raised during the work of the Preparatory Commission within the framework of the Working Group on Definitions and Elements of Crimes.[16] During the debate originated by the joint proposal of Switzerland and New Zealand to extend the competence of the Court

---

14. See Statement of the Minister of Justice of South Africa at the Diplomatic Conference on behalf of the Southern African Development Community (SADC) (Angola, Botswana, Democratic Republic of Congo, Malawi, Lesotho, Mozambique, Mauritius, Seychelles, Namibia, Swaziland, United Republic of Tanzania, Zambia, Zimbabwe and South Africa). Press release L/Rom/7, 15 June 1998. Joint statement of Afghanistan, Azerbaijan, Bosnia and Herzegovina, Croatia, Sierra Leone, *Terra Viva* Nr. 20 Rome 10 July 1998. In response to the question raised by the Chairman of the Committee of the Whole of the UN Diplomatic Conference of Plenipotentaries, Philippe Kirsch, 73 states declared themselves in favor of the extension of the competence of the International Criminal Court to crimes committed during non-international armed conflicts, whereas 16 states were opposed to it. *Terra Viva,* Nr. 21 Rome, 13 July 1998.

15. The position adopted by China and India amongst others.

16. C.K. Hall, 'The fifth Session of the UN Preparatory Committee on the establishment of an International Criminal Court', 92 *AJIL* (1998) p. 331.

to such crimes,[17] those in favour referred to the development of customary international law applicable in such conflicts.

The rules of customary international humanitarian law that extend to non-international armed conflicts were first identified in 1968 by a resolution by the United Nations General Assembly.[18] The adoption of the General Assembly resolution followed the XXth International Conference of the Red Cross held in Vienna in 1965, which examined the application of substantial rules of the law of The Hague during non-international armed conflicts. The General Assembly resolution adopted the three rules identified by the Conference, namely the rule limiting the choice of means to harm the enemy, the rules forbidding the launching of deliberate attacks against civilian populations, and the obligation to always distinguish between combatants and non-combatants.

Since then, the application of other rules has been extended by customary international law to non-international armed conflicts. The decision of the Appeals Chamber of the International Criminal Tribunal for the Former Yugoslavia on the Interlocutory Appeal on Jurisdiction in the *Tadić* case, delivered on 2 October 1995,[19] has the great merit of clarifying what parts of customary international law are applicable in non-international armed conflicts.[20] One can conclude from the *Tadić* decision that the law of The Hague and the provisions of the Geneva Conventions, except those whose violation is considered a 'grave breach' by these Conventions, are applicable in those conflicts.[21] Furthermore, one can assert that the key provisions of additional Protocol II can be considered as expressing a well-established custom. The obligation to protect cultural property included in Protocol II and the relevant provisions of the 1954 Hague Convention on the Protection of Cultural Property during Times of Armed Conflicts should also be included. Also applicable during non-international armed conflicts are prohibitions against specific methods of warfare, especially the use of certain weapons, such as chemical weapons and landmines, liable to cause unnecessary suffering. This rule stems from more general rules limiting the choice of means to harm the enemy,[22] from customary international law and from recent arms control treaties, such as the Chemical Weapons and Landmines Conventions and Amended Protocol II to the Certain Conventional Weapons Convention, which apply regardless of the nature of the conflict. The *Tadić* decisions importance deserves to be underlined all the

---

17. Switzerland-New Zealand Proposal. A/AC 249/1997/WG.1/DP.2 (1997).

18. A/RES 2444 (XXIII) 19 December 1968, 'Respect des droits de l'homme en période de conflits armés', and A/RES 2675 (XXV) 9 December 1970, 'Problèmes fondamentaux touchant la protection des populations civiles en période de conflits armés'.

19. *The Prosecutor* v. *Duško Tadić*, Case No. IT-94-1-AR72. Decision on the Defense Motion for Interlocutory Appeal on Jurisdiction (2 October 1995) Hereinafter *Tadić* Jurisdiction Decision.

20. Ibid., paras. 96-136.

21. Th. Meron, 'The Continuing Role of Custom in the Formation of International Humanitarian Law', 90 *AJIL* (1996) p. 243.

22. *Tadić*, Jurisdiction Decision, *supra* n. 19, at para. 126.

more because Protocol II did not include restrictions on the methods and means of warfare under its provisions.[23]

The Appeals Chamber of the ICTY, basing its findings on the development of customary international law in that field, declared itself, in accordance with Article 3 of the Tribunal's Statute, competent to judge persons guilty of violating international humanitarian law during a non-international armed conflict, a violation of which engages the international criminal responsibility of its author.[24] In its judgment of 7 May 1997, Trial Chamber II found Tadić guilty of violating Article 3 common to the four Geneva Conventions.[25]

It is generally agreed that this progressive extension of international humanitarian law to non-international armed conflicts only concerns a certain number of principles and rules governing international armed conflicts, and is limited to the essence of the rules, thus excluding the application of the details of the regulations. In the words of the Appeals Chamber in *Tadić*, it is not 'a full and mechanical transplant'.[26] For this reason, we must question whether the violation of these rules during non-international armed conflicts creates a real criminalization by customary international law.

Serious violations of the provisions of Article 3 common to the four Geneva Conventions and of Protocol II are not criminalized therein. Only the provisions of the Geveva Conventions and of their additional Protocol I, the violation of which is considered a grave breach, give rise to the principle of universal jurisdiction. Under these circumstances, and before criminalizing serious violations of international humanitarian law applicable in non-international armed conflicts, one has to be sure that the development of customary international law has extended the notion of individual criminal responsibility to these violations.

The contribution of the Security Council to the criminalization of the rules of international humanitarian law applicable in non-international armed conflicts has been even more decisive than that of the General Assembly.[27] The Security

---

23. *Tadić*, Jurisdiction Decision, *supra* n. 19, paras. 96-127. See C. Greenwood, 'International Humanitarian Law and the *Tadić* Case', 7 *EJIL* (1996) p. 278; H. Ascencio and A. Pellet, 'L'activité du Tribunal Pénal International pour l'ex Yougoslavie (1993-1995)', 41 *AFDI* (1995) p. 131.

24. *Tadić*, Jurisdiction Decision, ibid., para. 94. M.S. See, 'La première décision de la Chambre d'appel du Tribunal pénal international pour l'ex-Yougoslavie. *Tadić* (compétence)', 100 Revue Générale de Droit International Public (1996) p. 125 and Meron, loc. cit. n. 21 at p. 244.

25. *The Prosecutor* v. *Duško Tadić*, Opinion and Judgment, Case No. IT-94-1-T, 7 May 1997, para. 617.

26. *Tadić*, Jurisdiction Decision, *supra* n. 19, para. 126. See P. Bretton, 'Actualités du Droit International Humanitaire applicable dans les conflits armés', in *L'évolution du droit international Mélanges: offerts à Hubert Thierry* (Paris, Pédone 1998) p. 63.

27. Cf., Res. 3074 XXVII adopted on 30 November 1973 following the recommendation of the Economic and Social Council relative to the detection and punishment of individuals guilty of war crimes or crimes against humanity, foreseeing the application of the principle of *aut dedere aut judicare* for the presumed authors of those crimes. See E. David, 'Méthode et formes de participation des Nations Unies à l'élaboration du droit international humanitaire', in *The United Nations and International Humanitarian Law* (Paris, Pédone 1996) p. 92.

Council's extensive interpretation of the notion of threat against peace and international security has given this body a closer interest in non-international armed conflicts.[28] It could not remain insensitive to violations of international humanitarian law as a source of insecurity during these conflicts. The Security Council has not only urged the parties to diverse non-international armed conflicts to respect international humanitarian law, thus contributing to the development of the rules applicable in these conflicts,[29] but it has also committed itself to guaranteeing the suppression of the most serious violations of these rules, in order to avoid the success of several peace processes being seriously compromised by the impunity of those who are responsible for such violations.[30] Its calls upon states and humanitarian organizations to gather elements of proof, as well as the creation of Commissions of Inquiry, are the best evidence of the Security Council's will to incriminate the characterized violations of international humanitarian law during non-international armed conflicts.[31]

This is how, on the occasion of non-international armed conflicts breaking out in Afghanistan,[32] Somalia,[33] Burundi,[34] and Rwanda,[35] the Security Council asserted that the people who violate international humanitarian law, or the people ordering these violations, will be held personally responsible. The creation of the International Criminal Tribunal for Rwanda is obviously based on this premise.[36] One can thus assert that the principle of such criminal responsibility, at least for any violation of international humanitarian law rules concerning the conduct of hostilities during these conflicts, is well-established in customary international law.[37]

---

28. The Security Council considers serious violations of international humanitarian law, whether committed in non-international or international armed conflicts, as capable of constituting a threat to international peace and security. See for example, the Report of the Secretary-General Pursuant to Paragraph 2 of Security Council Resolution 808 (1993) (Presented 3 May 1993), S/25704, para. 10. Reprinted in *Basic Documents of the International Criminal Tribunal for the Former Yugoslavia* (United Nations 1995) pp. 157 at 163. Indeed, this argument was the legal basis used by the Secretary-General to create both *ad hoc* Tribunals. See L. Kama, 'Le Tribunal penal international pour le Rwanda and la repression des crimes de guerre', in *The United Nations and International Humanitarian Law*, ibid., p. 254.

29. SC Res. 693 (1991) Salvador; SC Res. 864 (1993) Angola; SC Res. 912 (Rwanda); and SC Res. 918 (Rwanda).

30. P. Tavernier, 'Vers une juridiction pénale internationale', in *Mutations internationales et evolutions des normes* (Paris, Presses Universitaires de France 1994) p. 149.

31. See SC Res. 771 (1992); SC Res. 1012 (1995).

32. UN SC Presidential Statement 1994/12.

33. SC Res. 794 (1992) para. 5 - SC Res. 814 (1993) para. 13.

34. SC Res. 1087 (1996).

35. SC Res. 935 (1994).

36. Th. Meron, 'International Criminalization of Internal Atrocities', 89 *AJIL* (1995) pp. 554-577.

37. T. Graditzky, 'La responsabilité pénale individuelle pour violation du droit international humanitaire applicable en situation de conflit armé non international', *RICR* no. 823 (1998) pp. 29-57.

3. THE VIOLATIONS OF INTERNATIONAL HUMANITARIAN LAW
DURING NON-INTERNATIONAL ARMED CONFLICTS
CRIMINALIZED BY THE STATUTE OF THE ICC

It is by taking into account the development of customary international law that the Statute of the International Criminal Court[38] qualifies as war crimes under its jurisdiction some serious violations of international humanitarian law applicable in non-international armed conflicts. Under the ICC Statute, the term applies to serious violations of common Article 3[39] and of minimum norms, as well as to serious violations of the laws and customs of war applicable in non-international armed conflicts within the established framework of international law.[40] In both cases, the exercise of the competence of the Court is subject to the fulfillment of the general conditions of the Statute regarding admissibility of the case.

3.1 Violations of common Article 3 and certain minimum norms applicable in non-international armed conflicts

The competence of the Court over serious violations of common Article 3 did not raise difficulties; the precedents of the ICTY and ICTR and the absence of controversy concerning the customary nature of these provisions made the work much easier for the negotiators of the Rome Statute. All the provisions of this article were adopted without notable change by the Statute, which qualifies their violations as war crimes under the jurisdiction of the Court.

On the other hand, the provisions of Article 4 of Protocol II, qualified as fundamental guarantees, are not included. These provisions mainly repeat but also develop and specify those listed in common Article 3, and constitute, according to the ILC, the minimal norms of treatment applicable to armed conflicts.[41] Thus, collective punishment is not incriminated by the Statute, even though it incontestably violates the provisions of common Article 3, violations otherwise qualified as war crimes by the Statute. In fact, such punishments necessarily aim at the dignity of the target people and obviously contradict the prohibition against conviction without previous trial by a regularly composed tribunal and with the judicial guarantees provided for in that article.

Regarding acts of terrorism, however, one could justify the refusal of the Statute to criminalize them by the absence of generally accepted definitions of such acts under general public international law.

---

38. Rome Statute of the International Criminal Court. A/CONF. 183/9, 17 July 1998.

39. Art. 8 para. 2 (c) of the Statute.

40. Art. 8 para. 2 (e) of the Statute.

41. Report of the Commission of International Law on the work of its 48th session. AG Doc. off. 51th session Supplement Nr. 10 Doc. (A/51/10) pp. 139-140. R. Abi-Saab, 'Human Rights and Humanitarian Law in Internal Conflicts', in D. Warner, ed., *Human Rights and Humanitarian Law* (The Hague, Kluwer Law International 1997) p. 114.

The criminalization of the prohibition against the recruitment of children drew the attention of the preparatory commission and of the Conference, following the proposal of certain states, supported by the ICRC and some non-governmental organisations, to raise from 15 to 18 the minimum age fixed by Protocol II[42] and by the United Nations Convention on the Rights of the Child of 20 November 1989.[43] These efforts mirrored those of a working group, established in the framework of the United Nations Human Rights Commission, which aims at the adoption of a protocol additional to the Convention on the Rights of the Child prohibiting the involvement of children under 18 in armed conflicts.[44] The increase in the number of children recruited, press-ganged or volunteering to take part in hostilities provides the impetus for the proposal. The opposition of certain states, especially the United States, which invoked their national legislation authorizing the enlistment of children younger than 18, was an obstacle to any modification of the existing regulation within the ICC Statute.[45] Thus, conscripting or enlistment children under 15 in the armed forces, or their active participation in hostilities, is a crime under the jurisdiction of the Court, whether committed in international or non-international armed conflicts.[46] The Statute excludes situations where the children are not directly engaged in the fighting but are in charge of support and logistics tasks.[47]

The refusal of the Conference to raise the age-limit is particularly regrettable given that, in conformity with the Statute, the Court does not have competence over an individual under the age of 18 at the moment of the presumed occurrence of a crime.[48] Under these conditions, any person between 15 and 18 years old will be considered as a legitimate combatant, free to commit war crimes, without risk of being prosecuted by the ICC, a fact which can only encourage warlords to recruit them and force them to commit atrocities.

3.2   Serious violations of the laws and customs of war applicable in non-international armed conflicts under the ICC Statute

It is necessary to distinguish between the provisions of Protocol II that can be considered as part of the laws and customs of war and those that cannot be. The provisions of Protocol II the violation of which has been qualified as a crime are those intended to assure a higher protection level to the population and to civilian property. Regarding protection of the population, two principles of international humanitarian law, identified by the General Assembly as applying to non-

---

42. Art. 4 para. 3 (c).
43. Art. 38 paras. 2 and 3.
44. 'L'implication des enfants dans les conflits armés', *RICR* no. 829 (1998) pp. 111-132.
45. *Terra Viva* no. 14, 2 July 1998.
46. Art. 8(2)(b)(xxvi) [international armed conflicts] and Art. 8(2)(e)(vii) [non-international armed conflicts].
47. Ibid.
48. Art. 26 of the Statute.

international armed conflicts, seem to exist: the principle prohibiting attacks on the civilian population as such and the obligation to distinguish between combatants and non-combatants and to spare the latter as much as possible. Recent practice of the Security Council is the best proof of the existence of an *opinio juris* relative to the criminalization of the violation of these rules during these conflicts.

It is on this basis that the Rome Statute qualifies as a crime the launching of deliberate attacks against the civilian population[49] and ordering its displacement, for reasons directly linked with the conflict, except in the case where its security or military imperatives require it.[50] It also defines as criminal a deliberate attack against civilian property, including buildings, equipment, medical units and transport and medical staff which use the distinctive emblems of the Geneva Conventions in conformity with international law.[51] This prohibition also applies to buildings devoted to religion, teaching, art, science or charitable action, historical monuments, hospitals and places where ill and wounded people are gathered, on condition that they are not used for military purposes.[52]

The Statute innovates by qualifying as war crimes the violation of certain provisions of international humanitarian law not included in Protocol II. Firstly, the destruction and seizing of an adversary's property unless this destruction is imperatively demanded by military necessity.[53] These acts are qualified as 'grave breaches' by the Geneva Conventions, when executed on a large scale, in an illicit and arbitrary way; conditions not required by the Statute for their incrimination.

While the criminalization of sexual violence during any type of non-international armed conflict did not cause any particular difficulty during the Rome Conference, the inclusion of forced pregnancy in the list of acts constitutive of these crimes was highly contentious. The Vatican and states whose legislation prohibits the termination of pregnancy, were strongly opposed to its inclusion, estimating that it would intrinsically be a legal justification for abortion. In order to overcome this obstacle, the Statute takes care to specify that the inclusion of this crime can in no way be interpreted as impacting on national laws prohibiting abortion. While one can question the practical effect of such a rule, the fact remains that this criminalization[54] is the result of the unanimous condemnation of the practice during the Yugoslav conflict of illegally detaining raped and pregnant women with the intention of modifying the ethnic composition of the population.[55]

The incrimination of deliberate attacks against humanitarian peace-keeping missions, particularly aimed at their staff, their installations, equipment and units as well as their vehicles, is similarly justified by a unanimous condemnation of these

---

49. Art. 8(2)(e)(i) of the Statute.
50. Art. 8(2)(e)(viii) of the Statute.
51. Art. 8(2)(e)(ii) of the Statute.
52. Art. 8(2)(e)(iv) of the Statute.
53. Art. 8(2)(e)(xii) of the Statute.
54. Art. 8(2)(e)(vi) of the Statute.
55. According to Art. 7(e) of the Statute, by forced pregnancy is meant the illegal detention of a pregnant woman by force, with the intention of modifying the ethnic composition of a population or committing any other serious violations of international law.

practices. All peacekeeping operations are covered, except those of a coercive nature taken within the framework of Chapter VII of the United Nations Charter. In the latter case, international humanitarian law applies.[56] This was also the solution adopted by the New York Convention of 9 December 1994 on the Safety of United Nations and Associated Personnel.[57] While the Draft Code of Crimes Against the Peace and Security of Mankind, adopted by the ILC during its second reading in 1996,[58] also criminalises such an attack, the customary basis of such an incrimination is still much debated.

4.   VIOLATIONS OF INTERNATIONAL HUMANITARIAN LAW APPLICABLE IN NON-INTERNATIONAL ARMED CONFLICTS NOT CRIMINALIZED BY THE STATUTE OF THE ICC

The absence of incrimination by customary international law has been evoked in order to justify the non-incrimination of certain rules of international humanitarian law applicable in non-international armed conflicts. In reality, the main obstacle to the enlargement of the competence of the Court has been of a political nature.

4.1   Violations of international humanitarian law applicable in non-international armed conflicts criminalized by customary international law and not included in the Statute

Among the prohibitive norms of international humanitarian law whose application in non-international armed conflicts seems to be clearly established but which have not been included in the Statute as the basis of individual criminal responsibility, two particularly deserve to be noted: the prohibition against the use of specific weapons and the starvation of the civilian population.

The freedom of combatants to choose means of harming the enemy is not unlimited. By relying on this fundamental principle of international law, now applicable in non-international armed conflicts, international humanitarian law has progressively extended to these conflicts the prohibition against using specific weapons, which, because of their nature, hit without distinction military and non-

---

56. In its Report dated 29 April 1999 (A/54/87), the Special Committee on Peacekeeping Operations stressed that all personnel associated with United Nations mandated peacekeeping operations should strictly observe the norms of international humanitarian law and urged the Secretariat to finalize appropriate guidelines for peacekeepers. These guidelines, entitled 'Observance by United Nations Forces of International Humanitarian Law', were released on 6 August 1999 as a Secretary-General's Bulletin. ST/SGB/1999/13. Reprinted at p. 563 of this volume.

57. M. Arsanjani, 'Defending the Blue Helmets: Protection of the U.N. Personnel in the U.N. and International Humanitarian Law', in *The United Nations and International Humanitarian Law*, loc. cit. n. 27, pp. 117-147.

58. Report of the Commission of International Law on the work of its 48th session. AG Doc. off. 51th session Supplement Nr. 10 Doc. N.U. (A/51/10) p. 125.

military targets and are intended to cause unnecessary suffering. Such is the case with asphyxiating weapons, whose use during non-international armed conflicts is prohibited. The basic principle of this prohibition being applicable to both categories of armed conflicts, one can assert that the prohibition also concerns non-international armed conflicts. The Institute of International Law took that view in 1969,[59] followed by the General Assembly, which, without making a distinction amongst armed conflicts, qualified as obvious violations of the Hague Convention of 1907 and of the Geneva Protocol of 1925 the use of these weapons and of biological weapons.[60]

It would in fact be contrary to common sense if a state could use on its own territory weapons forbidden by international humanitarian law during an international conflict in order to crush a rebellion led by its own people. It is this logic that led the Appeals Chamber of the ICTY to declare that '[w]hat is inhumane and consequently proscribed, in international wars, cannot but be inhumane and inadmissible in civil strife',[61] and to extend the application of the prohibition of specific weapons to non-international armed conflicts. This is also the reason why the conventional law developed over the last few years and relating to the prohibition of specific weapons applies to both categories of armed conflicts.[62]

Despite the fact that the use of illegal weapons has not been raised to the level of a grave breach by the Geneva Conventions of 1949, one can nevertheless assert that, henceforth, such an incrimination arises from customary international law. This is the argument on which the ICTY Appeals Chamber relied to extend the application of Article 3 of the Tribunal's Statute to non-international armed conflicts, and to criminalize the use of toxic weapons or other weapons intended to administrate unnecessary suffering, *inter alia*.[63] That being said, one must recognise that such a criminalization, even if in the framework of international armed conflicts, still raises difficulties, and that it has not been maintained by the Draft Code of Crimes in second reading.[64] This explains why the qualification as crimes of the use of such weapons during these conflicts by the Statute of Rome

---

59. See *Annuaire de l'Institut du droit international*, the Edinburgh session, Vol. 53 II, p. 375.

60. GA Res. 26 74 (XXV) para. 5.

61. *Tadić*, Jurisdiction Decision, *supra* n. 19 at para. 119.

62. This is the case with two recent Conventions, namely, the Paris Convention on the Prohibition of the Development of Chemical Weapons and their Destruction of 13 January 1993 and the Ottawa Convention on the Prohibition of the Use, Stockpiling, Production, and Transfer of Anti-Personnel Mines and On Their Destruction of 18 September 1997.

63. *Tadić*, Jurisdiction Decision, *supra* n. 19, para. 216. See E. David, 'Le Tribunal international pénal pour l'ex-Yougoslavie', 25 *Belgian Revue of international law* (1992) pp. 576-577

64. The draft articles for a Code of Crimes against the Peace and Security of Mankind adopted during the first reading incriminate the use of illegal weapons during armed conflicts without distinction. Article 22 of the draft code names war crimes of exceptional gravity. Report of the Commission of International Law on the work of its 43th session. AG Doc. off. 46th session. Supplement Nr. 10 Doc. (A/46/10) (1991), p. 270.

is not clearly established, and is conditioned on the acceptance of a general prohibition by way of amendment of that Statute.[65]

Article 14 of Additional Protocol II, entitled *protection of objects indispensible to the survival of the civilian population*, prohibits the starvation of civilians as a means of warfare. To that end, the Protocol prohibits the attack, destruction, removal or the rendering useless of objects indispensable to the survival of the population. Even if this instrument does not expressly prohibit the deliberate prevention of the delivery of indispensible objects by one of the parties to the conflict, the Security Council nevertheless strongly condemned this practice during the Somali conflict.[66] Moreover, the Council did not limit itself to asserting that such practice was contrary to international humanitarian law, but also held personally responsible the people who committed or ordered such action.

The failure of the ICC Statute to qualify certain acts committed during non-international armed conflicts as crimes under the jurisdiction of the Court obviously does not exclude such behavior from being qualified as such under international humanitarian law.[67] Indeed, the Statute takes care to specify it, to the satisfaction of those who were in favour of the inclusion of such violations under the jurisdiction of the Court.[68]

5. THE ARGUMENTS IN FAVOR OF AN EXTENSION OF THE COMPETENCE OF THE COURT TO CRIMES COMMITTED IN NON-INTERNATIONAL ARMED CONFLICTS

It is advisable to distinguish between the legal arguments and those more political than military, in favor of the extension of the competence of the Court.

5.1   The legal arguments

The key argument referred to throughout the preparatory stages of the Statute against the extension of the competence of the court to specific characterized violations of international humanitarian law during non-international armed conflicts was their lack of incrimination by customary international law. The International Military Tribunal (IMT) at Nuremberg was also faced with this argument. In fact, the Statute of the IMT had qualified as crimes specific violations of the Hague regulations without any incrimination by the latter.[69] Fifty years later, the Appeals

---

65. Art. 8 para. 2 (b) XX.

66. SC Res. 794 (1992) para. 5.

67. Art. 22 para. 3 of the Statute.

68. Art. 10 provides: 'Nothing in this Part shall be interpreted as limiting or prejudicing in any way existing or developing rules of international law for purposes other than this Statute.'

69. The trial of Major Criminals: Proceedings of the International Military Tribunal Sitting at Nuremberg, Germany, Part 22 at p. 447 (1950) cited in *Tadić,* Jurisdiction Decision, *supra* n. 19 at para. 128. C. Meindersma, 'Violations of Common Article 3 of the Geneva Conventions as violations of the Laws or Customs of War under Article 3 of the Statute of the International

Chamber of the ICTY had, in turn, to face a similar difficulty. Relying on the argumentation supported in the past, the Appeals Chamber found that 'general principles governing the conduct of hostilities (the so-called "Hague Law")' apply to non-international armed conflicts.[70] This was how it was able to find that criminal penal responsibility following upon the violation of a rule of international humanitarian law during this type of conflict does not need to be expressly foreseen by conventional law. In order to establish the existence of such responsibility, one has to be able to deduct from state practice that the intention to criminalize such behavior exists.[71]

The question one is bound to ask is whether at the present stage a practice in favor of the criminalization of all 'grave breaches' identified by the Geneva Conventions and Additional Protocol I committed during non-international armed conflicts exists? The Appeals Chamber of the ICTY, in the jurisdiction decision in *Tadić*, while recognizing the existence of a movement in favor of such an extension, using the expedient of the progressive development of customary international law, rejected the idea that one could qualify as grave breaches serious violations of international humanitarian law committed during non-international armed conflicts.[72] This conclusion was not shared by Judge Abi-Saab, who joined to the Decision a separate opinion. This considered that the practice and *opinio juris* of states confirms the extension of the regime of grave breaches to crimes committed during these conflicts[73] with all the consequences it brings about as far as the criminalization of this behavior is concerned. This also seems to be the position adopted by the United States in its *amicus curiae* brief presented during the *Tadić* case.[74]

One of the concrete signs of such an extension is a Belgian Law of 16 June 1993.[75] This law grants Belgium universal competence over grave breaches of international humanitarian law whether committed during internal or international armed conflicts.[76] While the penal codes of certain states had previously incriminated the violation of certain norms of international humanitarian law during armed conflicts, the Belgian law calls attention to itself by the fact that it specifically enumerates as war crimes certain serious violations of international humanitarian

---

Criminal Tribunal for the Former Yugoslavia', 42 *NILR* (1995) p. 380.

70. *Tadić*, Jurisdiction Decision, *supra* n. 19, paras. 118, 119-127.

71. *Tadić*, Jurisdiction Decision, ibid., n. 19 at para. 128.

72. *Tadić*, Jurisdiction Decision, ibid., para. 89. See Th. Meron, loc. cit. n. 21, p. 243.

73. A. Cassesse, 'The International Criminal Tribunal of the Former Yugoslavia and the implementation of International Humanitarian Law', in *The United Nations and International Humanitarian Law*, loc. cit. n. 27, p. 239.

74. T. Graditzky, loc. cit. n. 37, pp. 35-36.

75. Loi du 16 juin 1993 relative à la repression des infractions graves aux Conventions internationales de Genève du 12 août 1949 et aux Protocols I et II du 8 juin 1977, additionnels a ces Convention. Published in *Moniteur belge* (1993). Reprinted in an unofficial English translation at p. 541 of this volume.

76. E. David, 'La loi belge sur les crimes de guerre', 28 *Belgian revue of international law* (1995) pp. 668-671.

law committed in the course of an internal armed conflict. The Belgian example has since been followed by other states.[77] The *Brocklebank* case, a Canadian decision to prosecute certain Canadian blue helmets suspected of having violated international humanitarian law during the Somali conflict, is of great interest in the efforts to establish the existence of an *opinio juris* in the sense of the criminalization of severe violations of international humanitarian law during non-international armed conflicts.[78]

Also relevant are some recently adopted military manuals which no longer distinguish between the categories of armed conflicts, such as that of the armed forces of the Federal Republic of Germany, which qualifies as war crimes the violation of some of the provisions of Protocol II, including that prohibiting the use of starvation as a means of warfare.[79] In order to be considered as a decisive contribution in the determination of the existence of a customary law, one must of course make sure that in all cases the pertinent provisions of military manuals are supported by legislation in the relevant state, which does not always seem to be the case.

Finally, one should point out that the absence of abundant and followed practice by the Security Council in that field should not be interpreted as disproving the existence of an *opinio juris*. In fact, the intervention of that body, which the Charter has invested with the main responsibility of peace-keeping and international security, is commanded by these imperatives. The Security Council may however prefer not to intervene in a given non-international armed conflict, estimating that it does not threaten international peace.

5.2   The political arguments

From a political perspective, the intensity and unprecedented violence which characterized recent non-international armed conflicts, as well as their implications for the functioning of public institutions, justify the extension of the competence of the International Criminal Court to these crimes. States experiencing these kind of armed conflicts are usually unable to prosecute persons suspected of having violated the rules of international humanitarian law. Often, military operations have completely disturbed the normal functioning of judicial institutions, which sometimes cease to exist, making any judicial procedure extremely problematic.

---

77. Cf., Case of Spain and others cited by Thomas Graditzky, loc. cit. n. 37, pp. 39-44.

78. *Regina* v. *Brocklebank*, Court Martial Appeal Court of Canada, 2 April 1996 (Court File No. CMAC-383). 106 Canadian Criminal Cases (3d) at p. 234. For commentary thereon, see K. Boustany, 'Brocklebank: A Questionable Decision of the Court Martial Appeal Court of Canada', 1 *YIHL* (1998) p. 371.

79. Humanitarian Law in Armed Conflicts – Manual - Federal Ministry of Defense of the Federal Republic of Germany (August 1992) para. 1209. Starvation of the civilian population is also criminalised as a war crime in the Slovenian Penal Code, Art. 374, which applies in times of armed conflict or peace. Slovene Penal Code, Chapter 35, Criminal Offences Against Humanity and International Law. *Official Gazette of Slovenia* Nr. 63, 13 October 1994. Entered into force 1 January 1995.

Even where the judicial system still functions satisfactorily, its impartiality will be open to question. The chances are high that 'justice' will be controlled by one of the parties to the conflict. Knowing that, in most cases, conflicts have a religious, ethnic or tribal origin, any guarantee of independence of the judicial system is an illusion.[80] In many cases, impunity for those responsible will be the norm, generating in turn new atrocities. In these conditions, international justice will be better suited and more able to judge and punish people guilty of serious violations of international humanitarian law, and thus to strengthen the basis of a future peace.

One must hope that customary international law and its development will be taken into account during the Review Conference which will meet seven years after the coming into force of the Statute of Rome,[81] and which will be, *inter alia,* concerned with completing the list of war crimes under the jurisdiction of the Court. Until then, the Security Council will always be able to create new jurisdictional instances to deal with extreme situations and to supplant an International Criminal Court failing because of incompetence, for instance, by creating new *ad hoc* Tribunals.

6.   CONCLUSIONS

While the ICC Statute is not beyond criticism, its adoption incontestably constitutes an important step in the process of criminalization of serious violations of international humanitarian law during non-international armed conflicts. This is in fact the first time that an international instrument of universal reach qualifies as criminal such violations, and foresees an international system of repression to, if the case arises, judge and condemn specific behavior committed during these conflicts.

It has been regretted that the Statute does not apply to situations of internal tension or disturbances, such as riots.[82] The extension of the competence of the Court to violations of fundamental human rights in such a context seemed to be premature and aroused strong reservations on the part of many states, which are nonetheless committed to ensuring better protection to the people involved in such types of situations.[83]

One must point out that the definition given by the Statute to non-international armed conflicts is less restrictive than that appearing in Protocol II, which is incontestably a progression. The Statute, following the example of the Geneva Conventions, does not fix any restrictive criteria to define non-international armed

---

80. L. Kama, 'Le Tribunal pénal international pour le Rwanda et la répression des crimes de guerre,' in *The United Nations and International Humanitarian Law*, loc. cit. n. 27, pp. 225-257.

81. Art. 123.

82. A. Pellet, 'Pour la Cour pénale internationale quand même! Quelques remarques sur sa compétence et sa saisine', *L'observateur des Nations Unies* (1998) p. 154. See Art. 8 para. 2(d) and (f) of the Statute.

83. See D. Momtaz, 'Les règles humanitaires minimales applicables en période de troubles et de tensions internes', *IRRC* no. 831 (1998) pp. 487-495.

conflicts. Concerning serious violations of the laws and customs applicable in those conflicts, the Court will not be able to exercise its competence, unless the conflict is prolonged and occurs on the territory of a State Party between the governmental authorities of that state and organized armed groups.[84] It is not necessary under the Statute, as it is under Protocol II, that the armed groups exercise, on a part of the territory of the state engaged in an armed conflict, such a degree of control so as to enable them to carry out continuous and concerted military operations, or that they must be able to apply the pertinent provisions of international humanitarian law, conditions whose fulfillment is not always easy. The lowering of the threshold introduced by Protocol II can only ensure a higher protection of the civilian population. One can only welcome such a change.

Finally, it is hoped that the Statute of Rome will enter into force as soon as possible, and that the states which will be party to it will not have recourse to the opt-out clause contained in Article 124, under which a State Party may declare that it does not accept the competence of the Court over war crimes, including those committed on its territory or by its nationals, for a period of seven years starting from the entry into force of the Statute.

---

84. Art. 1 of Additional Protocol II.

WAR CRIMES IN INTERNAL CONFLICTS: ARTICLE 8 OF THE ICC STATUTE[1]

Darryl Robinson[2] and Herman von Hebel[3]

1.   INTRODUCTION

The development of rules governing non-international, or internal, armed conflicts[4] has long been characterized by a profound tension between concerns of sovereignty and concerns of humanity. Historically, strong sovereignty-oriented interests dictated a slow and cautious pace of progress in this sensitive area. In recent years, however, a growing humanitarian concern for the protection of victims has prompted rapid developments in the regulation of internal armed conflict. This transformation has been greatly assisted by the establishment of the two *ad hoc* Tribunals for the former Yugoslavia and Rwanda by the Security Council, in 1993 and 1994 respectively, and the operation of these bodies. Clear trends in this area include not only the articulation and recognition of a growing body of norms applicable in internal armed conflicts but also the expanding criminalization of violations of those norms.[5] In a world where most armed conflicts are of a non-international character, these developments are of the greatest significance.

From 15 June to 17 July 1998, delegations from 160 countries assembled in Rome to negotiate and adopt a Statute for an International Criminal Court (ICC), with jurisdiction over genocide, crimes against humanity and war crimes.[6]

---

1. © D. Robinson and H. von Hebel, 1999.

2. Darryl Robinson serves as a Legal Officer in the United Nations, Human Rights and Humanitarian Law section of the Canadian Department of Foreign and International Trade.

3. Herman von Hebel serves as a Legal Counsel to the Ministry of Foreign Affairs of the Netherlands, Directorate of Legal Affairs, International Law Division, and was coordinator for the definition of war crimes during the Diplomatic Conference and is now coordinator for Elements of Crimes in the Preparatory Commission negotiations.

4. While the term 'non-international armed conflict' is used in common Article 3 and Additional Protocol II, this paper will generally employ the term 'internal armed conflict'.

5. See Th. Meron, 'Is International Law Moving towards Criminalization?', 9 *EJIL* (1998) pp. 18 at p. 30.

6. As many delegations were strongly committed to a provision addressing aggression, despite their inability to agree on a suitable definition, Art. 5(1) also makes reference to the crime of aggression. Art. 5(2) provides that the ICC will exercise jurisdiction over this crime once an amendment to the Statute is adopted, articulating a definition of the crime and the applicable preconditions.

Delegations agreed that definitions of these crimes must be articulated in the Statute and that those definitions must reflect existing customary law.[7] The fact that the Statute adopted by the Rome Conference recognizes several offences applicable in internal armed conflict is a significant indication of the rapid development in this area.

This article will briefly survey the emergence of criminal responsibility under customary international law for war crimes in internal armed conflicts, and will then discuss the provisions of the ICC Statute governing war crimes in internal armed conflict. It will also touch upon some related aspects of the ICC Statute, and finally offer some concluding observations.

2.   BACKGROUND: EMERGENCE OF CRIMINAL RESPONSIBILITY IN INTERNAL CONFLICTS

Despite the elaboration of a detailed corpus of rules applicable in international armed conflicts, states have historically been reluctant to regulate internal armed conflict. This dichotomy reflects the inclination of sovereign states to focus on their own interests rather than community concerns or humanitarian demands.[8] Many states have tended to regard such conflicts as a matter of internal policy and national criminal law rather than a subject for international regulation.[9] Until the second half of this century, evidence of rules applicable in internal armed conflict could only be found in a smattering of resolutions, statements and military manuals.[10]

A number of factors have engendered an increased willingness to regulate internal armed conflict, particularly in the latter half of the twentieth century. These relate primarily to the changed nature of internal armed conflicts, and in particular to the fact that they have become more ruthless and brutal, as entire civilian populations are deliberately drawn into the line of fire, and greater in magnitude and longer in duration, making them more akin to inter-state wars. Such conflicts have also become more frequent, to the point where today they are the prevalent form of

---

7. See Report of the Preparatory Committee on the Establishment of an International Criminal Court, Vol. I, GAOR 51st Sess., Supp. No. 22 (A/51/22) [Report of the PrepCom (1996)] at paras. 51-54 and 78. See also H. von Hebel and D. Robinson, 'Crimes within the Jurisdiction of the Court', in R.S. Lee, ed., *Rome Statute of the International Criminal Court: Negotiating Process, Major Issues and Reaching Agreement on Substance* (New York, Kluwer 1999 (forthcoming)).

8. See *The Prosecutor* v. *Dusko Tadić a/k/a 'Dule'*, case No. IT-94-I-AR72, Decision on the Defence Motion for Interlocutory Appeal on Jurisdiction, 2 October 1995 [*Tadić* (Appeal on Jurisdiction)] at para. 96.

9. As Meron observes, 'The sovereignty of states and their insistence on maintaining maximum discretion in dealing with those who threaten their "sovereign authority" have combined to limit the reach of international humanitarian law applicable to non-international armed conflict.' In Th. Meron, 'International Criminalization of Internal Atrocities', 89 *AJIL* (1995) pp. 554 at 554.

10. See for example, the statements and resolutions canvassed in *Tadić* (Appeal on Jurisdiction), *supra* n. 8 at paras. 100-124. See also the Lieber Code, reproduced in D. Schindler and J. Toman, *The Laws of Armed Conflict: A Collection of Conventions, Resolutions and Other Documents*, 3rd edn., (Geneva, Henri Dunant Institute 1988) at p. 3.

armed conflict. These trends compel regulation of internal armed conflict if international humanitarian law is to remain relevant. Other influential factors, as noted by the International Tribunal for the Former Yugoslavia (ICTY), are the increasing interdependence of states, making it difficult for third states to remain aloof, and the advent of human rights and a human being-based approach to international legal developments.[11]

A major step forward came with Article 3 common to the Geneva Conventions of 1949 (common Article 3). While a number of states had concerns about laying down rules applicable in internal armed conflicts, agreement on common Article 3 was reached by focusing on a few basic rules of humanity.[12] These were eventually supplemented with the adoption of Protocol II Additional to the 1949 Geneva Conventions in 1977, the first international instrument entirely dedicated to international humanitarian law applicable in non-international armed conflicts.[13] The negotiating history of this Protocol was again characterized by intense debates between those seeking maximum regulation (as close as possible to the regulation of international armed conflicts) and those seeking minimal or no regulation.[14] While the Protocol was clearly an advancement on common Article 3, to secure agreement it was again necessary to include only the most essential principles accepted by the international community.[15]

The laws of internal armed conflict have lagged behind those relating to international armed conflict not only in the recognition of norms but also regarding criminal responsibility for violations of those norms. Individual criminal responsibility for violations of the norms applicable in international armed conflicts was firmly established in international law in the Nuremberg and Tokyo Judgments and was further elaborated by, for example, the grave breaches provisions of the Geneva Conventions of 1949 and of Additional Protocol I of 1977. No such treaty provisions existed with respect to internal armed conflicts,[16] which, until recently, left open the question whether there was a basis for individual criminal responsibility for violations of such norms. While the proposition has been subject to doubt,

---

11. *Tadić* (Appeal on Jurisdiction), *supra* n. 8 at para. 97.

12. This provision has often been referred to as 'a Convention in miniature' within the Geneva Conventions. See the *Commentary to Geneva Convention I* (Geneva, International Committee of the Red Cross 1952) at p. 48.

13. L.C. Green, *The contemporary law of armed conflict* (Manchester, Manchester University Press 1993) at pp. 57-58.

14. M. Bothe et al., *New Rules for Victims of Armed Conflict* (The Hague, Martinus Nijhoff 1982) at p. 605; H.S. Levie, *The Law of Non-International Armed Conflict* (Dordrecht, Martinus Nijhoff 1987) at pp. 27-90.

15. Bothe, op. cit. n. 14, at pp. 606-608; Sandoz et al., *Commentary on the Additional Protocols of 8 June 1977* (Geneva, ICRC/Dordrecht, Martinus Nijhoff 1987) at p. 1336. As part of this agreement, it was necessary to define armed conflict in a restrictive manner, to the regret of many delegations.

16. One may look in vain for grave breaches provisions relating to common Art. 3 or Additional Protocol II.

particularly with respect to conduct predating this decade,[17] it has been observed that there is no moral justification and no truly persuasive legal reasons for treating perpetrators of atrocities in internal conflicts more leniently than those who commit such acts in international wars.[18]

A few developments that had a particular influence on the drafting of the ICC Statute should be mentioned here. A first catalyst was the determination in 1986 by the International Court of Justice that common Article 3 was an expression of 'elementary considerations of humanity', applicable as 'a minimum yardstick' in all kinds of conflicts.[19] A similar line of reasoning was followed by the International Law Commission (ILC) in its first draft of the Code of Crimes against the Peace and Security of Mankind in 1991, which included 'exceptionally serious war crimes' that applied equally to all types of armed conflict.[20]

In 1993, the draft Statute of the ICTY was developed, with definitions of crimes deliberately limited to 'rules of international humanitarian law which are beyond any doubt part of customary law'.[21] In line with this careful approach, the war crimes provisions that were included had their basis in norms relating to international armed conflicts.[22] However, during the Security Council debate on the adoption of the Statute, France, the United Kingdom and the United States gave a much wider interpretation to the relevant provisions, so as to cover all norms of international humanitarian law to which the former Yugoslavia had been a party, including norms relating to internal armed conflict.[23]

Another major step forward was taken with the adoption of the Rwanda Tribunal (ICTR) Statute by the Security Council in 1994.[24] Article 4 of that Statute specifically recognizes criminal responsibility for serious violations of common Article 3 and elements of Additional Protocol II.

An instructive analysis appears in the 1995 decision of the Appeals Chamber of the ICTY on the motion of the defence for an interlocutory appeal on jurisdiction in the *Tadić* case.[25] In accordance with the statements made during the Security Council debate, the Chamber gave a wide interpretation to Article 3 of the Statute

---

17. See D. Plattner, 'The Penal Repression of Violations of International Humanitarian Law Applicable in Non-international Armed Conflicts', 30 *IRRC* (1990) pp. 409. See also the UN Report of the Group of Experts for Cambodia pursuant to GA Res. 52/135, annex to UN Doc. S/1999/231, 16 March 1999, pp. 20-21, concluding that violations of common Art. 3 could not be viewed as war crimes under customary international law as far back as 1975.

18. Meron, loc. cit. n. 9, at p. 561.

19. International Court of Justice, *Case Concerning Military and Paramilitary Activities in and against Nicaragua, ICJ Rep.* (1986) at p. 114.

20. Report of the ILC (1991) UN Doc. A/46/10 at p. 270 (commentary on draft Art. 22).

21. Report of the Secretary-General Pursuant to Paragraphs 1-2 of SC Res. 808 (1993) UN Doc. S/25704 (3 May 1993) at para. 34.

22. Art. 2 incorporates the grave breaches of the Geneva Conventions of 1949, and Art. 3 (violations of the laws or customs of war) was based on the Hague Regulations of 1907: UN Doc. S/25704 (3 May 1993) at paras. 34 and 41-44.

23. UN Doc. S/PV.3217 of 25 May 1993, p. 11 (France), p. 15 (US) and 19 (UK).

24. UN Doc. S/RES/955, annex (1994).

25. *Tadić* (Appeal on Jurisdiction), *supra* n. 8.

on the violations of the laws or customs of war. The provision was therefore regarded as a 'residual clause', covering all serious violations of humanitarian law not falling under Articles 2, 4 or 5 of the Statute. Furthermore, the Tribunal concluded that this provision encompasses internal as well as international armed conflicts.[26] On the basis of an extensive review of state practice, ICRC practice, resolutions of the General Assembly of the United Nations, unilateral statements by governments, national legislation and military manuals, the Tribunal concluded that many norms developed in the context of international armed conflicts are now recognized as applicable to internal armed conflicts as well. However, the Tribunal clearly indicated that '(i) only a number of rules and principles ... have gradually been extended to apply to internal conflicts' and '(ii) this extension has not taken place in the form of a full and mechanical transplant of those rules to internal conflicts; rather, the general essence of those rules, and not the detailed regulation they may contain, has become applicable to internal conflicts.'[27]

Following the Nuremberg precedent, the ICTY concluded that an absence of treaty provisions explicitly recognizing criminal responsibility for certain violations of international humanitarian law should not be interpreted as meaning that such criminal responsibility does not exist.[28] In practice, therefore, the question of whether criminal responsibility exists for a norm of international humanitarian law depends on factors such as clear and unequivocal recognition of the norm, state practice indicating an intention to criminalize the norm, the gravity of the acts, and the interest of the international community in their prohibition.[29]

3. INTERNAL ARMED CONFLICTS IN THE ROME STATUTE

3.1 The negotiating process

In preparing the draft Statute of the ICC, the ILC refrained from elaborating definitions of crimes and instead simply made reference to relevant precedents.[30] In its commentary on the laws and customs applicable in armed conflict, the ILC

---

26. Ibid., at paras. 87-94.

27. Ibid., at para. 126.

28. The Nuremberg Tribunal concluded that criminal responsibility existed for violations of the Hague Regulations, notwithstanding the lack of a provision to that effect in the Regulations themselves. Ibid., at para. 128.

29. Ibid., at paras. 128 and 129.

30. Report of the ILC on the work of its forty-sixth session, UN GAOR 49th Sess., Supp. No. 10 (A/49/10) at pp. 74-75. In the ILC draft Statute, a distinction was made between core crimes and treaty crimes. The former were based on customary international law, whereas the latter were based on treaties that would appear in an Annex to the Statute, allowing states parties to choose which treaty crimes they recognized. Thus, war crimes were addressed under two separate headings, with serious violations of the laws and customs applicable in armed conflict appearing with the core crimes, and grave breaches of the 1949 Geneva Conventions and of Additional Protocol I thereto appearing with the treaty crimes.

referred to grave breaches of the Geneva Conventions and Additional Protocol I, as well as to some norms drawn from the Hague Regulations,[31] but did not refer to common Article 3 or Additional Protocol II.[32]

The ILC draft Statute was considered by an *Ad Hoc* Committee in 1995, which concluded, *inter alia*, that the principle of legality required a clearer definition of crimes in the Statute.[33] The task of elaborating a definition was taken up in the following years by a Preparatory Committee (PrepCom) and then by the Rome Conference in June and July 1998. The availability of an abundance of precedents on war crimes[34] necessitated a process of selection to identify the norms to be included in the Statute. Debate centered on three inter-related questions; namely (i) which norms appearing in the precedents were generally regarded as customary international law, (ii) which of these norms gave rise to individual criminal responsibility under customary international law, and (iii) which of these norms were considered serious enough to merit inclusion in the Statute.[35]

With respect to *international* armed conflicts, agreement was relatively easily reached that the norms laid down in the Hague Conventions and Regulations and the grave breaches provisions of the 1949 Geneva Conventions gave rise to individual criminal responsibility under customary international law, while differences of view existed on the customary law status of Additional Protocol I and other significant norms.[36]

With respect to *internal* armed conflicts, it remained controversial throughout the negotiations whether war crimes in internal armed conflict should be included in the Statute at all. Some delegations strongly believed that the ICC Statute should not include such norms, as it was feared that ICC competence over such crimes would be an unacceptable intrusion on sovereignty and would undermine the general acceptability of the Statute.[37] However, from the outset of the preparatory negotiations, a clear majority of delegations supported the inclusion of war crimes

---

31. Regulations to Hague Convention IV Respecting the Laws and Customs of War on Land.

32. Report of the ILC (1994) at pp. 73-75.

33. Report of the Ad Hoc Committee, UN GAOR 50th Sess., Supp. No. 22 (A/50/22) at paras. 75 and 76; Report of the PrepCom, Vol. I, *supra* n. 7, paras. 52, 53, 55, 75 and 76. It was also agreed that the different categories in the ILC draft (serious violations of the laws and customs of war, grave breaches and so on) were to a considerable extent overlapping and could be replaced by a single concept, war crimes, which would cover the whole field of norms applicable in armed conflict.

34. These precedents included, *inter alia*, the Hague Convention IV of 1907, the 1949 Geneva Conventions, the 1954 Hague Convention on Cultural Property and the 1977 Additional Protocols to the Geneva Conventions.

35. As noted, these questions were closely related; for example, the degree to which a norm was considered fundamental influenced whether states regarded it as a norm-giving rise to individual criminal responsibility.

36. See von Hebel and Robinson, op. cit. n. 7.

37. Report of the Ad Hoc Committee, *supra* n. 33, at para. 74 and Report of the PrepCom (1996), *supra* n. 7, para. 78. This minority consisted of, *inter alia*, the following states: China, India and several other Asian states, several Arab states, the Russian Federation and Turkey.

in internal armed conflict.[38] It was noted that most of the armed conflicts that have raged around the world since World War II have been conflicts of a non-international character, and that it is precisely in internal armed conflicts that humanitarian considerations are most often brutally disregarded and national criminal justice systems least likely to adequately respond to violations. It was also noted that the Statute of the ICTR already contained norms of international humanitarian law expressly relating to internal armed conflicts.

The discussion of *which* norms might apply in internal armed conflicts was of course inseparable from the discussion on the desirability of including internal armed conflicts. A majority of delegations was of the opinion that common Article 3 gives rise to individual criminal responsibility under customary international law. A large number of these delegations also believed that other norms, such as those in Additional Protocol II, must be included, while others questioned the customary law status of that Protocol.

During the February 1997 session of the PrepCom, two major proposals for a definition of war crimes were put forward, one by the United States and one by New Zealand and Switzerland.[39] In the area of internal armed conflicts, both proposals included common Article 3, but the New Zealand/Switzerland proposal also included aspects of Additional Protocol II and other norms. Over subsequent inter-sessional and PrepCom meetings,[40] the general approach adopted to narrow these differences was to avoid language from the controversial Additional Protocol II and instead to identify comparable norms regarded as fundamental in character and therefore clearly applicable in internal armed conflict.[41] Following this approach, a broad agreement eventually emerged in favour of a structure including not only common Article 3 but also other fundamental norms, as will be explained below. However, a minority of delegations remained strongly opposed to jurisdiction over internal armed conflicts and proposed the deletion of the relevant provisions.

At the Rome Conference, a large and growing majority confirmed its commitment to inclusion of violations of common Article 3 and other serious

---

38. Report of the Ad Hoc Committee, ibid., at para. 74. See also the Report of the PrepCom 1996, ibid., at para. 78.

39. The US proposal, UN Doc. A/AC.249/1997/WG.1/DP.1 of 14 February 1997, was the outcome of informal discussions between France, Japan, the United Kingdom and the United States, whereas the New Zealand/Switzerland proposal, UN Doc. A/AC.249/1997/WG.1/DP.2 of 14 February 1997, reflected a working paper prepared by the International Committee of the Red Cross. The US paper relied more on Hague law, whereas the New Zealand/Switzerland proposal relied more on the Additional Protocols. Another difference was that the US proposal introduced a threshold provision, meaning that the Court could only exercise jurisdiction over war crimes committed as part of a systematic plan or policy or as part of a large-scale commission of such offences.

40. Germany took essential steps to narrow these differences by hosting inter-sessional meetings of experts from interested western states. The resulting 'Bonn paper', UN Doc. A/AC.249/1997/WG.1/CRP.8 of 5 December 1998, was accepted as a basis for discussion at the December 1997 PrepCom, with several new provisions and options added. See Report of the PrepCom of December 1997, UN Doc A/AC.249/1997/L.9/Rev.1 of 18 December 1997, at pp. 4-16.

41. Interestingly, this approach reflects the approach adopted in *Tadić* (Appeal on Jurisdiction), discussed above.

violations, but determined opposition from a number of delegations remained. Some delegations voicing opposition to jurisdiction over internal armed conflicts began to indicate some flexibility, at least with respect to common Article 3. Eventually, with the inclusion of threshold provisions clarifying the scope of the concept of internal armed conflict, the majority view prevailed, and, despite some initial concerns, the final package won a wide degree of acceptance.

The agreement on war crimes in internal armed conflicts consists of a number of elements. The offences based on common Article 3 are listed in Article 8(2)(c), and other serious violations of the laws and customs of non-international armed conflict are enumerated in Article 8(2)(e). Subparagraphs 8(2)(d) and (f) elaborate the concept of internal armed conflict, thereby clarifying the scope of application of sub-paragraphs (c) and (e) respectively. Article 8(3) reaffirms the responsibility of a state to maintain law and order and to defend its territorial integrity, by all *legitimate* means. Also relevant is Article 8(1), which contains a threshold provision that essentially exhorts the court to focus on the most serious war crimes.[42]

3.2   Observations on specific offences in internal conflicts

Sub-paragraph (c) encompasses serious violations of common Article 3, and therefore prohibits the following acts against persons taking no active part in the hostilities:

(i)   violence to life and person, in particular murder of all kinds, mutilation, cruel treatment and torture;
(ii)   committing outrages upon personal dignity, in particular humiliating and degrading treatment;
(iii)   taking of hostages; and
(iv)   the passing of sentences and the carrying out of executions without previous judgement pronounced by a regularly constituted court, affording all judicial guarantees which are generally recognized as indispensable.

As was noted above, the customary international law status of common Article 3 has been affirmed by the ICJ and ICTY.[43] Considering the *Tadić* decision and the fundamental character of these norms, a strong majority of states insisted on inclusion in the Statute of serious violations of common Article 3.

Section (e) enumerates other norms applicable in non-international armed conflicts. In selecting the norms, the approach adopted by states was to identify those provisions applicable in international armed conflict which are so fundamental in character that they must be considered as applicable in internal armed conflict as well. In this respect, the approach is consistent with that in *Tadić*. As a result, the norms are derived from various sources, including the Hague Regulations, the Geneva Conventions, Additional Protocol II and even Additional Protocol I. The

---

42. Each of these provisions will be discussed further in the following sections.
43. *Nicaragua* v. *USA* (Merits), *supra* n. 19 and *Tadić* (Appeal on Jurisdiction), *supra* n. 8.

list of offences in sub-paragraph (e) is, in general,[44] a shortened version of the list in sub-paragraph (b) (other serious violations applicable in international armed conflict), with modifications as necessary to fit the context of internal armed conflict. Ultimately, however, support for the provisions in sub-paragraph (e) may be found in the instruments relating to internal armed conflict, particularly Additional Protocol II. A review of the negotiation history and sources for each of the offences in Article 8(2)(e) would be beyond the scope of the present paper, but a few general observations will be offered here.

The first four clauses of Article 8(2)(e) deal with intentionally directing attacks at certain protected targets. Clause (i) protects civilians and the civilian population;[45] clause (ii) protects personnel, buildings and equipment using the distinctive emblems of the Geneva Conventions;[46] clause (iii) protects those involved in humanitarian aid and peacekeeping (provided they are entitled to civilian status);[47] and clause (iv) protects buildings dedicated to certain civilian purposes.[48] Each of these was regarded as an indispensable norm. For example, the prohibition on attacking civilian populations has long been established as a fundamental prohibition applicable in any armed conflict.[49] Although the provision on humanitarian assistance or peacekeeping

---

44. An exception is Art. 8(2)(e)(viii) (displacement of the civilian population), discussed below.

45. Intentionally directing attacks against the civilian population as such or against individual civilians not taking direct part in hostilities: Art. 8(2)(e)(i). This provision is identical to Art. 8(2)(b)(i) (international armed conflict), which is based on Additional Protocol I, Arts. 51 and 85(3)(a), but is also supported by Additional Protocol II, Art. 13. See also *infra* n. 49 on the customary law status of this norm.

46. Intentionally directing attacks against buildings, material, medical units and transport, and personnel using the distinctive emblems of the Geneva Conventions in conformity with international law: Art. 8(2)(e)(ii), which is identical to Art. 8(2)(b)(xxiv). The international community attaches great value to respect for these distinctive emblems (for example, the red cross or the red crescent): see Geneva Convention I at Art. 38 and related provisions; Geneva Convention II at Art. 41 and related provisions; Additional Protocol I at Arts. 8(e), 15, 18, 38 and Annex I. The subject is addressed in Additional Protocol II at Art. 12 (in conjunction with Arts. 9-11).

47. Intentionally directing attacks against personnel, installations, material, units or vehicles involved in a humanitarian assistance or peacekeeping mission in accordance with the Charter of the United Nations, as long as they are entitled to the protection given to civilians or civilian objects under the law of armed conflict: Art. 8(2)(e)(iii). This provision was inspired by the Convention on the Safety of UN and Associated Personnel, but as noted *infra* it does not purport to expand customary law but rather provides a specific illustration of forbidden attacks on civilian targets.

48. Intentionally directing attacks against buildings dedicated to religion, education, art, science or charitable purposes, historic monuments, hospitals and places where the sick and wounded are collected, provided they are not military objectives: Art. 8(2)(e)(iv) is drawn from Art. 8(2)(b)(ix). This offence is based on Arts. 27 and 56 of the Hague Regulations, but also finds support in Arts. 53 and 85(4)(d) of Additional Protocol I, Art. 16 of Additional Protocol II, and the 1954 Hague Convention for the Protection of Cultural Property in the Event of Armed Conflict.

49. See for example L. Doswald-Beck, 'The Value of the 1977 Geneva Protocols for the Protection of Civilians', in M. Meyer, ed., *Armed Conflict and the New Law* (London, British Institute of International and Comparative Law 1989), noting that the principle was established before World War II. This understanding is reflected in the official statements and resolutions of the General Assembly (and earlier, the Assembly of the League of Nations) which are helpfully canvassed in *Tadić* (Appeal on Jurisdiction), *supra* n. 8, at paras. 100-118.

may at first glance appear novel, the drafting of the provision ensures that this is simply a specific example of the general obligation not to attack civilian targets.[50] Thus, while the provision may be technically redundant, it has symbolic importance as a clear signal by the world community that attacks against such personnel are recognized as serious crimes of international concern.

Several of the offences are based on the Hague Regulations, such as the prohibitions on pillage,[51] killing or wounding treacherously,[52] declaring that no quarter will be given,[53] and unjustified destruction of property.[54] Although the Hague Regulations were drafted for the purpose of international armed conflict, these provisions have long been recognized as customary international law and were considered so well-established as to give rise to criminal responsibility even in internal armed conflict.

Other activities were regarded as so reprehensible as to deserve specific condemnation, even though the conduct would have fallen under more general provisions of common Article 3. Examples include the prohibition on physical mutilation and medical experimentation[55] and the prohibition on rape and other sexual violence.[56] The latter offence simply provides a more elaborate and modern

---

50. As Art. 8(2)(e) does not specifically address attacks on civilian objects, it would appear to be necessary to rely on the prohibition in the general laws of armed conflict.

51. Pillaging a town or place, even when taken by assault: Art. 8(2)(e)(v), drawn from Art. 8(2)(b)(xvi), which is based on Article 28 of the Hague Regulations, but also finds support in Additional Protocol II, Art. 4(2)(g).

52. Killing or wounding treacherously a combatant adversary: Art. 8(2)(e)(iv), based on Article 23(b) of the Hague Regulations. The term combatant adversary is used instead of the term appearing in the Hague Regulations and Art. 8(2)(b) (individuals belonging to the hostile nation or army) to make it appropriate for internal armed conflict.

53. Declaring that no quarter will be given: Art. 8(2)(e)(x), drawn from Art. 8(2)(b)(xii), based on Art. 23(d) of the Hague Regulations, also finding support in Additional Protocol I, Art. 40 and Additional Protocol II, Art. 4(1).

54. Destroying or seizing the property of an adversary unless such destruction or seizure be imperatively demanded by the necessities of the conflict: Art. 8(2)(e)(xii). The terms 'adversary' and 'conflict' are used instead of 'enemy' and 'war' – the terms appearing in Art. 23(g) of the Hague Regulations and Art. 8(2)(b)(xiii) of the Statute – to make it appropriate to internal armed conflict.

55. Subjecting persons who are in the power of another party to the conflict to physical mutilation or to medical or scientific experiments of any kind which are neither justified by the medical, dental or hospital treatment of the person concerned nor carried out in his or her interest, and which cause death to or seriously endanger the health of such person or persons: Art. 8(2)(e)(xi), drawn from Art. 8(2)(b)(x). The language is based on Art. 13 of Geneva Convention III, but similar prohibitions may be found in Additional Protocol I, Art. 11 and Additional Protocol II, Art. 52(e). The term 'another party to the conflict' was adopted to make the provision appropriate for internal armed conflicts.

56. Committing rape, sexual slavery, enforced prostitution, forced pregnancy, as defined in Art. 7(2)(f), enforced sterilization, and any other form of sexual violence also constituting a serious violation of common Art. 3: Art. 8(2)(e)(vi), drawn from Art. 8(2)(b)(xxii).

articulation of clearly prohibited forms of sexual violence, de-linked from antiquated terminology used in previous instruments.[57]

Special mention must be made of Article 8(2)(e)(vii), which prohibits '[c]on-scripting or enlisting children under the age of fifteen years into armed forces or groups or using them to participate actively in hostilities.'[58] The provision is derived from Additional Protocol I, Article 77(2), Additional Protocol II, Article 4(3)(c), and Article 38 of the Convention on the Rights of the Child. There was particularly strong support for this provision, and despite some initial concerns,[59] consensus was eventually reached to include this norm. Delegations concluded that its inclusion in the Statute was justified by the near-universal acceptance of the norm, the violation of which warranted the most fundamental disapprobation. A few delegations suggested raising the relevant age from 15 to 18, but this was rejected because there was not adequate support for it in customary international law.[60]

Finally, Art. 8(2)(e)(viii), governing the displacement of civilian population,[61] is unusual, as it is the only deviation from the general approach of incorporating offences from Article 8(2)(b). The provision is based on Article 17(1) of Additional Protocol II, which has no exact parallel in Additional Protocol I, although Article 85(4)(a) of that Protocol is similar (now reflected in Article 8(2)(b)(viii)). Article 49 of Geneva Convention IV is the most direct precedent in a context of international armed conflict. It was widely accepted as a serious norm warranting inclusion.

---

57. Earlier instruments encompassed such conduct under rubric such as 'outrages on personal dignity' or 'humiliating and degrading treatment', which is seen today as trivializing the severity of such conduct. The language used in Art. 8(2)(e)(vi) is based on declarations such as the Platform for Action and the Beijing Declaration of the Fourth World Conference on Women (UN Sales No. E.DPI/1766 (1996)); see also Geneva Convention IV, Art. 27; Additional Protocol I, Art. 76; Additional Protocol II, Art. 4(2)(e). The definition of forced pregnancy was carefully negotiated in order to fully capture this particular harm which has been inflicted on women, while making clear that it does not give rise to a right to abortion or undermine national legislation on the subject. The crime consists of the unlawful confinement of a woman forcibly made pregnant, with the intent of affecting the ethnic composition of any population or carrying out other grave violations of international law.

58. This provision is similar to Art. 8(2)(b)(xxvi) with minor modifications to suit the context of internal armed conflict. Art. 8(2)(e)(vii) is in fact broader than 8(2)(b)(xxvi) in that it includes groups as well as forces to reflect the nature of internal armed conflicts. This is consistent with Art. 4(3)(c) of Additional Protocol II. In addition, although in Art. 8(2)(b)(xxvi), the term 'national' modifies 'armed forces' to address the concerns of Arab states about the *intifadah*, this arrangement was not considered necessary in the context of internal armed conflict.

59. The United States initially had strong concerns about this provision, taking the view that it did not reflect customary international law and was more a human rights provision than a criminal law provision. The US concerns were addressed by adopting the terms 'conscripting' or 'enlisting' rather than 'recruiting'. Some Arab states initially had concerns, which were overcome by including the term 'national' before 'armed forces' with respect to international armed conflicts, see ibid.

60. Raising the age limit to 18 under conventional law is currently being considered in the context of a new protocol to the Convention on the Rights of the Child.

61. Ordering the displacement of the civilian population for reasons related to the conflict, unless the security of the civilians involved or imperative military reasons so demand: Art. 8(2)(e)(viii).

3.3   **Scope of application of the norms**

Support for inclusion of internal armed conflicts was bolstered by the inclusion of sections (d) and (f) of Article 8(2), which help to clarify the concept of an armed conflict not of an international character for the purpose of sections (c) and (e) respectively.

Section (d) states that:

> Paragraph 2(c) applies to armed conflicts not of an international character and thus does not apply to situations of internal disturbances and tensions, such as riots, isolated and sporadic acts of violence or other acts of a similar nature.

This provision is drawn from Article 1(2) of Additional Protocol II. It provides a negative definition of internal armed conflict, i.e., it explains that the term does not apply to mere disturbances and therefore clarifies that some degree of intensity is inherent in the notion of an armed conflict.[62]

Section (f) applies to other serious violations, and repeats the above-quoted language, with the addition of the following sentence:

> It applies to armed conflicts that take place in the territory of a State when there is protracted armed conflict between governmental authorities and organized armed groups or between such groups.

Therefore, in addition to the negative definition, section (f) also includes a positive definition, i.e., it describes what a non-international armed conflict entails. At first sight, one might conclude that this extra sentence poses a restrictive threshold. However, this sentence, which is based on Article 1(1) of Additional Protocol II,[63] deliberately deviates therefrom in some significant respects. First, Additional Protocol II applies only to internal armed conflicts in which governmental authorities are at least one of the participants, whereas section (f) encompasses conflicts between armed groups *inter se*. Furthermore, the Protocol requires that the armed groups exercise control over territory and have the capacity to carry out sustained and concerted military operations and to implement the Protocol. In

---

62. Indeed, Art. 1(2) of Additional Protocol II was based on an ICRC draft which was simply intended to clarify the concept of armed conflict. It was understood that such a requirement was also implicit in common Art. 3. See the Commentary of the ICRC, *supra* n. 12, at p. 1354; and Bothe et al., op. cit. n. 14, at pp. 624-625.

63. Art. 1(1) of Additional Protocol II refers to armed conflicts which take place in the territory of a High Contracting Party between its armed forces and dissident armed forces or other organized armed groups which, under responsible command, exercise such control over a part of its territory as to enable them to carry out sustained and concerted military operations and to implement this Protocol. Thus, there are a number of elements to be satisfied under Art. 1(1), which have always given rise to concerns that the provision is too restrictive: Bothe et al., op. cit. n. 14, at p. 625; ICRC, *supra* n. 12 at pp. 1349-1353; Levie, op. cit. n. 14, at pp. 23-90.

contrast, section (f) simply requires a protracted armed conflict, posing a much lower threshold.[64]

The additional sentence in section (f) reflects an effort to accommodate the suggestion by a number of Arab states that the whole of Article 1(1) of Additional Protocol II should be adopted with respect to section (e) (other serious violations). When it was proposed that a provision along those lines might be included,[65] the proposal met with broad and intense opposition on the basis that the threshold in Additional Protocol II was too restrictive. It was argued that such a provision would exclude, for example, the situation in Somalia a few years ago, in which different groups were fighting against each other without the presence of any central government. It is precisely in those situations that the likelihood of flagrant violations of fundamental humanitarian norms is greatest and the chances for adequate prosecution of such crimes by a national judicial organ practically nonexistent. The drafters of the Statute therefore adopted the more moderate 'protracted armed conflict' test espoused in Tribunal jurisprudence.[66]

3.4   Non-intervention

Finally, paragraph 3 of Article 8 clarifies that:

> Nothing in paragraphs 2(c) and (d) shall affect the responsibility of a Government to maintain or re-establish law and order in the State or to defend the unity and territorial integrity of the State, by all legitimate means.

This paragraph is based on Article 3(1) of Additional Protocol II, and was included once it was clear that norms applicable to internal armed conflicts would be included in the Statute. The provision is a compromise to help accommodate the concerns of some states, such as China and the Russian Federation, that the provisions on internal armed conflict might be used as a tool for unjustified interference in domestic affairs. (In this respect, see also the seventh and eight preambular paragraphs of the Statute, on the obligation to refrain from the use of force and the principle of non-intervention, which were included for similar purposes.) As the provision affirms the right of a state to act by all *legitimate* means, it in no way negates criminal responsibility for the commission of war crimes.[67]

---

64. This criterion was taken from ICTY jurisprudence, particularly *Tadić* (Appeal on Jurisdiction), *supra* n. 8.
65. UN Doc. A/CONF.183/C.1/L.59.
66. *Tadić* (Appeal on Jurisdiction), *supra* n. 8.
67. See the Commentary of the ICRC, *supra* n. 12 at p. 1363.

3.5   Related aspects of the Rome Statute

Although this article focuses on the definition of war crimes in internal armed conflicts developed at the Rome Conference, a few short comments on related aspects of the Rome Statute are in order.

First, the ICC itself will not necessarily deal with every isolated war crime but rather will focus on the most serious crimes of international concern.[68] Thus, Article 8(1) indicates that '[t]he Court shall have jurisdiction in respect of war crimes in particular when committed as part of a plan or policy or as part of a large-scale commission of such crimes.' The deliberate choice of the flexible phrase 'in particular' means that this provision is a guideline rather than a limitation on jurisdiction.[69]

Second, the war crimes listed in Article 8(2) of the Statute are not the only offences applicable in situations of internal armed conflict. Articles 6 (Genocide) and 7 (Crimes Against Humanity) are applicable in any context, including internal armed conflict. Article 6 encompasses certain harmful acts committed with the intent to destroy, in whole or in part, a national, ethnical, racial or religious group as such, and applies regardless of the existence of armed conflict.[70] The definition of crimes against humanity in Article 7 encompasses certain inhumane acts (such as murder, torture, and sexual violence) when committed as part of a widespread or systematic attack directed against any civilian population.[71] Although some delegations sought to restrict the concept of crimes against humanity to acts committed during armed conflicts, this view was rejected, so that the definition applies to any situation.

Third, Article 9 of the Statute contemplates the elaboration of Elements of Crime (Elements) which will assist the Court in the interpretation and application of the definition of crimes.[72] The Elements will be developed by a Preparatory Commission

---

68. See for example the fourth preambular paragraph, and Arts. 1, 5(1), 8(1), 17(1)(d), 53(1) and 53(2) of the ICC Statute.

69. The United States was strongly committed to a threshold clause to ensure a focus on the most serious crimes and to avoid overburdening the Court with minor or isolated cases. Other delegations were concerned about introducing an additional hurdle. Agreement was reached on the basis of the compromise text of Art. 8(1). See von Hebel and Robinson, op. cit. n. 7.

70. The definition of genocide in Article 6 mirrors the definition in the Genocide Convention, which is clearly recognized as customary international law.

71. The definition is derived from the relevant authorities, including international instruments and jurisprudence, and provides a rigorous test consistent with customary international law. See D. Robinson, 'Defining Crimes Against Humanity at the Rome Conference', 93 *AJIL* (1999) p. 43.

72. Although most delegations felt that further elaboration of Elements was unnecessary, the United States in particular attached the utmost importance to Elements, arguing that these were necessary to provide the requisite certainty and clarity. In the interest of reaching general agreement, the majority was willing to agree to the future elaboration of Elements, but Elements purporting to be binding on the judges were clearly unacceptable to most delegations. To indicate the non-binding nature of the Elements, Art. 9 deliberately avoids the term 'shall enter into force' (a term used with respect to Rules of Procedure) and merely states that the Elements 'shall assist the Court'. Art. 9(3) unequivocally requires that the Elements of Crimes 'shall be consistent with this Statute', which must ultimately be determined by the Court.

and adopted by the Assembly of States Parties, and must be consistent with the Rome Statute. It is to be hoped that the Elements will provide useful guidance on some of the concepts in Article 8.

Fourth, Article 10 of the Statute clarifies that '[n]othing in this Part shall be interpreted as limiting or prejudicing in any way existing or developing rules of international law for purposes other than this Statute.' Thus, the non-inclusion in the Statute of certain norms does not prejudice the status of those norms in customary international law, either at present or in the future.

Finally, although the focus of this paper concerns the definition of crimes, the jurisdictional provisions of the ICC Statute may also be mentioned in this context. The ICC may exercise jurisdiction with respect to an internal armed conflict where the matter is referred by the Security Council[73] or where the Court's jurisdiction has been accepted by the state of nationality of the accused or the state of the territory where the crime was committed ('territorial state'). Such acceptance could be provided on an *ad hoc* basis or could arise by virtue of being a state party to the ICC Statute.[74] In the case of an internal armed conflict, the state of nationality and the territorial state will likely be the same. Given that states experiencing internal armed conflict may be less likely to ratify the ICC Statute, it is expected that in its early years the Court will rely on Security Council referrals to obtain jurisdiction over internal armed conflicts. As time passes and more states ratify the ICC Statute, the ICC will eventually be better equipped to assume jurisdiction over internal armed conflicts without a Security Council referral.

---

73. The Security Council may refer a situation acting under Chapter VII of the UN Charter: Art. 13 of the ICC Statute. All member states of the UN, regardless of whether they have ratified the ICC Statute, are obliged to comply with decisions of the Security Council: Art. 25 of the Charter of the United Nations.

74. See Art. 12 of the ICC Statute. The ILC draft Statute featured an opt-in regime, allowing a state party to choose the crimes for which it would accept the Court's jurisdiction. In order to enhance the effectiveness of the Court, this approach was rejected and an automatic jurisdiction regime was adopted, whereby states parties must accept the Court's jurisdiction over all of the crimes. However, as part of the final compromise, a transitional provision allows a one-time, opt-*out*, for a limited period of seven years, with respect to war crimes only (Art. 124). This was a political concession made to those that preferred an opt-in regime. This provision was controversial, and it is not expected that many states will use this provision due to its political unpopularity. It might however have some utility in providing an opportunity for hesitant states to become familiar with the Court's operations before accepting jurisdiction over all crimes. States using the provision would remain bound by international humanitarian law and enforcement mechanisms, such as national prosecutions or Security Council action.

4.   CONCLUDING OBSERVATIONS

One of the major guiding principles in the elaboration of the definitions of the crimes was that these definitions should be reflective of customary international law.[75] This exercise was not without its challenges and dangers, particularly where those norms relate to a field of customary law that is undergoing rapid development. There was always the risk that, as a result of disagreement about the content of customary international law, the lowest common denominator would prevail. It is the view of the present authors that this risk has in practice hardly materialized. Instead, while respecting the parameters of customary international law, the Statute offers an extensive and modern list of offences.

The affirmation of individual criminal responsibility for war crimes committed during internal armed conflict is a particularly welcome step by the international community. Because of the profound tension between concerns of humanity and concerns of sovereignty, the offences applicable in internal armed conflict are restricted to the most serious offences only. This is consistent with the evolving trend in this area and the approach recognized in the jurisprudence of the ICTY, particularly the *Tadić* (Appeal on Jurisdiction) decision. This trend includes the transposition of norms applicable in international armed conflict to internal conflict, thereby gradually blurring the fundamental distinction between the two types of armed conflict, as well as the expanding criminalization for violations of the most fundamental norms, including in internal armed conflict.

Article 8 also contains threshold provisions, clarifying the concept of internal armed conflict, in order to help address the concerns of hesitant states. However, the ICC Statute deliberately deviates from the restrictive definition of an internal armed conflict laid down in Additional Protocol II, which would have excluded some serious situations of internal armed conflict, such as that in Somalia. The Statute instead contains a threshold more consistent with the natural meaning of armed conflict, drawn from Tribunal jurisprudence. The intense reaction by an overwhelming majority to the shortcomings of the Additional Protocol II definition, only twenty years after its adoption, is particularly interesting.

In some respects, the definition of war crimes in internal armed conflict falls short of what many had desired. For example, the failure to include deliberate infliction of starvation of civilians as a war crime in internal armed conflict is regrettable.[76] Likewise, the criminalization of the use of certain prohibited weapons had generated enormous political controversies in the context of international armed conflict, making delegations unwilling to re-enter the debate in the context of

---

75. The reason behind this approach was that the Court should operate only for crimes that are of concern to the international community as a whole. This implied that the Court's jurisdiction should include only those crimes universally recognized as such. An additional pragmatic reason was that becoming a party to the Statute would not be contingent on first becoming a party to other instruments containing the substantive norms.

76. The inclusion of this crime in the context of internal armed conflicts did not appear to garner sufficient support, notwithstanding that the prohibition is explicitly included in Art. 14 of Additional Protocol II.

internal armed conflicts.[77] It was also suggested that the Conference should do away completely with the distinction between international and internal armed conflict, but that suggestion clearly was a bridge too far for most delegations.

Thus, the ICC Statute is by no means the final word on war crimes in internal armed conflict; the Statute itself recognizes that customary international law is in no way frozen by the ICC Statute and may continue to evolve.[78] In the meantime, the ICC Statute provides a list of offences that captures the worst atrocities, and offers a persuasive indication of customary international law. As noted in the introduction, in the context of today's armed conflicts, it is essential that war crimes in internal armed conflict be addressed if international humanitarian law is to remain relevant in the protection of victims.

---

77. This debate centered on whether a prohibition on the use of nuclear weapons was established in existing international law, and the political ramifications of including some weapons of mass destruction while others were excluded. For further discussion, see von Hebel and Robinson, op. cit. n. 7.

78. Art. 10 of the ICC Statute, discussed above.

CURRENT DEVELOPMENTS

THE YEAR IN REVIEW[1]

Avril McDonald[2]

1.   INTRODUCTION

Nineteen ninety-nine was a year of taking stock. For humanitarian lawyers, this was facilitated by the fact that it was a year of anniversaries. As well as being the final year of the decade of international law, it was also the centenary of the first Hague peace conference and the first Hague Convention and the fiftieth anniversary of the 1949 Geneva Conventions, providing ample occasion for reflection on the successes and failures of this branch of international law over the past century. The tone of the various commemorative meetings was chastened rather than celebratory. As one commentator noted: 'At the end of a century which has seen so much of war and in which the laws of war have proven so comparatively ineffectual, it seems obvious that that law must be seen as deficient and the record of the last hundred years be adjudged one of failure rather than achievement. (...) Yet the principle conclusion is not that the world needs new law, or different law, but that the law which we have needs to be made more effective.'[3]

The major developments in international humanitarian law have closely tracked a century that has seen society and the nature and aims of warfare change dramatically. Developments in the law have been reactive rather than anticipatory and have built on a model that was designed in response to imperatives that were different than those faced today and those that will be faced in the future. The time has long since passed in many countries when the state has a monopoly on violence. Entire societies have been militarised, and in many areas war has been 'privatised' as 'mercenaries, rebels, mutinous gangsters emerge to exploit the decline of the state'.[4] The civilian population has become the battleground, and humanitarian law

---

1. © A. McDonald, 1999.

2. Ms. Avril McDonald, LL.B., MA., LL.M., Grad. Dip. Journalism, is Managing Editor of the *Yearbook of International Humanitarian Law* and a Ph.D. candidate in the field of International Law at The Queen's University of Belfast. The research assistance of Jann K. Kleffner is gratefully acknowledged. The review is based on the classification scheme used in the Documentation section, although the numbering differs.

3. Christopher Greenwood, 'International Humanitarian Law and the Laws of War', Revised Report for the Centennial Commemoration of the First Hague Peace Conference 1899 (May 1999) p. 3 (para. 1.6).

4. 'The century that murdered peace', *The Observer*, 12 December 1999.

is largely irrelevant to the people who matter most: those involved in the fighting, and the persons it is designed to protect, as was demonstrated in several major non-international armed conflicts in 1999. Where the *modus operandi* is to terrorise civilians, and particularly where the armed conflict is taking place in a lawless environment, there is little to persuade the paramilitary member or rebel that he will gain more from observing humanitarian law than from breaching it. Neither does humanitarian law foresee the types of warfare that will be used in the future, including, increasingly, information warfare. The key problem, however, and the major and seemingly insurmountable challenge for the new century remains compliance with existing law rather than the adequacy of the law itself or even the question of enforcement.

2.   CIVILIANS GENERALLY

The 1999 Report of the Secretary-General on the Protection of Civilians in Armed Conflict[5] painted a depressing picture of the reality for civilians in armed conflicts today and urged the United Nations to respond to atrocities with action stronger than speeches and reports. It called on the Security Council to create a standing mechanism through which it could seek expert advice on specific issues, including legal protection, prevention of conflicts and physical protection.

It offered 40 recommendations to better protect civilians in conflicts. In particular, steps must be taken to strengthen the UN's ability to plan and deploy rapidly, which includes enhanced participation in the United Nations Stand-by Arrangements System. The Council should also consider deploying preventive peacekeeping operations in certain cases. Second, the Council should establish a permanent technical review mechanism of UN and regional sanctions regimes to ascertain the impact of sanctions on civilians. Further, the Council should use targeted sanctions to deter and contain persons who commit serious violations of international humanitarian law and human rights, as well as those parties to the conflict which continually defy Council resolutions. The Council should also consider the scope of breaches of humanitarian law or human rights, the inability of the local authorities to uphold law and order or the identification of a pattern of complicity by local authorities, the exhaustion of peaceful or consent-based solutions to the conflict, the ability of the Council to monitor actions that are undertaken, and the limited and proportionate use of force, with attention to repercussions on civilian populations and the environment. Above all, the Council should tackle the root causes of conflict.

By unanimously adopted Resolution 1265 of 17 September 1999, the Security Council established a mechanism to review further the recommendations contained in the Secretary-General's report and to considered appropriate steps by April 2000.

---

5. UN SG's Report on the Protection of Civilians in Armed Conflict. S/1999/957 of 8 September 1999.

The resolution emphasised 'the responsibility of States to end impunity and to prosecute those responsible for genocide, crimes against humanity and serious violations of international humanitarian law', and affirmed 'the possibility, to this end, of using the International Fact-Finding Commission established by Article 90 of the First Additional Protocol (...)'. The Council noted with concern 'the erosion in respect for international humanitarian, human rights and refugee law and principles during armed conflicts, in particular deliberate acts of violence against all those protected under such law, and (...) the denial of safe and unimpeded access to people in need'. The Council also condemned attacks upon UN and associated personnel, and humanitarian organisations, and affirmed the need to hold accountable persons who commit such acts. The Council underlined the importance of the widest possible dissemination of and training in international humanitarian law, human rights and refugee law. The Council held several other meetings specifically on the subject of civilians and armed conflicts during the year.[6]

2.1   Children

Nineteen ninety-nine was the 10th Anniversary of the adoption of the Convention on the Rights of the Child (CRC), but there are more child soldiers than ever and more children at risk from conflict.[7] By the end of the year, there had still been no breakthrough on the adoption of an additional Protocol to the CRC which would raise the minimum age at which children can be recruited and involved in hostilities to 18 years, due primarily to the opposition of the USA, although there were hopes that a draft Optional Protocol could be concluded early in 2000. Attention on the problem was focussed not only within the Working Group on the Draft Optional Protocol to the Convention on the Rights of the Child on Involvement of Children in Armed Conflicts but also within the UN and at a regional level, indicating that concern about this issue is worldwide.

Several organs within the UN organisation dealt with the issue of child soldiers, including the UN Special Rapporteur on Extrajudicial, Summary or Arbitrary Executions,[8] the UN Commission on Human Rights,[9] and the Security Council. On 25 August, the Security Council adopted resolution 1261 (1999), which set out a number of measures for protecting children in armed conflict. Further, it stressed 'the responsibility of all States to bring an end to impunity and their obligation to prosecute those responsible for grave breaches of the Geneva Conventions (...)'.

---

6. See further 'Conflicts in Kosovo, Sierra Leone and Angola, Question of East Timor Key Elements of Security Council's Work for 1999', UN Press Release SC/6784, 18 January 2000.

7. A recent report stated that 300,000 children are currently serving as soldiers in current armed conflicts, in more than 30 countries. 'Promises Broken: An Assessment of Children's Rights on the 10th Anniversary of the Convention on the Rights of the Child' (New York, Human Rights Watch, December 1999).

8. Report of the Special Rapporteur, Ms. Asma Jahangir, submitted pursuant to Commission on Human Rights resolution 1998/68, E/CN.4/1999/39, para. 97, 6 January 1999. The report deals further with the issue of child soldiers at paras. 71-73.

9. Commission on Human Rights resolution 1999/80, 28 April 1999, part IV, paras. 14-19.

The Council requested the Secretary-General to submit to it by 31 July 2000 a report on the implementation of the resolution. The Council also discussed the need to raise the age of recruitment of children at its two-day meeting on protection of civilians in armed conflicts, held from 16-17 September. Moreover, in his report on civilians in armed conflict, discussed above, the SG recommended raising the age of recruitment of children and their involvement in hostilities to 18 years.[10]

The recruitment of children for use in armed conflict was condemned as one of 'the worst forms of child labour' by the International Labour Organisation (ILO) in its 'Convention Concerning the Prohibition and Immediate Action for the Elimination of the Worst Forms of Child Labour', which was adopted by the International Labour Conference at its 87th Session in Geneva, on 17 June 1999.[11] Article 3 characterises 'forced or compulsory recruitment of children for use in armed conflict' as a form of slavery or practice similar to slavery. All ILO members who ratify the Convention commit themselves, under Article 1, to take 'immediate and effective measures to secure the prohibition and elimination of the worst forms of child labour as a matter of urgency'.

There were a number of regional developments, with the Maputo Declaration being adopted by the African Conference held in Mozambique from 19-22 April and the Montevideo Declaration on the Use of Children as Soldiers of 8 July 1999[12] being adopted by the Latin American and Caribbean Conference, held in Uruguay from 5-8 July 1999. Both called for a prohibition on the recruitment and use of children younger than 18 in hostilities.[13] On 29 August 1999, the five Nordic states signed a declaration against the use of child soldiers. Regional Conferences were also held in Australia from 8-9 September and in Europe from 18-20 October.[14] The promotion of the rights of the child, including those of child soldiers, was one of the five thematic priorities for 1999 within the European Initiative for Democracy and Human Rights.

The African Charter on the Rights and Welfare of the Child,[15] adopted in 1990, entered into force on 29 November 1999. Article 22 obliges States Parties to take all necessary measures to ensure that no child (defined in Article 1 as anyone younger than 18) should be recruited or involved in armed conflicts.

The UN Working Group on the Draft Optional Protocol would hold its 6th session in Geneva starting 10 January 2000.

---

10. For more on relevant developments within the SC, see *supra* n. 6.
11. Convention 182.
12. http://www.igc.org/hrw/campaigns/crp/montedec.htm.
13. See 'Children of War', Rädda Barnen, No. 4/99, December 1999, p. 3.
14. 'Children of War', A newsletter on child soldiers from Rädda Barnen, No. 3/99, October 1999, p. 2.
15. OAU Doc. CAB/LEG/24.9/49 (1990).

3.   WAR CRIMES COMMISSIONS

Group of Experts for Cambodia: The three-person Group of Experts for Cambodia was established by the UN Secretary-General in accordance with resolution 52/135 in July 1998 to investigate the possibility of bringing leaders of the Khmer Rouge to justice, before an international or national jurisdiction.[16] The Group, headed by the Australian, Sir Ninian Stephen, presented its report on 18 February 1999. It recommended that an *ad hoc* international criminal tribunal be established by the UN Security Council (or, if not, the General Assembly) to try Khmer Rouge leaders for crimes against humanity and genocide committed between 17 April 1975 and 7 January 1979. The Tribunal's Chief Prosecutor should be the Prosecutor of the ICTY/ICTR, assisted by a specially-appointed Deputy Prosecutor. Since this report was delivered, some progress has been made in efforts to establish a Tribunal for Cambodia.

Commission for Kosovo: Under a Swedish initiative, an independent, international commission to investigate the crisis in Kosovo was formed in August 1999, consisting of 12 members and headed by the South African, Richard Goldstone. 'The commission's task is to try and ascertain what happened in the Kosovo crisis before, during and after the war … [and] analyze the war's effects on the victimization and driving out of people.'[17] The Commission, which is supported by the UN Secretary-General, began its work in September 1999 and will release its final report in September 2000.

Commission for East Timor: On 16 November 1999, the UN Economic and Social Council voted to establish a five-person international Commission of Inquiry to examine issues of respect for human rights and humanitarian law in East Timor, headed by the Costa Rican, Sonia Picado Sotela. The Commission's report will be presented to the Secretary-General in due course. During a visit to East Timor from 25 November to 8 December 1999, the Commission heard evidence of serious violations of humanitarian law committed during a systematic campaign of intimidation and terror, including killings, sexual abuse and rape and destruction of civilian property. It emphasised the need to act against impunity and for the continuation of the investigatory process into allegations of atrocities with a view to bringing those responsible to justice.[18]

---

16. Report of the Group of Experts for Cambodia, A/53/850, S/1999/231, para. 6.

17. 'Swedish MP announces formation of independent Kosovo investigation', Associated Press, 6 August 1999. The Commission's website is at http://Kosovocommission.org/.

18. 'International Commission of Inquiry on East Timor Concludes Session in Geneva', UN Press Release, HR/99/120, 14 December 1999.

4.   AMNESTIES, TRUTH AND RECONCILIATION COMMISSIONS

Algeria: A law of 13 July 1999[19] regarding the reestablishment of civil harmony grants concessions to persons implicated in terrorist or subversive acts, who convey their willingness to desist from further criminal acts. Chapter I, Article 2, provides that such persons shall benefit from either exoneration from punishment, the placing under probation, or the attenuation of penalties. However, the amnesty does not apply to persons who have been involved in murder, rape or bomb attacks on public areas.

Guatemala: On 26 February 1999, the truth commission established to investigate human rights and humanitarian law violations committed in Guatemala during the decades-long conflict published its report.[20] The Commission for Historical Clarification was established through the accord of Oslo on 23 June 1994 to clarify the history of the events of more than three decades of war. It could not name abusers and its findings have no judicial effect. Rather than focusing on individual criminal responsibility, it looked at institutional responsibility, particularly of the Guatemalan state and armed forces but also of the rebels and outside actors, including the US. The report concluded that an estimated 200,000 people were killed or disappeared. State forces were responsible for 93 percent of the violations documented, the guerrillas for three percent. Eighty-three percent of the victims were Mayan. Most importantly, the report found that agents of the state of Guatemala committed genocide against the Mayan people, during counterinsurgency operations, and that these acts were not investigated or punished by Guatemala, despite its obligations under the Genocide Convention. Finally, the report proposed a Guatemalan presidential commission to purge the military of human rights violators and called for justice in connection with crimes excepted from the 1996 Amnesty Law.

Sierra Leone: The Lomé Peace Agreement[21] was signed on 7 July 1999, ending eight and a half years of civil war. It grants an unconditional pardon and blanket amnesty to all combatants, including members of the government and rebel forces, and provides for power-sharing with the rebels. While the UN signed the Peace Agreement and has welcomed the end to the conflict, the UN's Special Representative, in signing the accord, made an oral disclaimer that the amnesties given in the Peace Agreement did not apply to crimes against humanity, genocide

---

19. Loi no. 99-08 du 29 Rabi El Aoul 1420 correspondant au 13 juillet 1999 relative au rétablissement de la concorde civile.

20. Guatemala: Memoria del Silencio. Available online at http://hrdata.aaas.org/ceh/index.html (Spanish only). An English language summary is available at http://hrdata.aaas.org /ceh/report/english/toc.html.

21. Peace Agreement between the Government of Sierra Leone and the Revolutionary United Front of Sierra Leone. Available online at http://www.sierra-leone.gov.sl/peace_agreement.htm.

and war crimes.[22] The Agreement also provides for the establishment of a national Truth and Reconciliation Commission,[23] which is in the process of being established, with the help of the UN High Commissioner for Human Rights. The UN is also considering establishing its own Commission of Inquiry for Sierra Leone, and has hinted that it might even undertake international prosecutions at a later stage.[24]

South Africa: The five-volume final report of the South Africa Truth and Reconciliation Commission (TRC) was presented to then-President Nelson Mandela on 29 October 1998. An additional volume will be added once the Amnesty Committee completes its report.

While the TRC Report does not attempt to identity the nature of the conflicts in southern Africa from the perspective of humanitarian law, it indicates that it was guided by the principles of humanitarian law. However, it does not qualify the violations committed during the course of the conflicts as breaches of humanitarian law but as violations of human rights.[25] The Commission makes findings on specific incidents, and refers to the commission of gross human rights violations, such as the use of fragmentation bombs in attacks on civilian targets. The language speaks of humanitarian law violations although there is no reference to violations of humanitarian law. The reason for the TRC's reluctance to qualify the crimes as humanitarian law violations may be explained by its view that humanitarian law was of itself inadequate to address all the problems with which it had to deal. 'The Commission found the Geneva Conventions and its various protocols to be of great assistance, but believes that there is still more that could be added.'[26]

---

22. UN Secretary-General Kofi Annan stated: 'I instructed my Special Representative to sign the agreement with the explicit provision that the United Nations holds the understanding that the amnesty and pardon in article IX of the agreement shall not apply to international crimes of genocide, crimes against humanity, war crimes and other serious violations of international humanitarian law'. UN Doc. S/1999/836, p. 2, para. 7.

23. Art. XXVI of the Peace Agreement calls for the establishment of a Truth and Reconciliation Commission to 'address impunity, break the cycle of violence, provide a forum for both the victims and perpetrators of human rights violations to tell their story, get a clear picture of the past in order to facilitate genuine healing.' The Truth and Reconciliation Act is at http://www.sierra-leone.org/trc.html.

24. See A. McDonald, 'Sierra Leone's Uneasy Peace: the amnesties granted in the Lomé Peace Agreement and the UN's dilemma', 13 *Humanitäres Völkerrecht* (2000), pp. 11-26.

25. TRC Report, Vol. 1, p. 76.

26. TRC Report, Vol. 5, p. 348. See further, J. Dugard at p. 254 of this volume.

5.   INTERNATIONAL TRIBUNALS

5.1   **The International Criminal Tribunal for the Former Yugoslavia**

The past year has seen the ICTY come into its own, with several more accused in custody, new indictments, and a number of new Judgements. There are several new faces at the top, with Carla del Ponte replacing Louise Arbour as Chief Prosecutor of both Tribunals,[27] and a new President, Claude Jorda.[28] Despite considerable progress, the Tribunal experienced ongoing problems of cooperation, with both the Federal Republic of Yugoslavia, Croatia and Bosnia and Herzegovina being reported to the Security Council for refusing to surrender indicted persons.[29]

On 27 May 1999, Louise Arbour announced the indictment of Slobodan Milosević under Article 7(1) and (3) for crimes against humanity and violations of the laws or customs of war for acts of murder, persecution and deportation committed in Kosovo. Four other senior Yugoslav figures were indicted.[30] Further indictments relating to events in Kosovo are expected, including possibly against the Kosovo Liberation Army.[31] The paramilitary leader, Zeljko 'Arkan' Raznatović was also indicted.[32]

SFOR arrested seven accused, including three Generals charged in secret indictments: Radislav Kristić, Momir Talić and Stanislav Galić, the latter two who were charged with genocide. Another accused, Vinko Martinović, aka 'Stela', was surrendered to the Tribunal by Croatia.

By the end of December 1999, the ICTY had custody of 33 indicted persons out of a total of 67 publicly accused. One accused, Drazen Erdemović, had been transferred to Norway to serve his sentence and two were released pending appeal: one, Zejnil Delalić, after being acquitted, and the other, Zlatko Aleksovski, because his time in detention on remand and during trial exceeded his sentence. Five judgements had been rendered (Tadić, Čelebići, Furundžjia, Aleksovski and Jelisić), and eight sentences (Erdemović, Tadić, Mucić, Delić, Landžo, Furundžjia, Aleksovski and Jelisić), although only the Erdemović case had been completely

---

27. She was appointed by the Security Council on 11 August 1999 and officially took up her post on 15 September 1999. SC Res. 1259 (1999), 11 August 1999.

28. He was sworn in on 24 November 1999.

29. See *inter alia*, 'Letter from President McDonald to the President of the Security Council Concerning Outstanding Issues of State Non-Compliance', ICTY Press Release, JL/P.I.S./444-E, The Hague, 2 November 1999; Letter from Judge Gabrielle Kirk McDonald, the President of the International Criminal Tribunal for the Former Yugoslavia, to the President of the United Nations Security Council, Concerning Croatia, JL/P.I.S./438-E, The Hague, 29 September 1999.

30. *Prosecutor* v. *Slobodan Milosević, Milan Milutinović, Nikola Sainović, Dragoljub Ojdanić* and *Vlajko Stojiljković,* IT-99-37, 23 May 1999.

31. A. Franco, 'Carla Del Ponte, procureur au TPIY, engage trois enquêtes au Kosovo, dont une sur l'UCK', *Le Monde*, 22 December 1999; Statement by Carla Del Ponte (...) on the Investigation and Prosecution of Crimes Committed in Kosovo, ICTY Press Release, PR/P.I.S./437-E, 29 September 1999; UN War Crimes Prosecutor Sets Out Kosovo Strategy', Reuters, 29 September 1999.

32. IT-97-27.

concluded. While an appeals decision was rendered in Tadić, he remained in Tribunal custody, appealing his new sentence. Eight accused had been convicted, and one acquitted.[33] The following outlines of the most recent decisions highlight their most interesting or significant points.

5.1.1   Čelebići *Decision and Sentences, 16 November 1998*

The four accused, three Bosnian Muslims and a Bosnian Croat, were charged in connection with crimes committed against Bosnian Serbs at the Čelebići detention camp. In a decision of 16 November 1998,[34] three of the four accused were convicted; one, Zejnil Delalić, who was charged solely under Article 7(3), was found not to have exercised superior control and was acquitted on all counts and released. Zdravko Mucić was found guilty under Article 7(1) and (3) and convicted on 11 out of 13 counts – two were dismissed – and sentenced to concurrent seven year sentences. Hazim Delić was convicted on 13 out of 38 counts, including four counts of rape as torture, found not-guilty on 22 counts and three counts were dismissed. The Trial Chamber found that he could not be held criminally liable as a superior as the Prosecutor had failed to show beyond a reasonable doubt that he 'lay within the chain of command in the Čelebići prison-camp, with the power to issue orders to subordinates or to prevent or punish criminal acts of subordinates'.[35] He received several concurrent sentences, the maximum being 20 years. Esad Landžo was found to have been personally responsible under Article 7(1) and convicted on 17 counts, found not guilty on four, and three were dismissed. He received several concurrent sentences, the maximum being 15 years. All three convicted and the Prosecution are appealing, the latter the acquittal of Delalić as well.

The decision of the Trial Chamber is significant for several reasons. It is the first decision of the Tribunal to pronounce on command responsibility – three of the four defendants were charged under Article 7(3) of the ICTY Statute for crimes committed by their subordinates. It is also the first to deal with rape, including rape as torture. There are many additional points of interest.

5.1.1.1   Nature of the conflict and the grave breaches regime

In considering the conditions for the applicability of Article 2 of the ICTY Statute, dealing with grave breaches, the Trial Chamber, taking note of the earlier recognition by the Appeals Chamber in *Tadić* that a change in the customary law scope of the grave breaches regime may be occurring,[36] seemed to go even further,

---

33. The latest figures are available online at http://www.un.org/icty/glance/fact.htm.

34. *Prosecutor* v. *Zejnil Delalić, Zdravko Mucić also known as "Pavo", Hazim Delić,* and *Esad Landžo also known as "Zenga"*, Case No. IT-96-21-T, Judgement, 16 November 1998.

35. Ibid., para. 810, p. 289.

36. *Prosecutor* v. *Tadić*, Decision on the Defence Motion for Interlocutory Appeal on Jurisdiction, 2 Oct. 1995, IT-94-1-AR72, para. 83.

if tentatively, stating that 'the possibility that customary law has developed the provisions of the Geneva Conventions since 1949 to constitute an extension of the system of "grave breaches" to internal armed conflicts should be recognised'.[37] However, the Chamber found it unnecessary to make a specific finding on the question of whether Article 2 can only be applied in international armed conflict, or whether it could also be applied in internal conflicts, as it found the conflict in Bosnia and Herzegovina as a whole to be an international armed conflict, primarily involving the Bosnian Serb Army (VRS), acting on behalf of the Federal Republic of Yugoslavia (FRY), and the Government of Bosnia and Herzegovina. Unlike the majority of the Trial Chamber in *Tadić*, which found the conflict in Bosnia between the VRS and the Bosnian Army to be an internal armed conflict, because Belgrade did not exercise the necessary control over the VRS, the Chamber in *Čelebići* recognised that the VRS was merely a cover for the Yugoslav Army.[38] Finding that the determination of the character of the conflict was not *res judicata*, and that it was not bound by earlier decisions of other Trial Chambers, the Chamber noted that it should also not rely on the findings of the ICJ in *Nicaragua*.[39] According to the Chamber, 'the question which arises is one of continuity of control of particular forces'.[40] The FRY never severed its link with the VRS, whose creation was a 'deliberate attempt to mask the continued involvement of the FRY in the conflict while its Government remained in fact the controlling force behind the Bosnian Serbs'.[41]

The Chamber also found the Bosnian Serb victims to be protected persons under the Fourth Geneva Convention, despite the fact that technically they were of the same nationality as the Bosnian Government forces who were detaining them. In applying the *Nottebohm* test of 'effective link', the Chamber stated that 'the International Tribunal may choose to refuse to recognise (or give effect to) a State's grant of its nationality to individuals for the purposes of applying international law'.[42] Even if the Bosnian Serbs had been given Bosnian nationality, there may be an insufficient link between the Bosnian Serbs and the state for them to be considered as Bosnian nationals. The Chamber emphasised 'the necessity of considering the requirements of article 4 of the Fourth Geneva Convention in a more flexible manner. The provisions of domestic legislation on citizenship in a situation of violent

---

37. See also *Čelebići* Judgement, *supra* n. 34 at para. 317, where the Chamber, in finding that violations of common Article 3 gives rise to individual criminal responsibility under Article 3 of the ICTY Statute, stated: 'Recognising that this would entail an extension of the concept of "grave breaches of the Geneva Conventions" in line with a more teleological interpretation, it is the view of this Trial Chamber that violations of common Article 3 may fall more logically within Article 2 of the Statute. Nonetheless, for the present purposes, the more cautious approach has been followed.'

38. Ibid., para. 226.

39. Ibid., para. 230.

40. Ibid., para. 231.

41. Ibid., para. 234.

42. Ibid., para. 259.

State succession cannot be determinative of the protected status of persons caught up in conflicts which ensue from such events.'[43]

5.1.1.2   Command responsibility

The Trial Chamber affirmed that 'the principle of individual criminal responsibility of superiors for failure to prevent or repress the crimes committed by subordinates forms part of customary international law'.[44] Superiors have a legal duty to 'take all necessary and reasonable measures to prevent the commission of offences by their subordinates or, if such crimes have been committed, to punish the perpetrators thereof'.[45]

The Chamber accepted that 'individuals in positions of authority, whether civilian or within military structures, may incur criminal responsibility under the doctrine of command responsibility on the basis of their *de facto* as well as *de jure* positions as superiors'.[46] Civilians can be held responsible as superiors 'only to the extent that they exercise a degree of control over their subordinates which is similar to that of military commanders', although this can be *de facto* or *de jure*.[47] The Chamber did not impose a standard of strict liability,[48] but noted that in order for the principle of superior responsibility to apply, 'it is necessary that the superior have effective control over the persons (...) in the sense of having the material ability to prevent and punish the commission of these offences'.[49]

As for the mental element, 'knew or had reason to know', the Trial Chamber found, based on customary international law, that 'a superior may possess the *mens rea* required to incur criminal liability where: (1) he had actual knowledge, established through direct and circumstantial evidence, that his subordinates were committing or about to commit crimes referred to under Articles 2 to 5 of the Statute, or (2) where he had in his possession information of a nature, which at the least, would put him on notice of the risk of such offences (...)'.[50]

5.1.1.3   Rape and sexual assault

Delić was charged under Article 7(1) with, *inter alia*, six counts related to acts of sexual violence: two grave breaches (torture) and four violations of the laws or customs of war (two torture; two cruel treatment). These charges arose out of the alleged rape and sexual abuse of two victims by the accused.

---

43. Ibid., para. 263.
44. Ibid., para. 343.
45. Ibid., para. 394.
46. Ibid., para. 354.
47. Ibid., para. 378.
48. Ibid., para. 383.
49. Ibid.
50. Ibid., para. 383.

Delić and two other accused, Delalić and Mucić, were additionally charged with superior responsibility under Article 7(3) for forcing two detainees to perform fellatio with each other. For their acts and omissions in relation to this incident, each of the three was charged with one grave breach of the Geneva Conventions (inhuman treatment) and one violation of the laws or customs of war (cruel treatment).

The Chamber found Delić guilty of a grave breach (torture) and a violation of the laws or customs of war (torture) in respect of each victim. Two counts of violations of the laws or customs of war (cruel treatment), one in respect of each victim, were dismissed as they were charged in the alternative.

The Chamber adopted the broad definition of rape given in the *Akayesu* Judgement of the ICTR. As to the more substantive question whether rape can constitute torture, the Chamber answered in the affirmative, guided by the jurisprudence of regional and international human rights bodies and the finding in *Akayesu*.[51] According to the Judgement, rape can constitute torture, either as a grave breach or a violation of common Article 3, and the characteristics of the offence do not differ in each case.[52] The prohibition on torture, including rape, is absolute and non-derogable in all circumstances. It is a norm of *jus cogens*.[53] The Chamber noted that 'it is difficult to envisage circumstances in which rape, by, or at the instigation of a public official, or with the consent or acquiescence of an official, could be considered as occurring for a purpose that does not, in some way, involve punishment, coercion, discrimination or intimidation. In the view of this Trial Chamber this is inherent in situations of armed conflict.'[54] Further, the violence suffered by the victims in the form of rapes and sexual violence was inflicted on them because they are women. '[T]his represents a form of discrimination which constitutes a prohibited purpose for the offence of torture'.[55]

As to the incident of fellatio, the Trial Chamber held that the act constituted 'at least, a fundamental attack on their [the victims'] human dignity. Accordingly, the Trial Chamber finds that this act constitutes the offence of inhuman treatment under Article 2 of the Statute, and cruel treatment under Article 3 of the Statute.' Finally, '[t]he Trial Chamber notes that the aforementioned act could constitute rape for which liability could have been found in the appropriate manner.'[56]

5.1.2   Furundžija *Decision and Sentence, 10 December 1998*

On 10 December 1998, Trial Chamber II rendered its judgement in the case of *Prosecutor* v. *Anto Furundžija*, a Bosnian Croat paramilitary leader accused of crimes against Bosnian Muslims.

---

51. Ibid., para. 489.
52. Ibid., para. 443.
53. Ibid., para. 454.
54. Ibid., para. 495.
55. Ibid., paras. 941, 963.
56. Ibid., para. 1066.

5.1.2.1   Rape and sexual assault

Originally charged with three counts of sexual violence, *inter alia*, these were reduced to two violations of the laws or customs of war (torture and outrages upon personal dignity including rape) after a grave breach charge of torture and inhumane treatment was withdrawn by the Prosecutor, 'in the interests of a fair and expeditious trial and the judicial economy of the Trial Chamber'.[57] The accused was found guilty on both of the charges. The Chamber found that the elements of torture were met, as were the elements of rape. In relation to the torture charge, while Furundžija did not personally rape the victim, he was found by the Trial Chamber to be 'a co-perpetrator by virtue of his interrogation of her as an integral part of the torture'.[58] Further, 'it is the view of the Trial Chamber that any form of captivity vitiates consent'.[59]

In relation to the second charge, the Trial Chamber was satisfied that the elements of rape were met. The Chamber found that the witness 'suffered severe physical and mental pain, along with public humiliation (…) in what amounted to outrages upon her personal dignity and sexual integrity'.[60] The accused did not personally rape the victim, so he could not be considered as a co-perpetrator for the purposes of liability for an outrage on human dignity, including rape. However, the Chamber found that '[t]he accused's presence and continued interrogation of Witness A encouraged Accused B and substantially contributed to the criminal acts committed by him.'[61] The Chamber thus found him guilty of aiding and abetting the rape.[62]

The Judgement noted that rape is criminalised as a crime against humanity in the ICTY Statute, but that it can also 'amount to a grave breach of the Geneva Conventions, a violation of the laws or customs of war or an act of genocide, if the requisite elements are met, and may be prosecuted accordingly'.[63] The Chamber departed from *Akayesu* and *Čelebiči* in defining rape narrowly. 'It is the sexual penetration, however slight, of the vagina, anus or mouth of the victim by the penis of the perpetrator or by any other object, by coercion or force or threat of force against the victim or a third person.'[64]

The Judges stated that not only rape but any serious sexual assault is punishable under international criminal law and that 'the distinction between them is one that is primarily material for the purposes of sentencing'.[65]

---

57. *Prosecutor v. Furundžija*, Case No. IT-95-17/1-T, Judgement, 10 December 1998, para. 7.
58. Ibid., para. 267.
59. Ibid., para. 271.
60. Ibid., para. 272.
61. Ibid., para. 273.
62. Ibid., para. 274.
63. Ibid., para. 172.
64. Ibid., para. 185.
65. Ibid., para. 186.

5.1.3   Aleksovski *Decision and Sentence, 7 May 1999*

On 7 May 1999, Trial Chamber I rendered its oral decision in the case of *Aleksovski*.[66] The accused, a Bosnian Croat camp commander, was charged on the basis of individual and command responsibility with two grave breaches (inhuman treatment and wilfully causing great suffering or serious injury to body or health) and one violation of the laws or customs of war (outrages upon personal dignity).

5.1.3.1   Nature of the conflict and the grave breaches regime

The two grave breaches were dismissed as the majority found the conflict to have been non-international in character and the victims not to have been protected persons. There must be 'some evidence of the control, direction or command of the State that is sufficiently strong to impute the rebel force's acts to it. The requisite degree of control depends on the circumstances of each case.'[67] However, the Prosecutor did not prove that 'during the time-period and in the place of the indictment, the HVO [Bosnian Croat Army] was in fact under the overall control of the HV [Croatian Army] in carrying out the armed conflict against Bosnia and Herzegovina. The majority (...) finds that the HVO was not a *de facto* agent of Croatia, and that there was no indirect involvement of that country in the armed conflict in Bosnia and Herzegovina.'

The majority also found that protected persons are those who are defined as such in Article 4 of the Geneva Conventions, that is, 'the victim must hold a nationality different from that of his captors'.[68] '[T]he majority of the Trial Chamber finds that the Bosnian Muslim civilian detainees were not protected persons within the meaning of Article 4 of Geneva Convention IV because they hold the same nationality as their captors'.[69]

Judge Rodrigues, dissenting, stated that the evidence supported finding that the conflict was international. However, even if this were not the case, the international character of the conflict is not a condition for Article 2 to apply.

Judge Rodrigues found that the conflicts in Bosnia and Herzegovina at the relevant time should be considered globally, as an international armed conflict, and concurred with the *Čelebiči* Judgment and the Dissenting Opinion of Judge McDonald in *Tadić* that the *Nicaragua* test was not the appropriate one to apply by a court charged with ascertaining individual criminal responsibility, rather than state responsibility.[70] In any event, the international character of the conflict is not

---

66. The written judgement and sentence were issued later: *Prosecutor* v. *Zlatko Aleksovski*, Case No. IT-95-14/1-T, Judgement, 25 June 1999.

67. Judgment, para. 14 of Joint Opinion of the Majority, Judge Vohrah and Judge Nieto-Navia, on the Applicability of Article 2 of the Statute pursuant to Paragraph 46 of the Judgment.

68. Ibid., para. 30.

69. Ibid., para. 34.

70. Paras. 21-22 of his Dissenting opinion.

a condition for Article 2 of the Statute to apply since it is autonomous in relation to the Geneva Conventions.[71] '[In] addition, (...) the development of the rules of customary law since 1949 tends to advocate the extension of the grave breaches system to internal conflicts and, accordingly, to reinforce the autonomy of Article 2 of the Statute in relation to the Geneva Conventions.'[72]

The Chamber found Aleksovski guilty under Article 7(1) and (3) for a violation of the laws or customs of war (outrages upon personal dignity), for the physical and psychological maltreatment of detainees. He was sentenced to two years and six months imprisonment. Considering that he had been in detention for two years, ten months and 29 days, he was immediately released, notwithstanding any appeal. The Prosecutor appealed.

5.1.4   Tadić *Appeals Decision and Sentence, 15 July 1999*

5.1.4.1   Nature of the conflict

On the nature of the conflict, the Appeals Chamber reversed the decision of the Trial Chamber of 7 May 1997, and found that it was an international armed conflict at the relevant time, the victims to be protected persons and Article 2 to be applicable. In order to consider the conflict as international, the Bosnian Serbs would have to be seen as belonging to a party to the conflict, in this case, the FRY. '[I]t appears that international rules and State practice therefore require control over them by a Party to an international armed conflict and, by the same token, a relationship of dependence and allegiance of these irregulars *vis-à-vis* that Party to the conflict'.[73]

As regards the degree of control necessary, the Appeals Chamber disagreed with the Trial Chamber, finding the test of 'effective control' enunciated in the *Nicaragua* case not to be persuasive. The Chamber distinguished between two situations: that of 'individuals acting on behalf of a State without specific instructions', and that of 'individuals making up *an organised and hierarchically structured group*, such as a military unit, or, in case of war or civil strife, armed bands of irregulars or rebels'. 'For the attribution to a State of acts of these groups it is sufficient to require that the group as a whole be under the overall control of the State.'[74] 'The control required by international law may be deemed to exist when a State (or, in the context of an armed conflict, the Party to the conflict) *has a role in organising, coordinating or planning the military actions* of the military group, in addition to financing, training and equipping or providing operational support to that group.'[75] If an organised group 'is under the overall control of a State, it must

---

71. Ibid., para. 42.

72. Ibid., para. 44.

73. *Prosecutor* v. *Duško Tadić*, Case No. IT-94-1-A, Appeals Chamber, Judgement, 15 July 1999, para. 94.

74. Ibid., para. 120.

75. Ibid., para. 137.

perforce engage the responsibility of that State for its activities, *whether or not each of them was specifically imposed, requested or directed by the State*.[76] This finding is supported by state practice.

Where the controlling state is not the territorial state where the armed conflict occurs, 'more extensive and compelling evidence is required to show that the State is genuinely in control of the units or groups not merely by financing and equipping them, but also by generally directing or helping plan their actions'.[77] However, '[w]here the controlling State in question is an adjacent State with territorial ambitions on the State where the conflict is taking place, and the controlling State is attempting to achieve its territorial enlargement through the armed forces which it controls, it may be easier to establish the threshold.'[78]

The Appeals Chamber found that the FRY, through the Yugoslav Army [VJ], had exercised the requisite overall control over the VRS,[79] and noted that the Trial Chamber had placed undue emphasis upon 'the ostensible structures and overt declarations of the belligerents, as opposed to a nuanced analysis of the reality of their relationship (…)'.[80] It warned that such an approach 'may tacitly suggest to groups who are in *de facto* control of military forces that responsibility for the acts of such forces can be evaded merely by resort to a superficial restructuring of such forces or by a facile declaration that the reconstituted forces are henceforth independent of their erstwhile sponsors'.[81]

As to whether the victims were protected persons, the Appeals Chamber found that while the Bosnian Serbs had the same nationality as the victims, nationality alone is not determinative. More important is allegiance to a state and diplomatic protection. In modern conflicts, such as those in the former Yugoslavia, 'ethnicity may become determinative of national allegiance'.[82] In this case, the Bosnian Serb forces owed allegiance to the FRY and 'acted as *de facto* organs of another State, the FRY. Thus, (…) the victims were "protected persons" as they found themselves in the hands of armed forces of a State of which they were not nationals.'[83] 'In granting its protection, Article 4 intends to look to the substance of relations, not to their legal characterisation as such.'[84]

5.1.4.2   Other findings

The Chamber found that the Trial Chamber erred in acquitting Tadić of the killing of five men in Jaskići. The Chamber held that Tadić could be held responsible for the murders, even though there was no evidence that the armed group to which

---

76. Ibid., para. 122.
77. Ibid., para. 138.
78. Ibid., para. 140.
79. Ibid., para. 156.
80. Ibid., para. 154.
81. Ibid.
82. Ibid., para. 166.
83. Ibid., para. 167.
84. Ibid., para. 168.

he belonged committed them, or that he had personally committed them, based on the doctrine of common purpose.[85]

The Chamber also overturned the finding by the Trial Chamber that a crime against humanity must not have been carried out for the purely personal motives of the perpetrator. To qualify acts as crimes against humanity under the ICTY Statute, the specific acts must be related to the attack upon the civilian population (during an armed conflict) and the perpetrator must know that his acts are so related.[86] However, the Appeals Chamber said that Article 5 did not require 'as a substantive element of *mens rea*, a nexus between the specific acts allegedly committed by the accused and the armed conflict, or to require proof of the accused's *motives*'.[87]

Finally, the Appeals Chamber also reversed the finding of the Trial Chamber that discriminatory intent is an element of all crimes against humanity and not just persecution. It found that '[s]uch an intent is an indispensible legal ingredient of the offence only with regard to those crimes for which this is expressly required, that is, for Article 5(h), concerning various types of persecution.'[88]

On 11 November 1999, the Trial Chamber handed down new sentences for the additional nine counts on which Tadić had been found guilty by the Appeals Chamber of between six and 25 years. These sentences, which will be served concurrently, increase Tadić's time in detention by five years. Tadić appealed the increase in his sentence.

5.1.5 Jelisić *Decision and Sentence, 19 October 1999*

Goran Jelisić, a *de facto* commander of the Luka detention camp, originally pleaded not-guilty to all the charges against him at his initial appearance on 26 January 1998. On 29 October 1998, he changed his plea, pleading guilty to all the counts of crimes against humanity and violations of the laws and customs of war, and not-guilty to genocide.

The accused was acquitted of genocide by the Trial Chamber *proprio motu* on 19 October 1999, in an oral judgment. The written decision was issued on 14 December.[89] The Chamber found that although the material basis of genocide had been established, namely, the murder of a given group, the Prosecutor had failed to prove beyond a reasonable doubt that Jelisić had acted with the required intent to destroy in whole or in part a national, ethnic or religious group.

According to the Trial Chamber, in order to establish Jelisić's genocidal intent, the Prosecutor had to prove that either Jelisić was an executioner, a participant to a genocidal project, or that he himself had committed genocide. However, the Trial Chamber found that neither had been established. The Chamber was not satisfied

---

85. Ibid., at paras. 185-229.
86. Ibid., para. 271.
87. Ibid., para. 272.
88. Ibid., para. 305.
89. *The Prosecutor* v. *Goran Jelisić,* Case No. IT-95-10-I, Judgement, 14 December 1999.

that genocide was carried out in the Brcko region.[90] However, it did note that 'international custom (…) admits the characterisation of genocide even when the exterminatory intent only extends to a limited geographic zone',[91] provided that a substantial part of the group is destroyed.[92] Further, Jelisić's declarations and actions could not be interpreted as an expression of specific genocidal intent. According to the Chamber, Jelisić's behaviour, while clearly odious and discriminatory, was 'opportunistic and inconsistent'[93] and that 'he killed arbitrarily rather than with the clear intention to destroy a group'.[94]

However, it found that he had sufficient discriminatory intent against Bosnian Muslims and Bosnian Croats to be guilty of persecution, a crime against humanity, and 30 other crimes against humanity and violations of the laws or customs of war, relating to 13 murders, the beating of four people and plunder.

It is interesting that the Chamber found Jelisić guilty of violations of the laws and customs of war despite the fact that there was no evidence that he had belonged to a police, military or paramilitary unit, and his status and link to the armed forces was unclear. Indeed, the question of the accused's position was not considered in any depth in the Judgement. While the Chamber found that Jelisić exercised *de facto* authority over the camp detainees, 'no element establishing the chain of command within which he operated [was] presented'.[95] It may be that the Chamber assumed that the fact that the crimes were committed against prisoners of war established a link between the accused and the conflict. However, the Judgement fails to explicate the Chamber's legal reasoning on this point.

Jelisić was sentenced to 40 years imprisonment, the stiffest sentence the Tribunal had handed down thus far. It found that the aggravating factors in his case, particularly the 'revolting, bestial and sadistic nature of his behaviour', and the fact that the self-designated 'Serb Adolf' had committed his crimes with such enthusiasm, outweighed mitigating factors such as his age at the time of the crimes, his young family, his personality disorder, and his guilty plea. The Judges were not convinced by his professions of remorse. The Judges diverged from the ICTY's sentencing practice up till then by issuing only a single sentence for all 31 counts, considering that although the crimes had been qualified as both crimes against humanity and war crimes, they were both part of a single set of criminal acts. Both the Prosecutor and the accused have appealed.

5.2   The International Criminal Tribunal for Rwanda

Business was also brisk at the Rwanda Tribunal. As of December 1999, the ICTR had taken custody of 38 accused persons while another two were awaiting transfer

---

90. Ibid., paras. 98, 108.
91. Ibid., para. 83.
92. Ibid., para. 82.
93. Ibid., at para. 105.
94. Ibid., para. 108.
95. Ibid., para. 96.

to the Tribunal. The accused and convicted include senior political leaders. An indictment against one accused, Bernard Ntuyahaga, was withdrawn at the request of the Prosecutor, and the accused's release was ordered.[96] Ntuyahaga, who surrendered himself to the Tribunal in July 1998, is wanted by both Rwanda and Belgium for the deaths of the ten Belgian peacekeepers of UNAMIR in 1994, the wilful killing of the then-Prime Minister of Rwanda, Mrs Agathe Uwilingiyimana, and crimes against other Rwandans, and is currently being held by Tanzania pending resolution of the extradition requests. Several arrests of high government officials were made, and by the end of the year, the Tribunal had custody of 11 members of the former Interim Government.

While the Prosecutor's application for a joint trial of 29 accused was rejected in March 1999, several joint trials will go ahead, including the so-called 'Politician's trial', which groups former Minister of the Interior, Edouard Karemera, and other government officials and which will be prosecuted by Carla Del Ponte herself; the 'media trial', which includes Ferdinand Nahimana and Hassan Ngeze, and the 'military trial' of Théoneste Bagasora, former Chef de Cabinet at the Rwandan Defence Ministry, and three other senior commanders in the Rwandan Army. On 6 October 1999, the Trial Chamber gave the green light for the so-called 'Butare' trial, the largest so far, consisting of six defendants. One of them, Pauline Nyiramasuhuko, became the first woman ever to be charged with rape by an international criminal court, when her indictment was amended to include charges of rape as a crime against humanity and a war crime on 10 August 1999.

Five judgements had been rendered by the Tribunal – in the cases of Akayesu, Kambanda, Serushago, Kayishema and Ruzindana and Rutaganda – leading to six convictions. All of the accused appealed.

5.2.1 Serushago *Sentencing Judgement, 5 February 1999*

On 5 February 1999, Omar Serushago, a former leader of the *Interahamwe* militia, who surrendered himself to police in the Ivory Coast in June of 1998, was sentenced to 15 years for genocide.[97] On 14 December 1998, he had pleaded guilty to four counts of genocide and three of crimes against humanity. Serushago pleaded not-guilty to a fifth count, for rape. That charge was then withdrawn by the Prosecutor. His sentence is in sharp contrast to the life sentence received by the only other accused to plead guilty, Jean Kambanda, the former prime minister. Judge Laity Kama said that Serushago deserved some clemency because of his voluntary surrender, his cooperation with the Prosecutor and his expression of remorse. Serushago appealed his sentence.

---

96. ICTR Press Release, ICTR/UPD/014, Arusha, 18 March 1999.
97. The Prosecutor v. Omar Serushago, Case no. ICTR 98-39-5, Sentence, 5 February 1999.

5.2.2   Kayishema and Ruzindana *Judgment, 21 May 1999*

In the second conviction at trial of the ICTR, the two accused were found guilty of genocide.[98] Clément Kayishema was convicted on four counts of genocide. He was acquitted of eight crimes against humanity (murder and extermination) because these charges were subsumed by the genocide charges, acquitted of four other crimes against humanity (other inhumane acts), four violations of common Article 3 of the Geneva Conventions and four violations of Additional Protocol II. Thus, Kayishema was convicted on only four out of a total of 24 counts. Obed Ruzindana was convicted on one of six charges against him. The Court found him guilty of genocide but not guilty of two crimes against humanity (murder and extermination), on the ground that these charges were fully subsumed by the genocide count. It also acquitted him of a further crime against humanity (inhumane acts), one violation of common Article 3 and one violation of Additional Protocol II. Ruzindana is currently awaiting a second trial on charges of genocide.[99]

Kayishema, the Prefect of Kibuye at the time of the genocide, was sentenced to four concurrent terms of life imprisonment for the remainder of his life, the first time the Tribunal has given such a sentence. This sentence is 'distinct from a "life sentence" under the laws of most national jurisdictions. The Chamber gives the phrase "remainder of his life" under Rule 101(A) its plain meaning.'[100] Ruzindana, formerly a commercial trader, was sentenced to 25 years imprisonment. It is worth looking at why the Chamber acquitted the accused of so many counts.

5.2.2.1   The relationship between the armed conflict, the crimes and the accused

As regards the counts alleging violations of Common Article 3 and the separate counts charging violations of Additional Protocol II, the Chamber found that the accused could not held guilty for several reasons. While there was an armed conflict in Rwanda at the time the crimes were committed, between the Government forces and the Rwandan Patriotic Front, and common Article 3 and Additional Protocol II were in fact applicable to the crimes committed during that conflict, the crimes ascribed to the accused were not related to the conflict, but were carried out in the course of the genocide. No direct link between the crimes and the conflict was established by the Prosecutor. Indeed, there was no armed conflict in Kibuye Prefecture, where the crimes were committed, and there was no evidence that the civilian population at the sites in question was affected by military operations which were underway in other parts of Rwanda. 'The term "nexus" should not be understood as something vague and indefinite. A direct connection between the alleged crimes, referred to in the Indictment, and the armed conflict should be established factually. The Prosecutor must show that material provisions of

---

98. *The Prosecutor* v. *Clément Kayishema and Obed Ruzindana,* Case No. ICTR-95-1-T, Judgement, 21 May 1999.

99. IT-96-10-T.

100. Ibid., para. 31 of Sentence.

Common Article 3 and Protocol II were violated and she has to produce the necessary evidence of these violations.'[101]

Furthermore, in order for Common Article 3 and Protocol II to be applicable, the accused must have had some connection with the armed conflict or the armed forces. However, neither of the accused were members of the armed forces, nor was there any evidence that they were in some other way supporting or involved in the armed conflict. 'It has not been shown that there was a link between the accused and the armed forces.'[102] Moreover, there was no evidence that the victims were connected to the armed conflict.[103]

5.2.2.2 Cumulative charging of crimes against humanity

On the question of cumulative charging, which resulted in Kayishema being acquitted of eight counts of crimes against humanity (murder and extermination), the Chamber found that in this case, the Prosecutor had relied on the same elements to prove these crimes as genocide. '[I]n the peculiar factual scenario in the present case, the crimes of genocide, extermination and murder overlap. Accordingly, there exists a *concur d'infractions par excellence* with regard to the three crimes in the present case.'[104] 'The scenario only allows for a finding of either genocide or extermination and/or murder. Therefore, because the crime of genocide is established against the accused persons, then they cannot simultaneously be convicted for murder and/or extermination, in this case. That would (…) amount to convicting the accused person twice for the same offence.'[105]

On the remaining crimes against humanity (other inhumane acts) charges, the Trial Chamber found that the Prosecutor had not discharged her burden. '[T]he Prosecutor failed to particularise the nature of the acts that she relied on for the charge of "other inhumane" acts.'[106] Nor did the Indictment specify the nature and extent of the accused's responsibility for the other inhumane acts. 'Accordingly, the fundamental rights of both the accused, namely to be informed of the charges against him [sic] and to be in a position to prepare his defence in due time with complete knowledge of the matter, has been disregarded in relation to all the counts of crimes against humanity for other inhumane acts. A right that is particularly important considering the gravity of the charges.'[107]

---

101. Ibid., para. 604.
102. Ibid., para. 623.
103. Ibid., para. 603.
104. Ibid., para. 647.
105. Ibid., para. 649.
106. Ibid., para. 584.
107. Ibid., para. 587.

5.2.2.3   Command responsibility

Kayishema was charged with command responsibility under Article 6(3) as well as individual criminal responsibility under Article 6(1). Ruzindana was charged only under Article 6(1).

Despite the fact that Kayishema was a civilian and not a military person, the Chamber found that he could be held responsible under Article 6(3).[108] The Chamber concurred with the *Čelebiá* Judgement that 'powers of influence not amounting to formal powers of command provide a sufficient basis for the imposition of command responsibility.'[109] The Chamber stressed the need to look beyond legal formalism at the actual facts of a particular situation.[110] '[A]cts or omissions of a *de facto* superior can give rise to individual criminal responsibility pursuant to Article 6(3) of the Statute. Thus, no legal or formal position of authority need exist between the accused and the perpetrators of the crimes. Rather, the influence that an individual exercises over the perpetrators of the crime may provide sufficient grounds for the imposition of command responsibility if it can be shown that such influence was used to order the commission of the crime or that, despite such *de facto* influence, the accused failed to prevent the crime.'[111]

The Chamber noted the approach taken in the *Čelebiá* case and in the Statute of the ICC, which is less strict than that adopted in the post-WWII cases. A distinction is drawn between military and non-military commanders. The former are subject to a more active duty to inform themselves of the activities of their subordinates when they, 'knew or, owing to the circumstances at the time, should have known that the forces were committing or about to commit such crimes. This is juxtaposed with the *mens rea* element demanded of all other superiors who must have, "[known], or consciously disregarded information which clearly indicated, that the subordinates were committing or about to commit such crimes."'[112] However, '[t]he principle of command responsibility must only apply to those superiors who exercise effective control over their subordinates. This material ability to control the actions of subordinates is the touchstone of individual responsibility under Article 6(3).'[113]

The Chamber found beyond a doubt that Kayishema 'exercised clear, definitive control, both *de jure* and *de facto*, over the assailants at every massacre site set out in the Indictment. It has also been proved beyond a reasonable doubt that Kayishema ordered the attacks or, knowing of their imminence, failed to prevent them.'[114]

---

108. Ibid., para. 213.
109. Ibid., para. 220.
110. Ibid., para. 230.
111. Ibid., para. 492.
112. Ibid., para. 227.
113. Ibid., para. 229.
114. Ibid., para. 515.

5.2.2.4   Genocide

The Court reiterated the finding in *Akayesu* that 'the crime of genocide is considered part of customary international law and, moreover, a norm of *jus cogens*.'[115] While genocide is a type of crime against humanity, it is different from other crimes against humanity insofar as it requires a special intent to exterminate a protected group in whole or in part.[116]

The *dolus specialis* (special intent) to commit genocide must be formed 'prior to the commission of the genocidal acts. The individual acts themselves, however, do not require premeditation; the only consideration is that the act should be done in furtherance of the genocidal intent'.[117] The Chamber concurred with the finding in *Akayesu* that the requisite intent 'can be inferred from either words or deeds and may be demonstrated by a pattern of purposeful action'. The number of victims from the group is also important.[118] '[A]lthough a specific plan to destroy does not constitute an element of genocide, it would appear that it is not easy to carry out a genocide without such a plan, or organisation. It is unnecessary for an individual to have knowledge of all details of the genocidal plan or policy.'[119] The Chamber concurred with the *Akayesu* judgement and the ILC in finding that the entire group need not be destroyed in order to show that the perpetrator intended to destroy a group in whole or in part.[120] However, 'both proportionate scale and total number are relevant'. It is necessary to destroy at least a substantial number of the group or a significant section, such as its leadership.[121] 'The "destroying" has to be directed at the group *as such*, that is *qua group*, as stipulated in Article 2(2) of the Statute.'[122]

5.2.3   Barayagwiza *Appeals Decision, 3 November 1999*

In a decision of 3 November 1999,[123] the Appeals Chamber of the ICTR/ICTY concluded that a combination of delays in the pre-trial phase of the case against Jean-Bosco Barayagwiza must result in the dismissal of the charges against him. The Rwandan Government reacted furiously to the decision to release Barayagwiza, suspending its cooperation with the Tribunal and refusing a visa to Carla Del Ponte, the Chief Prosecutor.[124] That decision was later reversed when Barayagwiza's release was suspended after Mrs Del Ponte took the unprecedented step of filing

115. Ibid., para. 88.
116. Ibid., para. 89.
117. Ibid., para. 91.
118. Ibid., para. 93.
119. Ibid., para. 94.
120. Ibid., para. 95.
121. Ibid., paras. 96-97.
122. Ibid., para. 99.
123. *Jean-Bosco Barayagwiza* v. *The Prosecutor*, Case No. ICTR-97-19-AR72, Decision of the Appeals Chamber [on release of Barayagwiza], 3 November 1999.
124. 'Rwanda snubs tribunal prosecutor', BBC World, 11 November 1999.

a Notice asking the Appeals Court to review its Decision, based on new facts. The Appeals Chamber of the Tribunal, normally based in The Hague, would sit in Arusha for three days in February 2000 to hear the Prosecutor's request.

The Appellant, the former political director of Rwanda's Ministry of Foreign Affairs during the genocide and founding member of Radio Television des Libre Mille Collines, was first arrested and taken into custody on 15 April 1996 by Cameroon, apparently at the behest of Rwanda and Belgium, on suspicion of having committed genocide, conspiracy to commit genocide and crimes against humanity in Rwanda in 1994. He remained in the custody of Cameroon until 19 November 1997, at different times at the request of the ICTR Prosecutor, Rwanda and Belgium. During the second period of his incarceration in Cameroon at the request of the ICTR Prosecutor, he was held for nine months, under first Rule 40, then Rule 40*bis* pending transfer to the Tribunal. Once there, he had to wait three months for his initial appearance. The Appeals Chamber stated: 'We cannot accept that the Prosecutor, acting alone under Rule 40, has an unlimited right to keep a suspect under provisional detention in a State, when Rule 40*bis* places time limits on such detention if the suspect is detained at the Tribunal's detention unit.'[125] At the time of writing, decisions on motions for release filed by three other detainees on similar grounds were pending.

5.2.4   Rutaganda *Judgement, 6 December 1999*

In its Decision of 6 December 1999, Trial Chamber I found George Anderson Nderubumwe Rutaganda, a leader of the *Interahamwe* militia, guilty of one count of genocide and two counts of crimes against humanity (murder and extermination). It found that he was individually criminally responsible for the crime of genocide under Article 6(1) of the ICTR Statute for having ordered, incited and carried out murders and for causing serious bodily or mental harm to members of the Tutsi ethnic group.[126]

Rutaganda was acquitted of violations of common Article 3 of the Geneva Conventions (under Article 4 of the ICTR Statute) on the grounds the Prosecutor had failed to establish that the accused's acts were committed in conjunction with the armed conflict. The Prosecutor had not 'proved beyond reasonable doubt that there existed a nexus between the culpable acts committed by the Accused and the armed conflict'.[127] Moreover, 'the Prosecutor cannot merely rely on a finding of Genocide and consider that, as such, serious violations of Common Article 3 and Additional Protocol II are thereby automatically established. Rather, the Prosecutor must discharge her burden by establishing that each material requirement of offences under Article 4 of the Statute are met.'[128] While he was not charged with

---

125. *Supra* n. 123, para. 46.
126. *The Prosecutor* v. *Georges Anderson Nderubumwe Rutaganda*, Case No. ICTR-96-3-T, Judgement and Sentence, 6 December 1999, para. 400.
127. Ibid., para. 444.
128. Ibid., para. 443.

violations of Additional Protocol II, the Chamber considered 'the material require-ments of Article 4 of the Statute to be indivisible, in other words, that Common Article 3 and Additional Protocol II must be satisfied conjunctively, before an offence can be deemed to be covered by Article 4 of the Statute'.[129] Rutaganda's acquittal on the Article 4 counts means that the Prosecutor has yet to have a successful prosecution for violations of common Article 3 or Additional Protocol II before the ICTR.

Rutaganda was also acquitted on two further counts of crimes against humanity (murder) as the Chamber found that the elements of murder were covered by the extermination charges, for which he had been found guilty. In this respect, the Chamber concurred with the judgements in the *Akayesu* and *Kayishema* and *Ruzindana* cases, which found that an accused should not be convicted of more than one offence in relation to the same set of facts where, as in this case, one offence is a lesser included offence of the other.[130] In this case, the same facts supporting the murder charge were included in the more serious crime of extermination, for which the accused was found guilty. However, *Rutaganda* was found guilty of a further charge of murder as a crime against humanity based on other facts.

Nonetheless, the Trial Chamber fully concurred with the dissenting opinion of Judge Khan in the *Akayesu* case, which endorsed the principle of cumulative charges. According to the Chamber, 'the offences covered under the Statute (...) have disparate ingredients and, especially that their punishment is aimed at protecting disparate interests. As a result, multiple offenses may be charged on the basis of the same acts, in order to capture the full extent of the crimes committed by an accused.'[131]

In sentencing Rutaganda to life imprisonment, the Tribunal stated that the aggravating factors in the case outweighed the mitigating ones, in particular, his senior position in the *Interahamwe* militia, his conscious and knowing participation in the crimes and his lack of remorse. Rutaganda is appealing the verdict and his sentence.

6. REGIONAL COURTS

6.1 Inter-American Commission

Not for the first time, the Inter-American Commission of Human Rights has directly applied international humanitarian law to a case before it, this time in January 1999,[132] concerning a petition filed by six Salvadoran farm workers against the state,

---

129. Ibid., para. 435.

130. Ibid., para. 421.

131. Ibid., para. 117.

132. Inter-American Commission on Human Rights, Report No. 1/99, Case 10.480, 27 January 1999.

alleging that the Salvadoran Army had detained and tortured them, as a result of which two died.

Noting that the incidents alleged occurred during an internal armed conflict and that it had earlier declared itself competent in situations of domestic armed conflicts to directly enforce rules of humanitarian law or interpret provisions of the American Convention using those rules as reference,[133] the Commission stated that: 'Human rights instruments contain norms of a higher level (Art. 27 of the American Convention) that, under circumstances such as those we are dealing with of armed conflict, need to be supplemented with interpretation in the light of the standards of International Humanitarian Law. (...) [G]iven that it was a known fact, both nationally and internationally, that at the time of the events in question (1989) El Salvador was engaged in an internal armed conflict, in addition to the rules of the American Convention, the rules of international humanitarian law for non-international armed conflicts are also applicable to the situation in El Salvador at the time, (...) particularly, Article 3 common to the four Geneva Conventions of 1949 and its Additional Protocol II of 1977, to which El Salvador is a party.'[134]

The Commission found the agents of the state had contravened common Article 3 and Article 4 of Protocol II, and the relevant provisions of human rights law, in particular the prohibitions of torture and cruel and inhumane treatment and summary execution.[135]

In its consideration of the 1993 Amnesty Law,[136] which the petitioners claimed violated their rights under the Convention, the Commission made some general observations on amnesties and impunity. It noted that it was competent to declare any amnesty law of a State Party to be in contravention of its obligations under the Convention, and it had already repeatedly indicated that the enforcement of amnesties renders null and void the international obligations imposed on States Parties by Article 1(1) of the Convention.[137] The Commission noted that the 1993 Amnesty Law applied to all violations of common Article 3 and Additional Protocol II, committed by agents of the state,[138] even though Article 6(5) of Protocol II providing for amnesty was never intended to apply to serious violations of international humanitarian law. The Commission found that the 1993 Amnesty Law violated petitioners' rights to judicial guarantees and protection, and did not allow for criminal investigation by the state in order to establish the objective truth.[139]

---

133. See Annual Report of the Inter-American Commission on Human Rights (1997), OEA Ser.L/II.98 Doc. 6 rev. 1 of 3 April, 1998, Report 55/97, Case 11.137 (Abella), Argentina, paras. 164-166. See also IACHR, Report 26/97, Case 11.142 ("La Leche"), Colombia, para. 132.

134. *Supra* n. 132 at para. 65.

135. Ibid., paras. 67, 82.

136. General Amnesty Law for the Consolidation of Peace (Decree 486), 20 March 1993.

137. *Supra* n. 132 at para. 107.

138. Ibid., para. 115.

139. Ibid., paras. 150-158.

7. NATIONAL COURTS

The recent interest shown by some states in indicting, arresting and prosecuting war criminals and retired dictators, *inter alia,* has been hailed by many as proof that the world has become a smaller place for such people and that impunity is finally on the wane. In fact, a closer look at some of the cases of the past year reveals how reluctant states still are to exercise universal jurisdiction.

There have been several instances of states undertaking prosecutions based on extraterritorial jurisdiction. Yet none of these were based on universal jurisdiction but required another basis for the exercise of jurisdiction. Most courts have shown extreme caution in these instances, sometimes even more than required by law. Under s. 6 of the Penal Code, German courts can exercise universal jurisdiction. But in the *Jorgić* case, while the Federal Supreme Court relied on s. 6, it narrowed it in two ways: first, by adding a requirement that the exercise of universal jurisdiction may not be prohibited under international law, and second, by requiring a 'legitimising link in every case establishing a direct relation to the prosecution' within Germany; only then is the application of internal (German) penal jurisdiction justified with regard to an act committed abroad. 'If such a link is missing, criminal prosecution contravenes the principle of non-intervention which follows from the internationally-required recognition of other states' sovereignty.'[140] The court elaborated on what might constitute a legitimising link: it held that the fact that the defendant resided in Germany was not sufficient in itself. Additionally, the criminal prosecution was also held to be in conformity with the 'military and humanitarian measures in which Germany participated together with other states as requested on behalf of the United Nations in Bosnia and Herzegovina'. The Court also relied on the fact that the ICTY and the territorial state which would have been competent to conduct the proceedings chose not to exercise their jurisdiction. This finding of the Court conforms with earlier decisions of the High Court. In the case of *Götzfried*, German criminal law was held to apply according to s. 7(2) No. 1 of the StGB (penal code), because the accused had acquired German citizenship.[141]

In other cases, faced with the statutory possibility of exercising universal jurisdiction, states have chosen not to exercise it. In Canada, the Immigration and Refugee Board found that Leon Mugesera, a protégé of Juvenal Habyarimana, Rwanda's former President at the time of the genocide in 1994, committed genocide.[142] While proceedings to strip him of his refugee status have been instigated, he will not be prosecuted. Canadian law recognizes universal jurisdiction, and Mugesera could be tried in Canada for incitement to genocide. But the Justice Department has decided not to prosecute based on universal jurisdiction, and to restrict Canadian action to deportation of foreign war criminals.[143]

---

140. *Jorgić* case, Decision of Federal Supreme Court, 30 April 1999, 3StR215/98, p. 5, at I. See further the comments of Lüder and Schotten in Correspondents' Reports at p. 367 of this volume.

141. *Götzfried* case, Regional Court of Stuttgart, Judgment of 20 May 1999 - 2 Js 61533/97.

142. In a Decision of 6 November 1998.

143. See further W. Schabas in Correspondents' Reports at p. 345.

While the continuing prosecution of a handful of former Nazis may show that history and the law have a habit of catching up with people, these prosecutions rely on traditional bases of jurisdiction, generally, territoriality or nationality. Britain's successful prosecution under the 1991 War Crimes Act, against Andrzej Sawoniuk, in respect of crimes committed in Nazi-occupied Belarus in 1942, only drew attention to the limitations of that law, which only allows it to undertake prosecutions against persons accused of crimes committed in German-held territory during the Second World War who have become UK nationals or residents.[144] Britain needs to implement legislation enabling it to prosecute all persons for violations of international humanitarian law, including non-nationals, and to conform with the provisions of the ICC Statute, which it has signed.

While not a criminal prosecution against non-nationals, a Court in Australia found that while genocide is a preemptory norm of customary international law, and that customary law imposes on all states the duty to extradite or prosecute persons found within its territory who appear to have committed genocide, universal jurisdiction, of itself, does not render an *erga omnes* crime justiciable under municipal law. Implementing legislation would have to be adopted to enable Australia to exercise jurisdiction.[145]

A rare example of judicial activism in this area was seen in Belgium, where a Judge in an extradition request in respect of General Pinochet found that he had jurisdiction over crimes against humanity, which had not at that time been incorporated into Belgian penal law, based on the customary incrimination of these crimes.[146] While the Belgian Code of Criminal Inquiry makes no general provision for universal competency, the Judge based his competence on the customary rules establishing universal jurisdiction for crimes against humanity. Since the case, Belgium has adopted a law giving it universal jurisdiction over genocide and crimes against humanity.[147]

A Spanish Court ruling on the question of jurisdiction over General Augusto Pinochet found that there was a basis for jurisdiction over Pinochet in Spanish law and in the fact that while the Genocide Convention does not explicitly provide for universal jurisdiction, this is not incompatible with the right of any State Party, such as Spain, to consider that it has the right to take measures against genocide that has taken place beyond the limits of jurisdiction of its territory. However, the Court seemed to have in mind more the prosecution of persons with some link to Spain who commit acts outside its territory than the exercise of jurisdiction over persons with no connection to Spain. In any event, the victims in this case were Spanish

---

144. *See* further I. Bryan and P. Rowe at p. 307 of this volume.

145. *Nulyarimma* v. *Thompson* [1999] Federal Court of Australia 1192 (1 September 1999). See further Correspondents' Reports at p. 331.

146. Decision of 6 November 1998 of the Brussels Tribunal of First Instance on extradition request in respect of Augusto Pinochet Ugarte. Ruling on Article 61 *quinquies* 5 C.I. Cr- request for an instrument of supplementary preliminary investigation. Dossier nr. 216/98. Notices nr. 30.99.3447/98.

147. Loi du 10 février 1999 relative à la répression des violations graves du droit international humanitaire, reprinted at p. 539 of this volume.

nationals and Spain could assert jurisdiction based on the passive personality principle.

General Pinochet is not the only former military officer to attract the attention of foreign Judges. In May, an Italian Judge indicted former Argentinian Army General Carlos Guillermo Suarez Mason and six associates for the murder of six Italian citizens and the disappearance of a child. The seven will be tried *in absentia*. Here the basis for extraterritorial jurisdiction was found in Article 8 of the Italian Penal Code, which allows courts to exercise jurisdiction over political crimes committed by or against Italian citizens anywhere in the world.

Despite the arrest of Pinochet, states are still reluctant to arrest serving or former heads of state. South Africa resisted pressure to arrest and try the former Ethiopian dictator Mengistu Haile Mariam when he visited there for medical treatment in November 1999, stating that to arrest him would be contrary to its policy of reconciliation. South Africa also refused a request of Ethiopia for extradition of Mengistu to face charges of genocide and crimes against humanity, on the basis that there was no extradition treaty between the two states.[148]

In August, Austria refused to arrest Izzat Ibrahim Al Douri, a member of the Iraq state leadership, who was visiting Vienna for medical treatment, expressing the view that he enjoyed immunity from arrest as a 'member of the Iraqi state leadership'.

What these cases, as well as all the ones that have not taken place, signal is that there is a pressing need for states to implement legislation enabling them to exercise jurisdiction over genocide, crimes against humanity and war crimes, *inter alia,* and then to exercise this competence. The adoption of such legislation will in any event be necessary to enable most states to take advantage of the principle of complementarity under the ICC Statute.

7.1   ICRC and the Federation

7.1.1   *The 27th International Conference of the Red Cross and Red Crescent*

The 27th International Conference of the Red Cross and Red Crescent met in Geneva from 31 October to 6 November 1999. It brought together 176 Red Cross and Red Crescent Societies from around the world, government representatives from the 188 signatories to the Geneva Conventions and the leadership of the ICRC and the Federation.[149] At the close of the Conference, a formal Declaration was made and a four-year Plan of Action was adopted, consisting of a series of proposed actions, linked to long-term goals. In particular, the Action Plan calls on States Parties to the Geneva Conventions and regional intergovernmental organisations, in the face of serious violations of international humanitarian law,

---

148. AP Worldstream, 19 November 1999; Greg Barrow, 'Ethiopians push SA for Mengistu extradition', BBC, 3 December 1999; 'Focus on mounting pressure to extradite former Ethiopian dictator', IRIN, 7 December 1999.

149. Joint Communication to the Press. ICRC No. 99/57, Federation No. 32/99, 26 October 1999.

to act, jointly or individually, in cooperation with the United Nations and in conformity with the United Nations Charter.[150] States are to vigorously prosecute persons who violate humanitarian law, and are to search out and prosecute all persons who commit grave breaches, regardless of their nationality and to contribute to the setting up of the ICC.[151] A strategic partnership, between the ICRC, the Federation, states and other actors should be pursued. The Plan of Action also addresses the role of the Red Cross and Red Crescent Movement, and cooperation between it, other humanitarian actors and states.

A new feature of this quadrennial Conference was the pledging, by the Red Cross and Red Crescent Movement, by states, by individuals and by the corporate sector. '[P]ledging can be considered as a means of turning goodwill into commitment for support, for resources, for ideas, for action. Calling for pledges from within and outside the Red Cross Red Crescent can strengthen relations and establish new links.' The pledges varied, from a specific promise to train new volunteers to broader aspirations.

7.1.2   *The People on War Project*

The People on War project, an international consultation on the rules to limit violence in warfare, involving over 20,000 people in 17 countries, was launched in late-1998. Billed as 'the most important and innovative body of social research on war ever carried out',[152] it involved in-depth interviews with civilians and combatants on a range of issues to ascertain their attitude to conflict, their knowledge of the Geneva Conventions and their understanding of why they are so often violated. The idea was to give a voice to civilians and combatants alike and to hear from them about the reality of war. The People on War Report, published in October 1999, focuses on the effects of war on civilians, and with trying to establish why combatants attack civilians and why the norms of humanitarian law tend to break down during conflicts. It provides a wealth of empirical information which could be used to try and address some of the problems identified. While it is clear from the study that conflict leaves no-one untouched, and much has to be done to improve knowledge of and respect for the Geneva Conventions, '[t]he experience has heightened consciousness of what is right and wrong in war. People in battle zones across the globe are looking for forces in civil society or their own State institutions or, if not them, international structures to assert themselves and impose limits that will protect civilians.'[153]

---

150. Action Plan, s. 6.
151. Ibid., s. 10.
152. ICRC Communication to the Press No. 99/56, 11 October 1999.
153. The People on War Report: ICRC worldwide consultation on the rules of war (Geneva, ICRC 1999) at p. vi.

7.1.3 *Immunity from testifying before ICTY for ICRC staff*

A decision of the ICTY in the *Simić and Others* case[154] gives immunity to ICRC personnel from testifying before the Tribunal. In this case, the Prosecutor wished to call as a witness a former employee of the ICRC who witnessed grave violations of international humanitarian law while working for the ICRC in the Former Yugoslavia. The ICRC objected, saying that past and present Red Cross employees may not testify before courts of law about information gathered while performing their duties in the field. This would, the ICRC argued, affect its perceived impartiality and limit its ability to perform its humanitarian role in armed conflicts. The Court decided that the testimony should not be given. 'The Trial Chamber noted the principles derived from the mandate entrusted to the ICRC by international law under the Geneva Conventions and Additional Protocols. In particular, the Trial Chamber focused on three fundamental principles that guide the movement, that is, impartiality, neutrality and independence, and considered that the right to non-disclosure of information relating to the ICRC's activities in the possession of its employees in judicial proceedings is necessary for the effective discharge by the ICRC of its mandate.' The Trial Chamber also came to the conclusion that 'customary international law provides the ICRC with an absolute right to non-disclosure of information relating to the work of the ICRC in the possession of an ICRC employee. Consequently, no issue arises as to balancing the ICRC's confidentiality interest against the interests of justice.'

8. INTERNATIONAL ORGANISATIONS AND INTERNATIONAL ACTIONS

8.1 **United Nations Organisation**

8.11 *Security Council Resolutions[155] and Statements by the President of the Security Council*

Increasingly, Security Council Resolutions and Presidential Statements refer to humanitarian law and condemn violations of the law by the Parties. At other times, in relation to armed conflicts, the Council fails to mention international humanitarian law when it is relevant. In some cases, but not in others, the Council calls for those responsible for humanitarian law violations to be held accountable. It is also

---

154. Decision on the prosecution motion under Rule 73 for a ruling concerning the testimony of a witness, 27 July 1999.

155. The intention is not to provide a comprehensive analysis of every relevant SC resolution but merely to draw attention to their humanitarian aspects and particularly, specific references to humanitarian law and to breaches of the law and the need for responsibility. Only resolutions that specifically refer to humanitarian law or relate to armed conflicts in some way are mentioned. For a good general overview of the SC's work in 1999, see *supra* n. 6.

noticeable that certain countries where there are armed conflicts and violations of humanitarian law are completely ignored by the Council. The gaps can be seen clearly when the resolutions are grouped according to country.

Abkhazia: The Council focused on Abkhazia twice in 1999, at no time specifically referring to violations of humanitarian law but alluding indirectly to violations. Resolution 1225 (1999) of 28 January 1999 expressed the Council's concern over the risk of renewed fighting in the region and the continued deadlock in reaching a political settlement. It demanded that both sides broaden their commitment to the United Nations-led peace process and a political solution to the status of Abkhazia, within the state of Georgia. It condemned the activities by armed groups, including the continued laying of mines, which endanger the civilian population and impede the work of humanitarian organisations. A further statement of 12 November 1999 by the President of the Security Council demanded that the parties deepen their commitment to the UN-led peace process. It condemned the hostage-taking of seven UN personnel on 13 October 1999, welcomed their release and stressed that the perpetrators of that act be brought to justice.

Afghanistan: Resolution 1214 (1998) of 8 December 1998 expressed the Council's grave concern at the continuing armed conflict in Afghanistan, which is increasingly of an ethnic nature and is the cause of 'a serious and growing threat to regional and international peace and security (...)'. It recalled that 'all parties to the conflict are bound to comply with their obligations under international humanitarian law and in particular under the Geneva Conventions (...), and that persons who commit or order the commission of breaches of the Conventions are individually responsible in respect of such breaches'. It expressed the Council's deep concern at the continuing discrimination against girls and women and at other violations of human rights and international humanitarian law in Afghanistan, and demanded an end to such practices. It encouraged the SG to continue his efforts to dispatch a mission to Afghanistan to investigate numerous reports of grave breaches and serious violations of international humanitarian law, in particular mass killings and mass graves of prisoners of war and civilians and the destruction of religious sites. It supported the SG's proposal to establish within the United Nations Special Mission to Afghanistan (UNSMA) a civil affairs unit with the primary objective of monitoring the situation, promoting respect for minimum humanitarian standards and deterring massive and systematic violations of human rights and humanitarian law in the future.

Resolution 1267 (1999) of 15 October 1999 reiterated the Security Council's 'deep concern over the continuing violations of international humanitarian law and of human rights, particularly discrimination against women and girls (...)'.

On 22 October 1999, a statement made by the President of the Security Council on behalf of the Council took note of the deteriorating humanitarian and human rights situation. It took note of the deliberate abuse and arbitrary detentions of civilians, the use of child soldiers, and indiscriminate bombing and other violations of human rights and international humanitarian law in Afghanistan. It called on all parties to, in particular, ensure the protection of civilians.[156]

Angola: Resolution 1212 (1998) of 3 December 1998 condemned the failure of UNITA to implement the Lusaka Protocol, including the complete demilitarisation of its forces, and expressed the Council's grave concern at the serious humanitarian impact of the impasse in the peace process and the deteriorating security situation, including the increase in minelaying activity. It called upon the Government of Angola and UNITA to, *inter alia*, respect international humanitarian, refugee and human rights law.

Resolution 1229 (1999) of 26 February 1999 expressed its concern at the humanitarian effects of the present situation on the civilian population and its view that lasting peace and reconciliation could only come through peaceful means.

Resolution 1237 (1999) of 7 May 1999 expressed the Council's alarm at 'the humanitarian effects of the present crisis on the civilian population of Angola', and condemned the indiscriminate attacks by UNITA against the civilian population. However, the resolution refrains from mentioning violations of international humanitarian law, nor does it call for the parties to respect humanitarian law treaties. Resolution 1268 (1999) of 15 October 1999 addressed the conflict in Angola and, while expressing the Council's 'concern at the humanitarian effects of the present situation on the civilian population', did not expressly refer to violations of international humanitarian law. It authorised the establishment of a United Nations Office in Angola (UNOA), for an initial period of six months until 15 April 2000.

Burundi: On 12 November 1999, the President of the SC made a statement on behalf of the Council concerning Burundi, in which it noted with concern the recent outbreak of violence and the delays in the peace process. It condemned the murder of UN personnel in Burundi in October and called on the Government to undertake and cooperate with investigations and for the perpetrators to be brought to justice. It condemned the attacks by armed groups against civilians and called for an end to these unacceptable incidents, without specifically referring to violations of humanitarian law.[157]

Democratic Republic of the Congo: Resolution 1234 (1999) of 9 April 1999 expressed the Council's 'concern at violations of human rights and international humanitarian law in the territory of the Democratic Republic of the Congo, including acts of and incitement to ethnic hatred and violence by all parties to the conflict'. It called on 'all parties (...) to protect human rights and to respect international humanitarian law, in particular as applicable to them, the Geneva Conventions of 1949 and the Additional Protocols of 1977, and the Convention on the Prevention and Punishment of the Crime of Genocide of 1948'. It condemned the massacres

---

156. S/PRST/1999/29 of 22 October 1999.
157. S/PRST/1999/31, 12 November 1999.

carried out in the DRC, and called for 'an international investigation into all such events, with a view to bringing to justice those responsible'.

Resolution 1258 (1999) of 6 August 1999 welcomed the signing of the Ceasefire Agreement of 1 August 1999 by the Movement for the Liberation of the Congo and expressed concern that the Congolese Rally for Democracy had not yet signed it, and called on all parties to cease hostilities. While not referring to violations of international humanitarian law, paragraph 11 urged all parties 'to respect strictly the relevant provisions of international humanitarian law'.

In resolution 1279 (1999) of 30 November 1999, the Security Council expressed its concern at 'continuing violations of human rights and international humanitarian law committed throughout the territory of the DRC.' It established the United Nations Organization Mission in the Democratic Republic of Congo (MONUC).

East Timor: Resolution 1264 of 11 June 1999 established the United Nations Mission in East Timor (UNAMET). Resolution 1264 of 15 September 1999 expressed the Council's 'concern at reports indicating that systematic, widespread and flagrant violations of international humanitarian and human rights law had been committed in East Timor, and stressed that persons committing such violations bear individual responsibility'. Acting under Chapter VII of the UN Charter, the Council 'condemn[ed] all acts of violence in East Timor, call[ed] for their immediate end and demand[ed] that those responsible for such acts be brought to justice', and authorised the establishment of a multinational force under a unified command structure. Resolution 1272 (1999) of 25 October 1999 established the United Nations Transitional Administration in East-Timor (UNTAET).

Ethiopia and Eritrea: Resolution 1226 (1999) of 29 January 1999 expressed grave concern over the risk of armed conflict between Ethiopia and Eritrea and the arms build-up along the border, and the Council's support for peace initiatives. It called on both sides to adopt urgent measures to improve the humanitarian situation and respect for human rights, and to exercise maximum restraint.

Resolution 1227 (1999) of 10 February 1999 stressed that the situation constituted a threat to peace and security and condemned the use of force by both parties. It demanded an immediate end to hostilities and a peaceful resolution to the conflict. Further, it called upon Ethiopia and Eritrea to 'ensure the safety of the civilian population and respect for human rights and international humanitarian law'.

FRY, including Kosovo: Security Council Resolution 1207 (1998) of 17 November 1998 condemned the failure to date of the FRY to arrest the three persons accused in the Vukovar Hospital indictment of the ICTY, and demanded their immediate and unconditional arrest and transfer to the Tribunal. It reiterated its call to the FRY, the leaders of the Kosovar Albanians and all others concerned to cooperate fully with the Prosecutor in the investigation of all possible violations within the jurisdiction of the Tribunal.

The President of the Security Council, on 29 January 1999, reiterated its concern about attacks on civilians in Kosovo and underlined the need for a full and unhindered investigation of such attacks. It called upon all the parties to fully respect their obligations under the relevant resolutions and to cease immediately all acts of violence and provocations.[158] No reference was made to possible humanitarian law violations.

Resolution 1239 (1999) of 14 May 1999, concerning assistance to countries affected by the refugee crisis in Kosovo, expressed grave concern at the humanitarian catastrophe in and around Kosovo as a result of the crisis. The only reference to humanitarian law was in the preamble, which stated that in adopting the resolution the Security Council had borne in mind, *inter alia,* the Geneva Conventions of 1949 and their Additional Protocols and other instruments of international humanitarian law.

Resolution 1244 (1999) of 10 June 1999 condemned acts of violence against the Kosovar population and terrorist acts by any party and reaffirmed the jurisdiction of the ICTY. It provided for the implementation of the 6 May principles, in particular, the deployment in Kosovo, under UN auspices, of international civil and security presences, with appropriate equipment and personnel as required, and the appointment of a Special Representative to control the implementation of the international civilian presence. KFOR's mandate does not expressly include the duty to apprehend war criminals.

Guinea-Bisseau: Resolution 1233 (1999) of 6 April 1999 expressed the Council's grave concern over the security and humanitarian situation in Guinea-Bisseau, and called upon all parties to 'respect strictly the relevant provisions of international law, including international humanitarian and human rights law' and to implement their undertakings under the Peace Agreement.

Sierra Leone: On 7 January 1999, the President of the Security Council expressed its grave concern at serious humanitarian consequences of the fighting and the attacks by armed rebels on the capital Freetown, and condemned the rebels' campaign of terror against the civilian population and especially the atrocities committed against women and children.[159]

Resolution 1231 (1999) of 11 March 1999 expressed the Council's concern over the continuing fragile situation and extended the mandate of UNOMSIL until 13 June 1999. It condemned 'the atrocities perpetrated by the rebels on the civilian population of Sierra Leone, including in particular those committed against women and children, deplor[ed] all violations of human rights and international humanitarian law which have occurred in Sierra Leone during the recent escalation of violence (…), including the recruitment of children as soldiers, and urge[d] the appropriate authorities to investigate all allegations of such violations with a view to bringing the perpetrators to justice'. The resolution called on 'all parties to the conflict in Sierra Leone fully to respect human rights and international humanitarian law and

---

158. S/PRST/1995/5 of 29 January 1999.
159. S/PRST/1991/1 of 7 January 1999.

the neutrality and impartiality of humanitarian workers, and to ensure full and unhindered access for humanitarian assistance to affected populations'.

On 15 May 1999, the President of the Security Council made a statement on behalf of the Council concerning Sierra Leone, in which it expressed its support for the Lomé peace process and condemned the recent killings, atrocities, destruction of property and other violations of human rights and international humanitarian law perpetrated by rebels against civilians.

Resolution 1245 (1999) of 11 June 1999 expressed the Council's continuing concern over the fragile situation in Sierra Leone and extended the mandate of UNOMSIL until 13 December 1999.

Resolution 1260 (1999) of 20 August 1999 welcomed the signing of the Lomé Peace Agreement and commended the Government of Sierra Leone for its courage. Despite the disclaimer made by the UN's Special Representative when signing the Peace Agreement on behalf of the UN, that the amnesties in the Agreement do not apply to genocide, crimes against humanity and war crimes, the Resolution did not specifically call for the prosecution of violators of humanitarian law but referred in a more oblique way to 'the urgent need to promote peace and national reconciliation and to foster accountability and respect for human rights (...)'. It welcomed the provisions for the establishment of a Truth and Reconciliation Commission and a Human Rights Commission in Sierra Leone. Paragraph 14 made the only direct reference to humanitarian law, calling on all parties (...) 'to respect strictly the relevant provisions of international humanitarian law'.

On 22 October 1999, acting under Chapter VII of the UN Charter, the Security Council, by resolution 1270 (1999), established the United Nations Mission in Sierra Leone (UNAMSIL), with immediate effect for an initial period of six months. The resolution highlighted the need for including in UNAMSIL personnel with appropriate training in international humanitarian law, human rights law and refugee law, particularly their provisions relating to children and women.

Refugees: Resolution 1208 (1998) of 19 November 1998 affirmed the 'primary responsibility of States hosting refugees to ensure the security and civilian and humanitarian character of refugee camps and settlements in accordance with international refugee, human rights and humanitarian law (...)'. The Secretary-General was requested to respond, as appropriate, to requests from African states, the OAU and subregional organisations for advice and technical assistance in the implementation of international refugee, human rights and humanitarian law relevant to the present resolution, including through appropriate training programs and seminars. The Secretary-General and member states involved in efforts to enhance Africa's peacekeeping capacity were also encouraged to ensure that training gives due emphasis to international refugee, human rights and humanitarian law.

International terrorism: Resolution 1269 of 19 October 1999 referred to the need to intensify the fight against international terrorism at the national level, and to strengthen international cooperation in this field, based on respect for international humanitarian law and human rights. The resolution also referred to the need to 'take appropriate measures in conformity with the relevant provisions of national and international law, including relevant standards of human rights, before granting refugee status, for the purpose of ensuring that the asylum-seeker has not participated in terrorist acts'. While it does not specifically refer to violations of humanitarian law as a basis for exclusion under Article 1(f) of the Refugee Convention, perpetrators could be excluded on this basis. The Netherlands is currently spearheading attempts to adopt a Europe-wide policy on exclusion under Article 1(f), including for acts constituting violations of international humanitarian law.[160]

Prevention of armed conflict: A two-day open debate of the Security Council from 29–30 November 1999 dealt with the prevention of armed conflict. The Council highlighted the importance of preventive action *vis-à-vis* situations of potential armed conflict, including conflict resolution mechanisms and preventive military and civilian deployments. Where conflicts do occur, the Council expressed its willingness to respond to situations where civilians are being deliberately targeted or where humanitarian assistance is being deliberately obstructed, and acknowledged the need to enhance the UN's capacity for rapid deployment. Humanitarian law, human rights and refugee law should be disseminated as widely as possible among the civilian police, the armed forces, the judiciary and legal profession, civil society and personnel of international and regional organisations.[161]

On 30 November 1999, at the end of the debate, the President of the Security Council made a statement on the 'Role of the Security Council in the prevention of armed conflicts' which affirmed its responsibility under the Charter to take action on its own initiative in order to maintain international peace and security, and the important role of the Secretary-General in the prevention of armed conflicts. The Council will consider preventive measures such as the establishment of demilitarised zones and preventive disarmament. Further, '[t]he Council underlines that the existing international criminal tribunals represent useful instruments to combat impunity and can, by helping to deter crimes against humanity, contribute to the prevention of armed conflicts.'[162]

8.1.2   *Secretary-General's Guidelines for UN forces*

By an executive order of 6 August 1999, UN Secretary-General Kofi Annan laid out guidelines for UN troops, which state that they must respect and observe the rules of international humanitarian law or face prosecution before their own national courts.

---

160. See Note by the Netherlands State Secretary of Justice to Parliament on Article 1F of the Refugee Convention, in Peter J. van Krieken, ed., *Refugee Law in Context: The Exclusion Clause,* (The Hague, TMC Asser Press 1999) pp. 300-312.

161. See *supra* n. 6.

162. S/PRST/1999/34 of 30 November 1999.

While not stipulating precisely which parts of international humanitarian law apply to UN forces, or all of it, the Guidelines state that the 'fundamental principles and rules of international law set out in the present bulletin are applicable to UN forces when in situations of armed conflict. They are accordingly applicable in enforcement actions, or in peacekeeping operations when the use of force is permitted in self-defence.' However, the guidelines for UN forces only apply to UN military operations and Security Council-authorised enforcement missions in which the United Nations commands the force, and would not apply, for example, to the peacekeeping mission in Kosovo, which is commanded by NATO, not the UN.[163]

The application of the guidelines does not affect UN forces' protection under the 1994 Convention on the Safety of United Nations and Associated Personnel or their status as non-combatants as long as they do not get involved in combat.[164] However, once UN troops become involved in hostilities, they lose their protection. The guidelines cover the broad areas of humanitarian law, including the protection of the civilian population and the principle of distinction, methods and means of combat, treatment of civilians and persons *hors de combat*, treatment of detained persons and protection of the wounded, the sick, and medical and relief personnel.

UN personnel who violate humanitarian law are subject to prosecution before national courts, in which case, the material basis for prosecution would presumably be violations of the Geneva Conventions and Additional Protocols, as incorporated into national law, rather than the guidelines themselves, as the latter have no legal status. While the guidelines have been criticised for not stating that grave breaches by peacekeepers give rise to universal jurisdiction, there is nothing in them that explicitly excludes prosecutions before international courts or the courts of third states exercising universal jurisdiction.

The guidelines entered into force on 12 August 1999. By stating that they are not an exhaustive list of principles and rules binding upon military personnel, they suggest that UN forces are indeed otherwise bound by international humanitarian law. UN forces also remain subject to national laws. Issued in the form of an order to troops, the guidelines would of course become binding for those troops as a matter of internal military discipline.

8.1.3   *UN report on Srebrenica*

On 15 November 1999, the Secretary-General released the UN's 'Srebrenica Report'.[165] The report is deeply critical of the UN's role in the fall of Srebrenica. 'Through error, misjudgement and an inability to recognize the scope of the evil confronting us, we failed to do our part to help save the people of Srebrenica from

---

163. This is stated in the guidelines. See also Nicole Winfield, 'UN peacekeepers bound to respect, protect civilians', Associated Press, 10 August 1999.

164. The Safety Convention entered into force on 15 January 1999 with the ratification of the 22nd State, in accordance with Article 27(1).

165. A/54/549, 15 November 1999. http://www.un.org/peace/srebrenica.pdf.

the Serb campaign of mass murder. No one regrets more than we the opportunities for achieving peace and justice that were missed. No one laments more than we the failure of the international community to take decisive action to halt the suffering and end a war that had produced so many victims.'[166]

The report criticises 'the prism of moral equivalency' between the Bosnian Serbs and the Bosnian Muslims through which the conflict was for too long viewed. It admits to 'persuasive ambivalence within the UN regarding the role of force in the pursuit of peace' and an 'institutional ideology of impartiality even when confronted with attempted genocide'.

8.1.4   *UN and French reports into Rwanda*

In March 1999, the UN commissioned its own inquiry into the UN's role in the 1994 genocide in Rwanda. The report, issued on 17 December 1999,[167] says that the UN and the international community was woefully unprepared and lacked the political resolve to stop the genocide. It laid the blame at the door of the Secretary-General, the Secretariat, the Security Council, UNAMIR and the broader membership of the United Nations. The report, by a three-member independent panel headed by former Swedish Prime Minister, Ingvar Carlsson, follows a nine-month investigation during which the panel had unrestricted access to documents.

Upon receiving the report, Kofi Annan voiced his 'deep remorse' over the UN's failure to stop the genocide and stated that '[a]ll of us must bitterly regret that we did not do more to prevent it. There was a United Nations force in the country at the time but it was neither mandated nor equipped for the kind of forceful action which would have been needed to prevent or halt the genocide. On behalf of the United Nations, I acknowledge this failure and express my deep remorse.'[168]

France has also conducted an inquiry into the role of its troops during the genocide. The report of the nine-month long French Parliamentary Inquiry[169] deflected blame away from the French Government towards the UN and the USA. Washington, it said, bore special responsibility for resisting demands to boost the UN monitoring force. France, it said, committed only some small errors, such as getting poor intelligence and wrongly assuming it could control the former Belgian colony as it could its own former colonies. The report denied that France had been involved when violence was unleashed, saying that while it had propped up the Hutu-government, it had withdrawn its support after the 1993 peace accords. While the French troops involved in 'Operation Turquoise' may have delayed the Rwandan Patriotic Front gaining power, it saved thousands of lives. However, as the recent,

---

166. Ibid., para. 503.

167. http://www.un.org/News/ossg/rwanda_report.htm. The report has no document number.

168. UN Press Release SG/SM/7263, AFR/196, 16 December 1999.

169. Rapport d'Information No. 1271 par la mission d'information de la commission de la Défense Nationale et des Forces Armées et de la Commission des Affaires Étrangères sur les operations militaires menées par la France, d'autres pays et l'ONU au Rwanda entre 1990 et 1994.

authoritative book of Alison Des Forges shows, France, and many other states, are far from blameless.[170]

9.   ARMS CONTROL AND DISARMAMENT

9.1   **Small arms and light weapons**

For most fighters today, small arms and light weapons are the weapons of choice,[171] indeed, they are 'particularly well-suited to the intrastate conflicts of the 1990s'.[172] In spite of efforts to control these weapons, the number of manufacturers of small arms increased by 25 percent between 1985 and 1995, to 300 companies in over 70 countries. While arms do not of themselves cause conflicts, an ICRC study concluded that 'arms availability can indeed facilitate violations of international humanitarian law and lead to a deterioration of the situation of civilians in armed conflicts'.[173]

On 8 July 1999, the Council met to consider the maintenance of international peace and security and post-conflict peace building, which must include disarmament, demobilization and reintegration of ex-combatants in a peacekeeping environment. In a statement following that meeting, the Council expressed concern that fighting among various parties and factions continued despite the conclusion of peace agreements by warring parties and the presence of UN peacekeepers. It recognised that a major contributing factor was the continued availability of arms, particularly small arms and light weapons. The Council stressed the need for the implementation of practical measures to promote the success of peacekeeping activities, including the prevention and reduction of the excessive and destabilising flow, accumulation and illegitimate use of small arms and light weapons.[174]

Security Council Resolution 1261 (1999) of 25 August 1999, addressing armed conflicts and children, recognised 'the deleterious impact of the proliferation of arms, in particular small arms, on the security of civilians, including refugees and other vulnerable populations, particularly children (...)'.

On 24 September 1999, the United Nations Security Council met at an inter-ministerial level to discuss the question of small arms. Among the issues raised was

---

170. A. Des Forges, *Leave None to Tell the Story* (New York, Human Rights Watch 1999); see also P. Gourevitch, *We Wish to Inform You that Tomorrow We Will Be Killed With Our Families: Stories from Rwanda* (New York, Farrar Straus & Giroux 1998).

171. A study of 101 conflicts fought between 1989 and 1996 found that small arms and light weapons were generally the weapon of preference or even the only weapon used. P. Wallensteen and M. Sollenberg, 'Armed Conflicts, Conflict Termination and Peace Agreements, 1989-1996', 34 *Journal of Peace Research*, quoted in Arms Availability and the Situation of Civilians in Armed Conflict, ICRC 1999.

172. Arms Availability and the Situation of Civilians in Armed Conflict, ICRC 1999, s. 2(e). http://www.icrc.org/icrceng.nsf/4d.../10805a47444523884125680f0034a72c?Open Document.

173. Ibid.

174. *Supra* n. 6.

that of effective implementation of arms embargoes imposed by Council resolutions. The Council President called on member states to provide the Council with information on violation of arms embargoes. The Council also called for measures to discourage arms flows to countries experiencing or emerging from armed conflict, and urged states to abide by national or regional moratoria on arms transfers.[175] The Council also welcomed the recommendations of the Group of Governmental Experts on Small Arms, which adopted a report on international progress in dealing with the issue, including the convening of an international conference on the illicit arms trade in all its forms no later than 2001. The Government of Switzerland has offered to host the meeting in Geneva.

---

175. S/PRST/1999/28, 24 September 1999.

SOUTH AFRICA'S TRUTH AND RECONCILIATION PROCESS AND INTERNATIONAL HUMANITARIAN LAW[1]

John Dugard[2]

1.   INTRODUCTION

Since its establishment in 1995, the South African Truth and Reconciliation Commission has captured the attention of an international community preoccupied with the problem of dealing with crimes of the past in divided societies. While the creation of a permanent international criminal court to punish those guilty of atrocities constituting international crimes has been the first priority, the international community has, albeit grudgingly, accepted that there may be circumstances in which amnesty and reconciliation hold out more hope for troubled societies than punishment. This realisation has led to the search for an acceptable alternative to punishment that does not result in absolute amnesty for those guilty of gross human rights abuses. The South African model, of conditional amnesty accompanied by the uncovering of the past, appears to offer such an alternative. This factor, together with the relief over the fact that apartheid has at last been laid to rest, accounts for the interest shown in the South African experience.

The present note will not attempt to describe and analyse the South African precedent in detail. Instead it will provide an overview of the history, establishment and work of the South African Truth and Reconciliation Commission (TRC); examine the significance of the Report of the TRC for international humanitarian law; and consider the status of amnesty under contemporary international law in the context of the South African experience.

2. THE TRUTH AND RECONCILIATION COMMISSION

Before 1990, when the South African national liberation movements[3] and the South African apartheid regime were locked in a conflict, both political and military, it

---

1. © J. Dugard, 1999.

2. Professor of Public International Law, University of Leiden; Emeritus Professor of Law, University of the Witwatersrand, South Africa.

3. The liberation movements were spearheaded by the African National Congress and the Pan-Africanist Congress.

was widely believed that, if the liberation movements were victorious in their efforts to overthrow the apartheid regime by force, the leaders of the regime would be tried in the same way that Nazi leaders had been tried at Nuremberg. The spectre of Nuremberg was thus held out as a threat by the liberation movements in exile. This threat was thwarted, however, by the abandonment of apartheid by the National Party regime. In February 1990, President F.W. de Klerk announced the end of apartheid, withdrew the ban on the African National Congress (ANC) and Pan-Africanist Congress (PAC), released Nelson Mandela from prison, and initiated a process of negotiation aimed at the establishment of a just political order in South Africa. To facilitate negotiations between the National Party regime and the ANC, the principal liberation movement, the National Party itself released political prisoners and granted temporary indemnity from prosecution to members of the ANC in exile for crimes committed in the course of their struggle against apartheid. The National Party government then attempted to extend this indemnity to its own security forces – a measure that proved to be ineffectual. Consequently, it was left to constitutional negotiations to decide on the question of dealing with the crimes of the past.

Politically there were only two options open to the negotiators of the new political order: unconditional, blanket amnesty, which understandably was favoured by the National Party, or conditional amnesty for individual applicants. The latter was chosen. In terms of this compromise, which was endorsed by both the Interim Constitution of 1993[4] and the 1996 Constitution[5] and given substance by the Promotion of National Unity and Reconciliation Act of 1995,[6] the following regime was established for dealing with the past.

In early 1996, a Truth and Reconciliation Commission of 17 members was appointed by the President, in consultation with the cabinet, to establish by means of public hearings and investigations, a complete picture of 'the gross violations of human rights' committed between 1960 and 1993; to facilitate the granting of amnesty; to restore the human dignity of victims by providing them with an opportunity publicly to relate their own accounts of the human rights abuses; and to prepare a report containing recommendations of measures to prevent the future violations of human rights. Broadly representative of the peoples of South Africa and presided over by Desmond Tutu, Nobel Peace Laureate and former Archbishop of Cape Town, it commenced the task of conducting public hearings into human rights violations. Although several members of the TRC were lawyers by training, the majority was drawn from church or community service backgrounds, emphasising the fact that the TRC did not purport to be a judicial body.

The TRC was given wide powers of investigation, including the power of search and seizure and the power to subpoena persons to appear before it. Its hearings were to be held in public unless special circumstances required an *in camera*

---

4. Act 200 of 1993.
5. Act 108 of 1996.
6. Act 34 of 1995.

hearing. Persons subpoenaed to appear before the TRC were entitled to legal representation.

There was no general amnesty. Instead, persons seeking amnesty for gross human rights violations were required to apply to the Committee on Amnesty, a quasi-judicial body linked to the TRC. Initially this Committee was to comprise five members but as the number of applicants swelled, the membership of the Committee was increased to seventeen. It now sits in several committees of three, made up of judges and senior lawyers. Entrusted with the task of granting or refusing amnesty, these committees play a pivotal role in the truth and reconciliation process.

An amnesty committee considers applications for amnesty and may grant amnesty if it is satisfied that the applicant has committed an act constituting 'a gross violation of human rights', and made 'a full disclosure of all relevant facts', and that the act to which the application relates is 'an act associated with a political objective committed in the course of conflicts of the past'.[7] The criteria to be employed for deciding whether the act is one 'associated with a political objective' are drawn from the principles used in extradition law for deciding whether the offence in respect of which extradition is sought is a political offence. The criteria include, *inter alia*, the motive of the offender; the context in which the act took place and, in particular, whether it was committed 'in the course of or as part of a political uprising, disturbance or event'; the gravity of the act; the objective of the act, and in particular, whether it was 'primarily directed at a political opponent or state property or personnel or against private property or individuals'; and the relationship between the act and the political objective pursued, and 'in particular the directness and proximity of the relationship and the proportionality of the act to the objective pursued'. A person granted amnesty shall not be criminally or civilly liable in respect of the act in question.[8]

The amnesty committees, like the TRC, conduct their hearings in public. Both applicants and victims are entitled to legal representation. An unusual feature of the process is that the inquiry into the events of the past is not limited to acts committed in furtherance of the apartheid state. Members of the liberation movements, notably the ANC and PAC, together with officers of the apartheid regime, fall within the terms of reference of the Commission.

The ANC and PAC, inevitably, were guilty of 'the gross violation of human rights' in the course of their attempts to overthrow the apartheid regime by force. Innocent civilians were killed and maimed by acts of violence directed at civilian targets. Moreover, suspected spies were brutally tortured in the military camps of the liberation movements in neighbouring territories. Despite this, the ANC had every right to claim that it occupied the moral high ground as it was engaged in a 'just war' of national liberation, legitimised or condoned by the United Nations. The Promotion of National Unity and Reconciliation Act, however, fails to distinguish between the moral culpability of the opposing sides and subjects the agents of both

---

7. Sections 10(1), 19(3)(b)(iii) of Act 34 of 1995.
8. Section 20 of Act 34 of 1995.

sides to the amnesty process. This even-handedness was a necessary consequence of the political compromise that led to the adoption of the amnesty law.

A surprising feature of the Truth and Reconciliation process is that it fails to provide for an investigation into the injustices of apartheid, i.e., systematic racial discrimination and domination, or to require the functionaries of the apartheid state to seek amnesty for their complicity in the international crime of apartheid. The 'gross violations of human rights' investigated by the TRC and the committees on amnesty are confined to 'the killing, abduction, torture or severe ill-treatment of any person'; that is, acts that were crimes under the apartheid legal order – such as murder, culpable homicide, kidnapping and assault.[9] There is no attempt to bring within the ambit of the inquiry acts that constituted a crime under international law but were not criminal under the law of apartheid.[10] To bring such acts within the purview of the truth and reconciliation process, it would have been necessary to denounce the validity of the laws of apartheid with retrospective effect, and this the legislature was not prepared to do out of respect for the political compromise that constituted the foundation of the process, the rule of law and the principle of legality. In its hearings, however, the TRC was not able to avoid examining the broader policies and practices of apartheid.

From 1996 to 1998, the TRC held open, televised hearings on individual human rights violations, patterns of human rights violations, the state structures and political leaders responsible for human rights violations, the conduct of the liberation movements and ANC leaders (such as Winnie Madikizela-Mandela), and the part played by institutions such as the press, the churches, business and the judiciary in the maintenance of the apartheid state.

The TRC completed its work in 1998 and submitted its Report and Recommendations in October 1998. This report is not accurately described as a final report as the amnesty committees have not completed their task and are unlikely to do so before the end of 1999. Of the over 7,000 applications received, 150 have been granted, almost 5,000 dismissed and 2,000 remain to be dealt with. These applications, mainly from members of the police force, and not the army, have provided, and continue to provide, a horrifying picture of brutality by the security forces, involving torture, murder, disappearances and repression. The picture will not be complete until these hearings are finished, at which time the TRC will add a codicil to its Report.

Those who have failed to obtain amnesty from an amnesty committee, or who failed to apply for amnesty, are exposed to prosecution. Some prosecutions have been completed, others are underway, and no doubt there will be more to come as

---

9. This meant, in the words of Desmond Tutu, that 'the Commission was restricted to examining only a fraction of the totality of human rights violations that emanated from the policy of apartheid'. *TRC Report, infra* n. 11, Vol. 1, p. 29.

10. Many of the lawfully prescribed practices of apartheid relating to systematic discrimination and persecution on racial grounds, but not involving physical violence to the person, might be categorized as crimes against humanity under customary international law or as crimes of apartheid under the 1973 Convention on the Suppression and Punishment of the Crime of Apartheid.

evidence of complicity in human rights violations becomes available. A special unit within the Prosecutor's office has been established for this purpose. This serves to emphasise that amnesty in South Africa is conditional.

3.   THE TRC REPORT AND INTERNATIONAL HUMANITARIAN LAW

The even-handedness of the TRC Report published on 29 October 1998 was evidenced by the opposition to its publication. Both former state President F.W. de Klerk and the ANC brought court applications to prevent publication of adverse findings. Mr De Klerk's application is still being considered, but the ANC application was dismissed out of hand. While President Mandela gave his support to the Report, the ANC has been less than enthusiastic about it.

Space does not permit a detailed account of the TRC Report.[11] In five volumes it records the gross human rights violations that occurred between 1960 and 1994. It finds that the leaders of the apartheid state were responsible for systematic torture, disappearances, judicial and extra-judicial killings and unlawful incursions into foreign states to kill opponents of apartheid. It condemns former state President P.W. Botha for his role in the facilitation of gross human rights violations. The perpetrators of human rights violations were named after being given prior notice of the TRC's findings of their complicity. The ANC does not escape blame. The Report finds that it was guilty of gross human rights violations in its conduct of the armed struggle, particularly in its targeting of civilians and in its torturing of suspected spies in its training camps in Angola. Mrs Winnie Madikizela-Mandela is found responsible for committing gross violations of human rights. The participation of business, the media, the health sector and the judiciary in the maintenance of the apartheid state is also condemned.

South Africa became a party to the Geneva Conventions of 1949 in 1952. It became a party to the Additional Protocols only after the fall of apartheid – in 1995. In 1980, the ANC deposited a declaration with the President of the International Committee of the Red Cross (and not the Swiss Federal Council, as required) in which it stated that it intended 'to respect and be guided by the general principles of international humanitarian law applicable in armed conflicts'.[12]

During the apartheid era, the South African army and police were involved in major military operations in Angola and northern Namibia; in counter-insurgency operations in pre-independence Zimbabwe; in cross-border raids into Lesotho, Botswana, Swaziland, Mozambique, Zimbabwe and Zambia; and in covert operations in the Seychelles and Comores. More people were killed by South African security forces in the maintenance of the apartheid state *outside* South

---

11. *Truth and Reconciliation Commission Report*, 5 volumes (Cape Town, Truth and Reconciliation Commission 1998).
12. 22 *IRRC* (1981) p. 20.

Africa than within.[13] In 1978, for instance, over 600 men, women and children were killed in a raid on the SWAPO base/refugee camp at Kassinga in Angola, 198 km north of the Namibian border.

During this period, it is not clear how the South African security forces saw their obligations under the Geneva Conventions. No clear policy statement was made on this subject in respect of external conflicts. The Angolan conflict, particularly in its initial phases when the South African army advanced to the outskirts of Luanda in 1975, could be described as an international armed conflict. The wars in northern Namibia and southern Angola, on the other hand, probably qualified as non-international armed conflicts to which common Article 3 of the Geneva Conventions was applicable. The low intensity conflict on South Africa's own northern borders, on the other hand, probably failed to meet the threshold of common Article 3. The South African government consistently treated members of SWAPO arrested in Namibia (and southern Angola) and members of the ANC and PAC arrested in South Africa (or neighbouring territories) as 'terrorists' and criminals who were not entitled to treatment as prisoners of war.[14]

The *TRC Report* makes no attempt to identify the nature of the conflicts in southern Africa from the perspective of international humanitarian law. However, it makes it clear that, in its assessment of the responsibility of both government and ANC forces for gross human rights violations in their military operations, it was guided by the principles of international humanitarian law contained in the Geneva Conventions and Additional Protocols and the Principles of International Law Recognized in the Charter of the Nuremberg Tribunal and in the Judgement of the Tribunal, adopted by the International Law Commission in 1950.[15] Invoking the distinction between 'combatants' and 'protected persons', it applies the following principles to the killing or ill-treatment of persons in armed conflict.

Those combatants who were killed or seriously injured while they were unarmed or out of combat, executed after they had been captured, or wounded when they clearly could have been arrested were held to be victims of gross violations of human rights, and those responsible were held accountable.

In cases where the Commission could not determine whether a combatant was out of combat, and therefore regarded as a protected person, it followed the precedent set by international humanitarian law. The commission gave the benefit of doubt to people

---

13. *TCR Report, supra* n. 11, Vol. 2, pp. 42-43.

14. Unsuccessful attempts were made to persuade South African and Namibian courts to accord special status to captured members of national liberation movements on the ground that Art. 1(4) of Additional Protocol I had become part of customary international law or was believed to be a customary rule by the combatants themselves. See J. Dugard, 'The Treatment of Rebels in Conflicts of a Disputed Character: The Anglo-Boer War and the 'ANC-Boer War' Compared', in A. Delissen and G.J. Tanja, eds, *Humanitarian Law of Armed Conflict. Challenges Ahead. Essays in Honour of Frits Kalshoven* (Dordrecht, Martinus Nijhoff Publishers 1991) p. 447.

15. 2 *ILC Yearbook* (1950) p. 374.

killed or seriously injured in uncertain circumstances and found them to be the victims of gross violations of human rights.[16]

Although the TRC acknowledges the distinction between international and non-international armed conflicts, and the distinction between grave breaches and common Article 3 protection, it makes no attempt to evaluate the conflicts in question because

> This distinction between international and internal armed conflicts is less relevant today, as the laws of war have evolved to regulate more closely the use of force in all situations of armed conflict.[17]

Guided by these principles, it found that the attack on Kassinga in 1978 resulted in the commission of gross human rights violations against the civilian occupants of Kassinga camp by reason of the use of fragmentation bombs in the initial air assault, which constituted an indiscriminate use of force, and the failure to take adequate care to protect the lives of civilians. The Commission made no finding on the killing of wounded persons although there was evidence that this had happened.[18] The TRC rejected the suggestion that this operation had been an exercise in legitimate self-defence on the ground that South Africa was in illegal occupation of Namibia.[19]

The TRC further found that the South African government's campaign in Angola between 1977 and 1988 'led to gross violations of human rights on a vast scale' and constituted 'a systematic pattern of abuse' for which the South African political and military leadership was responsible.[20]

The taking of prisoners-of-war by either side in the Angolan conflict was rare, although there were instances of it occurring.[21] In 1978, some 200 to 300 South West African refugees were captured during a raid on a base in Angola and taken to Namibia. There they were detained – and tortured – until 1984. The South African authorities did not treat them as prisoners of war because, from the South African perspective, there was no war! The TRC categorised this treatment as 'deportation to slave labour'.[22]

The TRC made findings of gross human rights violations on the part of the security forces in Namibia between 1966 and 1989.[23] Cross border raids on military targets in neighbouring territories were condemned as violations of international law

---

16. *TRC Report, supra* n. 11, Vol. 1, p. 76.
17. Ibid., Vol. 1, p. 75.
18. Ibid., Vol. 2, pp. 52-55.
19. Ibid.,Vol. 2, p. 53.
20. Ibid., Vol. 2, pp. 60-61.
21. In 1985 Captain Wynand du Toit was captured in the course of a commando operation in Cabinda (ibid. p. 6), while Cuban soldiers were taken prisoners of war in Southern Angola.
22. Ibid., Vol. 2, pp. 67-68.
23. Ibid., Vol. 2, p. 84.

and gross violations of human rights on the ground that those killed were killed in non-combat situations.[24]

The TRC's determination to act within the parameters of international law was further evidenced by its findings on crimes against humanity and just wars.

The TRC 'endorsed' the view that 'apartheid as a form of systematic racial discrimination and separation constituted a crime against humanity',[25] despite the fact that 'it was perfectly legal within [South Africa]'.[26] A special Appendix on the evolution of this crime in international law is included in the *TRC Report.*[27]

The TRC accepted that the liberation movements had been engaged in a 'just war' in their struggle against apartheid.[28] But it distinguished between the 'justice of war' and 'justice in war' and declared that 'the fact that the apartheid system was a crime against humanity does not mean that all acts carried out in order to destroy apartheid were necessarily legal, moral and acceptable'.[29] Torture, abduction and the killing and injuring of defenceless people (both civilians and soldiers out of combat) could not be regarded 'as morally or legally legitimate, even where the cause was just'.[30] 'Apartheid as a system was a crime against humanity' but acts carried out by *any* of the parties to the conflict in southern Africa could be classified as human rights violations.[31]

Acting on this premise,[32] the TRC found that the liberation movements had committed gross violations of human rights for which they were accountable.[33] These acts included the indiscriminate use of landmines, the killing of informers and spies and torture.

The TRC found that the principles of international humanitarian law did not adequately cover many of the problems it was required to address. Hence its recommendation that:

Renewed international consideration be given to:

— The way in which liberation wars and civil wars are conducted.
— The treatment of participants in armed combat in circumstances of war, civil war, revolutions, insurgency or guerrilla warfare.

In this era of international concern for human rights, it is necessary to examine whether it is acceptable for deserters or traitors to be executed, even if they have been tried by

---

24. Ibid., Vol. 2, p. 154.
25. Ibid., Vol. 5, p. 222.
26. Ibid., Vol.1, p. 102.
27. Ibid., Vol. 1, pp. 9-102. Cf., the 'Minority Position' submitted by Commissioner Wynand Malan, ibid., Vol. 5, pp. 448-450.
28. Ibid., Vol. 1, pp. 66-68; Vol. 2, p. 325.
29. Ibid., Vol. 2, p. 69.
30. Ibid.
31. Ibid.
32. Ibid., Vol. 5, p. 211.
33. Ibid., Vol. 2, p. 325.

a tribunal. It must be borne in mind that in many such circumstances it is not possible for tribunals to comply with all the present international requirements. Minimum acceptable standards should be devised, governing conditions of detention and fair trials. The Commission found the Geneva Convention and its various protocols to be of great assistance, but believes there is still more that could be added.[34]

4.   AMNESTY: FOREIGN RECOGNITION

Amnesty is a practice that has its roots in the early history of mankind. From time immemorial, successor regimes have sought to secure peace through pardon. It is unlikely that this practice will disappear simply because of the establishment of an International Criminal Court and the assertion that there is an obligation on states to prosecute or extradite those suspected of the crimes of genocide, war crimes, crimes against humanity or torture.[35] A powerful military may still stand unrepentant and eager to resume power in the shadow of civilian rule – as in Argentina and Chile in the 1980s. Or amnesty may be the price to be paid for a settlement – as in the case of South Africa. In these and similar circumstances, amnesty holds out more hope for peace, stability and reconciliation than prosecution before national or international courts.

Amnesty will, however, lose its appeal to the incumbent 'criminal' regime if it is not accompanied by some guarantee of international recognition. It is hardly to be expected that a military or political leadership accustomed to international travel will willingly surrender power if it knows that its days of foreign travel are over, and that by transferring power to a civilian, democratic regime it will sentence itself to confinement within its own territory. Here the obvious question must be asked: would Augusto Pinochet have accepted return to civilian rule if he could have predicted what was to befall him?

The South African TRC was sensitive to this issue. In its *Report* it makes the following appeal to the international community:

> The definition of apartheid as a crime against humanity has given rise to a concern that persons who are seen to have been responsible for apartheid policies and practices might become liable to international prosecutions. The Commission believes that international recognition should be given to the fact that the Promotion of

---

34. Ibid., Vol. 5, p. 348.

35. See D. Orentlicher, 'Settling Accounts: The Duty to Prosecute Human Rights Violations of a Prior Regime', 100 *Yale Law Journal* (1991) p. 2537. In *Azapo v. President of the Republic of South Africa* 1996 (4) *South African Law Reports* 562 (CC), the South African Constitutional Court found that international law imposes no such duty to prosecute. See further J. Dugard, 'Is the Truth and Reconciliation Process compatible with International Law? An Unanswered Question', 13 *South African Journal on Human Rights* (1997) p. 258; J. Dugard, 'Reconciliation and Justice: the South African Experience', 8 *Transnational Law & Contemporary Problems* (1998) p. 277.

National Unity and Reconciliation Act, and the processes of this Commission itself, have sought to deal appropriately with the matter of responsibility for such policies.[36]

This appeal is conveniently, and one suspects, deliberately, vague as it fails to indicate whether it applies to those who have secured amnesty from an amnesty committee or to the leadership of the apartheid regime, such as Mr F.W. de Klerk, whose crimes were limited to the imposition of systematic racial domination and discrimination – an international crime against humanity – which was approved by South African law and therefore did not fall within the scope of the amnesty process. It appears to cover the latter category, which suggests that its main purpose is to secure immunity from prosecution for leaders of the apartheid regime in States Parties to the Convention on the Suppression and Punishment of the Crime of Apartheid.

At the same time, the TRC made it clear that it did not favour blanket amnesty. It recommended prosecution of those who had not sought or had been denied amnesty and declared that 'in order to avoid a culture of impunity and to entrench the rule of law, the granting of general amnesty in whatever guise should be resisted'.[37]

Unfortunately, the Rome Statute of the International Criminal Court fails to provide for recognition of amnesty, despite the fact that this matter had previously been considered by the Preparatory Commission. This is a matter that requires attention, particularly in the light of the Pinochet experience. Clearly not all national amnesties will, or should, receive international recognition. When, as in the case of Chile, the military dictatorship grants itself unconditional, blanket amnesty for conduct that is criminal under both national and international law, it is impossible to expect foreign courts and international criminal tribunals to honour it. Where, however, amnesty is conditional upon full disclosure of the crime and determination by a judicial or quasi-judicial body, and accompanied by an enquiry into the crimes of the past, it is difficult to suggest that amnesty should not be recognised abroad. The South African Truth and Reconciliation process has demonstrated that there is a middle-path between prosecution and amnesia. It also serves to emphasise that there is a need to consider the international benefits of such a process in the form of international recognition of its amnesties.

---

36. *TRC Report, supra* n. 11, Vol. 5, p. 349.
37. Ibid., Vol. 5, p. 309.

NATIONAL IMPLEMENTING LEGISLATION FOR THE CHEMICAL WEAPONS CONVENTION: THE EXPERIENCE OF THE FIRST TWO YEARS[1]

Lisa Woollomes Tabassi[2]

1.   INTRODUCTION

> 'We are witnessing today an historic event. An entire category of weapons of mass destruction has been banned by the Chemical Weapons Convention ... Pause for a moment, if you will, and consider the symbolism, but more importantly the significance of this act. It is not merely a great step in the cause of disarmament and non-proliferation. It is not merely a signal of restraint and discipline in war. It is much more. It is a momentous act of peace.'

With these words United Nations Secretary-General Kofi Annan opened the First Session of the Conference of the States Parties, the principal organ of the Organisation for the Prohibition of Chemical Weapons (OPCW), in The Hague on 5 May 1997. An undercurrent of idealism has been a driving force in the negotiation and implementation of the Chemical Weapons Convention.[3] But as States Parties and the Technical Secretariat of the OPCW (the treaty's implementing body) have discovered, finding a sense of purpose in the work of the OPCW has been easier than translating the Convention into practical measures enforceable in domestic jurisdictions.

The Convention enjoyed remarkably wide adherence from the outset: 165 signatory states; 87 States Parties at the entry into force of the Convention on 29 April 1997 and 121 States Parties two years later.[4] Of the 121 States Parties, one-third (40) have met their obligation to notify the Secretariat that they have adopted necessary measures to implement the Convention. However, of the measures adopted, not all are complete: some of those 40 States Parties are continuing to draft or amend additional legislation or regulations that they deem necessary.

---

1. © L. Woollomes Tabassi, 1999.

2. Ms Lisa Woollomes Tabassi is Senior Legal Assistant in the Office of the Legal Adviser of the Technical Secretariat of the Organisation for the Prohibition of Chemical Weapons (OPCW). The views expressed are the author's own and do not necessarily reflect those of the Secretariat.

3. The Convention on the Prohibition of the Development, Production, Stockpiling and Use of Chemical Weapons and on Their Destruction, opened for signature on 13-15 January 1993 and entered into force on 29 April 1997. Text available at http://www.opcw.org.

4. For a list of States Parties to the Chemical Weapons Convention see Annex 1.

The reasons for this are explored below. The situation is of particular importance as the lack of national implementing legislation is hindering some States Parties from complying with all of their obligations under the Convention, and under international law, a state may not invoke the provisions of its internal law as justification for its failure to perform its treaty obligations.[5] More important still is the effect such failure could have, depending on the obligation not being met. Potentially it could affect the regime designed to ensure that toxic chemicals and precursors are used only for peaceful purposes or, ultimately, it could affect the ability to prosecute and punish offenders.

2.   BRIEF OVERVIEW OF THE CONVENTION REGIME[6]

Under Article I, paragraph 1, of the Convention, each State Party undertakes never under any circumstances:

(a) To develop, produce, otherwise acquire, stockpile or retain chemical weapons, or transfer, directly or indirectly, chemical weapons to anyone;
(b) To use chemical weapons;
(c) To engage in any military preparations to use chemical weapons;
(d) To assist, encourage or induce, in any way, anyone to engage in any activity prohibited to a State Party under this Convention.[7]

'Chemical weapons' are defined in Article II, paragraph 1, as:

(a) Toxic chemicals and their precursors, except where intended for purposes not prohibited under this Convention, as long as the types and quantities are consistent with such purposes;
(b) Munitions and devices, specifically designed to cause death or other harm through the toxic properties of those toxic chemicals specified in subparagraph (a), which would be released as a result of the employment of such munitions and devices;
(c) Any equipment specifically designed for use directly in connection with the employment of munitions and devices specified in subparagraph (b).

'Purposes not prohibited under this Convention' are defined in Article II, paragraph 9, as:

---

5. Art. 27 of the 1969 Vienna Convention on the Law of Treaties.

6. For comprehensive analysis see primarily, W. Krutzsch and R. Trapp, *A Commentary on the Chemical Weapons Convention* (Dordrecht, Martinus Nijhoff 1994); Hague Academy of International Law 1994 workshop, *The Convention on the Prohibition and Elimination of Chemical Weapons: a Breakthrough in Multilateral Disarmament*, (Dordrecht, Martinus Nijhoff 1995); M. Bothe, N. Ronzitti and A. Rosas, *The New Chemical Weapons Convention - Implementation and Prospects* (The Hague, Kluwer Law International 1998); and http://www.opcw.org.

7. The remainder of Art. I concerns the obligations of each State Party: to destroy its chemical weapons; to destroy chemical weapons it abandoned on other States Parties' territory; to destroy its chemical weapons production facilities; and not to use riot control agents as a method of warfare.

(a)Industrial, agricultural, research, medical, pharmaceutical or other peaceful purposes;

(b)Protective purposes, namely those purposes directly related to protection against toxic chemicals and to protection against chemical weapons;

(c)Military purposes not connected with the use of chemical weapons and not dependent on the use of the toxic properties of chemicals as a method of warfare;

(d)Law enforcement including domestic riot control purposes.

The definition of 'purposes not prohibited under this Convention' is an early indicator of the root of the Convention's complexity: the toxic chemicals used in chemical weapons and their precursors can have wide peaceful applications.[8] In contrast to previous arms control agreements, which affected only the military and government, the Chemical Weapons Convention can have an impact on the ordinary pursuits of civil society.[9]

The Convention affects several distinct spheres at once: the military (in respect of methods and means of warfare); the police (in respect of riot control agents and enforcement of laws and regulations); customs (in respect of control of trade in controlled chemicals); private industry (in respect of the production, processing or consumption of controlled chemicals); and government (in respect of its representation in the OPCW and the 'National Authority' which the state is required to establish to serve as a national focal point for effective liaison with the OPCW and other States Parties).

Not only does the Convention affect activities in those spheres, it gives rise to the responsibility to report relevant activities to the National Authority for the compilation of the State Party's initial[10] and annual national declarations to the OPCW. Declarations serve as the basis for the Convention verification regime (encompassing on-site inspections and monitoring by the Secretariat's inspectorate; it also includes provision of the data compiled to States Parties as required to assure them of continued compliance by other States Parties).   .

The declarations contain data concerning, *inter alia*, the State Party's possession (or not) of chemical weapons and its general plan for their destruction; old or abandoned chemical weapons on its territory, chemical weapons production facilities and its general plan for their destruction; other facilities designed, constructed or used primarily for development of chemical weapons, and the riot control agents it holds. Chemicals of particular relevance to the Convention are listed in three schedules annexed to the Convention. Initial and annual declarations

---

8. For example, in medical and pharmaceutical preparations, pesticides, defoliants, dyes, printing ink and ball point pen fluids, photography, paints, leather tanning, cement, metal plating, pesticides, toiletries and numerous others.

9. Private industry which is producing, processing or consuming controlled chemicals may find itself subject to new reporting requirements and may fall under the obligation to open its facilities or plants to on-site inspection by international inspectors. Traders may also find themselves subject to increased regulation. States have accepted that the objective of a world free of chemical weapons is worth the additional regulatory burden.

10. Due 30 days after entry into force of the Convention for the State Party.

are required to be submitted concerning Schedule 1 chemicals and the facilities that produce them. Initial and annual declarations also report: aggregate national data concerning Schedule 2 and 3 chemicals; the plant sites that produce, process or consume Schedule 2 chemicals; the plant sites that produce Schedule 3 chemicals; and the plant sites that produce by synthesis unscheduled discrete organic chemicals over a threshold amount. Since information contained in some declarations may consist of confidential business information pertaining to private industry, the Convention also sets forth strict requirements for protection of confidentiality which must be upheld by the Secretariat, by the other organs of the OPCW and by States Parties who receive information from the Secretariat.

Ongoing reporting is also required: all transfers of Schedule 1 chemicals must be reported 30 days in advance of the transfer. Schedule 1 chemicals may only be transferred between States Parties, may not be re-transferred, and both the exporting and the importing State Party must report the transfer to the Secretariat. Other trade restrictions embodied in the Convention are as follows: Schedule 2 chemicals (until 29 April 2000) and Schedule 3 chemicals may be transferred to states not party only upon the provision of an end-user certificate by the competent governmental authority of that state. From 29 April 2000, transfers of Schedule 2 chemicals to states not party will also be prohibited.

It is generally apparent from the above that regardless of the State Party's legal system,[11] legislation will be necessary to compel the submission of the information needed for an accurate national declaration and for export/import controls. Experience in the first two years has shown that comprehensive implementing legislation is the key to obtaining reliable, complete information.

3.   THE REQUIREMENT FOR LEGISLATION

Article VII is the basis for national implementing legislation:

1. Each State Party shall, in accordance with its constitutional processes, adopt the necessary measures to implement its obligations under this Convention. In particular, it shall:
(a) Prohibit natural and legal persons anywhere on its territory or in any other place under its jurisdiction as recognised by international law from undertaking any activity prohibited to a State Party under this Convention, including enacting penal legislation with respect to such activity;
(b) Not permit in any place under its control any activity prohibited to a State Party under this Convention; and

---

11. Principally, the state's position on the relationship of domestic law to international law. The two main theories are monism (in the event of a conflict between international law and domestic legislation, international law will prevail) and dualism (international law is applied within a state only if it has been incorporated into domestic legislation).

(c) Extend its penal legislation enacted under subparagraph (a) to any activity prohibited to a State Party under this Convention undertaken anywhere by natural persons, possessing its nationality, in conformity with international law.

2. Each State Party shall cooperate with other States Parties and afford the appropriate form of legal assistance to facilitate the implementation of the obligations under paragraph 1.

...

5. Each State Party shall inform the Organisation of the legislative and administrative measures taken to implement this Convention.

Article VI, paragraph 2, is the basis for regulating Schedules 1, 2 and 3 chemicals under that Article and under Parts VI to IX of the Verification Annex to the Convention.

2. Each State Party shall adopt the necessary measures to ensure that toxic chemicals and their precursors are only developed, produced, otherwise acquired, retained, transferred, or used within its territory or in any other place under its jurisdiction or control for purposes not prohibited under this Convention.

A review of existing legislation is specifically required under Article XI, paragraph 2:

2. Subject to the provisions of this Convention and without prejudice to the principles and applicable rules of international law, the States Parties shall:

...

(c) Not maintain among themselves any restrictions, including those in any international agreements, incompatible with the obligations undertaken under this Convention, which would restrict or impede trade and the development and promotion of scientific and technological knowledge in the field of chemistry for industrial, agricultural, research, medical, pharmaceutical or other peaceful purposes;

...

(e) Undertake to review their existing national regulations in the field of trade in chemicals in order to render them consistent with the object and purpose of this Convention.

Each State Party must assess whether steps are necessary to ensure that the treaty will be, and continue to be, implemented effectively and enforced in its jurisdiction. Depending upon the state's constitution, its existing laws and the extent of its chemical industry, the steps the State Party has to take may be very few, or may be quite extensive. In all cases a review of existing legislation is in order.

4.   OUTREACH BY THE SECRETARIAT

During the preparatory phase before entry into force[12] of the Convention, the Secretariat carried out a range of activities focused at facilitating the task of adopting national implementing legislation as early as possible. Workshops, seminars and, in some cases, bilateral assistance, were conducted and reference materials were developed. Examples of legislation drafted early on by a number of signatory states,[13] a manual[14] and a model act to implement the Convention[15] were widely disseminated.

Since the entry into force of the Convention, the Secretariat has continued those activities and has developed a 'Legislation Package' which includes: a prioritised checklist of general obligations for the National Authority;[16] a checklist for legislators[17]; a survey[18] of national implementing legislation comparing how states legislated in the three required areas[19] and 17 additional areas;[20] an Australian national paper on import/export controls; a Swedish national paper on review of existing national legislation in the field of trade in chemicals; and a Note by the Director-General entitled, 'Compliance with Article VII: Legislation, Cooperation and Legal

---

12. From January 1993 to May 1997, the Provisional Technical Secretariat of the Preparatory Commission for the OPCW was in existence and supported intensive work undertaken by signatory states.

13. Australia, Canada, Finland, Germany, Norway, Peru, South Africa, Sweden and Switzerland. Germany submitted its legislation in four languages (German, English, Russian and Spanish) for dissemination by the Provisional Technical Secretariat of the Preparatory Commission for the OPCW.

14. B. Kellman, E. Tanzman, D. Gualtieri and S. Grimes, *Manual for National Implementation of the Chemical Weapons Convention, 1993*, 2nd edn. (Chicago JL, International Criminal Justice and Weapons Control Centre, DePaul Univ. 1998). The project for the manual was initiated at the suggestion of the Preparatory Commission for the OPCW which also cooperated in the convening of a conference of a Committee of Legal Experts on National Implementation of the Chemical Weapons Convention in 1993 to comment on the penultimate draft of the manual.

15. Preparatory Commission Doc. PC-XI/7/Rev.1, dated 31 May 1996.

16. Aimed primarily at states that do not possess chemical weapons and that have little or no chemical industry relevant to the Convention. Such states usually will have allocated only limited resources for implementation of the Convention. Nevertheless, they still have a number of obligations which need to be met to be in compliance with the Convention. Several National Authorities have found it necessary to carry out significant research and outreach to ensure that all declarable facilities/plants are identified and the owners are aware of the obligations they are required to comply with under the Convention.

17. The Convention may impact several areas of law, depending upon the State Party's legal system, for instance: constitutional law, civilian and military statutes and penal codes, customs, immigration and administrative law, civil and criminal procedure.

18. OPCW Doc. S/85/98, dated 17 November 1998, available from http://www.opcw.org.

19. Prohibitions, penal provisions and extraterritorial application to its nationals.

20. Legal assistance; definition of chemical weapons; declaration obligations; the regime for scheduled chemicals (regulation of Schedule 1 production/use; criteria for Schedule 2 and 3 declarations; import/export controls); licensing of industry; access to facilities; inspection equipment; respect for inspectors' privileges and immunities; confidentiality; liability; mandate of the National Authority; enforcement powers of the National Authority; samples; and primacy of the Convention.

Assistance'.[21] The latter Note is aimed at focusing the attention of States Parties on the need to develop the framework within which the Article VII, paragraph 2 obligation to 'co-operate and provide legal assistance' can be carried out. This will primarily be necessary for the prosecution and punishment of offenders[22] with the necessary components in place: criminalising activities prohibited under the Convention, extraterritorial extension of penal legislation to acts committed by nationals abroad,[23] harmonising penalties, and inclusion of the offences as extraditable crimes in extradition treaties. Following distribution of the Director-General's Note, the Conference of the States Parties recently requested the Secretariat to conduct a workshop on this subject, which is in the planning stages.

By the end of 1998, most of the key players have legislation in place although some important ones are missing. Submissions under Article VII have dwindled[24]

---

21. OPCW Doc. C-III/DG.1/Rev.1, dated 17 November 1998. Available from http://www.opcw.org.

22. In parallel, significant advances have recently been made towards codifying and criminalising, at the international level, chemical attacks. Two instruments were opened for signature in 1998: the International Convention for the Suppression of Terrorist Bombings (which enhances international cooperation between states to prevent acts of terrorism and to prosecute and punish perpetrators) and the Rome Statute for the International Criminal Court (which defines the use of chemical weapons in international armed conflict as a war crime falling within the jurisdiction of the Court). A third multilateral instrument, the Convention to Prohibit Biological and Chemical Weapons under International Criminal Law, is currently being drafted at the initiative of the Harvard Sussex Program on CBW Armament and Arms Limitation. The draft Convention is aimed at making it an international crime of universal jurisdiction for any person anywhere to develop, produce, acquire, stockpile, retain or transfer biological or chemical weapons. This is a clear reflection of international determination not only to prohibit and prevent, but also to punish offenders. Important in this respect was the 1995 Appeals Chamber decision in the *Tadić* case before the International Criminal Tribunal for the former Yugoslavia (ICTY), which found that the customary international law prohibition of the use of chemical weapons in international armed conflict is also applicable in non-international armed conflict. Thus the basic prohibition of the use of chemical weapons would be binding upon all states, individuals and organisations in all situations.

23. Sweden has taken this a step further, by providing that, 'A crime against the Convention will be sentenced by Swedish law and at a Swedish court even if the crime is committed abroad and irrespective of the perpetrator's nationality.' (Chapter 2, Section 3 of the amended Criminal Code of Sweden), thus raising the offence, for Sweden, to the level of an international crime of universal jurisdiction.

24. It is noteworthy that the Ad Hoc Group of States Parties to the Biological and Toxin Weapons Convention, meeting in Geneva to negotiate a binding protocol to strengthen that Convention, is considering inclusion of a much more stringent obligation for implementing legislation in the Protocol than the one contained in the Chemical Weapons Convention ('inform the Organisation of ... measures taken'). The bracketed provision contained in Article III D of the January 1999 rolling text of the draft BWC Protocol would require each State Party to submit a legislation declaration within 180 days of entry into force and to notify any changes in legislation:

"[(K) National legislation and regulations

24. Each State Party shall submit to the Organisation, not later than [180] days after this Protocol enters into force for it, a declaration containing the titles of legislation, regulations, orders or other legal measures that govern, regulate, provide guidance on or otherwise control:

(a) Access to buildings or other structures in which pathogens or toxins are being produced, handled or stored;

(b) Access to buildings or other structures or areas in which an outbreak of infectious disease

and in examining this, a new aspect of the problem came to light, i.e., the struggle to avoid competing chemicals' legislation.

5.   OVERLAPPING TREATY REGIMES

In the course of workshop and regional seminar presentations on national implementing legislation, the Secretariat became increasingly aware that a number of States Parties were facing difficulties with their legislation because of overlapping treaty regimes. Most of the early submissions under Article VII, paragraph 5, of the Convention consisted of a sectoral approach to legislation, i.e., a comprehensive act to implement the Convention. The reference materials distributed by the Secretariat also followed that approach. However, other States Parties have been trying to draft legislation to implement several instruments[25] at once, all involving the regulation of chemicals, and they identified the need for assistance in adopting an integrated approach to avoid conflicts between legislative provisions.

---

affecting humans, animals or plants is suspected or is known to be occurring.

25. The State Party shall provide the Organisation on request with copies of any legislation, regulations, directives, orders or other legal measures declared under paragraph 24. The State Party shall notify changes in such legislation within [90] days of their entry into force or their being promulgated within the State Party.

26. Copies of the legislation shall be provided, where possible in one of the official languages of the United Nations.]"

The rolling text of the draft BWC Protocol is available from http://www.brad.ac.uk/acad/sbtwc.

25. Annex VII to the 1998 IOMC document, *Key Elements of a National Programme for Chemicals Management and Safety*, lists the major binding international agreements related to chemicals as: the 1974 Convention for the Prevention of Marine Pollution from Land-Based Sources; the 1985 Montreal Guidelines for the Protection of the Marine Environment from Land Based Sources of Marine Pollution; 1989 Montreal Protocol on Substances that Deplete the Ozone Layer; the 1992 Basel Convention on the Control of Transboundary Movements of Hazardous Wastes and their Disposal; the 1990 ILO Convention Concerning Safety in the Use of Chemicals at Work; the 1988 Convention Against Illicit Traffic in Narcotic Drugs and Psychotropic Substances; the 1971 Convention on Psychotropic Substances; the 1961 Single Convention on Narcotics, as amended by the 1972 Protocol; the 1992 Convention on the Transboundary Effects of Industrial Accidents; the 1993 Convention concerning the Prevention of Major Industrial Accidents; the 1993 Chemical Weapons Convention; the 1979 Convention on Long-range Transboundary Air Pollution; the 1986 ILO Convention on Asbestos; the 1971 ILO Convention on Benzene. Voluntary Agreements consist of: the 1989 Amended London Guidelines for the Exchange of Information on Chemicals in International Trade (UNEP); the 1994 Code of Ethics on International Trade in Chemicals (UNEP); the 1989 Amended International Code of Conduct on the Distribution and Use of Pesticides (FAO); and the 1975 Certification Scheme on the Quality of Pharmaceutical Products Moving in International Trade (WHO). Recently opened for signature is the 1998 Rotterdam Convention on the Prior Informed Consent (PIC) Procedure for Certain Hazardous Chemicals and Pesticides in International Trade and currently under negotiation is the International Legally Binding Instrument for Implementing International Action on Certain Persistent Organic Pollutants (POPs Convention). Further information is available at http://www.unep.org.

At the same time, the Secretariat became aware of activities in precisely that area undertaken by the IFCS,[26] the IOMC[27] and UNITAR[28] in connection with the preparation of National Profiles to assess national infrastructure for management of chemicals. UNITAR has reported that in the course of preparing national profiles, some countries identified more than 100 laws and decrees addressing chemicals which are often not consistent with each other. Those countries are aiming at overcoming an overly sectoral approach in legislating chemicals. Others wish to identify legislative measures and policy instruments which could result in efficient risk reduction with minimum administrative costs. Still others are working on developing a national legislative framework which will allow for (a) incorporation of international harmonisation efforts and (b) implementation of national obligations under the growing number of legally binding international instruments.

Exploring this initiative, the Secretariat is cooperating with IFCS, IOMC and UNITAR in a workshop in 1999.[29] It is primarily aimed as a forum for government officials in developing countries and countries with economies in transition, to exchange experiences and views but it will also be attended by representatives from countries with advanced chemicals legislation, non-governmental organisations, intergovernmental organisations and development cooperation agencies. The expected outcome of the workshop is 'to provide pragmatic and innovative ideas which countries can use in developing strategies to fit their national needs' and the Secretariat is hoping to find improved, practical ways[30] of assisting States Parties to the Chemical Weapons Convention with this task.

---

26. The Intergovernmental Forum on Chemical Safety (IFCS) was established by the International Conference on Chemical Safety in Stockholm in 1994. At its first meeting, the IFCS adopted a 'Priorities for Action' plan to implement the recommendations of Chapter 19 of Agenda 21 of the 1992 United Nations Conference on Environment and Development (UNCED) and recommended that National Profiles should be elaborated to indicate the current capabilities and capacities for management of chemical and the specific needs for improvement.

27. The Inter-Organization Programme for the Sound Management of Chemicals (IOMC) was established in 1995 by FAO, ILO, OECD, UNEP, UNIDO, WHO and joined by UNITAR in 1998. It was designed to serve as a mechanism for coordinating policies and activities pursued by the participating organisations, jointly and separately, related to the assessment and management of chemicals. The Secretariat is located at WHO, the administering organisation.

28. In 1996, the United Nations Institute for Training and Research (UNITAR) published, under the auspices of IOMC, a guidance document entitled 'Preparing a National Profile to Assess the National Infrastructure for Management of Chemicals: A Guidance Document' and has since been an integral part of the programme, assisting developing countries and countries in economic transition to prepare comprehensive national profiles.

29. Thematic Workshop on Developing and Strengthening National Legislation and Policies for the Sound Management of Chemicals, Geneva, 22 to 25 June 1999. The final report will be available from http://www.unitar.org and http://www.opcw.org.

30. Programmes and initiatives undertaken in other intergovernmental organisations are being viewed with interest, such as the laudable ICRC Advisory Service on International Humanitarian Law, the review of TRIPS laws by the WTO Council on Trade Related Intellectual Property Rights, and the WIPO/WTO joint initiative legal technical assistance programme related to the TRIPS Agreement for developing country members of either of the two organisations.

6.   CONCLUSION

A challenge even for a state with an elaborate institutional framework, the task of drafting effective legislation to implement the Chemical Weapons Convention in parallel with other chemicals regimes is daunting for a state with limited resources. For non-chemical weapons possessor states with little or no chemical industry relevant to the Convention, it is difficult for the state's government to assign priority and scarce resources to the task of implementing the Chemical Weapons Convention, despite its value as an instrument of international security, protection[31] (against the threat of use) and trade and economic development.[32]

From this effort, one factor is clearly emerging: the need for inter-ministerial and inter-sectoral coordination. The majority of National Authorities established under the Chemical Weapons Convention have been centred in the State Party's Ministry of Foreign Affairs. A few have been centred in Ministries of Industry, Economy or Defence, or elsewhere. It was interesting to note that the national co-ordinating agencies for the preparation of National Profiles in the IFCS/UNITAR/IOMC initiatives have largely been centred in the Ministries of Environment, Health, Labour and Agriculture.[33] Argentina, which is participating in the UNITAR/IOMC Pilot Programme,[34] has as its national coordinator the Ministry of Health, supported by the Ministry of Foreign Affairs, the Secretariat for Natural Resources and Sustainable Development, the Ministry of Labour, the Board of Industry, the Institute of Oil and Gas, and the Inter-American Association for Sanitary Engineering.[35] Slovenia, which is also participating in the UNITAR/IOMC Pilot Programme, has as its national coordinator the Ministry of Health, supported by the Intersectoral Committee on the Management of Dangerous

---

31. Under Art. X, Assistance and Protection Against Chemical Weapons, assistance means 'the coordination and delivery to States Parties of protection against chemical weapons, including, *inter alia*, the following: detection equipment and alarm systems; protective equipment; decontamination equipment and decontaminants; medical antidotes and treatments; and advice on any of these protective measures'. Para. 3 of Art. X provides that 'Each State Party undertakes to facilitate, and shall have the right to participate in, the fullest possible exchange of equipment, material and scientific and technological information concerning means of protection against chemical weapons.'

32. Art. XI, para. 2(b), provides that States Parties shall 'undertake to facilitate, and have the right to participate in, the fullest possible exchange of chemicals, equipment and scientific and technical information relating to the development and application of chemistry for purposes not prohibited under this Convention'.

33. UNITAR/IFCS Secretariat, *Preparation of National Profiles to Assess the National Infrastructure for the Sound Management of Chemicals,* document IFCS/ISG3/98.14B, section 5.

34. UNITAR/IOMC Pilot Programme to Assist Countries in Implementing National Action Programmes for Integrated Chemicals Management.

35. The Argentine National Authority for the Chemical Weapons Convention was established as the Interministerial Commission for the Prohibition of Chemical Weapons in the Ministry of Foreign Affairs, International Trade and Economy.   The Board of the Directors of the Inter-ministerial Commission is composed of representatives from the Ministry of Foreign Affairs, International Trade and Economy, the Ministry of Economy and Public Works and Services, the Ministry of Defence, and the Armed Forces Scientific and Technical Research Institute (CITEFA).

Chemicals.[36]   From the case study of national implementation measures of international humanitarian law in Zimbabwe, it was learned that the Zimbabwean Interministerial Committee for Human Rights was extended to become the Interministerial Committee for Human Rights and Humanitarian Law. 'This Committee facilitates coordination at ministerial level of all matters relating to international humanitarian law. It is composed of representatives of the Ministries of Foreign Affairs,[37] Defence, Home Affairs, Justice and Social Welfare and of the President's Office. Each authority has its own responsibilities and competence within the Committee, whose mandate is to advise on the ratification of new humanitarian law treaties and on national implementation ... [It] is also competent to advise on new implementing legislation ...'[38]

Although the above examples of Argentina, Slovenia and Zimbabwe would indicate the possibility that regulatory efforts under the Chemical Weapons Convention are being carried out in coordination with efforts under other regimes, it is not yet clear whether the responsible officials focusing on different aspects of chemicals management (export/import controls of dangerous chemicals; environmental regulations; war matériel) are actually talking to each other. Logically, a concerted approach would be the trend to encourage to achieve a coherent legal regime. Much work remains to be done, however. Adherence to the Convention is growing and implementation is incrementally improving. And although the Chemical Weapons Convention is aimed at preventing substances from falling into the hands of individuals who would use them illegally and at setting the framework within which States Parties will control toxic chemicals and their precursors, enforce prohibited acts and prosecute violators, it is only when States Parties have completed the steps they need to take within that framework that enforcement of the Convention will become universally effective.

---

36. The Slovenian National Authority for the Chemical Weapons Convention is located in the Ministry of Health.

37. The Zimbabwean National Authority for the Chemical Weapons Convention is located in the Ministry of Foreign Affairs.

38. M.T. Dutli, 'National Implementation Measures of International Humanitarian Law: Some Practical Aspects', 1 *YIHL* (1998) pp. 245 at 254.

Annex 1
Status of the Chemical Weapons Convention
as of 29 April 1999

Number of States Parties: 121
Number of Signatory States which have not yet ratified: 48

States Parties:

Albania	El Salvador	Mali	Slovakia
Algeria	Equatorial Guinea	Malta	Slovenia
Argentina	Ethiopia	Mauritania	South Africa
Armenia	Fiji	Mauritius	Spain
Australia	Finland	Mexico	Sri Lanka
Austria	France	Monaco	Suriname
Bahrain	Gambia	Mongolia	Swaziland
Bangladesh	Georgia	Morocco	Sweden
Belarus	Germany	Namibia	Switzerland
Belgium	Ghana	Nepal	Tajikistan
Benin	Greece	Netherlands	The former Yugoslav
Bolivia	Guinea	New Zealand	Republic of
Bosnia and	Guyana	Niger	Macedonia *
Herzegovina*	Hungary	Norway	Togo
Botswana	Iceland	Oman	Trinidad and
Brazil	India	Pakistan	Tobago *
Brunei Darussalam	Indonesia	Panama	Tunisia
Bulgaria	Iran (Islamic	Papua New Guinea	Turkey
Burkina Faso	Republic of)	Paraguay	Turkmenistan
Burundi	Ireland	Peru	Ukraine
Cameroon	Italy	Philippines	United Kingdom of
Canada	Japan	Poland	Great Britain and
Chile	Jordan *	Portugal	Northern Ireland
China	Kenya	Qatar	United Republic of
Cook Islands	Kuwait	Republic of Korea	Tanzania
Costa Rica	Lao People's Demo-	Republic of Moldova	United States of
Côte d'Ivoire	cratic Republic	Romania	America
Croatia	Latvia	Russian Federation	Uruguay
Cuba	Lesotho	Saint Lucia	Uzbekistan
Cyprus	Lithuania	Saudi Arabia	Venezuela
Czech Republic	Luxembourg	Senegal	Viet Nam
Denmark	Malawi	Seychelles	Zimbabwe
Ecuador	Maldives	Singapore	

*   accession

**   The most up-to date figures can be accessed at http://www.opcw.org.

Annex 2
National Implementing Legislation
(documents on file in the Office of the Legal Adviser,
Technical Secretariat of the OPCW)
as of 29 April 1999

State Party	Legislation in force
Argentina	1. Decree 920/97 dated 11 September 1997 [establishing the National Authority and granting it certain powers]; 2. Joint resolution No. 125/98 dated 22 January 1998, of the Ministers of Defence, Foreign Affairs, International Trade and Economy, Public Works and Services, modifying Decree No. 603 of 9 April 1992, to attach the CWC Schedules on Chemicals and the recommendations of the Australia Group; 3. Decree 603 dated 9 April 1992; 4. Decree 1291/93 dated 24 June 1993 on nuclear exports [regarding export licenses issued by the National Commission for the Control of Sensitive Exports and War Material, applicable to transfers of Schedules 2 and 3 chemicals]; 5. Resolution No. 475 dated 13 February 1998, appointing the Executive Secretary of the Interministerial Commission for the Prohibition of Chemical Weapons.
Australia	1. Chemical Weapons (Prohibition) Act 1994, Act No. 26 of 1994 as amended; 2. Chemical Weapons (Prohibition) Regulations (Statutory Rules 1997 No. 84); 3. Customs (Prohibited Exports) Regulations (Amendment) (Statutory Rules 1996 No. 281); 4. Customs (Prohibited Exports) Regulations (Amendment) (Statutory Rules 1996 No. 325); 5. International Organizations (Privileges and Immunities) Act 1963; 6. Chemical Weapons (Prohibition) Amendment Regulations 1998 (No. 1).
Austria	1. Bundesgesetzblatt III No. 38/1997 [Convention made an integral part of the Austrian legal system]; 2. Federal Act on the Implementation of the Chemical Weapons Convention (Federal Law Gazette I No. 28/1997 [translation]; 3. Decree 145/1997: Chemical Weapons Convention Act - CWCA Regulation (Federal Law Gazette 145/1997) [translation]; 4. Foreign Trade Act 1995 (Federal Law Gazette 172/1995, as amended by Federal Act, Federal Law Gazette 429/1996, and by Council Regulation (EC) No. 3381/94, OJ No. L 295 of 30 November 1993, p. 1, as amended by Council Regulation (EC) No. 837/95, OJ No. L 90 of 21 April 1995, p. 1); 5. S.177a of the Criminal Code (Federal Law Gazette 60/1974, as amended by Federal Act, Federal Law Gazette I 112/1997) and S.64 para. 1 No. 4 lit. b of the Criminal Code.

State Party	Legislation in force
Belarus	*Unofficial translations:* 1. Cabinet of Ministers Resolution No. 344 dated 27 May 1996 [appointing the MFA as the National Authority, enumerating the related functions; and stipulating that a Committee of Experts shall be established], as amended by Resolution No. 271 of 22 February 1999; 2. Council of Ministers Resolution No. 245 of 14 April 1994 on visits by foreign inspectors; 3. Law on Export Control, approved by the Council on 19 December 1997; 4. Council of Ministers Resolution No. 218 of 18 March 1997 on the imposition of prohibitions and restrictions on the transport of goods across the customs frontier; 5. Amendments to the Criminal Code, the Code of Criminal Procedure and the Corrective Labour Code, approved on 20 December 1997; 6. Council of Ministers Resolution No. 27 dated 10 January 1998 on improving State control of the transport of specific goods (works or services) across the customs frontier; 7. Article 213 of the Criminal Code; 8. Statute of the Committee of Experts attached to the National Authority dated 27 February 1999.
Brazil	*Summary:* Decree No. 2.074 dated 14 November 1996 (establishing the National Authority); Law No. 9.112 dated 10 October 1995 (export controls).
Chile	1. Decree No. 354 dated 13 April 1997. General Regulations, Executive Authority, Ministry of Foreign Affairs, Appointment of a National Authority [unofficial translation and original]; 2. Comptroller of the Republic, Legal Department, certifying the scope of Decree No. 364 of 1997 of the Ministry of Foreign Affairs, No. 21.142, Santiago, 4 July 1997 [unofficial translation and original].
China	1. Decree No. 190 by the State Council, promulgating the Controlled Chemicals Regulations, entered into force on 27 December 1995 [unofficial translation and original]; 2. Ordinance No. 11 by the Ministry of Chemical Industry, issuing the List of Controlled Chemicals by Category, effective 15 May 1996 [unofficial translation and original]; 3. Ordinance No. 12 by the Ministry of Chemical Industry promulgating the Detailed Rules and Regulations on Implementation of the Controlled Chemicals Regulations, entered into force on 10 March 1997 [unofficial translation and original].
Czech Republic	1. Act No. 19/1997 of 24 January 1997 on some measures concerning chemical weapons prohibition and on amendments to Act No. 50/1976 Coll. 'On Zone Planning and the Building Code' (Building Act), as amended, the Small Businesses Act No. 455/1991 Coll., as amended, and the Penal Code Act No. 140/1961 Coll., as amended [translation and original]; 2. Decree No. 50/1997 of the Ministry of Industry and Trade of the Czech Republic dated 27 March 1997, Implementing the Act on some measures concerning chemical weapons prohibition [containing the lists of chemical substances which are subject to the control regime] [translation and original];

State Party	Legislation in force
	3. Act No. 21/1997 Coll. of 24 January 1997 on control of exports and imports of goods and technologies subject to international control regimes [licensing] [translation and original]; 4. Decree No. 43/1997 Coll. dated 21 February 1997 implementing Act No. 21/1997 Coll. [licensing] [translation and original]; 5. Decree of the Ministry of Industry and Trade No. 44/1997 dated 21 February 1997 introducing a general licence for imports of controlled goods [translation and original].
Denmark	1. Danish Agency for Development of Trade and Industry, Executive Order No. 771 of 6 October 1997 on the Submission of Declarations, Control and Inspections pursuant to the United Nations Convention on the Prohibition of Chemical Weapons [translation]; 2. Act No. 470 of 10 June 1997: Act to amend Act on Inspections, Submission of Declarations and Control pursuant to the United Nations Convention on the Prohibition of Chemical Weapons (Transfer of competence from government customs and tax authorities to the Ministry of Business and Industry) [translation]; 3. Act No. 443 of 14 June 1995: Act on Inspections, Submission of Declarations and Control pursuant to the United Nations Convention on the Prohibition of Chemical Weapons [translation]; 4. Executive Order No. 297 of 30 April 1997 on the Entry into Force of Act on Inspections, Submission of Declarations and Control pursuant to the United Nations Convention on the Prohibition of Chemical Weapons [translation]; 5. *Bek nr 712 af 29/08/1995. Forskriftens fulde tekst Bekendtgørelse om våben og ammunition mv* [Executive Order No. 712 of 29 August 1995 on Weapons and Ammunition etc., section 11, cfr].

European Union (applicable to EU members)	1. Council Regulation 2455/92 concerning imports and exports of hazardous chemicals (OJ L251 of 29 August 1992, p. 13), amended by:
	   a) Council Regulation 3135/94 (OJ L332 of 22 December 1994, p. 1);
	   b) Commission Regulation 41/94 (OJ L8 of 12 January 1994, p. 1).
	 2. Council Regulation (EC) 3381/94 setting up a Community regime for the control of exports of dual use goods (OJ L367 of 31 December 1994, p. 1), amended by:
	   a) Council Regulation (EC) 837/95 dated 10 April 1995 (OJ L90 of 21 April 1995, p. 1).
	
	 which should be read together with:
	 3. Council Decision 94/942/CFSP on the joint action adopted by the Council on the basis of Article J.3 of the Treaty on the European Union concerning the control of exports of dual-use goods (OJ L367 of 31 December 1994, p.8) which contains the list of goods under control. This Decision has been amended by Council Decision 99/193/CFSP of 9 March 1999 which incorporates all amendments since 94/942/CFSP into a single consolidated text.

Finland	1. Act No. 346 on the approval of certain provisions of the Convention on the Prohibition of the Development, Production, Stockpiling and Use of Chemical Weapons and on their Destruction and on its Application [translation]; 2. Decree No. 348 on the Implementation of the Convention on the Prohibition

State Party	Legislation in force
	of the Development, Production, Stockpiling and Use of Chemical Weapons and on their Destruction and on the entry into force of the Act on the approval of certain provisions of the Convention [translation]; 3. Act No. 351 on the Amendment of the Penal Code [translation]; 4. Decree No. 352 on the Entry into Force of the Act on the amendment of the Penal Code [translation]; 5. Decree No. 353 on the amendment of the Decree on the application of Chapter 1, Section 7 of the Penal Code [translation]; 6. Extracts from the Penal Code [translation]: Chapter 38: Data and Communications Offences (21 April 1995/578); Chapter 40: Offences in office and offences by an employee of a public corporation (8 September 1989/972).
France	1. Law No. 98-467 of 17 June 1998 concerning the implementation of the Convention ... [unofficial translation and original].
Germany	1. Act implementing the Chemical Weapons Convention - CWCIA [implementing legislation of 2 August 1994 and regulation of 20 November 1996] [translations into English, Russian, and Spanish and original]; 2. Part Four, Sections 18, 20, 21, 22a, 22b, of the War Weapons Control Act of 20 April 1961 and its annex, the War Weapons List, as amended on 26 February 1998.
Ireland	1. Chemical Weapons Act 1997.
Italy	1. Law of 18 November 1995, No. 496: Ratification and implementation of the Convention [translation and original]; 2. Law of 4 April 1997, No. 93: rules for the implementation of and amendments to Law of 18 November 1995, No. 496 [translation and original]; 3. Decree of the President of the Republic, 16 July 1997 No. 289 - Regulation on the Prohibition . . . of Chemical Weapons and on their Destruction [translation and original].
Japan	1. [implementing legislation and new legislation to prohibit the production and possession of Sarin and other toxic chemicals (in Japanese)]; 2. [Official Gazette issue containing the implementing legislation, the cabinet order and the ministerial order (in Japanese)]; 3. [Law No. 65: Law on the Prohibition of Chemical Weapons and Regulation etc., of Special Chemicals (law amended after entry into force of the Convention - in Japanese].
Latvia	1. Regulations No. 421 (protocol No. 70 §25): Regulations on Control of Strategic Goods dated 16 December 1997 [translation]; 2. Regulations No. 429 (protocol No. 72 §2) dated 23 December 1997: Regulations of the Control Committee of Strategic Goods [translation]; 3. Regulations of the Control Committee of Strategic Export and Import (Regulations No. 167) [establishes the National Authority – unofficial translation].
Lithuania	1. Law on the Prohibition of Chemical Weapons No. VIII-864 (24 September 1998); 2. Article 137 of the Constitution of the Republic of Lithuania; 3. Article 13 of the Law on the Control of Arms and Ammunitions (2 July

State Party	Legislation in force
	1996); 4. Law on the Control of Export, Import and Transit of Strategic Goods and Technology (5 July 1995); 5. Article 13(1) of the Law on Enterprises (8 May 1990) [licensing]; 6. Articles 4, 6, 7(1), 66, and 232 of the Penal Code; 7. Articles 21 and 21(1) of the Code of Penal Procedure; 8. Article 189(9) of the Code of Administrative Offences (8 January 1998).
Luxembourg	1. Law of 10 April 1997 approving the Convention ...[unofficial translation and original].
Malta	1. Act No. V of 1997, Supplemental Gazette of the Government of Malta, No. 16,447, 28 April 1997, authorising ratification of the CWC, establishment of the National Authority, enacting implementing legislation, annexing the text of the Convention and providing that "it shall form part and be enforceable as part of the laws of Malta". 2. Government Notice No. 532, Ratification of the Chemical Weapons Act, 1997 (Act No. V of 1997), National Authority for the Implementation of the Chemical Weapons Convention, published in *The Malta Government Gazette* No. 16,488 dated 15 July 1997).
Netherlands	1. Bulletin of Acts and Decrees 1995. No. 338: Act of 8 June 1995 containing rules on the implementation of the Convention ... (Chemical Weapons Convention Implementation Act) [translation]; 2. Bulletin of Acts and Decrees 1997. No. 181: Order of 24 April 1997, issued by the Minister of Justice, for the publication in the Bulletin of Acts and Decrees of the text of the Chemical Weapons Convention Implementation Act, as last amended by the Decree of 22 April 1997, Bulletin of Acts and Decrees 179 [translation]; 3. Text of the Chemical Weapons Convention Implementation Decree, as amended by Royal Decree of 22 April 1997 (Bulletin of Acts and Decrees 179) [translation]; 4. Chemical Weapons Convention Implementation Ordinance [of the Netherlands Antilles] (Country Ordinance of 21 April 1997, Official Bulletin A 1997 No. 122); 5. Chemical Weapons Convention Implementation Decree [of the Netherlands Antilles] (Country Decree, Containing General Measures, of 21 April 1997 containing rules on the implementation of the Country Ordinance to implement the Chemical Weapons Convention, Official Bulletin A 1997 No. 141).
New Zealand	1. 1996, No. 37: An Act to Implement in the Law of New Zealand the Convention ..., 24 June 1996.
Norway	1. Act No. 10 of 6 May 1994 relating to the implementation of the Convention; 2. Royal Decree of 16 May 1997: Regulations relating to the implementation of the Convention; 3. Export Control List I (includes scheduled chemicals which are not dual-use chemicals); 4. Export Control List II (which corresponds to the Dual-Use List of the European Union) as amended to include all scheduled dual-use chemicals (a new item 1C450 in Control List II constitutes the amendment); 5. Amendment to the General Civil Penal Code (Act No. 10 of 22 May 1902),

State Party	Legislation in force
	section 12, items 3e and 4b and section 13.
Oman	1. Sultan's Decree No. 21/97 on the regime for the implementation of the Convention [translation and original]; 2. Regime for the Implementation of the Convention [translation and original].
Panama	1. *Asamblea Legislative Ley N. 48 (de 15 de julio de 1998) "Por la cual se aprueba la Convención ... (Gaceta Oficial No. 23,589, 20 July 1998)* [incorporates the Convention into the domestic law of Panama].
Peru	1. Law No. 26672 dated 7 October 1996, establishing the National Authority for the Prohibition of Chemical Weapons CONAPAQ (20 October 1996) [unofficial translation and original].
Republic of Korea	1. Act on the Control of the Production, Export, Import, etc. of Specific Chemicals for the Prohibition of Chemical Weapons (enacted by Act No. 5162, 16 August 1996) [translation and original].
Romania	1. Act No. 56/1997 on implementing the provisions of the Convention (enacted by Parliament on 24 March 1997 as Law No. 56 and promulgated by Decree No. 148 of the President of Romania on 15 April 1997) [translation].
Slovakia	1. Amendment to Decree No. 23/1994 of the Ministry of Economy [including Schedules 1, 2 and 3 chemicals in the control regime]. 2. *129. Zákon o zákaze chemickych zbrani a o zmene a oplneni niektorych zákono* [law approved by the National Council on 1 April 1998].
South Africa	1. Government Gazette dated 2 July 1993 (Vol. 337, No. 14919: No. 1159 dated 2 July 1993: Act No. 87 of 1993: Non-Proliferation of Weapons of Mass Destruction Act, 1993; 2. Government Gazette dated 23 May 1997 (Vol. 383, No. 18013): No. 704 dated 23 May 1997: Non-Proliferation of Weapons of Mass Destruction Act, 1993 (Act No. 87 of 1993): Declaration of certain goods to be controlled goods and the control measures applicable to such goods; 3. Government Gazette dated 23 May 1997 (vol. 383, No. 18014): No. R. 705 of 23 May 1997: Non-Proliferation of Weapons of Mass Destruction Act, 1993 (Act No. 87 of 1993): Schedule: Regulations relating to the implementation and administration of the Chemical Weapons Convention in the Republic.
Sweden	1. Act on Inspections according to the Chemical Weapons Convention (1994:118) [translation]; 2. Ordinance on Inspections according to the Chemical Weapons Convention (1997:121) [summary in English]; 3. Amendment to the Criminal Code [translation]; 4. Amendments to the Act on Immunity and Privileges in Certain Cases (1976:661) [translation]; 5. Amendments to the Strategic Products Act (1991:341) [translation]; 6. Amendments to the Ordinance relating to Strategic Products (1994:2060) [translation]; 7. Amendments to the Military Equipment Act (1992:1300) [translation]; 8. Amendments to the Military Equipment Ordinance (1992:1303) [translation].
Switzerland	1. Federal Order concerning the implementation of the Chemical Weapons Convention No. 515.08 of 3 October 1994 (as at 1 January 1997) [unofficial translation and original];

State Party	Legislation in force

	2. Weaponry [unofficial translation and original]
	    I. Federal law of 13 December 1996 on weaponry (LFMG);
	    II. Order of 25 February 1998, amending the clause on the conferment of powers in the law on weaponry;
	    III. Order of 25 February 1998 on weaponry (OMG);
	3. Dual use goods [unofficial translation and original]
	    I. Federal law on the inspection of chemicals which can be used for both civilian and military purposes (Law on goods inspections, LCB);
	    II. Order on the inspection of chemicals which can be used for both civilian and military purposes (Order on the inspection of chemicals, OCPCh);
	    III. DFEP Order on controls of chemicals which can be used for both civilian and military purposes (DFEP Order on control of chemicals, OCPCh-DFEP).

Turkey	*Summary:* 1. Amendment of 25 January 1997 to the Law on Control of the Industrial Companies which produce war related equipment, ammunition and explosive (Law No. 3763 dated 1940); 2. Regulation dated 6 January 1996; 3. Regulation dated 8 October 1997; 4. Regulation by the Turkish Central Bank dated 15 October 1997; 5. Regulation by the Undersecretariat of Foreign Trade dated 6 November 1997; 6. Regulation dated 6 May 97.
United Kingdom of Great Britain and Northern Ireland	1. Chemical Weapons Act 1996; 2. Chemical Weapons Act 1996 (Commencement) Order 1996 (SI 1996/2054); 3. Chemical Weapons (Notification) Regulations 1996 (SI 1996/2503); 4. Chemical Weapons (Notification) (Amendment) Regulations 1996 (SI 1996/2669); 5. Chemical Weapons (Licence Appeal Provisions) Order 1996 (SI 1996/3030); 6. Amendment No. 148 to the Open General Import Licence dated 4 December 1987 granted by the Secretary of State and coming into force 29 April 97; 7. Dual Use and Related Goods (Export Control) Regulations 1996 (SI 1996/2721) and the Dual-Use and Related Goods (Export Control) (Amendment No. 2) Regulations 1997 (SI 1997/1007) which implement the controls on the export of dual-use goods contained in European Council Decisions 96/613/CFSP and 97/100/CFSP; 8. Export of Goods (Control) Order 1994 (SI 1994/1191); 9. Export of Goods (Control) (Amendment No. 2) Order 1997 (SI 1997/1008).
United States of America	1. Bill H.R. 4328, signed by the President of the United States on 21 October 1998; 2. Congressional Record dated 19 October 1998 (extract) [text contained in the Conference report, agreed by the House on 20 October 1998 and by the Senate on 21 October 1998 and sent to the President on 21 October 1998].

THE FIRST AND SECOND SESSIONS OF THE PREPARATORY COMMISSION FOR THE INTERNATIONAL CRIMINAL COURT[1]

Knut Dörmann[2]

1.   BACKGROUND

The adoption of the Statute of the International Criminal Court in July 1998 in Rome was the culmination of years of effort by the international community. Under Article 126, the Statute will enter into force once it is ratified by 60 states. As many states will have to enact national legislation or even change their constitutions before ratification to comply with the obligations of the Statute, the required number of ratifications will probably not be reached in the short term.

Besides, a number of tasks still remain to be undertaken by states, as indicated in the Statute itself, namely, drafting of a document called 'Elements of Crimes' (EOC),[3] drafting of the Rules of Procedure and Evidence (RPE) and reaching agreement on the definition of the crime of aggression. Therefore, the UN General Assembly[4] has mandated a Preparatory Commission (PrepCom) to prepare draft texts of the RPE and EOC and proposals for a provision on aggression, including its definition, elements and the conditions under which the International Criminal Court (ICC) shall exercise its jurisdiction with respect to this crime. The drafts of the EOC and RPE must be finalized by 30 June 2000, when they should be formally adopted. The definition of aggression does not have to be agreed on until the first review conference seven years after the entry into force of the Statute. In addition to these tasks, which this article will describe in greater detail, the PrepCom will work on a relationship agreement between the Court and the United Nations, basic principles governing a headquarters agreement and financial regulations and rules.

---

1. © Knut Dörmann, 1999.

2. Knut Dörmann is Legal Advisor at the Legal Division of the International Committee of the Red Cross (ICRC), Geneva. The opinions expressed are those of the author and do not necessarily reflect the views of the ICRC.

3. These elements are intended to help the Court interpret the provisions on crimes, Article 9 ICC Statute.

4. See UN GA Res. 53/105 of 8 December 1998 and Res. F adopted by the United Nations Diplomatic Conference on the Establishment of an International Criminal Court on 17 July 1998.

Yearbook of International Humanitarian Law
Volume 2 - 1999 - pp. 283-306

2.   THE FIRST PREPCOM

The PrepCom met in New York at UN Headquarters from 16 to 26 February 1999 for its first session. Given that the author has been involved mainly in the negotiations on the elements of war crimes, the primary focus of this section will be the description of the work done in the Working Group on EOC.

2.1   **Working group on elements of crimes**

2.1.1   *General remarks*

The basis for the work on the EOC is to be found in Article 9 of the ICC Statute.[5] This provision stipulates that the EOC 'shall assist the Court in the interpretation and application of Articles 6 [genocide], 7 [crimes against humanity] and 8 [war crimes]', thereby clearly indicating that the elements themselves are not binding upon judges. These Elements must 'be consistent with this Statute'.

The Working Group on EOC held eight meetings. The negotiations were mainly based on a comprehensive United States document[6] defining the elements of all crimes listed in the ICC Statute and a joint Swiss/Hungarian document[7] containing proposals for elements of war crimes defined in Article 8(2)(a), that is, the war crimes derived from the grave breaches provisions of the Geneva Conventions. The negotiations were supported by an analytical Spanish document[8] and the first part of an ICRC study[9] relating to the crimes listed in Article 8(2)(a). The ICRC paper, introduced at the request of six states (Belgium, Costa Rica, Finland, Hungary, South Africa and Switzerland), presented relevant sources based on an exhaustive research and analysis of international humanitarian law instruments and the relevant case law of international and national war crimes trials (Leipzig Trials after the First World War, post-Second World War trials, including the Nuremberg and Tokyo Trials, as well as national case law and decisions from the *ad hoc* Tribunals for the former Yugoslavia and Rwanda), as well as human rights law instruments and the respective case law of the UN Human Rights Committee, the European Court of Human Rights and the Inter-American Court of Human Rights.

During the first stage of the discussions, the Working Group considered the elements of the crime of genocide (Art. 6), as well as the elements of war crimes listed in Article 8(2)(a), on the basis of the proposals before it. The discussions in the Working Group focussed mostly on substantive issues. Based on the views expressed in the Working Group and the written proposals, the Coordinator, Herman von Hebel (Netherlands), prepared discussion papers PCNICC/WGEC/RT.1 to 3 for the elements of the crime of genocide and for the elements of war crimes

---

5. All Articles referred to below are of the ICC Statute, unless otherwise specified.
6. PCNICC/1999/DP.4 and Add.1–3.
7. PCNICC/1999/DP.5.
8. PCNICC/1999/DP.9 and Add.1 and 2.
9. PCNICC/1999/WGEC/INF.1.

listed in Article 8(2)(a)(i) to (iii). The discussion papers reflect the substantive considerations on the elements of the crimes mentioned, without prejudice to the eventual structure of the final document on EOC. Mainly, the views of delegations were divided as to the appropriateness of the use of footnotes, comments and introductory general paragraphs. Further discussion is necessary in order to design a structure acceptable to delegations.

2.1.2   *Elements of genocide*

The negotiations on the elements of genocide, which were largely based on the US working document, led to two discussion papers prepared by the Coordinator. The first discussion paper containing the elements[10] repeats most of the proposed

---

10. 'Art. 6(a): Genocide by killing - Elements
1. The accused intended to destroy, in whole or in part, a national, ethnical, racial or religious group, as such.
2. The accused killed one or more persons of that group in furtherance of that intent.
3. The accused knew or should have known that the conduct would destroy, in whole or in part, such group or that the conduct was part of a pattern of similar conduct directed against that group.
    Art. 6(b): Genocide by harming - Elements
1. The accused intended to destroy, in whole or in part, a national, ethnical, racial or religious group, as such.
2. The accused caused serious bodily or mental harm to one or more persons in that group in furtherance of that intent.
3. The accused knew or should have known that the harm caused would destroy, in whole or in part, such group or was part of a pattern of similar conduct directed against that group.
    Art. 6(c): Genocide by inflicting conditions of life - Elements
1. The accused intended to destroy, in whole or in part, a national, ethnical, racial or religious group, as such.
2. The accused inflicted certain conditions of life upon the group or members of the group in furtherance of that intent.
3. The conditions of life were calculated to physically destroy that group, in whole or in part.
4. The accused knew or should have known that the conditions inflicted would destroy, in whole or in part, such group or were part of a pattern of similar conduct directed against that group.
    Art. 6(d): Genocide by preventing births - Elements
1. The accused intended to destroy, in whole or in part, a national, ethnical, racial or religious group, as such.
2. The accused imposed measures upon one or more persons within that group in furtherance of that intent.
3. The measures imposed were intended to prevent births within that group.
4. The accused knew or should have known that the measures imposed would destroy, in whole or in part, such group or were part of a pattern of similar conduct directed against that group.
    Art. 6(e): Genocide by transferring children - Elements
1. The accused intended to destroy, in whole or in part, a national, ethnical, racial or religious group, as such.
2. The accused forcibly transferred one or more persons from that group to another group in furtherance of that intent.
3. The person or persons were, and the accused knew or should have known that the person or persons were, under the age of 18 years.
4. The accused knew or should have known that the forcible transfer or transfers would destroy, in whole or in part, such group or were part of a pattern of similar conduct directed against that group.'

elements from the US paper, taking into account the critiques expressed within the Working Group. The major changes from the US proposals are the following:

— The mental element was drafted in a more precise way with the intention of covering all potential perpetrators (superiors, military commanders, those who aid, abet or otherwise assist, and those who execute). The formulation 'in conscious furtherance of a widespread or systematic policy or practice' contained in the US paper was rejected because many delegations were of the opinion that this threshold was too high and did not reflect the Genocide Convention properly. Instead, the formulation, 'The accused knew or should have known that the conduct would destroy, in whole or in part, such group or that the conduct was part of a pattern of similar conduct directed against that group', was chosen.

— Concerning genocide by inflicting conditions of life and genocide by preventing births, the discussion paper dropped the elements requiring that the imposed measures produce a result ('That the conditions of life contributed to the destruction of that group' and 'That the measures imposed had the effect of preventing births within that group'). In conformity with the Genocide Convention, it is sufficient that the measures were imposed with the described aim.

— Moreover, it has been accepted that the maximum age of children whose forcible transfer may constitute an act of genocide is 18 rather than 15 years.

The substance of this document seemed to be widely acceptable to delegations. The second discussion paper[11] contains commentaries which previously had not been the subject of detailed discussions. Among other things, the commentary clarifies that 'rape and sexual violence may constitute genocide in the same way as any other act, provided that the criteria of the crime of genocide are met'. Some delegations expressed doubts as to the value and necessity of such commentaries.

2.1.3   Elements of war crimes

The negotiations on the elements of war crimes as derived from the grave breaches provisions of the 1949 Geneva Conventions were based in particular on the US document and the Swiss/Hungarian proposal. The negotiations led to one discussion paper prepared by the Coordinator, which is based on the results of an informal working group of interested states, dealing with the following crimes: wilful killing; torture or inhuman treatment, including biological experiments; and wilfully causing great suffering, or serious injury to body or health.[12] The document contains several footnotes reflecting, on the one hand, specific understandings of the drafters of this text,[13] and on the other hand, the diverging views of various delegations. It starts with a general introduction. The drafters of the document thought it useful

---

PCNICC/1999/WGEC/RT.1 (PCNICC/1999/L.3/Rev.1), pp. 20 et seq.

11. PCNICC/1999/WGEC/RT.3.

12. PCNICC/1999/WGEC/RT.2.

13. Again, some delegations contested the value and the necessity of commentaries and footnotes containing points of substance.

to address in this introductory commentary general elements applicable to all crimes dealt with at the first PrepCom. It reads as follows:

'The following general paragraph would be included as an introduction:
"Consistent with the general principles of law defined in article 30, it is presumed that all actions described in the elements must be intentionally committed and the elements do not repeat the general intent implied for each action. Likewise, the elements presume that the conduct is not otherwise legally justified under applicable law referred to in article 21, paragraph 1 (b) and (c) of the Statute. Hence, the element of 'unlawfulness' that exists in the jurisprudence of many of these offences has not been repeated in the elements of crimes. Absence of a lawful justification for a particular action need not be proved by the Prosecutor unless the issue is raised by the accused."'

The reference to Article 21(1)(b) and (c) of the Statute[14] is of particular interest. It was introduced in order to clarify that the lawfulness of a certain conduct has to be determined in accordance with international law. The latter has primacy over diverging national law, which may only be invoked under the conditions set forth in sub-paragraph (c).

One area of controversy was whether the mental element should be defined for every crime. The compromise found refers back to the Statute, to the definition contained in Article 30, and leaves the issue to the future judges to resolve. Reading the wording of Article 30 of the Statute,[15] one may have some doubts about whether it incorporates the view expressed by many delegations that the definition includes the concept of recklessness (common law countries) or *dolus eventualis* (civil law systems), as recognized in some recent decisions of the *ad hoc* Tribunals for the Former Yugoslavia (ICTY) and for Rwanda (ICTR).[16]

The proposed elements contain two general elements describing the material and personal scope of application. They are repeated with identical formulation for each crime. Both elements are derived from the *chapeau* of Article 8(2)(a): 'Grave

---

14. Art. 21 of the Statute reads as follows:
'1. The Court shall apply:
(a) In the first place, this Statute, Elements of Crimes and its Rules of Procedure and Evidence;
(b) In the second place, where appropriate, applicable treaties and the principles and rules of international law, including the established principles of the international law of armed conflict;
(c) Failing that, general principles of law derived by the Court from national laws of legal systems of the world including, as appropriate, the national laws of States that would normally exercise jurisdiction over the crime, provided that those principles are not inconsistent with this Statute and with international law and internationally recognized norms and standards.'
15. '2. For the purposes of this article, a person has intent where:
(a) In relation to conduct, that person means to engage in the conduct;
(b) In relation to a consequence, that person means to cause that consequence or is aware that it will occur in the ordinary course of events.'
16. For example *The Prosecutor* v. *Zejnil Delalić, Zdravko Mucić, also known as 'Pavo', Hazim Delić, Esad Landžo also known as 'Zenga'* (Čelebići), IT-96-21-T, Opinion and Judgment [hereinafter, Čelebići Opinion and Judgment], 16 November 1998, paras. 434 et seq., p. 159.

breaches of the Geneva Conventions of 12 August 1949, namely, any of the following acts against persons or property protected under the provisions of the relevant Geneva Convention.' The first common element reads as follows: 'The conduct took place in the context of and was associated with an international armed conflict.' It reflects the understanding that grave breaches as defined in the Geneva Conventions of 1949 can only be committed in an international armed conflict. The formulation 'in the context of [...] an international armed conflict' is based on the jurisprudence of the two *ad hoc* Tribunals.[17] The words 'and was associated with' were added. It was the understanding of the drafters that this formulation encompasses all acts linked to an armed conflict, including those committed after the cessation of active hostilities[18] and excluding acts committed for purely personal motives.[19] However, some delegations were of the view that the words 'and was associated with' were unnecessary because they either were implied in the words 'in the context of' or they limited the scope of these words.

The second common element is drafted in the following way: 'Such person or persons were protected under one or more of the Geneva Conventions of 1949 and the accused was aware of the factual circumstances that established this status.' The first part defines those who may be victims of a war crime in the sense of Article 8(2)(a) of the Statute. The second part is intended to emphasise the rule that only ignorance of facts may be an excuse and not ignorance of law. The agreed understanding of the drafters is further clarified in a footnote as follows: 'This element specifies the requisite factual knowledge while clarifying that ignorance of the Geneva Conventions is not an excuse.'

In addition to those two common elements, the following specific elements are included in the Coordinator's discussion paper (footnotes omitted):

---

17. Ibid., para. 201, p. 76.

18. Concerning the time frame, the ICTY stated that '(i)nternational humanitarian law applies from the initiation of such armed conflicts and extends beyond the cessation of hostilities until a general conclusion of peace is reached.' *The Prosecutor* v. *Duško Tadić*, Decision on the Defence Motion for Interlocutory Appeal on Jurisdiction [hereinafter, *Tadić* Jurisdiction Decision], IT-94-1-AR72, 2 October 1995, para. 70, p. 37. In this regard, see for example the First Geneva Convention (Art. 5), the Third Geneva Convention (Art. 5) and the Fourth Geneva Convention (Art. 6), which are applicable until protected persons who have fallen into the power of the enemy have been released and repatriated. See also in this context Art. 3(b) Additional Protocol I.

19. This limitation was clearly expressed by the ICTR in *The Prosecutor* v. *Jean-Paul Akayesu*, ICTR-96-4-T, Judgment [hereinafter, *Akayesu,* Judgment], 2 September 1998, para. 636. With respect to the necessary nexus between the acts of the accused and the armed conflict, the ICTY held the following:
'For a crime to fall within the jurisdiction of the International Tribunal, a sufficient nexus must be established between the alleged offence and the armed conflict which gives rise to the applicability of international humanitarian law.'
'For an offence to be a violation of international humanitarian law, therefore, this Trial Chamber needs to be satisfied that each of the alleged acts was in fact closely related to the hostilities.'
The Prosecutor v. *Duško Tadić*, IT-94-1-T, Opinion and Judgement, 7 May 1997, paras. 572 et seq., p. 207. See also *Tadić*, Jurisdiction Decision, ibid., para. 69, p. 37.

— 'Article 8(2)(a)(i): War crime of wilful killing

[...] 2. The accused killed one or more persons. [...]

— Article 8(2)(a)(ii)–1: War crime of torture

[...] 2. The accused inflicted severe physical or mental pain or suffering upon one or more persons. [...]

4. The accused inflicted the pain or suffering for the purpose of: obtaining information or a confession, punishment, intimidation or coercion, or obtaining any other similar purpose.

— Article 8(2)(a)(ii)–2: War crime of inhuman treatment

[...] 2. The accused inflicted severe physical or mental pain or suffering upon one or more persons. [...]

— Article 8(2)(a)(ii)–3: War crime of biological experiments

[...] 2. The accused subjected one or more persons to a particular biological experiment. [...]

4. The intent of the experiment was non-therapeutic and was neither justified by medical reasons nor carried out in such person's or persons' interest.

5. The experiment seriously endangered the physical or mental health or integrity of such person or persons.

— Article 8(2)(a)(iii): War crime of wilfully causing great suffering

[...] 2. The accused caused great physical or mental pain or suffering to or serious injury to body or health of one or more persons. [...]'

Concerning the special elements of these crimes, major disagreement persists with regard to the elements of 'torture' being part of the crime as defined under Article 8(2)(a)(ii). The Swiss/Hungarian proposal was largely based on the definition of torture as contained in Article 1(1) of the 1984 Convention Against Torture and Other Cruel, Inhuman or Degrading Treatment or Punishment (the 'Torture Convention').[20] The ICTY considered this definition as representing customary international law[21] and defined the elements accordingly.[22]

---

20. 'For the purpose of this Convention, the term 'torture' means any act by which severe pain or suffering, whether physical or mental, is intentionally inflicted on a person for such purposes as obtaining from him or a third person information or a confession, punishing him for an act he or a third person has committed or is suspected of having committed, or intimidating or coercing him or a third person, or for any reason based on discrimination of any kind, when pain or suffering is inflicted by or at the instigation of or with the consent or acquiescence of a public official or other person acting in an official capacity. It does not include pain or suffering arising only from, inherent in or incidental to lawful sanctions.'

21. *Čelebiċ*, Judgment, *supra* n. 16, para. 459, p. 167.

22. Ibid., and para. 494, p. 178: '(i) There must be an act or omission that causes severe pain or suffering, whether mental or physical, (ii) which is inflicted intentionally, (iii) and for such purposes as obtaining information or a confession from the victim, or a third person, punishing the victim for an act he or she or a third person has committed, intimidating or coercing the victim or a third person, or for any reason based on discrimination of any kind, (iv) and such act or omission being committed by, or at the instigation of, or with the consent or acquiescence of, an official or other person acting in an official capacity.'

In the *Furundžija* Judgment, the ICTY described some specific elements that pertain to torture as

However, some delegations expressed the fear that the element, 'The perpetrator was himself an official, or acted at the instigation of, or with the consent or acquiescence of, an official or person acting in an official capacity', as contained in the Swiss/Hungarian paper, essentially reproducing the ICTY's formulation in the *Čelebići* case, would exclude acts of torture committed by irregular forces, whereas such conduct would be covered by the Geneva Conventions. Therefore, this element was dropped. However, some delegations are still in favour of keeping the element. With respect to future discussions, the reasoning of the ICTY in this regard should be recalled. In the *Čelebići* case it held:

> 'Traditionally, an act of torture must be committed by, or at the instigation of, or with the consent or acquiescence of, a public official or person acting in an official capacity. In the context of international humanitarian law, this requirement must be interpreted to include officials of non-State parties to a conflict, in order for the prohibition to retain significance in situations of internal armed conflicts or international conflicts involving some non-State entities.'[23]

This understanding could eventually reconcile the two approaches if it could be reflected in an adequate wording.

Another unresolved question concerns the following proposed element, as contained in the Coordinator's discussion paper: 'The accused inflicted the pain or suffering for the purpose of: obtaining information or a confession, punishment, intimidation or coercion, or obtaining any other similar purpose.' Some delegations held the view that torture could be committed for a variety of reasons. According to this view, a prohibited purpose should not be an element of the crime. However, it must be indicated that this element is based to a large extent on the jurisprudence of the ICTY,[24] although in its present form it seems to be a little more restrictive. As well as requiring a prohibited purpose as an element of torture (see n. 22), the ICTY in *Čelebići* added:

> 'The use of the words 'for such purposes' in the customary definition of torture [the definition contained in the Torture Convention], indicates that the various listed

---

'considered from the specific viewpoint of international criminal law relating to armed conflicts'. Thus, the Trial Chamber considers that the elements of torture in an armed conflict require that torture: '(i) consists of the infliction by act or omission of severe pain or suffering, whether physical or mental; in addition; (ii) this act or omission must be intentional; (iii) it must aim at obtaining information or a confession, or at punishing, intimidating, humiliating or coercing the victim or a third person; or at discriminating, on any ground, against the victim or a third person; (iv) it must be linked to an armed conflict; (v) at least one of the persons involved in the torture process must be a public official or must at any rate act in a non-private capacity, e.g., as a de facto organ of a State or any other authority-wielding entity.'

The Prosecutor v. *Furundžija*, Judgment [hereinafter, *Furundžija,* Judgment] IT-95-17/1-T, 10 December 1998, para. 162, pp. 63 et seq.

23. *Čelebići*, Judgment, *supra* n. 16, para. 473, p. 172.

24. See *supra* n. 22 for the findings of the *Čelebići* and *Furundžija* Judgments on the element of purpose. The ICTY defined the element of purpose slightly differently in each case.

purposes do not constitute an exhaustive list, and should be regarded as merely representative.'[25]

In addition, the ICTY emphasised that

'there is no requirement that the conduct must be solely perpetrated for a prohibited purpose. Thus, in order for this requirement to be met, the prohibited purpose must simply be part of the motivation behind the conduct and need not to be the predominant or sole purpose.'[26]

In the *Furundžija* case the ICTY drafted this element in a slightly different way (see n. 22). With respect to the addition of the purpose 'humiliating', which the ICTY mentioned in this case, it stated that it is

'warranted by the general spirit of international humanitarian law; the primary purpose of this body of law is to safeguard human dignity. The proposition is also supported by some general provisions of such international treaties as the Geneva Conventions and Additional Protocols, which consistently aim at protecting persons not taking part, or no longer taking part, in the hostilities from "outrages upon personal dignity". The notion of humiliation is, in any event close to the notion of intimidation, which is explicitly referred to in the Torture Convention's definition of torture.'[27]

The formulation 'for the purpose of: [...] obtaining any other similar purpose' in the Coordinator's discussion paper was chosen as a compromise, in order to show that the explicitly mentioned purposes do not constitute an exhaustive list.

Another controversial point concerned the elements of 'inhuman treatment'. Some delegations expressed the view that the reprehensible conduct should not be limited to the infliction of severe physical or mental pain, but should include conduct constituting 'a serious attack on human dignity'. This opinion seems to be well founded, since the ICTY has recognized this element in various decisions.[28]

The proposals concerning the elements of the remaining offences in Article 8(2)(a) were only the subject of a general exchange of views within the Working Group. No work resulting in a discussion paper was undertaken.

---

25. *Čelebići*, Judgment, *supra* n. 16, para. 470, p. 170. But the ICTR seems to suggest an exhaustive list by formulating 'for one or more of the following purposes', *Akayesu*, Judgment, *supra* n. 19 at para. 594.

26. *Čelebići*, Judgment, *supra* n. 16, para. 471, p. 171.

27. *Furundžija*, Judgment, *supra* n. 22, para. 163, p. 64.

28. According to the ICTY, 'all acts found to constitute torture or wilfully causing great suffering or serious injury to body or health would also constitute inhuman treatment'. However, inhuman treatment is not limited to acts described by the other two offences. It 'extends further to other acts which violate the basic principle of humane treatment, and particularly the respect for human dignity'. *Čelebići*, Judgment, *supra* n. 16, para. 544, p. 194.

2.2   Working Group on the Rules of Procedure and Evidence

The Working Group on RPE held nine meetings. It had before it quite comprehensive proposals by the Australian and French delegations.[29]

The Working Group considered various proposals submitted in connection with Part 5 of the Statute, dealing with the following subject matters:

a. Commencement of investigation and proceedings, including notification of the decisions of the Prosecutor, procedure to be followed in the event of an application for review of a decision not to proceed with an investigation or not to prosecute and supervision by the Pre-trial Chamber of decisions of the Prosecutor taken in the interests of justice;

b. Conduct of investigation and proceedings, including measures to restrict or deprive a person of liberty;

c. Disclosure;

d. Closure of the pre-trial phase, including proceedings on confirmation of charges in the presence of the person;

e. Consequences of the decisions taken by the Pre-trial Chamber, final decisions on confirmation, amendment of the charges, transition from the pre-trial phase to the trial and confirmation proceedings in the absence of the person charged.

On the basis of the written proposals and the views expressed in the Working Group as well as in informal consultations, the Coordinator, Silvia Fernandez de Gurmendi (Argentine), proposed four discussion papers for consideration at future sessions of the PrepCom:

a. PCNICC/1999/WGRPE/RT.1 on commencement of investigations and proceedings;

b. PCNICC/1999/WGRPE/RT.2 on the procedure to be followed in the event of an application for review of a decision by the Prosecutor not to proceed with an investigation or not to prosecute, as well as the review by the Pre-trial Chamber of decisions of the Prosecutor under Article 53(1)(c) or 2(c);

c. PCNICC/1999/WGRPE/RT.3 on proceedings with regard to the confirmation of the charges; and

d. PCNICC/1999/WGRPE/RT.4 on disclosure.

The numbering of the rules in these discussion papers is of a provisional nature, pending a decision regarding the structure of the Rules of Procedure and Evidence.

2.3   Definition of the crime of aggression

The question of the definition of the crime of aggression was dealt with in one plenary session. The debate was limited to interventions of a more general charac-

---

29. PCNICC/1999/DP.1   (Australia)   and   PCNICC/1999/DP.2,   PCNICC/1999/DP.3, PCNICC/1999/DP.6, PCNICC/1999/DP.7 and Add.1 and 2, PCNICC/1999/DP.8 and Add.1 and 2, PCNICC/1999/DP.10 and Add.1 (France).

ter. Concerning the substance, some delegations referred to the legal bases that need to be taken into account for the drafting of a definition, in particular UN General Assembly Resolution 3314 (1974). All delegations taking the floor expressed the great importance they attach to this question.

3.   THE SECOND PREPCOM

During its second session, held in New York at UN Headquarters from 26 July to 13 August 1999, the PrepCom continued its efforts to prepare draft texts of the RPE and the EOC as well as a proposal for a provision on aggression, including its definition, elements and the conditions under which the ICC shall exercise its jurisdiction with respect to this crime.

3.1   **Working Group on Elements of Crimes**

3.1.1   *General remarks*

With regard to the EOC, the PrepCom focussed on the elements of war crimes, Article 8 of the ICC Statute. The Working Group, which held ten meetings, resumed consideration of those war crimes that it had already begun to consider at the first session but could not complete. It had before it several proposals in addition to those that had been tabled at the first session of the PrepCom. The proposals submitted at the second session are contained in documents PCNICC/1999/WGEC/DP.8 to DP.27; and PCNICC/1999/WGEC/INF.2 and Add.1-2.

In the same way as at the first session, the negotiations at the second session were mainly based on the comprehensive US document defining the elements of all crimes listed in the ICC Statute,[30] and a joint Swiss/Hungarian/Costa Rican document containing proposals for elements of war crimes contained in Article 8(2)(a), (b), (c) and parts of (e) of the ICC Statute.[31] A Japanese proposal covered the crimes contained in Article 8(b)(i)-(xvi).[32]

The negotiations were supported by some other proposals, for example, by the Spanish and Colombian delegations as well as parts II-VI of an ICRC study relating to the crimes listed in Article 8(2)(c), (b) and parts of (e) of the ICC Statute.[33] The follow-up of the ICRC paper submitted at the first session of the PrepCom, introduced at the request of seven states (Belgium, Costa Rica, Finland, Hungary, Republic of Korea, South Africa and Switzerland) again presented relevant sources, based on an exhaustive research and analysis of international humanitarian law instruments and the relevant case law of international and national war crimes trials,

---

30. *Supra* n. 6.
31. PCNICC/1999/WGEC/DP.8, 10, 11, 20, 22.
32. PCNICC/1999/WGEC/DP.12.
33. PCNICC/1999/WGEC/INF.2 (Parts II-IV) and Add.1-2 (Parts V-VI).

as well as human rights law instruments and the respective case law. The ICRC study once again formed the basis for the Swiss/Hungarian/Costa Rican proposals. To facilitate discussion, the remaining war crimes provisions were divided into nine clusters based on the possible commonality of their elements, as follows:

I.   Humanitarian/human rights provisions
    1. Article 8(2)(c)
    2. Article 8(2)(b)(x), (xxi), (xxii)
    3. Article 8(2)(b)(viii), (xiii), (xvi)
    4. Article 8(2)(b)(xiv), (xv), (xxvi)
II. Hague law provisions
    5. Article 8(2)(b)(vi), (vii), (xi), (xii)
III. Conduct of hostilities provisions
    6. Article 8(2)(b)(i), (ii), (iii)
    7. Article 8(2)(b)(iv), (v), (ix), (xxiv)
    8. Article 8(2)(b)(xxiii), (xxv)
IV   Weapons provisions
    9. Article 8(2)(b)(xvii), (xviii), (xix), (xx)

The Working Group discussed all the proposals for Article 8(2)(b) and (c) of the ICC Statute in the Plenary. However, there was not sufficient time for the Coordinator to prepare discussion papers on the elements of all of the provisions of war crimes. Based on the written proposals and on the views expressed in the Working Group as well as in informal consultations, the Coordinator prepared discussion papers PCNICC/WGEC/RT.4 to 10 for the elements of war crimes contained in the remainder of Article 8(2)(a)(iv) to (viii), Article 8(2)(c), Article 8(2)(b)(i)-(iii), (vi), (vii), (x)-(xvi), (xxi), (xxii) and (xxvi).[34] The discussion papers reflect the provisional agreement of the Working Group and are without prejudice to the eventual structure of the document on the EOC. Informal discussions on clusters 7-9 did not take place. Therefore, no discussion papers on elements of these offences could be produced.

3.1.2   Elements of War Crimes

This overview of the substantial negotiations is not intended to be exhaustive. Thus, in the following, only some main points of controversy will be described. The choice of some aspects does not mean that the Working Group thus far has reached

---

34. PCNICC/1999/WGEC/RT.4 on elements of Art. 8(2)(a); PCNICC/1999/WGEC/RT.5/Rev.1 on elements of Art. 8(2)(c); PCNICC/1999/WGEC/RT.6 on elements of Art. 8(2)(b)(xxii); PCNICC/1999/WGEC/RT.7 on elements of Art. 8(2)(b)(xiii)-(xvi) and (xxvi); PCNICC/1999/WGEC/RT.8 on elements of Art. 8(2)(b)(x) and (xxi); PCNICC/1999/WGEC/RT.9 on elements of Art. 8(2)(b)(i)-(iii); and PCNICC/1999/WGEC/RT.10 on elements of Art. 8(2)(b)(vi), (vii), (xi) and (xii).

perfect solutions in all the other fields. It is understood that the definition of all EOC still needs careful examination.

3.1.2.1 Mental element

More than during the first session of the PrepCom, quite different views were expressed on the relation between Articles 6-8 of the ICC Statute containing the definition of crimes, and Part 3 of the Statute, containing general principles of criminal law, such as inchoate offences, the definition of the mental element or mistake of law. This controversy is reflected to a certain extent in the Coordinator's discussion papers on EOC of Article 8 of the ICC Statute, which include elements that might easily be derived directly from the provisions in Part 3.

This general problem may be illustrated with respect to the interpretation of Article 30 of the ICC Statute defining the mental element. Although the introductory paragraph, which was drafted at the first session of the PrepCom and which remained almost identical after the second session,[35] still refers back to Article 30 of the ICC Statute, the question is not settled whether the mental element should be defined for every crime, whether a reference to Article 30 is sufficient or whether the judges should make their own determination. Considerable differences in national conceptions made it impossible to address the mental element of war crimes in a consistent manner. To illustrate the difficulties, it is useful to have a closer look at Article 30 of the Statute, which reads as follows:

'1. Unless otherwise provided, a person shall be criminally responsible and liable for punishment for a crime within the jurisdiction of the Court only if the material elements are committed with intent and knowledge.

2. For the purposes of this article, a person has intent where:

(a) In relation to conduct, that person means to engage in the conduct;

(b) In relation to a consequence, that person means to cause that consequence or is aware that it will occur in the ordinary course of events.

3. For the purposes of this article, "knowledge" means awareness that a circumstance exists or a consequence will occur in the ordinary course of events. "Know" and "knowingly" shall be construed accordingly.'

---

35. With a slight modification emphasised in italics it reads as follows:
'The following general paragraph would be included as an introduction *to the Elements of article 8:* "Consistent with the general principles of law defined in article 30, it is presumed that all actions described in the elements must be intentionally committed and the elements do not repeat the general intent implied for each action. Likewise, the elements presume that the conduct is not otherwise legally justified under applicable law referred to in article 21, paragraph 1(b) and (c) of the Statute. Hence, the element of 'unlawfulness' that exists *in the Statute and* in the jurisprudence of many of these offences has not been repeated in the elements of crimes. Absence of a lawful justification for a particular action need not be proved by the Prosecutor unless the issue is raised by the accused."'

The first problematic issue relates to what is meant by 'unless otherwise provided', because it raises the question of which other legal sources are relevant in this context. For example, does this formulation mean that Article 30 of the ICC Statute defines exclusively the mental element for every crime unless the Statute otherwise provides, even if it is more restrictive than customary international law? Or does the formulation mean that the mental element might also be specifically defined in the EOC?

In addition to this problem of interpretation of this part of Article 30, at the end of the second session of the PrepCom, no agreement could be reached on what constitutes 'general' intent as defined in Article 30 (see also the wording of the introductory paragraph) and what is meant by 'specific' intent, which would be relevant only for some crimes and should therefore be explicitly defined. This uncertainty is enhanced by the fact that some crimes in Article 8(2)(b) and (e) contain the word 'intentionally'. One might ask whether this term only refers back to the definition of 'intent' in Article 30 or whether a specific intent requirement was introduced. All these aspects explain why the Coordinator's discussion papers contain both the introductory paragraph and mental elements for some war crimes but not for others.

The other problem with regard to the interpretation of Article 30 concerns the question of which non-mental elements require knowledge, which intent (general or specific) and which require no mental element.

With a view to clarifying the notions of Article 30 and to facilitating future negotiations, the delegation of Samoa introduced two informal papers. Basically, the papers, entitled 'elements of The Elements: A Very Informal Discussion Paper from the Delegation of Samoa' and 'Structure of Elements in Article 30 of ICC Statute', indicated that Article 30 describes three types of non-mental elements and specifies different types of mental elements with respect to those non-mental elements. The non-mental elements were:

— Article 30(2)(a): conduct, i.e., acting or failing to act where there is a duty (for example: a person pulls the trigger);
— Article 30(2)(b): consequence, i.e., result, harm brought about by conduct (as a result of pulling the trigger, a person is killed);
— Article 30(3): circumstance, i.e., state of affairs or background (existence of an international armed conflict or that a victim was not taking part in hostilities).

According to the Samoan papers, Article 30 of the Statute ('default rule') defines three types of mental elements linked to these non-mental elements:

— intent in relation to conduct, i.e., the perpetrator 'means to engage in the conduct' (e.g., means to pull the trigger);
— intent in relation to a consequence, i.e., the perpetrator 'means to cause that consequence or is aware that it will occur in the ordinary course of events' (e.g., if the person pulls the trigger, the person means the victim to die, or at least knows 'that death is certain [almost certain? fairly certain?] to happen'); and
— knowledge, i.e., 'awareness that a circumstance exists' (e.g., awareness that a victim was not taking part in hostilities).

The delegations took note of these conceptual submissions but did not adopt any position. It was agreed that the issue of the mental elements should be resolved in a consistent manner for all crimes after the first reading of the complete draft on EOC.

3.1.2.2   Remainder of Article 8(2)(a) of the ICC Statute

The discussions on Article 8(2)(a)(iv) – Extensive destruction and appropriation of property, not justified by military necessity and carried out unlawfully and wantonly – are to a certain extent very significant for the negotiations on crimes derived from the grave breaches provisions of the Geneva Conventions (GC).

Article 8(2)(a) repeats established language from the GC; nevertheless it proved to be difficult to draft the elements. This might have been the case because the grave breaches provisions refer back to various provisions in the GC which establish different levels of protection. In the case of appropriation or destruction, the GC define different standards for specific protected property. This may be illustrated with respect to the protection of civilian hospitals on the one hand and property in occupied territories on the other, as follows:

Article 18 of GC IV defines the protection of civilian hospitals against attacks, i.e., against destruction, in the following terms:

'Civilian hospitals organized to give care to the wounded and sick, the infirm and maternity cases, may in no circumstances be the object of attack but shall at all times be respected and protected by the Parties to the conflict. [...]'

Article 19 of GC IV specifies the strict conditions under which such civilian hospitals may nevertheless be attacked:

'The protection to which civilian hospitals are entitled shall not cease unless they are used to commit, outside their humanitarian duties, acts harmful to the enemy. Protection may, however, cease only after due warning has been given, naming, in all appropriate cases, a reasonable time limit, and after such warning has remained unheeded.'

Article 53 GC IV defines the protection of property in occupied territory in a different manner:

'*Any destruction* by the Occupying Power of real or personal property belonging individually or collectively to private persons, or to the state, or to other public authorities, or to social or cooperative organizations, *is prohibited, except where such destruction is rendered absolutely necessary by military operations.*' (emphasis added)

Considering these examples, the drafting of EOC had to be done in a way that both standards are properly reflected. The meaning of 'not justified by military necessity', as contained in Article 8(2)(a)(iv) of the ICC Statute, is crucial in this regard. It is important to indicate that military necessity covers only measures that are lawful in accordance with the laws and customs of war. Consequently, a rule of the law of armed conflict cannot be derogated from by invoking military necessity unless this possibility is explicitly provided for by the rule in question. It is desirable that this understanding be clearly expressed in the document on EOC.

With regard to the war crime of 'Taking of hostages' (Art. 8(2)(a)(viii)), it is worth indicating that the elements of this offence are largely based on the definition taken from the 1979 International Convention against the Taking of Hostages, which is not a treaty of international humanitarian law and was drafted in a specific legal context. However, as in the case of the crime of torture, the definition was adapted by the Working Group to the context of the law of armed conflict. The Hostage Convention defines hostage-taking in Article 1.1 as

'any person who seizes or detains and threatens to kill, to injure or to continue to detain another person (the 'hostage') in order to compel a third party, namely a State, an international organisation, a natural or judicial person, or a group of persons, to do or abstain from doing any act as an explicit or implicit condition for the release of the hostage.'

Taking into account the case law from the Second World War, this definition was considered to be too narrow. Therefore, the Coordinator's text defines the specific mental element in the following terms, adding the emphasised element:

'The accused intended to compel a State, an international organisation, a natural or legal person or a group of persons, to act or refrain from acting as an explicit or implicit condition for *the safety or* the release of such person or persons.'

3.1.2.3   Article 8(2)(c) of the ICC Statute

The proposed elements for the crimes listed in Article 8(2)(c) contain two general elements repeated for each crime describing the material and personal scope of application. Both elements are derived from the *chapeau* of Article 8(2)(c): 'In the case of an armed conflict not of an international character, serious violations of article 3 common to the four Geneva Conventions of 12 August 1949, namely, any of the following acts committed against persons taking no active part in the hostilities, including members of armed forces who have laid down their arms and those placed *hors de combat* by sickness, wounds, detention or any other cause.' The first common element reads as follows: 'The conduct took place in the context of and was associated with an armed conflict not of an international character.'

The second common element is drafted in the following way: 'Such person or persons were either *hors de combat*, or were civilians, medical personnel, or religious personnel taking no active part in the hostilities, and the accused was aware of the factual circumstances that established this status.' This part defines those who may be victims of a war crime in the sense of Article 8(2)(c). The wording differs from that of common Article 3 GC and the *chapeau* of Article 8(2)(c). However, many states took the view that this formulation reflects the true interpretation of common Article 3 GC and avoids ambiguity. It was the understanding of the drafters in informal consultations that the term *hors de combat* should not be narrowly interpreted. In addition to the examples contained in common Article 3 GC, reference was made especially to Articles 41 and 42 of the First Additional Protocol to the GC (AP I).

The specific elements of many war crimes listed under Article 8(2)(c) are defined more or less in the same manner as in Article 8(2)(a). It was the view of states that there can be no difference between wilful killing and murder, between inhuman and cruel treatment, between torture or taking of hostages in an international and a non-international armed conflict. This approach seems to be in conformity with ICTY case law.[36]

Concerning the special elements of these crimes, disagreement persists to the same extent as in the context of Article 8(2)(a). Any change at a later stage will also affect the EOC of Article 8(2)(c) which describe the same criminal conduct.

With regard to Article 8(2)(c)(iv) of the ICC Statute, 'The passing of sentences and the carrying out of executions without previous judgement pronounced by a regularly constituted court, affording all judicial guarantees which are generally recognized as indispensable' it is worth indicating that the drafting of its elements was largely influenced by the content of Article 6(2) of the Second Additional Protocol to the Geneva Conventions (AP II). The specific elements in the rolling text now read as follows:

— 'Article 8(2)(c)(iv): War crime of sentencing or execution without due process [...] 2. The accused passed sentence or executed one or more persons. [...]

4. There was no previous judgment pronounced by a court, or the court that rendered judgment was 'not regularly constituted', that is it did not afford the essential guarantees of independence and impartiality, or the court that rendered judgment did not afford all other guarantees generally recognized as indispensable under international law.

---

36. The ICTY concluded – with regard to any difference between the notions of 'wilful killing' in the context of an international armed conflict on the one hand, and 'murder' in the context of a non-international armed conflict on the other hand – that there 'can be no line drawn between "wilful killing" and "murder" which affects their content'. *Čelebiĝi*, Judgment, *supra* n. 16, paras. 422 and 423, p. 154. See also ICTY, The Prosecutor's Pre-trial Brief, *The Prosecutor* v. *Slavko Dokmanović*, IT-95-13a-PT, p. 23. According to the Tribunal, 'cruel treatment constitutes an intentional act or omission, that is an act which, judged objectively, is deliberate and not accidental, which causes serious mental or physical suffering or injury or constitutes a serious attack on human dignity. As such, it carries an equivalent meaning and therefore the same residual function for the purpose of common article 3 of the Statute, as inhuman treatment does in relation to grave breaches of the Geneva Conventions'. *Čelebiĝi*, Judgment, para. 552, p. 196. Concerning any difference between the notion of 'torture' in the context of an international armed conflict on the one hand, and in the context of a non-international armed conflict on the other hand, the ICTY concluded that '[t]he characteristics of the offence of torture under common article 3 and under the "grave breaches" provisions of the Geneva Conventions, do not differ'. Ibid., para. 443, p. 162.

5. The accused was aware of the absence of a previous judgment or of the denial of relevant guarantees and the fact that they are essential or indispensable to a fair trial.'

On the basis of Article 6 of AP II, the term 'regularly constituted court' as contained in common Article 3 and thus Article 8(2)(c)(iv) of the ICC Statute was defined as a court that affords the essential guarantees of independence and impartiality. Besides, it was controversial whether a list of fair trial guarantees should be included on the basis of the Swiss/Hungarian/Costa Rican proposal.[37] Some states feared that even an illustrative list would suggest that omitted rights were not indispensable, others feared that there could be a discrepancy between this list of fair trial guarantees and those contained in the Statute, and a third group took the view that violation of only one right would not necessarily amount to a war crime. Instead of weakening the value of such a list of fair trial guarantees by an introductory paragraph defining what is to be considered indispensable, states preferred not to include such a list. In addition, the concerns of the third group of states are reflected in a footnote which reads as follows:

'With respect to elements 4 and 5, the Court should consider whether, in the light of all relevant circumstances, the cumulative effect of factors with respect to guarantees deprived the person or persons of a fair trial.'

3.1.2.4   Article 8(2)(b) of the ICC Statute

The crimes defined in Article 8(2)(b) of the ICC Statute cover other serious violations of the laws and customs applicable in international armed conflict.

Particular problems arose with regard to those offences that reproduce language from the Hague Regulations, rather than the 'modern' language of AP I. The Working Group had to determine to what extent this new language may be used in the drafting of EOC.

For example, the crime of killing or wounding treacherously individuals belonging to a hostile nation or army as derived from the Hague Regulations is to a certain extent linked with Article 37 AP I on the prohibition of perfidy. The concept of perfidy in Article 37 is both more extensive and more narrow. Article 37 AP I covers not only the killing or wounding, but also the capture of an adversary by means of perfidy. The latter is clearly not included in Article 23(b) of the Hague Regulations. However, the Hague Regulations seem to also cover acts of assassination[38] not included in Article 37 AP I.

---

37. PCNICC/1999/WGEC/DP.8.

38. See for example Oppenheim, *International Law, A Treatise*, Vol. II, 7th edn. (London, Longmans 1952) p. 342, who indicates the following examples of treacherous conduct: 'no assassin must be hired, and no assassination of combatants be committed; a price may not be put on the head of an enemy individual; proscription and outlawing are prohibited; no treacherous request for quarter must be made; no treacherous simulation of sickness or wounds is permitted.'

The impact of Article 37 AP I on the traditional rule as formulated in the Hague Regulations is not clear. Ipsen, for example, concludes:

'The fact that Article 37 has been accepted by the vast majority of States indicates that there is no customary international law prohibition of perfidy with a wider scope than that of Article 37.'[39]

However, both terms are used on equal footing in the original 1980 Protocol on Prohibitions or Restrictions on the Use of Mines, Booby-Traps and Other Devices in Article 6 dealing with certain types of booby traps, and in its amended form of 1996 in Article 7.

After some discussions, the Coordinator's discussion paper reproduces, for the most part, the definition of perfidy as contained in Article 37 of AP I, but excludes the capture of an adversary.

With regard to other crimes derived from the Hague Regulations, the Working Group decided on a case by case basis whether or not the language of AP I could be used to clarify the EOC. One positive example in this regard is the Rolling Text for the elements of killing or wounding a combatant who, having no longer means of defence, has surrendered at discretion (Article 8(2)(b)(vi) of the ICC Statute). This text departs from the old Hague language in that it incorporates the concept of Article 41 of AP I, and probably Article 42 of AP I as well.

Also problematic was the drafting of the elements of the crime 'Making improper use of a flag of truce, of the flag or of the military insignia and uniform of the enemy or of the United Nations, as well as of the distinctive emblems of the Geneva Conventions, resulting in death or serious personal injury' (Article 8(2)(b)(vii)). The Working Group realized after some debate that the definition in the Statute is not very well drafted since it treats emblems, signs and symbols of a different character and governed by different legal standards in a single crime. Therefore, it was decided to define the elements for each category in a distinct manner. The term 'improper use' was understood as meaning that the use of signs and symbols was prohibited under international law. Considerable discussion focussed on the question of what level of knowledge the perpetrator must have with regard to the prohibited nature of such use. Some delegations insisted that the perpetrator must know that the use was illegal, thereby accepting that a mistake of law would be a defence. Other delegations pointed out that such a standard would, for example, encourage states not to teach how to use the distinctive emblem of the Red Cross and Red Crescent. As a compromise, the following standards were agreed upon: with regard to the flag of truce, the flag or the military insignia and uniform of the enemy as well as the distinctive emblems of the Geneva Conventions, the perpetrator 'knew or should have known of the prohibited nature of such use'; with regard to the flag or the military insignia and uniform of the United Nations, the perpetrator must have known of the prohibited nature. The latter standard was

---

39. K. Ipsen, 'Perfidy', in R. Bernhardt, ed., 3 *Encyclopedia of Public International Law* (1997) p. 980.

accepted because many states referred to the complexity of UN regulations on the use of its flags, military insignia and uniforms. A standard of negligence expressed by the 'should have known' formula therefore would not be more appropriate.

Much time was devoted by the Working Group to the gender crimes defined in Article 8(2)(b)(xxii). The task was quite difficult because very little case law exists thus far. Even where case law exists, it is not always uniform. For example, the *ad hoc* Tribunals for Rwanda and the former Yugoslavia defined the EOC of rape in different ways.

In the *Furundžija* case the Trial Chamber of the ICTY found that the following may be accepted as the objective elements of rape:

'(i) the sexual penetration, however slight:
(a) of the vagina or anus of the victim by the penis of the perpetrator or any other object used by the perpetrator; or
(b) of the mouth of the victim by the penis of the perpetrator;
(ii) by coercion or force or threat of force against the victim or a third person.'[40]

However, the Trial Chamber of the ICTR defined rape in the *Akayesu* case as a physical invasion of a sexual nature, committed on a person under circumstances which are coercive.[41] The delicate compromise found now reads as follows:

[…] 2. The accused invaded the body of a person by conduct resulting in penetration, however slight, of any part of the body of the victim or of the perpetrator with a sexual organ, or of the anal or genital opening of the victim with any object or any other part of the body.
3. The invasion was committed by force, or by threat of force or coercion, such as that caused by fear of violence, duress, detention, psychological oppression or abuse of power, against such person or another person, or by taking advantage of a coercive environment, or the invasion was committed against a person incapable of giving genuine consent.

A footnote to element 3 clarifies that '[i]t is understood that a person may be incapable of giving genuine consent if affected by natural, induced or age-related incapacity.'

The formulation 'invaded [...] by conduct resulting in penetration' in element 2 was chosen in order to draft the elements in a gender-neutral way and to also

---

40. *Furundžija*, Judgment, *supra* n. 22, para. 185, p. 73. See also the definition by the ICTY Prosecution quoted in that judgement (para. 174, p. 68): 'rape is a forcible act: this means that the act is "accomplished by force or threats of force against the victim or a third person, such threats being express or implied and must place the victim in reasonable fear that he, she or a third person will be subjected to violence, detention, duress or psychological oppression". This act is the penetration of the vagina, the anus or mouth by the penis, or of the vagina or anus by other object. In this context, it includes penetration, however slight, of the vulva, anus or oral cavity, by the penis and sexual penetration of the vulva or anus is not limited to the penis.' (Footnote omitted).

41. *Akayesu*, Opinion and Judgment, *supra* n. 19, paras. 597 et seq.

cover rape committed by women. Element 3, including the above-cited footnote, largely reflects the findings of the ICTR in the *Akayesu* case, taking into account the effect of special circumstances of an armed conflict on the victim's will:

> '[C]oercive circumstances need not be evidenced by a show of physical force. Threats, intimidation, extortion and other forms of duress which prey on fear or desperation may constitute coercion, and coercion may be inherent in certain circumstances, such as armed conflict or the military presence [...].'[42]

Another point of major controversy in this cluster of crimes was how to distinguish enforced prostitution from sexual slavery, especially whether or not the following fact was an element of enforced prostitution: the 'accused or another person obtained or expected to obtain pecuniary or other advantage in exchange for or in connection with the acts of a sexual nature'. After long debates, states answered in the affirmative.

Finally, considerable difficulties existed with regard to the war crime of sexual violence due to the formulation contained in the Statute 'also constituting a grave breach of the Geneva Convention'. While some delegations took the view that this formulation should only indicate that gender crimes could already be prosecuted as war crimes, others thought that the conduct must constitute one of the crimes defined in Article 8(2)(a) – the specifically named grave breaches of the GC – and involve violent acts of a sexual nature. However, the majority, in an attempt to reconcile the wording of the Statute with its aim, considered the formulation as an element of the crime that introduces a specific threshold. Therefore, the compromise reads as follows:

> '[...] The accused committed an act of a sexual nature against one or more persons or caused such person or persons to engage in an act of a sexual nature by force, or by threat of force or coercion, such as that caused by fear of violence, duress, detention, psychological oppression or abuse of power, against such person or persons or another person, or by taking advantage of a coercive environment or such person or persons' incapacity to give genuine consent.
> 3. The conduct was of a gravity comparable to that of a grave breach of the Geneva Conventions.'

Looking at element 3, one might come to the conclusion or at least have the impression that a higher threshold was introduced for this 'capture' war crime than for rape and the other gender crimes where no reference is made to a gravity comparable to that of grave breaches.

The most difficult negotiations so far concerned the war crime of transfer, directly or indirectly, by the Occupying Power of parts of its own civilian population into the territory it occupies, or the deportation or transfer of all or parts of the population of the occupied territory within or outside this territory as defined

---

42. Ibid., para. 688.

in Article 8(2)(b)(viii). The crime of transferring, directly or indirectly, by the Occupying Power of parts of its own civilian population into the territory it occupies caused particular controversy. Although intensive informal negotiations took place, no provisional agreement was reached. This deadlock was manifested in a document compiled by the Coordinator that reproduced all the different written proposals on the table.[43] The main points of controversy were the following:

— is this crime limited to forcible transfers, although the Statute uses the formulation 'transfer, directly or indirectly'?
— is this crime limited to transfer of population on a large scale?
— must the economic situation of the local population be worsened and their separate identity be endangered by the transfer?
— what link must there be between the perpetrator and the Occupying Power?

Although negotiations seemed to stall on these questions, most delegations took the view that the problems might be resolved at a later session of the PrepCom.

To summarize, while substantial progress was made during this session of the Working Group on Article 8, further consideration of this article would be undertaken at the following session of the Working Group to ensure the formulation of generally acceptable EOC on Article 8, as part of a complete set of EOC for all crimes laid down in the Statute. Despite all efforts by the Coordinator and the Subcoordinator as well as the delegations, the very demanding goal to finish Article 8 was not achieved. The work on Article 8 would continue at the third PrepCom and negotiations on Article 7 would begin.

3.2   Working Group on the Rules of Procedure and Evidence

With respect to the RPE, the PrepCom focussed on rules pertaining to the following parts of the ICC Statute: Part 4 (Composition and Administration of the Court); Part 5 (Investigation and Prosecution); Part 6 (The Trial); and Part 8 (Appeal and Revision). The Working Group held 12 meetings and had before it several new proposals, in addition to those which were made at the first session of the Prep-Com.[44]

It has to be emphasised that the inter-sessional meeting on victims' access to the ICC, hosted by the Government of France in Paris from 27 to 29 April 1999, and the informal inter-sessional meeting hosted by the International Institute of Higher Studies in Criminal Sciences in Siracusa, Italy from 21 to 27 June 1999, made very valuable contributions to the negotiations. The Working Group considered proposals related to Parts 6 and 8 of the Statute in plenary meetings and in informal consultations, as well as to Part 5, which the PrepCom had begun to consider during its first session.

---

43. PCNICC/1999/WGEC/INF/3.

44. The proposals submitted at this second session are contained in the following documents: PCNICC/1999/DP.7/Add.1/Rev.1; PCNICC/1999/DP.8/Add.1/Rev.1; PCNICC/1999/WGRPE/INF.2 and Add.1; PCNICC/1999/DP.8/Add.2/Rev.1; and PCNICC/1999/WGRPE/DP.5-38.

On the basis of the written proposals and the views expressed in the Working Group and in informal consultations, the Coordinator proposed three discussion papers for consideration at the next session of the PrepCom.[45]

The Working Group on RPE dealing with provisions of Part 4 of the Statute completed the discussion on all issues related to organization and composition of the Court. However, due to time constraints, a Coordinator's discussion paper could only be produced on more limited issues, such as removal from office and disciplinary measures.[46]

3.3   Definition of the crime of aggression

The question of the definition of the crime of aggression was dealt with in two plenary sessions. The debate was limited to interventions of a more general character. As at the first session of the PrepCom, the views concerning the organization of the future work were quite divided. Certain states advocated the creation of a working group for upcoming sessions of the PrepCom in order to reach a definition of this crime as quickly as possible. Other states underlined the fact that the PrepCom is obliged to finalize the work on RPE and EOC before 30 June 2000. Therefore, they preferred to use the limited time primarily for these issues. However, after consultations undertaken by the bureau of the PrepCom with interested states, the PrepCom agreed on the following arrangements concerning the question of the crime of aggression:

(a) A working group on the crime of aggression will be established at the outset of the next session of the Preparatory Commission;

(b) At the next and the following sessions of the Preparatory Commission, the plenary traditionally held each Monday morning will be maintained, but will be significantly shorter, essentially limited to brief reports by the coordinators;

(c) A meeting of the working group on the crime of aggression will follow each of the Monday morning plenary meetings, until the end of the morning;

(d) Informal consultations on the crime of aggression will be conducted at other times where possible and appropriate, it being understood that this should be without prejudice to the requirements of the work on subjects which must be completed by 30 June 2000. Within the limits of what is practicable, the Secretariat will endeavour to provide the best possible facilities for those informal consultations;

(e) The above arrangements are based on a clear and general understanding that they will remain unchanged until 30 June 2000, and that no additional requests concerning organization of the work with respect to the crime of aggression will be made before that date.[47]

---

45. PCNICC/WGRPE/RT.5/Rev.1, Add. 1 and Corr.1, and Add. 2 and 3 on rules related to Part 6 of the Statute; PCNICC/WGRPE/RT.6 on rules related to Part 5 of the Statute; and PCNICC/WGRPE/RT.7 on rules related to Part 8 of the Statute.

46. PCNICC/1999/WGRPE(4)/RT.1.

47. PCNICC/1999/L.4.

The Coordinator Tuvaku Manongi (Tanzania) prepared a compilation of various proposals on a definition in order to further the upcoming negotiations.[48]

4.   CONCLUSIONS

As during the first session of the PrepCom, the negotiations linked to the EOC and RPE were held in a very constructive and cooperative atmosphere, determined by the wish to complete the PrepCom's mandate within the established deadlines. However, the discussions during the second session became much more intense and controversial. The debate on the transfer by the Occupying Power of parts of its own population into occupied territory is just one example.

Although considerable progress has been made, a major effort has to be undertaken to proceed with the necessary speed in order to complete a draft before 30 June 2000. According to the assessment of the Chair, Philippe Kirsch from Canada, the PrepCom has already expended 65 percent of its time, but only accomplished 45 percent of its work on RPE and EOC. Therefore, he encouraged further inter-sessional consultations and meetings.

The third session of the PrepCom was from 29 November to 17 December 1999.[49]

---

48. PCNICC/1999/INF.2.

49. Reports on the outcome of PrepComs Three and Four will be included in Volume 3 of the *YIHL.*

THE ROLE OF EVIDENCE IN WAR CRIMES TRIALS: THE COMMON LAW AND THE YUGOSLAV TRIBUNAL[1]

Ian Bryan[2] and Peter Rowe[3]

1.   INTRODUCTION

With the passing into law of the War Crimes Act of 1991,[4] the United Kingdom joined common law states such as Canada and Australia in conferring upon its domestic courts jurisdiction to try individuals suspected of having committed war crimes in Europe during the Second World War.[5] Under the 1991 Act, proceedings for murder, manslaughter or culpable homicide may be brought, with the consent of the Attorney-General, against any person who, on 8 March 1990 or later, became a British citizen or resident in the United Kingdom, providing that the offence charged is alleged to have been committed between 1 September 1939 and 4 June 1945 in a place which was, at the material time, part of Germany or under German occupation.[6] The Act further provides that the offence charged must have constituted a violation of the laws and customs of war under international law at

---

1. © I. Bryan and P. Rowe, 1999.

2. Lecturer in Law, University of Lancaster, UK.

3. Professor of Law and Head of the Department of Law, University of Lancaster, UK.

4. War Crimes Act, Chapter 13. Enacted 9 May 1991. The Act gives UK courts jurisdiction 'in respect of certain grave violations of the laws and customs of war committed in German-held territory during the Second World War and for connected purposes'.

5. For the equivalent legislative provisions in Australia see, War Crimes Act, 1945, as amended by the War Crimes Amendment Act, 1988; for Canada see, Criminal Code, RSC, 1985, ss. 7 (3.71) - (3.77). Currently, there is no provision under US law for the criminal prosecution of US citizens suspected of having committed war crimes during the Second World War. However, such individuals may be denaturalised and extradited to a second country where that second country seeks the prosecution of the individual for war crimes and where a valid extradition treaty exists between the US and the second county. See L.J. Del Pizzo, 'Not Guilty - But Not Innocent: An Analysis of the Acquittal of John Demjanjuk and Its Impact on the Future of Nazi War Crimes Trials', 18 *Boston College International & Comparative Law Review* (1995) p. 176. Under US law, an alleged war criminal may be denaturalised on proof that the individual had obtained entry into the United States either by a wilful misrepresentation or by the concealment of a material fact which, if disclosed at the time of entry, would have made the application for entry ineligible. see *US* v. *Demjanjuk*, 518 *F Supp.* 1362 (ND Ohio, 1981); *US* v. *Demjanjuk*, 680 *F* 2d 32 (6th Cir., 1982); *Demjanjuk* v. *US*, 459 *US* 1036 (1982); and *Demjanjuk* v. *Petrovsky*, 776 *F* 2d 571 (6th Cir., 1985), cited in Del Pizzo, *supra*. For the problems faced in Australia and Canada, see respectively, *Polyukhovich* v. *The Commonwealth of Australia* (1991) 172 *CLR* 501 and *R* v. *Finta* [1994] 1 *SCR* 701.

6. War Crimes Act 1991, ss. 1(1), 1(1)(a), 1(2) and 1(3).

the time it was committed.[7] In addition, the Act stipulates that the nationality of the alleged offender at the time the alleged offence was committed is immaterial.[8]

On 1 April 1999, Anthony (Andrzej) Sawoniuk became the first person to be convicted under the 1991 Act.[9] The conviction followed an eight-week trial before a jury at the Central Criminal Court in London, into allegations that Sawoniuk had murdered several Jewish civilians when, in late 1942 – following the Nazi invasion of Poland and the small, now Belarussian, town of Domachevo in June 1941 and Sawoniuk's recruitment by the occupying Germans forces to the local police force – he took part in 'search and kill' operations directed towards those who had escaped the mass slaughter of some 2,900 Jewish civilians in September 1942 on the Jewish festival of Yom Kippur.[10]

Beyond its significance as the first case to result in a conviction under the 1991 Act, the case of *R* v. *Sawoniuk*[11] provides an opportunity to assess the role played by rules of evidence in securing a fair trial for, and testing the case against, war crimes suspects. In light of the *Sawoniuk* case, this article considers whether and to what extent, evidential and procedural rules generally associated with common law legal systems and as applied in domestic, common law trials of suspected war criminals, present barriers to conviction distinct from those discernible in war crimes trials before international criminal tribunals.[12]

---

7. Ibid., s. 1(1)(b).

8. Ibid., s. 1.

9. Though the first to be convicted, Sawoniuk was the second person to be prosecuted under the 1991 Act. In April 1996, Szymon Serafinowicz was indicted for the murder of Jewish civilians in Belarus. However, the case against Serafinowicz collapsed in January 1997 after a jury at the Central Criminal Court found the defendant unfit to stand trial. The Attorney-General then entered a *nolle prosequi* (a permanent stay on the prosecution) due to Serafinowicz's failing mental health, reported to be dementia brought on by Alzheimer's disease. Serafinowicz subsequently died, aged 86, in August 1997. See Hansard, House of Lords, Vol. 596, 11 January 1999, Written Answers, col. *WA 9*. See also *The Times*, 3 September 1997; *The Times*, 2 April 1999.

10. Though implicated in the murder of many Jewish civilians, *The Times*, 9 and 11 February 1999, Sawoniuk went to trial facing four individual counts of murder. He was not alleged to have participated in the massacre of Jews in September 1942. Under English law, where an indictment carries several charges of murder, each count in the indictment must relate to the killing of a single person.

11. Unreported. The authors would like to thank Smith Bernal Reporting Ltd. for providing them with a copy of the trial Judge's summing-up and sentencing remarks.

12. This article will consider, in particular, the International Criminal Tribunal for the Former Yugoslavia (ICTY), see below part 7. For an evaluation of the contention that common law systems employ evidential and procedural rules which present higher barriers to conviction than trial procedures recognised in civil law legal systems see M. Damaška, 'Evidentiary Barriers to Conviction and Two Models of Criminal Procedure: A Comparative Study', 121 *University of Pennsylvania Law Review* (1973) p. 506

2.   CRIMINAL EVIDENCE AND TRIAL BY JURY

As a preliminary to appraising the manner in which particular rules of evidence were brought to bear in *Sawoniuk*, it may usefully be observed that, whether before a domestic criminal court displaying features consistent with the common law adversarial model, or before a tribunal exhibiting features associated with the civil law inquisitorial model,[13] any case involving a formal inquiry into serious criminal offences will, and indeed must, be determined on the basis of evidence.[14] Although this is a far from controversial observation, it raises the question of whether, or how far, rules governing the means by which disputed facts are resolved in trials on indictment under English law, in such cases as *Sawoniuk,* find expression in proceedings before international criminal tribunals.

As to criminal proceedings under English law, it is important to acknowledge the general rule that, in trials on indictment, it is for the jury to decide whether the accused is guilty of the offence or offences charged and for the Judge to settle questions of law. Furthermore, with regard to evidential issues, the Judge is responsible for deciding questions of relevance, admissibility and, where a piece of evidence is legally admissible, whether it is sufficient to be considered by the jury.[15] The jury, on the other hand, determines the credibility and value or weight to be attached to the evidence legally adduced.[16] These key features in the process of law-application and fact-finding under the adversarial mode of trial are greatly influenced by and, in turn, greatly influence the structure of the law of criminal evidence in English criminal trials.[17] They may be seen to operate in *Sawoniuk*.

3.   ADMISSIBILITY OF EVIDENCE IN *SAWONIUK*

The jury in *Sawoniuk* was asked to return verdicts upon charges relating to events which took place in Eastern Europe some 57 years before the case came to trial. As the evidence supporting the charges was based, almost exclusively, on testimony tendered by elderly witnesses, both Judge and jury were confronted with the problem of evaluating oral evidence from witnesses whose memories of distant events might not be reliable.

---

13. The more salient features of common law, adversarial criminal proceedings and of civil law, non-adversarial criminal proceedings are considered in Damaška, ibid., pp. 513-589. See also K. Mann, 'Hearsay Evidence in War Crimes Trials', 24 *Israel Yearbook on Human Rights* (1994) pp. 311-313 at 297.

14. See Damaška, loc. cit. n. 12, pp. 513, 521, 536, 545, 551; Mann, ibid., pp. 310-311, 314.

15. See *R* v. *Sang* (1979) 69 *Cr.App.R* 282, p. 290.

16. For a discussion of the general rule respecting the division of functions between judge and jury in English criminal cases and exceptions to the general rule, see C. Tapper, *Cross and Tapper on Evidence,* 8th edn. (London, Butterworths 1995) pp. 177-190; A.A.S. Zuckerman, *The Principles of Criminal Evidence* (Oxford, Clarendon 1989) pp. 29-46.

17. See Zuckerman, ibid., pp. 13-16. See also Damaška, loc. cit. n. 12, pp. 510-511.

Sawoniuk had been indicted on four individual counts of murder, each of which was alleged to have been committed in 1942 during the German occupation of the defendant's native town of Domachevo, and each, it was alleged, constituted a 'violation of the laws and customs of war'.[18] The first count charged the defendant with the murder of a unnamed Jewess; the second alleged that he murdered a Jewish male known as Schlemko; the third related to the murder of another unnamed Jewess and the fourth count accused him of the murder of a second Jewish male known as Mir Barlas.

At the close of the prosecution's case, Potts J, directed the jury to return 'not guilty' verdicts in respect of counts two and four since, as he made clear, the jury could not safely convict the defendant of murder on either count.[19] The trial Judge issued this direction after forming the view that no reasonable jury could convict Sawoniuk of the offences outlined in the two counts.[20]

It is clear from remarks made by the Judge during his summing-up that count two rested upon the evidence of a single witness. The witness in question gave evidence purporting to identify the defendant as the policeman involved in the murder of Schlemko. However, the evidence depended on what the witness claimed he was told by the defendant's brother two days after the alleged murder.[21] The Judge, therefore, ruled that as the witness' evidence depended on hearsay, it should be disregarded.

Here, the common law rule against hearsay worked to prevent the jury from considering the evidence given by the witness of what a second party had allegedly said to that witness. The scope of the common law hearsay rule in English criminal proceedings is such that 'an assertion other than one made by a person while giving oral evidence in the proceedings is inadmissible as evidence of any fact asserted'.[22] Put simply, the evidence from the witness was held to fall within the exclusionary rule on the basis that the defendant's brother was not present at the trial and, therefore, could not be cross-examined on the truth or falsity of what was alleged to have been said to the witness.[23]

With respect to the Judge's direction to the jury on count four, again the evidence in issue depended on a single witness. In this instance, the Judge appears to have exercised a discretion, either under common law or statute, to direct the jury to disregard what the witness deposed the defendant had said to him about the fate of the person named in count four. The witness, in his evidence-in-chief,

---

18. War Crimes Act, 1991, s. 1(1)(b).

19. Transcript of Summing-up, Smith Bernal Reporting Ltd., (hereafter, Transcript), 29 March 1999, p. 27.

20. Ibid. The common law rule which obliges a trial Judge to issue such a direction is discussed in *DPP* v. *Stonehouse* [1978] *AC* 55 and in *R* v. *Galbraith* (1981) 1 *WLR* 1039.

21. Transcript, 29 March 1999, p. 27.

22. Tapper, op. cit. n. 16, p. 46. This formulation of the rule was approved by the House of Lords in *R* v. *Sharp* [1988] 1 *All ER* 65, p. 86.

23. On the operation of the hearsay rule in the Israeli war crimes trial of John Demjanjuk see Mann, loc. cit. n. 13, pp. 312-313, 318-322. For discussion of how this issue is handled by the ICTY, see below.

claimed that he witnessed an elderly Jewish civilian named Mir Barlas, being handed over to the defendant and two other policemen who then marched him off in the direction of the local sand hills. He further claimed that, some days later, he asked the defendant what had happened to Barlas. According to the witness, the defendant replied that Barlas had been courageous when he died.[24] At trial, the Judge ruled that this evidence could not safely be regarded as a confession to murder.[25] The 'confession', therefore, was to be disregarded.

The admissibility of confession evidence in criminal proceedings is governed by the Police and Criminal Evidence Act 1984.[26] The Act provides that a confession – defined as including 'any statement wholly or partly adverse to the person who made it, whether made to a person in authority or not and whether in words or otherwise'[27] – may not be received in evidence if obtained either by oppression of the person who made it or in consequence of anything said or done which was likely to render any confession made unreliable.[28] A judge has no discretion in the matter; if the prosecution fails to show that a confession was not obtained by oppression or is not likely to be unreliable, that confession must be excluded. However, where a confession is not excluded for oppression or possible unreliability, a Judge may, nevertheless, exclude the confession in the exercise of his statutory or common law discretion. The statutory discretion permits exclusion if it appears that, having regard to all the circumstances, including the circumstances in which the evidence was obtained, the admission of the evidence would have such an adverse effect on the fairness of the proceedings that the court ought not to admit it.[29] The common law discretion, which is preserved in the 1984 Act,[30] may be exercised in favour of exclusion in order to prevent the appearance of injustice.[31] While the actual basis upon which the Judge in *Sawoniuk* directed the jury to disregard the evidence advanced in support of count four is not entirely clear, his view on the matter appears to have been informed by a concern to ensure the defendant received a fair trial.

---

24. *The Times*, 24 and 25 February 1999; Transcript, 30 March 1999, p. 15.

25. Transcript, 29 March 1999, pp. 27-28.

26. Police and Criminal Evidence Act, 1984, ss. 76, 78 and 82(3).

27. Ibid., s. 82(1).

28. Ibid., s. 76(2)(a) and (b). The burden of proof to show that the confession is admissible is upon the prosecution. Compare Rule 92 of the Rules of Procedure and Evidence (1994, as amended) of the ICTY, where the burden of proof on the issue is on the defendant.

29. Ibid., s. 78(1). The application of this section is not limited to confession evidence; it applies to any evidence on which the prosecution proposes to rely, *R* v. *Mason* (1988) 86 *Cr.App.R* 349, p. 354.

30. Police and Criminal Evidence Act, 1984, s. 82(3). As with the s. 78(1) discretion, the common law discretion to exclude is not limited to confession evidence.

31. *R* v. *Sat-Bhambra* (1989) 88 *Cr.App.R* 55.

4.   THE EVIDENCE AGAINST SAWONIUK

Turning to the remaining two counts, each relating to the murder of a single Jewess, it should be emphasised that, as a matter of law, the burden of proving guilt in such cases rests on the prosecution.[32] As Potts J pointed out to the jury, to discharge the burden of proof in respect of each of the two counts, the prosecution had to make the jury 'sure' of the defendant's guilt.[33] The prosecution had contended that the defendant was a willing executioner of Nazi policy when he shot the individuals referred to in counts one and three. The defendant's case was one of complete denial of the charges contained in the counts.[34] The counts in question centred on the evidence of two principal witnesses, AB and FZ, who gave evidence identifying the defendant as the person who carried out the shootings.

AB gave evidence that he was 13 years-old when he and a friend, who had since died, were caught by the defendant and other local police officers as they scavenged for clothes in the ghetto area of Domachevo two or three days after the massacre in September 1942. The defendant, who was known to the witness as Andrusha, herded them towards the site of the massacre. There, he saw two Jewish men, aged about forty, and a Jewish woman, aged about twenty-five, being guarded by two other policemen as they stood near an open pit. The defendant, who was carrying a pistol, ordered the three Jews, who were wearing yellow patches on the back and front of their clothes, to undress. The men undressed but the woman would not remove all her clothing. The defendant threatened to beat her with a truncheon. She then complied. Standing behind each of the three Jews, the defendant shot them. As they fell, the defendant levered them into the pit by raising his knees. After the executions, the defendant and the other policemen searched the clothes of the dead. After this, the witness and his friend were ordered to shovel earth over the bodies and return the shovel to the police station.[35] During cross-examination, the witness denied being mistaken about the defendant's presence at the scene of the murder, saying: 'I remember it beautifully. Andrusha gave the orders for that

---

32. The general common law rule that in criminal cases the legal burden of proving any fact essential to the prosecution's case rests on the prosecution and remains on the prosecution throughout the case was laid down in *Woolmington* v. *DDP* [1935] *AC* 462.

33. Transcript, 29 March 1999, pp. 35, 48. In stating that the jury should return a guilty verdict only if the prosecution could make them 'sure' of the defendant's guilt, Potts J was alluding to the standard of proof to be met by the prosecution in discharging the legal burden. In English law, whenever the prosecution carries the legal burden of proving an issue, the standard of proof or sureness to be met is 'beyond reasonable doubt'. However, as Denning J observed in *Miller* v. *Minister of Pensions* [1947] 2 *All ER* 372, p. 373: 'Proof beyond reasonable doubt does not mean proof beyond the shadow of doubt ... If the evidence is so strong against a man as to leave only a remote possibility in his favour which can be dismissed with the sentence 'of course it is possible, but not in the least probable', the case is proved beyond reasonable doubt, but nothing short of that will suffice.' See Art. 21.3 of the Statute of the ICTY.

34. Transcript, 29 March 1999, pp. 31-32, 46.

35. Transcript, 30 March 1999, pp. 28-37. See *The Times*, 19 February and 6 March 1999.

execution. He shot the Jews and ordered us to fill the grave. He marched us to the site. There is no mistake.'[36]

FZ, who at the time of the trial was over 75 years-old, stated that he knew the defendant as Andrusha, and that he, FZ, and the defendant had been at school together.[37] FZ deposed that in the autumn of 1942, a few days after the September massacre, he was walking through the woods near the town of Domachevo when he heard crying and shouting. He went to investigate and, from his hiding place in the undergrowth, he saw no fewer than 15 women by a pit getting undressed. The women were asked to turn and face the pit. The defendant was alleged to have shot the women with a machinegun.[38]

Other evidence, more circumstantial in nature, was given by a number of other witnesses to provide the jury with a backdrop against which to consider events surrounding the charges faced by the accused. The witnesses, all of advanced years, gave the jury accounts of such matters as: day-to-day life in the predominantly Jewish town of Domachevo prior to and following the German invasion of the town; the confinement of Jews to the local ghetto; the activities of the local police established by the occupying Germans; the recruitment of local men for police service; the role of the local police in the September 1942 massacre of Jews; the defendant's role and status in the local police; activities of 'search and kill' squads; sites where alleged crimes were committed;[39] and acts of brutality allegedly committed by the defendant.

Expert testimony – that is, evidence from a witness having specialised knowledge or skill rather than direct experience of a subject matter not within the knowledge or experience of the trier of fact[40] – was also tendered for the prosecution. Based

---

36. Ibid., p. 37. It is a common feature of war crimes trials that witnesses' testimony has to be translated. It is unlikely that a native English speaker would use the expression 'I remember it beautifully' in such a context.

37. Ibid., p. 43.

38. Ibid., pp. 47-49. See *The Times*, 10, 12 February, and 16 March 1999.

39. The court in *Sawoniuk* – including the jury of eight men and four women, the trial Judge, counsel and court staff – made British legal history when it travelled to Domachevo, in February 1999, in order to better understand the nature of the town, the terrain and relevant sites. This was the first time a British criminal court had convened on foreign soil, see *The Times*, 9 and 17 February 1999.

40. It is a matter for the judge to decide whether the jury could be assisted by expert evidence and whether the expert in question has the expertise to so assist, *R. v. Stockwell* (1993) 97 *Cr.App.R* 260, p. 264. It was emphasised by the Court of Appeal in *Stockwell*, at p. 266, that where expert evidence is received by a trial court, the trial Judge 'should make clear to the jury that they are not bound by the expert's opinion and that the issue is for them to decide'. Expert evidence will not be admissible where the triers of fact can form their own opinion without the assistance of an expert, see *R. v. Turner* [1975] *QB* 834; *R. v. Weightman* (1991) *Cr.App.R* 291. Expert evidence and the opinion of an *amicus curiae* are more readily admitted in trials before a trial chamber of the ICTY because the triers of fact are professional Judges and not a jury.

on a number of World War II documents and reports written by the Germans,[41] the witness, an historian and expert on the Holocaust, gave the jury background information on such matters as: the German advance into Soviet-occupied territory in 1941; actions by German troops against civilian populations; orders from within the German military for the liquidation of potential enemies, including Jews; the setting up of a civilian administration in Domachevo; the recruitment of policemen from the local population; and the role of the local police in the enforcement of Nazi occupation policy.[42] The defence did not dispute this evidence.[43]

5.   THE DEFENDANT'S CASE

In his evidence, the 78 year-old defendant claimed that at all times he was a friend of the Jews and asserted that the witnesses who gave evidence against him were liars in league with the KGB and Scotland Yard.[44] He admitted to having joined the local police as a volunteer soon after the German occupation of Domachevo but denied that local Jews were ever confined to a ghetto. He also stated that, though he was a policeman at the material time, he had left Domachevo two or three days before the Yom Kippur massacre and returned two or three days later, at which time he was told of the incident. In addition, he denied participating in searches for Jewish survivors of the massacre, denied carrying out acts of brutality against civilians, denied knowing AB and FZ, denied that he left Domachevo in July 1944 with the retreating Germans and, finally, denied killing any Jews.[45]

When interviewed by Scotland Yard police officers, in April 1996, the defendant had denied serving as a police officer in Domachevo.[46] At trial, however, he admitted that he had served as a volunteer policeman in the town at the relevant time and that others regarded him as a senior officer in the local police force. He, nevertheless, maintained that there were no restrictions on local Jews and that he did not leave Domachevo in company with the retreating Germans in July 1944. He also maintained that he had no prior knowledge of the September 1942 massacre and that he was not guilty of murder.[47] The prosecution contended that the defendant had lied to the British police in order to conceal the part he played in the offences outlined in the case against him and that this lie was but one of many told by the defendant.[48]

---

41. The testimony of an expert witness will, invariably, be founded on hearsay or multiple hearsay since much of the witness' expertise will be derived from sources such as documents, reports and books. This, however, is not a basis in English law for excluding expert testimony, see *R* v. *Abadom* (1983) 76 *Cr.App.R* 48.

42. Transcript, 29 March 1999, pp. 42, 51-62.

43. Ibid., pp. 42-43.

44. Ibid., 29 March 1999, p. 32; 30 March 1999, p. 55.

45. Ibid., 29 March 1999, pp. 37, 66-72; 30 March 1999, pp. 37-38, 54-55, 71-74, 79-81.

46. Ibid., 29 March 1999, p. 38; 30 March 1999, pp. 57, 61-62.

47. Ibid., 29 March 1999, pp. 67-68; 30 March, 1999, pp. 1-4.

48. Ibid., 30 March 1999, pp. 62, 74.

This aspect of the case draws attention to common law rules governing the treatment of lies told by a defendant, which are admitted as such by the defendant. Where it is found by a criminal court that the defendant has lied, either during or prior to trial, and where those lies are relied on by the prosecution to support its case, the trial Judge is obliged to issue an appropriate direction to the jury. The direction acknowledges that there is 'a natural tendency for a jury to think that if an accused is lying, it must be because he is guilty, and accordingly convict him without more ado'.[49] It is in recognition of this danger that the direction, commonly referred to as a '*Lucas* direction', is given.[50] Such a direction should make the point that the mere fact that the defendant lied is not, in itself, evidence of guilt since defendants may lie for entirely innocent reasons.[51]

In accordance with the terms of a '*Lucas* direction', the jury in *Sawoniuk* were told that they were to decide whether the defendant lied and that if they were sure he had, they were to ask themselves why he did so.[52] To this, Potts J added, 'the mere fact that a defendant tells a lie is not in itself evidence of guilt. A defendant may lie for many reasons, and they may be innocent ones which do not indicate guilt of the offences charged'.[53] The Judge then adverted to the defendant's explanation of his lies. The defendant claimed he lied to the investigating officers not to conceal offences but for fear of being deported.[54] Potts J directed the jury that if they thought there may be some innocent explanation for the lies told they should disregard those lies.[55] The Judge emphasised to the jury that only if they were sure that the defendant did not lie for innocent reasons could they regard his lies as going to the proof of his guilt.[56] He also advised the jury that, when assessing the credibility of the defendant as a witness, they were entitled to take into account discrepancies between his evidence and that of other witnesses as to when the defendant left Domachevo.[57]

---

49. *Broadhurst* v. *R* [1964] *AC* 441, p. 453, *per* Lord Devlin.

50. *R* v. *Lucas* [1981] 2 *All ER* 1008. See also *R* v. *Goodway* [1993] 4 *All ER* 894. It is not appropriate to issue a '*Lucas* direction' when the defendant's lies are irrelevant to the prosecution's case, *R* v. *Landon* [1995] *Crim. LR* 338; *R* v. *Mussell and Dalton* [1995] *Crim. LR* 887; *R* v. *Keeton* (1995) 2 *Cr.App.R* 241; *R* v. *Harron* (1996) 2 *Cr.App.R* 457. Furthermore, a '*Lucas* direction' will be inappropriate where the prosecution's case gives rise to the conclusion that the defendant is lying. This is because the defendant's lies must be considered separately from the main issue at trial, *R* v. *House and Meadows* [1994] *Crim. LR* 682.

51. See *R* v. *Lucas* ibid. at p. 1011; *R* v. *Burge* [1996] 1 *Cr.App.R* 163, pp. 173-174.

52. Transcript, 29 March 1999, p. 38.

53. Ibid.

54. Ibid., 30 March 1999, p. 61.

55. Ibid., 29 March 1999, p. 39.

56. Ibid., 29 March 1999, pp. 39-40; 30 March 1999, p. 62.

57. Ibid., 29 March 1999, pp. 40-42.

6.   ASSESSING THE WEIGHT OF THE EVIDENCE

Once the Judge in a trial on indictment has resolved questions of relevance and admissibility, the jury, as triers of fact, must assess the evidence presented and decide whether that evidence is sufficiently reliable to be accepted. At this stage, then, it is for the jury to determine the weight to be accorded to the evidence. In *Sawoniuk*, the main witnesses gave direct testimony of long-distant events. These witnesses testified to having known the defendant at the time of the alleged offences; one deposed that he was standing next to the defendant when the defendant shot three Jews, the other, that he observed the defendant shooting a number of Jewesses from a distance of 127 paces.[58] The defendant's case was not that these incidents, the subjects of counts one and three, did not take place; it was his contention that he was not present. It is to the approach taken in English law to such evidence that this article now turns.[59]

The English Court of Appeal, in the leading case of *Turnbull*,[60] laid down guidelines to assist courts in cases where visual identification is disputed. The *Turnbull* guidelines make clear, firstly, that a trial Judge should warn the jury of the special need for caution whenever the prosecution's case depends wholly or substantially on evidence of visual identification. Secondly, that the Judge should explain why caution is needed. Thirdly, that the Judge should make reference to the circumstances in which the disputed identification came to be made. Finally, the guidelines direct that the Judge should point out that a convincing witness might be mistaken in his or her identification evidence.[61] Should a Judge, in any criminal case which hinges on the allegedly mistaken visual identification of the defendant, fail to follow the *Turnbull* guidelines it is likely that any conviction gained will be quashed by the Court of Appeal.[62]

Thus, in cases such as *Sawoniuk*, where the identity of the defendant as the offender is at issue, the trial Judge is required to instruct the jury that a truthful witness may be mistaken in his or her identification of the defendant, particularly when recalling events from long ago. And where the identification of the defendant by one witness might conceivably support the identification evidence of another witness, the Judge should bring this to the attention of the jury, making clear that even a number of honest witnesses can be mistaken in their identification of the

---

58. Transcript, 29 March 1999, pp. 35, 37.

59. For a discussion of the part played by disputed identification evidence in the Israeli trial and subsequent acquittal of John Demjanjuk, see Mann, loc. cit. n. 13, pp. 298-309. For a discussion of the problems posed by disputed identification evidence before the ICTY, see below.

60. *R* v. *Turnbull* [1977] *QB* 224.

61. Ibid., p. 228.

62. Ibid., p. 231, *per* Lord Widgery. See also *R* v. *Keane* (1977) 65 *Cr.App.R* 247; *R* v. *Hunjan* (1978) 68 *Cr.App.R* 99; *R* v. *Tyson* [1985] *Crim. LR* 48; *Reid* v. *R* [1990] *AC* 363.

defendant.[63] In *Sawoniuk*, the trial Judge appears to have followed the *Turnbull* guidelines scrupulously.[64]

The jury, originally of four women and eight men but reduced to eleven after one woman fell ill,[65] returned guilty verdicts in respect of the two counts in question. On count one the jury delivered a unanimous verdict. With regard to count three, the jury found the defendant guilty by a majority of ten-to-one.[66]

In sentencing Sawoniuk, at the close of the eight-week trial, Potts J referred to the testimony of a witness who had described how the defendant became a man of power, a master, a lord. The Judge commented that:

> No word of mine can add anything of value to those already written and spoken about the events in which you played a part. I only say this, that though you held a lowly rank in the hierarchy of those involved in liquidating Jews in eastern Europe, to the Jews of Domachevo it must have seemed otherwise. [One witness] said of you that when you became a policeman you became a man of power, a master and a lord. I am sure from the evidence that we have heard in this trial that he was right when he said that.
>
> You have been convicted of charges properly brought, you have had a fair trial, no jury could have given closer attention to the issues raised by this case than the one that has tried you. You have been convicted of 2 charges of murder on clear evidence in my judgment.
>
> I pass upon you the sentence fixed by law on each count which is one of life imprisonment.[67]

---

63. *R* v. *Weeder* (1980) 71 *Cr.App.R* 228; *R* v. *Breslin* (1984) 80 *Cr. App. R* 226.

64. During his summing-up, Potts J warned the jury of the need for caution, with such comments as: 'There is special need for caution when considering evidence of identification and convicting a defendant in reliance on it ... it is possible that an honest witness may make a mistaken identification. ... An apparently convincing witness can be mistaken ... examine carefully the circumstances in which the identification ... was made. ... Please, members of the jury, be careful. Many years have passed. It is not easy to remember [events from] all those years ago. ... Again, ladies and gentlemen, remember, it was a long time ago ... Approach the evidence with care. Do not act on it unless it makes you absolutely sure. ... Even if you are satisfied, so as to be sure that [a given witness] was not lying, that he was doing his best to tell the truth, you would still have to be sure that his evidence was accurate and reliable. ... [P]eople do, after a time, speak forcefully of having seen things when close enquiry shows that their recollection must be wrong.' Transcript, 29 March 1999, pp. 36-38, 85; 30 March 1999, pp. 11, 24, 38, 39.

65. A Judge is given authority to discharge individual members of the jury by section 16(1) of the Juries Act, 1974. The section provides that where any member of the jury dies or is discharged through illness, but the number of its members is not reduced below nine, the jury shall nevertheless be considered as remaining for all the purposes of that trial properly constituted, and the trial shall proceed and a verdict may be given accordingly.

66. By section 17(1)(a) of the Juries Act 1974, the verdict of a jury need not be unanimous in a case where there are not less than 11 jurors, 10 of which agree on the verdict. The procedure to be followed by the Judge in taking majority verdicts is set out in *Practice Direction (Crime: Majority Verdicts)* [1967] 1 *WLR* 1198.

67. Transcript, Sentencing Remarks, 1 April 1999, p. 32. By section 1(1) of the Murder (Abolition of the Death Penalty) Act 1965, an offender aged 21 or over who is convicted of murder must be sentenced to imprisonment for life. Thus, since the abolition of the death penalty in the UK, life

7.   THE ADMISSIBILITY OF EVIDENCE BEFORE INTERNATIONAL
      WAR CRIMES TRIBUNALS

The circumstances surrounding the crimes committed by Sawoniuk were not dis-similar to those surrounding the crimes committed, for example, by Tadić, Delić, Furundžija or Akayesu. They were, however, different from most 'ordinary' criminal activity. Charges usually involve more than one killing,[68] witnesses are often traumatised as a result of their experiences, prosecution and defence witnesses are usually confined to their respective ethnic group making inherent bias a real risk, witnesses' evidence has to be translated and oral evidence is given some years after the events.

As noted, the *Sawoniuk* trial was before a Judge and jury, the form of criminal trial generally adopted in common law systems, and the laws of evidence applied were those that would govern the trial of a thief or a burglar, or indeed, any other person tried on indictment. The procedure (by which term is included the laws of evidence) applying to criminal trials will vary from state to state. The procedure chosen is often a product of history or an adoption of another state's system with national variations. Providing the basic form of criminal process conforms with international standards,[69] it is difficult to determine which system is more or less likely to lead to a defendant receiving a fair trial, the objective of any criminal trial process.

International tribunals established to try alleged war criminals have had to adopt their own rules without the luxury of developing them over a period of time or of testing their efficacy in trial after trial of 'ordinary' criminals. Procedures of such tribunals must win the acceptance of the world community and thus must not be seen as merely a reflection of the criminal procedures of one particular group of states (such as common law or civil law). Moreover, the Judges will have to be drawn from a variety of legal systems. The procedure selected by an international tribunal will have a profound effect on the admissibility of evidence and the way in which evidential issues are decided. Like any national criminal court, the objective will be to ensure that an accused receives a fair trial.

The International Criminal Tribunal for the Former Yugoslavia (ICTY) faces these issues. Article 20 of its Statute requires 'Trial Chambers [to] ensure that a trial is fair and expeditious ... with full respect for the rights of the accused', while Article 21 develops further the notion of the rights of the accused. Article 22 directs the Tribunal to provide its own rules of procedure and evidence, which it did in

---

imprisonment is the mandatory sentence for murder. Under section 1(2) of the 1965 Act, a Judge can make a recommendation as to the minimum period that the convicted offender should serve in prison before being released on licence.

68. 'Duško Tadić stood trial for the murder of thirteen people and the torture of nineteen others. In the United States, he would have been considered among the nation's worst mass murderers, (...).' Michael Scharf, *Balkan Justice* (Durham NC, Carolina Academic Press 1997) p. 222.

69. For example, Art. 14 of the Covenant on Civil and Political Rights 1966 or the European Convention on Human Rights 1950.

'two months'.[70] The procedure selected in the Statute of the Tribunal was trial by three Judges, as judges of fact and law. The evidential provisions decided upon by the Judges could therefore reflect this chosen form of criminal process. Thus, evidence is to be admissible if it is relevant and deemed to have 'probative value'.[71] Conversely, evidence can be excluded if 'its probative value is substantially outweighed by the need to ensure a fair trial'.[72]

The form of deciding guilt or innocence adopted by the ICTY is quite different from the common law system under which Sawoniuk was tried and the basis upon which evidence is admitted is therefore also different. Under the common law system, the Judge acts as a gatekeeper, keeping away from the jury all evidence that he or she thinks is irrelevant or inadmissible. Evidence will generally be inadmissible simply because of its potential to prejudice a jury or because of its inherent unreliability or irrelevance. Once facts are admitted in evidence, generally through the giving of testimony, the weight to be attached to them is for the jury alone. In the ICTY, however, everything is decided by the Judges alone. The judicial input in a trial switches from admissibility to weight.[73] But the issue is not as simple as this, since if this were the case two serious disadvantages would flow. First, the investigation of a case against an individual would be very inefficient. If the investigators do not know what will ultimately be considered as evidence having probative value by the Trial Chamber they will either take too long in securing a mass of potential evidence or they will need to seek guidance from a trial chamber by way of interlocutory motion. Secondly, the effectiveness of the Appeals Chamber will be curtailed in so far as it might be able to judge whether the defendant was rightly convicted. This is because the weight of evidence is a question of fact and not law. The trial Judges will have seen and heard the witnesses and will, in consequence, have been in a better position to weigh their credibility than five Appeals Chamber Judges who have not. The Judges in the Trial Chambers have therefore had to redress the balance more in favour of developing, as the issues have arisen, rules as to the admissibility of evidence.

Experience has shown that reliance upon the reception of 'probative' evidence alone may not be sufficient. Hearsay is generally excluded, with important exceptions, in common law jurisdictions. The defence in the *Tadić* case sought a ruling that hearsay evidence should be excluded before the ICTY. In a decision of 5 August 1996, the Trial Chamber decided that hearsay was not to be excluded as a general rule but that its reliability was to be assessed in determining whether

---

70. See Scharf, op. cit. n. 68, p. 67.

71. Rule 89 of the Rules of Procedure and Evidence (as revised and amended). Under English law evidence is said to be 'probative' if it 'tends to render probable the existence or non-existence of any fact', Criminal Law Revision Committee, *Evidence (General)*, 11th Report, 1972, *Cmnd.* 4991, para. 14.

72. Ibid., Rule 89D.

73. This can be seen under English law in the general admissibility of hearsay in non-criminal cases which are tried by a Judge alone.

it possessed probative value within the meaning of Rule 89(c).[74] This ruling adds little to the solution of the problem of uncertainty as to the weight which will be given by the Judges to hearsay evidence. If oral[75] testimony (the most common form of evidence before the ICTY) is challenged, how can its reliability be tested if it is an out-of- court statement[76] not subjected to cross-examination? When it is borne in mind that most (if not all) witness statements tendered by the prosecutor will be made by individuals of a different ethnic group, against whom serious crimes are alleged to have been committed by the defendant, any attempt to assess their credibility in these circumstances will either be very difficult, or impossible. There is some force in the argument that a trial before three Judges is different from a trial before a Judge and jury, with the exclusion of hearsay being justifiable only in the latter form of trial. Whether it is enough, however, merely to treat such evidence 'with caution'[77] may be questionable. Scharf concludes, after analysing in detail the evidence presented in the *Tadić* case, that 'at times the Tribunal tread dangerously close to denying Tadic a fair trial, most conspicuously by its decision to allow certain witnesses to testify anonymously and by *permitting the prosecution to base so much of its case on hearsay'*.[78]

Problems of disputed identification evidence give rise to similar concerns, especially where the identifying witness has not known the accused beforehand. What degree of probative value can such evidence possess, given the *sui generis* nature of the crimes charged? At best, it may be circumstantial evidence, showing that the defendant was in the area at the time when the crimes were committed. Those committing serious war crimes will often try to ensure that there are no witnesses (of the 'opposite side') to the actual events themselves. Like hearsay evidence, this type of evidence should also be treated with caution by Trial Chambers. It may be argued, however, that this, in itself, is not sufficient. The trial Judges will, of course, have to rely upon vigorous cross-examination by the defence, but there is a real risk of a wrongful conviction unless the trial Judges themselves are seen to be drawing attention to the inherent dangers of disputed identification evidence.[79]

---

74. *Tadić*, The Jurisprudence, 5. Decision on Hearsay. Factors such as whether it is 'voluntary, truthful and trustworthy' should be considered.

75. Documentary evidence may well be treated differently, especially where it is in the form of an official record. See the 'duty rosters' as evidence in the *Tadić* case, Scharf, op. cit. n. 68, p. 194.

76. Rule 89E is directed to the form of the statement and not its content.

77. See *Prosecutor* v. *Akayesu* 37 *ILM* (1998) p. 1399, at para. 24 (ICTR).

78. Op. cit. n. 68, p. 220, emphasis supplied. For the issue of anonymous witnesses, see Christine Chinkin, 'Amicus Curiae Brief on Protective Measures for Victims and Witnesses', 7 *Criminal Law Forum* (1996) p. 179 and compare Monroe Leigh, Editorial Comment: Witness Anonymity is Inconsistent with Due Process, 91 *AJIL* (1997) pp. 80-82.

79. A rule of mandatory corroboration is not the answer and the ICTY has (rightly) rejected this, see *Prosecutor* v. *Akayesu*, *supra* n. 77 at para. 24.

The power given to trial chambers to exclude evidence 'if its probative value is substantially outweighed by the need to ensure a fair trial'[80] has not been interpreted by trial chambers so as to create a rule of admissibility of evidence. This is due, largely, to the difficulty of defining the requirements of a 'fair trial', beyond the minimum principles of a fair trial.[81] Is the reception of anonymous evidence, or of oral hearsay, or of poor quality disputed identification evidence such as to contribute (at least) to the denial of a fair trial? Only if its probative value is not assessed properly by the trial chamber Judges[82] and set against the story being told by the defendant. The judges would be very unlikely to come to the conclusion that they could not assess it fully and properly. In consequence, Rule 89D is unlikely to have any practical significance.

8.   CONCLUSION

The Statute, Rules of Procedure and Evidence and the decisions of the ICTY are seen to be important in setting a 'standard for proceedings before ... a permanent criminal court'.[83] The results are not, however, encouraging. The *Sawoniuk* trial in London took eight weeks from the start of the trial itself to judgment and sentencing. By way of contrast, the trial of Tadić took seven months,[84] that of the four defendants in the *Čelebići* case took 19 months and that of *Blaškić* 25 months.[85] In some trials, the Trial Chamber had to adjourn while motions were heard separately and to enable other proceedings to be started when the number of court-rooms was inadequate.

---

80. Rule 89D. See also Rules 92 (confessions) and 95 (improper methods of obtaining evidence), both of which are likely to be more significant than Rule 89D in excluding evidence. See for some discussion, *Prosecutor* v. *Delalić et al.*, Decision on the Motion of the Prosecution for the Admissibility of Evidence, 19 January 1998, para. 22. For decisions on evidential issues, *Prosecutor* v. *Delalić et al.*, Judgment, 16 November 1998, dealing with the admissibility of an alleged confession, para. 69 and self-incrimination, at para. 66.

81. These are stated in the Statute of the ICTY, see Articles 10, 20, 21 and 23. See also the Rules of Procedure and Evidence, in particular, Section 3. Compare Articles 99, 100, 101, 103, 105 and 106 of Geneva Convention III, 1949 and Article 75, Additional Protocol I, 1977. The suggestion by Presiding Judge McDonald in *Prosecutor* v. *Delalić*, Decision on the Prosecutor's Motion Requesting Protective Measures for Victims and Witnesses, 10 August 1995, that the ICTY was 'comparable to a military tribunal, which often has limited rights of due process and more lenient rules of evidence' (at para. 28) is, with respect, misleading. Where modern military tribunals (in most countries) are dealing with serious offences, as compared with mere breaches of military discipline, this is most unlikely to be the case.

82. 'The trials before the International Tribunal are conducted before professional judges, who by virtue of their training and experience are able to consider each piece of evidence which has been admitted and determine its appropriate weight,' *Prosecutor* v. *Delalić et al.*, Decision on the Motion of the Prosecution for the Admissibility of Evidence, 19 January 1998, para. 20.

83. Ibid., para. 25.

84. A further 5 months passed before the verdict was delivered, see Scharf, op. cit. n. 68, p. 214.

85. The trial ended on 30 July 1999. The verdict was delivered on 3 March 2000.

Why is there such a disparity in the time taken to try an individual, when Article 20 of the Statute requires a trial to be 'expeditious'? To some extent, the Trial and Appeal Chambers had to mould a new criminal trial system, an 'innovative amalgam' of the common law and civil law systems,[86] as they went along. There were important practical differences between the precedents of the International Military Tribunal at Nuremberg and at Tokyo. Unlike during those trials, the prosecutor's case would be based upon large numbers of witnesses and upon relatively few documents.[87] The difficulties posed by the reception of oral evidence at a war crimes tribunal were, it is argued, not fully foreseen when the Judges drafted the Rules of Procedure and Evidence and, particularly, the rules of evidence. They have a far greater significance at The Hague than at Nuremberg or Tokyo. Yet the rules of evidence are not dissimilar.[88]

One consequence of this minimalist approach to the rules of evidence has been delays in the start of trials. Trials have had to be adjourned while prosecution or defence motions concerning evidence issues are decided upon, and it may be that at the investigation stage there was no clear view of what would be the most relevant evidence to secure.[89] In addition, the trial Judges have been put under the most enormous pressure. They have been faced with large numbers of witnesses, most of whom have had to give their evidence through a translator, and a very large volume of transcripts, compiled over a long period of time, during which they have also had to deal with other trials and issues.

It is interesting to speculate whether these same difficulties would have presented themselves if the Judges, in drawing up the rules of evidence, had been much more specific as to what would or would not be admissible, in much the same way as Judges before national courts. By not doing so they have made their task much

---

86. *Prosecutor* v. *Delalić*, Decision on the Prosecutor's Motion Requesting Protective Measures for Victims and Witnesses, 10 August 1995, para. 22; *Prosecutor* v. *Delalić et al.*, Decision on the Motion of the Prosecution for the Admissibility of Evidence, 19 January 1998, at para. 15.

87. See generally, Evan Wallach, 'The Procedural and Evidentiary Rules of the Post-World War II War Crimes Trials: Did They Provide an Outline For International Legal Procedure?', 37 *Columbia Journal of Transnational Law* (1999) p. 851; Richard May and Marieke Wierda, 'Trends in International Criminal Evidence: Nuremberg, Tokyo, The Hague, and Arusha', 37 *Columbia Journal of Transnational Law* (1994) at p. 725.

88. Cf., Art. 19 of the Charter of the International Military Tribunal at Nuremberg with Rule 89 of the ICTY Statute.

89. See the paper given by Major-General Gordon Risius at the Meeting of Common Law Experts in International Humanitarian Law and Criminal Law and Procedure, Geneva 1998, to be published by the ICRC, who emphasises the 'need for specialist investigators who understand what is likely to be admissible and what is likely to be excluded'. Although General Risius was referring to the common law system, his view that there is a link between the investigation of offences and the rules of evidence in the trial itself cannot be gainsaid.

more difficult.[90] It is suggested, with respect, that the Judges of the International Criminal Court should not fall into the same trap.

---

90. A Judge may sit without a jury to decide serious criminal offences in Northern Ireland if they are 'terrorist type offences', s. 2 Northern Ireland (Emergency Provisions) Act, 1973. He or she is, however, obliged to give reasons for any conviction. These reasons appear to be much more detailed than those given by a trial chamber of the ICTY, principally because the Judge gives reasons why a particular piece of evidence is or is not believed.

CORRESPONDENTS' REPORTS

A guide to state practice concerning
International Humanitarian Law

CORRESPONDENTS' REPORTS[1]
A guide to state practice
concerning International Humanitarian Law

---

1. Correspondents' Reports is compiled and edited by the Managing Editor, Avril McDonald, primarily from information provided to the *YIHL* by its correspondents but also drawing on other sources. The research assistance of Jann K. Kleffner is gratefully acknowledged. It does not purport to be a fully inclusive compilation of all international humanitarian law-related developments in every state, reporting in this volume developments mainly since the beginning of 1998 until 1 December 1999 that have come to the Yearbook's attention. Legal developments that were noted in volume 1 of the *YIHL* are not repeated here. Readers are thus advised to consult this section in conjunction with Correspondents' Reports in volume 1. We apologise for this inconvenience. Some humanitarian law-related developments from 1998 and earlier came to our attention after volume 1 went to press and could not be noted there; for the sake of completeness we have included them here. While the *YIHL* apologies for any omissions, it cannot accept responsibility for them. Where citations or dates have not been provided, they were not available or obtainable. Where not otherwise specified, comments are by Avril McDonald and Jann Kleffner. The *YIHL* invites readers interested in becoming correspondents to contact the Managing Editor at A.McDonald@asser.nl.

Editor's Note: The Yearbook has decided not to include information concerning signings or ratifications of treaties. This information, constantly updated and referring to over 91 IHL treaties, is provided by the ICRC at its IHL database: http://www.icrc.org. Current information regarding ratifications, as well as full texts of reservations and declarations, is also available from the UN Treaty Website at http://www.un.org/Depts/Treaty/.

ARGENTINA[2]

Pending projects[3]

☞ Project of Law of Civil Protection (including in case of war). Senator Antonio Berhongaray. Presented 2 March 1998

☞ Project of the Deputy Jorge Yoma in order to put crimes against humanity in Chapter VII, Title I, Book 2 of the Argentine Penal Code. Presented 6 May 1998.

☞ Project of the Executive Power concerning the implementation by the internal law of certain aspects of the Convention of the Prohibition, Development, Production, Warehousing and Use of Chemical Weapons and on Their Destruction. Presented 3 July 1998

☞ Project to modify the study plans of the Formation Institutions of the Armed Forces, Policy Forces and Security Forces, including in the teaching programs special instructions about the law of armed conflict. Senator José María García Arecha. Presented 29 July 1998

☞ Project to include in the instruction of the armed forces which participate in Peace Missions or Multinational Missions concepts about the imperatives of international humanitarian law. Senator José María García Arecha. Presented 29 July 1998

CORRECTION

☞ Volume 1 of the *YIHL* reported that Argentina ratified the Convention on the Non-Applicability of Statutory Limitations to War Crimes and Crimes Against Humanity without reservations.[4] In fact, Argentina has not yet ratified this Convention. The Argentine Congress has approved but the Executive Power has not yet ratified the Convention because of some internal political opposition.

AUSTRALIA[5]

Landmines

☞ Anti-Personnel Mines Convention Act 1998, No. 126 of 1998, Acts of the Parliament of the Commonwealth of Australia 1998, Australian Government Publishing Service, Canberra 1999 [http://scaleplus.law.gov.au/]

☞ Anti-Personnel Mines Convention Bill 1998: Explanatory Memorandum, 1998, The Parliament of the Commonwealth of Australia: House of Representatives [Tabled in Parliament on 12 November 1998. Copy on file with the *YIHL*.]

☞ The Minister for Foreign Affairs, Hon. Alexander Downer MP, Reply to Question, (1998) 223 *Parliamentary Debates (House of Representatives),* 26 November 1998, 745-748 [http://www.aph.gov.au/hansard/reps/dailys/dr261198.pdf]

---

2. Information provided by Professor José Alejandro Consigli, Assistant Professor of Public International Law, University of Buenos Aires, Member of the Institute of International Law of the Argentine Council for International Relations, and Gabriel Valladares, Assistant Professor of International Humanitarian Law, University of Buenos Aires, Member of the Institute of International Law of the Argentine Council for International Relations.

3. There is no guarantee that these projects will become law.

4. See p. 401.

5. Information and comments provided by Professor Tim McCormack, Australian Red Cross Professor of International Humanitarian Law, University of Melbourne, member of the Board of Editors, *Yearbook of International Humanitarian Law.*

The Anti-Personnel Mines Convention Act of 1998 implements Australia's obligations pursuant to the Ottawa Landmines Convention[6] into domestic law. The legislation applies throughout Australian territory and extraterritorially to the acts of Australian citizens and Australian Defence Force Personnel. Section 7(1) criminalises the placement, possession, development, production, acquisition, stockpiling or transfer of anti-personnel mines, and the legislation also prescribes serious penalties for a refusal to surrender anti-personnel landmines to the authorities. The Act also provides for the implementation of the Convention compliance monitoring regime, including privileges and immunities for inspectors undertaking an international fact-finding mission and the empowerment of magistrates to issue search warrants for premises that are the subject of a mission.

Section 7 includes two key exceptions to the list of offences in Section 7(1): a) Section 7(2), which incorporates the exception envisaged in the Convention itself – the maintenance of a small stockpile of anti-personnel landmines for training in mine detection, clearance, destruction and/or mine deactivation techniques; and b) Section 7(3), which allows an exception for the 'mere participation' in military activities conducted in combination with armed forces not party to the Convention, and which engage in activities prohibited under the Convention.

Some concerns were expressed domestically in Australia in response to the inclusion of Section 7(3) in the Act. Unfortunately, the Foreign Minister's Explanatory Memorandum for the legislation, far from explaining the intention behind Section 7(3), introduced ambiguity about the scope of the exception in stating that 'Subclause 7(3) would provide that the prohibition would not extend to activity done in conjunction with the armed forces of a country that was in breach of the Convention but was not a State Party to the Convention.'

The possible interpretation that Section 7(3) legitimises Australian action in a joint operation that would be prohibited in a unilateral operation was dismissed in a statement of clarification by the Honourable Alexander Downer MP, Minister for Foreign Affairs, in response to a question in Parliament. The Minister stated that the exception was 'not intended to be construed as a blanket decriminalisation of the activities listed in section 7(1)'. Rather, Section 7(3) ensures that a member of the Australian Defence Force would not be subject to prosecution merely by reason of his participation in a combined operation. However, the Minister clarified the Australian Government's intention for Section 7(3) when he stated that the exemption 'does not provide a defence where a person *actually carries out a prohibited activity in the course of combined operations*'.

TIM McCormack

Peacekeeping/Scope of Application of the Fourth Geneva Convention
☛ Australian Government Statement for Meeting of Contracting Parties to the Fourth Geneva Convention, Geneva, 27-29 October 1998[7]

---

6. Convention on the Prohibition of the Use, Stockpiling, Production and Transfer of Anti-personnel Landmines and on Their Destruction, opened for signature 18 September 1997, 36 *ILM* (1997) 1507; 1 *YIHL* (1998) p. 539 (entered into force on 1 March 1999). As of 1 October 1999, there were 90 States Parties.

7. Reprinted *infra* at p. 450

During the deployment of the Australian Defence Force (ADF) contingent to Baidoa, Somalia as part of the UN-sanctioned Operation 'Restore Hope', the ADF legal adviser argued that the Fourth Geneva Convention applied *de jure* to the ADF's partial occupation of Somali territory. In an unprecedented approach to the scope of application of the Fourth Convention, the ADF legal adviser suggested that the second paragraph of Article 2 of the Convention extends to non-belligerent occupations, including in the context of multilateral peace operations and particularly in the situation of so-called 'failed states' where a significant public security function is expected of peace operation contingents. In Baidoa, the acceptance of this argument created an array of rights and obligations for the ADF contingent arising pursuant to the provisions of the Convention.

The approach adopted in Baidoa has now been adopted as official Australian Government policy in relation to deployment in complex peace operations without the consent of the 'occupied' state. This innovative approach to the application of the Fourth Convention breaks new ground in the debate about the law applicable to personnel deployed in complex peace operations. As the Australian Statement to the meeting of States Parties to the Fourth Geneva Convention shows, the Australian Government is actively promoting international consideration of this approach.

TIM MCCORMACK

Cases
☛ *Nulyarimma* v. *Thompson* [1999] Federal Court of Australia 1192 (1 September 1999) [http://www.austlii.edu.au/Federal Court of Australia]

The case was an appeal of two decisions from the Supreme Court of the Australian Capital Territory by representatives of Australia's Aboriginal community, who claimed that certain Commonwealth Ministers and members of Parliament had engaged in genocide. The Court dismissed the appeal. While accepting that genocide is a peremptory norm of customary international law, and that customary law imposes on all states the duty to extradite or prosecute persons found within its territory who appear to have committed genocide, the Court found that universal jurisdiction, of itself, does not render a crime giving rise to obligations *erga omnes* justiciable under municipal law. 'In the absence of enabling legislation, the offence of genocide is not cognisable in the courts of the Australian Capital Territory.'[8] Merkel J, *contra*, found that genocide is a universal crime under both international and municipal law because crimes against humanity, including genocide, could be considered as crimes under the common law of Australia.[9] However, he also dismissed the case, stating that 'the conduct complained of in the Application is plainly not capable of constituting genocide under international or municipal law'.[10] The case provides an in-depth examination of the status of international law, and particularly customary international law, within the Australian legal system.

---

8. Per Wilcox J, para. 32; see also Whitlam J, para. 56.
9. Per Merkel J, paras. 185-186.
10. Per Merkel J, para. 231.

AUSTRIA[11]

International Criminal Court
☛ Declaration of the Austrian Representative at the Conference on the Establishment of an International Criminal Court on behalf of the European Union, 17 July 1998. Published in *Außenpolitische Dokumentation* 1998/4, p. 109
☛ Declaration of the Presidency on behalf of the European Union on the Establishment of an International Criminal Court, 22 July 1998. Published in *Außenpolitische Dokumentation* 1998/4, p. 112
☛ Draft resolution of the Parliament concerning the ratification of the Statute of the International Criminal Court [Entschließungsantrag der Abgeordneten Dr. Martina Gredler, Partnerinnen und Partner betreffend die Ratifizierung des Statuts des Internationalen Strafgerichtshofs]. Proposed on 16 December 1998. Published in 987/A *BlgNR* [*Beilagen zu den Stenographischen Protokollen des Nationalrates*] 20.*GP* [*Gesetzgebungsperiode*]

The purpose of the draft resolution is to call upon the Federal Government to initiate the process of ratification of the Statute of the International Criminal Court as soon as possible. Furthermore, the Federal Minister for Foreign Affairs is requested to promote, within the framework of the European Union and in bilateral negotiations, the signature of the ICC Statute by states which have not yet done so, in particular China, India, Iraq, Libya and the United States of America.

THOMAS DESCH and PETER KUSTOR

Anti-Personnel Landmines
☛ Speech by the Federal Minister for Foreign Affairs, Vice-Chancellor Dr. Wolfgang Schuessel, on the occasion of the signature of the Convention on the Prohibition of the Use, Stockpiling, Production and Transfer of Anti-Personnel Mines and on their Destruction, Ottawa 3 December 1997. Published in *Außenpolitische Dokumentation* 1998/1, p. 64
☛ Text, draft translation into German and Explanatory Memorandum concerning the Convention on the Prohibition of the Use, Stockpiling, Production and Transfer of Anti-Personnel Mines and on their Destruction [Regierungsvorlage betreffend das Übereinkommen über das Verbot des Einsatzes, der Lagerung, der Herstellung und der Weitergabe von Antipersonenminen und über den Vernichtung samt Erklärung der Republik Österreich]. Published 24 March 1998 in *RV* [*Regierungsvorlage*]. 1088 *BlgNR* 20.*GP*

When ratifying the Landmines Convention on 29 June 1998, Austria declared, in accordance with Article 18 of the Convention, that it will provisionally apply paragraph 1 of Article 1 pending the Convention's entry into force. This provisional application was possible as the prohibitions under Article 1(1) were already effective in Austria on the basis of the Federal Law on the Prohibition of Anti-Personnel Mines, which entered

11. Information and commentaries by Dr. Thomas Desch, Federal Ministry of Defence, Vienna, and Mag. Peter Kustor, Federal Chancellery, Vienna.

into force on 1 January 1997.[12] The text of the Landmines Convention, which entered into force in Austria on 1 March 1999, and of the Austrian Declaration as well as of the respective German translations have been published in *BGBl.* III Nr. 38/1999.

THOMAS DESCH and PETER KUSTOR

➤ Text, draft translation into German and Explanatory Memorandum concerning the Protocol on Prohibitions or Restrictions on the Use of Mines, Booby-Traps and Other Devices as Amended on 3 May 1996 (Protocol II of the UN Convention on Prohibitions or Restrictions on the Use of Certain Conventional Weapons Which May Be Deemed To Be Excessively Injurious or to Have Indiscriminate Effects, 1980) [Protokoll über das Verbot oder die Beschränkung des Einsatzes von Minen, Sprengfallen und anderen Vorrichtungen in der am 3. Mai 1996 geänderten Fassung (Protokoll II in der am 3. Mai 1996 geänderten Fassung) zu dem Übereinkommen vom 10. Oktober 1980 über das Verbot oder die Beschränkung des Einsatzes bestimmter konventioneller Waffen, die übermäßige Leiden verursachen oder unterschiedslos wirken können samt Erklärung]. Published 11 May 1998 in *RV* 1107 *BlgNR* 20.*GP*

When ratifying amended Protocol II, on 27 July 1998, Austria declared in respect of Article 1 that it is her understanding that the provisions of the amended Protocol which by their contents or nature may also be applied in peacetime, shall be observed at all times. In respect of Article 2(3), Austria declared that it is her understanding that the word 'primarily' is included in Article 2(3) of the amended Protocol to clarify that mines designed to be detonated by the presence, proximity or contact of a vehicle as opposed to a person and that are equipped with anti-handling devices are not considered anti-personnel mines as a result of being so equipped. The text of the Protocol, which entered into force for Austria on 27 January 1999, the Austrian declarations and the respective German translations have been published in *BGBl.* III Nr. 17/1999.

THOMAS DESCH and PETER KUSTOR

Blinding Laser Weapons

➤ Text, draft translation into German and Explanatory Memorandum concerning the Additional Protocol on Blinding Laser Weapons (Protocol IV) to the Convention on Prohibitions or Restrictions on the Use of Certain Conventional Weapons Which May Be Deemed to Be Excessively Injurious or to Have Indiscriminate Effects [Protokoll über blindmachende Laserwaffen (Protokoll IV) zu dem Übereinkommen vom 10. Oktober 1980 über das Verbot oder die Beschränkung des Einsatzes bestimmter konventioneller Waffen, die übermäßige Leiden verursachen oder unterschiedslos wirken können]. Published 11 May 1998 in *RV* 1107 *BlgNR* 20.*GP*

When ratifying Protocol IV on 27 July 1998, Austria declared in respect of Article 1 that it is her understanding that the provisions of Protocol IV which by their contents or nature may be applied also in peacetime shall be observed at all times. The Protocol entered into force for Austria on 27 January 1999. Its text, the Austrian Declarations, as well as the respective German translations have been published in *BGBl.* III Nr. 17/1999.

THOMAS DESCH and PETER KUSTOR

---

12. See 1 *YIHL* (1998) pp. 410 and 561.

☛ Federal Law on the Prohibition of Blinding Laser Weapons[13]

Biological Weapons

☛ Response of the Federal Minister for Foreign Affairs to a parliamentary request concerning the progress in the negotiations on an Additional Protocol to the Convention on the Prohibition of the Development, Production and Stockpiling of Bacteriological (Biological) and Toxin Weapons and on their Destruction [Antwort des Bundesministers für auswärtige Angelegenheiten auf die schriftliche parlamentarische Anfrage der Abgeordneten Dr. Martina Gredler, Partnerinnen und Partner an den Bundesminister für auswärtige Angelegenheiten betreffend Fortschritte in den Verhandlungen zu einem Zusatzprotokoll zum B-Waffenübereinkommen] (30 June 1998). Published in *AB [Ausschußbericht]* 4075 Blg Nr 20.GP

This response deals with the Austrian position towards the negotiations on an additional Protocol to the Bacteriological (Biological) Weapons Convention, the Austrian contributions to solving outstanding problems, in particular during the Austrian EU presidency, and the results of the meeting of experts in Vienna, 28-29 May 1998.

THOMAS DESCH and PETER KUSTOR

☛ Declaration by the State-Secretary in the Federal Ministry for Foreign Affairs, Dr. Benita Ferrero Waldner, at the meeting of Ministers concerning the Convention on the Prohibition of the Development, Production and Stockpiling of Bacteriological (Biological) and Toxin Weapons and on their Destruction, 23 September 1998. Published in *Außenpolitische Dokumentation* 1998/5, p. 146

In her Declaration, the State-Secretary strongly supported the creation of a legally binding Protocol to the Biological Weapons Convention concerning the future compliance regime and the speeding-up of the negotiations within the Ad Hoc Group in Geneva. For the key elements to be included in such a Protocol, she referred to the respective Common Position of the European Union of 4 March 1998.

THOMAS DESCH and PETER KUSTOR

Criminal Complaint

☛ Criminal Complaint against *Izzat Ibrahim Al Douri*

On 16 August 1999, Vienna city councilman Peter Pilz filed a criminal complaint against Izzat Ibrahim Al Douri, deputy chairman of Iraq's ruling Revolutionary Command Council, for his alleged involvement in the 1990 Iraqi invasion of Kuwait, in the bloody crackdown against Iraqi Kurds and in the torture and murder of Iraqi citizens. Al Douri was issued a month's visa by the Austrian authority for medical treatment at a private clinic in Vienna. However, he was not arrested. While the State Prosecutor Erich Wetzer was

---

13. See 1 *YIHL* (1998) pp. 410-411.

quoted as saying that '[T]here was no urgency' to do so, the Austrian Foreign Ministry expressed the view that he enjoyed immunity from arrest as a 'member of the Iraqi state leadership'. Al Douri left Austria on 18 August 1999.[14]

BELGIUM[15]

Repression of genocide and crimes against humanity
☞ Law of 10 February 1999 relating to the repression of serious violations of international humanitarian law [Loi du 10 février relative à la répression des violations graves du droit international humanitaire]. Published in *Moniteur belge*, 23 March 1999[16]

Cases
A. Re. Belgium peacekeepers in Somalia
☞ Decision of Military Court, Brussels, 17 December 1997. Published in *Journal des tribunaux,* 4 April 1998, pp. 286-289
☞ Decision of Military Court, Brussels, 7 May 1998

B. Re. General Pinochet
☞ Decision of 6 November 1998 of the Brussels Tribunal of First Instance on extradition request in respect of Augusto Pinochet Ugarte. Ruling on Article 61 quinquies 5 C.I. Cr- request for an instrument of supplementary preliminary investigation. Dossier nr. 216/98. Notices nr. 30.99.3447/98. Published in *Journal des tribunaux*, 1999, pp. 308-311[17]

The British authorities' decision to place the former Chilean dictator under house arrest and the three rulings issued by the House of Lords in the *Pinochet* case[18] have been welcomed with some degree of approval by numerous commentators. However, well before the first ruling was issued by the House of Lords, a complaint lodged against Augusto Pinochet by several plaintiffs with a view to obtaining his extradition to Belgium for criminal offences had already given rise to an Order, delivered on 6 November 1998, of particular interest for international criminal law.

In this Order, Judge Vandermeersch did not issue the warrant of arrest claimed by the plaintiffs,[19] deeming that the case required further investigation, but on the other hand, he did not hesitate to affirm his competency by virtue of the customary rules of international criminal law.

14. 'Iraqi Official Accused in Austria', Associated Press, 16 August 1999; 'Saddam Deputy Escapes Arrest in Austria for Torture Crimes', *The Independent*, 19 August 1999.
15. Information provided by Professor Eric David, Centre de droit international, Institut de Sociologie, Brussels.
16. Unofficial translation reprinted *infra* at p. 539.
17. Unofficial translation reprinted *infra* at p. 475.
18. See under UK, *infra* p. 419; for analysis of these decisions, see C. Warbrick et al., p. 91.
19. He was, however, to do so subsequently.

1. *Competency* ratione personae *and the denial of sovereign immunity granted to foreign heads of state*

The Magistrate first proceeded to examine his competency *ratione personae,* i.e., whether Augusto Pinochet might voice a claim to sovereign immunity granted to former heads of state for the offences he committed. With this end in view, the Judge distinguished two elements, viz., (A) the General's status as a head of state, and (B) the nature of the offences with which he had been charged.

(A)The Judge declared that the judicial inquiry would need to assess the extent to which the Belgian state actually acknowledged Augusto Pinochet's status as the lawful head of state of Chile, in order to determine whether he might avail himself of the right to immunity accruing to this status.

Whereas it is legitimate to wonder whether Augusto Pinochet actually fulfilled the functions of head of the Chilean state and to determine the moment at which he started fulfilling these functions, the issue whether Belgium recognised Augusto Pinochet as a lawful head of state is, on the other hand, irrelevant to the question of whether he might be entitled to sovereign immunity; in contrast to American jurisdictions, which have grounded their decisions on the recognition or absence of recognition by the US government of the defendant's official status,[20] Belgian jurisdictions could not rely on a similar argument, considering that Belgium, like a number of other countries, recognises only new states, not new governments. In this respect, the Belgian policy has been invariant since 1965.[21] The government's position is justified by the fact that the practice [of recognising governments rather than states] might be perceived as interference in another state's internal affairs, inasmuch as it might appear as a judgment of the legitimacy of its system of government.[22] This policy has effectively been pursued in the case of Chile, where the seizure of power by Augusto Pinochet in 1973 was not subject to any recognition by Belgium.[23]

(B) Subsequently, the Judge declared that the defendant in question could voice no claim to personal immunity, considering the nature of the offences imputed to him. He underscored that, on the one hand, if the offences imputed to Augusto Pinochet were

---

20. An American jurisdiction has resorted to this argument to reject the exception relied on by General Noriega, Panama's former Commander in Chief of the Armed Forces, prosecuted in the US for drug trafficking, money laundering, racketeering, etc., who claimed sovereign immunity granted to foreign heads of state. The jurisdiction argued that Noriega had never been recognised as a lawful head of state by the US (US Distr. Crt., S.D. Fla., *US* v. *Noriega and Others,* 8 June 1990, 99 *ILR,* pp. 161 and 162). By the same token, in the *Lafontant* v. *Aristide* case, the Court approached the issue of the immunity of the Haitian head of state in terms of his recognition as a lawful head of state by the US (US Distr. Crt., EDNY, 27 January 1994, 103 *ILR* p. 587).

21. Cf., Jean Salmon, 'La jurisprudence belge en matière de reconnaissance', in *Liber Amicorum Elie Van Bogaert* (Antwerpen, Kluwer Rechtswetenschappen 1985) p. 235.

22. Translated from 'Position de principe du gouvernement belge', reprinted in 'La pratique du pouvoir exécutif et le contrôle des chambres législatives en matière de droit international', 1 *Revue belge de Droit International* (1976) p. 339.

23. Shortly after the Chilean coup, the Belgian Minister of Foreign Affairs issued a press release 'following rumours according to which Belgium is alleged to have recognised the new Chilean regime', in which he voiced a reminder that 'in accordance with the diplomatic practice prevailing in most European countries, Belgium does not recognise governments or regimes [...]; consequently, a change of government in a state recognised by Belgium has no legal effect upon the recognition of the state' (transl. from Chronique n° 940, 1 *Revue belge de Droit International* (1975) p. 351).

considered as established, they would not normally pertain to a head of state's functions, and on the other hand, that the immunity granted to heads of state is not applicable to offences under international law such as war crimes, crimes against peace or against humanity.

International customary law indisputably establishes this exception to the principle of sovereign immunity for war crimes, crimes against peace or against humanity. The principle has been repeatedly restated, including in Article 227 of the Versailles Treaty, under which the German Emperor William II was publicly arraigned by the Allies; in Article 7 of the Charter of the Nuremberg Tribunal; Article 6 of the Charter of the Tokyo Tribunal; the Statutes of the *ad hoc* Tribunals for the Former Yugoslavia and Rwanda; and in Article 27 of the Statute of the International Criminal Court.[24] Moreover, the exception to the principle of sovereign immunity for war crimes, crimes against peace or against humanity has been further established by jurisprudence[25] as well as by the International Law Commission.[26]

2. *Competency* ratione materiae: *prosecutions based on the criminalization of crimes against humanity*

Judge Vandermeersch explained why the facts alleged by the plaintiffs are liable to constitute crimes against humanity and examined (A) the question whether local law makes provision for criminalization of crimes against humanity, and (B) the question whether a Belgian judge may claim universal competence in the matter.

(A) As the notion of a crime against humanity does not exist in Belgian penal law, it is necessary first to address the question whether the criminalization of crimes against humanity exists in international law, and subsequently to establish whether this criminalization may be regarded as immediately applicable within the Belgian legal system. Judge Vandermeersch addressed these issues in his Order.

While up to the time of the charges of crimes against humanity brought before the Nuremberg and Tokyo Courts the fact of crimes against humanity being part of international criminal law may have been open to question,[27] after Nuremberg the existence of the criminalization is beyond doubt, and appears in many instruments of international law. The Statutes of the *ad hoc* Tribunals for the former Yugoslavia and Rwanda criminalize crimes against humanity[28] without there being any objection in the *travaux préparatoires* suggesting that it might infringe the principles of the legality of the offence and of non-retroactivity. The same may be observed *vis-à-vis* the Statute of the International Criminal Court.[29] Thus, the Judge rightfully recognised the existence

---

24. Cf., the Secretary-General's Report, drawn up in conformity with para. 2 of SC Res. 808 (1993) presented on 3 May 1993 (S/25704), which comprises proposals relative to the establishment of a court for former Yugoslavia (§55).

25. Cf., notably the Nuremberg judgment (*Procès des grands criminels de guerre devant le Tribunal militaire international, Doc. Off.* (Nuremberg 1947) Vol. I, p. 235).

26. Cf., Art. 7 of the project for a code relative to war crimes, crimes against peace or against humanity approved in 1996 (Rapport de la C.D.I. sur les travaux de sa 48ème session, 6 mai-26 juillet 1996, *A.G., Doc. Off.,* 51 session, Suppl. n° 10, (A/51/10), pp. 56 et seq).

27. E. David, *Eléments de droit pénal international,* 7th edn. (Brussels, Presses Universitaires de Bruxelles 1994) n° 13.300 et seq.

28. Art. 5 of the Statute of the ICTY and Art. 3 of the Statute of the ICTR.

29. Arts. 5 and 7 of the Statute of the International Criminal Court.

of a customary criminalization of crimes against humanity in international law. The customary origin of the criminalization of crimes against humanity is not contrary to the legality of the offence (*nullum crimen sine lege*), which must be understood to address the material rather than the formal legality of the offence. This conclusion emerges from a study of the relevant provisions contained in the international instruments for the protection of human rights[30] as well as of Belgian practice. This may be documented by means of the two examples referred to in the Order by Judge Vandermeersch himself. On the one hand, the Belgian legislator has recognised the existence of the Statutes of the *ad hoc* International Criminal Tribunals and integrated them into the internal legal system, while those Statutes establish the criminalization of crimes against humanity applied to acts committed before the Statutes came into effect.[31] On the other hand, when ratifying the Genocide Convention, Belgium did not deem it necessary to adapt its internal legislation, considering that 'the principles included in the Convention [could] be regarded as already belonging to the Belgian legal system'.[32] More examples may be adduced. Thus, after the end of World War II, while neither the Belgian Criminal Code nor particular laws knew the criminalization of war crimes, this did not impede criminal prosecutions and judgments on this account after the liberation. Like war crimes in 1940-1945, crimes against humanity constitute an international customary criminalization which finds its source in Nuremberg law.[33] The principle and the legality of the offences could thus be expressed by the adage *nullum crimen sine jure,* wherein *jure* comprises customary law.[34]

Finally, the Magistrate argued that, at any rate, the crimes against humanity imputed to Augusto Pinochet are also punishable offences under internal law, by provision of common criminal law. Indeed, the facts invoked by the plaintiffs qualify as offences according to Articles 347 *bis*, 393, 394, 398, 434 and 438 of the Belgian Code of Criminal Law.[35]

(B) The request submitted to Judge Vandermeersch by the plaintiffs raised the question whether the Belgian judge could prosecute and sanction charges brought against a foreigner for acts committed against foreigners in a foreign country, and qualified as crimes against humanity. The competency to do so is tantamount to universal competency. The Belgian Code of Criminal Inquiry makes no general provision for

---

30. Cf., Art. 11(2) of the *Universal Declaration of Human Rights,* Art. 7(1) of the European Convention on Human Rights and Art. 15(1) of the International Covenant on Civil and Political Rights.

31. Loi du 22 mars 1996 relative à le reconnaissance du Tribunal penal international pour l'ex-Yougoslavie et du Tribunal pour le Ruanda, et à la cooperation avec ces Tribunaux, *Moniteur belge,* 27 avril 1996.

32. Exposé des motifs du projet de loi d'approbation de loi Convention sur le Genocide, Doc. Parl., Chambre 1950, 201-1, 4.

33. Cf., E. David, 'L'actualité de Nuremberg', in *Le procès de Nuremberg: Conséquences et actualisation. Actes du Colloque international, 27 mars 1987* (Brussels, Bruylant/Editions de l'Université de Bruxelles 1988) paras. 61, 80 and 105.

34. S. Glaser, *Droit international pénal conventionnel* (Brussels, Bruylant 1970) p. 24.

35. J. Burneo Labrin and H.-D. Bosly, Comment on the Ruling of the Examining Judge, 6 November 1998, 'La notion de crime contre l'humanité et le droit pénal interne', *Revue de droit pénal et de criminologie* (1999) p. 291.

universal competency.[36] The Magistrate did not hesitate to infer the foundation of his competency from the customary rules establishing universal competency for crimes against humanity. This position, though apparently audacious, is in accordance with doctrine[37] and jurisprudence[38] as well as practice.[39] It has, moreover, been implicitly recognised by the Statutes of the *ad hoc* Tribunals and the International Criminal Court when these established the complementarity of competencies of international jurisdictions and national Courts and Tribunals.[40]

3. *The judge's competency* ratione temporis: *the imprescriptibility of crimes of international law*

The magistrate rejected the arguments according to which the charges brought against Augusto Pinochet were covered by prescription, recognizing the existence of a customary rule establishing the imprescriptibility of crimes against humanity. Several instruments of international law support this reasoning, such as law N° 10 of the Allied Control Council and the United Nations Convention of 26 November 1968 as well as the Convention of the European Council of 25 January 1974 on the imprescriptibility of war crimes and crimes against humanity. Even if it can be said that, on this issue, the reasoning of the Judge is uncertain, national legislative,[41] governmental[42] and jurisprudential[43] practices confirm the customary imprescriptibility of crimes against humanity.[44]

---

36. The notion has, however, entered into Belgian internal law. It has been established by the Law of 16 June 1993 relative to the punishment of serious violations of the international Conventions of Geneva of 12 August 1949 and to the Protocols I + II of 8 June 1977 additional to these Conventions (reprinted at p. 541 of this volume) as well as by the Law of 13 April 1995 regarding the human slave trade and child pornography.

37. From the same perspective, cf., S.R. Ratner, 'The Schizophrenias of International Criminal Law', 33 *Texas ILJ* (1998) p. 255, and ref. to Demjanjuk; Final Report of the Commission of Experts Established Pursuant to Security Council Resolution 780 (1992) at pp. 20-21, UN Doc. S/1994/674 (1994); H.M. Osofsky, 'Domesticating International Criminal Law: Bringing Human Rights Violators to Justice', 107 *Yale LJ* (1997) p. 219.

38. Cf., notably *Eichmann Case,* Supreme Court of Israel, 29 May 1962, *ILR* 36, pp. 298-300; Canada, High Court of Justice, 10 July 1997, *Regina* v. *Finta, ILR* (1982) p. 444.

39. A.G., Résolution 3074 du 3 décembre 1973.

40. Art. 10 of the Statute of the ICTY; Art. 8 of the Statute of the ICTR; 10th preamble to the Statute of the ICC. On this point, cf., L. Reydams, 'Universal Jurisdiction over Atrocities in Rwanda: Theory and Practice', 4 *European Journal of Crime, Criminal Law and Criminal Justice* (1996) p. 32.

41. Cf., notably, Art. 213-5 of the French Criminal Code, Art. 12 of Israeli law S-710 of 1950, Art. 37 of Rwandan law 8/96 of 30 August 1996.

42. Cf., notably, the decision of France's Minister of Foreign Affairs on 15 June 1979 delivered in the *Barbie* case.

43. Cf., notably, the French Court of Cassation, 26 October 1982, *Leguay, Bulletin des arrêts de la Cour de Cassation en matière criminelle,* 1982, n° 231, and Cour de Cassation Française, 6 October 1983, *Barbie, JDI* (1984) pp. 308 et seq.

44. Cf., A. Weyembergh, 'Sur l'Ordonnance de Juge d'Instruction Vandermeersch rendue dans l'affaire Pinochet et le 6 novembre 1998', 1 *Revue belge de droit international* (1999).

4. Conclusion

The Order delivered on 6 November 1998 by Judge Vandermeersch in the *Pinochet* case contributes a welcome development in international criminal law. The magistrate sought to establish the existence of customary rules in international law which would provide a foundation for his competency. He found himself competent *ratione personæ* by ruling out the sovereign immunity granted to former heads of state; competent *ratione materiæ* by recognising the direct application in Belgian internal law of the criminalization of crimes against humanity as established by international law; and competent *ratione temporis* by observing the imprescriptibility of crimes against humanity.

However, since 10 February 1999 and the adoption of the Law relating to the repression of serious violations of international humanitarian law (*supra*), Belgian Judges no longer need to exert themselves to establish their competence through recourse to customary international law. The law aims at bringing crimes of genocide and crimes against humanity within the scope of the Belgian Law of 16 June 1993 relative to the sanctioning of heavy infractions of the Geneva Conventions of 12 August 1949 and their Additional Protocols I and II of 8 June 1977. It introduces into Belgian law an explicit incrimination for crimes against humanity. The *travaux préparatoires* clearly stipulate that this is no more than a confirmation of existing customary law, seeking to give it increased visibility.[45] This law also establishes the universal competency of Belgian Judges to hear such crimes, the imprescriptibility of these crimes and the rejection of any plea of defence based on sovereign immunity for similar crimes.

LAURENCE WEERTS[46] and ANNE WEYEMBERGH[47]

BOSNIA AND HERZEGOVINA[48]

Cases

☞ *Zuhdija Rizvić* and *Mustafa Odobasić*, Bihac Cantonal Court, Decision Number K-7/97-RZ, 27 May 1997 and Supreme Court of the Federation of Bosnia Herzegovina, Decision Number Kz-373/97, 13 January 1998, unreported

The defendants, members of the forces of the 'AP-ZB', a unit of the Bosnian Serb Army, in May 1995 detained a member of the Bosnian Army in the North-Western Veliki Kladusa municipality of Bosnia and Herzegovina. Odobasić subsequently tortured and beat the detainee and when the latter tried to escape, he ordered Zuhdija Rizvić to kill him. The latter obeyed the order and shot the victim dead.

The Bihac Cantonal Court found the two defendants guilty of violations of Article 3(1)(a) (violence to life and person, in particular murder of all kinds, mutilation, cruel treatment and torture) and Article 13 (prohibition of inhumane treatment) of the Third Geneva Convention relative to the Treatment of Prisoners of War. Mustafa Odobasić

---

45. *Doc. Senat.*, 1 - 749/3 - 1998/1999, (20).

46. Researcher at the Centre for International Law at the Free University of Brussels (U.L.B.).

47. Research assistant at the Institute for European Studies at the Free University of Brussels (U.L.B.).

48. Information provided by Tonia Gillett, office of the High Representative, Bosnia and Herzegovina. Ongoing cases and cases currently under appeal are not included due to limited space. They will be included in the forthcoming volumes of the *YIHL* once completed.

was also found guilty of violations of the aforementioned provisions of the Third Geneva Convention for hitting and subsequently shooting another prisoner of war in March of the same year. A third defendant, the commander of the army unit, who was charged with participation in torturing one of the victims, was acquitted.

The court classified the acts as criminal acts under Article 144[49] of the 1977 Inherited Criminal Law (ICL)[50] (war crimes against prisoners of war) and sentenced Mustafa Odobasić to 15 and Zuhdija Rizvić to 12 years imprisonment.

The defendants appealed against the judgment on procedural and factual grounds and against the sentence. The Bosnian Supreme Court rejected the appeal and confirmed the judgment. The appeal of the prosecutor against the acquittal of the commander of the army unit was also rejected. The Supreme Court held that there was no evidence that, during the critical event in May 1995, he committed any action related to the event in which the prisoner was killed, nor evidence that he ordered his subordinates to act in violation of international humanitarian law. The Supreme Court reasoned that the defendant could not be held responsible for 'self-initiated and unpredictable excesses of his subordinates'[51] and rejected the prosecutor's view that the victim was tortured and killed 'with agreement' of the defendant.

The case touches upon several issues: First, both courts applied common Article 3 alongside Article 13 of the Third Geneva Convention despite the fact that the former provision relates to armed conflicts not of an international character while the latter is applicable to international armed conflicts. Second, the considerations leading to the acquittal of the commander of the army unit apparently did not involve the question of command responsibility for omissions, i.e., the failure to prevent the commission of violations of international humanitarian law. The judgments are silent on whether the defendant knew or should have known that the crime was being or was going to be committed and whether he took all feasible measures to prevent the criminal conduct or to put a stop to it, as required under Article 86(2) of Additional Protocol I.

JANN K. KLEFFNER

☞ *Drago Ilić*, Tuzla Cantonal Court, Decision Number K: 177/96, 31 October 1997 and Supreme Court of the Federation of Bosnia Herzegovina, Decision Number: Kz-612/97, 19 May 1998, unreported

During the war in Bosnia and Herzegovina, Drago Ilić served, between October 1992 until the end of 1993, as a military police officer in the 3rd Battalion of the Eastern-Bosnian Corps of the Bosnian Serb Army in the Batković concentration camp, established at the agricultural estate of Semberija in the Eastern Bijeljina municipality, where up to 1,700

---

49. Art. 144 reads: 'Whoever, in violation of the rules of international law, orders murders, tortures or inhuman treatment of prisoners of war, including therein biological experiments, causing of great sufferings or serious injury to the bodily integrity or health, compulsive enlistment into the armed forces of an enemy power, or deprivation of the right to a fair and impartial trial, or who commits some of the foregoing acts, shall be punished by imprisonment for not less than five years or by the death penalty.'

50. The ICL was applied until the new Criminal Codes of the Federation of Bosnia and Herzegovina came into force in November 1998. It is still applied in the Republika Srpska, as the adoption of the new Criminal Codes was delayed by the Republika's National Assembly.

51. Unofficial translation.

mainly Muslims and Croats were interned. The accused was alleged to have beaten and terrorised imprisoned civilians and captured members of the Bosnian Army, treated them inhumanely, inflicted great suffering and serious injury to body and health and exposed them to forced labour, in one case in the first front lines of the battlefields, and in another case, despite certifications of the International Red Cross that the individual concerned was incapable of working.

The court of first instance (Tuzla Cantonal Court) found the defendant guilty of violating Geneva Conventions III and IV and 1977 Protocol I in conjunction with Articles 142[52] and 144 (war crime against civilians and prisoners of war) of the Inherited Criminal Law and sentenced him to seven years imprisonment. The court emphasised that the relevant acts were committed during an international armed conflict and during the partial occupation of Bosnia and Herzegovina, relying, *inter alia*, on Security Council Resolution 752 of 18 May 1992.

As regards the treatment of civilians (count 1), it held that '[A]ll acts and omissions [of] Drago Ilić ... are serious violations ... according to Article 147 of the IV Geneva Convention ...'[53] '[A]ll the prisoners were unlawfully detained civilians, that is to say there was not legal ground for their imprisonment, except the fact that they were of Muslim and Croat nationality. ... [W]hile working as a policeman in the concentration camp during the war [the defendant] was obliged to follow ... the Geneva Convention [IV] and the 1977 Additional Protocol I ... and to work in accordance with the above-mentioned provisions and treat them as captured civilians.' The court further held that the persons mentioned in relation to count 1 were civilians according to Article 147 of the Fourth Geneva Convention and Article 50 of the 1977 Additional Protocol I.[54] Consequently, the defendant was found guilty of violations of international humanitarian law, namely war crimes against civilians punishable under Article 142(1) of the Inherited Criminal Law.

As regards count 2 (war crimes against prisoners of war), the court determined that the defendant had repeatedly beaten captured members of the Bosnian Army while interrogating them, and refused medical treatment to some wounded POWs. The prisoners were accommodated together with civilians and were also exposed to forced labour. Moreover, they were tried, although the court did not specifically consider whether such trials were in violation of Article 99 of the Third Geneva Convention. The

---

52. Art. 142 reads: 'Whoever in violation of rules of international law effective at the time of war, armed conflict or occupation, orders that civilian population be subject to killings, torture, inhuman treatment, biological experiments, immense suffering or violation of bodily integrity or health; dislocation or displacement or forcible conversion to another nationality or religion; forcible prostitution or rape; application of measures of intimidation and terror; taking hostages; imposing collective punishment; unlawful bringing in concentration camps and other illegal arrests and detention; deprivation of rights to fair and impartial trial; forcible service in the armed forces of enemy's army or in its intelligence service or administration; forcible labour, starvation of the population; property confiscation; pillaging; illegal and self-willed destruction and stealing on a large scale of a property that is not justified by military needs; taking an illegal and disproportionate contribution or requisition; devaluation of domestic currency or the unlawful issuance of currency; or who commits one of the foregoing acts, shall be punished by imprisonment for not less than five years or by the death penalty.'

53. Unofficial translation.

54. This is despite the fact that the status as civilians under Geneva IV is determined according to Arts. 4 and 13 and not according to Art. 147.

court stated that all persons mentioned in count 2 were POWs according to Article 4 of the Third Geneva Convention and Article 44 of 1977 Additional Protocol I. It concluded that by treating them inhumanely and inflicting severe suffering and serious injury to body and health, the defendant committed war crimes against prisoners of war, punishable under Article 144 of the Inherited Criminal Law. However, the court rejected the allegation of the indictment relating to the forced labour of the POWs, the living conditions in the camp as regards food, medical attention and heating, 'since neither were within the competence of Drago Ilić as a policeman nor did they depend on him; they depended on the camp commander and his deputy'.

In determining the adequate sentence, the court took into consideration the defendant's partial confession, his family situation and his correct behaviour in court as mitigating factors, while considering his police record to constitute an aggravating circumstance. In conclusion, the judges determined seven years imprisonment to be 'proportional to the level of social danger of the crime committed ...' and stated its belief 'that this penalty will have a correctional influence on the defendant not to commit crimes in the future'.

The subsequent appeals of Drago Ilić, on procedural and factual grounds and against the sentence, and of the public prosecutor, on procedural, factual and substantive grounds, were rejected by the Supreme Court of Bosnia and Herzegovina. However, with regard to the conviction for war crimes against POWs, the Supreme Court clarified that, '[T]he number of mistreated persons is not important ..., a single person mistreated for the same motives is sufficient to realize elements of the ... criminal acts'. As to the mental element with regard to the crimes in question, it also stated that, as a rule, they could only be committed with direct intent (*dolus directus*) and only exceptionally with indirect intent (*dolus eventualis*). Moreover, the perpetrator 'does not have to be aware of the fact that with his acts he violates rules of international law'. The court thus rejected mistake of law as a ground for excluding criminal responsibility, in line with Article 32(2) of the ICC Statute.

JANN K. KLEFFNER

☛ *Ferid Halilović*, Modrica Municipal Court, Decision Number K-43/97, 23 October 1997 and Doboj District Court, Decision Number Kz-46/98, 10 August 1998, unpublished

Halilović was a member of the Croatian Defence Council (HVO) between June and August 1992 and served as a prison guard at detention centres in Ozdak, Novi Grad and Bosanski Brod, in which mainly Serb civilians were kept. The first instance court held that the accused, individually and together with other guards, commanders of the camp and unknown soldiers, had taken part in ill-treating inmates and killing four of them. Halilović was convicted and sentenced to 15 years imprisonment. The defendant was found guilty by the Modrica Municipal Court of war crimes against the civilian population under Article 142(1) of the Criminal Law of the Republika Srpska.

Both the defendant and the public prosecutor appealed against the judgment, the former alleging procedural violations, violations of the criminal law, incorrectly and incompletely established facts and challenging the sentence; the latter claiming that the court had overestimated the mitigating circumstances and consequently had sentenced the defendant too leniently.

The Doboj District Court rejected the complaints of both parties. The court briefly elaborated on the Modrica Municipal Court's decision on sentencing. It stated that the first instance court correctly took into consideration as mitigating circumstances the fact that the accused had no previous convictions and that he has a family. On the other hand, the acts of the defendant represented violations of international law and it was held that the Municipal Court correctly considered that fact to be an aggravating circumstance. Others were the 'great persistence'[55] displayed by the defendant and the fact that he committed several acts, as well as the fact that these acts were 'of great social danger'. However, the court also stated, that 'one also has to keep in mind that the accused was working in the camps as a guard, so he did some forbidden acts at orders of superiors and especially at orders of the camp warden ...'.

JANN K. KLEFFNER

Amnesties

On 3 March 1999, only three days before he was dismissed from the position as the Republika Srpska President by the High Representative Carlos Westendorp, Nikola Poplasen granted amnesty to three persons who were found guilty of war crimes by courts of the Federation of Bosnia and Herzegovina. The persons granted amnesty are Savo Ivanić, sentenced to 15 years imprisonment, Dusko Pasalić, sentenced to 10 years imprisonment, and Milan Hrvacević, sentenced to 12 years imprisonment. All three served their time in prisons of the Federation of Bosnia and Herzegovina but were exchanged on 19 January 1999 and subsequently returned to the Republika Srpska on the basis of a special protocol under the condition that they continue serving their time in prison.[56]

CAMBODIA

Indictment
☞ Indictment of *Ta Mok* for acts of genocide, Phnom Penh Military Court, 7 September 1999

A former Khmer Rouge guerilla chief, *Ta Mok,* was charged with genocide on 7 September 1999 under a new law that permits keeping suspects in custody for up to three years if they have been charged with genocide, war crimes or crimes against humanity.[57] *Ta Mok* was arrested in March 1999 and is one of two high-ranking Khmer Rouge officials awaiting trial.

---

55. Unofficial translation.
56. 'Nikola Poplasen amnestied war criminals', *Daily Voice* (Bosnian national daily from Sarajevo), 17 May 1999.
57. 'Cambodia Raises Genocide Charge', *International Herald Tribune*, 8 September 1999.

CANADA[58]

☞ *Extradition*

Extradition Act. Bill C-40, 1st Session, 36th Parliament, 46-47 Eliz. II, 1997-98. [http://www.parl.gc.ca/36/1/parlbus/chambus/house/bills/government/C-40/C-40_3/C-40_cover-E.html]

Canada's new Extradition Act was passed by the House of Commons on 1 December 1998 and is currently being studied by the Senate, the final step prior to proclamation. The Act facilitates cooperation between Canada and the *ad hoc* International Criminal Tribunals, and was also drafted with a view to compatibility with the International Criminal Court. The Act provides for extradition to a 'State or entity', and section 2 of the Act defines an 'entity' as 'an international criminal court or tribunal'. The new Act will also simplify extradition where there is no treaty in force between Canada and a requesting state.

WILLIAM A. SCHABAS

Cases

☞ *Mugesera*. Decision of the Immigration and Refugee Board (Appeal Division), 6 November 1998

The Immigration and Refugee Board (Appeal Division) of Canada denied the appeal of Leon Mugesera, a protégé of Juvenal Habyarimana, Rwanda's former president of the interim government at the time of the genocide in 1994. At that time, Mugesera was an adviser in the Ministre de la famille et de la promotion feminine, and vice-president of the MRND party in Gisenyi prefecture. A speech given by Mugesera in November 1992 inciting genocide against the Tutsi minority has been widely regarded as a defining moment in the build-up to the genocide, and was cited by the International Criminal Tribunal for Rwanda in the *Akayesu* judgment of 2 September 1998.[59] Mugesera fled Rwanda for Canada in 1993. An adjudicator of the Immigration and Refugee Board stripped him of his permanent resident status on 11 July 1996. The ruling held Mugesera responsible for a violation of Article III(c) of the 1948 Convention for the Prevention and Punishment of the Crime of Genocide. The 6 November 1998 decision of the Appeal Division upheld that ruling. Mugesera has been recognized as a refugee, and further proceedings are required to strip him of that status. He cannot be tried by the International Criminal Tribunal for Rwanda because the crimes of which he is accused took place in 1992 whereas the Tribunal's jurisdiction *ratione temporis* begins on 1 January 1994.

Canadian law recognizes universal jurisdiction, and Mugesera could be tried in Canada pursuant to s. 318 of the Criminal Code[60] for incitement to genocide. However, since 1995 the Department of Justice has taken a policy decision not to prosecute under universal jurisdiction, and to confine Canadian efforts to expulsion of foreign war criminals. It concluded that the principles laid down by the Supreme Court of Canada in the *Finta*

---

58. Information and comments by Professor William Schabas, University of Quebec at Montreal and Senior Research Fellow, United States Institute of Peace.

59. *The Prosecutor v. Jean-Paul Akayesu*, Case No. ICTR-96-4-T, 2 September 1998.

60. R.S.C. 1985, C-46.

decision of 1994[61] make it extremely difficult to obtain convictions for war crimes and crimes against humanity. Rwanda has made an extradition request to Canada for Mugesera. The apparent absence of an extradition treaty has been invoked by Canadian authorities for the failure to extradite. A new Extradition Act (*supra*) will entitle Canada to extradite even if there is no treaty in force. However, Canadian officials are concerned about petitions by Mugesera to international human rights bodies alleging that he cannot get a fair trial in Rwanda.

WILLIAM A. SCHABAS

Ongoing cases
☛ *Nicholas Ribich*, Ottawa

In the first Canadian case of its kind, a Canadian of Serb descent who joined the Bosnian Serb Army as a volunteer, *Nicholas Ribich,* is facing four counts of hostage-taking for his alleged involvement in the abduction of four military observers who were used as human shields during NATO bombings in Bosnia in May 1995. The Canadian Criminal Code was amended in 1989 to allow for prosecutions of hostage-takings committed abroad. The defendant was arrested in Germany in February 1999 and subsequently extradited to Canada in May 1999. The hearing for his trial has been set for May 2000.[62]

Implementation
☛ The Canadian National Committee on International Humanitarian Law was created in March 1998 pursuant to a memorandum of 18 March 1998 between the Departments of Foreign Affairs and International Trade, National Defence and Justice, the Royal Canadian Mounted Police, the Canadian International Development Agency and the Canadian Red Cross Society.[63]

CHILE[64]

Cases
☛ Supreme Court, 9 September 1998, Rol 469-98 concerning the illegal detention of Pedro Poblete Córdova

This decision of the Supreme Court, the highest tribunal in the Republic of Chile, implies a radical change in its jurisprudence concerning the application of international humanitarian law, and particularly common Article 3 of the 1949 Geneva Conventions, to the period included in Executive Decree N° 2191 of 1978, as well as with respect to its hierarchy in the national legal order. The 1978 Act conceded amnesty to all persons having participated in offences between 11 September 1973 and March 1978.

---

61. *Regina* v. *Finta*, Supreme Court of Canada, 88 C.C.C. 3d 417, 24 March 1994.

62. Richard Roik, 'City Man's Hearing Set', *The Edmonton Sun*, 28 September 1999; Peter Hum, 'Canadian Serb released on bail: Man faces trial in soldier's abduction in Bosnia', *The Ottawa Citizen,* 19 May 1999.

63. Information provided by the Advisory Service on International Humanitarian Law, ICRC.

64. Information and commentaries provided by Professor Hernán Salinas Burgos, Professor of International Law, University of Santiago, Chile. The case is reprinted at p. 485.

Article 1 of Executive Decree N° 5 of September 1973 issued by the 'Junta Militar de Gobierno', which took power in Chile the previous day (11/9/73) declared that the State of Siege decreed by the existing internal disorder in those days should be understood as 'State of Time of War' in the application of Penal Law by the Military Courts. In the extant case, the Supreme Court has determined the application of common Article 3 as an enforceable international instrument in Chile when the offense motivating the Judgement was committed (19 July 1974). As well as declaring, for the first time, the application of these Conventions during the indicated period, the Supreme Court also declares its application over the mentioned Amnesty Law.

The argument of the Court is based on Article 5 of the 1980 Constitution of the Republic of Chile which guarantees essential human rights. In this way, the Court has stated in several decisions that from the history of the establishment of Article 5 of the Constitution, it is clearly established that the sovereignty of the state of Chile is limited by the recognition of the essential rights arising from human nature. These values are above all norms that may be decreed by state authorities, including the legislative power in its constitutional capacity, impeding the violation of these rights.

HERNÁN SALINAS BURGOS

Indictments

☛ Indictments against *Humberto Gordon, Riberto Schmiedt* and *Sergio Arellano,* Ruling of the Court of Appeals, 22 September 1999, unpublished

On 22 September 1999, the Court of Appeals rejected the request of the defendants, three retired army generals, to overturn the indictments against them for the assassination in 1982 of a dissident labour leader and the deaths of 72 dissidents that took place during the military dictatorship of General Augusto Pinochet.[65]

COLOMBIA[66]

Military Criminal Code

☛ New Military Criminal Code, Law No. 522 of 12 August 1999. [Ley número 522 del 12 de agosto de 1999 'por la cual se expide el Código penal militar']. Published in the *Diario oficial (D.O.)* No. 43.665 of 13 August 1999[67]

The new Military Criminal Code not only reforms the military criminal justice system but also streamlines the civilian jurisdiction. It also expressly introduces the topic of human rights into military or martial legislation. The new Code is the result of a long process of debate at the national and international levels between state entities and non-governmental organisations starting in 1993. It contains important new provisions, for example, with regard to the military and police *fœros,* i.e., the criteria for deciding on ordinary or military jurisdictional competence. It means that the members of the armed

---

65. Chilean Generals Rebuffed, *International Herald Tribune*, 23 September 1999.

66. Information provided by Professor Frits Kalshoven, President of the International Fact-Finding Commission; the Embassy of Colombia, The Hague; and Rafael A. Prieto Sanjuán, Ph.D. candidate at University of Paris II, MA (Political science), LL.M.

67. http://www.minjusticia.gov.co:9090/ows-bin/owa/pagina_diario?p_idioma=Español.

forces must be tried either before ordinary or military courts depending on the nature of the crime. Consequently, only those so-called 'proper' military infractions will be tried before military courts. Genocide, forced disappearance and torture shall fall exclusively under the jurisdiction of ordinary courts. With respect to such crimes, the defense of the line of duty or of superior orders is categorically excluded. Another advance in the new Military Criminal Code is reflected in the provisions relating to the duties of commanders. First, the judicial role of commanders in proceedings regarding their subordinates – criticised in the past as a source of impunity – has been eliminated. Secondly, *due obedience* is admitted as a ground to exclude criminal responsibility, but it can solely be claimed for legitimate orders issued by the competent authorities. Finally, the civil dimension is increased in military criminal trials, because it includes the participation of civil advocacy in the search for the truth and compensation for victims.

RAFAEL A. PRIETO SANJUÁN

Investigations into IHL and Human Rights Violations
- Presidential Decree No. 2429 of 1 December 1998 establishing a Special Committee for the oversight of investigations into human rights violations and infractions of international humanitarian law [Comité de seguimiento a las investigaciones sobre los casos más graves a las violaciones de los Derechos Humanos e infracciones al Derecho Internacional Humanitario]. Published in *D.O.* No. 43444 of 4 December 1998[68]
- 1998-2004 Presidential "Policy on the Promotion, Guaranteeing and Respect for Human Rights and the Application of International Humanitarian Law" of 12 August 1999 [Política de Promoción, Respeto y Garantía de los Derechos Humanos y de Aplicación de Derecho Internacional Humanitario. 1998-2000]

The main instruments adopted by Colombia for the last year have been, on the one hand, the approval by the Congress of the new Military Criminal Code and on the other hand, the Government's setting up of a special supervisory committee for the investigation of violations of human rights and international humanitarian law in accordance with the Presidential Policy on Human Rights and IHL (1998-2004).[69]

Its task of supervising and coordinating the work of other state and non-state institutions active in the field of human rights includes the taking up of cases of serious violations of IHL. Moreover, it is to facilitate their satisfactory judicial conclusion in order not only to punish guilty persons but also by seeking restitution for victims of those violations. Certainly, progress can be expected but it can also be seen as an important

---

68. Available at http://www.minjusticia.gov.co:9090/ows-do/43444/434442.htm. One week before, a special commission for the department of Arauca was created by presidential decree n° 2391 of 24 November 1998 [Por el cual se crea la Comisión Interinstitucional de Seguimiento a las Investigaciones que se adelantan por violación a los derechos humanos (Comisión especial para el Departamento de Arauca)]. Published in *D.O.* No. 43440, 30 November 1998. http://www.minjusticia.gov.co:9090/ows-do/43440/434401.htm.

69. The priority areas of work defined are: fight against illegal armed groups, security of human rights defenders and people under threat, attention to displaced populations, special measures to promote IHL (protection of women and minors, as well as eradication of anti-personnel mines), improvement of the administration of justice, and a national action plan on human rights and IHL.

step in the framework of reaching 'amicable solutions' before the Inter-American Commission on Human Rights.[70]

Aside from the international instruments that should be ratified, the legislative agenda seeks to include in the Penal Code breaches of IHL as autonomous crimes (a bill on the military penal justice structure is expected to be introduced in Congress, to ensure that it is adapted to the new regulations of the approved Code).

RAFAEL A. PRIETO SANJUÁN

Recognition and Status of Belligerency

☞ Ministry of External Affairs of Colombia, Vice-Ministry of External Relations. Zone of Hostilities, Lack of Belligerent Status [Ministerio de Relaciones Exteriores de Colombia. Viceministerio de Relaciones Exteriores'. La Zona de Distension. No es "Status" de Beligerancia]. Por Ernesto Borda Medina. 4 *Correa Diplomatico por la Paz*, 16 June/Junio 1999

☞ Ministry of External Affairs of Colombia.

Response of Minister of External Affairs, Guillermo Fernandez de Soto on his competence, the drafted question and the proposition of No. 142. Recognition of Belligerence of the FARC [Ministerio de Relaciones Exteriores de Colombia. Vice-ministerio de Relaciones Exteriores. Respuesta del Senor Ministro de Relaciones Exteriores Guillermo Fernandez de Soto en lo de su Competencia, Al Cuestionario Formulado en la Proposcion de Citacion No. 142. Reconocimiento de Beligerancia a Las Farc]. 4 *Correo Diplomatico por la Paz,* 16 June/Junio 1999. Reprinted at p. 440.

Red Cross Emblem[71]

☞ Presidential Decree No. 860 of 8 May 1998 relating to the protection and use of the name and emblem of the Red Cross, to protect its activities and facilitate its humanitarian services [Decreto por el cual se reglamenta lo relativo a la protección y el uso que debe darse al nombre y el emblema de la Cruz Roja, se protegen sus actividades y se facilita la prestación de los servicios humanitarios en Colombia]. Published in the *Diario Oficial (D.O.)* No. 43.298 of 13 May 1998

Cases[72]

☞ Judgement of Constitutional Court [Sentencia C-340/98] of 8 July 1998. Military Service for Minors, voluntary enrolment and prohibition of participation in war zones

---

70. See for example, the Report No. 45/99. Case 11.525 *(Roison Mora Rubiano)* and the Report No. 46/99. Case 11.531 *(Faride Herrera Jaime et al.)*, both of 9 March 1999, whose friendly settlement implied an act of reparation (compensation and signification). The legal base in the internal order to compensate victims for damages established by some human rights organisations is set up by the Law No. 288 of 5 July 1996 [Por la cual se establecen instrumentos para la indemnización de perjuicios a las víctimas de violaciones de Derechos Humanos en virtud de lo dispuesto por determinados órganos internacionales de Derechos Humanos]. Published in the *Gaceta del Congreso* n 276/96 and *D.O.* n 42826, 9 July 1996.

71. The most important documents regarding state statements and implementation may be consulted at the Internet site of the Colombian human rights network: http://www.rdh.gov.co.

72. National jurisprudence may be consulted in the Colombian network on human rights and on the Internet site of the judicial branch: http://www.fij.edu.co/homepage.htm.

Military or national service is an obligation under Colombian law, but only for males over 18 years old. As far as young people under this age who have completed high school are concerned, they are obliged to define their military situation at this moment (Art. 13 of Law 418/97). With regard to the latter provision, the plaintiff considered that it violates, *inter alia,* the international obligations of the state. Such obligations particularly comprise Article 38 of the Convention on the Rights of the Child, to which Colombia made a reservation that elevates the minimum age for recruitment from 15 to 18 years old. The Court considered that the law is clear in allowing the recruitment of minors, as well as their voluntary service, provided that their parents approve and provided that they express their true and free will. Furthermore, they cannot be deployed for tasks or to areas of risk, e.g. participation in war zones. Considering that military service does not represent *per se* a risk of war and a violation of the right to life of minors, the Court gave a material interpretation (regarding activities) rather than a formal one (enlistment) of what constitutes 'military recruitment', assimilating it to a social service in the case of minors. In other words, the fact of serving in the army does not necessarily mean being enrolled in its ranks for war.

RAFAEL A. PRIETO SANJUÁN

Pending Legislation
☛ Law to implement the Landmines Convention. A law was approved at first reading in the Senate's Second Committee and is currently awaiting the procedure for plenary session debate.

CONGO (BRAZZAVILLE)

Legislation
☛ Law No. 8-98 of 31 October 1998 on the definition and the repression of genocide, war crimes and crimes against humanity[73]

Articles 1 and 3 of the Congolese law penalise the same acts as genocide as do Articles 2 and 3 of the 1948 Genocide Convention except that the Congolese law extends the protection against genocide to any other group 'determined by any other arbitrary criterion' ['...groupe déterminé à partir de tout autre critère arbitraire']. Article 2 requires the death penalty for genocide. As far as the definition of war crimes is concerned, the law sets forth a general reference to grave breaches of the Geneva Conventions, other grave violations of the laws and customs of war applicable in international armed conflicts within the established framework of international law, grave violations of common Article 3 and other grave violations recognised as applicable in non-international armed conflicts within the established framework of international law.[74] Articles 6-9 deal with crimes against humanity. These are defined in conformity with Article 7 of the ICC Statute to comprise the enumerated acts 'when committed as part

---

73. Source: ICRC Advisory Service on International Humanitarian Law; available at: http://www.icrc.org/ihl-nat.nsf/WebLAW?OpenView&Start=1&Count=30&Expand=6.2#6.2.

74. Art. 4 of the Congolese law. All following references are to the Congolese law unless stated otherwise.

of a widespread or systematic attack directed against any civilian population, with knowledge of the attack'.[75] While the definition reproduces most of the acts enumerated in the ICC's Statute, the two provisions differ in certain respects. The Congolese law does not require persecution to be committed 'in connection with any act referred to [in paragraph one of Article 7 of the ICC Statute] or [genocide or war crimes]' as is required under the Rome Statute.[76] It thus does away with the nexus requirement. Moreover, the Congolese law does not mention specifically the crime of apartheid,[77] but instead refers to 'the crime of discrimination: tribal, ethnic or religious' which appears to be broader than apartheid as defined in Article 2 of the 1973 Convention on the Suppression and Punishment of the Crime of Apartheid. The law also adds a non-exhaustive list of 'other inhumane acts of a similar character intentionally causing great suffering to mental or physical health'[78] and does not adopt the definitions under paragraphs 2 and 3 of Article 7 of the ICC Statute. Articles 7 to 9 enumerate those acts constituting crimes against humanity for which the death penalty is prescribed.

The final provisions relate to the criminal responsibility of those who have inspired or given orders to commit genocide, war crimes or crimes against humanity[79] and provide for additional sentences and measures that can be adopted against persons who have committed one of these crimes.[80] The law also provides that criminal responsibility cannot be excluded by the mere fact that the author or accomplice of one of the crimes committed an act which is prescribed or authorised by legislative or regulatory provisions or which was ordered by the legitimate authorities. However, such fact shall be taken into consideration in determining the sentence.[81] The law also provides that public action with regard to the prosecution and repression of the crimes as well as pronounced sentences are imprescriptible[82] and that the provisions of the law are applicable even with respect to crimes committed before the promulgation of the law, and thus that they have retroactive effect.[83]

JANN K. KLEFFNER

Case Law
☛ Opinion of the Supreme Court in re: Draft law on the definition and repression of genocide, war crimes and crimes against humanity, Decision No. 007/CS/98, 24 March 1998 [Avis émis par la Cour Suprême, Affaire: Projet de loi portant définition et répression des crimes contre l'Humanite, Cour Suprême decision No. 007/CS/98][84]

---

75. Art. 6.
76. Compare Art. 7(1)(h) ICC Statute.
77. Art. 7(1)(j) ICC Statute.
78. Art. 6(k); cf., Art. 7(1)(k) ICC Statute.
79. Art. 10.
80. Arts. 11 and 12.
81. Art. 13.
82. Art. 14.
83. Art. 15. Cf. Article 15(2) of the 1966 International Covenant on Civil and Political Rights, which provides that the prohibition of retroactive legislation does not 'prejudice the trial and punishment of any person for any act or omission which, at the time when it was committed, was criminal according to the general principles of law recognised by the community of nations'.
84. Source: ICRC Advisory Service on International Humanitarian Law. Available at: http://www.icrc.org/ihl-nat.nsf/WebCASE?OpenView&Start=1&Count=30&Expand=5#5.

Asked by the Ministry of Justice to give an opinion on the constitutionality of a draft of the above-mentioned law, the Supreme Court declared the draft law to be in complete conformity with the Basic Law of the country and international treaty law binding upon the Congo.

CROATIA[85]

Landmines
- ☛ Decree of 19 February 1998 establishing the Croatian Demining Centre, Published in *Narodne novine*, No. 24/1998
- ☛ Law on Demining (amended), 1998. Published in *Narodne novine*, No. 86/1998

In accordance with the 1996 Law on Demining (*Narodne novine*, No. 19/1996), as amended in 1998, the Government of the Republic of Croatia established by its Decree of 19 February the Croatian Demining Center, a public institution with the following main tasks: to collect and analyse relevant data, to estimate risks in the mined areas, to propose a Demining Plan to the Government, to undertake research on demining technology and to coordinate the work of international experts (Art. 3 of the Decree).

MAJA ŠERSIĆ

Use of Weapons (symposium)
In 1998, a useful initiative emerged from an international symposium hosted by the Croatian Defence Ministry. One of the conclusions of the symposium 'Eco-terrorism – Chemical and Biological Warfare without Chemical and Biological Weapons', held in Dubrovnik, Zagreb, from 25-30 October, was that attacks on chemical/biological facilities (e.g., industrial plants processing chemicals) by conventional weapons were not covered by international humanitarian law. Since such attacks could have similar consequences as the use of chemical weapons, explicit prohibition of attacks against such facilities, analogous to those of 1977 Protocols I (Art. 56) and II (Art. 15) to the Geneva Conventions, which protect works and installations that could act as dangerous forces, is needed. It was decided to forward the proposal to that effect to the competent international bodies, such as Organisation for the Prohibition of Chemical Weapons.

MAJA ŠERSIĆ

Cases
- ☛ Miro Bajramović and Branko Sarić-Kosa, unpublished

In the first trial of ethnic Croats in a Croatian court on charges of committing war crimes against members of the Serb minority in 1991, the two defendants were found guilty and sentenced to 20 months imprisonment for house breaking and extortion at gunpoint (Miro Bajramović) and one year imprisonment for illegally detaining and assaulting a Serb villager (Branko Saric-Kosa). Four other defendants were acquitted of all charges brought against them. The court dismissed the other charges of murder, attempted murder and kidnapping for lack of evidence in the cases of all six men who were accused of being

---

85. Information and commentaries by Maja Šersić, Professor of International Law, University of Zagreb, Croatia.

part of a group involved in the deaths of up to 100 ethnic Serbs in the area of Pakrac, 100 km south-east of Zagreb.[86]

☛ *Dinko Sakić,* Zagreb County Court, case No. DO-K-141/98, judgment of 4 October 1999, unpublished[87]

After his extradition to Croatia from Argentina in June 1998,[88] an indictment against Dinko Sakić was issued by the County Prosecutor in Zagreb on 18 December 1998.[89] The charges were that the defendant 'in the events of World War II when, pursuant to the implementation of Nazi and racial laws and legal provisions against political opponents between 1941 and 1945, tens of thousands of civilians, mostly Jews, Roma, Serbs and Croats, were abused, tortured and killed in the Jasenovac camp, in the territory of the then "Independent State of Croatia", after he had become a member of the "Ustasha Defense" on 18 February 1942 and working as head of the "General Section" and Deputy and Vice-Commandant at the headquarters of the "Stara Gradiska" and Jasenovac camps until April 1944 at the time when executions were carried out in these, and having become commandant of the Jasenovac camp in the beginning of April 1944, [he] continued until November 1944 by commanding and otherwise managing, taking and implementing decisions, with the abuse, torture and killing of internees by personally issuing orders and participating in their implementation and at the same time by not undertaking anything to prevent the other members of the "Ustasha Defense" from doing the same.'[90] The indictment concluded that 'therefore, in breach of the rules of international law in times of war, he ordered and carried out torture, inhuman treatment and killing of civilians and ordered and carried out measures aimed at intimidating, terrorizing and forcing civilians to forced labour, as well as starving and collectively punishing them and by such acts – he committed a crime against humanity and international law – a war crime against the civilian population - recognized by, and punishable under, Article 120, Paragraph 1 of the Basic Penal Code of the Republic of Croatia.'

The Prosecutor amended the factual description of the criminal offence on 8 July 1999. He added that Sakić, '[F]rom April to November 1944, as the commander of the Jasenovac Camp, [acted] contrary to the principles and provisions of Articles 46[91] and 50[92] of the [Hague] Convention (IV) on the Laws and Customs of War on Land (1907) and while commanding the camp and performing other tasks of administrating, making and enforcing decisions, he abused, tortured and killed the internees by personally issuing orders and participating in their implementation and at the same time by not undertaking

---

86. '*Croats convicted of war crimes*', BBC World, Europe, 1 June 1999.

87. Information and documents on the trial are available at: http://pubwww.srce.hr/sakic/.

88. See 1 *YIHL* (1998) pp. 429-430.

89. No. DO-K-141/98.

90. Office of the County Public Prosecutor in Zagreb, Document No. DO-K-141/98, Zagreb, 18 December 1998.

91. The provision reads: 'Family honour and rights, the lives of persons, and private property, as well as religious convictions and practice, must be respected. Private property cannot be confiscated.'

92. The provision reads: 'No general penalty, pecuniary or otherwise, shall be inflicted upon the population on account of the acts of individuals for which they cannot be regarded as jointly and severally responsible.'

anything to prevent the directly subordinated members of the 'Ustasha Defence' from doing the same ...' The legal qualification of the criminal offence, i.e., war crimes against the civilian population according to Article 120, Paragraph 1 of the Basic Penal Code, remained unchanged.[93]

The trial began on 15 March 1999. The main proceedings comprised 56 trial days during which substantial evidence was presented and 34 witnesses were heard. The proceedings for the presentation of evidence were terminated on 20 September 1999, after which the parties presented their closing arguments. The latter stage of the proceedings was terminated on 29 September 1999.[94]

On 4 October 1999, the court found Dinko Sakić guilty of all charges and sentenced him to a maximum of 20 years imprisonment. The court rejected Sakić's defense lawyers' argument that the defendant merely obeyed his superiors' orders.

JANN K. KLEFFNER

Ongoing cases
☞ Criminal proceedings against *Radivoje Jakovljević* and 21 others, Vukovar County Court, No. K-86/98

On 25 May 1999, criminal proceedings for acts of genocide and war crimes against the civilian population took place against 22 defendants – 21 of them *in absentia* – before the County Court in Vukovar. The allegations relate to events that took place in November and December 1991 in Vukovar, namely in the district of the company 'Velepromet', in the prisoner-of-war camp in 'Stajičevo' and in the prison Sremska Mitrovica. The defendants, mostly ethnic Serbs, are accused of killing members of Croatian and other non-Serbian ethnic groups, causing them serious bodily harm and expelling them, with the intention of the complete extinction of Croatian and other non-Serbian ethnic groups. The allegations further include that the accused violated international law during the partial occupation of Croatia's territory by killing, torturing and treating inhumanely the civilian population, and gradually depopulating the area, by intimidating and terrorising them, by taking people to the concentration camp and robbing them of their property.

Criminal Investigations
☞ Criminal investigations against *Dragisa Cancarević,* Zagreb County Court

On 20 April 1999, the public prosecutor in Zagreb ordered the investigation of a Serb police commander, Dragisa Cancarević, arrested for war crimes against civilians and maltreatment of prisoners of war in contravention of the Geneva Conventions allegedly committed in Vukovar in 1991. The alleged crimes took place in the period after Croatia declared independence from Yugoslavia in summer 1991. Dragisa Cancarević commanded

---

93. Office of the County Public Prosecutor in Zagreb, Document Number: DO-K-141/98, Zagreb, 8 July 1999.

94. Republic of Croatia, County Court in Zagreb, Office of the President of the Court, Communique 20, 1 October 1999.

a camp for civilian and military prisoners set up in the Vukovar suburb of Borovo Naselje.[95]

CZECH REPUBLIC[96]

Cooperation with the International Committee of the Red Cross
- Agreement on Cooperation Concerning the Dissemination of Humanitarian Law and Universal Humanitarian Principles Concluded Between the International Committee of the Red Cross and the Ministry of Defence of the Czech Republic, Prague, 4 May 1999

This five-Article Agreement provides for the dissemination and introduction of appropriate humanitarian law and universal humanitarian principles in the Czech Army by the International Committee of the Red Cross chiefly by: providing documentation, organizing workshops, seminars, basic courses, lectures and round tables on this issue; assisting in the preparation of the relevant documentation and visual aids; contributing financially, when appropriate, to the participation of the members of the Czech Army and its civilian components in international courses and meetings; and participation of ICRC staff, at the invitation of the Czech military authorities, in the planning of military exercises with a view to ensuring practical cooperation between humanitarian and military bodies.

JAN HLADIK

War graves
- Agreement between the Government of the Czech Republic and the Government of the Russian Federation on the Mutual Upkeep of War Graves, Moscow, 15 April 1999. Entered into force 11 August 1999

The main purpose of this nine-Article Agreement is to regulate issues related to the upkeep of war graves of Czech, Czechoslovak or Austro-Hungarian citizens of Czech origin in the Russian Federation and war graves of Russian or former Soviet citizens in the Czech Republic.

The Preamble refers to the principles and norms of international humanitarian law and, in particular, to the provisions of the Geneva Conventions 1949 and their Additional Protocols 1977. It also refers to Article 21 of the 1993 mutual bilateral treaty on friendly relations and cooperation.

The Contracting Parties are requested to ensure the protection of war graves situated in their territory and their relevant upkeep (Art. 2). In conformity with their national legislation, the Contracting Parties are obliged to permit access of the citizens of the other Contracting Party to graves located in their territory so that those citizens may pay honours to the deceased. The Contracting Parties are also required to grant the respective diplomatic and consular authorities as well as bodies to be set up under Article 7 the right to monitor the state of war graves. Finally, the Contracting Parties are obliged to inform

---

95. 'Croatia targets police chief in war crimes probe', *Reuters*, 21 April 1999.

96. Information and commentaries provided by Jan Hladik, Programme Specialist, International Standards Section of the Division of Cultural Heritage, UNESCO, Paris.

each other of crimes committed against war graves of the other Contracting Party, to restore those graves, and to notify the other Party of this designated body.

At the time of writing this Agreement had not yet entered into force. A similar agreement with the Slovak Republic is being prepared.

JAN HLADÍK

DENMARK

Extradition proceedings in Re. Pinochet

☛ Request of the Prime Minister, Poul Nyrup Rasmussen, to the Minister of Justice, Frank Jensen, to study the possibility of asking for the extradition of the former head of state of Chile, December 1998[97]

ESTONIA[98]

Implementation

☛ The Implementation of Humanitarian Law in National Defence Forces, Regulation of Defence Minister Andrus Oeöevel No. 2 of 10 July 1998. Published in *Riigi Teataja* [national gazette] annex 1998, 238/239, 1000, 30 July 1998

Problems surrounding the implementation of international humanitarian law within the national Defence Forces of Estonia centre on the above regulation, whose legal grounds are the decision of 24 August 1992 of the Supreme Council of the Republic of Estonia on the accession of Estonia to the Geneva Conventions and their Additional Protocols[99] and the Government of the Republic Act.[100] The Regulation consists primarily of the translation and a brief summary of the most important legal instruments on humanitarian law.

The Estonian Republic contracted international legal obligations after the passing of the accession documents to the depositary. The decision of the Supreme Council of the Republic of Estonia cites the Geneva Conventions and their Additional Protocols. However, the texts of the Conventions have not yet been published in the *Riigi Teataja,* raising the question of the status of Geneva treaty norms in our internal legal order.

Paragraph 3 of the Estonian Constitution, which was adopted by means of a referendum on 28 June 1992,[101] indicates that Estonia is a monistic state. Paragraph 3 of the Constitution provides that, 'The powers of state shall be exercised solely pursuant to the Constitution and laws which are in conformity therewith. Generally recognized principles and rules of international law are an inseparable part of the Estonian legal system.' The question is whether 'generally recognized principles and rules of international law' bind an individual if the legislator has not made them known to him.

---

97. Source: Amnesty International: *The Pinochet case – Universal Jurisdiction and the absence of immunity for crimes against humanity*, AI Index: EUR 45/01/99, January 1999, at p. 17.

98. Information and commentary by Mr T. Kerikmäe, LL.M, LL.Lic., lecturer in international law at Tartu University, Estonia.

99. *Riigi Teataja* (1992) pp. 34, 447.

100. 1 *RT* (1998) p. 28.

101. 1 *RT* (1992) pp. 26, 349.

Paragraph 3(2) of the Constitution states: 'Laws shall be published in the prescribed manner. Only published laws have obligatory force.' Despite the recognition of the supremacy of ratified international treaties over Estonian laws or other legislative acts by paragraph 123 of the Constitution, the formal requirements of publication for conformance with this condition cannot be disregarded.

The Law on Legal Acts of Estonia[102] provides the procedure for publication of international treaties besides other legal acts. Paragraph 5(10) reaffirms the principle that: 'An international treaty enters in force on the date prescribed by the treaty.' Paragraph 9(2) states that in the second part of the Legal Acts of Estonia, the 'international agreements named in paragraph 2(3) of the present law' are published (by this the international treaties ratified by the Riigikogu [Parliament] and entered by the Government of the Republic are meant).

The texts of the Geneva Conventions have not yet been published in the Legal Acts of Estonia. Paragraph 10 of the Law on Legal Acts of Estonia states the requirements for the publication of international treaties. Paragraph 4(2) contains the only exception to publication which can be made by decision of the State Secretary: only the annex of an international treaty could remain unpublished if, due to technical reasons or the great volume of material, it becomes unreasonable.

The National Court of Estonia, referring to Article 24(1) of the Vienna Convention on Law of International Treaties,[103] has declared that international treaties are enforced as it is determined by the treaty. The National Court has therefore concluded that 'the publication of an international treaty must not be the pre-condition for its enforcement'.[104] However, the question in the current case is not the enforceable nature of 'Geneva law' but its interesting 'competition' with the Regulation of the Defence Minister, and the implementation methods of humanitarian law in the Estonian legal order.

Avoiding the tricky question of to what extent international humanitarian norms are compulsory in the internal legal order (above all, for the defence forces), the Minister of Defense has 'skillfully' solved the problem by issuing the Regulation, imposing an obligation on members of the armed forces to respect the norms of international humanitarian law.

The first problematic issue is that the material legal basis of the Regulation is narrower as compared to that used therein. If the Regulation is issued on the basis of the above-mentioned decision of 1992, then it is interesting to note that the contents of the decision is the accession to the Geneva Conventions and Additional Protocols. The Regulation on the other hand points to the other international humanitarian agreements. For example, paragraph 6 of the Regulation provides that 'the rights and obligations of the soldier in an armed conflict are stated in the Hague 1907 agreements, ... of which the most important are ...'.

It remains unclear and questionable how a mere regulation, having a lower position in the hierarchy of legal norms, may determine the implementation area of international law and its 'importance'. It seems to be an obvious contradiction with the (above-mentioned) terms of paragraph 3 of the Constitution.

---

102. 1 *RT* (1999) pp. 10, 155.
103. 2 *RT* (1993) pp. 13, 16.
104. Case 3-4-1-1, 10 May 1996.

Furthermore, the other legal ground of the Regulation, the Government of the Republic Act,[105] is also inadequate and gives rise to numerous legal problems. Paragraph 49(1)(3), dealing with 'the competence of a Minister as a Head of a Ministry', states that the Minister 'decides issues belonging to the sphere of competence of the ministry ...'. It is clear that the Ministry of Defence has no competence to legislate provisions for determining the position of international law. Paragraph 50(1) also manifests evident contradiction, as 'a Minister makes regulations ... on the basis of law and for enforcement'. The Minister of Defence has no such competence with regard to the aforesaid Regulation deriving from Estonian legislation or/and the Constitution.

Estonia is a party to other international Conventions not mentioned in the aforementioned decision of the Supreme Council 1992. However, the texts of these Conventions are published according to the formal requirements. So, the 1968 UN Convention on Non-retroactivity of War Crimes and Crimes against Humanity[106] and the Hague Convention of 1954 on the Protection of Cultural Property in Armed Conflict[107] are published in Estonian in *Riigi Teataja*.

In conclusion, it is clear that 'Geneva Law' is part of our legal system. However, the implementation methods seem to be in contradiction with the Estonian Constitution and may cause confusion in determining the legal rights and duties of individuals (especially members of the Defence Forces). Where there is 'competition' between the conventional law and the Regulation (as 'transformer' and 'interpreter'), reference to Article 27 of the Vienna Convention on the Law of Treaties must be made.

TANEL KERIKMÄE

FRANCE[108]

Landmines

➡ Law 98-542 of 1 July 1998 authorising the ratification of the Convention on the Prohibition of the Use, Stockpiling, Production and Transfer of Anti-personnel Mines and on Their Destruction of 18 September 1998 [Loi n° 98-542 of 1 juillet 1998 autorisant la ratification de la Convention sur l'interdiction de l'emploi, du stockage, de la protection et du transfert des mines antipersonnel et sur leur destruction du 18 septembre 1998]. Published in *Journal Officiel*, 2 juillet 1998, p. 10/078

➡ Law 98-564 of 8 July 1998 for the Elimination of Anti-personnel Mines [Loi n° 98-564 of 8 juillet 1998 tendant à l'élimination des mines antipersonnel]. Published in *Journal Officiel*, 9 juillet 1998, p. 10/456

The latter was adopted unanimously by the French National Assembly on 25 June 1998, supplementing the Act of 1 July above. It came into effect on 1 July 1999, the same day as the Landmines Convention's entry into force and is based expressly on the Landmines

---

105. 1 *RT* (1998) 28.

106. 2 *RT* (1994) 16/15, 50

107. 2 *RT* (1995) 7, 32. At the same time, the Regulation contains a special chapter on the protection of cultural heritage.

108. Information and commentaries provided by Professor Paul Tavernier, Centre de Recherches et D'Etudes Sur les Droits de l'Homme et le Droit Humanitaire (CREDHO), Faculté Jean Monet, Université de Paris-Sud.

Convention. The Act prohibits absolutely the development, manufacture, stockpiling, supply, transfer and use of anti-personnel landmines and stipulates that all stocks of such mines must be destroyed by 31 December 2000. A national committee for the banning of anti-personnel landmines will monitor enforcement of the Act.

Chemical Weapons
- ☛ Law 98-467 of 17 June 1998 concerning the Application of the Convention of 13 January 1993 on the Prohibition of the Development, Manufacture, Stockpiling and Use of Chemical Weapons and on their Destruction [Loi n° 98-467 du 17 juin 1998 relative à l'application de la convention du 13 janvier 1993 sur l'interdiction de la mise au point, de la fabrication, du stockage et de l'emploi des armes chimiques et sur leur destruction]. Published in *Journal Officiel de la République française,* 18 June/juin 1998, p. 9247
- ☛ Decree 99-64 of 27 January 1999 concerning certain international verification systems required by the Law of 17 June 1998 concerning the application of the Convention of 13 January 1993 on the Prohibition of the Development, Manufacture, Stockpiling and Use of Chemical Weapons and on their Destruction [Decret n° 99-64 du 27 janvier 1999 concernant certaines vérifications internationales systématiques prévues par la loi n° 98-467 du 17 juin 1998 relative à l'application de la convention du 13 janvier 1993 sur l'interdiction de la mise au point, de la fabrication, du stockage et de l'emploi des armes chimiques et sur leur destruction]. Published in *Journal Officiel de la République française,* 30 January/janvier 1999, p. 1565

Constitutional Law (concerning ratification of the ICC Statute)
- ☛ Constitutional Law n° 99-568 of 8 July 1999, adopted by the Congress on 28 June 1999, inserting into the Constitution an Article 53(2) on the International Criminal Court [loi constitutionnelle n° 99-568 du 8 juillet 1999 insérant au titre VI de la Constitution un article 53(2) et relatif a la Cour pénale internationale]. Published in *Journal Officiel* n° 157 of 9 July 1999, p. 10175

Parliamentary Documents Concerning Ratification of the ICC Statute
- ☛ Bill (projet de loi constitutionnelle), doc. National Assembly, n° 1462, 11 March 1999
- ☛ Report of Alain Vidalies (National Assembly), n° 1501, 31 March 1999
- ☛ *Journal Officiel* (Doc. Assemblée Nationale, Débats, séance du 6 avril 1999)
- ☛ Information report (Rapport d'Information) of André Dulait (Commission on Foreign Affairs, Senate n° 313, 12 April 1999) on the International Criminal Court (with hearings of Prof. Mario Bettati, Prof. Thierry de Montbrial, Prof. Hervé Cassan and Mr Romy Abraham, Head of the Legal Services in the French Ministry of Foreign Affairs
- ☛ Report of Robert Badinter (Senate n° 318, 28 April 1999)
- ☛ *Journal Officiel* (Doc. Sénat, Débats, séance du 29 avril 1999)

Military Operations in Rwanda
- ☛ Report of the French National Assembly n° 1271 about the Information mission of the Department of Defence, the Armed Forces and the Department of Foreign Affairs on the military operations undertaken by France, other countries and the UN in Rwanda between 1990 and 1994 [Rapport d'Information n° 1271 par la mission d'information de la commission de la Défense Nationale et des Forces Armées et de

la Commission des Affaires Étrangères sur les operations militaires menées par la France, d'autres pays et l'ONU au Rwanda entre 1990 et 1994]. [www.assemblee-nationale.fr/2/2rwanda.html]

This voluminous report of 413 pages contains four parts devoted to the history of Rwanda, the events from 1990 to 1994, the analysis of responsibilities and the proposals of the Information mission. While the report includes a wealth of information, it reflects the fact that the mission did not have extensive powers belonging to a commission of inquiry. It held 110 hours of debates on 35 meetings and heard 88 civilian and military persons. Its rapporteurs met in New York at the seat of the United Nations and at Washington with the US authorities. They were also received by the representatives of the Belgian government and parliament, in particular by the Commission of Inquiry of the Belgian Senate regarding the events in Rwanda in April 1994. Belgium for its part has been profoundly traumatised.

The conclusions of this report received a mixed reception. It examines in length the qualification of genocide as applied to the Rwandan case (pp. 286 et seq. of the report). The third part (pp. 351 et seq.) analyses the different responsibilities, of Rwanda, 'the author of its own history', France and the international community. The mission underlines the absence of relations between France and the 'Interahamwe' militias and reveals that the French soldiers did not participate in any way in the formation of the militias. The mission emphasises the powerlessness of the United Nations, paralysed by its deficiencies and its errors, but also by the obstruction of the United States.

The proposals of the mission appear to be quite weak considering the gravity of the situation. They are limited to recommending more transparency and coherence in the mechanisms for crisis management in France, enhanced parliamentary control and the improved efficiency of interventions to maintain or restore peace of the United Nations. The information mission also pronounces to be in favour of an early ratification by France of the Statute of the International Criminal Court, being an 'essential element of measures for the prevention and settlement of crises'.

PAUL TAVERNIER

Cases

☛ Decision no. 98-408 DC of 22 January 1999 concerning the Statute of the International Criminal Court [Décision n° 98-408 DC du 22 janvier 1999: Traité portant statut de la Cour pénale internationale]. Published in French in *L'Actualité juridique – Droit administratif*, 20 March/mars 1999, p. 266 (with commentary by Jean-Eric Schoettl at p. 230)[109]

The Constitutional Council (*Conseil Constitutionnel*), seized by both the President of the Republic and by the Prime Minister on 24 December 1998, rendered an important decision on 22 January 1999 in which it announced that 'the authorisation to ratify the Statute of the International Criminal Court requires a revision of the constitution'. The *Conseil Constitutionnel* addressed some of the contradictions between the Rome Statute and the French Constitution after having examined in depth the international undertaking which was submitted to it.

---

109. Unofficial English language translation at p. 493 of this volume.

As far as the object of the Statute is concerned, the *Conseil Constitutionnel* rejected the reservation of reciprocity as provided for under Article 55 of the French Constitution[110] and it considered the constitutional principles applicable to criminal law and criminal procedure not to be questioned, namely as regards the non-application of statutory limitations (provided for in French law only for genocide and crimes against humanity but not for war crimes), the presumption of innocence, the legality of crimes and sentences, the non-retroactivity of criminal law, procedural equality and the independence of the Judge. It also underlined the role of the preliminary chamber/ *chambre préliminaire*.

The *Conseil Constitutionnel* held that the Rome Statute is contrary to the French Constitution with respect to three points:

1) Article 27 of the Statute (irrelevance of official capacity): the Constitution provides for a specific regime governing the responsibility of the President of the Republic (jurisdictional immunity and privileges with respect to the *Haute Cour de Justice*/High Court of Justice: Article 86), of members of the government (jurisdictional privileges with respect to the *Cour de Justice de la Republique*/Court of Justice of the Republic: Article 68-1), and of members of parliament (immunities: Article 26). These provisions are incompatible with Article 27 of the Statute, which does not allow for any distinction based on official capacity.

2) Article 17 of the Statute (principle of complementarity): The *Conseil Constitutionnel* does not criticise the regime established by the Rome Statute as such. The latter does not threaten the 'essential conditions for the exercise of national sovereignty', except in the case where 'France, apart from a lack of willingness or from the inability of the State, could be compelled to arrest and surrender to the Court a person on the basis of facts covered by an amnesty or statutory limitation under French law'. Despite these slight restrictions, the *Conseil Constitutionnel* thus preserves the principle of complementarity, which is the basis of the Statute.

3) Article 99 of the Statute (investigative powers of the Prosecutor): While the *Conseil Constitutionnel* admitted that the provisions relating to international cooperation, to judicial assistance and to the investigative powers of the Prosecutor in their entirety are in conformity with the Constitution, it nevertheless considered the application of paragraph 4 of Article 99 to be susceptible to influence the essential conditions for the exercise of national sovereignty as far as 'the Prosecutor can, even apart from the case where the national judicial system is unavailable, proceed with certain investigative acts without the presence of the required authorities of the State and on the territory of the latter'. In contrast, the regime for the execution of sentences does not influence French sovereignty.

In conclusion, the decision of the *Conseil Constitutionnel* did not close in any way the path to a ratification of the Statute of the International Criminal Court by France. It implied a prior revision of the Constitution. Two possibilities were envisageable: either to revise the different provisions of the Constitution which were declared incompatible with the Rome Statute (namely Articles 26 and 68), but this would have entailed certain difficulties, or to adopt a constitutional law which includes a general formula allowing

---

110. The provision reads: 'Regularly ratified or approved treaties or agreements take superior priority over laws, from the date of their publication, provided that each treaty or agreement is applied by the other party.'

for ratification by France. The second possibility was chosen. The Constitutional Law of 8 July 1999 inserted into Title VI of the Constitution a revised Article 53-2 which reads: 'The Republic can recognise the jurisdiction of the International Criminal Court under the conditions provided for in the treaty signed on 18 July 1998.' This ambiguous formula is imprecise, because the treaty was adopted and not signed on that date. Furthermore, even though the *Conseil Constitutionnel* did not have the final text of the Rome Statute at its disposal, it left open the possibility that an eventual modification of the Statute could require a new revision of the Constitution (in this sense: report of Alain Vidalies, Assemblée Nationale, n° 1501, 31 March 1999). One can regret it.

PAUL TAVERNIER

Pending proceedings
☛ Proceedings against *Alois Brunner*, Decision of Investigative Judge of 1 September 1999

In a decision of 1 September 1999, Investigative Judge Herve Stephan recommended that Alois Brunner be tried for the deportation of 250 French-Jewish children to the Auschwitz concentration camp, where most of them subsequently died. The French Investigative Judge recommended that the indictee, a close aide of Adolf Eichmann believed to live in Syria, be tried *in absentia* as he was for other crimes relating to the deportation of Jews in 1954 and 1956, which led to his conviction and sentencing to death. The trial is expected to begin in early 2000.[111]

GEORGIA

Commission for Humanitarian Law
☛ Presidential Decree No. 327 of 22 June 1998 on the establishment of an interministerial commission for international humanitarian law. Amended by Presidential Resolution No. 495 of 14 August 1998. Entered into force 22 June 1998. Published in *Collection of Decrees and Resolutions of the President of Georgia*, No. 12
☛ Presidential Resolution No. 494 of 24 August 1998 approving the Statutes of the Interministerial Commission for International Humanitarian Law
☛ Statutes of the Interministerial Commission for International Humanitarian Law. Adopted 31 August 1998. Entered into force 24 August 1998. Published in *Collection of Decrees and Resolutions of the President of Georgia*, No. 16

GERMANY[112]

Landmines
☛ Convention on the Prohibition of the Use, Stockpiling, Production and Transfer of Anti-Personnel Mines and on their Destruction of 18 September 1997 Act [*Gesetz zu*

---

111. 'France to Prosecute Alleged Nazi', Associated Press (1 September 1999).

112. Information and commentaries provided by Sascha Rolf Lüder and Gregor Schotten, Research Associates at the Institute for International Law of Peace and Armed Conflict (IFHV), Ruhr-Universität Bochum, and Jann K. Kleffner, Assistant Editor of the *Yearbook of International Humanitarian Law*.

dem Übereinkommen über das Verbot des Einsatzes, der Lagerung, der Herstellung und der Weitergabe von Antipersonenminen und über deren Vernichtung vom 18. September 1997]. Published in II *Bundesgesetzblatt* (1998) pp. 778 et seq.

On 1 March 1999, the Convention on the Prohibition of the Use, Stockpiling, Production and Transfer of Anti-Personnel Mines and on Their Destruction of 18 September 1997 (Landmines Convention) entered into force for Germany. Germany ratified this Convention in May 1998.[113] Earlier, on 3 December 1998, 1996 amended Protocol II of the Certain Conventional Weapons Convention of 1981 entered into force for Germany.

SASCHA ROLF LÜDER and GREGOR SCHOTTEN

Chemical Weapons
☞ Statement by German Government regarding Chemical Weapons [*Antwort der Bundesregierung auf die Kleine Anfrage der Fraktion der F.D.P., 'Verzicht auf den Ersteinsatz von Atomwaffen und NATO-Einsätze ohne VN-Mandat'*]. 28 December 1998. Published in 14 *Bundestags-Drucksache* p. 241

Small Arms and Light Weapons
☞ Speech by the German Minister of Foreign Affairs at the German Africa Foundation [*Rede des Bundesministers des Auswärtigen beim Jahresempfang der Deutschen Afrika-Stiftung*], Bonn, 27 January 1999. Federal Foreign Office, Press Release of 27 January 1999

The widespread availability of small arms and light weapons in conflicts, particularly those of a non-international character, has become a growing concern of the German Government. The German Minister of Foreign Affairs criticised the uncontrolled transfer and use of these weapons and called for control mechanisms. In the German Parliament, several factions have charged the German Government with actively supporting initiatives within the framework of the United Nations to establish effective control mechanisms for small arms and light weapons.[114]

SASCHA ROLF LÜDER and GREGOR SCHOTTEN

International Criminal Tribunal for Rwanda
☞ Act for Co-operation with the International Criminal Tribunal for Rwanda of 4 May 1998 [*Gesetz über die Zusammenarbeit mit dem Internationalen Strafgerichtshof für*

---

113. Concerning the negotiation and ratification process of the Landmines Convention in Germany, see, H. Fischer, 'Some Aspects of German State Practice Concerning IHL', 1 *YIHL* (1998) pp. 380 et seq. at 329.

114. *Antrag der Fraktion der SPD, 'Abrüstung von Kleinwaffen', 25 November 1997.* Published in *Bundestags-Drucksache* 13/9248; *Antrag der Fraktionen der CDU/CSU und F.D.P., 'Internationale Kontrolle und Abrüstung von Kleinwaffen',* 4 March 1998. Published in *Bundestags-Drucksache* 13/10026. For possible international, national and regional measures to be taken, see the Summary Report of the PrepCom - Preparatory Committee for a Global Campaign on the Spread and Unlawful Use of Small Arms and Light Weapons, Meeting of Experts on Arms Availability, Violations of International Humanitarian Law and the Deteriorating Situation of Civilians in Armed Conflict, 11 *Humanitäres Völkerrecht - Informationsschriften* (1998) pp. 252 et seq.

Ruanda (Ruanda-Strafgerichtshof-Gesetz) vom 4. Mai 1998]. Published in I *Bundesgesetzblatt* (1998) pp. 843 et seq.

The 1998 Act for Co-operation with the International Criminal Tribunal for Rwanda, along with the earlier Act for Co-operation with the International Criminal Tribunal for the Former Yugoslavia,[115] necessitated an amendment of the Act on International Assistance in Criminal Matters (IRG),[116] which was primarily concerned with judicial assistance to other states.

According to s. 67a of the IRG, part V of the amended act, dealing with the permissibility of legal assistance other than transfer assistance and assistance regarding the execution of foreign judgements, such rules also apply in respect of international and supranational organisations. Furthermore, s. 74a of the IRG gives permission to German authorities to address requests for legal assistance to those organisations.

SASCHA ROLF LÜDER and GREGOR SCHOTTEN

Characterisation of the Conflict in Kosovo and Support for Investigations
☛ Federal Foreign Office, Statement on the Legality of Deportations in Kosovo under International Law [*Zur völkerrechtlichen Beurteilung der Deportationen im Kosovo*] (1999)
☛ Federal Foreign Office, Press Release of 12 May 1999

The German Federal Foreign Office has argued that there were two kinds of armed conflict during the 1999 Kosovo conflict. First, the NATO air attacks against the Federal Republic of Yugoslavia had to be qualified as an international armed conflict; second, the conflict between the Yugoslav Federal Army and the Kosovo Liberation Army had to be characterized as an armed conflict of a non-international character.

Notwithstanding its finding that violations of international humanitarian law applicable in non-international armed conflicts had been committed by the Yugoslav forces, the Federal Foreign Office qualified the forced displacements of the civilian population in Kosovo as genocide and crimes against humanity. The existence of an armed conflict is not necessary to commit those crimes.

The German Government has played an active role in documenting atrocities committed in Kosovo and in providing financial support for investigations. On 12 May 1999, the Federal Foreign Office presented further evidence to the International Criminal Tribunal for the Former Yugoslavia. Simultaneously, the German Government questioned refugees who stayed in Germany about human rights violations. Finally, the Federal Armed Forces interviewed people in Kosovo on-site.

SASCHA ROLF LÜDER and GREGOR SCHOTTEN

---

115. Act for Co-operation with the International Criminal Tribunal for the Former Yugoslavia of 10 April 1995 [*Gesetz über die Zusammenarbeit mit dem Internationalen Strafgerichtshof für das ehemalige Jugoslawien vom 10. April 1995*]. Published in *Bundesgesetzblatt* (1995) I, pp. 428 et seq.

116. Act on International Assistance in Criminal Matters of 23 December 1982 [*Gesetz über die internationale Rechtshilfe in Strafsachen vom 23. Dezember 1982*]. Published in I *Bundesgesetzblatt* (1994) pp. 1537 et seq.

Child Soldiers
☞ Statement of German Minister of Foreign Affairs before the 55th session of the United Nations Commission on Human Rights. Federal Foreign Office, Press Release of 23 March 1999

Before the 55th session of the United Nations Commission on Human Rights, the German Minister of Foreign Affairs condemned the recruitment of children in armed conflicts and requested that it be universally banned. Germany has supported the negotiation process of an Optional Protocol to the Convention on the Rights of the Child, on Involvement of Children in Armed Conflicts. One of the most contested provisions of the Protocol is the prohibition on the recruitment of children under the age of 18. The German government had earlier criticised the current age limit of 15[117] during the ratification process of the Convention in 1992.[118] When ratifying the Convention, the German Government made a formal declaration annexed to the declaration of ratification stating that the age limit of 15 was incompatible with other provisions of the Convention seeking to guarantee the protection of children. It also declared that Germany would not recruit soldiers under the age of 18. In the German Parliament, several initiatives undertaken by different factions called upon the German Government to advocate for the incorporation of a prohibition on recruiting children under the age of 15 in the Optional Protocol to the Convention on the Rights of the Child.[119]

SASCHA ROLF LÜDER and GREGOR SCHOTTEN

Humanitarian Assistance and Safety of Humanitarian Personnel
☞ Statement by the German Permanent Representative to the United Nations before the United Nations 53rd General Assembly regarding the conflict in Afghanistan. Permanent Mission of Germany to the United Nations, Press Release of 9 December 1998
☞ Statement of German Minister of Foreign Affairs re. humanitarian assistance to Kosovo. Federal Foreign Office, Press Release of 6 April 1999
☞ Coordinated Statement by Foreign Ministers of Germany, France, Great Britain, Italy and the United States. Federal Foreign Office, Press Release of 7 April 1999

Several recent statements acknowledge Germany's support for effective protection of humanitarian personnel and unimpeded access to humanitarian assistance. During a debate in the United Nations General Assembly in December 1998, the German Representative deplored attacks against international aid workers and criticised the denial of access to victims by warring factions in Afghanistan. He underlined that '(...) safety

---

117. Art. 38, para. 3 of the Convention.

118. Memorandum to the Convention on the Rights of the Child of 20 November 1989 Draft Act [*Entwurf eines Gesetzes zu dem Übereinkommen vom 20. November 1989 über die Rechte des Kindes, Denkschrift zu dem Übereinkommen*]. Published in *Bundestags-Drucksache* 12/42, p. 51.

119. Antrag der Fraktion der CDU/CSU, 'Gegen den Mißbrauch von Kindern als Soldaten', 26 January 1999. Published in *Bundestags-Drucksache* 14/310, p. 2; Antrag der Fraktion der PDS, 'Einsatz von Kindern als Soldaten wirksam verhindern', 17 March 1999. Published in *Bundestags-Drucksache* 14/552, p. 1; Antrag der Fraktionen der SPD und Bündnis '90/Die Grünen, 'Gegen den Einsatz von Kindern als Soldaten in bewaffneten Konflikten', 21 April 1999. Published in *Bundestags-Drucksache* 14/806, p. 1.

and security (of humanitarian personnel) was a non-negotiable issue and a prerequisite for the delivery of humanitarian assistance'.

In April 1999, the German Minister of Foreign Affairs called upon the President of the Federal Republic of Yugoslavia, Slobodan Milošević, to guarantee that humanitarian assistance could reach Kosovo and those who were on the verge of starvation. In a coordinated statement, the Foreign Ministers of Germany, France, Great Britain, Italy and the United States declared that an interruption of NATO air strikes and a cease-fire depended on the fulfillment of several conditions by the Yugoslav government. One of these conditions was unimpeded access for humanitarian aid to Kosovo.

These statements can be added to an already significant German practice indicating its acceptance of a customary principle that states have to grant access to humanitarian organisations in armed conflicts of an international and non-international character if the situation of the civilian population so requires.

SASCHA ROLF LÜDER and GREGOR SCHOTTEN

International Criminal Court
➤ Signature of the Rome Statute for the International Criminal Court on 10 December 1998. Federal Foreign Office, Press Release of 10 December 1998
➤ Statement of the Commissioner for Human Rights and Humanitarian Aid at the Federal Foreign Office regarding the ratification process of the International Criminal Court. Federal Foreign Office, Press Release of 23 April 1999
➤ Speech of the German Minister of Justice at the Conference of the Institut de Droit International [*Rede der Bundesministerin der Justiz bei der Tagung des Institut de Droit International*], Berlin, 17 August 1999. *Presse- und Informationsdienst der Bundesregierung: Regierungsbulletin* (1999) pp. 537 et seq.

The German Minister of Justice declared that Germany will ratify the Rome Statute for the International Criminal Court during the months to come and will simultaneously change those provisions of the GG[120] which are imperatively necessary for ratifying the Rome Statute.

Irrespective of the ratification of the Rome Statute as such, it remains to be seen how far the provisions of the Statute will be incorporated into German criminal law. As the general provisions of international humanitarian law are complex, the process of incorporation should be well planned. The Federal Ministry of Justice has asked an expert group to assist its legislative work.

SASCHA ROLF LÜDER and GREGOR SCHOTTEN

Cases
➤ *Sokolović* case, Higher Regional Court at Dusseldorf, Judgment of 29 November 1999 [*Oberlandesgericht Düsseldorf, Urteil vom 29 November 1999* - 2 StE 7/97]
➤ *Jorgić* case, Federal Supreme Court, Judgment of 30 April 1999 [*Bundesgerichtshof, Urteil vom 30. April 1999)* - 3 StR 215/98]

---

120. Basic Law for the Federal Republic of Germany of 23 May 1949 [*Grundgesetz für die Bundesrepublik Deutschland vom 23. Mai 1949*]. Published in I *Bundesgesetzblatt* (1949) pp. 1 et seq.

On 30 April 1999, the Federal Supreme Court (*Bundesgerichtshof*/BGH) held in its Appeals Judgment in the *Jorgić* case that, according to s. 6(1) of the StGB,[121] German domestic courts have only limited jurisdiction over persons accused of genocide (s. 220a of the StGB). *Nikolai Jorgić* had been the leader of a paramilitary group in the region of Doboj in Bosnia. Together with officials of the Bosnian Serbs, he had taken part in terrorist attacks against Bosnian Muslims in order to strengthen the Serbian policy of ethnic cleansing. *Jorgić* and others had assaulted and executed Bosnian Muslims, including the elderly and the handicapped.

Referring to the provisions of the Convention on the Prevention and Punishment of the Crime of Genocide, as implemented in Germany,[122] the Federal Supreme Court held that German courts only have jurisdiction where there is a special link between the offence which has been committed abroad and Germany. In the extant case, the Federal Supreme Court assumed such a link because the accused had lived in Germany from 1969 to 1982 and was still registered there. Moreover, his wife and daughter still lived in Germany. Furthermore, *Jorgić* had been arrested on German territory.[123]

The *Jorgić* Appeals Judgment confirmed an earlier decision of the Federal Supreme Court in the *Tadić* case, where the Court limited German jurisdiction over genocide by stipulating that there must be a special link between the offence which has been committed abroad and Germany.[124] This is in spite of the fact that in the StGB, the principle of universal jurisdiction is applied for genocide and violations of international humanitarian law.

The Federal Supreme Court also implicitly upheld the Higher Regional Court's findings as regards the classification of the Bosnian conflict. While the Higher Regional Court did not enquire whether or not the specific acts committed by the accused or other Bosnian Serbs had been ordered by the authorities of the Former Republic of Yugoslavia, it nevertheless determined the conflict to be international in character on the basis that the Bosnian Serbs fighting against the central authorities of Sarajevo had acted on behalf of the Federal Republic of Yugoslavia. The Court supported the finding in emphasising that Belgrade financed, organised and equipped the Bosnian Serb army and paramilitary units and that there existed between the JNA and the Bosnian Serbs a close personal, organisational and logistical interconnection, which was considered to be a sufficient basis for regarding the conflict as international. The view was expressly confirmed in the *Tadić* Appeals Judgment of the International Criminal Tribunal for the Former Yugoslavia of 15 July 1999.[125]

In another decision, the Higher Regional Court at Dusseldorf (*Oberlandesgericht Düsseldorf*/OLG Düsseldorf) held in the *Sokolović* case that, according to s. 6(9) of the

---

121. German Penal Code of 15 May 1871 [*Strafgesetzbuch vom 15. Mai 1871*]. Published in *Bundesgesetzblatt* (1987) pp. 1160 et seq.

122. Convention on the Prevention and Punishment of the Crime of Genocide of 9 December 1948 Act [*Konvention über die Verhütung und Bestrafung des Völkermordes vom 9. Dezember 1948*]. Published in *Bundesgesetzblatt* (1954) II, pp. 730 et seq.

123. In another recent case, the Federal Supreme Court rejected such a link. *Bundesgerichtshof, Beschluß vom 11. Dezember 1998* - 2 ARs 499/98.

124. *BGH-Ermittlungsrichter, Beschluß vom 13. Februar 1994* - BGs 100/94.

125. *The Prosecutor* v. *Duško Tadić*, Case No. IT-94-1T, Judgment of 15 July 1999, at paras. 137 and 145.

StGB, read with the relevant provisions of the GC,[126] German domestic courts have jurisdiction over grave breaches of the GC committed in the former Yugoslavia. The Court was of the opinion that German law is applicable when there is an armed conflict of an international character and the victims are protected persons under the provisions of the GC. The accused Bosnian Serb *Maksim Sokolović* had taken part in terrorist attacks against Bosnian Muslims and had participated in their execution.

Both judgments are problematic in part. In *Jorgić,* the Federal Supreme Court failed to notice that, according to international law, the scope of jurisdiction for genocide is universal. The domestic courts act in the interest of the international community when a criminal is punishable. In these cases, international law broadens domestic criminal jurisdiction in its enforcement with regard to the offence, the criminal or both. Consequently, the domestic courts prosecute instead of international bodies. According to this point of view, the domestic courts act as instruments of a decentralised enforcement of international law, of which the Convention on the Prevention and Punishment of the Crime of Genocide is a typical example.[127] Further, the Federal Supreme Court's decision in *Jorgić* and the decisions of other domestic courts explicitly refer to genocide. It is to be questioned if this limitation of jurisdiction can also be connected with war crimes and crimes against humanity.

In the *Sokolović* case, it was not sufficiently clear to what extent German courts should have jurisdiction over breaches of international humanitarian law applicable in non-international armed conflicts. On the one hand, breaches of international humanitarian law could not be prosecuted under Article 2 of the ICTY Statute when committed in an armed conflict of a non-international character. On the other hand, German courts could have jurisdiction to prosecute persons who violate the laws or customs of war according to Article 3 of the Statute which includes wrongful acts committed in internal conflicts, accepting that Article 3 of the Statute expresses a principle of customary international law. According to Article 103(2) of the GG, an act may be punishable only if it constitutes a criminal offence under written law. Therefore, although customary international law can be incorporated into German domestic law as such, customary law rules cannot be a legal basis for perpetrating a criminal offence under German domestic law. In contrast, a violation of common Article 3 of the four GC or of Article 4 of AP II,[128] which contain the fundamental guarantees of humane treatment in internal conflicts, can support a domestic criminal prosecution because of their written character.

---

126. Geneva Conventions of 12 August 1949 [*Genfer Abkommen vom 12. August 1949*]. Published in *Bundesgesetzblatt.* (1954) II, pp. 783 et seq.

127. See for example, R. Wolfrum, 'The Decentralized Prosecution of International Offences Through National Courts', in Y. Dinstein, and M. Tabory, eds., *War Crimes in International Law* (The Hague, Martinus Nijhoff Publishers 1996) pp. 233 et seq., at 236.

128. Protocols Additional to the Geneva Conventions of 12 August 1949 and Relating to the Protection of Victims of Armed Conflicts of 8 June 1977 [*Zusatzprotokolle zu den Genfer Abkommen vom 12. August 1949 über den Schutz der Opfer bewaffneter Konflikte vom 8. Juni 1977*]. Published in *Bundesgesetzblatt* (1990) II, pp. 1551 et seq.

Due to the fact that most current armed conflicts are of a non-international character, the scope of German jurisdiction for breaches of international humanitarian law applicable in those conflicts is still not broad enough.[129]

SASCHA ROLF LÜDER and GREGOR SCHOTTEN

☞ *Götzfried* case, Regional Court of Stuttgart, Judgment of 20 May 1999 [*Landgericht Stuttgart, Urteil vom 20. Mai 1999 - 2 Js 61533/97*]

In 1997, the Head Office in the State of Northrhine-Westphalia for the Prosecution of National Socialist Mass Crimes at the Department of Public Prosecution at Dortmund [*Zentralstelle im Lande Nordrhein-Westfalen für die Bearbeitung von national-sozialistischen Massenverbrechen bei der Staatsanwaltschaft Dortmund*] started investigations against *Alfons Götzfried* on the grounds of his alleged role in the execution of Jews in a Nazi concentration camp in Poland during World War II.[130] Accusations of having participated in 17,000 counts of aiding and abetting murder were subsequently laid against *Götzfried*. On 20 May 1999, the Regional Court of Stuttgart [*Landgericht Stuttgart/LG Stuttgart*] found *Götzfried* guilty of all 17,000 counts of aiding and abetting murder [*'Beihilfe'*] and sentenced him to ten years imprisonment for his role in the execution of at least 17,000 Jews in the Majdanek concentration camp on 3 November 1943. On that day, the so-called 'Operation Harvestfeast' [*'Aktion Erntefest'*] was carried out on the order of Himmler. This mass execution was the largest massacre during the so-called 'Operation Reinhard', the codename for the systematic extermination of Jews in Polish occupied territory. *Götzfried,* a Ukrainian-born man of German origin, belonged to the execution squad and shot approximately 500 of the victims. After he was unable to continue with the shooting because he felt sick, he refilled ammunition magazines for the executions.

The Court held that *Götzfried* participated in the mass execution conscious of the fact that the victims were killed out of an emotionless and merciless motivation and that they suffered severely, physically and mentally. He thereby aided and abetted the intentional killing of the victims, which, being committed cruelly and out of 'low motives' [*'niedrige Beweggründe'*], constitute murder according to s. 211(2) of the StGB. Despite the fact that *Götzfried* had himself killed approximately 500 victims, he could only be convicted for aiding and abetting as he found himself at the end of the chain of command, did not have any decision-making capacity, and had no overall control over and no individual interest in the commission of the crimes. The Court held that the same result is warranted by applying s. 47(1), sentence 2, No. 2 of the Military Penal Code.[131] The provision states that subordinates following orders are punishable for aiding and abetting if they know that the order of the superior concerns an action which constitutes a common or military crime. The Court rejected the defence of duress as the accused was not threatened by danger to life or limb if he had failed to comply with the orders. The Court emphasised that refusing to follow such orders in the said circumstances generally did not involve

---

129. See also, K. Ambos, 'Aktuelle Probleme der deutschen Verfolgung von 'Kriegsverbrechen' in Bosnien-Herzegowina', 19 *Neue Zeitschrift für Strafrecht* (1999) pp. 226 et seq.

130. *Staatsanwaltschaft Dortmund* – 45 Js 2/97.

131. Military Penal Code of 10 October 1940 [*Militärstrafgesetzbuch vom 10. Oktober 1940*]. Published in *Reichsgesetzblatt* (1940) pp. 1347 et seq.

a danger to life or limb, as exemplified by historical and expert research in the area. German criminal law was held to apply according to s. 7(2) No. 1 of the StGB, because the accused had acquired German citizenship after he had moved to Germany in 1991. The judgment is currently under appeal.

JANN K. KLEFFNER

Pending cases
☛ *Zepezaunes* case, Department of Public Prosecution at Braunschweig, Preliminary Proceedings [*Staatsanwaltschaft Braunschweig, Ermittlungsverfahren* - 703 Js 19606/97]

In 1997, the Head Office in the State of Northrhine-Westphalia for the Prosecution of National Socialistic Mass Crimes at the Department of Public Prosecution at Dortmund started investigations against *Zepezaunes* on the grounds of suspected murder. The Head Office suspects *Zepezaunes* of taking part in the execution of 42,000 civilians in the concentration camp of Majdanek concentration camp in Poland in 1943.[132] Meanwhile, the proceedings against *Zepezaunes* have been submitted to the Department of Public Prosecution at Braunschweig.

SASCHA ROLF LÜDER and GREGOR SCHOTTEN

☛ *Kusljić* case, Decision of State Court of Bavaria, 15 December 1999

On 15 December 1999, a court in Bavaria found Djuradj Kusljić guilty of genocide for ordering the killings of Bosnian Muslims. Kusljić, a former police chief who was arrested in Munich in 1998, was jailed for life.

GREECE
International Criminal Tribunals
☛ Law 2665 of 15/17 December 1998 Implementing Resolutions 827 (25 May 1993) and 955 (6 November 1995) of the United Nations Security Council establishing the International Criminal Tribunals for the Former Yugoslavia and Rwanda, respectively. Published in *Government Gazette* vol. A, p. 279

Law 2665/1998 purports to fulfil Greece's obligation to abide by the resolutions of the UN Security Council concerning the International Criminal Tribunals.[133] The promulgation of such a law was not inevitable as Greece has already a statute on the implementation of Security Council resolutions in the domestic legal order: Necessity Law 92/1967 was adopted in the aftermath of the Rhodesia crisis and has constituted the legal basis of all implementation actions for sanctions imposed by the Security Council ever since.[134] Although, admittedly, the creation of these two *ad hoc* Criminal Tribunals does not fall

---

132. *Staatsanwaltschaft Dortmund* – 45 Js 1/97.

133. Art. 25 of the Charter as ratified by Necessity Law 585/1945, GG A 242 and 286.

134. See for instance, Jenny Stavridi, 'Actes et positions de la Grèce en 1997, Implementation by Greece of Security Council Resolutions adopted within the framework of Chapter VII of the UN Chapter', 50 *RHDI* (1997) pp. 290-291; idem, 51 *RHDI* (1998).

into any of the traditional types of enforcement action envisaged in Chapter VII of the Charter, it could still be argued that the two-tiered procedure[135] established by Necessity Law 92/1967 could be adapted to the necessities of the present case.

Alternatively, Greece could have joined a number of other states[136] which have declared that no implementing legislation is required in order to cooperate with the Tribunal. Indeed a request by the Tribunal for assistance under Article 29 of the ICTY Statute is, after all, but a specific measure under Chapter VII of the UN Charter,[137] a mandatory resolution of the Security Council with superlegislative force in the domestic legal order according to Article 28 of the Constitution.[138] Moreover, the Tribunal itself has further prescribed particular implementation procedures in its own, perennially modified, Rules of Procedure and Evidence.[139] Indeed, the former President of the ICTY, Antonio Cassese, has repeatedly declared that the obligation of states to enact implementing domestic legislation is but an 'obligation of means',[140] the lack of which does not relieve a state from its duty to comply with the requests and orders issued by the Tribunal.[141] Such a construction would also help cover some obvious inadequacies of the implementing law, which, in a rather embarrassing omission,[142] makes no reference to Security Council Resolution 1166/1998, whereby a third Trial Chamber of the International Tribunal for the former Yugoslavia was established. Strictly speaking, the International Tribunal recognised by the Greek legal order is one comprised of two Trial Chambers and one Appeals Chamber.[143]

The procedure established by Law 2665/1998 follows what seems to be a rather general pattern. Thus, Article 5 recognises the general principle of the primacy of the Tribunal

---

135. On the particulars of this procedure see M. Gavouneli, 'The introduction and implementation of UN Security Council resolutions in the Greek legal system', 51 *RHDI* (1998) pp. 219-230.

136. Among them, the Russian Federation, the Republic of Korea, Venezuela and Singapore; see *Report of the International Tribunal for the Prosecution of Persons Responsible for Serious Violations of International Humanitarian Law committed in the Territory of the Former Yugoslavia since 1991*, A/53/219, S/1998/737, 10 August 1998 [http://www.un.org/icty/rapportan/rapport5-e.htm].

137. See para. 4 of Res. 827/1993 and para. 2 of Res. 955/1995. This was also *per* President Cassese in ICTY, *Prosecutor* v. *Duško Tadić*, Case No. IT-94-1-AR72, *Decision on the Defence Motion for Interlocutory Appeal on Jurisdiction*, paras. 33-36; see also ICTR, *Prosecutor* v. *Joseph Kanyabashi*, Case No. ICTR-96-15-T, *Decision on the Defence Motion on Jurisdiction*, 18 June 1997, 18 *HRLJ* (1997) pp. 343-347.

138. On the status of international law in the Greek legal order see Emmanuel Roucounas, Grèce, in Pierre-Marie Eisemann, ed., *L'intégration du droit international et communautaire dans l'ordre juridique national* (The Hague, Kluwer Law International 1996) pp. 287-315.

139. For instance, the procedure for the execution of arrest warrants is described in Rule 55(B) whereas Rule 40*bis* provides for the provisional arrest and detention of suspects and their transfer to the Tribunal.

140. ICTY, *Prosecutor* v. *Blaškić*, Case No. IT-95-14-T, para. 8. *Decision on the objection of the Republic of Croatia to the issuance of subpoena duces tecum*, 18 July 1997.

141. See also the President's *Memorandum on the Obligation of States to Pass Legislation Implementing the Tribunal's Statute*, March 1996 and most recently a letter dated 8 September 1998 from the President of the International Tribunal for the Prosecution of Persons Responsible for Serious Violations of International Humanitarian Law Committed in the Territory of the Former Yugoslavia to the President of the Security Council, UN Doc. S/1998/839.

142. The truth of the matter seems to be that the necessary preparatory acts had been concluded a long time in advance and the bill was presented to Parliament without updating.

143. Art. 11 of the Statute.

over the domestic legal order, whereas Article 4 requires that criminal charges brought in Greece against a person already sought by or appearing before the International Tribunal shall be declared inadmissible. All actions further envisaged by the implementing legislation constitute manifestations of that same principle:

1. *Transfer order.* According to Article 7 of Law 2665/1998, a request by the International Tribunal for the surrender of a person shall be addressed to the Minister of Justice, who in turn refers the case to the Public Prosecutor at the Athens Court of Appeal. Upon receipt of the application, the Public Prosecutor issues a warrant for the arrest of the person wanted, who, once apprehended, is brought before the Judicial Council of the Court of Appeal. The procedure thus established attests to the willingness of the legislator to comply with such requests in a speedy and summary manner. The Judicial Council is a panel of Judges usually deciding *in camera,*[144] although in this case the hearing is conducted in public. Their decisions must be reasoned like all court decisions[145] and the whole procedure is carried out under the same requirements of judicial independence and impartiality as in any other trial. Appeal against a decision of the Judicial Council is allowed before *Areios Pagos*.

The Judicial Council is called to effectively carry out two types of review. The first, set out in Article 10(1), constitutes a fairly typical example of 'legality review':[146] the Chamber ascertains whether the person arrested is actually the same person as the person whose transfer is requested[147] and whether the typical prerequisites of temporal and territorial jurisdiction of the Tribunal actually concur in the case under consideration. Once these questions are answered in the affirmative, the Judicial Council has no alternative but to surrender the defendant to the International Tribunal.

The second type of review, however, relates to the merits of the case and raises a number of issues, since it is perhaps in direct contravention of the principle of primacy over domestic jurisdiction established both by Article 9(2) of the ICTY Statute and Article 5 of Law 2665/1998. The investigation of alleged crimes and the accumulation of sufficient evidence against a person that would justify his indictment falls, according to Article 18 of the Statute, under the primary responsibility of the Office of the Prosecutor, who has 'the power to question suspects, victims and witnesses, to collect evidence and to conduct on-site investigations'. It is difficult to argue that a request for the surrender of a person, which is the result of such an elaborate procedure with the full guarantees of the rule of law, could be effectively subjected to a review of the merits by a national

---

144. In ordinary criminal investigations the procedure before the Judicial Councils constitutes a phase of the pre-trial stage. Once the ordinary investigation is completed, the prosecutor reports to the Judicial Council with a motion either to refer the case to trial or to acquit the defendant. For a general overview of the Greek criminal procedure system see Dionyssios D. Spinellis, 'Criminal Law and Procedure' in Konstantinos D. Kerameus and Phaedon J. Kozyris, eds., *Introduction to Greek Law*, 2nd edn. (Deventer, Kluwer 1993) pp. 339-365, 359.

145. Art. 93(3) of the Constitution.

146. See also Photini Pazartzis, Loi no. 2665/1998. Application des résolutions 827/25-5-1993 et 955/8-11-1994 du Conseil de sécurité de l'organisation des Nations Unies instituant deux Tribunaux pénaux internationaux chargés de juger des violations graves du droit international humanitaire commis sur les territoires de l'ex Yougoslavie et du Rwanda, 52 *RDHI* (1999).

147. A case of mistaken identity was already addressed by the ICTY Prosecutor: Case No. IT-95-8-T, Decision, Order for the Withdrawal of the Charges against the Person named Goran Lajić and for his Release, 17 June 1996.

judge without full knowledge of the facts of the case. Yet Article 10(2) of Law 2665/1998 grants to the Judicial Council at the Court of Appeal the authority to appoint an investigating magistrate, a *juge rapporteur*, who would be charged with the compilation of any additional evidentiary material.

Much more problematic is the second prerequisite of this review of the merits: the double criminality question,[148] which brings the concepts and preconceptions of the national legal order to the fore. Thus, not only may the Judicial Council refuse a request for the surrender of a person, if the act for which he stands accused is not punishable under Greek law, but also a sentence imposed by the International Tribunal may not be recognised and thus carried out in Greece.[149] In practice, all four categories of crimes falling within the ambit of the Tribunal are punishable under Greek law: crimes of war and crimes against humanity are sanctioned both in the Criminal Code and the Military Criminal Code[150] whereas Greece has ratified both the 1948 Convention on the Prevention and Punishment of the Crime of Genocide[151] and the 1949 Geneva Conventions[152] and 1977 Additional Protocols I[153] and II[154] thereto. It is interesting to note, however, that scarcely a national implementing law exists that would not include a similar 'national review clause' under some guise.

2. *Judicial assistance*. The Tribunal has been at great pains to emphasise that all acts of cooperation and assistance requested by states, including the surrender of the suspect or the defendant, do not amount to extradition and thus the established extradition procedures do not apply, not even *mutatis mutandis* – the traditional prohibition of extraditing nationals being the major stumbling block.[155] However, almost all national legislatures and implementing statutes – including the Greek one – have used extradition as a point of reference. True to this universal trend, the procedure set out in Article 10 of Law 2665/1998 on the review of an arrest warrant refers expressly to Articles 448 and 450 of the Code of Criminal Procedure on extradition. Even the right of appeal against the legality review of a decision or warrant, under Article 5(2), is modelled on the same procedure used under Article 451 of the Code of Criminal Procedure during extradition proceedings.

As regards reluctant witnesses, the Law extends to them the application of domestic rules compelling their appearance at court[156] or before the investigating magistrate.[157] The provisions on false testimony and perjury[158] are also applicable for acts committed before the ICTY. There is, however, no special provision for the protection of witnesses

---

148. In spite of the fact that the criminality of conduct brought to the attention of the International Tribunal is to be judged solely on the basis of international law; ILC, *Report to the General Assembly*, UN Doc. A/47/10, Annex; UN Doc. A/48/10, Annex 4.

149. Art. 13 para. 2(b) of Law 2665/1998.

150. See Maria Gavouneli, Military Criminal Code, 1 *YIHL* (1998) pp. 445-449.

151. Ratified by Legislative Decree 3091/1954.

152. Ratified by Law 3481/1956.

153. Ratified by Law 1786/1988.

154. Ratified by Law 2015/1992.

155. Indeed, going even further, in a formulation to be found in all Greek Constitutions since the independence of the modern Greek State, Art. 5(2)(b) of the Constitution stipulates: 'The extradition of a foreigner, prosecuted for its activity for freedom, is prohibited.'

156. Art. 353 of the Code of Criminal Procedure.

157. Art. 229 of the Code of Criminal Procedure.

158. Arts. 224-228 of the Criminal Code.

willing to testify before the International Tribunal, although the ICTY has already developed a certain practice on the subject.[159] Should the need arise, one could well envisage the conclusion of an agreement similar to that with the United Kingdom for the relocation of witnesses endangered by testifying at the Tribunal.[160]

3. *Enforcement of sentences*. According to Article 27 of the Statute, sentences imposed by the Tribunal may be served in the territory of a state which has indicated to the Security Council its willingness to accept convicted persons. Greece joins a host of states which, although they have included in their implementing legislation provisions for the enforcement of sentences in their territory,[161] have made no such formal announcement to either the Security Council or the Tribunal. The actual service of the sentence is to be carried out according to the national legislation of the state concerned, subject to the supervision of the International Tribunal,[162] which has recently elaborated a series on codes of conduct applicable to persons held by the Court pending procedures against them:[163] it is to be expected that the gist of these provisions would also apply to conditions of imprisonment in national penitentiary institutions.

The latter are fully safeguarded in the domestic legal order. Article 13(2) of Law 2665/1998 sets out a procedure for the 'recognition' of the convicting decision and the 'conversion' of the sentence imposed to the system of penalties provided for in the Greek legal system: incarceration for a maximum of five years for misdemeanours[164] and imprisonment for a longer period, including life, for crimes.[165] There is no provision for the death penalty neither in the Statute[166] nor in the Greek legal order.[167]

As to the duration of the sentence, the Statute itself provides in Article 28 for the commutation of the sentences imposed or even the granting of pardon to the person convicted. Article 14 of the implementing law reproduces almost verbatim this provision, recognising the competence of the International Tribunal to have the final word on the subject.

MARIA GAVOUNELI

---

159. See most recently *Decision of Trial Chamber I on the protective measures for General Philippe Morillon, witness of the trial chamber*, 12 May 1999.

160. ICTY Doc. CC/PIU/258-E, 7 November 1997.

161. These include the Netherlands, Sweden, Switzerland, Belgium, Spain and Austria.

162. Art. 27 of the Statute and Rules 103-104 of the Rules of Procedure and Evidence.

163. See for instance, *Rules of Detention*, Rev. 7, 17 November 1997; *Regulations to govern the supervision of visits to and communications with the detainees*, Rev. 3, July 1999. A similar agreement has been concluded between the International Criminal Tribunal for the Former Yugoslavia and the International Committee of the Red Cross on procedure of visiting persons held on the authority of the Tribunal, *IRRC* no. 311 (1996) p. 238.

164. Art. 53 of the Criminal Code.

165. Art. 52 of the Criminal Code.

166. Art. 24 para. 1 of the Statute.

167. Greece ratified the 1966 International Covenant on Civil and Political Rights, the Optional Protocol and the Second Optional Protocol thereto on the Abolition of the Death Penalty by Law 2462/1997, Art. 2 of which contains a reservation as to the availability of the death penalty in times of war and only for an extremely grave offence of a military nature.

HUNGARY[168]

Cases

☛ Decisions of the Supreme Court on the Applicability of the Geneva Conventions. Decisions of 5, 10 and 17 November 1998. [Decisions not published officially but can be obtained from the Court in xerox form using these identification numbers: Bf.V.1344/1998/3; Bf.V.1759/1998/3; and bf.V.1760/1998/3]

☛ Decision of 28 June 1999 of the Revision Panel of the Supreme Court,[169] cancelling the three above-mentioned decisions

The *Yearbook of International Humanitarian Law* (1998 pp. 451-455) presented the interpretation of the Constitutional Court of the status of the 1949 Geneva Conventions in the Hungarian constitutional system. Footnote 102 of the commentary referred to criminal proceedings directed against those charged with war crimes committed during their participation in the repression of the 1956 uprising.

Because the district courts in the referred cases did not accept the applicability of common Article 3 of the 1949 Geneva Conventions to the above-mentioned atrocities, the state attorney submitted an appeal and the cases were sent to the Supreme Court, which rendered its decisions on the 5th, 10th and 17th of November 1998 in three analogous cases with similar reasoning.[170]

In fact, three acts were put before the Supreme Court: the shootings in the towns of Tiszakécske (27/10/1956), Kecskemét (26/10/1956) and Tatabánya (27/10/1956). As was shown in the commentary in the 1998 *YIHL,* the real issue was the question of prescription. Murder was already covered by prescription, but war crimes are imprescriptible in international law and also in the Hungarian legal system.

The Supreme Court stated correctly that 'common article 3 of the 1949 Conventions does not say precisely what is the real content of a non-international armed conflict'. But it then made the same legal error as the above-mentioned district courts, that is, confusion of the scope of application of Additional Protocol II of 1977 with that of common Article 3 of 1949.

The Supreme Court correctly identified that there is no definition of a non-international armed conflict in common Article 3, but there is without a doubt a formal definition of such a conflict in Article 1 of Additional Protocol II.[171]

---

168. Information and commentary provided by Péter Kovács, Professor of International Law, Péter Pázmány Catholic University of Budapest and Miskolc University, Hungary. Unofficial translations of the decisions have been made by Professor Kovács.

169. The Hungarian Code of Criminal Procedure recognises the 'revision' of a *res judicata* in case of an error in law committed by the Court of final instance (§ 284 of the Code of Criminal Procedure). The revision can be proposed by the condemned, his counsel or (in case of a death in custody) a family member or his attorney (§ 284(A)). The Revision Panel is normally composed of three Judges of the Supreme Court. It is composed of five Judges of the Supreme Court if the challenged sentence was passed by the Supreme Court (§ 287). If the Revision Panel declares the motion to be well-founded, the penal procedure should be relaunched at the first instance (§ 291). In this case, the revision was formally initiated by the Office of the Chief State Attorney.

170. The quoted excerpts of the Supreme Court decisions are the same in all three cases.

171. Art. 1 provides:

1. This Protocol, which develops and supplements Art. 3 common to the Geneva Conventions of 12 August 1949 without modifying its existing conditions of application, shall apply to all armed conflicts which are not covered by Art. 1 of the Protocol Additional to the Geneva Conventions of

The Supreme Court started from highly dubious premises: 'To develop and supplement a treaty means, without any doubt – on the basis of the grammatical interpretation of these notions – that the Court has to base its decision on an examination of both of the treaties, i.e., the basic one and the supplementing one. Any legal interpretation should be exercised only by the common interpretation of both instruments. The Supreme Court arrived at the conclusion that there is only one possible interpretation [of common Article 3 of 1949] and that is the one which is enshrined in Article 1(1-2) of the Protocol.'

As a logical consequence thereof, the Supreme Court stated that no precise territory was seized in 1956, no concerted military operations were carried out by insurgents and thus international humanitarian law was not applicable. That is, no grave humanitarian law breaches occurred during the events in Tiszakécske, Kecskemét and Tatabánya and no war crimes were committed. The shootings should be considered as 'simple' murder, already covered by prescription.

The decision was criticised in the scientific literature, *inter alia*, because the Supreme Court's interpretation had no solid basis in public international law. Neither in customary law nor in the 1969 Vienna Convention on the Law of Treaties can one find such an alleged rule of interpretation as mentioned in the rulings of the Supreme Court. Further, the grammatical interpretation given by the Supreme Court to the terms of Protocol II of 1977 was very strange. Finally, the interpretation of an *anterior* treaty on the basis of a *posterior* treaty is hardly reconcilable with the principle of *effet intertemporel*.

In sum, the interpretation given by the Supreme Court seemed to be too far removed from that which is taught in humanitarian law textbooks, and which shows the link between common Article 3 and the Second Protocol as being like two concentric circles: from the point of view of the scope of application of the two instruments, the greater circle is common Article 3 of 1949 and the smaller one is Protocol II. The ruling of the Supreme Court, however, was based on the following logic: if the object that is in my hand is not an apple, it is certain that it cannot be a fruit.

The author of the current commentary sent a scientific article to the presidency of the Supreme Court, pointing out the serious errors in interpretation. Some articles were also published in the media and a critical colloquium was held by an organisation called Független Jogászfórum (Independent Forum of Lawyers).

This much-criticised *dictum* was not the last-word on the matter, however. On 28 June 1999, the Revision Panel of the Supreme Court annulled its previous decision, with the following explanation: 'The Supreme Court had erroneously interpreted the relationship between common Article 3 and Protocol II of 1977 and it made a mistake in the analysis of the scope of application of these instruments. The Court committed in this way an error when it declared that humanitarian law was applicable in the given circumstances.'

---

12 August 1949, and relating to the Protection of Victims of International Armed Conflicts (Protocol I) and which take place in the territory of a High Contracting Party between its armed forces and dissident armed forces or other organized armed groups which, under responsible command, exercise such control over a part of its territory as to enable them to carry out sustained and concerted military operations and to implement this Protocol.

2. This Protocol shall not apply to situations of internal disturbances and tensions, such as riots, isolated and sporadic acts of violence and other acts of a similar nature, as not being armed conflicts.

This decision of the Revision Panel cancels not only the decisions of the Supreme Court but also those of the District Courts. The cases will now return to the District Court for retrial, based on a correct interpretation of public international law.

PÉTER KOVÁCS

INDIA

Education and Training

The Association of Indian Universities, in consultation with experts in international humanitarian law, drafted model syllabi on international humanitarian law for undergraduate law courses at all Indian Universities. Humanitarian Law will form part of a compulsory subject in the law course, namely, 'Human Rights and International Law'. The Association also drafted a model syllabus of a full paper on IHL for Masters of Arts in Defence and Strategic Studies courses of Indian Universities. Both the syllabi have been recommended by the Association to all the Indian Universities for inclusion in their courses of study. Most of the universities have followed the recommendations of the Association.

The National Law School of India, Bangalore, organised a two-week long South Asian Teaching Session on International Humanitarian Law and Refugee Law in May 1999 in collaboration with the International Committee of the Red Cross and the Office of the United Nations High Commissioner for Refugees. The session was aimed at post-graduate students, researchers and young lecturers in international law, human rights and international relations from South Asia. Thirty persons from Bangladesh, Bhutan, India, Nepal and Pakistan participated in the teaching session.

Finally, the Indian Academy of International Law established by the Indian Society of International Law has launched a one-year Diploma programme in Human Rights, Humanitarian Law and Refugee Law from August 1999.

SARAH KHAN[172]

IRAN[173]

Chemical Weapons

☛ Bill authorising Iran to ratify the Chemical Weapons Convention, passed by the Iranian Parliament on 27 July 1997

☛ Instrument of ratification/Letter of Deposition of Iran's Instrument of ratification of the Chemical Weapons Convention with accompanying Declaration, 3 November 1997

On 27 July 1997, the Iranian parliament – the Islamic Consultative Assembly – approved a bill authorising the Iranian government to join the Convention on the Prohibition of the Development, Production, Stockpiling and Use of Chemical Weapons and on Their Destruction (CWC), which it signed on 13 January 1993. This was followed by the deposition of Iran's instrument of ratification of the CWC with the UN Secretary-General,

---

172. Sarah Khan is with the Indian Red Cross Society.

173. Information and comment by Mehrdad Rezaeian, Director for International Affairs, Dadpajooh Institute for legal studies and services.

the depositary of the CWC, on 3 November 1997. Annexed to this instrument of ratification was a declaration on Iran's position regarding this Convention.

To realise the importance of the ratification of the CWC by Iran, certain factors should be taken into account. First, it should be noted that although Iran is a State Party to the 1925 Geneva Protocol for the Prohibition of the Use in War of Asphyxiating, Poisonous or Other Gases, and of Bacteriological Methods of Warfare, it has been one of the major victims of the use of chemical weapons in recent decades. During the Iran-Iraq War (1980-1988), such weapons were used repeatedly and on a massive scale against Iranian soldiers and civilians, a fact affirmed by the missions dispatched by the UN SG to investigate the matter, and later reflected in SC Res. 620 of 26 August 1988.

Second, Iran is among those states that actively participated in the negotiations held in the framework of the Committee, and then the Conference on Disarmament on chemical weapons, which ultimately resulted in the adoption of the CWC on 13 January 1993. The positions expressed in the declaration annexed to its instrument of ratification are, to a large extent, influenced by the positions of the Iranian representatives during these negotiations.

Another factor which signifies the importance of the ratification of the CWC by the Iranian Government is that Iran has been subject to various accusations over the last 20 years, mainly by the United States and Israel, concerning its political and military ambitions. Acting on such beliefs, some countries have restricted their trade with Iran of certain materials and technologies that are considered to help it develop its arsenal of nuclear and chemical weapons. Denying such accusations and stressing the fact that Iran itself has been a victim of the use of chemical weapons, the Iranian government has on many occasions stated its policy against acquiring or developing such weapons. In this atmosphere, the Iranian authorities found it necessary to take a step such as the ratification of the CWC to confirm their determination and commitment not to acquire, develop or use weapons of mass destruction, including chemical weapons.

A number of aspects of the Declaration are worth noting. First, paragraph 1 quotes the text of the legislation passed by the Iranian parliament. The wording used in paragraph 2, providing for the withdrawal from the CWC in certain situations, differs from the usual phraseology employed by Iran in similar cases where a treaty was ratified. It is evident that, in view of Article 16 of the Convention, it adds nothing to what the Iranian government is in principle entitled to do. But taken together with paragraphs 2-7 of the Declaration annexed to the instrument of ratification, it indicates the situations that Iran believes would justify its withdrawal.

It should also be noted that the substantive debate in the Islamic Consultative Assembly on the ratification of the CWC was held on 8 June 1997. Although a decision to that effect was taken on that date, the Council of Guardians – an organ responsible for deciding on the conformity of the Assembly's legislation with the Constitution and Islamic tenets – returned the Bill to the Assembly for certain modifications to be applied in the single article legislation, regarding which authority has the power to decide on withdrawing from the CWC. In the decision of 8 June 1997, it was provided that upon the proposal of the Ministry of Foreign Affairs, the Council of Ministers should have the power to decide on withdrawing from the CWC. In the Act of 27 July 1997, however, such power was declared as vested in the Supreme National Security Council, after a proposition to that effect by the Council of Ministers. This change was mainly due to the powers and authority vested in the Leader of the Islamic Republic of Iran, the highest authority in accordance with the Iranian Constitution.

Secondly, Article 11 of the CWC on economic and technological development in the field of chemical activities seems to be of great importance for the Iranian authorities. In view of the specific language of this Article, which may be differently interpreted by different states, Iran is stating its understanding and interpretation of this matter. Although no explicit obligation on industrialised countries to provide chemicals and technological information to other countries is envisaged in Article 11, the Iranian government believes that such an obligation can be deduced from the principles of 'promoting free trade and international cooperation' envisaged in the preamble and Article 11. Indeed, this was one of the main reasons why the Iranian government decided to ratify the Convention. Speaking at a plenary meeting of the Islamic Consultative Assembly on 8 June 1997, Dr. Zarif, the Iranian Deputy Foreign Minister on Legal and International Affairs, stated that 'in accordance with Article 11:

> . . . the [States] Parties to the Convention have a duty to cooperate in the transfer of technological information and data and materials necessary for chemical industry, which is of special importance for the Islamic Republic of Iran . . . Non-membership of States in the Chemical Weapons Convention shall be a pretext to impede the export of chemical materials . . .'[174]

It therefore appears from the Iranian declaration that States Parties to the Convention should not be able to impose any trade restrictions against Iran based on their national policy, except action decided upon in the framework of the CWC. It is not certain, however, that this interpretation is accepted by those states which, in Iran's opinion, are obliged to furnish chemical and technological information to countries like Iran after they become Parties to the Convention.

The third point to be mentioned here concerns the principle of non-discrimination in the implementation of the Convention. In that regard, there is a strong belief in Iran that the policy adopted by the so-called 'Group of Australia' to impose restrictions on their trade of chemical materials and relevant technological information with certain countries that may, in the opinion of members of the Group, use such materials and information in the development and manufacturing of chemical weapons, is not applied on a transparent and impartial basis. In accordance with this view, while Iran has been subject to such restrictions on the basis of unproven accusations, no action has been taken against countries like Israel that have not acceded to the Convention and which have created an arsenal of chemical and other weapons of mass destruction. In this regard, CWC ratification seems to endanger Iran's national security.

Representing those who are of this point of view, Mr Yahyavi, one of the Iranian Parliament Deputies who spoke out against the Bill on the CWC ratification when it was discussed in the Islamic Consultative Assembly, stated that '. . . as long as our enemies are producing and stockpiling such weapons, we have to make efforts to acquire the same weapons. (. . .) If we join this Convention, we will tie our own hands in confronting

---

174. Verbatim Records of the Islamic Consultative Assembly annexed to the Official Gazette of the Islamic Republic of Iran, No. 15270, 8 June 1997, p. 38.

those enemies that would use such weapons against us and have not signed [the Convention] and are publicly announcing that "we will not do so".'[175]

In spite of this opposition, the majority of the Parliament approved the ratification bill along with the declaration. This means that the majority was of the view that, with participation in the OPCW's activities, Iran will be able to draw the attention of the international community to its peaceful and humanitarian policies. But it remains to be seen whether Iran would be able to act in accordance with its declaration, that is, to withdraw from the Convention, if the conditions stipulated in the declaration are not realised. In such a situation, one could expect a strong reaction on the part of other states, especially certain members of the UN Security Council, as happened in the case of North Korea when it tried to withdraw from the Nuclear Non-Proliferation Treaty.

MEHRDAD REZAEIAN

IRELAND[176]

Implementing Legislation (Additional Protocols)
☛ Geneva Conventions (Amendment) Act 1998 (1998 No. 35). Published in *Irish Current Law Statutes,* Round Hall/Sweet & Maxwell, 1998

The purpose of this Act is to enable Ireland to ratify the two Additional Protocols adopted in 1977 to the four Geneva Conventions of 1949. The new Act operates mainly by way of amendment to legislation adopted earlier in order to ratify the Geneva Conventions.[177] That it took over 20 years to give effect to the Protocols in Irish law is a reflection of the low priority attached to international humanitarian law responsibilities by successive Irish governments.

In most respects, the 1998 Act makes no more than the minimum changes required to translate the requirements of the two Protocols into Irish law, but in one significant respect it goes further: Section 4 provides for criminal sanctions not only for grave breaches of the Geneva Conventions and Protocol I but also for breaches of Protocol II, and for minor breaches of the Geneva Conventions and Protocol I (i.e., breaches other than grave breaches), without there being an international law obligation to do so. This seems to be in line with an emerging trend to criminalise violations of international humanitarian law committed in non-international armed conflicts, as seen in the Statute of the ICTR and the jurisprudence of both *ad hoc* International Criminal Tribunals, as well as the Statute of the ICC.

Unlike the situation in respect of grave breaches, where universal jurisdiction applies, jurisdiction in respect of minor breaches is variously based on territoriality and nationality. Under section 4 of the Geneva Conventions Act 1962, as amended by Section 4 of the 1998 Act, jurisdiction within the state, both in respect of the commission of minor breaches and of the failure to prevent their commission, extends over any person 'whatever his or her nationality'. Extraterritorial jurisdiction in relation to such offences

---

175. Ibid. p. 34.

176. Information provided by Professor Colm Campbell, University of Ulster and Mr Ray Murphy, National University of Ireland, Galway.

177. The Geneva Conventions Act 1962 ('the Principal Act'), the Red Cross Act 1954 and the Prisoner of War and Enemy Aliens Act 1956.

extends only to Irish citizens. While the section refers to 'minor breaches' of Protocol II, this is to be taken to refer to any 'contravention' of the Protocol by virtue of Subsection 4(4) of the 1962 Act as substituted by Subsection 4(1)(g) of the 1998 Act.

Section 5 facilitates the proof of application of any of the Conventions or of Protocols I and II in court proceedings by way of certificate from the Minister for Foreign Affairs. In effect, it dispenses with the need for formal proof of ratification. Where the question of applicability is raised in appropriate proceedings, the Minister shall determine the issue. Such a question might involve complex questions of law and fact and could be expected to be subject to judicial review.

Section 6 inserts a new section (5A) into the Geneva Conventions Act 1962 that allows judicial notice to be taken of a report of the International Fact-Finding Commission provided for under Protocol I. Article 90(2) of Protocol I permits High Contracting Parties to declare that they recognise *ipso facto* the competence of the Commission to inquire into certain allegations. Provision in the Act that judicial notice be taken of a report of the Commission facilitates domestic proceedings by dispensing with the formal proofs which would otherwise be required in respect of such reports.

Sections 9, 10, 11, 12 and 13 deal with administrative matters in relation to the use of signs, emblems and information cards. The thrust of Section 14 of the 1998 Act is to extend the category of those subject to the regime governing the detention of prisoners of war (POWs) in the Prisoner of War and Enemy Aliens Act 1956, in response to the changes introduced by Protocol I. The 1956 Act, which was introduced as a result of Ireland having signed the Third and Fourth Geneva Conventions in 1949, provides for the internment of prisoners of war and enemy aliens. Section 14 provides that reference to POWs in the 1956 Act is to include reference to unprivileged combatants. It is submitted that the effect of this is not to grant POW status to this category but rather to subject them to the same detention regime as that provided for POWs. This view is buttressed by the fact that section 1(2A) of the 1956 Act (as inserted by the 1998 Act) stipulates that reference to POWs is to include 'reference to mercenaries (within the meaning of Article 47 of Protocol I)', despite the fact that Article 47 stipulates that 'A mercenary shall not have the right to be a combatant or a prisoner of war.' The implication is that while such unprivileged combatants and mercenaries could be tried for their actions, they would otherwise be treated as equivalent to POWs.

Section 15 contains an important provision restricting the application of Section 12 of the Extradition Act 1965, which requires that extradition not be granted for offences under military law which are not offences under ordinary criminal law. The effect of Section 15 is to ensure that this exception in respect of military offences does not extend to a grave or minor breach of the Conventions or of Protocol I, or to minor breaches of Protocol II. Under the provision of the Conventions, which also apply in respect of Protocol I, States Parties are obliged under the principle *aut dedere aut iudicare* either to extradite or to try those suspected of grave breaches. Section 15 is calculated to ensure that this obligation can be discharged, but goes further than required in that it extends beyond grave breaches to include minor breaches of Protocols I and II. The reference to 'minor breaches' of Protocol II must be read in light of Section 4 of the 1998 Act so that the definition of 'minor breach' in that section includes 'a contravention of Protocol I'. The reference to 'minor breach of Protocol II' in Section 14 of the 1998 Act is therefore intended to refer to any breach of Protocol II, since by virtue of Subsection 18(2) of the 1998 Act, the Geneva Convention Act 1962 and the 1998 Act are to be construed together as one.

Section 18(5) provides that the Act shall come into operation on such day as the Minister for Foreign Affairs may appoint by order. The two instruments of ratification were lodged with the Swiss government in Bern on 19 May 1999, and a commencement order must be published and take effect six months after the date of lodgment, i.e., 19 November 1999. Section 8 of the Act enables the Minister for Foreign Affairs to publish in a statutory instrument any reservation or declaration made by the state in relation to Protocols I and II. No indication was given in the course of the Parliamentary debates as to the nature of any declaration or reservation that might be made. There are a number of proposed declarations and reservations, but these have not yet been published.

RAY MURPHY and COLM CAMPBELL

International Criminal Tribunals
☛ International War Crimes Tribunal Act, 1998 (1998, No. 40). Published in *Irish Current Law Statutes*, Round Hall/Sweet & Maxwell, 1998

The purpose of the Act is to enable Ireland to fulfil its obligations to cooperate with the ICTY and ICTR in the performance of their functions relating to the prosecution and punishment of serious violations of international humanitarian law.

While the Act deals specifically with the ICTY and the ICTR, Section 37 enables regulations to be made to apply the provisions of the Act to any other war crimes tribunal or court that may be established by the UN in the future. This is a significant provision, which may be invoked by the Minister to comply with the requirements arising from the establishment of similar *ad hoc* international tribunals as the need arises.

Part II of the Act contains some of its more important provisions and is concerned with the arrest and surrender of those accused or convicted by an international tribunal of the kind covered by the Act. The broad architecture of the provisions follows that in the Extradition Acts 1965 to 1994, though unlike the arrangements that apply in relation to conventional extradition, arrested persons are to be brought, in the first instance, before the High Court rather than the District Court. This reflects the legal complexities inevitably involved in recourse to the Act.

Section 19 provides for a time lapse before surrender so as to ensure that a person who is being sought for trial or imprisonment cannot be surrendered until he or she has the opportunity to exhaust all the domestic legal remedies provided for in the Act. Section 26 deals with the *non bis in idem* provisions in the Statutes of the ICTY and ICTR. Subsection (1) provides that, subject to Subsection (2), the person will not be surrendered where final judgement has already been passed in this state or in another state for the same conduct.

The provisions of Part IV of the Act provide for other forms of assistance and they too arise from the obligation to cooperate fully with the Tribunals and their organs in accordance with the Security Council resolutions establishing the Tribunals and their respective Statutes.

As there is no commencement date, all provisions came into force on 10 November 1998 on signature by the President. The issue is not crucial as, under Section 3, it is deemed to apply in relation to international tribunal crimes committed, or alleged to have been committed, before or after the commencement of the Act.

RAY MURPHY and COLM CAMPBELL

Peace Process
☛ Criminal Justice (Release of Prisoners) Act, 1998 (No. 36 of 1998). Published in *Irish Current Law Statutes*, Round Hall/Sweet & Maxwell, 1998

This Act provides for the phased release of 'qualifying prisoners' whose crimes were politically motivated in the context of the Northern Ireland conflict. Under the 'Agreement Reached in the Multi-Party Talks' (the Belfast Agreement) of 10 April 1998, the Irish and British governments agreed to put in place mechanisms to implement the commitment to early prison release. The Act provides for a 'Release of Prisoners Commission' to advise the government, and it is the intention that all 'qualifying prisoners' will be released within two years of the coming into effect of the scheme. The equivalent UK statute is the Northern Ireland (Sentences) Act, 1998 (c. 35). Paramilitary prisoners belonging to organisations that do not declare and maintain a ceasefire are not eligible. Release is conditional on keeping the peace and good behaviour. While the release of prisoners was a controversial aspect of the Belfast Agreement, its implementation has not proven an obstacle to the peace process to date.

RAY MURPHY and COLM CAMPBELL

Pending Legislation
☛ Criminal Justice (United Nations Convention Against Torture) Bill, 1998
The Bill n.r., when enacted, will enable Ireland to ratify the UN Convention against Torture and other Cruel, Inhuman and Degrading Treatment or Punishment. The Convention was signed by Ireland on 28 September 1992.
☛ Safety of United Nations Personnel and Punishment of Offenders Bill, 1999

ISRAEL[178]

Compensation for IHL violations
☛ Draft Law Concerning Suits Arising from Security Force Activities in Judea, Samaria and the Gaza Strip, 5757-1997[179] [http://www.btselem.org/]

According to information provided by the Israeli Ministry of Justice, the above-mentioned law provides an exception to the Civil Wrongs Law (the Responsibility of the State) 1952, which exempts acts carried out by Israeli security forces in the framework of 'combatant activities' from civil liability. Under the draft law, the state may be liable to pay compensation for damage caused by members of the security forces in some cases, while still regarding the acts as combatant activites. The proposed law establishes, notwithstanding the immunity from civil liability for damages caused by 'combatant activity', that the court may determine that the plaintiff should receive compensation if it has determined that the circumstances of the case contain justified humanitarian considerations. The proposed law does not therefore provide a new defence for the state, but rather clarifies and delimits the extent of the immunity that exists under the current law. The proposed law proposes that a claim may be exempt from civil liability in three instances: where the alleged damage was sustained as a result of serious hostile activity,

---

178. Information provided by B'Tselem.
179. Jewish name for West Bank.

carried out by the plaintiff himself against the security forces or civilians; where the plaintiff has been convicted of severe terrorist acts; or where the state was not given suitable opportunity to defend itself against the claim, due to a violation on the part of the Palestinian Authority of the Interim Agreement regarding legal cooperation.

The Israeli authorities deny that Article 3 of the Hague Convention IV of 1907 applies to the present situation, as they consider that the activities of the security forces are activities for restoring and ensuring public order and security, which it claims are legitimate under Article 43 of the Hague Regulations of 1907.[180]

Cases

☞ Case concerning Legality of the General Security Services Interrogation Methods H.C. 5100/94; H.C. 4054/95; H.C. 6536/95; H.C. 5188/96; H.C. 7563/97; H.C. 7628/97; H.C. 1043/99, Supreme Court of Israel, sitting as the High Court of Justice 6 September 1999 [http://www.israel-mfa.gov.il/]

In which case, nine Supreme Court justices unanimously ruled that the interrogation methods of the General Security Service (GSS) which involve the use of physical force are not legal.

ITALY[181]

Peacekeeping

☞ Law No. 77 of 29 March 1999 regarding Urgent Measures for International Peace Missions Abroad

Law No. 77 of 29 March 1999 embodies and amends Law Decree No. 12 of 28 January 1999 setting urgent measures in the field of international peace missions abroad. The Act authorised, for the whole of 1999, the participation of a contingent of 150 officials in the OSCE Observers' mission in Kosovo pursuant to UN SC Res. 1203 of 24 October 1998. A mission of 250 soldiers to Macedonia was also authorised.

Article 2(6) of the Act subjects the persons engaged with the contingents to the discipline set by the Italian Military Penal Code in Time of Peace. This is a derogation from Article 9 of the Military Penal Code in Time of War, which states that Italian troops operating abroad, yet in time of peace, should apply the norms of the latter.

As for the presence of the numerous Italian military contingents in the territories of the former Yugoslavia previously assured by Law No. 270 of 3 August 1998, Law No. 77/1999 limits itself to extending until 24 June 1999 the terms of stay of the following corps: Troops from the Italian Army; *Carabinieri* engaged as part of MSU (Multinational Specialised Unit), MAPE (Multinational Advisory Police Element) and IPTF (International Police Force in Bosnia); *Guardia di Finanza* and *Polizia di Stato* engaged in MAPE.

The act also extended to 24 June 1999 the presence of 31 military units engaged with TIPH (Temporary International Presence in Hebron).

LIANA PECORANO[182]

---

180. Cf., a Palestinian view on the draft law, *infra* p. 394.

181. Information provided by Professor Sergio Marchisio and the staff of the Instituto di Studi Giuridici sulla Comunita' Internazionale (ISGCI), Rome.

182. Liano Pecorano is a consultant at ISGCI, Rome.

☛ Conclusive Report on the Investigation of Behaviour of the Italian Military Contingent in Somalia in the context of the UN Mission 'Restore Hope', Rome, 2 June 1999

The Conclusive Report by the Commission for Defence of the Senate concerns the acts of violence perpetrated between 1993 and 1994 against Somali civilians by soldiers of the Italian military contingent engaged with the operation IBIS-ITALFOR, in the context of the international missions UNITAF and UNOSOM II. The Report follows the Report presented on 8 August 1997 by the Governmental Commission on the facts in Somalia[183] and the one presented by the Commission of the General Staff of the Army, established for taking disciplinary actions.

The Report from the Senate intended to examine the circumstances behind the operations of the Italian contingent in Somalia in order to clarify the general conditions and factors that made the acts of violence possible. The Commission did not intend to ascertain individual responsibilities; that was the task of the Commission of the Army General Staff for the disciplinary profile, and of the competent Judicial Offices in Milan, Livorno and Turin, in front of which criminal trials are currently being held in order to determine the existence of any penal responsibility.

On the basis of the Governmental Report, the Senate Commission acknowledges that acts of violence are ascertained in three episodes. It however deems that events of the sort alleged constitute isolated cases, and expresses an overall positive appreciation of the Italian participation in the two missions in Somalia. The Commission also identified the causes of the acts under examination in the absence of appropriate control by superiors and military police corps.

In conclusion, the Report recommends that military police corps be present in any mission of Italian contingents abroad, with the sole tasks of military and judicial police activities and assigned to no operational task of any other sort. The Commission also recommends the insertion of the offence of torture in the Italian Penal Code and in the Military Penal Code.

FABIO RASPADORI[184]

Cases

☛ Corte dei Conti, Joint Sections, Judgment No. 6 of 16 February 1998

The judgement clarifies the requisites to qualify a Nazi concentration camp as an 'extermination camp: KZ Konzentrations Zone'. From perspective of Italian law, the qualification is relevant to the possibility to grant, in favour of prisoners, economic benefits provided for by Law 791/80 for those who survived deportation.

The Court identifies two crucial elements. The first is the cause of deportation, which must have been determined on the basis of political reasons, specifically (see decree of

---

183. See N. Lupi, 'Report by the Enquiry Commission on the Behaviour of Italian Peace-Keeping Troops in Somalia', 1 *YIHL* (1998) p. 375.

184. Fabio Raspadori is a researcher at the ISGCI, Rome and a part-time professor of human rights at the University of Perugia.

the President of the Republic 2043/63), religion, ideology or race, or acts of resistance or sabotage against German production. KZ camps are thus to be considered those which held political enemies of the regime.

The second requisite for KZ qualification of a camp is the control of imprisonment directly by the Gestapo or SS. The investigation carried out by the Judge to qualify a Nazi camp as a 'KZ extermination camp' is not limited to verification whether the camp is included in official documents, such as the lists published in the *Official Journals of the Federal Republic of Germany*, but can extend to any other means of evidence, such as documents of the Specialised Archives of the International Committee of the Red Cross, International Service Arolsen Research or witnesses, from which the existence of the two requisites above emerge.

MARIO CARTA[185]

☛ Court of Cassation, I Penal Section, Judgement of 22 April 1998

This judgement cancels a previous judgement '*de plano*' by the Judge of Preliminary Investigations (GIP) of Rome, dated 13 November 1997. The latter declared the existence of an evident circumstance of estoppel, preventing judicial action against the defendants charged with the crimes of genocide and multiple murder aggravated by '*infoibamento*' (killing by launching in fissures of Karst-soil).

The Court's decision censors the GIP's judgement on the ground that it was adopted in violation of the principle imposing the *contraddittorio* (the adversary system) on facts not characterised by macroscopic evidence. The Italian Code of Penal Procedure, in fact, considers such evidence as an essential condition for issuing a decision without the help and the approval of parties in the trial.

The first fact to escape a satisfactory examination in the cancelled judgement was the question of jurisdictional competence of the Italian Judge for those crimes committed in the part of national territory afterwards ceded to Yugoslavia (Gimino and Pisino after 8 September 1943, and Fiume, in May of the same year, now Croatia). Furthermore, the GIP of Rome failed to adequately examine the problem of the applicability of the crime of genocide, which was not sanctioned, at the time, by Italian legislation. In fact, the crime was introduced into the Italian legal system with Law No. 962 of October 1967.

According to the Court of Cassation, these elements necessarily require, from both their international and national regime and legal qualification perspectives, the intervention and dialectic contribution of all parties involved with the trial in order for the Judge to attain a complete conviction. This did not occur in relation to the decision cancelled.

MARIO CARTA

☛ Court of Cassation, I Penal Section, Judgement No. 1560 of 23 June 1999

The Judgement of 23 June 1999 of the Court of Cassation is another chapter in the long-running judicial saga concerning Erich Priebke, an SS official found guilty and sentenced

---

185. Mario Carta is a consultant at the ISGCI, Rome and part-time professor at the European Communities Law programme of the School of the Ministry of the Interior, Rome.

in 1998 in Italy for the massacre at the Ardeatine caves in Rome, committed by the Nazis on 24 March 1944 during their occupation of Italy as a reprisal to the attack in Via Rasella on 24 March 1944 when a group of partisans exploded a device killing 42 Nazi soldiers and two Italian civilians.

In the judgment under examination, the Court of Cassation overruled an appeal filed by Erich Priebke and Karl Hass against the Order of 16 April 1998 given by the Judge for Preliminary Investigations of the Tribunal of Rome (GIP). The Order qualified the attack by the Partisans in Via Rasella as a crime of slaughter but it found that it did not give rise to penal consequences because, having been committed for patriotic goals, it was covered by the amnesty granted by Legislative Decree n. 96 of 1944.

In the view of the respondents, the attack could not be considered a crime for it constituted, on the grounds of Legislative Decree No. 194 of 1945, an operation carried out by patriots in the context of the struggle against the Nazis and was thus to be regarded as a legitimate act of war. As a consequence of the above, the GIP's Order was requested to be annulled for absolute groundlessness.

The Court granted the request of the respondents in consideration of the fact that an act of amnesty involves the extinction of the offence: the 1945 Decree, in fact, cancelled the nature of offence of the attack in Via Rasella, which would otherwise be considered an 'act of war'.

As for the contrast with international law of war norms that, according to the GIP, would not permit equating the partisan group with the voluntary corps mentioned in Article 1 of the 1907 Hague Convention, the Court held that, on the ground of the 13 October 1943 declaration of the state of war against Germany by the legitimate government of Italy, the attack in Via Rasella can also be attributed to the Italian state, for the group of partisans operated as a *de facto* organ of it.

FABIO RASPADORI

Pending Cases

☛ Indictments against seven Argentinian military, *General Carlos Guillermo Suarez Mason, Santiago Omar Riveros, Juan Carlos Gerardi, Alejandro Puertas, Roberto Julio Rossin, Héctor Maldonado and José Luis Porchetto*

On 20 May 1999, an Italian Judge indicted former Argentinian Army General *Carlos Guillermo Suarez Mason* for the murder of six Italian citizens and the disappearance of a child, and six other military men for the murder of two other Italian citizens during the 'dirty war' in Argentina. All accused reside in Argentina but Italian criminal procedure allows for trial *in absentia*. The basis for extraterritorial jurisdiction is to be found in Article 8 of the Italian Penal Code, which allows courts to exercise jurisdiction over political crimes committed by or against Italian citizens anywhere in the world. The case was originally filed in 1983. The trial is set to start on 21 October 1999.[186]

---

186. Derechos Human Rights, Press Release, 21 May 1999. More information on the case is available in Spanish at: http://www.derechos.org/lidlip/grusol/.

Pending Legislation

☛ Draft-Law of the Senate No. 2984 on Adaptation of Italian Penal Military Legislation in the field of humanitarian law to international law, on enactment of the Additional Protocols to the 1949 Geneva Conventions

This draft-law, submitted by the Government, aims at adapting the Italian legal system to the norms of the international laws of war through abrogation and modification of specific norms of the Military Penal Code of War.

The international Acts referred to by the draft, i.e., the four Geneva Conventions on Humanitarian Law of 12 August 1949 and the two Additional Protocols of 8 June 1977 have been ratified and in force in Italy since the 1950s, in the case of the Conventions, and the 1980s, regarding the Protocols.[187] Hence, the draft-law deals with limited interventions concerning sanctions and ignores issues related to judicial procedure. The choice is also based on the fact that a global reorganisation of the wartime military judicial system, envisaged by an *ad hoc* governmental Commission some time ago, is currently being programmed.

In the first place, the draft provides for the application of norms of the Code regarding crimes against the laws and customs of war independently from the declaration of the state of war (Art. 2). It does not deal with internal disturbances; the Italian legislation already permits the application of laws of war in time of peace in circumstances of emergency and grave disturbance of peace.

In accordance with international norms, new crimes are created (Art. 4), such as acts of racial discrimination, apartheid, torture and inhuman and degrading treatment, unlawful transfers and deportations (such offences are punished up to five-years imprisonment). For the crime of capture of hostages, imprisonment terms of 25 to 30 years are prescribed.

Furthermore, the draft-law limits the possibility of resorting to the reciprocity condition, and provides that judicial action against such crimes be waged and exercised by the Prosecutor *ex officio*. Lastly, the abrogation of stipulations in contrast with international norms is proposed, particularly by Articles 183 and 241 of the Military Penal Code of War (Art. 7) and the power of a commander thereupon to order, in given cases, immediate executions.

FABIO RASPADORI

JAPAN[188]

Landmines

☛ Law relating to the prohibition of the production and the regulation of the possession of anti-personnel mines [taijin jirai no seizo no kinshi oyobi shoji no kisei tou ni kansuru horitsu]. Law No. 116 of 7 October 1998. Published in Japanese Law Gazette [*Horei Zensho*] of October 1998, pp. 42-44

---

187. Law No. 1739 of 27 October 1951 for the Conventions; Law No. 762 of 11 December 1985 for the Protocols.

188. Information and commentaries provided by Professor Hideyuki Kasutani, Professor of International Law, Setsunan University, Japan.

Japan ratified the Convention on the Prohibition of the Use, Stockpiling, Production and Transfer of Anti-Personnel Mines and on their Destruction of September 1997 on 30 September 1998. In order to implement the treaty obligations as a State Party, Japan enacted the Law relating to the prohibition of the production and the regulation of the possession of anti-personnel mines. Its main purpose is to prohibit the production of anti-personnel mines and to regulate the activities prohibited by the Convention in domestic law. One of its features is that it regards acquiring, stockpiling and retaining of anti-personnel mines as possession [shoji] of them, which is subject to the permission of the Minister of International Trade and Industry [Tsusan-daijin]. It prohibits the possession of anti-personnel mines in principle but allows their possession in certain exceptional circumstances under the control of the government, considering Article 3 of the Convention (Exceptions).

HIDEYUKI KASUTANI

UN Peacekeeping Operations
☛ Law amending a part of the Law relating to the cooperation with UN peace-keeping operations and others [kokusairengo heiwaijikatsudo tou ni taisuru kyoryoku ni kansuru horitsu no ichibu wo kaiseisuru horitsu] (Law No. 102 of 12 June 1998). Published in Japanese Law Gazette [*Horei Zensho*] of June 1998, p. 80

Law No. 102 of 12 June 1998 has amended the Law relating to the cooperation with UN peace-keeping operations and others (Law No. 79 of 1992) in some respects. The monitoring of elections is added to the activities to which this law is applicable. Under the old law, these activities were premised on the existence of a cease-fire agreement between the parties to the conflict. However, the new law enables international humanitarian relief activities conducted by certain international organisations, such as UNHCR, even in the absence of a cease-fire agreement. Further, the use of weapons by the officers of Self-Defense Forces who are engaged in the services of international peace operations is permitted, except in cases of emergency, only by the order of superiors in the field.

HIDEYUKI KASUTANI

Cases (for compensation arising out of activities during WWII)
☛ *Korean ex-'comfort women'* v. *Japanese Government*. Yamaguchi District Court, 27 April 1998. Reported in *Hanrei Jiho*, No. 1642, pp. 24-88
☛ *Filipino ex-'comfort women'* v. *Japanese Government*. Tokyo District Court, 9 October 1998, not yet reported
☛ *English ex-prisoners of war et al.* v. *Japanese Government*. Tokyo District Court, 26 November 1998, not yet reported
☛ *Dutch ex-prisoners of war et al.* v. *Japanese Government*. Tokyo District Court, 30 November 1998. Reported in *Hanrei Taimuzu*, No. 991, pp. 262-277

The first case is one of several in which Korean women have sued the Japanese government for an apology and compensation because it forced them to be sexual slaves – so-called 'comfort women' – during WWII. The Court ordered the government to pay compensation of 300,000 yen to each plaintiff. This judgement is noteworthy to the extent that it is the first recognition by a Japanese court that the system of 'comfort women' was an extreme case of sexual and ethnic discrimination, as well as the first recognition of the involvement of the Japanese military in the operation of this system. However, this judgment does not examine problems relating to international humanitarian law, such as war crimes or crimes against humanity, because these were not the main arguments invoked by the plaintiffs.

The second case is similar to the first and was filed by Filipino 'comfort women' for compensation. However, the Court dismissed the case, holding that, with respect to Article 3 of the 1907 Hague Convention respecting the Laws and Customs of War on Land, a state is not liable to directly compensate individual victims of other belligerent states. The Court also rejected the plaintiff's argument that it is well-established international practice that a state is liable to directly compensate individual victims if its nationals perpetrated a crime against humanity. The Court finally held that the plaintiff's claim for compensation was barred by the twenty-year statute of limitations in the Japanese Civil Code, even if the Japanese government was liable.

The third case was filed by former English prisoners of war and others, while the fourth was brought by former Dutch prisoners of war and others. Plaintiffs in both cases claimed compensation on the basis that some members of the Japanese military had abused plaintiffs in the POW camps during WWII, in breach of international humanitarian law, especially Article 3 of the 1907 Hague Convention Respecting the Laws and Customs of War on Land and the 1929 Geneva Convention. The Court dismissed the third case without finding the alleged facts. The Court also dismissed the fourth case in spite of recognizing that there were abuses by the Japanese military in breach of international humanitarian law. The Court rejected the plaintiffs' claim that individual victims could demand compensation against the Japanese government directly under Article 3 of the 1907 Hague Convention respecting the Laws and Customs of War on Land or international customary law of the same substance, standing on the same reasoning in both cases. In the fourth case the Court stated that international law is basically a legal system which is valid between states, and a treaty must have a provision which specifies the rights and duties of individuals in order for it to be directly applicable before domestic courts. On this premise, the Court interpreted Article 3 of the Hague Convention as providing only for international responsibility of a state which has violated Hague rules. Therefore, the Court concluded that individual victims could not claim compensation against the state to which military personnel violating international humanitarian law belong based on Article 3 of the Hague Convention.[189]

HIDEYUKI KASUTANI

KAZAKHSTAN

Penal Code

☛ Penal Code of Kazakhstan.[190] Adopted 16 July 1997; entered into force 1 January 1998

---

189. For a similar finding by a US court, see *infra* p. 427.
190. Reprinted in an unofficial English translation at p. 552 of this volume.

LATVIA

Cases

☛ *Case of Mikhail Farbtukh*, Judgment of 27 September 1999, unpublished

Former Soviet state security official Mikhail Farbtukh was convicted and sentenced to seven years imprisonment for acts of genocide committed in 1941, after Latvia was annexed by the Soviet Union in 1940 as part of the Molotov-Ribbentrop pact. As deputy chief of a regional unit of the predecessor to the Soviet KGB, he had collected information on 31 Latvian families who were subsequently arrested and deported by the Soviets in June 1941. Farbtukh's case was the second conviction for genocide, following the case of Alfons Noviks. Two other former Soviet security officials are awaiting trial on charges of genocide.[191]

THE NETHERLANDS[192]

Cases

☛ District Court of The Hague (Arrondissementsrechtbank te 's-Gravenhage). Decision KG 99/69, 18 March 1999
☛ District Court of The Hague. Decision KG 99/339, 7 April 1999

On 18 March 1999, a few days before the start of the NATO bombardment of the Federal Republic of Yugoslavia (FRY), a decision was rendered by the District Court in The Hague on the direct effect of Article 2(4) of the UN Charter. In this case, three Dutch antimilitarist associations and 139 citizens of several countries, including Serbia, demanded that the Netherlands abstain from the threat or the use of force against the FRY. Claimants argued that the Dutch state was acting in breach of Article 2(4) of the UN Charter by its association with the NATO threat to use force against the FRY. Furthermore, claimants accused the Dutch Prime Minister of war crimes in respect of his participation in the NATO decision-making process concerning a future attack on the FRY. For this, he was alleged to be individually responsible under the Dutch War Crimes Act of 1952.[193] By arguing this, claimants seemed to confuse two separate bodies of law, *ius in bello* and *ius ad bellum*. After all, the illegal resort to force does not of itself constitute a war crime.

The Court rejected claimants' petition, arguing that, as no actual force had been deployed at the time of filing the complaint, Article 2(4) of the UN Charter has no direct effect and appeal could not be made to it. With the same argument the Court considered the Dutch War Crimes Act as inapplicable. The case was dismissed. Claimants lodged an appeal that had not been heard at the time of writing.

On 7 April 1999, after the commencement of the NATO bombardment, the same Court rendered a decision in a similar case. Aleksander Daniković and eight other Serbs living in Serbia and awaiting mobilization requested a Court order putting an immediate end to the Dutch participation in the NATO bombing campaign in the FRY. Claimants argued that the Dutch actions at NATO-level were unlawful as they constituted a crime against peace and violated customary international law. Moreover they claimed that the

---

191. 'Former Latvian KGB official gets 7-year jail term for genocide', *Agence France Press*, 27 September 1999.
192. Information and commentary by Elies van Sliedregt, Research Fellow, University of Tilburg.
193. Wet Oorlogsstrafrecht, 10 July 1952.

Netherlands acted in breach of the Dutch War Crimes Act. Referring to the case of 18 March, claimants argued that the Dutch War Crimes Act can be appealed to as actual force had been deployed. Again, claimants did not seem to be aware of their erroneous argument that an illegal resort to force constitutes a war crime.

Referring to a decision of the Dutch Supreme Court in which the direct effect of Article 2(4) of the UN Charter was not explicitly rejected,[194] the Court admitted that in some cases the ban on the use of force and the principle of non-intervention can have direct effect. It believed that arguments for this can be found in Article 15(2) of the European Convention on Human Rights which allows an exception to the right to life laid down in Article 2 of the Convention, namely, only if the death results from 'lawful acts of war'. The reference of the Court to Article 15(2) of the European Convention seems to be based on the Court's assumption that, when confronted with an appeal to the right to life, the European Court will sometimes have to test against Article 2(4) of the UN Charter to establish if it was a case of 'lawful acts of war'. Consequently Article 2(4) would have direct effect in these cases.

Assuming that Article 2(4) of the UN Charter can have direct effect, the Court examined the lawfulness of the Dutch actions against the FRY under international law. It closely examined Security Council Resolution 1199, as the defendant asserted that this resolution legitimized the military action in Kosovo. Pointing at the legal basis of Resolution 1199 – Chapter VII of the UN Charter, allowing the use of force – and at the factual situation in Kosovo, the Court decided that the Dutch participation in the NATO bombing was not unlawful under international law. Furthermore, the Court stated that the fact that it was not the Security Council but the NATO Council which had decided upon the resort to force did not necessarily entail the unlawfulness of the decision. As to claimants' appeal to the Dutch War Crimes Act, the Court found that it was not valid as this law only deals with crimes committed by individuals. Unlike the first case, no individual was summoned in the second case; only the Dutch state as such stood trial.

All in all, the Court did not consider the Dutch participation in the NATO bombing campaign to be in breach of Article 2(4) of the UN Charter. The Court dismissed the case. Claimants lodged an appeal that had not been heard at the time of writing.

In the first case, the Court dismissed the appeal to Article 2(4) of the UN Charter, contending that no armed force had been employed yet. As a result, the Court did not explicitly go into the accusation of war crimes. In the second case, the Court argued that under certain circumstances Article 2(4) can have direct effect but that, in spite of this, the Dutch War Crimes Act is not applicable as it only applies to individuals. In both cases, claimants' misunderstanding over *ius in bello* and *ius ad bellum* was not cleared up by the Court. Instead, the Court rejected claimants' appeal to the Dutch War Crimes Act by concentrating on (some of) the requirements that trigger the applicability of the Dutch War Crimes Act: armed conflict and individual responsibility. This reasoning was not necessary as the Dutch War Crimes Act was not applicable anyway. Even if the Dutch Prime Minister had been summoned in the second case, he could not have been charged under the Dutch War Crimes Act for having illegally resorted to force.

---

194. Supreme Court of the Netherlands (De Hoge Raad der Nederlanden). Decision No. 13698, 10 November 1989. *NJ* (1991) p. 248 (with annotation by Professor Kooymans) and *NYIL* (1991) p. 453.

The Netherlands, however, seemed to be aware of the strict division between *ius in bello* and *ius ad bellum,* arguing in its plea in the second case that: '(…) Even if NATO bombardments would constitute a breach of Article 2(4) of the UN Charter it does not necessarily entail a breach of international humanitarian law.'

ELIES VAN SLIEDREGT

NEW ZEALAND[195]

Landmines

☛ Anti-Personnel Mines Prohibition Act 1998, No. 111 of 1998. *The Statutes of New Zealand 1998*, Government of New Zealand, Wellington 1999 [http://www.knowledge-basket.co.nz/gpprint/acts/public/text/1998/an/111.html]

This legislation implements New Zealand's obligations as a State Party to the Ottawa Anti-Personnel Landmines Convention. Section 7 makes it a criminal offence to use, develop, produce, transfer or possess anti-personnel landmines. However, this list of offences is subject to the same exceptions included in the Australian legislation referred to above (p. 329), namely, the use of mines by officers for detection and deactivation training and the possession of a mine by an officer pending destruction. Section 8(d) includes a similar exception to the Australian legislation related to interoperability between New Zealand Defence Force personnel and the armed forces of a non-State Party to the Convention.

The New Zealand Section 8(d) is clearer in the scope of the exception than the equivalent Section 7(3) of the Australian legislation. This New Zealand provision only excuses the participation by a member of the New Zealand armed forces in military activities with a state not party to the Convention and which engages in prohibited conduct where 'that participation does not amount to active assistance in the prohibited conduct'. Despite the different constructions of this exemption in the Australian and New Zealand legislation, the Australian Foreign Minister's clarification of the intended scope of Section 7(3) makes it evident that the two provisions are intended to have the same effect.

TIM MCCORMACK

Peacekeeping

☛ Crimes (Internationally Protected Persons and Hostages) Amendment Act 1998, No. 36 of 1998. The Statutes of New Zealand 1998, Government of New Zealand, Wellington 1999 [http://www.knowledge-basket.co.nz/gpprint/acts/public/text/1998/an/036.html]

The legislation amends the *Crimes (Internationally Protected Persons and Hostages) Act 1980* to include New Zealand's obligations under the *Convention on the Safety of United Nations and Associated Personnel 1994*.[196] The amendment to the principal Act

---

195. Information and commentaries by Professor Tim McCormack, *supra* note 5.

196. The original Act gives effect to the Convention on the Prevention and Punishment of Crimes Against Internationally Protected Persons, including Diplomatic Agents, 1973 and the Convention Against the Taking of Hostages 1979.

includes a change to its title to reflect the extension of protection to new categories of personnel. The new title is the *Crimes (Internationally Protected Persons, United Nations and Associated Personnel, and Hostages) Act* 1980. The amending legislation gives universal jurisdiction to New Zealand courts for the prosecution of alleged offences. However, despite the potentially broad application of the legislation, there is a high threshold subjective test in that alleged offenders must have directed their act or omission against a person whom they knew to be a 'person protected by a convention'. Furthermore, the alleged act or omission must also be one that constitutes (or would constitute, if done or made in New Zealand) a crime referred to or described in existing New Zealand legislation.

The extension of existing categories of protected persons to include UN and associated personnel excludes operations sanctioned pursuant to Chapter VII of the UN Charter in which UN personnel are engaged as combatants against organised armed forces and where the law of international armed conflict applies.

TIM MCCORMACK

OCCUPIED PALESTINIAN TERRITORIES[197]
Compensation for IHL violations
☞ Draft Law Concerning Suits Arising from Security Force Activities in Judea, Samaria and the Gaza Strip,[198] 5757-1997[199] [http://www.btselem.org/][200]

On 30 July 1997, the Israeli parliament started debating the above draft law concerning liability for injuries and deaths inflicted by Israeli security forces in the Occupied Palestinian Territories (hereinafter OPTs). The draft law was further discussed in the Constitution and Law Committee of the Israeli parliament on 16 December 1997. The Constitution and Law Committee discussed the draft law again on 20 July 1998, when Committee members were divided on the issue, and amendments were requested before the draft is further debated.[201]

Amongst the supporters of rapid passing of the draft law have been Justice Minister, Tsahi Hanigbi, and former Defense Minister, Yitzhak Mordechai. The draft has been opposed by Arab and minor leftist parties. Though there has been no publicly-known progress on the draft law since it was rejected by the Constitution and Law Committee of the Israeli parliament on 20 July 1998, Israeli law permits revival of the draft at any time as far as it has been transferred for consideration at committee level.

---

197. Information and commentaries provided by Mustafa Mari, LL.B.; LL.M.; Researcher, Peace Processes Project, National University of Ireland, Galway; Head of the Legal Department of the Palestinian Independent Commission for Citizens' Rights (PICCR). Formerly, Head of the Legal Department of Al-Haq, West Bank Affiliate of the Geneva-based International Commission of Jurists.

198. Jewish name for West Bank.

199. For a detailed examination of the Israeli draft law see Mustafa Mari and Munir Pujara, *In Light Of The Israeli Draft Law On Denying Compensation To Palestinians: Accountability Of The Israeli Occupier For Violations Of Palestinians' Rights* (Ramallah, Al-Haq 1998).

200. For an Israeli perspective on this draft law, see Israeli report, *supra* p. 383.

201. See Gideon Alon, 'Government yanks "Intifada law" for rewrite', *Haaretz*, 21 July 1998.

Israel has rarely properly investigated attacks committed by its forces in the OPTs. It has thus far refused to properly address issues pertaining to humanitarian law and human rights abuses committed by its forces, and its judiciary has generally accepted the government's arguments as to the legality of security policies and practices, such as the use of force against detainees and damage to and seizure of property. However, a recent decision of the High Court of Justice found the use of force by the security services during interrogations to be illegal.[202] Civil liability for such attacks has generally been the only way for Palestinians to hold the Israeli government accountable. The draft law in question would permanently and retroactively exempt Israel of much of its liability arising out of injuries inflicted by its troops upon Palestinians in the OPTs. By attempting to do so, the draft law contravenes applicable provisions of both international human rights and humanitarian law,[203] according to which Israel is under a duty to pay damages to Palestinians for such violations as house demolition, confiscation of land, torture, etc.[204]

The right to compensation is guaranteed by provisions which have arguably become part of customary international law. Israeli courts have repeatedly decided that Israel is bound by the provisions of the Hague Convention of 1907, which forms part of customary international law.[205]

MUSTAFA MARI

Training and Education of Security Forces
Palestinian NGOs, the ICRC, and the Palestinian Independent Commission for Citizens' Rights (PICCR – Palestinian National Human Rights Institution) train members of security agencies, set up after the establishment in 1994 of the PNA, on human rights and humanitarian law issues. Training by the NGO community is done in the framework of assisting the Palestinian armed forces to transform into a civilian police force, while the ICRC's involvement is part of its world-wide activities aimed at promotion of humanitarian law and dissemination of relevant material. Though most training provided by Palestinian NGOs is focused on international human rights law, international humanitarian law is generally addressed in order to make the distinction between the two sets of laws, and the conditions surrounding their applicability, clear.[206] Though

---

202. See *supra* p. 384
203. See Mustafa Mari, '*Guarantees for Respect of Human Rights in Palestine: Present Problems and Future Prospects*', (Jerusalem, LAWE 1997) pp. 25-27. See also Linda Bevis, '*Applicability of Human Rights Law to Occupied territories: The Case of the Occupied Palestinian Territories*', (Ramallah, Al-Haq 1994).
204. For details and thorough discussion of these and other forms of violations of the rights of Palestinians committed by Israeli occupation forces, see publications by human rights organizations, including *A Nation Under Siege: Al-Haq's annual report on Israel's violations of human rights in the OPTs* (Ramallah, Al-Haq 1989); *Punishing A Nation* (Ramallah: Al-Haq, 1988), *Protection Denied*, (Ramallah, Al-Haq 1991) and *"Awda' motaghairah wa intihakat mostamirah"* (Changing context and continuing violations), (Ramallah, Al-Haq 1995).
205. See for example *Elon Moreh* case, High Court case 390/79, reported in 1 *Palestine Yearbook of International Law* (1984) pp. 134-157, especially at p. 156.
206. The issue of providing training for the Palestinian police force proved controversial during the past few years since establishment of the PNA. Many NGOs working in the field of strengthening the rule of law and promotion of human rights stress the importance of such training, but argue that the government is duty bound to provide it for members of the police force. Others, while agreeing

the ICRC does not have a program for training Palestinian security forces members in the field of international humanitarian law, members of its mission to the OPTs have on several occasions lectured members of the security forces on international humanitarian law. The ICRC also cooperates with the Palestinian Ministry of Education and Palestinian universities through organizing a number of seminars on various international humanitarian law themes.

The PA Ministry of Higher Education decided in 1998 to include within the future curricula of all Palestinian universities a compulsory course on democracy, human rights and humanitarian law. A technical committee, composed of representatives of civil society organizations, universities and the Ministry, and the ICRC, discussed the issue, and though there were calls for separating democracy and human rights education from education in the field of humanitarian law, the committee's final decision was to teach the three subjects within one course. It is expected that teaching will start in 1999/2000.

According to ICRC officers based in the PA, the ICRC's awareness/dissemination programs include not only distribution of texts of international humanitarian law instruments, and lecturing on international humanitarian law rules to police/national security forces, but also outreach activities through various civil society organs that include seminars and exhibits in rural areas. These seminars discuss a wide range of issues such as humanitarian values and equality (within a society and among nations).

MUSTAFA MARI

PARAGUAY[207]

National Defense and Internal Security Law
➤ Law No. 1337/99 Law of national defense and internal security. Enacted by the Congress on 15 September 1998, vetoed by the Executive Power on 23 October 1998. The veto was rejected by the Congress, which confirmed the original version on 30 December 1998. The law entered into force in April 1999

The above-mentioned law establishes the so-called National Defense Council as a consultative organ to the President of the Republic. Likewise the new law enshrines the prerogatives of the President of the Republic in cases of international conflicts and defines the obligations of civilians and the applicable sanctions regarding national defense. Regarding civilians, the Law states that foreigners with permanent residence in the territory of Paraguay could be called to contribute to the defense of the country. As far as internal security is concerned, the law creates a consultative body, the Internal Security Council.

It is noteworthy that the law contains a chapter dedicated to the international aspects of national defense. This chapter recognizes the principles that shall rule the implementation of national defense, which include, *inter alia*, the principle of self-deter-

---

in principle with the said argument, have taken a more pragmatic approach, in order to accommodate the dire need for such training during the period of transition. Example of the first category of NGOs is Law Society and the Palestinian Centre for Human Rights, while the PICCR falls in the second category.

207. Information and commentaries provided by Professor Alfonso Velázquez, Professor of International Law, Catholic University of Asunción.

mination, the principle of solidarity and international cooperation, the condemnation of dictatorship and colonialism, and the international protection of human rights. Moreover, Article 34 states that the Republic of Paraguay could propose or join regional or global treaties and alliances in order to assure an international order based on democratic values, the defense of human rights, freedom and justice. In addition, Article 35 refers to the possibility of joining international peacekeeping missions promoted by international organizations.

ALFONSO VELÁZQUEZ

Penal Procedural Code
☛ Law No. 1286/98, Penal Procedural Code. Enacted by the Congress on 18 June 1998. Entered into force on 9 July 1999

The enactment of this Code represents a significant change in Paraguay's penal system. The previous Procedural Code was in force since 1890. The new legislation completely modifies the rules and procedures applicable to criminal cases. The former written procedure is replaced by a system of oral and public procedures which will guarantee the principle of immediacy, and will therefore allow the judge to make a better evaluation of the claims.

ALFONSO VELÁZQUEZ

Status of Military Personnel
☛ Law No. 1115/97, Status of Military Personnel. Enacted by the Congress on 13 August 1997. The law entered into force in August 1997

THE PHILIPPINES[208]

Peace Agreements
A. Between the Government of the Republic of the Philippines (GRP) and the National Democratic Front (NDF or NDFP)
☛ Comprehensive Agreement on Respect for Human Rights and International Humanitarian Law (CARHRIHL) between the Government of the Republic of the Philippines (GRP) and the National Democratic Front of the Philippines (NDFP), 16 May 1998
☛ Communiqué on the Memorandum of Agreement (MOA) on the Release of AFP Brig. General Victor Obillo, AFP Captain Eduardo Montealto, PNP Major Roberto Bernal and AFP Sergeant Alipio Lozada, 17 March 1999[209]
☛ NDFP Position on the Prisoners of War and the GRP-NDFP Peace Negotiations (Press Release by NDFP National Council, 18 March 1999)

---

208. Information and commentaries provided by Professor Alberto T. Muyot, Associate Professor at the University of the Philippines College of Law and the Director of the Institute of Human Rights, and Vincent Pepito F. Yambao, Jr., a junior researcher at the Institute. The two prepared the Philippines Country Report on Customary International Law commissioned by the ICRC.

209. The contents of the Memorandum of Agreement is deemed highly confidential to 'ensure effective implementation of the release procedure and the safety of the captives and their custodians'.

☛ Presidential Statement on the Release of Abducted Government Personnel (issued by the Office of the President, 22 March 1999)

On 16 May 1998, the negotiating panels of the GRP and the NDF signed the CARHRIHL in The Hague, the Netherlands.[210] The Agreement is the first of the four substantive matters contained in the 1992 Hague Joint Declaration signed by the parties on 1 September 1992, to wit: (1) respect for human rights and humanitarian law; (2) socio-economic reforms; (3) political and economic reforms; and (4) cessation of hostilities and disposition forces.

The agreement is very lengthy and technical. It consists of several parts, namely: (1) preamble; (2) declaration of principles; (3) bases, scope and applicability; (4) respect for human rights; (5) respect for international humanitarian law; (6) joint monitoring committee; and (7) final provisions.

Governed by the framework of national sovereignty, democracy and social justice as stipulated in The Hague Joint Declaration[211] and other subsequent agreements, the parties have agreed to the following:

1. recognition of the crucial importance and necessity of the respect for human rights and IHL in laying the ground for a just and lasting peace;

2. consideration of the current human rights situation in the Philippines, as well as the historical experience of the Filipino people;

3. affirmation of the universal application of the principles of human rights and IHL;

4. acknowledgement of the necessity of the application of the principles of human rights and IHL in the prolonged armed conflict in the Philippines; and

5. reaffirmation of the continuing commitment of the both parties, as well as the assumption of separate duties and responsibilities in holding, protecting and promoting the principles of human rights and IHL.

More concretely, the Parties have agreed to uphold, protect and promote the full scope of human rights and fundamental freedoms as embodied in international instruments such as the UN Covenant on Civil and Political Rights and the 1984 UN Convention Against Torture. Notably, most of these rights and freedoms are already guaranteed by the 1987 Philippines Constitution.

Of great importance are the Agreement's provisions on IHL. Both Parties have agreed to be bound by the generally accepted principles and standards of IHL, and to assume separate duties and responsibilities toward this end. Specifically, the Parties intend to apply the provisions of IHL to the following persons:

---

210. Hereafter cited as CARHRIHL.

211. The Hague Joint Declaration provided that (a) formal peace negotiations between the GRP and the NDF shall be held to resolve the armed conflict; (b) the common goal of the aforesaid negotiation shall be the attainment of a just and lasting peace; (c) such negotiations shall take place after the parties have reached agreement on substantive issues in the agreed agenda through the reciprocal working committees to be separately organized by the GRP and the NDF; (d) the holding of the peace negotiations must be in accordance with mutually acceptable principles, including national sovereignty, democracy and social justice and no precondition shall be made to negate the inherent character and purpose of the peace negotiations; (e) preparatory to the formal negotiations, the parties have agreed to recommend specific measures of goodwill and confidence-building to create a favorable climate for peace negotiations.

1. civilians or those taking no active part in the hostilities;
2. members of armed forces who have surrendered or laid down their arms;
3. those placed *hors de combat* by sickness, wounds of any other cause;
4. persons deprived of their liberty for reasons related to the armed conflict; and
5. relatives and duly authorized representatives of above-named persons.[212]

The protections given to the aforementioned persons under the Agreement are a substantial reiteration of the 1949 Geneva Conventions and the Additional Protocol Relating to Non-International Armed Conflict (Protocol II). Finally, civilians are given the right to demand appropriate disciplinary actions against abuses arising from the failure of the parties to the armed conflict to observe the principles and standards of IHL.[213] To this end, a Joint Monitoring Committee is created to ensure implementation of the Agreement.[214] Moreover, the Parties have agreed to carry out educational campaigns on IHL, especially among the people involved in the armed conflict.[215]

However, barely ten months after the GRP and the NDF signed the CARHRIHL, the New People's Army (NPA), NDF's armed component, abducted Brig. Gen. Victor Obillo, commander of a Mindanao-based engineering brigade, and his aide, Capt. Eduardo Montealto, outside Davao City on 17 Feb. 1999. Later, the NPA, abducted Chief Insp. Roberto Bernal in Sorsogon and Army Sgt. Alipio Lozada in Surigao del Sur. The NDF asserted that NPA members were holding the captive officers as 'prisoners of war'.[216]

In reaction to these events, President Joseph Estrada suspended the peace talks between the GRP and the NDF on 24 February 1999, and refused to give in to the rebels' demand to withdraw and halt government's military operations in at least five provinces. The President likewise refused to endorse a private mission to the Netherlands led by Roman Catholic bishops to negotiate with the exiled NDF head, Jose Ma. Sison.

Meanwhile, the NDF negotiating panel and the private humanitarian mission headed by Archbishop Fernando Capalla and Sen. Loren Legarda executed a Memorandum of Agreement on 17 March in the Netherlands for the release of the captive officers between 22 March and 19 April for 'humanitarian reasons'.[217] The NDF likewise expressed its willingness to resume peace negotiations with the GRP if the latter respects their bilateral agreements.[218]

In light of these developments, President Estrada ordered the unilateral suspension of military operations effective on 'Palm Sunday [28 March] until the date of the actual release [of the captive officers], and a reasonable and sufficient time thereafter'.[219]

ALBERTO MUYOT and VINCENT PEPITO F. YAMBAO

---

212. Ibid., Part IV, Art. 2.
213. Ibid., Part IV, Art. 4 (5)
214. Ibid., Part V.
215. Ibid., Part IV, Art 14.
216. The Question of Releasing Prisoners of War is Necessary and Appropriate Subject in Peace Negotiations. NDFP Press Statement (18 March 1999). In the said document, the NDFP stated that the 'taking of the prisoners of war is a legitimate and necessary part of the war between the armies of the GRP and the NDFP'. The NDFP likewise stated that the captives are afforded 'respect and treatment required by international humanitarian law'. [http/www.geocities.com/~cpp-ndf/]
217. Op. cit. at p. 397.
218. Ibid.
219. Office of the President. *Presidential Statement on the Release of Abducted Government Personnel* (22 March 1999).

B. Between the Government of the Republic of the Philippines (GRP) and the Moro Islamic Liberation Front (MILF)

☛Agreement (To Sustain the Quest for Peace), 6 February 1998
☛Agreement (Creating a Quick Response Team), 11 March 1998
☛Agreement of Intent (27 August 1998)
☛ Resolution No. 2 (Creation of a Joint Monitoring Contingent) 16 October 1998
☛ Resolution No. 3 (Immediate Cessation of Hostilities in Datu Piang, Shariff Aguak and Talayan, Maguindanao, 24 October 1998)

Peace remains elusive in the southern part of Mindanao despite the start of the formal peace talks between the Government of the Republic of the Philippines (GRP) and the Moro Islamic Liberation Front (MILF). Early in 1999, the Armed Forces of the Philippines (AFP) engaged the MILF in a series of encounters following MILF leader Hashim Salamat's statement that he wanted complete independence for Mindanao and not mere autonomy.[220] The said encounters claimed the lives of 60 people and wounded many others, most of whom were civilians. Around 90,000 people were rendered homeless.[221]

It should be noted that two months before the said incident, the GRP and the MILF agreed to the cessation of hostilities in Datu Piang, Sahriff Aguak and Talayan, Maguindanao, the same towns where the encounters of January 1998 took place.[222] The GRP and the MILF entered into an Agreement for General Cessation of Hostilities on 18 July 1997, which signaled the opening of the formal peace talks. Subsequently, the Parties have entered into several agreements, among them the creation of a Quick Response Team[223] and of a Joint Monitoring Contingent.

ALBERTO MUYOT and VINCENT PEPITO F. YAMBAO

Landmines
☛ *Philippine Country Report:* Measures for Monitoring and Advancing the Implementation of the Ottawa Treaty (submitted by Philippine Campaign to Ban Landmines, 12-14 June 1998)
☛ Instrument of Ratification [of the Ottawa Treaty] submitted by (former) President Fidel V. Ramos to the Philippine Senate (30 January 1998)

The Philippines signed the Ottawa Treaty on December 1997. However, by December 1999, the Philippine Senate had not yet ratified the Treaty despite the issuance by (former) President Fidel V. Ramos of the Instrument of Ratification on 30 January 1998.

---

220. A. Lopez, 'Mindanao's Chance', *Asia Week,* 5 March 1999, p. 26.

221. According to the Department of Social Welfare and Development (DSWD), about 52,000 people from Matanog, Datu Piang, Shariff Aguak and other towns were forced from their homes because of the said encounters. Officials of the Autonomous Region of Muslim Mindanao (ARMM) estimated that as many as 90,000 to 100,000 persons had sought refuge in evacuation centers.

222. Resolution No. 3 (24 October 1998).

223. The Quick Response Team was established 'on account of the confrontations/conflicts on the ground between the elements of the GRP and the MILF despite the Agreement on the General Cessation of Hostilities (AGCH) signed by the GRP and the MILF Panels on 18 July 1997 in Cagayan de Oro City'.

The 1998 Country Report prepared by the Philippine Campaign to Ban Landmines noted that the use of landmines in the armed conflicts between the Government Forces and the different rebel groups (National Democratic Front, the Moro National Liberation Front, and the Moro Islamic Liberation Front (MILF)) is at a relatively low-level. Moreover, it clarified that the Armed Forces of the Philippines (AFP) is not producing landmines nor does it use them in counter-insurgency operations. The AFP however admitted that it is using landmines for training.[224] On the other hand, it was alleged that the rebel groups produce or manufacture 'homemade' mines.[225] The prohibition on the use of landmines is contained in peace agreements between the Government of the Republic of the Philippines and the National Democratic Front,[226] as well as that of the government and the MILF.[227]

ALBERTO MUYOT and VINCENT PEPITO F. YAMBAO

International Criminal Court
☞ Administrative Order No. 387 dated 24 March 1998, 'Providing for the Creation of a Task Force on the Proposed Establishment of the International Criminal Court'

This Administrative Order signified the Philippine government's support for the establishment of the International Criminal Court as a 'legal mechanism that would enhance international criminal justice enforcement.' Hence, a Task Force was created to undertake the following duties and functions:
(1) undertake studies and researches pertaining to the establishment of the International Criminal Court;
(2) formulate policy recommendations to serve as inputs in the review and consolidation of the Philippine Government's position in the Preparatory Committee meetings of the ICC and the United Nations General Assembly;
(3) identify and recommend legislative measures necessary for the furtherance of the foregoing;
(4) serve as a forum for the resolution of issues and concerns pertaining to the establishment of the ICC; and
(5) pursue other related functions which may be deemed necessary by the President.[228]
At the time of writing, however, the Philippines has not yet signed the ICC Statute.

ALBERTO MUYOT and VINCENT PEPITO F. YAMBAO

---

224. See also Letter to Colonel Denwill Lee, Chief, JUSMAG Philippines, from Captain Artemio Arugay, DCS for Plans, 2 October 1995.
225. See also Memorandum for the Chief of Staff, AFP, from Capt. Artemio Arugay, DCS for Plans, J5, Re: On Landmines Production Issue, 2 October 1995.
226. CARHRIHL, Part III, Art. 2(15)
227. Art. I sec. 3(a). Implementing Operational Guidelines of the GRP-MILF Agreement on the General Cessation of Hostilities, 14 November 1997.
228. Sec. 3, A.O. No. 387 (24 March 1998).

Prisoners of War

☛ Decree of the President of the Russian Federation, 'On the Presidential Commission of Russian Federation on Prisoners of War, Interned and Missing' of 27 February 1997, No. 133 (as amended by Decrees of the President of Russian Federation No. 574 of 14 June 1997; No. 162 of 12 February 1998; And No. 163 of 30 January 1999), entered into force on the day of its signing. [УКАЗ Президента РФ от 27.02.97 N 133   (последняя ред. от 30.01.99)   'О КОМИССИИ ПРИ ПРЕЗИДЕНТЕ РОССИЙСКОЙ ФЕДЕРАЦИИ ПО ВОЕННОПЛЕННЫМ, ИНТЕРНИРОВАННЫМ И ПРОПАВШИМ БЕЗ ВЕСТИ'.] Published *in Sobranye Zakonodatielstva RF*, No. 9. 3 March 1997 at p. 1089

(As Part of the Decree are additional annexes: the Regulation of the Commission on POWs; Annex 1 containing the list of members of the Commission; and Annex 2 containing an additional list of members that are Deputies of the Russian Parliament.)

On 27 February 1997, by a Presidential decree (which was slightly amended in 1998 and in 1999; the consolidated version of the decree dates from September 1999), a Presidential Commission of the Russian Federation on POWs, Interned and Missing, was created to replace another of the same name created in 1994 (see para. 4 of 1997 decree).

   Although its work seems to be focused primarily on the conflict in Chechnya (see para. 3 of decree), the scope of the competence of the Commission is broad enough to encompass not only the case of Russian nationals, but also of those foreigners (see heading provisions of decree) considered missing (if any) in the territory of Russia.

As nothing is said about the timeframe in which these Russian and foreign nationals are considered missing, it can be deemed as encompassing the period of World War Two.

IGOR BLISHCHENKO and JOSE DORIA

Cultural Property (moveable)/Reparations

☛ Federal Russian Act of 15 April 1998 on Cultural Property Transferred into the USSR, in Consequence of World War II and being found in the Territory of the Russian Federation. Adopted by GosDuma (Lower Chamber of the Russian Parliament) in 5 February 1997, approved by the Soviet of Federation (the upper Chamber of the Russian Parliament) on 5 March 1997, signed by Russian President on 15 April 1998 [ФЕДЕРАЛЬНЫЙ ЗАКОН РФ от 15 апреля 1998г. "О КУЛЬТУРНЫХ ЦЕННОСТЯХ, ПЕРЕМЕЩЕННЫХ   В СОЮЗ ССР В РЕЗУЛЬТАТЕ ВТОРОЙ МИРОВОЙ ВОЙНЫ И НАХОДЯЩИХСЯ НА ТЕРРИТОРИИ РОССИЙСКОЙ ФЕДЕРАЦИИ"]. Entered into force on 20 April 1998, the day of its official publication in *Sobranya Zakonodatyelstva RF* 20 April 1998, No. 16 at p.1799, Moscow

In April 1998, a new Russian Federal Act was adopted to deal with issues of moveable cultural property (i.e., paintings) brought to Russia from abroad (mainly from Germany) as a result of World War Two. This act deals with the highly controversial issue of rights

---

229. Information and commentaries provided by Professor Igor Blishchenko, Professor of International Law, Russian University of Friendship, Moscow, and Associate Professor Jose Doria, Russian University of Friendship, Moscow.

to this property, which is seen by the Russian Parliament as part of a just reparation from Germany.

The preamble of the Act states that it was adopted with the objective 'to protect the transferred culture property from its plundering, staving off illegal removal from Russian territory, to protect from its illegal transmission to whomever he may be, with the purpose to create the necessary legal conditions for actual use of this property in Russia, as partial compensation of damage to Russian cultural property by Germany and its military allies during World War Two, to protect the interests of Russia when resolving conflicts with other states on the basis of the principle of reciprocity, and to create ideal conditions for progressive development of international cooperation in the sphere of education, science and culture'.

However, certain provisions of the Act are so controversial that then-President Yeltsin, initially refused to sign it, and when this veto was bypassed by the Parliament in second voting procedure, he maintained his opposition to it, and filed a claim with the Constitutional Court of Russia, so that this organ could clarify it. The most important provisions of this Act are analyzed below in connection with the decision of the Constitutional Court concerning this Act.

IGOR BLISHCHENKO and JOSE DORIA

Cases

☛ Russian Constitutional Court Decision of 20 July1999 concerning verification of the constitutionality of the Federal Act 'on cultural property transferred into USSR, in consequence of World War Two, and being found in territory of the Russian Federation'. N 12-P [ПОСТАНОВЛЕНИЕ КОНСТИТУЦИОННОГО СУДА РОССИЙСКОЙ ФЕДЕРАЦИИ от 20 июля 1999 г. N 12-П ПО ДЕЛУ "О ПРОВЕРКЕ КОНСТИТУЦИОННОСТИ ФЕДЕРАЛЬНОГО ЗАКОНА ОТ 15 АПРЕЛЯ 1998 ГОДА "О КУЛЬТУРНЫХ ЦЕННОСТЯХ, ПЕРЕМЕЩЕННЫХ В СОЮЗ ССР В РЕЗУЛЬТАТЕ ВТОРОЙ МИРОВОЙ ВОЙНЫ И НАХОДЯЩИХСЯ НА ТЕРРИТОРИИ РОССИЙСКОЙ ФЕДЕРАЦИИ"] Published in the *Sobranya Zakonodatyelstva RF,* No. 30, 26 July 1999 at p. 3989, Moscow

Hearings in this case were instituted following submissions from the President of the Russian Federation, in which the validity of the whole Act in the face of (in the opinion of the President) serious violation of rules of procedure concerning conditions to bypass the veto of the president by Parliament, as well as the constitutionality of Articles 3, 5-10,16 and 18 of the said Federal Act are questioned.

It is important to note that, under the Act, the definitions of the following terms are used (under Art. 4 of the Act):

Cultural Property – property of religious and temporal character with historic, scientific or other cultural meaning: works of art, books, manuscripts, incunabula, material of archives, components and fragments of architecture, history, and art monuments, as well as monumental art, familiar relics and others similar items.

Compensatory Restitution – a form of material international legal responsibility of an aggressor state applied in cases in which the responsibility of this state cannot be incurred in the common form of Restitution, and which consists in the obligation of this state to compensate the material damage caused to another state, by ways of transfer to the victim state (or by ways of confiscation by victim state in its favor) of objects of the same nature as those plundered and illegally removed by the aggressor state from the territory of the victim state.

Former Enemy States – Germany and its allies during World War Two, namely, Bulgaria, Hungry, Italy, Romania and Finland.

Transferred cultural property – Cultural property transferred in realization of compensatory restitution from the territory of Germany and its military allies, named above, into the territory of the USSR, on the basis of military orders of the military Command of the Russian Army, of the Soviet Military Administration in Germany, and of the Instructions of other competent organs of the USSR, and which (this property) are found presently in the territory of the Russian Federation.

Property of Former Enemy States – the property public or private, of municipalities, public and other organizations and societies in former enemy states.

Interested States – States (other than the Russian Federation and other former Soviet Republics), the territory of which totally or in part has been occupied by forces of former enemy states (for example, the Netherlands, Poland, Belgium, Austria and others).

Property of Interested States – the property, public or private, of municipalities, public and other organizations and societies in the interested states.

Articles 3, 5, and 6 of the Act state that all transferred cultural property, being found in the territory of Russia, is considered the property of Russia, and that from the point of view of its former state of origin, is composed of: cultural property which was property of former enemy states; cultural property which was property of 'Interested States', who lost their property rights in consequence of non-exigency of their restitution from former enemy states in time; cultural property for which state origin is not established (property in abeyance).

It should be remembered that, in 1997, President Yeltsin refused to sign this Federal Act and demanded that Articles 3, 5-10, 16, 18 be revised according to the Constitution of the Russian Federation and international law. The 1993 Constitution of Russia states that to bypass the President's veto, a majority of 2/3 of the deputies of the GosDuma is needed. In the opinion of President Yeltsin, the procedure to bypass the veto of the President was not fulfilled: on 4 April 1997, the day of the vote, as there were less then the 300 Deputies needed to make 2/3 present in the Room of the House of the Parliament, some of the remaining Deputies, to make the needed majority of 2/3, used the deputy cards of up to 20 absent deputies to vote, in violation of Article 41 of the 1994 Regulation of the GosDuma, which states that there must be personal voting for each and every deputy.

On this matter, the Constitutional Court asserted as lawful the allegations of the President, but then it refused to declare unlawful the whole Act. The Court stated that materials presented by the parties show that the practice of voting instead of absent deputies has become so common at the Russian Parliament that almost all Acts adopted up to now have been done in the same way, without any opposition from the President or from any of the deputies. In this situation, declaring this Act unconstitutional would amount, in the opinion of the court, to declaring all the previous Acts adopted in the same way also unconstitutional, and 'this in turn would be contrary to doing justice'. But the Court warned that unless deputies change their regulations concerning voting procedure, all protests based on this fact will in the future be considered valid.

Turning to the second point of the submissions of President Yeltsin, demanding declaration of the unconstitutionality of Articles 3, 5-8 (property rights), 16, 18 (procedure of property conflicts) and 9, 10 (time-limits), the court found it necessary to state, firstly, that the Act in question is only concerned with cultural property transferred into the former USSR (from former enemy states Germany, and its allies Finland, Bulgaria, Romania, Hungary and Italy) and found in the territory of Russia, by way of compensatory restitution, that is, according to international agreements signed by the parties and orders of the Soviet Supreme Command during the period of 1945-1949. Consequently, it does not deal with issues arising out of any other cultural property found in the territory of Russia today, which was transferred not by way of compensatory restitution, such as property imported not from the territory of enemy states but that of interested countries, that imported it illegally from enemy states, bypassing or abusing orders of the Soviet Supreme Command, and the origin state of which is unknown. That means issues concerning this property is ruled by another norm, such as the 1994 Civil Code of Russia, and applicable norms of international law. And consequently, each and every Russian individual to which this property belongs, lawfully asserts, in relation to it, all the rights of owners.

Consequently, the provisions of Article 3(6) stating that every cultural property transferred from abroad and being found in the territory of Russia is Federal property regulated under said Act is void.

According to the Court, the rights of Russia to cultural property imported into Russia from former enemy states (Germany and its allies) by way of compensatory restitution are well founded in international law, mainly the 1944 Agreement between the Governments of US, Great Britain, and USSR on the control mechanism in Germany; the 1945 Declaration on the defeat of Germany in the war and on the establishment of the supreme Authority thereon of the Governments of US, GB, USSR and France; the 1945 Agreement between US, GB, USSR and France concerning additional demands from Germany; the 1946 Sentence of the Nuremberg Tribunal; the Acts based on the rights and supremacy of occupying Authorities in Germany during the period 1945-1949; and the 1947 Peace Agreements with Bulgaria, Hungary, Romania, Italy and Finland. These acts deal with the international responsibility of former enemy countries, including by way of reparation and restitution.

In the opinion of the Court, the obligation of former enemy states to compensate their victims in the form of common restitution and compensatory restitution is based on the well-established principle of international law recognized well before World War Two, concerning international legal responsibility of an aggressor state. Moreover, the legal validity of actions taken against former enemy states is confirmed by Article 107 of the UN Charter.

In light of these norms of international law, former enemy states have lost whatever rights to that cultural property which had previously belonged to them and which was transferred into the USSR by way of compensatory restitution. The irrevocability of all property actions taken against Germany is confirmed in the Joint Communiqué of the Governments of the Federal Republic of Germany and the Democratic Republic of Germany of 15 June 1990 on the regulation of unsolved property issues, which is part of the 1990 Agreement on Unity between FRG, and the export of this property to former enemy states can only be made by way of exchange of each other's property under international agreements to be signed, or as a gift of Russia to those former enemy states, seen as a gesture of friendship and humanism from Russia.

Consequently, those provisions of the Act in Articles 3, 5 and 6 concerning property of former enemy states transferred into Russia by way of compensatory restitution are lawful.

But, according to the Court, the same cannot be said of the property of interested states (that is, those under partial or full occupation by enemy states during the war), which, in the Act, is also considered the property of Russia, and in respect of which no claims had been raised in time (that is until 1950 for Germany and until 1948 for its allied states) by those interested states. The Court found these provisions of the Russian Federal Act absurd, first because the time-limits referred to in those acts engaged only former enemy states and interested states and not Russia, and thus they do not concern possible claims against Russia for transferring into its territory property of interested states alongside property of enemy states transferred by way of compensatory restitution, and secondly, because it would amount to the imposition of sanctions against victim states contrary to international law if the property of a victim of aggression, as those interested states are themselves, could be seen as permissible objects to take by way of compensatory restitution by Russia.

Consequently, those provisions in the Act (Arts. 3, 5, 6, 9) concerning property rights of Russia over cultural property of interested states are void. Any decisions taken in relation to this property supposedly by way of compensatory restitution are illegal. Only cultural property of enemy states could be seen as the object of action, said the Court.

As for the so-called Property in abeyance, that is, the property whose state of origin is unknown, which the Act also considers as Federal Property, the Court found it even more difficult to accept that it could have been lawfully transferred to Russia. Firstly, because its origin is unknown, it could not have been transferred into Russia legally as a form of sanction against former enemy states. In fact, this property may even belong to interested states. Secondly, because its origin is unknown, consent to these actions could not even be given legally by enemy states themselves. Thirdly, the origin of this property is unknown only to Russia but not to its owners.

For this reason, in the opinion of the Court, once information regarding this 'unknown' property is made public, and nobody claims it, it is to be considered 'unknown' and thus part of Russian property. Consequently, the respective provisions of the Act (Arts. 3, 5, 6, 18) are also void.

The court further considered the provisions of Article 16, in which it is stated that a special body of the government to deal with property issues will be created, decisions of which are final and whose revocation are possible only by another act of the same body. The court found these provisions unlawful, stating that decisions of a special body of the government can be constitutionally revoked by a decision of the full government itself, and by decision of a civil court.

The court considered provisions of Article 18(1), in which it is stated that only foreign governments have the right to file claims concerning property issues, including on behalf of their citizens, and that these claims should be addressed only to the government of Russia. No claims will be received from individuals and organizations. The court said that the intergovernmental (diplomatic) way of solving property issues in case of restitution and reparations may sometimes be the easiest way for citizens to recover their goods, but it cannot be understood as denying access to whomever wants to follow the normal judicial procedure. Consequently, access to the court for individual foreigners is still open, under international law and the Russian Constitution.

Finally, turning to the question of time-limits (Arts. 9 and 10), the court has found it necessary to state firstly that, in its opinion, the time-limit of 18 months stated in those Articles is valid not only for the non-judicial (diplomatic) but also for the judicial procedure, the 1994 Russian Civil Code's provision for a period of three years (in Art. 196), notwithstanding.

As for the time this period should run from (according to the Act itself, from the moment of its publication, that is from 20 April 1998), the Court disagreed. In the opinion of the Court, this period runs only from the time when interested countries and former enemy states (due consideration given to the provisions of this decision of the Constitutional Court), take official notice of their property which is found in the territory of Russia. For this purpose, the government (states the Court) must provide a catalogue of everything transferred from abroad for its correct identification and the filing of claims by foreigners. The time-limit of one and a half years for claims will only run from the moment of official publication of these catalogues.

According to Article 79 of the 1994 Federal Constitutional Act 'on the Russian Constitutional Court', decisions of the Russian Constitutional Court are final and binding, no appeal is possible and they come into effect immediately after their announcement and directly, bypassing any contrary provisions of the Act in question.

In approaching this Decision of the Russian Constitutional Court in the case of 'the Cultural Property transferred into Russia from abroad during the Second World War', it is important to note that it finally regulates all remaining problems in the controversial issue of cultural property in Russia transferred from abroad in consequence of the Second World War.

It is important that the court has made clear that only cultural property legally transferred from the territory of former enemy states is Federal property of Russia. This includes only property of enemy states proper. Property of interested states transferred even with consent of former enemy states does not form part of this property.

Besides this legally transferred property of enemy states, in the form of compensatory restitution, the ownership of every other sort of cultural property of former enemy states found in the territory of Russia, in factual possession of the Russian government or individuals, may be questioned, to ascertain to whom it belonged prior to the war. This includes the so-called 'property of unknown state of origin', even if it is found to be property of former enemy states, as not all the cultural property of former enemy states was to be transferred to Russia as compensatory restitution.

It is also significant that the Court has made clear that the time-limit runs not from the date of publication of the Act (April 1998), but from the time when foreigners can potentially know that their cultural property has been found in Russia, that is, as for the property in the possession of the Russian government, when respective catalogues will be made officially public in Russia. Time limits do not affect questions of cultural property illegally in the hands of individual Russian owners (not the government). In these cases, the time will still be according to the 1994 Russian Civil Code, that is, three years from the moment foreigners know that their property was illegally transferred into USSR from abroad during the Second World War, and is in Russia, in the hands of private entities or of individuals.

We agree with almost everything stated by the Court in its decision, except for two aspects. First, the period of 18 months stated in the Act is true only for the non-judicial (diplomatic) procedure. The judicial procedure was not even envisaged in the Act (one of the reasons for the President's refusal to sign it). Thus, if the Court came to the conclusion that judicial procedure is always possible, and if it is not expressly stated in the Act, the time-limit is that of the 1994 Russian Civil Code, that is, three years. The function of the Court is to interpret norms as they are found in the Acts according to the Russian Constitution and other laws and not to create instead of the Parliament new norms. The interpretation of the Court becomes more clearly erroneous when we see that in the Act itself there is another situation for which no time-limit is provided at all, that is, the filing of claims by foreigners in respect of familiar relics (familiar archives, photos, medals, portraits, etc.) of former enemy states (Arts. 12 and 19).

Second, it looks very artificial for the Court to deny invalidation of the Act for failure to comply with rules of procedure by the Parliament, because it would invalidate other Acts adopted in the same manner. Under the 1994 Act 'on the Constitutional Court', the Court does not interpret Acts of its own initiative. That means invalidation could be possible only in relation to each and every Act presented for this purpose to the Constitutional Court. This was the first time it happened, and only after a Presidential veto because of disagreement with issues in the subject-matter of the Act. Secondly, as the Court itself states, on no other ordinary occasions have any claims been made. Consequently there is no reason, in our opinion, to believe that in the future it could happen, as the President, as well as the deputies are in agreement as regards the subject matter of the said other Acts, which are thus 'illegal', only with respect to the procedure of their adoption.

It is also noteworthy that the Russian Federal Act as well as the Decision of the Court uses the term 'Compensatory Restitution' which is not found in the 1996 International Law Commission's Draft Articles on State Responsibility (Articles 42-46).

IGOR BLISHCHENKO and JOSE DORIA

Military Courts

☞ Act on Military Courts of the Russian Federation, adopted by GosDuma on 20 May 1999, approved by Soviet of the Federation on 9 June 1999, signed by the President on 23 June 1999 [ФЕДЕРАЛЬНЫЙ КОНСТИТУЦИОННЫЙ ЗАКОН РФ "О ВОЕННЫХ СУДАХ РОССИЙСКОЙ ФЕДЕРАЦИИ" от 23 июня 1999г.]. In force from the time of its official publication in the *Sobranya Zakonodatyelstva RF* of 26 June, 1999, Moscow

On 23 of June of 1999, a new Russian Federal Act on the Russian System of Military Courts was adopted. This Act states that Russian Military Courts are the only competent bodies in Russia to deal with crimes committed by serving military personnel. As nothing more is said in this respect, the question remains whether international crimes such as war crimes, crimes against humanity, genocide and the crime of aggression, if committed by Russian military officials, are also included.

IGOR BLISHCHENKO and JOSE DORIA

SIERRA LEONE

Peace Agreement

☛ Peace Agreement between the Government of Sierra Leone and the Revolutionary United Front of Sierra Leone. 7 July 1999 [http://www.sierra-leone.gov.sl/peace_agreement.htm]

A peace agreement between Sierra Leone's largest rebel group, the Revolutionary United Front of Sierra Leone (RUF/SL), and the government was signed on 7 July 1999, ending eight and half years of war. The agreement provides for the permanent cessation of hostilities, disarmament and demobilisation, power-sharing and the transformation of the RUF into a political party, *inter alia*. One of the most controversial aspect of the agreement is its provision for blanket amnesties for members of the rebel groups, the Sierra Leone Army and the Civil Defence Forces who may have committed violations of international humanitarian law. However, the UN special representative for Sierra Leone, when signing the agreement on behalf of the organisation, made an oral disclaimer that 'the United Nations holds the understanding that the amnesty and pardon provision in Article IX of the agreement shall not apply to international crimes of genocide, crimes against humanity, war crimes and other serious violations of international humanitarian law'.[230]

SOUTH AFRICA[231]

Mercenaries

☛ The Regulation of Foreign Military Assistance Act 15 of 1998. Published in the *Republic of South Africa Government Gazette* [Staatskoerant van die Republiek van Suid-Afrika], Vol. 395, No. 18912, Capetown, 20 May 1998

This Act gives effect to the main provisions of the 1989 International Convention Against the Recruitment, Use, Financing and Training of Mercenaries by making it an offence to 'recruit, use or train persons for or finance or engage in mercenary activity' (ss. 2 and 8). 'Mercenary activity' is defined as 'direct participation as a combatant in armed conflict for private gain' (s. 1(iv)). South African courts are given jurisdiction over such an offence committed extraterritorially, except where a foreign citizen commits the offence 'wholly outside the borders of the Republic' (s. 9). 'Armed conflict' is defined as: 'any conflict between – (a) the armed forces of foreign states; (b) the armed forces of a foreign state and dissident armed forces or other armed groups; or (c) armed groups'.

The Act does not incorporate the 1989 Mercenaries Convention into South African Law. Further, it fails to enact the Convention's provisions dealing with international cooperation in the suppression of crimes or to provide for the extradition of offenders.

The Act provides for the authorization of the rendering of foreign military assistance to 'any State or organ of State, group of persons or other entity or persons' by the National Conventional Arms Control Committee (ss. 3-5). Foreign military assistance is

---

230. Report of the Secretary-General to the Security Council, S/1999/836, p. 2, para. 7.

231. Information provided by Professor John Dugard, Professor of Public International Law, University of Leiden, the Netherlands; member of the International Law Commission; associate member of the Institute of International Law; member of the board of editors, *YIHL*.

defined in s. 1(iii). The conditions when foreign military assistance would not be authorised are set out in s. 7(1).

JOHN DUGARD

Peacekeeping/peace enforcement
☛ Parliamentary debates regarding the South African National Defence Force intervention in Lesotho in response to the urgent appeal for help by the Prime Minister of Lesotho, P.B. Mosisli, to the presidents of South Africa, Zimbabwe, Botswana and Mozambique. *Debates of Parliament* (National Assembly), 22 September 1998 cols. 676306778), and ibid. 3 November 1998 cols. 7317-7329. See also 23 *South African Yearbook of International Law* (1998) pp. 320-331

SPAIN[232]

Cases (concerning crimes committed in Chile and Argentina)[233]
A. Claims and Orders
☛ Claim filed against those responsible for genocide and terrorism in Chile (1973-1990). [The case went to National Court, Central Trial Court No. Six, Madrid (Judge Manuel García Castellón).] 5 July 1996
☛ Order of Judge Manuel García Castellón accepting to proceed with the case. 6 February 1997
☛ Central Trial Court No. Five (Judge Baltasar Garzón) attaching the Operation Condor to the Argentina Case. Order of Judge Garzón affirming competence on the Operation Condor. Appealed for amendment by the public prosecutor. 15 September 1998
☛ Order of Judge Garzón rejecting the motion of the public prosecutor. New appeal by the public prosecutor. 1 October 1998
☛ Order of Judge Garzón accepting the enlargement of the accusation against General Pinochet. 16 October 1998
☛ Order of Judge Garzón of provisional warrant for the arrest of General Pinochet in UK, to enable his extradition to Spain. 16 October 1998
☛ (Second) Order of Judge Garzón of provisional warrant for the arrest of General Pinochet in UK. 18 October 1998
☛ Order of Judge García Castellón, stating his lack of competence in the Chile Case and transferring proceedings to Central Trial Court No. Five. 20 October 1998
☛ Order of Judge Garzón accepting transfer and joining the proceedings in the Argentina and Chile Cases. Appealed for amendment by the public prosecutor. 20 October 1998
☛ Order of Judge Garzón of request for extradition of General Pinochet relating in Spanish Law to genocide, to torture and to terrorism. 3 November 1998
☛ Order of Judge Garzón of indictment against General Pinochet. 10 December 1998[234]

---

232. Information and commentary by Antoni Pigrau i Solé, Professor of Public International Law, Rovira i Virgili University, Tarragona, Spain.
233. The following is a list of some of the extant documents and decisions of Spanish Judges concerning events in Chile and Argentina. It is not complete; references for orders from the period February 1997 to August 1998 are missing.
234. Reprinted in excerpted form at p. 515 *infra.*

☛ Order of Judge Garzón enlarging the indictment against General Pinochet. 24 December 1998

☛ Order of Judge Garzón enlarging the indictment against General Pinochet. 26 March 1999

☛ Order of Judge Garzón enlarging the indictment against General Pinochet. 5 April 1999

☛ Order of Judge Garzón enlarging the indictment against General Pinochet. 27 April 1999

☛ Order of Judge Garzón enlarging the indictment against General Pinochet. 30 April 1999

B. Decisions

☛ Decision of the National Court's Division One (Criminal), plenary session, Appeal Record 84/98, Summary of Proceedings 19/97, Central Trial Court No. Five, Madrid, 4 November 1998 [Audiencia Nacional, Sala de lo penal, Pleno, Rollo de Apelación 84/98, Sumario 19/97, Juzgado Central de Instrucción No. Cinco, Madrid, 4 de noviembre de 1998]. Not yet reported

☛ Decision of the National Court's Division One (Criminal), plenary session, Appeal Record 173/98, Summary of Proceedings 1/98, Central Trial Court No. Six, Madrid, 5 November 1998 [Audiencia Nacional, Sala de lo penal, Pleno, Rollo de Apelación 173/98, Sumario 1/98, Juzgado Central de Instrucción No. Seis, Madrid, 5 de noviembre de 1998].[235] Not yet reported

As a result of the claims filed in 1996 against those responsible for grave violations of human rights in Argentina (1976-1983) and Chile (1973-1990), proceedings were initiated in Central Trial Courts Nos. Five and Six of the National Court. The charges were torture, murder and kidnapping in connection with the crimes of genocide and terrorism. Despite the fact that the public prosecutors claimed that the proceedings should be terminated, both Judges repeatedly stated that Spanish justice was competent to deal with these crimes. Once the appeal for amendment had been rejected by both Judges, the public prosecutor's appeal reached the plenary session of the National Court's Division One (Criminal), composed of twelve magistrates.

On 4 and 5 of November 1998, they unanimously decided to make two rulings which were identical in structure and similar in content: they dismissed the public prosecutor's appeal in both proceedings (Appeal Record 84/98, Division One, summary of proceedings 19/97, Central Trial Court No. Five and Appeal Record 173/98, Division One, summary of proceedings 1/98, Central Trial Court No. Six) and confirmed Spanish jurisdiction to judge the events which were the object of the proceedings.

Two facts must be known if the whole process, and particularly these decisions, are to be understood in context. The first is that Article 23.4 of the Judiciary Act, 1985 (*Ley Orgánica del Poder Judicial*)[236] states that Spanish courts are competent to 'hear cases related to acts committed by Spaniards or aliens outside national territory which can be classified under Spanish criminal law as one of the following: a) genocide, b) terrorism,

---

235. Reprinted *infra* at p. 505.

236. *6 Ley Orgánica del Poder Judicial* 1 July 1985, *Boletín Oficial del Estado*, No. 157 of 2 July and No. 264 of 4 November. *BOE* is the official publication of legislation passed and public notices and appointments.

c) hijacking or the illegal takeover of aircraft, d) counterfeiting foreign currency, e) crimes related to prostitution, f) illegal trafficking of psychotropic, toxic or narcotic drugs, [and] g) any other crime which should be prosecuted in Spain according to international treaties and conventions'. The second is that the Spanish Criminal Code of 1995,[237] which is currently in force,[238] does not include the category of crimes against humanity.

The decisions taken by the National Court belong to an area in which the judicial precedents in Spain are minimal, and are related to cases of considerable international significance; their importance, therefore, is obvious. There are many points of juridical interest, the most significant of which are discussed below.

1. *The 1948 Convention on Genocide and competent jurisdiction*

According to the Court, it would be contrary to the spirit of the Convention,[239] whose main aim is to take measures against genocide and prevent exemption from punishment for genocide, to consider that this article limits the exercise of jurisdiction and excludes all jurisdictions other than the ones envisaged in the legal provision.

Although the Convention makes no provision for the universal obligation to pursue genocide, this is not incompatible with the right of any State Party, such as Spain, to consider that it has the right to take measures against genocide that has taken place beyond the limits of jurisdiction of its territory:

> It would be unthinkable that, as a result of applying the Convention for the Prevention and Punishment of the Crime of Genocide, Spain, for example, could not punish a Spanish national responsible for genocide who had committed the crime outside Spain and was currently in our country, provided the requirement specified in Article 23(2) of the Judiciary Act was met.

According to the Court, the Convention on Genocide establishes:

> accessory action by jurisdictions other than those envisaged in the legal provision, and thus the jurisdiction of a State should abstain from exercising jurisdiction regarding events constituting genocide which are the object of prosecution by the courts of the country in which they took place or by an international criminal court.

2. *On the classification of events as genocide*

The Criminal Court did not follow the letter of Article II of the Convention on Genocide but adopted a wider ranging concept which it regarded as being 'understood on a social level' by the international community. The concept is the following: 'Genocide is a crime consisting of the total or partial extermination of a human race or group, by killing or neutralizing its members.'

The Court stated that the parallel events in Chile and Argentina were an act of persecution intended to destroy a certain sector of the population which was heterogeneous, but which could be distinguished by a political preconception: the group of

---

237. *Ley Orgánica* [Criminal Code Act] 10/95 of 23 November.
238. See also 1 *YIHL* (1998) pp. 502-505 and 636-640.
239. Spain acceded to the Genocide Convention on 13 September 1968; *BOE*, 8 February 1969.

citizens who did not respond to the type pre-established by the promoters of repression as appropriate for the new order which was sought to be imposed in the country.

This assumption was then fitted into the concept of 'national group' and an evolutionary interpretation was provided of the text of the Convention on Genocide which 'requires that the phrase "national group" means not "a group of persons who form part of the same nation", but simply a national human group, a human group distinguished by a certain characteristic and which forms part of a greater group'.

The conclusion is that, at the time of the events and in both countries, the events constituted genocide because 'efforts were made to destroy a national group which had certain features, namely those who could not be included in the national reorganization plan or those who, according to the persecutors, did not fit in'.

3. *On the classification of the events as terrorism*

The Court considered that those events resulting in death, injury, coercion and illegal arrest, and which may be classified as genocide, can also be classified as terrorism since they have all the elements of this type of crime: persons who constitute an armed group, stable organization, the generation of fear or alarm in the population as a whole and the objective of subverting the constitutional order or of severely disturbing public peace.

The last of these elements was specifically discussed by the public prosecutor who considered that the constitutional order mentioned should be understood as referring to the Spanish constitutional order. On this point, the Criminal Court's response was categorical: 'The subversive tendency relates to the legal or social order of the country in which the crime of terrorism is committed or which is directly affected by it as the target of the attack.' Indeed, the fact that terrorism is included in the paragraph in Article 23 of the Judiciary Act, relative to universal jurisdiction, and not in paragraph 2, relative to the principle of protection of the state, makes it difficult to argue against this interpretation.

4. *On the crimes of torture*

On this point, the Criminal Court did not deem it necessary to go into detail since it understood that the alleged crimes of torture form part of the greater crime of genocide or terrorism, for which jurisdiction had already been established according to Spanish Law, independently of the validity of the Convention of 10 December 1984 against Torture or other cruel, inhuman or degrading treatment,[240] which provides an extra jurisdictional base for crimes of this nature.

5. *On the applicability of the regulation which establishes universal jurisdiction*

The Criminal Court considers that Article 23.4 of the Judiciary Act is applicable to those events prior to its coming into force. According to the Court, the said article does not define any action or omission, but extends Spanish jurisdiction for prosecuting crimes which are already defined by other laws. The principle of legality states that acts constitute a crime when they take place but not that the jurisdiction and the procedural provision be prior to the triable action: 'Jurisdiction is the premise of the prosecution, not of the crime.'

ANTONI PIGRAU I SOLÉ

---

240. Spain ratified the Torture Convention on 19 October 1987; *BOE*, 9 November 1987.

☛ Case on Chile, Decision of the National Court's Division One (Criminal), plenary session. Dismissing the appeal of public prosecutor on the joining of proceedings on Argentina and Chile Cases. 23 November 1998

SWEDEN

Cases

☛ Preliminary investigations against Augusto Pinochet for allegations of murder, torture and other crimes, Public Prosecutor of Stockholm, 9th Chamber, Decision of 4 May 1999, Document Number C9-1-1631-98

After the arrest of Augusto Pinochet in the United Kingdom in October 1998, approximately 165 criminal complaints were filed against him in Sweden for the same crimes as are subject to the proceedings for his extradition to Spain, i.e., acts of murder, torture and other crimes committed during the period when Augusto Pinochet was the Head of State of Chile. The Public Prosecutor decided that preliminary investigations should not be initiated, as Swedish authorities must bow to the interpretation of international law as adopted by the House of Lords in its decision of 24 March 1999.[241] Accordingly, only acts of torture committed after 8 December 1988 could be considered to constitute extraditable offences. None of the criminal complaints filed in Sweden related to acts after that date and Sweden thus lacked jurisdiction.

SWITZERLAND[242]

Nuclear Weapons

☛ Message of the Federal Council to the Federal Assembly [Message concernant le Traité d'interdiction complète des essais nucléaires] dated 9 September 1998 relative to the Comprehensive Test Ban Treaty. Published in *Feuille fédérale* (1999) pp. 607-697

By a message of 9 September 1998, the Federal Council invited the Parliament to approve the Comprehensive Test Ban Treaty (CTBT) of 10 September 1996. Switzerland signed this instrument on 24 September 1996, the day it opened for signature.

Switzerland is a party to both the Partial Test Ban Treaty (1963) and the Nuclear Non-Proliferation Treaty (1968). By ratifying the CTBT, Switzerland would confirm its disarmament and nuclear non-proliferation policies. Indeed, the Treaty contributes to a global security policy by making it more difficult both to develop nuclear weapons and to modernise existing stocks. In addition, Switzerland's ratification of the Treaty would facilitate its entry into force.

---

241. See Colin Warbrick, Elena Martin Salgado and Nicholas Goodwin, in this volume *supra* at p. 9.

242. Information provided by Anne-Marie La Rosa, International Labour Office, Freedom of Association Branch, Geneva and A.D. Henchoz, Swiss Department of Foreign Affairs, Bern. The report covers 1998 only; 1999 developments will be covered in *YIHL* Vol. 3.

Switzerland, through its station for the measurement of seismic activity in Davos, will be integrated into the international surveillance system, a network of 321 national measurement stations, whose role is to supervise the application of the Treaty.

ALAIN-DENIS HENCHOZ and ANNE-MARIE LAROSA

Conventional Weapons

☞ Federal Law on War Equipment, Modification, 31 March 1998 [Loi fédérale sur le matériel de guerre, Modification du 20 mars 1998]. [Amending Federal Law on War Equipment dated 31 December 1996 entered into force 1 April 1998.[243] Published in *Feuille fédérale*, 31 March 1998, p. 1159. Not yet entered into force. The aim of this modification is to bring the definition of anti-personnel mines contained in Article 2 of the 1996 law in line with that contained in Article 8 of the Landmines Convention.

First Periodical Meeting of the States Parties to the Geneva Conventions (19-23 January 1998)

i. Preparatory Documents of the ICRC

☞ Respect for and Protection of the Personnel of International Humanitarian Organisations

☞ Armed Conflicts Linked to the Disintegration of State Structures

ii. Swiss documents

☞ Working Paper on the Respect for and Security of the Personnel of Humanitarian Organisations

☞ Working Paper on Armed Conflicts linked to the Disintegration of State Structures

☞ Statements of the Swiss Delegation on the Respect for and Security of the Personnel of Humanitarian Organisations, 19 and 20 Janauary 1998, and on Armed Conflicts linked to the Disintegration of State Structures, 21 January 1998

☞ Report of the Meeting's Chairman

The XXVIth International Conference of the Red Cross and Red Crescent (1995) had recommended that Switzerland, as depository of the Geneva Conventions, convene periodical meetings of the States Parties to consider general problems regarding the application of international humanitarian law. In principle, such meetings would be held in the interval between two conferences of the Red Cross and the Red Crescent.

The first Periodical Meeting was held in Geneva from 19 to 23 January 1998. Ambassador Lucius Caflisch, Legal Adviser to the Swiss Ministry of Foreign Affairs, chaired the meeting, which was attended by 129 state representatives and 36 observer delegations. A preparatory meeting due to take place on 27 and 28 November 1997 had to be cancelled as political differences – regarding notably the participation of a state and a particular entity – could not be resolved in time.

During the Meeting, experts dealt in an informal manner with the following two themes: Respect for and protection of the personnel of international humanitarian organizations and Armed conflicts linked with the disintegration of state structures. Delegates had at their disposal documents prepared by the ICRC and by Swiss authorities. At the close of the meeting, the Chairman drew up and presented his conclusions, which were

---

243. See 1 *YIHL* (1998) p. 510.

included in a report to be issued to State Parties to the Geneva Conventions and the XXVIIth International Conference of the Red Cross and Red Crescent (1999). The report was also communicated to the United Nations Secretary-General, who was responsible for the preparation of a report on the protection of humanitarian personnel.

States unanimously condemned the acts of violence committed against humanitarian personnel. Such acts put at risk the protection and the survival of civilian populations, the very rationale of humanitarian law. Where civilian populations are particularly targeted by acts of violence, the disintegration of state structures and of the common values of a society can have particularly serious consequences. The discussion highlighted both the complexity of the topics addressed and the need to have recourse to concrete solutions to solve the issues identified. These solutions are not to be found solely in humanitarian law. They comprise also political, economic and social facets. They may be implemented therefore before, during or after a conflict. The participants underlined the importance of heightened cooperation between humanitarian organisations, as well as between the latter and political and military bodies, and the need to be more sensitive to the specificities of local situations and customs. Finally, the need to establish, as soon as possible, an international criminal court of a permanent nature was stressed.

ALAIN-DENIS HENCHOZ and ANNE-MARIE LAROSA

Meeting of Experts on Problems regarding the Fourth Geneva Convention (Geneva, 9-11 June 1998 and 27-29 October 1998)
☛ Press release on the meeting held at Villa Sarasin from 9 to 11 June 1998
☛ Report of the ICRC in view of the Meeting of 27-29 October 1998

Statements by the Swiss delegation at the October 1998 Meeting:
☛ Déclaration de la délégation suisse sur le thème de la protection des populations civiles dans les conflits armés en général, le 27 octobre 1998
☛ Déclaration de la délégation suisse sur le thème des mesures envisageables pour rémedier aux problèmes généraux identifiés et des mesures de mise en oeuvre, le 28 octobre 1998
☛ Déclaration de la délégation suisse sur le thème de la protection des populations civiles dans des territories occupés, le 28 octobre 1998
☛ Report of the Meeting's Chairman, 11 December 1998

The United Nations General Assembly adopted at its tenth emergency special session a number of resolutions on respect for the Fourth Geneva Convention in the Israeli occupied Palestinian territories. It recommended that state parties convene a conference to examine the measures necessary to ensure respect for the Convention in the above-mentioned territories. It invited Switzerland, as depository of the Geneva Conventions, to undertake the necessary preparatory steps, including the convening of a meeting of experts (see in particular General Assembly Resolution ES-10/5).

After a long consultation process, Switzerland drew up a package consisting of two measures. The first one was a closed meeting of representatives from Israel and the Palestinian Liberation Organisation, in the presence of ICRC representatives and under the chairmanship of Switzerland. The meeting was to deal specifically with problems relating to the application of the Fourth Geneva Convention in the Israeli occupied

Palestinian territories. It took place in Geneva from 9 to 11 June 1998. The second part of the package consisted of the convening of a Meeting of Experts on the Fourth Geneva Convention, to examine general problems in the implementation of the Convention in general and, in particular, in occupied territories. The meeting was held in Geneva from 27 to 29 October 1998 and was chaired by Ambassador Walter Gyger, Permanent Representative to the International Organisations in Geneva. One hundred and eighteen state representatives and 15 observer delegations took part. In terms of its organisation and its objective, the Meeting was based on the model of the first Periodical Meeting on International Humanitarian Law (see *supra*).

The convening of this meeting raised a number of politically-related questions concerning, *inter alia,* the participation of a state and a particular entity, and the relationship between the Meeting and the follow-up to General Assembly Resolution ES-10/5.

States categorically condemned violations of the Fourth Geneva Convention throughout the world. Such violations affect the protection and survival of civilian populations. The discussions highlighted the complexity of the topics addressed. The participants identified a series of problems and solutions. Certain solutions correspond to those highlighted at the first Periodical Meeting on International Humanitarian Law. One of these is the possibility of convening meetings or conferences to deal with specific situations.

At the end of the meeting, the Chairman drew up a report which summarised the debates. The latter was transmitted to State Parties to the Convention, to the United Nations Secretary-General and to the observers invited to take part in the Meeting.

ALAIN-DENIS HENCHOZ and ANNE-MARIE LAROSA

International Criminal Court
- Statement of Secretary of State Jakob Kellenberger, delivered 18 June 1998 (at the Rome Conference)
- Statement of Ambassador Lucius Caflisch, delivered 21 October 1998 (before the Sixth Committee of the United Nations General Assembly)

From the outset, Switzerland actively supported the project for an International Criminal Court. It participated both at the Rome Conference and in its preparation.

Switzerland favoured the creation of a strong court with compulsory jurisdiction and the ability to act independently. It considered that the Court's jurisdiction should not be weakened by reservations or by the need for state authorisations or those of relevant United Nations organs. The definition of the offences over which the Court would have jurisdiction needed to be adapted to contemporary international law. States, the Security Council or the Court Prosecutor should be in a position to instigate proceedings. The jurisdiction of the Court should be complementary to that of states and cases are deferred to it only if the latter are unwilling or unable to fulfil their obligations.

Switzerland welcomed the adoption of the Rome Statute. It considers that it contains a number of positive elements. It would have preferred a more complete list of war crimes, a system of automatic or inherent Court jurisdiction, more flexibility in the criteria governing the choice of Judges and more precision in the definition of penalties and that the Statute be more easily amended.

Switzerland signed the Statute on 18 July 1998. The Federal Council hopes to ratify the instrument as soon as possible.

ALAIN-DENIS HENCHOZ and ANNE-MARIE LAROSA

Cases
➤ Sonabend case: Press release of the Federal Department of Finance, dated 19 February 1998
➤ Spring case: Press release of the Federal Department of Finance, dated 23 June 1998

The Federal Law on the Responsibility and the Liability of the Swiss Confederation, its Authorities' Members and its Civil Servants, of 14 March 1958 (Loi fédérale sur la responsabilité de la Confédération, des membres de ses autorités et de ses fonction-naires), provides that the Confederation shall be responsible for damage caused to a third person by its authorities' members or its civil servants in the exercise of his or her functions, notwithstanding any fault. Responsibility is excluded if the injured party does not introduce his or her claim in the year following the day upon which the harm was known, and in any event, within ten years from the date upon which the act causing the harm occurred. The claim filed with the Federal Department of Finance (Département fédéral des finances) is to be examined by the Federal Council. A further proceeding may be introduced before the Federal Tribunal.

Two claims asserting responsibility were recently brought against the Confederation concerning Switzerland's asylum policy with respect to Jewish refugees during the Second World War.

The first was brought by Mr Charles Sonabend, a British citizen. His parents had unsuccessfully sought asylum in Switzerland in 1942. After being forced to leave Switzerland, they were arrested by a German patrol and were deported. They died in Auschwitz. The claimant sought compensation of CHF 100,000 in moral damages.

The second claim was from Mr Joseph Spring, an Australian resident who had twice sought refuge in Switzerland at the age of 16. After his second attempt in November 1943, he was handed over to a German patrol and was deported to Auschwitz. He too claimed compensation of CHF 100,000 in moral damages.

These claims received considerable publicity in Switzerland. Beyond their political and moral dimension, they raised legal questions. These related, in particular, to the identification of the applicable standards of international law in light of which the purported acts were to be assessed, the characterisation of these crimes (were they war crimes, crimes against humanity or genocide, was there complicity or violations of the principle of non-refoulement?) and the possible submission of such alleged violations to a statute of limitations.

The Federal Council examined the two requests, basing itself on the above-mentioned Law. Whilst expressing its sympathy and regrets, it rejected the claims on legal grounds. In particular, it considered that there had been no violation of the law in force at the relevant time and that the legal deadlines for the filing of claims had expired. The Federal Council's reasoning was not published. In conformity with the 1958 Law, the claimants brought their claims before the Federal Court (Tribunal fédéral), which, at the time of writing, had not yet handed down a judgement on the matter.

ALAIN-DENIS HENCHOZ and ANNE-MARIE LAROSA

TAJIKISTAN

Penal Code

☛ On 21 May 1998, Tajikistan adopted a new Penal Code containing various provisions regarding the implementation of IHL. Articles 403 to 405 punish grave breaches of IHL committed in either international or non-international armed conflicts. Article 333 states that abuse of the emblem and name of the Red Cross/Red Crescent is a punishable offence. The Code entered into force on 1 September 1998

UNITED KINGDOM

Cases

☛ *R* v. *Sawoniuk*, Central Criminal Court, Verdict delivered 1 April 1999. Unreported[244]

Pinochet

a. Divisional Court

☛ *R* v. *Bow Street Metropolitan Magistrate*, ex parte *Pinochet Ugarte*, 28 October 1998. Unreported

b. House of Lords[245]

☛ *R* v. *Bow Street Metropolitan Magistrate*, ex parte *Pinochet Ugarte* (Amnesty International and others intervening) (No. 1) [1998] 4 *All ER* 897, 25 November 1998

☛ *R* v. *Metropolitan Magistrate*, ex parte *Pinochet Ugarte* (No. 2) 1 *All ER* 577 [parte *Pinochet Ugarte* (Amnesty International and others intervening) [1998] 4 *All ER* 897a, 15 January 1999

☛ *R* v. *Metropolitan Stipendiary Magistrate and others*, ex parte *Pinochet Ugarte* (Amnesty International and others intervening)(No 3) 2 *All ER* 97 [parte *Pinochet Ugarte* (Amnesty International and others intervening) [1998] 4 *All ER* 897, 24 March 1999

[All of the judgements issued in the *Pinochet* case are available online at http://www.derechos.org/nizkor/chile/juicio/eng.html]

UNITED STATES OF AMERICA

Landmines

☛ The White House: Statement by the Press Secretary re. the Amended Mines Protocol to the Convention on Conventional Weapons, 25 May 1999[246]

☛ US Senate's advice and consent to ratification of Amended Protocol II subject to a reservation, understanding and conditions, Congressional Record: 20 May 1999, pp. S5780-S5782

On 25 May 1999, the President signed the US instrument of ratification of Amended Protocol II to the 1980 United Nations Convention on Prohibitions or Restrictions on the Use of Certain Conventional Weapons Which May be Deemed to be Excessively

---

244. For analysis, see Rowe, at p. 307 of this volume.
245. For analysis see Warbrick, et al. at p. 91
246. Reprinted at p. 472 *infra*.

Injurious or to Have Indiscriminate Effects, concerning Mines, Booby-Traps and Other Devices.

In accordance with the US Senate's resolution of advice and consent to ratification, the ratification was accompanied by one reservation and nine statements of understanding. The resolution also contained 13 'conditions' directed to the President. The conditions do not purport to alter or construe international legal obligations, and are principally of domestic political concern.

The reservation provides that 'the United States reserves the right to use other devices ... to destroy any stock of food or drink that is judged likely to be used by an enemy military force, if due precautions are taken for the safety of the civilian population'. Under the Protocol, 'other devices' are manually emplaced munitions that are detonated by a timer, manually or by remote control. From a legal standpoint, this reservation is interesting primarily because it establishes a much lower threshold for the destruction of foodstuffs than that in Article 54 of the First Protocol Additional to the Geneva Conventions. Article 54 would allow destruction of food and drink that are to be used 'solely' by members of the enemy forces, a restriction that commentators have construed as applying only to supplies already in the hands of those forces. Again, the United States appears to be deliberately deviating from the restrictions of Protocol I.

Some of the statements of understanding repeat interpretations adopted upon ratification of the original (1980) Protocol II. Several of the new understandings are interesting from a juridical standpoint. An understanding to Article 14, which for the first time requires penal legislation to implement the Protocol, spells out more clearly the mental element required for any offense. Specifically, it is the US understanding that penal liability should attach only if the accused:

(1) knew, or should have known, that his action was prohibited under the Protocol;

(2) intended to kill or cause serious injury to a civilian; and

(3) knew, or should have known that the intended victim was a civilian.

This understanding reflects the widely-held US sensitivity over spurious war crimes changes against US personnel, as does another understanding to the effect that nothing in Article 14 authorizes trial before an international criminal tribunal. To ensure that the point is driven home, the understanding goes on to state that '[t]he United States shall not recognize the jurisdiction of any international tribunal to prosecute a United States citizen for a violation of the Protocol or the Convention on Conventional Weapons.'

It should be noted that implementing legislation for Article 14 was enacted in 1998, prior to US ratification of the Amended Protocol. Section 2441 of Title 18, United States Code, includes the following in the definition of war crimes punishable under federal law: '[conduct] of a person who, in relation to an armed conflict and contrary to the provisions of the Protocol on Prohibitions or Restrictions on the Use of Mines, Booby-Traps and Other Devices as amended at Geneva on 3 May 1996 (Protocol II as amended on 3 May 1996), when the United States is a party to such Protocol, willfully kills or causes serious injury to civilians.'

In relation to Article 5, an understanding was filed on paragraph 6, which was specifically included to authorize continued use of the US hand-emplaced above-ground Claymore mine. Such mines may continue to be used in the immediate proximity of the unit that emplaced them, and if the area is, in the words of the Protocol, 'monitored by military personnel to ensure the effective exclusion of civilians'. A US understanding states that 'the maintenance of observation over avenues of approach [to the mined area]

... constitutes one acceptable form of monitoring to ensure the effective exclusion of civilians'. In other words, monitoring does not require the presence of sentries on the lines of approach, but can be done by observation.

Finally, the Senate added understandings to the effect that 'trip-wired hand grenades' shall be considered 'booby-traps' rather than mines or anti-personnel mines. They may thus be used outside perimeter-marked and monitored areas, and need not have self-destruction or self-deactivation devices.

BURRUS M. CARNAHAN

Weapons Causing Unnecessary Suffering and Superfluous Injury
☛ Letter of 23 September 1998 from Uniformed Services University of the Health Services to the American Medical Association[247]

The Office of International Medicine of the American Medical Association wrote letters to the Surgeons General of the armed forces, concerning the SIrUS Project of the International Committee of the Red Cross. On behalf of the Surgeons General, the Uniformed Services University of the Health Sciences replied, recommending that the Association not endorse the SIrUS Project. The letter noted that the SIrUS Project attempted to determine which weapons caused unnecessary suffering or superfluous injury based almost exclusively on medical data. International law, on the other hand, required weighing medical data against the military necessity for a weapon, the comparable wounding effects of other weapons, and other variables. The letter noted that this process could only be authoritatively carried out by states, rather than by non-governmental organizations.

BURRUS M. CARNAHAN

Revised Directive on the Law of War
☛ Department of Defence: Directive 5100.77, 9 December 1998

This document replaces the original directive from 1979.[248] The most significant changes relate to responsibility for investigating violations of the law. The earlier directive had assigned responsibility for only two situations: violations committed by a member of the US armed forces or violations committed by the enemy against US personnel. The new directive also provides for possible investigation of incidents committed by or against allied personnel, or by or against other persons during a conflict in which the United States is not a combatant party. These changes probably result from US Army experience during the 1991 Persian Gulf War. During and after that conflict, the United States assisted in the investigation of Iraqi war crimes against Kuwaiti and other allied nationals.

BURRUS M. CARNAHAN

---

247. Reprinted *infra* at p. 439.
248. DoD Directive 5100.77, 'DoD Law of War Program', 10 July 1979, reprinted *infra* at p. 534.

Cultural Property
☛ The White House: Submission of the Hague Convention on Cultural Property to the Senate: Presidential Message, Congressional Record, 6 January 1999, pp. S35-S36

On 6 January 1999, President Clinton submitted the 1954 Hague Convention on Protection of Cultural Property in Armed Conflict to the US Senate for advice and consent to ratification. The Protocol to the Convention was submitted for advice and consent to accession. The President's letter of transmittal noted that 'United States military policy and the conduct of operations are entirely consistent with the Convention's provisions.' The President also emphasized that, '[i]n conformity with the customary practice of nations, the protection of cultural property is not absolute. If cultural property is used for military purposes, or in the event of imperative military necessity, the protection afforded by the Convention is waived, in accordance with the Convention's terms.' This emphasis suggests that if the United States becomes a party to the Convention, it will resist efforts to amend the convention to remove the military necessity clauses.

BURRUS M. CARNAHAN

Radio Operators as Protected Medical Personnel
☛ Department of Defense, Office of General Counsel: Memorandum for Defense Human Resources Activity. Subject: Geneva Convention Cards for Medical Personnel, 4 August 1998[249]

The Defense Human Resources Activity requested advice on whether radio operators assigned to an Air Force medical unit could be issued identification cards bearing the Red Cross and documenting their status as personnel 'exclusively engaged in the administration of medical units and establishments' under Article 24 of the First Convention. Colonel Philip A. Johnson, Associate Deputy General Counsel, concluded that '[t]he administrative staff category would appear to be broad enough to cover radio operators, so long as they are exclusively engaged in supporting a medical unit or establishment in the performance of its medical mission.' The cards could therefore be issued. The final paragraph issued two cautionary statements. First, it noted that commanders have discretion not to issue medical identification cards and Red Cross armbands to particular categories of personnel, such as those likely to be called upon to perform additional duties besides supporting a medical unit or establishment. Second, it noted that if the cards were issued to radio operators, they should be given special training in their duties as exclusive medical administrative staff. These caveats were probably aimed at the danger that medical radio operators might be called upon to transmit intelligence or operational information (perhaps at the request of one of the military patients). This might be an act 'harmful to the enemy' that could endanger the protected status of the entire unit. There is also the danger that a radio operator might be suddenly transferred to a combat unit, where he or she would be subject to capture before a new identification card could be issued. This would be a technical violation by the United States of Article 44 of the First Convention, prohibiting use of the distinctive

---

249. Reprinted *infra* at p. 449.

emblem except to identify persons entitled to protection under the Convention. The individual carrying the erroneous card at the time of capture would be in an awkward situation if asked by the detaining power to verify the card's accuracy. The Code of Conduct in which all US military personnel are trained states that, beyond providing name, rank service number and date of birth, as required by the Third Convention, a service member should avoid answering further questions to the best of his ability. These and similar issues will have to be faced in developing training materials for any radio operators issued with these cards.

BURRUS M. CARNAHAN

Attacks by US on Sudan and Afghanistan: Application of Customary Law
- The White House: Presidential Address, 20 August 1998
- Department of Defence: Press Conference by Secretary of Defense William S. Cohen, 20 August 1998
- 'Why the U.S. Bombed', by Sandy Berger, *The Washington Times,* 16 October 1988

On 20 August 1998, United States' cruise missiles attacked what the government identified as terrorist training camps in Afghanistan and a chemical weapons plant in Sudan. All were asserted to be connected with Osama bin Laden, whom the United States believed was involved in attacks on US embassies in Africa. He was also believed to be planning new attacks on US nationals. The international law of war would probably apply to these attacks, since the targets were in the territory of states that did not consent to the US use of force. On that assumption, the documents illustrate how the United States applies certain rules of the customary law of war.

1. *Minimizing Civilian Casualties: Specific Measures:*
The President, in announcing the attacks, emphasized that 'every possible effort to minimize the loss of innocent life' had been made. General Shelton, Chairman of the Joint Chiefs of Staff, identified one of the specific measures adopted to this end – timing the attacks at night (7:30 PM in Sudan and 10:00 PM in Afghanistan). In the newspaper column written almost two months after the attacks, the President's National Security Adviser stated that the US government verified that no night shift was at work in the Sudanese plant. Defense Secretary Cohen also indicated that the possibility of an airborne 'plume' of toxic chemicals from the plant had been taken into account in an effort to minimize civilian casualties.

2. *Identification of Military Targets: No Presumption:*
Although the United States is not a party to Protocol I Additional to the Geneva Conventions, it generally accepts Article 52(2) of the Protocol as an accurate definition of lawful military objectives under customary law. The United States has not, however, agreed with Article 52(3), which states that 'in case of doubt whether an object which is normally dedicated to civilian purposes, such as a place of worship, a house or other dwelling or a school', is a military objective, 'it shall be presumed not to be so used'.

Instead of this presumption, the United States has stressed that a commander must make a reasonable and good faith judgement as to whether an object is a military objective based on all the information available at the time. The information on which targeting decisions are made is often classified; the August attack on Sudan provides a rare public illustration of the process. National Security Adviser Berger conceded that the plant was a 'dual-use' facility, i.e., one capable of supporting either civil or military production. The Sudanese government described it as a pharmaceutical plant, arguably an 'object normally dedicated to civilian purposes'. The information upon which the United States based its decision to attack the plant included:

— Discovery of traces of a precursor to nerve gas (VX) near the plant;
— This precursor chemical did not occur in nature and had no civilian use;
— Close ties between Osama bin Laden and the Sudanese government;
— Financial ties between Osama bin Laden and the enterprise owning the plant; and
— Interest by Osama bin Laden in acquiring chemical weapons.

While these circumstances were suspicious, it cannot be said that there was no 'doubt' as to the military use of the plant. Nevertheless, based on all the facts and circumstances, including the nature of the threat, it was decided that the plant should be considered a valid military objective.

3. *Targeting Individuals: Assassination*

The law of war prohibits assassination. Within the US government, an Executive Order issued by President Reagan prohibits assassination by any government agency in peace or war. The rule against assassination does not, however, prohibit attacks, by regular military forces, on specific individuals who are themselves legitimate military targets. In this case the President noted that the attack on the camps in Afghanistan were carried out on 20 August because of evidence that a meeting of 'key terrorist leaders' was being held there. When Secretary of Defense Cohen was asked whether Osama bin Laden was himself a legitimate target, he replied 'to the extent that he or his organization have declared war against the United States or our interests, then he certainly is engaged in an act of war', implying that this individual was a legitimate target of military action.

BURRUS M. CARNAHAN

International Criminal Court

☛ US Department of State, Daily Press Briefing No. 88, 20 July 1998
☛ Testimony of David J. Scheffer, Ambassador-at-Large for War Crimes Issues and Head of the US Delegation to the UN Diplomatic Conference on the Establishment of a Permanent International Criminal Court, before the Senate Foreign Relations Committee, Washington DC, 23 July 1998

In the initial press conference, three reasons were given for US rejection of the Treaty. All these objections were explicitly related to concern that US officials and military personnel might be subjected to frivolous or politically motivated prosecutions. Ambassador Scheffer's testimony contains a more technical discussion of these objections, and adds a few additional US problems unrelated to concern over abusive prosecutions.

The three primary objections were: 1) The Treaty would extend the Court's jurisdiction to nationals of states not parties to it; 2) The Treaty should have given the parties an opportunity to assess the Court's impartiality and effectiveness before subjecting their nationals to its jurisdiction; and 3) The Court's prosecutor could initiate investigations and prosecutions on his or her own authority (with the consent of two judges); this could involve the court in 'controversy, political decision-making and confusion'. (Ambassador Scheffer)

In connection with the first two objections, the State Department also announced that, as long as it remained a non-party, the United States would not recognize the court's jurisdiction over US nationals.

This position raises an interesting question about the United States' general policy on jurisdiction over war crimes and crimes against humanity. From the end of World War II to 1998, the United States had consistently supported the doctrine that, under customary international law, jurisdiction over war crimes and crimes against humanity was universal. That is, any state could properly bring a person accused of those crimes before its own courts for trial, regardless of whether its nationals, territory or other interests were involved in the alleged crime. By supporting this doctrine, the United States implicitly accepted that any other state could lawfully try a US national for war crimes or crimes against humanity. Logically, it should follow that if universal jurisdiction could be lawfully exercised by a state through its own courts, that state could also delegate that jurisdiction to an international tribunal.[250] Yet the United States has now expressly rejected any exercise of jurisdiction by the International Criminal Court over US nationals, even though the offenses within the Court's competence are those traditionally subject to universal jurisdiction.

Do these developments mean that, as of July 1998, the United States no longer recognizes universal jurisdiction over war crimes and crimes against humanity? While a literal reading of the official documents might suggest this, a more cautious assessment is probably warranted. It should be noted that the documents contain no express reference to the exercise of universal jurisdiction by *states*. Indeed, their purpose is not to express general policy on criminal jurisdiction, but rather to explain the US policy towards a specific treaty. In his testimony, Ambassador Scheffer noted that the Rome conference had, after consideration of the issue, decided *not* to confer universal jurisdiction on the International Criminal Court, though it did include language that could confer jurisdiction over some offenses by nationals of non-party states. It is therefore premature to conclude that the United States has now repudiated its long-standing support for universal jurisdiction over war crimes and crimes against humanity. The more likely conclusion is that the United States position relates to the specific court created by the Rome conference. The United States therefore appears to take the position that the International Criminal Court was not intended by the negotiating parties to exercise

---

250. For example, the United States, Britain, France and the Soviet Union delegated part of their national jurisdiction over Nazi war crimes to the International Military Tribunal at Nuremberg in the 1945 London Agreement.

universal jurisdiction in even a partial form, and that any exercise of jurisdiction over nationals of non-parties would be *ultra vires* for that court.

The true basis of United States' opposition to the International Criminal Court appears to lie in the third reason: the independence of the prosecutor. It may be difficult to understand why institutional independence should be considered a cause for suspicion rather than confidence. The United States position is not, however, without a basis in its history. Sweeping, politically-motivated war crimes charges were leveled against American prisoners of war in both the Korean (1950-1953) and Southeast Asian (1965-1975) conflicts. The European experience with international institutions has differed from that of the United States. With the growing power of the European Union over the last 40 years, Europeans have grown to accept the general legitimacy and impartiality of supranational institutions; the United States government and people have no similar experience.

Finally, differences in legal culture appear to have aggravated misunderstandings at the Rome conference. Like all international penal tribunals, the International Criminal Court will mix procedures from both the continental civil law tradition and the Anglo-American common law tradition. In the civil law tradition, an independent, apolitical prosecutor is one of the fundamental components of a fair system of penal procedure. The common law system, particularly as it has evolved in the United States, is more comfortable with prosecutors as political officials, either elected or appointed. For protection against politically-motivated prosecutions, this system places reliance on the independent jury and a vigorous role for the defense counsel. Given these fundamental differences in legal culture, it is easy to understand why many European delegations to the Rome conference insisted on an independent, powerful prosecutor, and why the American government would view that proposal with suspicion.

BURRUS M. CARNAHAN

Cases

(A) Under the ACTA and TVPA

☞ *Jane Doe* v. *Islamic Salvation Front (FIS) and Anwar Haddam*, 993 *F.* Supp. 3 (D.C. Cir. 1998)

Plaintiffs are eight anonymous Algerian and French female citizens and the Rassemblement Algerien de Femmes Democrates (RAFD), a non-governmental organization of Algerian women with its headquarters in Algiers. The defendants are the Islamic Salvation Front (FIS) and Mr. Anwar Haddam (a native and citizen of Algeria), whom the plaintiffs alleged served as a high-ranking official in the FIS. The plaintiffs asserted that the defendants participated in and conspired to commit crimes against humanity, war crimes, highjacking, summary execution, rape, mutilation, sexual slavery, murder, and numerous other violations of international law in violation of the Alien Tort Claims Act (ATCA) and the Torture Victim Protection Act (TVPA).

The context of this case is the civil war in Algeria. In 1991-1992 the FIS won Algeria's first free elections, but the military declared the election invalid and banned the FIS. The result was civil strife. Mr Haddam won a seat in the National Assembly in 1991, but in 1992 when the military regime banned the FIS, Mr Haddam fled Algeria and sought political asylum in the United States. Plaintiffs alleged that Mr Haddam established an office in Washington, DC, where he acted as an official spokesman for the FIS, and conspired, aided and abetted, and participated in other violent activities of the FIS. Over the defendants' motion to dismiss, the court found that there was personal jurisdiction, proper service of process, justiciability (at least under the ATCA), and that the RAFD has standing to sue. The court's analysis and discussion of subject matter jurisdiction under the ATCA is important.

The ATCA, initially enacted in 1789, provides that '[t]he district court shall have original jurisdiction of any civil action by an alien ... committed in violation of the law of nations or a treaty of the United States.' Mr Haddam claimed that the violation of the law of nations must be state action – an act under actual or apparent authority, or color of law, of a foreign state. Citing *Kadić* v. *Karadžić*,[251] the court held: 'We do not agree that the law of nations, as understood in the modern era, confines its reach to state action. Instead, we hold that certain forms of conduct violate the law of nations whether undertaken by those acting under the auspices of a state or only as private individuals.'[252] The court concluded by noting that the acts alleged to have been suffered by the plaintiffs violate international law as evidenced by common Article 3 of the 1949 Geneva Conventions, ratified by over 180 states.

Regarding the TVPA, the court found that the statute does require state action, but that the state action requirement does not require that a particular government is officially recognized. A private group could constitute a *de facto* state, in which case members of that group could be held liable under the TVPA. The court reserved its ruling on whether the FIS was a *de facto* state pending further development of the facts.

RONALD D. NEUBAUER

(B) Compensation for IHL violations
☞ *Fishel* v. *BASF Group, et al.*, Civil No. 4-96-CV-10449, Lexis 21230 (S.D. Iowa 1998)

The plaintiff, on behalf of himself and the purported Class, sought compensation for forced labor provided through German labor camps between 1942 and 1945. Plaintiff also sought monetary damages for alleged war crimes and other statutory violations. The defendants (BASF Group, Hoechst AG, Bayer Group, Daimler-Benz AG, and Frid Krupp BMBH) are alleged successors-in-interest to firms the plaintiffs alleged to have worked in concert with the German government to force plaintiff and others to perform slave labor. For example, Plaintiff alleged that he and others were forced to perform slave labor for Herman Goering Works (a missile manufacturer) and Messerschmitt (an aircraft manufacturer), predecessors-in-interest to Daimler-Benz AG. Among other claims, the plaintiff also alleged a cause of action for breach of contract for failure to pay wages under the Convention Respecting the Laws and Customs of War on Land of 1907 (Hague Convention) and that the defendants' acts in violation of the Hague Convention were war crimes.

The Court granted defendants' combined motion to dismiss the case. First, and dispositive, the court held that plaintiff did not make the required showing that any of

251. 70 F.3d 232 (2d Cir. 1995).
252. Ibid., at p. 239.

the defendants had the requisite 'quality and quantity of contacts with Iowa necessary to support the exercise of general personal jurisdiction'. The court also noted that the cases are 'unanimous . . . in holding that nothing in the Hague Convention even impliedly grants individuals the right to seek damages for violation of [its] provisions'.[253]

RONALD D. NEUBAUER

Ongoing Cases
☛ Civil Law Suit of *two unnamed Kosovar Albanians* v. *Slobodan Milošević,* his wife and senior members of his government, Boston District Court

On 25 May 1999, two Kosovar Albanians filed a lawsuit under the Alien Tort Claims Act in the Boston District Court against Slobodan Milošević, his wife and senior members of his government for acts of genocide and war crimes. In the civil action, the plaintiffs allege that as a part of a 'deliberate campaign of "ethnic cleansing"' the defendants violated laws of the United States as well as international law. The lawsuit relates to the killings of relatives of the two plaintiffs by Serbian policemen and members of the 'White Tigers', the paramilitary unit headed by Zeljko Raznjatović, also known as 'Arkan'. Defendants include the latter, the foreign minister and the minister of information of Yugoslavia, a former Yugoslav diplomat in Washington who is now spokesman for the foreign ministry, the chief of staff of the Yugoslav army and several military and police commanders.[254]

Pending Legislation
☛ Anti-Atrocity Alien Deportation Act, sponsored by Senators Patrick Leahy (D-Vermont) and Orrin Hatch (R-Utah)

On 4 November 1999, the US Senate passed legislation to facilitate the deportation of war criminals and expand the mandate of the Justice Department's Office of Special Investigations' (OSI) which, since its founding in 1979, has been confined to tracking down former Nazis and their allies who slipped into the United States after World War II. The bill would expand the duties of the OSI to investigate, prosecute and remove any alien who participated in torture or genocide abroad. It would also amend the Immigration and Nationality Act to authorize direct deportation of any aliens who have engaged in such acts. The new law would add torture to the criminal criteria for excluding or deporting an immigrant, but it is silent about other crimes. The bill now has to be approved by the House of Representatives.[255]

---

253. A similar finding was reached by a court in Japan. See *supra* pp. 390 et seq.

254. Raymond Bonner, 'Civil Action Accuses Yugoslavs of War Crimes', *New York Times*, 26 May 1999.

255. War Criminal Deportation Bill OK'd', Associated Press, 4 November 1999; Steve Fainaru, 'New pursuit seen on war criminals living in US', *Boston Globe*, 29 October 1999.

YEMEN[256]

Military Penal Code
☛ Law 21 of 25 July 1998 concerning military infractions and penalties.[257]

---

256. Information provided by the ICRC Advisory Service.
257. Reprinted *infra* p. 558.

DOCUMENTATION

The Documentation section is compiled and edited by the Managing Editor, Avril McDonald, from materials provided to the *YIHL* by its correspondents, *inter alia*. Restricted space forces us to be selective in the documents included. The *YIHL's* general policy is to prefer documents to which access might otherwise be difficult, in particular regarding state practice. In general, we will tend not to publish documents that are easily and widely available, such as UN Documents or jurisprudence of the *ad hoc* Tribunals, although we may make exceptions. Readers are invited to send documents to the Managing Editor for inclusion in this section. Please note that, in order to save space, documents may appear in a more condensed format than the original, and some changes may have been made to the form, though not the content, in order to conform with the Yearbook's house style. The titles of documents listed in the table of contents on pp. 437-438 may not be the exact titles. The latter appear alongside the particular documents.

CLASSIFICATION OF DOCUMENTS

NOTE: Many international and national documents related to international humanitarian law are available on the Internet through an on-line access to the ICRC IHL database (ICRC website: http://www.icrc.org). This database now contains 91 treaties and texts on the conduct of hostilities and the protection of victims of war (dating from 1856 to the present); the commentaries on the four Geneva Conventions and their Additional Protocols; an up-to-date list of signatures, ratifications, accessions or successions to IHL treaties; and the full text of reservations. Constantly updated, this data is also regularly replicated on a CD-ROM that can be obtained from the ICRC (Public Information Division, 19, av. de la Paix, CH-1202 Geneva; e-mail; webmaster.gva@icrc.org; Fax: ++ 41 22 733 20 57; CHF 49.- or USD 39.-). National implementing legislation (Geneva Conventions Acts, extracts from Penal Codes, laws related to the protection of the emblem, laws on co-operation with the international Tribunals, etc.) and jurisprudence are also available for an increasing number of countries.

DOCUMENTS

1.22   SUPERFLUOUS INJURY AND UNNECESSARY SUFFERING

☛ **USA: Letter of 23 September 1998 from Uniformed Services University of the Health Services to the American Medical Association**

Uniformed Services University of Health Science
4501 Jones Bridge Road
Bethseda, Maryland

Ms. Ellen Waterman
Office of International Medicine
American Medical Association
515 North state street
Chicago, IL 60610
September 23, 1998

Dear Ms. Waterman

Thank you for your letter of August 27, 1998, concerning the SirUS Project of the International Committee of the Red Cross (ICRC), and the British Medical Association's proposed resolution to the World Medical Association Assembly (WMA) to be held in October. I am responding to your letter and the letters addressed to the military Surgeons General on behalf of the AMA section Council on Federal and Military Medicine.

A medical study of the physical effects of military weapons may be worthwhile if conducted to advance the medical knowledge that improves the quality of medical care for weapons injuries. Physicians need to be aware of the types of injuries caused by different weapons in order to be better prepared to treat them. Accordingly, we feel that a project that attempts to study the effects of weapons in order to contribute to improve medical care should be supported.

To a limited degree, we are comfortable with the goal of identifying medical information that may be useful to governments in discharging their respective responsibilities to ensure that the weapons their military forces employ do not violate the law of war prohibition of weapons that may cause superfluous injury or unnecessary suffering. However, the responsibility for making a determination as to whether a weapon may cause unnecessary suffering is a treaty obligation of governments. In this regard, the United States has had a long-standing requirement for the legal review of all new weapons to ensure that they are consistent with its law of war and arms control obligations. It would be inappropriate for the ICRC or other private organizations to endeavour to usurp a treaty obligation of governments.

In this respect, we have some difficulty with the suggestion made in the executive summary of the SirUS Project in the article by Dr. Coupland (provided as an attachment to the communication on the (SirUS Project) that much of the human toll in Twentieth Century wars is the result of the use of weapons that cause superfluous injury or unnecessary suffering. The law of war principle of unnecessary suffering constitutes acknowledgement that, in war, there is necessary suffering. Serious injury or death in war is regrettable, but is not prohibited by the law of war. Nor is it necessarily unjustifiable or morally wrong. The greater cause of unnecessary deaths, such as civilian deaths, is due to the unlawful use of lawful weapons rather than the use of illegal weapons. The SirUS Project seemingly fails to take into account this very important distinction.

We do not object to the SirUS Project's collection of objective and relevant material that, once validated, can be made available to governments and others. However, it appears that the SirUS Project attempts to do more than this. According to the 'summary points' in Dr. Coupland's article, SirUS would rely exclusively on medical data to determine whether a weapon causes unnecessary suffering, and, therefore, is illegal.

This appears to place authority for determining the legality of weapons in the hands of a medical body or organisation, and to rely almost exclusively on medical data in determining what constitutes superfluous injury or unnecessary suffering. We believe that this is an extremely complex determination reserved to governments that requires weighing a number of medical, ethical, scientific, technical and other variables. Although in some instances, such as biological weapons, governments have agreed to the express prohibition of weapons, in most cases a law of war weapon review requires consideration of the military necessity for a weapon – a foundation law of war principle that is not mentioned in the SirUs Project. Nor does the SirUS Project provide for governments to take into consideration the comparable wounding effect of other lawful weapons when determining the legality of a particular weapon, as permitted by the law of war and manifested in State practice.

For these reasons and in conclusion, we must reluctantly recommend that the American Medical Association not endorse the SirUS Project.

Emmanuel G. Cassimatis, MD
COL, MC, USA
Chair, AMA Section Council on Federal and Military Medicine

2.1   TYPES OF CONFLICT

☛ **Colombia: Statement of Government of Colombia regarding the Status of FARC, 16 June 1999**

Ministry of Foreign Affairs of Colombia
Vice-ministry of Foreign Affairs of Colombia
Diplomatic Exchange concerning the Peace No. 4
16 June 1999

Answer of H.E. the Minister of Foreign Affairs Guillermo Fernando to the questions as posed in the proposal of summons no. 142

Recognition of state of war respecting the FARC
(Fuerzas Armadas Revolucionarias de Colombia)

The Government has not and will not recognise the state of war with any subversive groupings, which operate within the country. In the framework of the negotiations undertaken to come to a peaceful solution in Colombia, a political status has been conferred on the FARC, which is different from the state of belligerence.

The institution of belligerence, which is part of the international customary law, is in practise obviously in disuse.

International law provides certain minimum requirements for the recognition of the belligerent character of irregular groupings, which operate within the territory of a state, namely:

— That the grouping is actually in possession of part of the territory of the state;

— That their leaders effectively exercise jurisdiction and control over that territory;

— That their troops are somehow organised and conduct their battles according to the rules and customs of warfare.

In relation to the first two points: the reason that the scene of the negotiations with the FARC is set in a part of Colombian territory, is because this situation was given by a facultative and non-compulsory administrative act, based on the Constitution and Law 418 of 1997, and not in the course of armed combat. Thus is this unilateral and temporary decision of the Government based on the recognition of the national law and the integration of the sovereignty over the whole territory of the nation and in particular over the zone of détente. It should be kept in mind that in this zone the mayors and certain government agencies are functioning according to their competence.

As far as the third point is concerned: no deeds should be committed, that are so evidently forbidden by the Law of Human Rights, such as the recruitment of minors, killing of civilians and the taking of hostages.

It will be remembered that at the beginning of this year there was some speculation, if indeed certain utterances of the President of Venezuela would have the juridical consequence, that the FARC would implicitly be recognised as a belligerent grouping. The Government of Venezuela denied emphatically that this was their intention and clearly indicated that the Government of Colombia continued to be their only valid interlocutor and that the remarks of the President should be taken as purely a matter of speech.

Finally, it should be clear that the concept of recognition of belligerence is entirely foreign to the application of International Human Rights (IHR). Since the adoption of the Conventions of Geneva 1949 it is internationally accepted that the application of this norm does not in any way affect the juridical status of the parties in conflict, as was shown convincingly during the procedure that led to the endorsement by Colombia of the Additional Protocol II of 1977. Likewise are undoubtedly all the guerrilla groupings, operating in Colombia obliged to comply with the rules of the IHR, but this does not make them subjects of international law. Under Art. 3 of the Conventions of Geneva and under Protocol no. II, these groupings have the status of 'parties in conflict' and as such they are obliged to respect the most elementary humanitarian rules laid down in these treaties.

☛ Resolution adopted by the Institute of International Law at its Session in Berlin from 17–20 August 1999 concerning the Application of International Humanitarian Law and Fundamental Human Rights in Armed Conflicts in which Non-State Entities are Parties

(Fourteenth Commission, Rapporteur: Mr Milan Sahović)

The Institute of International Law,

Recalling its Resolutions 'Droits et devoirs des Puissances étrangères, au cas de mouvement insurrectionnel, envers les gouvernements établis et reconnus qui sont aux prises avec l'insurrection' (Neuchâtel session, 1900), 'The Principle of Non-Intervention in Civil Wars' (Wiesbaden session, 1975) and 'The Protection of Human Rights and the Principle of Non Intervention in Internal Affairs of States' (Santiago de Compostela session, 1989);

Recalling further its Resolutions on the 'Conditions of Application of Humanitarian Rules of Armed Conflict to Hostilities in which United Nations Forces May Be Engaged' (Zagreb session, 1971) and on the 'Conditions of Application of Rules, Other than Humanitarian Rules, of Armed Conflict to Hostilities in which United Nations Forces May Be Engaged' (Wiesbaden session, 1975);

Considering that armed conflicts in which non-State entities are parties have become more and more numerous and increasingly motivated in particular by ethnic, religious or racial causes;

Noting that, as a consequence, the civilian population is increasingly affected by internal armed conflicts and ultimately bears the brunt of the resulting violence, causing great suffering, death and privation;

Noting that armed conflicts in which non-State entities are parties do not only concern those States in which they take place, but also affect the interests of the international community as a whole;

Bearing in mind that, in the last fifty years, the principles of the United Nations Charter and of human rights law have had a substantial impact on the development and application of international humanitarian law;

Recalling the ruling of the International Court of Justice that the obligation laid down in Article 1 common to the Geneva Conventions 'to respect' the Conventions and to 'ensure respect' for them 'in all circumstances' derives from general principles of international humanitarian law, with the consequence that it has acquired the status of an obligation of customary international law;

Emphasizing the ruling of the International Court of Justice that Article 3 common to the Geneva Conventions of 1949 reflects 'elementary considerations of humanity' and that the fundamental rules of humanitarian law applicable in armed conflicts 'are to be observed ... because they constitute intransgressible principles of international customary law';

Considering the ruling of the International Criminal Tribunal for the Former Yugoslavia whereby many principles and rules previously applicable only in international armed conflicts are now applicable in internal armed conflicts and serious violations of international humanitarian law committed within the context of the latter category of conflicts constitute war crimes;

Supporting the prosecution and punishment by national jurisdictions of those responsible for war crimes, crimes against humanity, genocide or other serious violations of international humanitarian law, as well as the establishment of international tribunals entrusted with this task;

Recognizing that, under Article 7 of the Rome Statute of the International Criminal Court, crimes against humanity can be committed by persons acting for States or non-State entities;

Noting that the actions undertaken by the Security Council under Chapter VII of the Charter in armed conflicts in which non-State entities were parties confirm that respect for international humanitarian law is an integral element of the security system of the world organization;

Welcoming the United Nations Secretary General's regulation of 6 August 1999 on the Observance by United Nations Forces of international humanitarian law which reaffirms their obligation to comply strictly with humanitarian law, in particular as to the protection of the civilian population, and provides for the possibility of prosecuting members of the military personnel of such Forces in case of violations of humanitarian law, in particular in situations of internal armed conflicts;

Welcoming also the important role played by the International Committee of the Red Cross in recent conflicts to which non-State entities were parties in seeking to ensure humanitarian protection for all victims and in inviting the parties to such conflicts to abide by elementary principles of humanity, notably to spare the civilian population the effects of violence and devastation;

Considering that it is desirable that international humanitarian law be reconsidered and adapted to new circumstances, so as to reinforce respect for this law and the protection of victims in aimed conflicts in which non-State entities are parties,

Adopts this Resolution:

I. For the purposes of this Resolution:

— the expression 'armed conflicts in which non-State entities are parties' means internal armed conflicts between a government's armed forces and those of one or several non-State entities, or between several non-State entities; also included are internal armed conflicts in which peacekeeping forces intervene;

— the expression 'non-State entities' means the parties to internal armed conflicts who oppose the government's armed forces or are fighting entities of a similar nature and who fulfil the conditions set forth in Article 3 common to the Geneva Conventions of 1949 on the Protection of Victims of War or in Article I of the 1977 Protocol Additional to the Geneva Conventions and relating to the Protection of Victims of Non-International Armed Conflicts (Protocol II).

II. All parties to armed conflicts in which non-State entities are parties, irrespective of their legal status, as well as the United Nations, and competent regional and other international organizations have the obligation to respect international humanitarian law as well as fundamental human rights. The application of such principles and rules does not affect the legal status of the parties to the conflict and is not dependent on their recognition as belligerents or insurgents.

III. Respect for international humanitarian law and fundamental human rights constitutes an integral part of international order for the maintenance and reestablishment of peace and security, in particular in armed conflicts in which non-State entities are parties.

IV. International law applicable to armed conflicts in which non-State entities are parties includes:

— Article 3 common to the Geneva Conventions of 1949 as basic principles of international humanitarian law;

— Protocol II and all other conventions applicable to non-international armed conflicts;

— customary principles and rules of international humanitarian law on the conduct of hostilities and the protection of victims applicable to internal armed conflicts;

— the principles and rules of international law guaranteeing fundamental human rights;

— the principles and rules of international law applicable in internal armed conflicts, relating to war crimes, crimes against humanity, genocide and other international crimes;

— the principles of international law 'derived from established custom, from the principles of humanity and from dictates of public conscience.'

V. Every State and every non-State entity participating in an armed conflict are legally bound *vis-à-vis* each other as well as all other members of the international community to respect international humanitarian law in all circumstances, and any other State is legally entitled to demand respect for this body of law. No State or non-State entity can escape its obligations by denying the existence of an armed conflict.

VI. In cases of serious violations of international humanitarian law or fundamental human rights, the United Nations and competent regional and other international organizations have the right to adopt appropriate measures in accordance with international law.

VII. Without prejudice to the functions and powers which the Charter attributes to the organs of the United Nations, in case of systematic and massive violations of humanitarian law or fundamental human rights, States, acting individually or collectively, are entitled to take diplomatic, economic and other measures towards any party to the armed conflict which has violated its obligations, provided such measures are permitted under international law.

VIII. Any serious violation of international humanitarian law in armed conflicts in which non-State entities are parties entails the individual responsibility of the persons involved, regardless of their status or official position, in accordance with international instruments that entrust the repression of these acts to national or international jurisdictions. The competent authorities of a State on the territory of which is found a person against whom is alleged a serious violation of international humanitarian law committed in a non-international armed conflict are entitled to prosecute and try such a person before their courts; they are urged to do so.

IX. In order to achieve a better protection for the victims in armed conflicts in which non-State entities are parties and taking into account the experience of recent armed conflicts of a non-international character the following measures should be considered:

— the conclusion by the parties to such conflicts of special agreements, in accordance with Article 3 paragraph 2 common to the Geneva Conventions of 1949, on the application of all or part of the provisions of the Conventions;

— the support of States, the United Nations, the International Committee of the Red Cross as well as other international bodies of a humanitarian character for measures to verify and oversee the application of international humanitarian law in internal armed conflicts; furthermore, should the State concerned claim that no internal armed conflict has broken out, the authorisation given to the United Nations or any other competent regional or international organisation to establish impartially whether international humanitarian law is applicable;

— the application of Protocol II in all non-international armed conflicts, without waiting for its formal revision;

— the amendment of Protocol II, with a view to complementing its rules and in particular so as:

(a) to establish an impartial and independent international body designed to investigate respect for international humanitarian law (cf. Article 90 of Protocol I);

(b) to add a grave breaches provision addressing, in particular, issues of jurisdiction, extradition and surrender to an international criminal jurisdiction.

X. To the extent that certain aspects of internal disturbances and tensions may not be covered by international humanitarian law, individuals remain under the protection of international law guaranteeing fundamental human rights. All parties are bound to respect fundamental human rights under the scrutiny of the international community.

XI. The Institute welcomes and encourages the progressive adaptation of the principles and rules relating to internal armed conflicts to the principles and rules applicable in international armed conflicts. Therefore it is desirable and necessary that States, the United Nations and competent regional and other international organizations, drawing special inspiration from the important work done by the International Committee of the Red Cross in this field, draft and adopt a convention designed to regulate all armed conflicts and protect all victims, regardless of whether such conflicts are international, non-international or of a mixed character.

XII. All States and non-State entities must disseminate the principles and rules of humanitarian law and fundamental human rights, which are applicable in internal armed conflicts.

2.231   MERCENARIES

☛ Republic of South Africa: Law No. 15 of 1998: Regulation of Foreign Military Assistance Act 1998[1]

Act
To regulate the rendering of foreign military assistance by South African juristic persons, citizens, persons permanently resident within the Republic and foreign citizens rendering such assistance from within the borders of the Republic; and to provide for matters connected therewith.

Preamble
The Constitution of the Republic of South Africa, 1996, provides in section 198(b) that the resolve to live in peace and harmony precludes any South African citizen from participating in armed conflict, nationally or internationally, except as provided for in the Constitution or national legislation. In order to implement aspects of this provision and in the interest of promoting and protecting human rights and fundamental freedoms, universally, it is necessary to regulate the rendering of foreign military assistance by

---

1. Provided by the South African Embassy, The Hague.

South African juristic persons, citizens, persons permanently resident in the Republic and foreign citizens who render such assistance from within the borders of the Republic.

Be it enacted by the Parliament of the Republic of South Africa, as follows:

Definitions
1. In this Act, unless the context indicates otherwise-
(i) 'armed conflict' includes any armed conflict between-
    (a) the armed forces of foreign states;
    (b) the armed forces of a foreign state and dissident armed forces or other armed groups; or
    (c) armed groups;
(ii) 'Committee' means the National Conventional Arms Control Committee as constituted by the National Executive by the decision of 18 August 1995;
(iii) 'foreign military assistance' means military services or military-related services, or any attempt, encouragement, incitement or solicitation to render such services, in the form of-
    (a) military assistance to a party to the armed conflict by means of-
        (i) advice or training;
        (ii) personnel, financial, logistical, intelligence or operational support;
        (iii) personnel recruitment;
        (iv) medical or paramedical services; or
        (v) procurement of equipment;
    (b) security services for the protection of individuals involved in armed conflict or their property;
    (c) any action aimed at overthrowing a government or undermining the constitutional order, sovereignty or territorial integrity of a state;
    (d) any other action that has the result of furthering the military interests of a party to the armed conflict, but not humanitarian or civilian activities aimed at relieving the plight of civilians in an area of armed conflict;
(iv) 'mercenary activity' means direct participation as a combatant in armed conflict for private gain;
(v) 'Minister' means the Minister of Defence;
(vi) 'person' means a natural person who is a citizen of or is permanently resident in the Republic, a juristic person registered or incorporated in the Republic, and any foreign citizen who contravenes any provision of this Act within the borders of the Republic;
(vii) 'Republic' means the Republic of South Africa;
(viii) 'register' means the register of authorisations and approvals maintained in terms of section 6.

Prohibition on mercenary activity
2. No person may within the Republic or elsewhere recruit, use or train persons for or finance or engage in mercenary activity.

Rendering of foreign military assistance prohibited
3. No person may within the Republic or elsewhere

(a) offer to render any foreign military assistance to any state or organ of state, group of persons or other entity or person unless he or she has been granted authorisation to offer such assistance in terms of section 4;

(b) render any foreign military assistance to any state or organ of state, group of persons or other entity or person unless such assistance is rendered in accordance with an agreement approved in terms of section 5.

Authorisation for rendering of foreign military assistance
4. (1) Any person who wishes to obtain the authorisation referred to in section 3(a) shall submit to the Committee an application for authorisation in the prescribed form and manner.

(2) The Committee must consider any application for authorisation submitted in terms of subsection (1) and must make a recommendation to the Minister that such application be granted or refused.

(3) The Minister, in consultation with the Committee, may refuse an application for authorisation referred to in subsection (2), or may grant the application subject to such conditions as they may determine, and may at any time withdraw or amend an authorisation so granted.

(4) Any authorisation granted in terms of this section shall not be transferable.

(5) The prescribed fees must be paid in respect of an application for authorisation granted in terms of subsection (3).

Approval of agreement for rendering of foreign military assistance
5. (1) A person who wishes to obtain the approval of an agreement or arrangement for the rendering of foreign military assistance, by virtue of an authorisation referred to in section 3(b) to render the relevant military assistance, shall submit an application to the Committee in the prescribed form and manner.

(2) The Committee must consider an application for approval submitted to it in terms of subsection (1) and must make a recommendation to the Minister that the application be granted or be refused.

(3) The Minister, in consultation with the Committee, may refuse an application for approval referred to in subsection (2), or grant the application subject to such conditions as they may determine, and may at any time withdraw or amend an approval so granted.

(4) Any approval granted in terms of this section shall not be transferable.

(5) The prescribed fees must be paid in respect of an application for approval granted in terms of subsection (3).

Register of authorisations and approvals
6. (1) The Committee shall maintain a register of authorisations and approvals issued by the Minister in terms of sections 4 and 5.

(2) The Committee must each quarter submit reports to the National Executive, Parliament and the Parliamentary Committees on Defence with regard to the register.

Criteria for granting or refusal of authorisations and approvals
7. (1) An authorisation or approval in terms of sections 4 and 5 may not be granted if it would-

(a) be in conflict with the Republic's obligations in terms of international law;

(b) result in the infringement of human rights and fundamental freedoms in the territory in which the foreign military assistance is to be rendered;

(c) endanger the peace by introducing destabilising military capabilities into the region where the assistance is to be, or is likely to be, rendered or would otherwise contribute to regional instability and would negatively influence the balance of power in such region;

(d) support or encourage terrorism in any manner;

(e) contribute to the escalation of regional conflicts;

(f) prejudice the Republic's national or international interests;

(g) be unacceptable for any other reason.

(2) A person whose application for an authorisation or approval in terms of section 4 or 5 has not been granted by the Minister may request the Minister to furnish written reasons for his or her decision.

(3) The Minister shall furnish the reasons referred to in subsection (2) within a reasonable time.

Offences and penalties

8. (1) Any person who contravenes any provision of section 2 or 3, or fails to comply with a condition with regard to any authorisation or approval granted in terms of section 4 or 5, shall be guilty of an offence and liable on conviction to a fine or to imprisonment or to both such fine and imprisonment.

(2) The court convicting any person of an offence under this Act may declare any armament, weapon, vehicle, uniform, equipment or other property or object in respect of which the offence was committed or which was used for, in or in connection with the commission of the offence, to be forfeited to the State.

Extraterritorial application of Act

9. Any court of law in the Republic may try a person for an offence referred to in section 8 notwithstanding the fact that the act or omission to which the charge relates, was committed outside the Republic, except in the instance where a foreign citizen commits any offence in terms of section 8 wholly outside the borders of the Republic.

Regulations

10. The Minister, in consultation with the Committee, may make regulations relating to-

(a) any matter which is required or permitted in terms of this Act to be prescribed;

(b) the criteria to be taken into account in the consideration of an application for an authorisation or approval in terms of section 4 or 5;

(c) the maintenance of the register; and

(d) any other matter which may be necessary for the application of this Act.

Exemptions

11. The Minister, in consultation with the Committee, may exempt any person from the provisions of sections 4 and 5 in respect of a particular event or situation, and subject to such conditions as he or she may determine.

Short title

12. This Act shall be called the Regulation of Foreign Military Assistance Act, 1998, and shall come into operation on a date fixed by the President by proclamation in the Gazette.

3.133   MEDICAL AND RELIGIOUS PERSONNEL

☛ USA: Eligibility of Radio Operators Assigned to Medical Units for Geneva Conventions Cards

Department of Defense Office of General Counsel,
1600 Defense Pentagon,
Washington, DC 20301-1600
4 August 1998

Memorandum for Defense Human Resources activity. Attention: Sheila L. Ford
Subject: Geneva Convention Cards for Medical Personnel

Some time ago you asked for our opinion on whether the radio operators assigned to an Air Force medical unit are eligible to be issued DD Form 1934, Geneva Convention Identity Card for Medical and Religious Personnel, and Auxiliary Medical Personnel. We delayed our reply awaiting what we anticipated would be the imminent publication of a USAF directive that we are told will address this subject, but we have decided not to wait any longer for its publication.

The issue is whether personnel who are assigned to medical units, but who are not directly engaged in the delivery of medical care, may be issued DD Form 1934. We believe they may.

Article 24 of the Geneva Convention for the Amelioration of the Condition of the Wounded and Sick in Armed Forces in the Field of August 12, 1949 (GWS) provides, 'Medical personnel exclusively engaged in the search for, or the collection, transport or treatment of the wounded or sick, or in the prevention of disease, staff exclusively engaged in the administration of medical units and establishments, as well as chaplains attached to the armed forces, shall be respected and protected in all circumstances.' The administrative staff category would appear to be broad enough to cover radio operators, so long as they are exclusively engaged in supporting a medical unit or establishment in the performance of its medical mission.

Section 7.004 of the DoD Law of War Manual currently being written by the DoD Law of War Working Group takes the position that the term 'medical personnel' as used in the Geneva Conventions includes individuals with a non-medical occupation specialty assigned to a medical unit or establishment. While this publication has not yet been published, this provision reflects the consensus of the representatives to the DoD Law of War Working Group from DoD/GC, OCJCS/LC, and each of the military services.

Article 40, GWS states that the personnel designated in Article 24 shall wear armlets with the distinctive Red Cross symbol and that they shall carry a special identity card bearing the distinctive emblem. DoD Instruction 1000.1, Identity Cards Required by the Geneva Conventions, January 30, 1974, provides for the issuance of DD Form 1934 to U.S. medical personnel to comply with Article 40. For your information, the United States has adopted the position that – despite the mandatory nature of the term 'shall' in GWS – the military services and commanders have the authority to make discretionary judgements as to whether or not to issue armbands and distinctive ID cards to particular categories of personnel or units. Among the military considerations a service or commander may consider in making such a judgement are the effect of brightly-colored armbands on unit camouflage and the likelihood that certain types of personnel will be called upon to perform additional duties outside of supporting their medical unit or establishment in the performance of its medical mission.

Medical personnel are granted certain protections by the law of war on the premise that they are not combatants. Accordingly, military personnel who wear an emblem or carry an identification card designating them as medical personnel must be trained concerning the law of war obligations of medical personnel, including especially the obligation of medical personnel not to engage in combatant acts except for the limited right to defend themselves and their patients against enemy law of war violations.

> Phillip A. Johnson, Colonel USAF Associate Deputy General Counsel
> (International Affairs)

3.22   OCCUPATION

☛ Australia: Government Statement for the Meeting of Contracting Parties to the Fourth Geneva Convention, Geneva, 27-29 October 1998

Mr Chairman,

Australia welcomes the opportunity to participate in this examination of issues relating to application of the Fourth Geneva Convention, and in particular, discussion of the application of the Convention in occupied territories. We believe it is timely that such discussion should take place, not only because it is always appropriate to assess how international laws have kept pace with the changing times but also because this instrument has become relevant to a far wider context than was foreseen when the Convention was first drafted. The Fourth Convention has in fact become increasingly relevant because of the recent trend toward intervention in disrupted/collapsed States and the establishment of so-called 'safe havens'.

This statement will first outline the relevance of the Fourth Geneva Convention in these situations, and then provide some practical suggestions based on Australia's experience of the implementation of the Convention. In situations involving intervention in collapsed States, an array of factors add to the complexity of the intervention and pose difficult questions as to the most appropriate legal framework to be applied. In recent experience, one of the challenges has been that of addressing the reduction or disappearance of the public security function, which commonly accompanies the collapse of states. It is often the case that the security instruments of the State were part of the reason for the internal disorder occasioning the collapse of the State. Accordingly, when the regime is overthrown there is no remaining acceptable foundation upon which to rebuild. For intervening forces, the issue therefore arises as to how to provide some basis for the regulation of their relationship with the local population and how to restore some level of public order and security.

Recent experience has also taught us that where such a vacuum exists there is a need to promote the application of International Humanitarian Law. This helps to discourage incidents where the intervening troops are left to believe that there is no other option to restore and maintain order than to deliver summary justice. This can lead forces to act in a way that results in the loss of support for the local population and ultimately the failure and/or the discrediting of the mission as a whole.

The Australian approach has been to regard the Fourth Convention as applying to a wider range of circumstances than international armed conflicts. Article 2 paragraph 2 of the Convention states that it shall apply not only to armed conflict but also to all cases of the partial or total occupation of the territory of a High Contracting Party, regardless of whether there is any armed resistance. This means the Convention applies not only in international armed conflicts but also wherever foreign forces find themselves in control of the territory of another State where there is no consent from a State government apparatus for them to be there.

The Convention was framed this way as a result of experience in World War II, where Allied forces found themselves in occupation of territory that belonged to States with which they were not at war. The Allies were, nevertheless, required to perform administrative functions including maintaining order in these territories. It also reflected the legal tradition of the law of non-belligerent occupation that existed prior to the introduction of the Convention. It is important to remember that the Geneva Conventions of 1949 were attempting to deal with de facto situations and to regulate them, rather than to base the application of the law on the technical legal determination of the basis for the de facto situation. The concern was with the elimination of the legal argument as to whether state of war existed and over the justness of the war.

The Fourth Convention is a good model to use in peace operations involving deployment without consent as it is geared to take account of the exigencies of attempting to administer or restore order in war-like conditions as opposed to a peace time human rights regime. Australian troops in Somalia found this to be the case when they were deployed into, and given responsibility for, the Bay Province during Operation Restore Hope in 1993. Following a determination that the Fourth Convention applied to that intervention, the Australian force relied on the Convention to provide answers to, and a framework for, many initiatives. These included the rehabilitation of the justice administration, from the police to the criminal investigation division and the judiciary. It also included the facilitation of trials against warlord and bandit figures who had been guilty of serious crimes against humanity. Underpinning these initiatives was a community consultation strategy involving formation of a committee of representatives of community elders, which met regularly with the Australian Civil Military Operations team.

This Australian approach had many positive outcomes including encouragement of the local population to renew economic activity and increased confidence in the responsible leadership to step forward. It also started the people on the road to self-reliance, built a good relationship between the force and the people, enhanced the security of the Australian force, aided in the acquisition of good intelligence and decreased the burden on the force for the provision of public security. It also had a good effect on the morale of the troops as they could see the benefits of their work and they knew that if they apprehended a bandit that person would be dealt with by due process and, with sufficient evidence, convicted and removed as a problem.

As a result of these recent experiences, we believe it is a pressing issue for common standards to be developed in the application of force and the Laws of Armed Conflict in general for all troops that are nominated to become part of a peace operation with a public security dimension. To this end we believe it would be useful for a training package to be created with the involvement of the ICRC and other organisations. This package could focus on the application of the Fourth Convention in circumstances often found in contemporary peace operations. This would not be a 'Code of Conduct' as such, but a formal training program. Ideally, this package could then be provided to every prospective troop contributing nation and a training regime commenced for those forces that have been nominated as part of the stand by force arrangements between the UN and participating countries. The UN could have a permanent training officer and monitor the standards attained. The advice of this officer could then be obtained as to whether a contingent being offered for a mission had achieved a satisfactory level of training in this respect. Such a package could form the basis of a general standard applicable to all armed forces.

We look forward to hearing the comments of other participants at this meeting concerning their experience of practical applications of the Fourth Geneva Convention.

Thank you, Mr Chairman.

4.11111   LANDMINES

☛ **USA: US Senate's Advice and Consent to Ratification of Amended Protocol II of the 1981 Certain Conventional Weapons Convention Subject to a Reservation, Understanding and Conditions, Congressional Record, 20 May 1999, pp. S5780-S5782**

Congressional record (Senate – May 20,1999)
[Page: S5780]

Mr. Hatch. I ask unanimous consent that the Senate proceed to executive session to consider the following treaty on today's Executive Calendar: No. 2. I further ask unanimous consent that the treaty be considered as having passed through its various parliamentary stages up to and including the presentation of the resolution of ratification; that all committee provisos, reservations, understandings, declarations be considered agreed to; that any statements be printed in the Congressional Record as if read; I further ask consent that when the resolution of ratification is voted upon the motion to reconsider be laid upon the table; the President be notified of the Senate's action and that following the disposition of the treaty, the Senate return to legislative session.
The Presiding Officer. Without objection, it is so ordered.

The treaty will be considered to have passed through its various parliamentary stages up to and including the presentation of the resolution of ratification.

The resolution of ratification is as follows:

Amended Mines Protocol
Resolved (two-thirds of the Senators present concurring therein),
[Page: S5781]

Section 1. Senate Advice and Consent Subject to a Reservation, Understanding and Conditions

The Senate advises and consents to the ratification of the Amended Mines Protocol (as defined in section 5 of this resolution), subject to the reservation in section 2, the understandings in section 3, and the conditions in section 4.

Section 2. Reservation

The Senate's advice and consent to the ratification of the Amended Mines Protocol is subject to the reservation, which shall be included in the United States instrument of ratification and shall be binding upon the President, that the United States reserves the right to use other devices (as defined in Article 2(5) of the Amended Mines Protocol) to destroy any stock of food or drink that is judged likely to be used by an enemy military force, if due precautions are taken for the safety of the civilian population.

Section 3. Understandings

The Senate's advice and consent to the ratification of the Amended Mines Protocol is subject to the following understandings, which shall be included in the United States instrument of ratification and shall be binding upon the President:

(1) United States Compliance. – The United States understands that –
(A) any decision by any military commander, military personnel, or any other person responsible for planning, authorizing, or executing military action shall only be judged on the basis of that person's assessment of the information reasonably available to the person at the time the person planned, authorized, or executed the action under review, and shall not be judged on the basis of information that comes to light after the action under review was taken; and
(B) Article 14 of the Amended Mines Protocol (insofar as it relates to penal sanctions) shall apply only in a situation in which an individual –
(i) knew, or should have known, that his action was prohibited under the Amended Mines Protocol;
(ii) intended to kill or cause serious injury to a civilian; and
(iii) knew or should have known, that the person he intended to kill or cause serious injury was a civilian.
(2) Effective Exclusion. – The United States understands that, for the purposes of Article 5(6)(b) of the Amended Mines Protocol, the maintenance of observation over avenues of approach where mines subject to that Article are deployed constitutes one acceptable form of monitoring to ensure the effective exclusion of civilians.
(3) Historic Monuments. – The United States understands that Article 7(1)(i) of the Amended Mines Protocol refers only to a limited class of objects that, because of their clearly recognizable characteristics and because of their widely recognized importance, constitute a part of the cultural or spiritual heritage of peoples.
(4) Legitimate Military Objectives. – The United States understands that an area of land itself can be a legitimate military objective for the purpose of the use of landmines,

if its neutralization or denial, in the circumstances applicable at the time, offers a military advantage.

(5) Peace Treaties. – The United States understands that the allocation of responsibilities for landmines in Article 5(2)(b) of the Amended Mines Protocol does not preclude agreement, in connection with peace treaties or similar arrangements, to allocate responsibilities under that Article in a manner that respects the essential spirit and purpose of the Article.

(6) Booby-Traps and Other Devices. – For the purposes of the Amended Mines Protocol, the United States understands that –

(A) the prohibition contained in Article 7(2) of the Amended Mines Protocol does not preclude the expedient adaptation or adaptation in advance of other objects for use as booby-traps or other devices;

(B) a trip-wired hand grenade shall be considered a 'booby-trap' under Article 2(4) of the Amended Mines Protocol and shall not be considered a 'mine' or an 'anti-personnel mine' under Article 2(1) or Article 2(3), respectively; and

(C) none of the provisions of the Amended Mines Protocol, including Article 2(5), applies to hand grenades other than trip-wired hand grenades.

(7) Non-Lethal Capabilities. – The United States understands that nothing in the Amended Mines Protocol may be construed as restricting or affecting in any way non-lethal weapon technology that is designed to temporarily disable, stun, signal the presence of a person, or operate in any other fashion, but not to cause permanent incapacity.

(8) International Tribunal Jurisdiction. – The United States understands that the provisions of Article 14 of the Amended Mines Protocol relating to penal sanctions refer to measures by the authorities of States Parties to the Protocol and do not authorize the trial of any person before an international criminal tribunal. The United States shall not recognize the jurisdiction of any international tribunal to prosecute a United States citizen for a violation of the Protocol or the Convention on Conventional Weapons.

(9) Technical Cooperation and Assistance. The United States understands that –

(A) no provision of the Protocol may be construed as affecting the discretion of the United States to refuse assistance or to restrict or deny permission for the export of equipment, material, or scientific or technological information for any reason; and

(B) the Amended Mines Protocol may not be used as a pretext for the transfer of weapons technology or the provision of assistance to the military mining or military countermining capabilities of a State Party to the Protocol.

Section 4. Conditions

The Senate's advice and consent to the ratification of the Amended Mines Protocol is subject to the following conditions, which shall be binding upon the President:

(1) Pursuit deterrent munition:

(A) Understanding. – The Senate understands that nothing in the Amended Mines Protocol restricts the possession or use of the Pursuit Deterrent Munition, which is in compliance with the provisions in the Technical Annex.

(B) Certification. – Prior to deposit of the United States instrument of ratification, the President shall certify to the Committee on Armed Services and the Committee on Foreign Relations of the Senate and to the Speaker of the House of Representatives that the Pursuit Deterrent Munition shall continue to remain available for use by the United States

Armed Forces at least until January 1, 2003, unless an effective alternative to the munition becomes available.

(C) Effective alternative defined. – For purposes of subparagraph (B), the term 'effective alternative' does not mean a tactic or operational concept in and of itself.

(2) Humanitarian demining assistance. – The Senate makes the following findings:

(A) United states efforts. – The United States contributes more than any other country to the worldwide humanitarian demining efforts, having expended more than $153,000,000 on such efforts since 1993.

(B) Development of detection and clearing technology. – The Department of Defense has undertaken a program to develop improved mine detection and clearing technology and has shared this improved technology with the international community.

(C) Expansion of United States humanitarian demining programs. – The Department of Defense and the Department of State have expanded their humanitarian demining programs to train and assist the personnel of other countries in developing effective demining programs.

(3) Limitation on the scale of assessment:

(A) Limitation on assessment for cost of implementation. – Notwithstanding any provision of the Amended Mines Protocol, and subject to the requirements of subparagraphs (B) and (C), the portion of the United States annual assessed contribution for activities associated with any conference held pursuant to Article 13 of the Amended Mines Protocol may not exceed $ 1,000,000.

(B) Recalculation of limitation:

(i) In general. – On January 1, 2000, and at 3-year intervals thereafter, the Administrator of General Services shall prescribe an amount that shall apply in lieu of the amount specified in subparagraph (A) and that shall be determined by adjusting the last amount applicable under that subparagraph to reflect the percentage increase by which the Consumer Price Index for the preceding calendar year exceeds the Consumer Price Index for the calendar year three years previously.

(ii) Consumer price index defined. – In this subparagraph, the term 'Consumer Price Index' means the last Consumer Price Index for all-urban consumers published by the Department of Labor.

(C) Additional contributions requiring congressional approval:

(i) Authority. – Notwithstanding subparagraph (A), the President may furnish additional contributions for activities associated with any conference held pursuant to Article 13 of the Amended Mines protocol which would otherwise be prohibited under subparagraph (A) if –

(I) the President determines and certifies in writing to the appropriate committees of Congress that the failure to make such contributions would seriously affect the national interest of the United States; and

(II) Congress enacts a joint resolution approving the certification of the President under subclause (I).

(ii) Statement of reasons. – Any certification made under clause (i) shall be accompanied by a detailed statement setting forth the specific reasons therefor and the specific activities associated with any conference held pursuant to Article 13 of the Amended Mines Protocol to which the additional contributions would be applied.

(4) United States authority for technical cooperation and assistance. – Notwithstanding any provision of the Amended Mines Protocol, no funds may be drawn from the

Treasury of the United States for any payment or assistance (including the transfer of in-kind items) under Article 11 or Article 13(3)(d) of the Amended Mines Protocol without statutory authorization and appropriation by United States law.

(5) Future negotiation of withdrawal clause. – It is the sense of the Senate that, in negotiations on any treaty containing an arms control provision, United States negotiators should not agree to any provision that would have the effect of prohibiting the United States from withdrawing from the arms control provisions of that treaty in a timely fashion in the event that the supreme national interests of the United States have been jeopardised.

(6) Land mine alternatives. – Prior to the deposit of the United States instrument of ratification, the President shall certify to Congress that –

(A) the President, in pursuing alternatives to United States anti-personnel mines or mixed anti-tank systems, will not limit the types of alternatives to be considered on the basis of any criteria other than those specified in subparagraph (B); and

(B) in pursuit of alternatives to United States anti-personnel mines, or mixed anti-tank systems, the United States shall seek to identify, adapt, modify, or otherwise develop only those technologies that –

(i) are intended to provide military effectiveness equivalent to that provided by the relevant anti-personnel mine, or mixed anti-tank system; and

(ii) would be affordable.

(7) Certification with regard to international tribunals. – Prior to the deposit of the United States instrument of ratification, the President shall certify to Congress that, with respect to the Amended Mines Protocol, the Convention on Conventional Weapons, or any future protocol or amendment thereto, the United States shall not recognize the jurisdiction of any international tribunal over the United States or any of its citizens.

(8) Tactics and operational concepts. – It is the sense of the Senate that development, adaptation, or modification of an existing or new tactic or operational concept, in and of itself, is unlikely to constitute an acceptable alternative to anti-personnel mines or mixed anti-tank systems.

(9) Funding regarding the international humanitarian crisis – The Senate finds that – (A) the grave international humanitarian crisis associated with anti-personnel mines has been created by the use of mines that do not meet or exceed the specifications on detectability, self-destruction, and self-deactivation contained in the Technical Annex to the Amended Mines Protocol; and

(B) United States mines that do meet such specifications have not contributed to this problem.

(10) Approval of modifications. – The Senate reaffirms the principle that any amendment or modification to the Amended Mines Protocol other than an amendment or modification solely of a minor technical or administrative nature shall enter into force with respect to the United States only pursuant to the treaty-making power of the President, by and with the advice and consent of the Senate, as set forth in Article 11, section 2, clause 2 of the Constitution of the United States.

(11) Further arms reduction obligations. – The Senate declares its intention to consider for approval an international agreement that would obligate the United States to reduce or limit the Armed Forces or armaments of the United States in a militarily significant manner only pursuant to the treaty-making power as set forth in Article 11, section 2, clause 2 of the Constitution of the United States.

(12) Treaty interpretation. – The Senate affirms the applicability to all treaties of the constitutionally-based principles of treaty interpretation set forth in condition (1) of the resolution of ratification of the INF Treaty, approved by the Senate on May 27, 1988, and condition (8) of the resolution of ratification of the CFE Flank Document, approved by the Senate on May 14, 1997.

(13) Primacy of the United States Constitution. – Nothing in the Amended Mines Protocol requires or authorizes the enactment of legislation, or the taking of any other action, by the United States that is prohibited by the Constitution of the United States, as interpreted by the United States.

[Page: S5782]

Section 5. Definitions
As used in this resolution:

(1) Amended mines protocol or protocol. – The terms 'Amended Mines Protocol' and 'Protocol' mean the Amended Protocol on Prohibitions or Restrictions on the Use of Mines, Booby-Traps and Other Devices, together with its Technical Annex, as adopted at Geneva on May 3, 1996 (contained in Senate Treaty Document 105-1).

(2) CFE flank document. – The term 'CFE Flank Document' means the Document Agreed Among the States Parties to the Treaty on Conventional Armed Forces in Europe (CFE) of November 19, 1990, done at Vienna on May 31, 1996 (Treaty Document 105-95).

(3) Convention on conventional weapons. – The term 'Convention on Conventional Weapons' means the Convention on Prohibitions or Restrictions on the Use of Certain Conventional Weapons Which May be Deemed to be Excessively Injurious or to Have Indiscriminate Effects, done at Geneva on October 10, 1980 (Senate Treaty Document 103-25).

(4) United States instrument of ratification. – The term 'United States instrument of ratification' means the instrument of ratification of the United States of the Amended Mines Protocol.

4.11122   CHEMICAL WEAPONS

☛ **Iran: Declaration made by the Iranian Government upon Ratification of the Chemical Weapons Convention. Annex to Instrument of Ratification deposited with the UN SG on 3 November 1997**

Ministry of Foreign Affairs of the Islamic Republic of Iran
In the Name of God, The Compassionate, The Merciful

No. 641

Whereas, the Convention on the Prohibition of the Development, Production, Stockpiling and Use of Chemical Weapons and on their destruction was opened for signature at Paris on 13 January 1993;

Whereas, said Convention was signed on behalf of the Government of the Islamic Republic of Iran on the same date;

Whereas, Article 19 of the aforesaid Convention provides that the convention is subject to ratification by the signatory states;

And whereas, the formalities of ratification of the said Convention have been completed in conformity with the Constitution of the Islamic Republic of Iran;

Now therefore, the Government of the Islamic Republic of Iran, having considered and approved the aforementioned Convention, hereby ratifies the same and undertakes faithfully to fulfil and carry out the stipulations therein contained.

In Witness Whereof, I, Kamal Kharrazi, Minister of Foreign Affairs of the Islamic Republic of Iran, have signed this Instrument of Ratification,

Tehran, 3 November 1997
Dr. Kamal Kharrazi, Minister of foreign Affairs of the Islamic Republic of Iran

The Islamic Republic of Iran, on the basis of the Islamic principles and beliefs, considers chemical weapons inhuman, and has consistently been on the vanguard of the international efforts to abolish these weapons and prevent their use.

1. The Islamic Consultative Assembly (the Parliament) of the Islamic Republic of Iran approved the bill presented by the Government to join the Convention on the Prohibition of the Development, Production, Stockpiling and Use of Chemical Weapons and on Their Destruction (CWC) on 27 July 1997, and the Guardian Council found the legislation compatible with the Constitution and the Islamic tenets on 30 July 1997, in accordance with its required Constitutional process. The Islamic Consultative Assembly decided that:

The Government is hereby authorised, at an appropriate time, to accede to the Convention on the Prohibition of the Development, Production, Stockpiling and Use of Chemical Weapons and on Their Destruction – which was opened for signature in Paris on 13 January 1993 – as annexed to this legislation and to deposit its relevant instrument.

The Ministry of Foreign Affairs must pursue in all negotiations and within the framework of the Organisation of the Convention, the full and indiscriminate implementation of the Convention, particularly in the areas of inspection and transfer of technology and chemicals for peaceful purposes. In case the aforementioned requirements are not materialised, upon recommendation of the Cabinet and approval of the Supreme National Security Council, steps aimed at withdrawing from the Convention shall be put in motion.

2. The Islamic Republic of Iran attaches vital significance to the full, unconditional and indiscriminate implementation of all provisions of the Convention. It reserves the right to withdraw from the Convention under the following circumstances:

— non-compliance with the principle of equal treatment of all States Parties in implementation of all relevant provisions of the Convention;

— disclosure of its confidential information contrary to the provisions of the Convention;

— imposition of restrictions incompatible with the obligations under the Convention.

3. As stipulated in Article XI, exclusive and non-transparent regimes impeding free international trade in chemicals and chemical technology for peaceful purposes should be disbanded. The Islamic Republic of Iran rejects any chemical export control mechanism not envisaged in the convention.

4. The Organisation for the Prohibition of Chemical Weapons (OPCW) is the sole international authority to determine the compliance of States Parties regarding chemical weapons. Accusations by States Parties against other States Parties in the absence of a determination of non-compliance by OPCW will seriously undermine the Convention and its repetition may make the Convention meaningless.

5. One of the objectives of the Convention as stipulated in its preamble is to 'promote free trade in chemicals as well as international co-operation for purposes not prohibited under the Convention in order to enhance the economic and technological development of all States Parties'. This fundamental objective of the Convention should be respected and embraced by all States Parties to the Convention. Any form of undermining, either in words or in action, of this overriding objective, is considered by the Islamic Republic of Iran a grave breach of the provisions of the Convention.

6. In line with the provisions of the Convention regarding non-discriminatory treatment of States Parties:
— inspection equipment should be commercially available to all States Parties without condition or limitation;
— the OPCW should maintain its international character by ensuring fair and balanced geographical distribution of the personnel of its Technical Secretariat, provision of assistance to and co-operation with States Parties, and equitable membership of States Parties in subsidiary organs of the Organisation.

7. The implementation of the Convention should contribute to international peace and security and should not in any way diminish or harm national security or territorial integrity of the States Parties.

4.142   CULTURAL PROPERTY AND PLACES OF WORSHIP

☛ Second Protocol to the Hague Convention of 1954 for the Protection of Cultural Property in the Event of Armed Conflict, The Hague, 26 March 1999

The Parties,
Conscious of the need to improve the protection of cultural property in the event of armed conflict and to establish an enhanced system of protection for specifically designated cultural property;
Reaffirming the importance of the provisions of the Convention for the Protection of Cultural Property in the Event of Armed Conflict, done at the Hague on 14 May 1954, and emphasizing the necessity to supplement these provisions through measures to reinforce their implementation;
Desiring to provide the High Contracting Parties to the Convention with a means of being more closely involved in the protection of cultural property in the event of armed conflict by establishing appropriate procedures therefor;
Considering that the rules governing the protection of cultural property in the event of armed conflict should reflect developments in international law;
Affirming that the rules of customary international law will continue to govern questions not regulated by the provisions of this Protocol;
Have agreed as follows:

Chapter 1   Introduction

Article 1   Definitions

For the purposes of this Protocol:

(a) 'Party' means a State Party to this Protocol;

(b) 'cultural property' means cultural property as defined in Article 1 of the Convention;

(c) 'Convention' means the Convention for the Protection of Cultural Property in the Event of Armed Conflict, done at The Hague on 14 May 1954;

(d) 'High Contracting Party' means a State Party to the Convention;

(e) 'enhanced protection' means the system of enhanced protection established by Articles 10 and 11;

(f) 'military objective' means an object which by its nature, location, purpose, or use makes an effective contribution to military action and whose total or partial destruction, capture or neutralisation, in the circumstances ruling at the time, offers a definite military advantage;

(g) 'illicit' means under compulsion or otherwise in violation of the applicable rules of the domestic law of the occupied territory or of international law;

(h) 'List' means the International List of Cultural Property under Enhanced Protection established in accordance with Article 27, sub-paragraph 1(b);

(i) 'Director-General' means the Director-General of UNESCO;

(j) 'UNESCO' means the United Nations Educational, Scientific and Cultural Organization;

(k) 'First Protocol' means the Protocol for the Protection of Cultural Property in the Event of Armed Conflict done at The Hague on 14 May 1954;

Article 2   Relation to the Convention

This Protocol supplements the Convention in relations between the Parties.

Article 3   Scope of application

1. In addition to the provisions, which shall apply in time of peace, this Protocol shall apply in situations referred to in Article 18 paragraphs 1 and 2 of the Convention and in Article 22 paragraph 1.

2. When one of the parties to an armed conflict is not bound by this Protocol, the Parties to this Protocol shall remain bound by it in their mutual relations. They shall furthermore be bound by this Protocol in relation to a State party to the conflict which is not bound by it, if the latter accepts the provisions of this Protocol and so long as it applies them.

Article 4   Relationship between Chapter 3 and other provisions of the Convention and this Protocol

The application of the provisions of Chapter 3 of this Protocol is without prejudice to:

(a) the application of the provisions of Chapter I of the Convention and of Chapter 2 of this Protocol;

(b) the application of the provisions of Chapter II of the Convention save that, as between Parties to this Protocol or as between a Party and a State which accepts and applies this Protocol in accordance with Article 3 paragraph 2, where cultural property has been granted both special protection and enhanced protection, only the provisions of enhanced protection shall apply.

Chapter 2   General provisions regarding protection

Article 5   Safeguarding of cultural property
Preparatory measures taken in time of peace for the safeguarding of cultural property against the foreseeable effects of an armed conflict pursuant to Article 3 of the Convention shall include, as appropriate, the preparation of inventories, the planning of emergency measures for protection against fire or structural collapse, the preparation for the removal of movable cultural property or the provision for adequate *in situ* protection of such property, and the designation of competent authorities responsible for the safeguarding of cultural property.

Article 6   Respect for cultural property
With the goal of ensuring respect for cultural property in accordance with Article 4 of the Convention:
(a) a waiver on the basis of imperative military necessity pursuant to Article 4 paragraph 2 of the Convention may only be invoked to direct an act of hostility against cultural property when and for as long as:
(i) that cultural property has, by its function, been made into a military objective; and
(ii) there is no feasible alternative available to obtain a similar military advantage to that offered by directing an act of hostility against that objective;
(b) a waiver on the basis of imperative military necessity pursuant to Article 4 paragraph 2 of the Convention may only be invoked to use cultural property for purposes which are likely to expose it to destruction or damage when and for as long as no choice is possible between such use of the cultural property and another feasible method for obtaining a similar military advantage;
(c) the decision to invoke imperative military necessity shall only be taken by an officer commanding a force the equivalent of a battalion in size or larger, or a force smaller in size where circumstances do not permit otherwise;
(d) in case of an attack based on a decision taken in accordance with sub-paragraph (a), an effective advance warning shall be given whenever circumstances permit.

Article 7   Precautions in attack
Without prejudice to other precautions required by international humanitarian law in the conduct of military operations, each Party to the conflict shall:
(a) do everything feasible to verify that the objectives to be attacked are not cultural property protected under Article 4 of the Convention;
(b) take all feasible precautions in the choice of means and methods of attack with a view to avoiding, and in any event to minimizing, incidental damage to cultural property protected under Article 4 of the Convention;
(c) refrain from deciding to launch any attack which may be expected to cause incidental damage to cultural property protected under Article 4 of the Convention which would be excessive in relation to the concrete and direct military advantage anticipated; and
(d) cancel or suspend an attack if it becomes apparent:
(i) that the objective is cultural property protected under Article 4 of the Convention;
(ii) that the attack may be expected to cause incidental damage to cultural property protected under Article 4 of the Convention which would be excessive in relation to the concrete and direct military advantage anticipated.

Article 8   Precautions against the effects of hostilities
The Parties to the conflict shall, to the maximum extent feasible:
(a) remove movable cultural property from the vicinity of military objectives or provide for adequate *in situ* protection;
(b) avoid locating military objectives near cultural property.

Article 9   Protection of cultural property in occupied territory
1.   Without prejudice to the provisions of Articles 4 and 5 of the Convention, a Party in occupation of the whole or part of the territory of another Party shall prohibit and prevent in relation to the occupied territory:
(a) any illicit export, other removal or transfer of ownership of cultural property;
(b) any archaeological excavation, save where this is strictly required to safeguard, record or preserve cultural property;
(c) any alteration to, or change of use of, cultural property which is intended to conceal or destroy cultural, historical or scientific evidence.
2.   Any archaeological excavation of, alteration to, or change of use of, cultural property in occupied territory shall, unless circumstances do not permit, be carried out in close co-operation with the competent national authorities of the occupied territory.

Chapter 3   Enhanced Protection
Article 10   Enhanced protection
Cultural property may be placed under enhanced protection provided that it meets the following three conditions:
(a) it is cultural heritage of the greatest importance for humanity;
(b) it is protected by adequate domestic legal and administrative measures recognising its exceptional cultural and historic value and ensuring the highest level of protection;
(c) it is not used for military purposes or to shield military sites and a declaration has been made by the Party, which has control over the cultural property, confirming that it will not be so used.

Article 11   The granting of enhanced protection
1.   Each Party should submit to the Committee a list of cultural property for which it intends to request the granting of enhanced protection.
2.   The Party, which has jurisdiction or control over the cultural property, may request that it be included in the List to be established in accordance with Article 27 sub-paragraph 1(b). This request shall include all necessary information related to the criteria mentioned in Article 10. The Committee may invite a Party to request that cultural property be included in the List.
3.   Other Parties, the International Committee of the Blue Shield and other non-governmental organisations with relevant expertise may recommend specific cultural property to the Committee. In such cases, the Committee may decide to invite a Party to request inclusion of that cultural property in the List.
4.   Neither the request for inclusion of cultural property situated in a territory, sovereignty or jurisdiction over which is claimed by more than one State, nor its inclusion, shall in any way prejudice the rights of the parties to the dispute.
5.   Upon receipt of a request for inclusion in the List, the Committee shall inform all Parties of the request. Parties may submit representations regarding such a request to

the Committee within sixty days. These representations shall be made only on the basis of the criteria mentioned in Article 10. They shall be specific and related to facts. The Committee shall consider the representations, providing the Party requesting inclusion with a reasonable opportunity to respond before taking the decision. When such representations are before the Committee, decisions for inclusion in the List shall be taken, notwithstanding Article 26, by a majority of four-fifths of its members present and voting.

6.   In deciding upon a request, the Committee should ask the advice of governmental and non-governmental organisations, as well as of individual experts.

7.   A decision to grant or deny enhanced protection may only be made on the basis of the criteria mentioned in Article 10.

8. In exceptional cases, when the Committee has concluded that the Party requesting inclusion of cultural property in the List cannot fulfil the criteria of Article 10 sub-paragraph (b), the Committee may decide to grant enhanced protection, provided that the requesting Party submits a request for international assistance under Article 32.

9. Upon the outbreak of hostilities, a Party to the conflict may request, on an emergency basis, enhanced protection of cultural property under its jurisdiction or control by communicating this request to the Committee. The Committee shall transmit this request immediately to all Parties to the conflict. In such cases the Committee will consider representations from the Parties concerned on an expedited basis. The decision to grant provisional enhanced protection shall be taken as soon as possible and, notwithstanding Article 26, by a majority of four-fifths of its members present and voting. Provisional enhanced protection may be granted by the Committee pending the outcome of the regular procedure for the granting of enhanced protection, provided that the provisions of Article 10 sub-paragraphs (a) and (c) are met.

10. Enhanced protection shall be granted to cultural property by the Committee from the moment of its entry in the List.

11. The Director-General shall, without delay, send to the Secretary-General of the United Nations and to all Parties notification of any decision of the Committee to include cultural property on the List.

Article 12   Immunity of cultural property under enhanced protection
The Parties to a conflict shall ensure the immunity of cultural property under enhanced protection by refraining from making such property the object of attack or from any use of the property or its immediate surroundings in support of military action.

Article 13   Loss of enhanced protection
1. Cultural property under enhanced protection shall only lose such protection:
(a) if such protection is suspended or cancelled in accordance with Article 14; or
(b) if, and for as long as, the property has, by its use, become a military objective.
2.   In the circumstances of sub-paragraph 1(b), such property may only be the object of attack if:
(a) the attack is the only feasible means of terminating the use of the property referred to in sub-paragraph 1(b);
(b) all feasible precautions are taken in the choice of means and methods of attack, with a view to terminating such use and avoiding, or in any event minimising, damage to the cultural property;

(c) unless circumstances do not permit, due to requirements of immediate self-defence:
(i) the attack is ordered at the highest operational level of command;
(ii) effective advance warning is issued to the opposing forces requiring the termination of the use referred to in sub-paragraph 1(b); and
(iii) Reasonable time is given to the opposing forces to redress the situation.

Article 14   Suspension and cancellation of enhanced protection
1.   Where cultural property no longer meets any one of the criteria in Article 10 of this Protocol, the Committee may suspend its enhanced protection status or cancel that status by removing that cultural property from the List.
2.   In the case of a serious violation of Article 12 in relation to cultural property under enhanced protection arising from its use in support of military action, the Committee may suspend its enhanced protection status. Where such violations are continuous, the Committee may exceptionally cancel the enhanced protection status by removing the cultural property from the List.
3.   The Director-General shall, without delay, send to the Secretary-General of the United Nations and to all Parties to this Protocol notification of any decision of the Committee to suspend or cancel the enhanced protection of cultural property.
4.   Before taking such a decision, the Committee shall afford an opportunity to the Parties to make their views known.

Chapter 4   Criminal responsibility and jurisdiction
Article 15   Serious violations of this Protocol
1.   Any person commits an offence within the meaning of this Protocol if that person intentionally and in violation of the Convention or this Protocol commits any of the following acts:
(a) making cultural property under enhanced protection the object of attack;
(b) using cultural property under enhanced protection or its immediate surroundings in support of military action;
(c) extensive destruction or appropriation of cultural property protected under the Convention and this Protocol;
(d) making cultural property protected under the Convention and this Protocol the object of attack;
(e) Theft, pillage or misappropriation of, or acts of vandalism directed against cultural property protected under the Convention.
2.   Each Party shall adopt such measures as may be necessary to establish as criminal offences under its domestic law the offences set forth in this Article and to make such offences punishable by appropriate penalties. When doing so, Parties shall comply with general principles of law and international law, including the rules extending individual criminal responsibility to persons other than those who directly commit the act.

Article 16   Jurisdiction
1.   Without prejudice to paragraph 2, each Party shall take the necessary legislative measures to establish its jurisdiction over offences set forth in Article 15 in the following cases:
(a) when such an offence is committed in the territory of that State;
(b) when the alleged offender is a national of that State;

(c) in the case of offences set forth in Article 15 sub-paragraphs (a) to (c), when the alleged offender is present in its territory.

2. With respect to the exercise of jurisdiction and without prejudice to Article 28 of the Convention:

(a) this Protocol does not preclude the incurring of individual criminal responsibility or the exercise of jurisdiction under national and international law that may be applicable, or affect the exercise of jurisdiction under customary international law;

(b) Except in so far as a State which is not Party to this Protocol may accept and apply its provisions in accordance with Article 3 paragraph 2, members of the armed forces and nationals of a State which is not Party to this Protocol, except for those nationals serving in the armed forces of a State which is a Party to this Protocol, do not incur individual criminal responsibility by virtue of this Protocol, nor does this Protocol impose an obligation to establish jurisdiction over such persons or to extradite them.

Article 17 Prosecution

1. The Party in whose territory the alleged offender of an offence set forth in Article 15 sub-paragraphs 1 (a) to (c) is found to be present shall, if it does not extradite that person, submit, without exception whatsoever and without undue delay, the case to its competent authorities, for the purpose of prosecution, through proceedings in accordance with its domestic law or with, if applicable, the relevant rules of international law.

2. Without prejudice to, if applicable, the relevant rules of international law, any person regarding whom proceedings are being carried out in connection with the Convention or this Protocol shall be guaranteed fair treatment and a fair trial in accordance with domestic law and international law at all stages of the proceedings, and in no cases shall be provided guarantees less favorable to such person than those provided by international law.

Article 18 Extradition

1. The offences set forth in Article 15 sub-paragraphs 1 (a) to (c) shall be deemed to be included as extraditable offences in any extradition treaty existing between any of the Parties before the entry into force of this Protocol. Parties undertake to include such offences in every extradition treaty to be subsequently concluded between them.

2. When a Party which makes extradition conditional on the existence of a treaty receives a request for extradition from another Party with which it has no extradition treaty, the requested Party may, at its option, consider the present Protocol as the legal basis for extradition in respect of offences as set forth in Article 15 sub-paragraphs 1 (a) to (c).

3. Parties which do not make extradition conditional on the existence of a treaty shall recognise the offences set forth in Article 15 sub-paragraphs 1 (a) to (c) as extraditable offences between them, subject to the conditions provided by the law of the requested Party.

4. If necessary, offences set forth in Article 15 sub-paragraphs 1 (a) to (c) shall be treated, for the purposes of extradition between Parties, as if they had been committed not only in the place in which they occurred but also in the territory of the Parties that have established jurisdiction in accordance with Article 16 paragraph 1.

Article 19   Mutual legal assistance

1.   Parties shall afford one another the greatest measure of assistance in connection with investigations or criminal or extradition proceedings brought in respect of the offences set forth in Article 15, including assistance in obtaining evidence at their disposal necessary for the proceedings.

2.   Parties shall carry out their obligations under paragraph 1 in conformity with any treaties or other arrangements on mutual legal assistance that may exist between them. In the absence of such treaties or arrangements, Parties shall afford one another assistance in accordance with their domestic law.

Article 20   Grounds for refusal

1.   For the purpose of extradition, offences set forth in Article 15 sub-paragraphs 1 (a) to (c), and for the purpose of mutual legal assistance, offences set forth in Article 15 shall not be regarded as political offences nor as offences connected with political offences nor as offences inspired by political motives. Accordingly, a request for extradition or for mutual legal assistance based on such offences may not be refused on the sole ground that it concerns a political offence or an offence connected with a political offence or an offence inspired by political motives.

2.   Nothing in this Protocol shall be interpreted as imposing an obligation to extradite or to afford mutual legal assistance if the requested Party has substantial grounds for believing that the request for extradition for offences set forth in Article 15 sub-paragraphs 1 (a) to (c) or for mutual legal assistance with respect to offences set forth in Article 15 has been made for the purpose of prosecuting or punishing a person on account of that person's race, religion, nationality, ethnic origin or political opinion or that compliance with the request would cause prejudice to that person's position for any of these reasons.

Article 21   Measures regarding other violations

Without prejudice to Article 28 of the Convention, each Party shall adopt such legislative, administrative or disciplinary measures as may be necessary to suppress the following acts when committed intentionally:

(a) any use of cultural property in violation of the Convention or this Protocol;

(b) any illicit export, other removal or transfer of ownership of cultural property from occupied territory in violation of the Convention or this Protocol.

Chapter 5   The protection of cultural property in armed conflicts not of an international character

Article 22   Armed conflicts not of an international character

1.   This Protocol shall apply in the event of an armed conflict not of an international character, occurring within the territory of one of the Parties.

2.   This Protocol shall not apply to situations of internal disturbances and tensions, such as riots, isolated and sporadic acts of violence and other acts of a similar nature.

3.   Nothing in this Protocol shall be invoked for the purpose of affecting the sovereignty of a State or the responsibility of the government, by all legitimate means, to maintain or re-establish law and order in the State or to defend the national unity and territorial integrity of the State.

4. Nothing in this Protocol shall prejudice the primary jurisdiction of a Party in whose territory an armed conflict not of an international character occurs over the violations set forth in Article 15.

5. Nothing in this Protocol shall be invoked as a justification for intervening, directly or indirectly, for any reason whatever, in the armed conflict or in the internal or external affairs of the Party in the territory of which that conflict occurs.

6. The application of this Protocol to the situation referred to in paragraph 1 shall not affect the legal status of the parties to the conflict.

7. UNESCO may offer its services to the parties to the conflict.

Chapter 6 Institutional Issues

Article 23 Meeting of the Parties

1. The Meeting of the Parties shall be convened at the same time as the General Conference of UNESCO, and in co-ordination with the Meeting of the High Contracting Parties, if such a meeting has been called by the Director-General.

2. The Meeting of the Parties shall adopt its Rules of Procedure.

3. The Meeting of the Parties shall have the following functions:

(a) to elect the Members of the Committee, in accordance with Article 24 paragraph 1;

(b) to endorse the Guidelines developed by the Committee in accordance with Article 27 sub-paragraph 1(a);

(c) to provide guidelines for, and to supervise the use of the Fund by the Committee;

(d) to consider the report submitted by the Committee in accordance with Article 27 sub-paragraph 1(d);

(e) to discuss any problem related to the application of this Protocol, and to make recommendations, as appropriate.

4. At the request of at least one-fifth of the Parties, the Director-General shall convene an Extraordinary Meeting of the Parties.

Article 24 Committee for the Protection of Cultural Property in the Event of Armed Conflict

1. The Committee for the Protection of Cultural Property in the Event of Armed Conflict is hereby established. It shall be composed of twelve Parties, which shall be elected by the Meeting of the Parties.

2. The Committee shall meet once a year in ordinary session and in extra-ordinary sessions whenever it deems necessary.

3. In determining membership of the Committee, Parties shall seek to ensure an equitable representation of the different regions and cultures of the world.

4. Parties members of the Committee shall choose as their representatives persons qualified in the fields of cultural heritage, defence or international law, and they shall endeavour, in consultation with one another, to ensure that the Committee as a whole contains adequate expertise in all these fields.

Article 25 Term of office

1. A Party shall be elected to the Committee for four years and shall be eligible for immediate re-election only once.

2. Notwithstanding the provisions of paragraph 1, the term of office of half of the members chosen at the time of the first election shall cease at the end of the first ordinary

session of the Meeting of the Parties following that at which they were elected. These members shall be chosen by lot by the President of this Meeting after the first election.

Article 26 Rules of procedure
1.   The Committee shall adopt its Rules of Procedure.
2.   A majority of the members shall constitute a quorum. Decisions of the Committee shall be taken by a majority of two-thirds of its members voting.
3.   Members shall not participate in the voting on any decisions relating to cultural property affected by an armed conflict to which they are parties.

Article 27 Functions
1.   The Committee shall have the following functions:
(a) to develop Guidelines for the implementation of this Protocol;
(b) to grant, suspend or cancel enhanced protection for cultural property and to establish, maintain and promote the List of Cultural Property under Enhanced Protection;
(c) to monitor and supervise the implementation of this Protocol and promote the identification of cultural property under enhanced protection;
(d) to consider and comment on reports of the Parties, to seek clarifications as required, and prepare its own report on the implementation of this Protocol for the Meeting of the Parties;
(e) to receive and consider requests for international assistance under Article 32;
(f) to determine the use of the Fund;
(g) to perform any other function which may be assigned to it by the Meeting of the Parties.
2. The functions of the Committee shall be performed in co-operation with the Director-General.
3. The Committee shall co-operate with international and national governmental and non-governmental organizations having objectives similar to those of the Convention, its First Protocol and this Protocol. To assist in the implementation of its functions, the Committee may invite to its meetings, in an advisory capacity, eminent professional organizations such as those which have formal relations with UNESCO, including the International Committee of the Blue Shield (ICBS) and its constituent bodies. Representatives of the International Centre for the Study of the Preservation and Restoration of Cultural Property (Rome Centre) (ICCROM) and of the International Committee of the Red Cross (ICRC) may also be invited to attend in an advisory capacity.

Article 28 Secretariat
The Committee shall be assisted by the Secretariat of UNESCO, which shall prepare the Committee's documentation and the agenda for its meetings and shall have the responsibility for the implementation of its decisions.

Article 29 The Fund for the Protection of Cultural Property in the Event of Armed Conflict
1. A Fund is hereby established for the following purposes:
(a) to provide financial or other assistance in support of preparatory or other measures to be taken in peacetime in accordance with, *inter alia*, Article 5, Article 10 sub-paragraph (b) and Article 30; and

(b) to provide financial or other assistance in relation to emergency, provisional or other measures to be taken in order to protect cultural property during periods of armed conflict or of immediate recovery after the end of hostilities in accordance with, *inter alia*, Article 8 sub-paragraph (a).

2. The Fund shall constitute a trust fund, in conformity with the provisions of the financial regulations of UNESCO.

3. Disbursements from the Fund shall be used only for such purposes as the Committee shall decide in accordance with the guidelines as defined in Article 23 sub-paragraph 3(c). The Committee may accept contributions to be used only for a certain programme or project, provided that the Committee shall have decided on the implementation of such programme or project.

4. The resources of the Fund shall consist of:

(a) voluntary contributions made by the Parties;

(b) contributions, gifts or bequests made by:

(i) other States;

(ii) UNESCO or other organizations of the United Nations system;

(iii) other intergovernmental or non-governmental organizations; and

(iv) public or private bodies or individuals;

(c) any interest accruing on the Fund;

(d) funds raised by collections and receipts from events organized for the benefit of the Fund; and

(e) all other resources authorized by the guidelines applicable to the Fund.

Chapter 7   Dissemination of Information and International Assistance

Article 30   Dissemination

1.   The Parties shall endeavour by appropriate means, and in particular by educational and information programmes, to strengthen appreciation and respect for cultural property by their entire population.

2.   The Parties shall disseminate this Protocol as widely as possible, both in time of peace and in time of armed conflict.

3.   Any military or civilian authorities who, in time of armed conflict, assume responsibilities with respect to the application of this Protocol, shall be fully acquainted with the text thereof. To this end the Parties shall, as appropriate:

(a)   incorporate guidelines and instructions on the protection of cultural property in their military regulations;

(b)   develop and implement, in cooperation with UNESCO and relevant governmental and non-governmental organizations, peacetime training and educational programmes;

(c)   communicate to one another, through the Director-General, information on the laws, administrative provisions and measures taken under sub-paragraphs (a) and (b);

(d)   communicate to one another, as soon as possible, through the Director-General, the laws and administrative provisions which they may adopt to ensure the application of this Protocol.

Article 31   International cooperation

In situations of serious violations of this Protocol, the Parties undertake to act, jointly through the Committee, or individually, in cooperation with UNESCO and the United Nations and in conformity with the Charter of the United Nations.

Article 32   International assistance

1.   A Party may request from the Committee international assistance for cultural property under enhanced protection as well as assistance with respect to the preparation, development or implementation of the laws, administrative provisions and measures referred to in Article 10.

2.   A party to the conflict, which is not a Party to this Protocol but which accepts and applies provisions in accordance with Article 3, paragraph 2, may request appropriate international assistance from the Committee.

3.   The Committee shall adopt rules for the submission of requests for international assistance and shall define the forms the international assistance may take.

4.   Parties are encouraged to give technical assistance of all kinds, through the Committee, to those Parties or parties to the conflict who request it.

Article 33   Assistance of UNESCO

1.   A Party may call upon UNESCO for technical assistance in organizing the protection of its cultural property, such as preparatory action to safeguard cultural property, preventive and organizational measures for emergency situations and compilation of national inventories of cultural property, or in connection with any other problem arising out of the application of this Protocol. UNESCO shall accord such assistance within the limits fixed by its programme and by its resources.

2.   Parties are encouraged to provide technical assistance at bilateral or multilateral level.

3.   UNESCO is authorized to make, on its own initiative, proposals on these matters to the Parties.

Chapter 8   Execution of this Protocol

Article 34   Protecting Powers

This Protocol shall be applied with the co-operation of the Protecting Powers responsible for safeguarding the interests of the Parties to the conflict.

Article 35   Conciliation procedure

1.   The Protecting Powers shall lend their good offices in all cases where they may deem it useful in the interests of cultural property, particularly if there is disagreement between the Parties to the conflict as to the application or interpretation of the provisions of this Protocol.

2.   For this purpose, each of the Protecting Powers may, either at the invitation of one Party, of the Director-General, or on its own initiative, propose to the Parties to the conflict a meeting of their representatives, and in particular of the authorities responsible for the protection of cultural property, if considered appropriate, on the territory of a State not party to the conflict. The Parties to the conflict shall be bound to give effect to the proposals for meeting made to them. The Protecting Powers shall propose for approval by the Parties to the conflict a person belonging to a State not party to the conflict or a person presented by the Director-General, which person shall be invited to take part in such a meeting in the capacity of Chairman.

Article 36   Conciliation in absence of Protecting Powers

1.   In a conflict where no Protecting Powers are appointed the Director-General may lend good offices or act by any other form of conciliation or mediation, with a view to settling the disagreement.

2.   At the invitation of one Party or of the Director-General, the Chairman of the Committee may propose to the Parties to the conflict a meeting of their representatives, and in particular of the authorities responsible for the protection of cultural property, if considered appropriate, on the territory of a State not party to the conflict.

Article 37   Translations and reports

1.   The Parties shall translate this Protocol into their official languages and shall communicate these official translations to the Director-General.

2.   The Parties shall submit to the Committee, every four years, a report on the implementation of this Protocol.

Article 38   State responsibility

No provision in this Protocol relating to individual criminal responsibility shall affect the responsibility of States under international law, including the duty to provide reparation.

Chapter 9   Final Clauses

Article 39   Languages

This Protocol is drawn up in Arabic, Chinese, English, French, Russian and Spanish, the six texts being equally authentic.

Article 40   Signature

This Protocol shall bear the date of 26 May 1999. It shall be opened for signature by all High Contracting Parties at The Hague from 17 May 1999 until 31 December 1999.

Article 41   Ratification, acceptance or approval

1.   This Protocol shall be subject to ratification, acceptance or approval by High Contracting Parties, which have signed this Protocol, in accordance with their respective constitutional procedures.

2.   The instruments of ratification, acceptance or approval shall be deposited with the Director-General.

Article 42   Accession

1. This Protocol shall be open for accession by other High Contracting Parties from 1 January 2000.

2.   Accession shall be effected by the deposit of an instrument of accession with the Director-General.

Article 43   Entry into force

1.   This Protocol shall enter into force three months after twenty instruments of ratification, acceptance, approval or accession have been deposited.

2.   Thereafter, it shall enter into force, for each Party, three months after the deposit of its instrument of ratification, acceptance, approval or accession.

Article 44   Entry into force in situations of armed conflict

The situations referred to in Articles 18 and 19 of the Convention shall give immediate effect to ratifications, acceptances or approvals of or accessions to this Protocol deposited by the parties to the conflict either before or after the beginning of hostilities or occupation. In such cases the Director-General shall transmit the communications referred to in Article 46 by the speediest method.

Article 45   Denunciation

1.   Each Party may denounce this Protocol.

2.   The denunciation shall be notified by an instrument in writing, deposited with the Director-General.

3.   The denunciation shall take effect one year after the receipt of the instrument of denunciation. However, if, on the expiry of this period, the denouncing Party is involved in an armed conflict, the denunciation shall not take effect until the end of hostilities, or until the operations of repatriating cultural property are completed, whichever is the later.

Article 46   Notifications

The Director-General shall inform all High Contracting Parties as well as the United Nations, of the deposit of all the instruments of ratification, acceptance, approval or accession provided for in Articles 41 and 42 and of denunciations provided for Article 45.

Article 47   Registration with the United Nations

In conformity with Article 102 of the Charter of the United Nations, this Protocol shall be registered with the Secretariat of the United Nations at the request of the Director-General.

In faith whereof the undersigned, duly authorized, have signed the present Protocol.

Done at The Hague, this twenty-sixth day of March 1999, in a single copy which shall be deposited in the archives of the UNESCO, and certified true copies of which shall be delivered to all the High Contracting Parties.

☛ **USA: The White House: Submission of Hague Convention on Cultural Property to Senate: Presidential Message, Congressional Record, 6 January 1999, pp. S35-S36**

Removal of Injunction of Secrecy – Treaty Doc. No. 106-1 (Senate – 6 January 1999) [Page: S35]

Mr. Lott. Mr. President, as in executive session, I ask unanimous consent that the injunction of secrecy be removed from the following treaty transmitted to the Senate on January 6, 1999, by the President of the United States: The Hague Convention and Hague Protocol, Treaty Document No. 106-1.

I further ask that the treaty be considered as having been read the first time; that it be referred, with accompanying papers, to the Committee on Foreign Relations and ordered to be printed; and the President's message be printed in the Record.

The Presiding Officer. Without objection, it is so ordered.

The message of the President is as follows:

To the Senate of the United States:
I transmit herewith, for the advice and consent of the Senate to ratification, the Hague Convention for the Protection of Cultural Property in the Event of Armed Conflict (the Convention) and, for accession, the Hague Protocol, concluded on May 14, 1954, and entered into force on August 7, 1956. Also enclosed for the information of the Senate is the report of the Department of State on the Convention and the Hague Protocol.

I also wish to take this opportunity to reiterate my support for the prompt approval of Protocol II Additional to the Geneva Conventions of 12 August 1949, concluded at Geneva on June 10, 1977 (Protocol II). Protocol II, which deals with non-international armed conflicts, or civil wars, was transmitted to the Senate for advice and consent to ratification in 1987 by President Reagan but has not been acted upon.

The Hague Convention

The Convention was signed by the United States on May 14, 1954, the same day it was concluded; however, it has not been submitted to the Senate for advice and consent to ratification until now.

The Hague Convention, to which more than 80 countries are party, elaborates on obligations contained in earlier treaties. It also establishes a regime for special protection of a highly limited category of cultural property. It provides both for preparations in peacetime for safeguarding cultural property against foreseeable effects of armed conflicts, and also for respecting such property in time of war or military occupation. In conformity with the customary practice of nations, the protection of cultural property is not absolute. If cultural property is used for military purposes, or in the event of imperative military necessity, the protection afforded by the Convention is waived, in accordance with the Convention's terms.

Further, the primary responsibility for the protection of cultural property rests with the party controlling that property, to ensure that the property is properly identified and that it is not used for an unlawful purpose.

The Hague Protocol, which was concluded on the same day as the Convention, but is a separate agreement, contains provisions intended to prevent the exportation of cultural property from occupied territory. It obligates an occupying power to prevent the exportation of cultural property from territory it occupies, requires each party to take into its custody cultural property exported contrary to the Protocol, and requires parties to return such cultural property at the close of hostilities. However, as described in the report of the Secretary of State, there are concerns about the acceptability of Section I of the Hague Protocol. I therefore recommend that at the time of accession, the United States exercise its right under Section III of the Hague Protocol to declare that it will not be bound by the provisions of Section I.

The United States signed the Convention on May 14, 1954. Since that time, it has been subject to detailed interagency reviews. Based on these reviews, I have concluded that the United States should now become a party to the Convention and to the Hague Protocol, subject to the understandings and declaration contained in the report of the Department of State.

United States military policy and the conduct of operations are entirely consistent with the Convention's provisions. In large measure, the practices required by the Convention to protect cultural property were based upon the practices of US military forces during World War II. A number of concerns that resulted in the original decision not to submit the Convention for advice and consent have not materialized in the decades of experience with the Convention since its entry into force. The minor concerns that remain relate to ambiguities in language that should be addressed through appropriate understandings, as set forth in the report of the Department of State.

I believe that ratification of the Convention and accession to the Protocol will underscore our long commitment, as well as our practice in combat, to protect the world's cultural resources.

I am also mindful of the international process underway for review of the Convention. By becoming a party, we will be in a stronger position to shape any proposed amendments and help ensure that U.S. interests are preserved.

I recommend, in light of these considerations, that the Senate give early and favorable consideration to the Convention and the Protocol and give its advice and consent to ratification and accession, subject to the understandings and declaration contained in the report of the Department of State.

Protocol II Additional

In his transmittal message dated January 29, 1987, President Reagan requested the advice and consent of the Senate to ratification of Protocol II. The Senate, however, did not act on Protocol II. I believe the Senate should now renew its consideration of this important law-of-war agreement.

Protocol II expands upon the fundamental humanitarian provisions contained in the 1949 Geneva Conventions with respect to internal armed conflicts. Such internal conflicts have been the source of appalling civilian suffering, particularly over the last several decades. Protocol II is aimed specifically at ameliorating the suffering of victims of such internal conflicts and, in particular, is directed at protecting civilians who, as we have witnessed with such horror this very decade, all too often find themselves caught in the crossfire of such conflicts. Indeed, if Protocol II's fundamental rules were observed, many of the worst human tragedies of recent internal armed conflicts would have been avoided.

Because the United States traditionally has held a leadership position in matters relating to the law of war, our ratification would help give Protocol II the visibility and respect it deserves and would enhance efforts to further ameliorate the suffering of war's victims – especially, in this case, victims of internal armed conflicts.

I therefore recommend that the Senate renew its consideration of Protocol II Additional and give its advice and consent to ratification, subject to the understandings and reservations that are described fully in the report attached to the original 29 January 1987, transmittal message to the Senate.

William J. Clinton
The White House, January 6, 1999

6.33   NATIONAL COURTS

☞ **Belgium: In re *Pinochet Ugarte*. District of Brussels *Tribunal of first instance* (…) Ruling Article 61 quinquies 5 C.I. Cr -request for an instrument of supplementary preliminary investigation**[2]

Dossier nr. 216/98
Notices nr. 30.99.3447/98

We, Damiaen Vandermeersch,
Examining magistrate at the tribunal of first instance of Brussels,
In accordance with article 61 quinquies of the Code of Criminal procedure;
Considering the documents of the proceedings which we are preparing in the case of:
Mr. Augusto Pinochet Ugarte;
Accused of a crime of international law;
Considering the request filed on 4 November 1989 by:
1. Mr. Rosario Lilian Aguilar Diaz,
2. Mr. José Ponce Vicencio;
3. Mrs. Georgina Jorquera Leyton;
4. Mrs. Sandra Fernandez Maturana;
5. Mrs. Maria Soledad Lopez Marambio;
6. Mr. Jorge Palma Donosa;

parties civiles in this present case in accordance with article 61 quinquies of the Code of Criminal Procedure.
Having regard to the closing speech of the King's Public Prosecutor of 5 November 1998 in accordance with article 61 quinquies paragraph 2, considering that it is not necessary, at this stage, to make a claim concerning the request of the plaintiffs.

1. Object of the request
The object of the request is the granting of an instrument of supplementary preliminary investigations based on article 61 quinquies of the Code of Criminal Procedure, namely to 'issue against Mr. Augusto Pinochet Ugarte, at present detained provisionally in the United Kingdom in the Grovelands Priory Hospital because of the request for extradition issued by Spain, for the urgent need of examination an international arrest warrant so that he could be extradited to Belgium as soon as possible.'
In their request, the *parties civiles* ask for this decision to be taken within 48 hours.

2. The admissibility of the request
The petitioners in this case have the status of *parties civiles* and thus are authorised to request the examining magistrate to carry out a supplementary preliminary investigation.
The issuance of an arrest warrant by default after the charge in order to obtain the extradition of an accused constitutes an act of preliminary investigation which comes

---

2. Translation by Ms. Louise Beschoor Plug.

within the competence of the examining magistrate on the occasion of the submission of the case before the court.

3. The competence of the examining magistrate to prepare the case to which he is referred
The examining magistrate is the magistrate upon whom the responsibility falls to issue an arrest warrant in all matters relevant to the common jurisdiction in criminal matters. He can only issue an arrest warrant against persons submitted to his jurisdiction.

Before ruling on the question of the issuance of an arrest warrant by default, the examining magistrate has to determine his competence as could result from the indications of the offences submitted to him.

If the final assessment of the competence of the examining magistrate falls within the competence of the jurisdictions of investigation and of the jurisdiction of verdict, the examining magistrate is nevertheless able to provisionally determine his competence to investigate the facts submitted to him before deciding on the acts of investigation relevant to his competence and, more specifically before issuing an arrest warrant against the accused (see notably, Cass., 31 May 1995, *Rev. dr. pen. crim.*, 1996, p. 198)

3.1. The personal competence and the question of recognised immunities of foreign heads of state
Mr. Augusto Pinochet came to power in September 1973 following a coup through which the then-ruling President Allende was overthrown and lost his life. Then, he *de facto* carried out the duties of head of state in Chile, which can be verified. General Pinochet Ugarte did not retire from his position as head of the army until March 1998.

Firstly it would be convenient, as part of the present investigation, to determine to what extent the Belgium state has attributed to Mr. Pinochet this position of legal head of state of Chile.

Then, if the position of head of state should be attributed to the person concerned, it would be convenient to examine whether this position actually grants him personal immunity.

As a rule, a foreign head of state while in office enjoys an absolute immunity of jurisdiction and execution (see, regarding this issue, J. Salmon, *Manuel de droit diplomatique*, Bruylant 1994, pp. 591 and following). However, it appears that Mr. Pinochet no longer holds the position of head of state in office.

Concerning a person that holds the position of former head of state, he ceases to enjoy the immunities attributed to the exercising of his position when this comes to an end. This person however continues to enjoy immunity for all the acts fulfilled while exercising his position as head of state as long as this immunity is not lifted by the state that sent him. (J. Salmon, *Manuel de droit diplomatique*, Bruylant 1994, p.602).

If the crimes at present attributed to Mr. Pinochet should be considered as established, you could not, however, consider that they have been committed in the line of his duties: such criminal acts cannot be supposed to fall under the regular exercise of his function as head of state, of which one of the tasks consists of precisely guaranteeing the protection of his citizens.

In addition, the immunity extended to heads of state does not seem to apply to the subject of crimes under international law, such as war crimes, crimes against peace or crimes against humanity (E. David, *Elements de droit penal international*, 1997-1998, Presses Universitaires de Bruxelles, p.36-37).

'The protection which international law extends to heads of state could not apply to criminal acts. The authors of these acts cannot invoke their official position in order to escape the regular procedure and to shelter from punishment' (Tribunal militaire international de Nuremberg, 1 October 1946, cited by J. Salmon, *Manuel de droit diplomatique*, Bruylant 1994, p. 603).

3.2. The application of the Act of 16 June 1993 to the facts of the case

The complaint with the institution of *parties civiles* proceedings of the applicants is based on crimes of international law as aimed at by the Act of 16 June 1993 regarding the repression of serious offences against the international Conventions of Geneva of 12 August 1949 and by the Protocols I and II of 8 June 1977 additional to these Conventions (*Moniteur belge* of 5 August 1993).

The Act of 16 June 1993 includes both regulations on material criminal law (specific incriminations, ...) as well as rules regarding the criminal procedure (universal competence, imprescriptibility, ...).

3.2.1. The universal jurisdiction

Article 7 of the Act of 16 June 1993 attributes to the Belgian judge a universal competence whatever the place where the offence has been committed. No complaint or official recommendation of the authorities of the country where the offence has been committed is required to justify the competence of the Belgian judge (Art. 7 paragraph 2 of the Act).

This regulation infringes upon the rule as set by Article 12 of the preliminary title of the Criminal Procedures Code in which the intention to prosecute depends on the condition that the accused is in Belgium. The preamble of the Act of 16 June 1993 actually specifies that the Belgian jurisdictions are competent 'even in the case where the presumed author of the offence is not on Belgian territory' (Doc. parl. Senat, 1317-1, 1990-1991, p.16; see also A. Andries, E. David, C. van den Wijngaert and J. Verhaegen, 'Commentaire de la loi du 16 juin 1993 relative a la repression des infractions graves au droit international humanitaire', *Rev. dr. pén. crim.* 12994, 1173).

As it concerns a rule of competence and, therefore, of criminal procedure, Article 7 of the Act of 16 June 1993 is of direct application; it applies to offences committed before its coming into force (Art. 3 of the Judiciary Code: Cass., 24 December 1973, Pas., 1974, 1, 447; Cass., 16 October 1985, *Rev. dr. pén. crim.,* 1986, p. 406).

Moreover this principle was accepted by the Belgian legislator when he recognised the international *ad hoc* tribunals and integrated them in our internal legal order (Act of 22 March 1996 relating to the recognition of the international Tribunal for the Former Yugoslavia and the international Tribunal for Rwanda – *Moniteur belge* of 27 April 1996). This act recognises the competence of these international jurisdictions *vis-à-vis* offences committed before their creation.

Finally, it remains to be pointed out that Mr. Pinochet comes under the competence of non-political law; a foreign soldier is considered, actually, as a civilian with regard to the rules of distribution of competence between the non-political legal jurisdictions and the military jurisdictions.

3.2.2. The question of the retroactivity of material law of the Act of 16 June 1993

The Act of 16 June 1993 has instituted a whole system of specific incrimination of offences aimed at by international humanitarian law. The Act addresses various serious infractions aimed at by the Conventions of Geneva and the Additional Protocols and lays down the sanctions applicable to these offences.

The Act came into force on 15 August 1993.

Pursuant to the general principle of non-retroactivity of criminal laws (Art. 2 of the criminal Code), the new offences introduced by the Act of 16 June 1993 cannot apply to acts committed before the coming into force of the Act if these acts have not been criminalised before.

Insofar as the offences addressed in the Act of 16 June 1993 were already punishable under internal law before the coming into force of the Act, notably on the basis of regulations of criminal non-political law such as those criminalising assassination, murder, beatings and injuries, detention with torture, hostage taking..., the principle of the legality of the offences, such as provided for in Article 2 of the Criminal Code, does not seem to be opposed to the institution of prosecution for such offences under the classification of crimes under international law on the understanding that the applicable punishments will be those that were in force at the moment of the commission of the offences pursuant to the criminal law under the restriction of the possibly more favourable character of the new punishments (principles of legality of the punishments and of retroactivity of the mildest punishment).

Finally it should be noted that within the framework of the application of Additional Protocol II (internal armed conflicts), it is agreed that the prosecutions are submitted to the principle of legality and more specifically to the condition of double incrimination (A. Andries, E. David, C. van den Wijngaert and J. Verhaegen, 'Commentaire de la loi du 16 juin 1993 relative à la repression des infractions graves au droit international humanitaire', *Rev. dr. pén. crim.* 1994, 1175). In this case, it is reasonable to believe that the facts attributed to Mr. Pinochet were criminalised at the time of the facts in Chilean law and in Belgian law.

3.2.3. Existence of an armed conflict, condition of application of the Act of 16 June 1993. The Act of 16 June 1993 refers explicitly to serious offences under the international Conventions of Geneva of 12 August 1949 and Additional Protocols I and II of 8 June 1977, and its field of application coincides with that of the international instruments pursuant to which the Act criminalises the offences. As a result, the application of the Act of 16 June 1993 requires the acknowledgement of the existence of an international armed conflict or of an internal armed conflict under article 1 of Additional Protocol II. (On these issues of international armed conflict and non-international armed conflict, A. Andries, E. David, C. van den Wijngaert and J. Verhaegen, 'Commentaire de la loi du 16 juin 1993 relative à la repression des infractions graves au droit international humanitaire,' *Rev. dr. pén. crim.*, 1994, pp. 1123 a 1135).

Article 1 of Additional Protocol II defines a non-international armed conflict as follows: 1. The present Protocol II, which further develops and supplements Article 3 common to the Conventions of Geneva of 12 August 1949 without modifying its present conditions of application, shall apply to all armed conflicts which are not covered by Article 1 of the Protocol Additional to the Conventions of Geneva of 12 August 1949 and relating to the Protection of Victims of International Armed Conflicts (Protocol I), and which takes place in the territory of a High Contracting Party between its armed forces and dissident armed forces or organised armed groups which, under responsible command, exercise such control over a part of its territory as to enable them to carry out sustained and concerted military operations and to implement this Protocol.

2. The present Protocol shall not apply to situations of internal disturbances and tensions, such as riots, isolated and sporadic acts of violence and other acts of a similar nature, as not being armed conflicts.

The question of the existence of an international armed conflict or of an internal armed conflict under Protocol II additional to the Conventions of Geneva comes under the supreme decision of the judge of first instance (Doc. parl., Senat, 481-5, S.E. 1991-1992, p.12).

Although the preliminary investigation has to be continued in this respect and under the reservation of elements which could disclose the continuation of the investigation, it does not appear at this moment that the condition of the existence of an international armed conflict or of an internal armed conflict under Protocol II additional to the Conventions of Geneva are fulfilled in this case. It follows that, under reservation of the later decision of the competent jurisdictions, the Act of 16 June 1993 will not apply to this case.

3.3. The grounds for the prosecution on the basis of the incrimination of crimes against humanity

When offences of international law do not come under the field of application of the Act of 16 June 1993, however, one ought to check whether the offences could be considered equivalent to a crime against humanity and fall within the provisions of other international crimalisations that tie Belgium out of custom or convention, such as crimes against humanity (See, on this matter, A. Andries, E. David, C. van den Wijngaert and J. Verhaegen, 'Commentaire de la loi du 16 june 1993 relative a la repression des infractions graves au droit international humanitaire', *Rev. dr. pén. crim.* 1994, pp. 1133 and 1135).

The examining magistrate, to whom the case is referred, is not bound by the classification given to the facts in the indictment for the preliminary investigation or in the act of institution of civil action (Cass., 11 décembre 1990, *Pas.,* 1991, 1, 355).

The classification given to the facts in the prosecution is only provisional, the responsibility for the qualification lies constitutionally and legally with the judge. Thus, the examining magistrate, the examining jurisdictions and the King's Prosecutor during the final drawing up of its requisitions, are free to substitute a correct classification for a classification that appears incorrect (M. Rigaux and P. E. Trousse, 'Les problemes de qualification', *Rev. dr. Pén. crim.,* 1948-1949; pp. 716 and 721-722; A. de Nauw, 'Het adieren van de onderzoeksrechter', in A. de Nauw; J. D'Haenens and M. Storme, *Actuele problemen van strafrecht,* Antwerpen, Kluwer, 1988, p. 11).

In this case, one ought to examine whether the facts of the case, which has been referred to us, could be reclassified as crimes against humanity and to base on that qualification the prosecution under Belgian law.

3.3.1 The principles of crimes against humanity

Crimes against humanity have been sanctioned in the Statute and the Judgement of the Nuremberg Trials as well as in the Act nr.10 of the Control Council for Germany. Article 11 of the Act nr.10 Control Council defines crimes against humanity as follows:

'c) Crimes against humanity – Atrocities and offences including, without this list being exhaustive, assassination, extermination, enslavement, deportation, imprisonment, torture, rape or all other inhuman acts committed against a civilian population and persecutions for motives of a political, racial or religious nature, whether or not the aforementioned crimes have constituted a violation of the national law of the country where they have been perpetrated'. (International Law Reports, Volume 36, p.31; on the genesis of Crimes against humanity see International Criminal Tribunal for Rwanda (Chamber 1), 2 September 1998, *in casu* Akayesu Jean-Paul, case nr. ICTR-96-4-T, pp. 228-241).

Crimes against humanity are directed against any civilian population and are punishable whether or not they have been committed during an armed conflict, international or internal. (Report of the General Secretary established in accordance with paragraph 2 of resolution 808 (1993-S/25704), nr.47, quoted by the International Criminal Tribunal for Rwanda (Chamber 1), 2 September 1998, *in casu* Akayesu U Jean-Paul, case nr. ICTR-96-4-T, P.229).

In the Eichmann, Barbie, Touvier and Papon cases, the principle of crimes against humanity has been taken up and specified (see, on this subject, C. Grynfogel, 'The concept of crimes against humanity – Yesterday, today and tomorrow', *Rev. dr. pen. crim.*, p.13 and following and the International Criminal Tribunal for Rwanda (Chamber 1), 2 September 1998, *in casu* Akayesu Jean-Paul, case nr. ICTR-96-4-T, pp.229 to 233).

Article 212-1 of the French Criminal Code (1994) defines crimes against humanity as 'deportation, taking into slavery or mass and systematic practice of summary executions, of abduction of persons followed by their disappearance, of torture or of inhuman acts, inspired by political, racial or religious motives and organised in accordance with the plan devised against a group of the civilian population.'

The international *ad hoc* tribunals (Criminal Tribunal for Yugoslavia and the Criminal Tribunal for Rwanda) have also accepted in their respective Statutes the incrimination of crimes against humanity.

Article 7 of the International Criminal Court takes up the incrimination of crimes against humanity, including notably, murder, extermination, enslavement, deportation, imprisonment, torture, forced disappearance of persons, persecution of a group or of a community for political, racial, national, ethnical, cultural or religious reasons. . . .

According to E. David (Elements of international criminal law, 1997-1998, Presses Universities de Brussels, p.552), crimes against humanity have the following in common:

'— these are acts of serious violence committed against persons;

— these persons are civilians but can also be combatants;

— these acts are massive (committed on a large scale);

— according to the texts, these acts have to be committed entirely or partially for political, racial or religious purposes;

— these acts can be committed in times of peace as well as in times of war;

— the sources of the incrimination are conventional, customary and institutional;

— the incrimination appears direct;

— The competence is universal.'

From the preceding it follows that the facts claimed by the civil parties are susceptible to constitute crimes against humanity in accordance with customary international law.

3.3.2. The incrimination of crimes against humanity in internal law
The question should be asked here in order to know whether the incrimination of crimes against humanity, as it is sanctioned in international law, should be considered as directly applicable in our internal legal order.

Our internal criminal law does not know the principle of crimes against humanity. However some acts that fall under the definition of crimes against humanity can correspond to certain incriminations under common law (such as assassination, murder, beatings and injuries, detention with torture, hostage-taking...).

If one accepts that custom is the result of a practice whereby the states concerned show that they have believe they should conform to what amounts to a legal rule, the incrimination of crimes against humanity appears as customary (E. David, *Elements of international criminal law*, 1997-1998, Presses Universitaires de Bruxelles, p. 540).

As has been outlined above, the concept of crimes against humanity has been taken up in various international instruments but these texts could only have sanctioned an incrimination already existing in customary law. We offer as proof the fact that several of these legal instruments have only been created *a postiori* after the commission of the facts and that if these incriminations were not pre-existing in customary law, then their application would have conflicted with the principle of non-retroactivity of criminal law.

One has to recall here that the Belgian legislator has recognized the existence and the Statutes of the international *ad hoc* tribunals and has integrated them in our internal legal order (Act of 22 March 1996 concerning the recognition of the International Tribunal for the former Yugoslavia and the International Tribunal for Rwanda – *Moniteur belge* of 27 April 1996). However, these Statutes sanction the incrimination of crimes against humanity regarding facts that have been committed before their coming into force.

As a consequence, there are grounds to consider that before being codified into treaties or acts, crimes against humanity were sanctioned by international custom and are, as such, part of the international *jus cogens* which imposes itself on the internal legal order with restrictive effect 'erga omnes' (see, concerning this subject, Cherif BASSIOUNI, *Crimes against humanity in international law*, Martinus Nijhoff Publishers, Dordrecht, 1992, pp. 489 to 499).

International customary law is a source of international law just as a treaty is and it can be applied directly in the Belgian legal order (J. Salmon, 'The role of the Belgian court of Cassation regarding international custom', in Melanges Ganshof van der Meersch, Bruylant, Bruxelles, pp. 220 and following.) International criminal law is a section of international public law. It is a customary law and, to some extent, a law with a conventional base. It expresses a rule superior to the will of States and exists as such notwithstanding all contrary regulations of national law. Thus, the racist and religious persecution, although in keeping with the internal legal order of the Third Reich, constitute crimes against humanity and can constitute war crimes. (W. J. Ganshof van der Meersch, *Justice and international criminal law*, J. T., 1961, 539).

It is worth pointing out here that at the time of the ratification of the Genocide Convention, Belgium did not deem it necessary to have to adapt its internal legislation, considering that 'the principles included in the Convention (could) be considered as already being a part of the Belgian legal system'. (Report on the motives of the Bill of approval of the Convention on genocide, Doc.parl. chambre, 1950, 201-1, p. 4, quoted by E. David, *Elements of international criminal law,* 1997-1998, Presses Universitaires de Bruxelles, p. 550). Similar reasoning can be applied regarding crimes against humanity, that there are grounds to consider them as already being part of our legal order.

Finally, insofar as crimes against humanity are also punishable in internal law on the basis of regulations of common criminal law such as those incriminating assassination, murder, beatings and injuries, detention with torture, hostage-taking..., the principle of legality of the incriminations such as provided for in article 2 of the criminal code does not appear to oppose itself to the institution of prosecution for such offences under the classification of crimes against humanity with the understanding that the applicable punishments would be those that were in force at the time of the committing of the offences by virtue of the common criminal law (principle of the legality of the punishments).

3.3.3. The competence of the Belgian judge on the basis of the classification of crimes against humanity

The question of the competence of the Belgian judge to have jurisdiction over the prosecution of a foreigner not found in Belgium on the charge of crimes against humanity committed in a foreign country against foreigners or Belgians is discussed and is worth considering.

Up until now, the question of the competence of the judge to have jurisdiction over the crimes against humanity committed beyond the borders has been examined mainly in terms of the obligation of the state authorities to prosecute such crimes and not in terms of the choice to prosecute.

The judicial authorities of several states have often given the impression that as far as crimes against humanity are concerned, they looked more for motives and juridical pretexts so as not to prosecute such crimes rather than check to what extent international law and internal law would allow them to institute such prosecutions.

And yet there is a consensus at an international level to consider that it is the responsibility of states to take the necessary measures to assure the suppression of crimes against humanity.

Let us recall here that the first duty of justice is to dispense justice and that this applies *a fortiori* for the most serious crimes, namely the crimes of international law.

Now, in humanitarian law, the risk does not seem to lie as much in the fact that the national authorities exceed their competence but rather in the reflex with which they look for pretexts to justify their lack of competence, leaving the door wide open to the impunity of the most serious crimes (which is definitely contrary to the *raison d'etre* of the rules of international law).

The general principle of international law 'aut dedere, aut judicare' (obligation of prosecution in the absence of extradition) constitutes one of the expressions on the necessity not to leave crimes of international law unpunished and on the responsibility of state authorities to assure the suppression of such crimes regardless of the place where they have been committed.

It has got to be one thing or the other: either crimes of humanity are just incriminations among many other ones that do not transcend borders and their suppression is left to the discretion of each state, or these crimes are of an unspeakable and unacceptable nature and the responsibility for their repression is shared by all.

According to this last hypothesis, all states and humanity as a whole could be considered as having a legal interest is repressing such crimes: the result of this is that apart from all conventional ties, the national authorities have the right and even under certain circumstances the obligation to prosecute the authors of such crimes irrespective of where they are found.

The fight against impunity of authors of crimes under international law falls therefore within the responsibility of all states of which the national authorities have the obligation or, at the very least, the right to take all measures in order to assure the prosecution and the repression of crimes against humanity.

As such, resolution 3074 (XXVIII) of 3 December 1973 entitled 'Principles of international cooperation concerning the tracking down, the arrest, the extradition and the punishment of individuals guilty of war crimes and of crimes against humanity' sets out as a first principle:
'War crimes and crimes against humanity, wherever they have been committed and whenever they have been committed, have to be the subject of an investigation and the individuals against whom there is proof establishing that they have committed such crimes have to be tracked down, arrested, brought to justice and, if admitted guilty, punished'. (Extract cited by E. David, *Elements of international penal law,* 1997-1998, Presses Universitaires de Bruxelles, p. 553).

From the moment this resolution of which the formulation is normative ('should') – sanctions a practice where the concerned states show that they are willing to comply with that which amounts to a legal rule, it is the expression of a rule of custom: 'A resolution can constitute proof of customary law or of one of its constitutive elements (creative practice of custom, *opinio juris*), particularly when such has been the intention of the states when they adopted the resolution or when the procedures that have been followed have led to the development of the wording of a rule of law ' (Resolution 20 of the 13th Commission of the Institute de Droit international, cited by E. David, *Droit des organizations internationales,* vol. II, P.U.B., 1997-1998, p.199).

In view of the above, we believe that a rule of custom exists of the right of the people, or even of imperative law, recognizing the universal competence and authorizing the national state authorities to prosecute and to bring to justice, in all circumstances, the persons suspected of crimes against humanity (See, on this matter, E. David, 'L'actualite juridique de Nuremberg', in *Le Proces de Nuremberg, consequences et actualisation,* Bruylant, 1988, pp. 169 and 170).

4.   The prescription and the issue of imprescriptibility of crimes of international law
The principle of imprescriptibility of war crimes and crimes against humanity is widely recognized in international law; it has been stated in Article 11, paragraph 5, of Control Council Law Number 10 of the Allied Council in Germany, the rule of imprescriptibility is sanctioned by the first article of the Convention of the United Nations of 26 November1968 on the imprescriptibility of war crimes and of crimes against humanity as well as by the first article of the Convention of the Council of Europe of 25 January 1974 on the imprescriptibility of war crimes and of crimes against humanity.

If these two above-mentioned instruments have not been ratified by Belgium and if no internal disposition provides for the imprescriptibility of crimes against humanity

(Art. 8 of the act of 16 June 1993 sanctions the imprescriptibility of serious offences against the Conventions of Geneva and to the Additional Protocols) then one ought to examine if the principle of imprescriptibility of crimes against humanity should perhaps be considered as a rule of custom of international law applicable in internal law.

To the extent that international criminal law ignores prescription in general and to the extent that it is incompatible with the nature of the incriminated facts, one should consider that crimes against humanity should be declared imprescriptible (E. David, *Elements de droit penal international,* Presses Universitaires de Bruxelles, 1997-1998, p. 438).

So if one has to consider that the imprescriptible nature of crimes against humanity is the result of the nature itself of these crimes, one ought to determine the existence of a rule of custom of international law that sanctions the imprescriptibility of crimes against humanity and that this rule is applicable in internal law.

The example given by France is eloquent on this subject: the French Act of 26 December 1964 is entitled 'The act aiming at ascertaining the imprescriptibility of crimes against humanity'.

It has been judged that 'crimes against humanity are imprescriptible by nature'; their imprescriptibility can be deduced from the general principles of law recognised by nations as a whole as well as from the International Military Tribunal annexed to the agreement of London of 8 August 1945; the Act of 26 December 1964 has been limited to confirming that this imprescriptibility has already been acquired, in internal law, by the effect of the international texts which France had joined. And thus, although committed more than thirty years ago, before the setting in motion of the public action, the crimes against humanity are not covered by prescription. (Cass. fr. (crim.), 26 January 1984, Bull. Crim. number 34, JCP, 11, 20197, J.D.I., 1984, pp. 314-3150).

From what has been stated above, one could consider that the principle of imprescriptibility of crimes against humanity is sanctioned by a rule of custom of international law applicable to internal law (see on this matter E. David, *Elements de droit penal international,* Presses Universitaires de Bruxelles, 1997-1998, p.555). The unpardonable nature of crime against humanity follows from its imprescriptibility (ibidem).

Furthermore, one could ask oneself the question whether prescription has not been suspended during the whole period that Mr. Pinochet occupied the position as head of state in office given the fact that this position would have extended immunity which constituted an obstacle to the proceedings.

5. The foundation of the request

The object of the request is to issue against Mr. Augusto Pinochet Ugarte an international arrest warrant within 48 hours so that he can be extradited to Belgium as soon as possible.

The issue of an international arrest warrant in view of extradition is governed by Article 34 of the Act of 20 July 1990 regarding preventive detention.

As this arrest warrant by default could constitute a title for preventive detention, the issue of such warrant is also submitted to the conditions attached to Article 16 of the Act of 20 July 1990.

When the accused is not detained on national territory, no legal regulation will set a period within which the examining magistrate will be held to issue an arrest warrant.

The preliminary investigation being led under the direction and responsibility of the examining magistrate, it is up to him to assess, without appeal, the most opportune moment to give a ruling on the question of the issue of an arrest warrant in view of the extradition.

The present preliminary investigation has been opened on the first of November 1998 following the institution of civil action proceedings of the applicants.

The undersigning magistrate has diligently carried out his various duties of the investigation. At this stage, the case is essentially based on the initial complaint and on the confirmation of the complaint by the *parties civiles*.

It is important to actively pursue the investigation in order to verify the unilateral declarations of the plaintiffs and to gather the maximum of information.

This continuation of the investigation seems to us essential to be able to give a ruling, with full knowledge of the facts, on the possible issue of an international arrest warrant. In this respect,

In view of the above, the request, as worded by the applicants, seems premature with regard to a good administration of justice and has to, as a result, be declared groundless because the measure will be, at the present stage of the investigation, detrimental to the investigation.

On these grounds,
We declare the request of the requesting party aiming at the granting of an instrument of supplementary preliminary investigation admissible but groundless.

Made and provided with our seal, in Brussels, on 6 November 1998. (. . .)

☞ Chile: Supreme Court, 9 September 1998, Rol 469-98 concerning the illegal detention of Pedro Poblete Córdova

Whereas:
This case roll no. 895-90 of the Higher Military Court of Santiago, dealt with before the Military Attorney, is, by the decision of first instance after thorough investigation, dismissed with prejudice, conform art. 408.5 of the Code of Penal Procedure (CPP), as the penal liability has been extinguished by the granting of amnesty to the persons, who took part in the events that befell Pedro Enrique Córdova, when he was taken prisoner. To this date his whereabouts are unknown.

The Military Court of the Army, Airforce and Carabineros has confirmed this decision in first instance; a decision against which the injured party represented by his lawyer, Sergio Concho Rodriguez has lodged an appeal for cassation.

Per doc. 981 the Advocate General of this Supreme Court in his compulsory conclusion is of the opinion that the appeal should be admitted. The relevant documents were brought forth.

Considering:
1. that appellant persists in his objection based on art. 546 par.6 of the CPP; that in his opinion the decision to dismiss the case with prejudice would mean violating the law by qualifying the circumstances as falling under art. 408 par. 5 in conjunction with art. 413 and 279 *bis* and with arts. 93.3 of the Penal Code (PC) and decree 2.191 on amnesty.

2. That, according to the appellant, the miscarriage of justice was brought about in the following manner:

a. By reaching a conclusion without first identifying that particular person that is the suspect in the case, which is an essential requirement according to art. 408.5 of the CPP.

b. By basing its decision on amnesty, as laid down in art. 93.3 of the PC by applying art.1 of decree 2.191, which contains a legislative benefit, that only becomes operative in the final phase of the criminal procedure and should be preceded by determining the crimes committed and the persons who committed them.

c. By coming to a conclusion without the investigation as laid down in arts. 279 *bis* and 413 of the CPP being completed whilst there are still fundamental measures to be taken.

d. By referring in the process to kidnapping and not to illegal arrest, as defined respectively in arts. 14 and 148 of the PC. That, given the more permanent character of the first crime, the disappearance of the victim has largely transgressed the time limit of the amnesty in question and

e. By not applying the international treaties on this matter, in particular art. 15.2 of the International Pact on Human Rights, whereby the state of Chile has committed itself concerning the investigation and punishment of persons who committed offences against human rights. These texts have constitutional primacy according to the amendment of art. 5 of the Constitution of the Republic and take precedence over the internal legislation in case of disparity as is the case with the amnesty in question;

3. That in the procedure it was established that on 19 July 1974 Pedro Enrique Poblete Córdova left his house and took off in the direction of his work, a metallurgic workshop, situated on the Panamericana Norte Rd. in Santiago, where he did not arrive and neither did he return home. Later did unknown persons inform his family that he was held up that day by persons in civilian clothes and was taken in custody in Cuatro Alomos, but his permanent whereabouts are unknown.

4. That art.1 of Decree 2.191 1978 has granted amnesty to all persons who have partaken in punishable offences between 11 September 1973 and 10 March 1978. As long as they were not involved in a criminal procedure or condemned, with the exception of some offences, they are of no relevance in this process.

5. That to begin with it is enough to point out that our judicial system is, as far as penalising is concerned, founded in the investigation of the facts, that form the basic elements of the crime for the application of sanctions on those persons, who are reproachable of guilty conduct. Consequently the penal procedure in the case of crime or simple misdemeanour aims in the first stage of the summary to determine the punishable fact and the person who committed it. However, it is allowed exceptionally ad initium according to arts. 91 and 102 of the PPC to abstain from such an investigation, but in every other later decision it is supposed that the conditions have been met as required for establishing the identity of the suspect by arts. 107, 403 and particularly 408.5 of the CPP, which makes a definite dismissal of the case possible 'as soon as the penal liability of the suspect has lapsed'.

6. That, although a dismissal of the case can be decided on in every stage of the process, special attention must be given in the case of a dismissal with prejudice, whether the investigation is completed in the way, as mentioned before, required in art. 76 of the Section Code and of the Code of Military Law. In this way it is possible to suspend the

proceedings because of lack of information, but on no condition is it allowed to close the case prematurely, with the result that new interrogations are prevented from the moment the sentence is in force. And as long as the investigation is not closed, it is possible to continue and find out exactly what happened and identify the criminals. By deciding otherwise the judges in first instance have made a judicial error by wrongly applying the norm of art. 408.5 of the PCC, in conjunction with art. 93.3 of the PC, contravening in that way especially what is laid down in art. 413 of the CPP, mentioned here in connection with facts, that came to light in the investigation, which makes it necessary to actuate the numerous rulings laid down in docs. 811, 833, 837, 842, 857, 867, 870, 872, 878, 897, all of which tend to elucidate the circumstances in which Pedro Poblete Córdova disappeared and where he was held and which may also lead to the identification of the persons responsible therefore.

7. That the text of the decree 2.191, 1978 is not contrary to what is said before, because it repeatedly uses the word 'persons' when referring to the ones to who its five rulings apply. And this is, moreover, in accordance with the character of the institution of amnesty, as described in the trustworthy history of its makings in art. 93.3 of the PC, published in 1874. It refers clearly to: 'persons involved'. (Session no. 139, 19 May 1873 of the Revisory Committee).

8. Hence to grant amnesty, the person who committed the crime must be unequivocally identified, because that is the only way that penal action for his part in the crime can be stopped. Of the foregoing it may be concluded that by applying a ground for termination of penal liability, that does not have power to decide the case, the judges again have violated justice.

9. That, considering the next point, it should be kept in mind that after 11 September 1973, the day the Armed Forces deposed the government and assumed power, which they claimed included the constitutive, legislative and executive power. This was laid down in decree no. 5 of 12 September 1973. Article 1 of the said decree declared to have interpreted art. 418 of the code of Military Law and ascertained that the state of affairs brought about by internal commotion (a situation which lasted till 19 July 1974) should be understood as 'a state or times of war', as far as the application of penalty those days was concerned as laid down in the aforementioned code, just like other penal laws of the same legislative. Undisputedly were in this legislation the Geneva Conventions of 1949 in force ratified by Chile and published in the Official Gazette of 17-20 April 1951. Article 3 (relative to the protection of civilians in times of war) compels the partaking nations in the case of an armed internal conflict, to the use of humane treatment, even to those who have laid down their arms, without discrimination, forbidding at any time or place among other things a. attempts on life or bodily integrity b. attempts on personal dignity. That international instrument, likewise, mentions in art.146 the engagement between the signatories to take the necessary legislative measures to decide on penalties to be applied to persons who commit or order to commit any of the infringements as defined in the Convention. The signatories are also compelled to track down such persons and bring them up to their own tribunals and to take measures to stop any contrary acts. The terms of the convention clearly indicate that in all circumstances the accused will benefit from the guarantee of a fair process and of a defence, that should come up to the standard as laid down in arts. 205 and following of the Geneva Convention of 12 August 1949 about the treatment of prisoners of war. In art. 147 is described

what is understood by serious infringements, e.g. homicide, torture, inhuman treatment, violating physical integrity, deportation and illegal detention.

10. That, consequently, under the terms of the Convention, the state of Chile has undertaken to guarantee the safety of those, who might have taken part in armed conflicts within the territory, especially if they have been taken prisoner, whilst it remains forbidden to use means to conceal the offences, that have been committed against certain persons or even to get exemption from punishment for the offenders, whilst keeping in mind that the international agreements should be executed in good faith. And as the object of the agreement is to guarantee the essential human rights, special attention should be given, in view of the fact that this Supreme Court has proclaimed on several occasions, that from the trustworthy history of the making of our Constitution, as laid down in art. 5 of the fundamental law, it is clear that the internal sovereignty of the state of Chile recognises her limit to the rights that stem from human nature – values that are superior to every norm, that the state may have at its disposal, the constitution included, as everybody knows. (Fallos del Mes no. 446, sección Criminal , pg. 2066.4).

Under these circumstances, not applying aforementioned provisions brings about a violation of the law, that must be put right through this appeal, in particular if it is kept in mind that according to the principles of International Law, international treaties must be interpreted and executed in good faith. From this it may be deduced that internal law must adjust itself to these and the legislator must assimilate the new norms as laid in these international instruments. He may not infringe on its principles, without first denouncing the treaty.

11. That, from an other perspective, it should be taken into consideration that the acts have been committed on 19 July 1974 and that up to this day the whereabouts of Pedro Poblete Córdova are unknown. For this reason it may be that the offender or offenders, still to be identified, fell outside the timing and motive set for the granting of amnesty under decree 2.191.

12. As has been said before, dismissing the case without prejudice was an erroneous application of the penal law, in particular of the arts. 93.3 and 148 of the PC and art.1 of the decree 2.191, 1978 related to what has been laid down in art 413 of the CPP and the Geneva Conventions of 1949. These faulty applications of the law form the motive of the cassation conform art. 546.6 of the code of criminal procedure, because of the erroneous interpretation of the circumstances as worded in art. 408.5 of the same code, namely the extinction of penal liability through amnesty. For these reasons persists the injured party in his appeal for cassation (fs. 973), as does the prosecutor.

Also taking into consideration, what is provided in arts. 535, 546 and 547 of the CPP and in arts. 764, 765, 772 and 785 of the Code of Civil Procedure.

We Declare:
That the appeal in cassation as filed per doc. 973 by the injured party is admitted against the sentence of January 19th last (doc. 965). This sentence is annulled and will be replaced by one that will be pronounced separately.

Agreed by majority vote against the Auditor General of the Army, Señor Torres, who wished to reject the appeal on the following grounds:

1. That from the previous evidence it has become obvious that Pedro Poblete Córdova was detained in a public road on 19 July 1974 by officials of the Direction of National

Intelligence and transferred to various locations, belonging to this organisation, whilst up to this moment his whereabouts are unknown.

2. That, as is indicated in the sentence of the second instance, in the court findings the delict can be classified as described, together with punitive measure in art. 148 of the penal code, that is to say: the illegal detention of Poblete Córdova by officials, pertaining to the Directorate of Intelligence of that moment.

3. That in April 1978 the Decree 2.191 was published, a legal document in which, in art. 1, amnesty was granted to all those persons, who in the quality of author, accomplice or fence might have committed punishable offences during the period from 11 September 1973 until 10 March 1978, provided they were not involved in a process or condemned at the moment of publication of the decree. Likewise the decree in art. 3 names certain punishable offences that will not benefit from amnesty, but among those are not mentioned: illegal or arbitrary detention, as in this case, and consequently they benefit fully from the grant of amnesty.

4. That, therefore, the case was dismissed with prejudice by virtue of the compelling command of art. 408.5 of the CCP, where it say that a dismissal with prejudice follows, when the penal liability has been extinguished on the ground of art.93.3, that is to say on the ground of amnesty.

5. That it should not be forgotten, that the institution of amnesty within the penal law, came into existence to resolve the serious difficulties, that emerged in conditions of profound political and social changes since a long time, in particular times of revolution, that made it imperative, that the state temporarily waived its power to judge and punish certain criminal offences for the sake of superior issues at stake, like national order and peace.

6. In this way the doctrine has unanimously been understood, as has the jurisprudence, from before the promulgation of the Decree no. 2.191, in the sense that once a law of amnesty is published, the criminal aspect of an act must be suspended and every penal consequence regarding the guilty party annulled. Therefore, if amnesty is pronounced before the beginning of the process, no penal action may be taken against those who are entitled to amnesty.

7. In our legislation, amnesty is legally laid down as motive for the cessation of penal liability in art. 93.3 of the penal code, because it completely ends the penalisation and its consequences, which in processes has its concretion in art. 408.5 of the CPP as ground for dismissal of the case with prejudice. Moreover, in art. 107 of the code of penal procedure, the legislator rules that before passing on to penal action, the judge must make certain from the background information if the penal liability of the accused indeed has ceased. Refusal to pass judgement must be done by writ with motive if there is one.

8. From what has been said before, it may be concluded, that the real meaning, scope and enforcement of art. 413 of the CPP, is a thorough research of those grounds for dismissal, that are not fully tested, but when there is question of a motive for ceasing the liability, accredited objectively, as is the case with amnesty, an exhaustive investigation to try to prove the crime and the participation of the ones responsible is useless, because the acts committed have ceased to be crimes. This makes the search for the ultimate aim of every criminal trial as mentioned in art. 108 of the CPP, useless and inefficient.

9. That, from another viewpoint, it is not a generally accepted opinion that those offences, which carry a more permanent character, should be excepted from the benefit

of amnesty on the supposition that the punishable conduct is still being committed, as long as the victims are not localised.

10. Indeed, it is certain that kidnapping has a permanent character and will continue to do so as long as the criminal activity has not ceased. Therefore it has to be determined, if Osvaldo Romo Mena – one of the two suspects – still partook in the crime after 10 March 1978, of which appellant accuses him.

11. Therefore the following facts must be kept in mind:

a. that, as maintained under point 1, is has been established from the records, that Pedro Poblete Córdova was detained on 19 July 1974, that is within the period covered by the decree 2.191 of 1978. It is possible that Osvaldo Romo Mena was partly responsible for the detention.

b. Nothing in this process leads to suppose that the detention of Poblete Córdova overstepped the date of 10 March 1978.

c. That, moreover, from document 67 of case no. 282-96 of the roll of the military court of appeal, it is established by means of a resolution issued by the Court-martial of 20 September 1994, that Osvaldo Romo Mena left the national territory on 16 October 1975, that he returned between 1 April 1976 and 12 June of the same year, according to doc.465 of the case roll no. 159-465 of the third criminal court of Santiago, and that he was arrested on 16 november 1992, according to the documents 287 of process no.130.923 of the same court.

And thus: the aforementioned facts lead to the conclusion, that it is very improbable that the accused, as he had left the country on the date indicated, could have gone on with the kidnapping that he is charged of. In any case as far as the other accused are concerned, nothing prevents the application of amnesty for the period it was in force and on the other hand concerning the hypothetical continuation of the crime after 10 March 1978, this must be made credible by proof, as our judicial system requires.

12. In the appeal in question is maintained, that the application of the decree no. 2.191 does not prevail over international law incorporated in the internal judicial system of the country. The appellant adds, that this is the consequence of the subscription and ratification by Chile of international treaties regarding investigation and punishment of offences against human rights. On this particular point, it must be made clear, that the basic judicial corps on which all the positive legislation is based and sustained, is the Constitution of the Republic, to which all international treaties, that our country subscribes, must adjust. In particular, it cannot possibly be maintained that the state of war as decreed in Chile between 11 September 1973 and 11 September 1974, because of the internal conflict of 1973, resembles that to which the Geneva Conventions, subscribed and ratified by us, refers to. The Decree no.5 of September 1973, rules that state or times of war or a state of siege, because of internal commotion, should be understood as only concerning the application of penalisation as laid down in the Code of Military Justice and other penal laws and this goes for all the consequences of this legislation. That is to say, we are dealing with the interpretation of art. 418 of the Code of Military Justice only with the purpose of applying wartime legislation whilst in reality the presuppositions do not meet the legal text. On the other hand, arts. 3 and 4 of the Geneva Conventions rule that conflicts regulated by them concern cases of declared international war and situations of in internal armed conflicts that may arise in the territory of one of the subscribing states. They state clearly, that in that case the situation should be treated as a real war, as is particularly indicated in art. 1 of the

Additional Protocol of the Geneva Conventions, concerning the protection of victims of internal armed conflicts, however on condition that these conflicts take place on the territory of a High Contracting Party between its regular army and a dissident army or armed groupings, who under the leadership of a responsible commander, exercise such a control, that allows them to mount an organised military operation. This Protocol does not apply to situations of internal tensions.

Thus, from the reading this Protocol, it cannot possibly be concluded that the crimes to which the Geneva Conventions refer are excepted from amnesty. In any case art. 6.5 recommends that at the conclusion of the hostilities, the authorities in power grant amnesty on the largest possible scale to those persons who have taken part in the armed conflict.

13. Concerning the application of other international agreements and treaties, which the appellant thinks should prohibit the application of amnesty in this case, although he knows the contents of art. 5 of the Constitution of the Republic, they are in this case not applicable, because in the reverse case authorisation should be given to reactivate a criminal law to the disadvantage of the accused, an eventuality, that is forbidden by virtue of another constitutional rule, contained in art. 19.3 par. 4 of our Charter, embodied explicitly in the PC in art. 18, that only admits the exception to the principle: suspect has the benefit of the doubt, a situation which in this case does not arise. At the same time it should be emphasised that the Vienna Treaties, as published in our country in the Official Gazette of 22 July 1981, about the application of the treaties says in art. 28 the following: the provisions of the treaty carry no obligation for the signatory for any act that has been committed before the treaty came into force. Moreover, the appellant should know, that there exists no international agreement or treaty, in force in Chile, that limits or restrains the power of the State to dictate laws of amnesty, bearing in mind, that it is in the power of the legitimate government to dictate laws of this nature as is explicitly laid down in the Political Constitution in art. 60.16.

14. Without prejudice to the legal basis of the motive for exemption of penal liability, there is also question of the extinguishing of the right to penal action, because the punishable facts, substance of the summary, were committed in July 1974, whilst the case was temporarily dismissed in October 1975. And so the claim of the appellant in cassation lacks foundation, because to move for an appeal whatsoever, it is required that the resolution he is trying to amend, annul or cancel should cause injury or damage to the person who lodges the appeal and such a circumstance must come from a body which prevented, a decision being given, as the one who lodged the appeal aimed at.

15. Consistent with foregoing, this same High Tribunal has drawn up jurisprudence with the purpose of habitually rejecting appeals of cassation filed by the injured party in lawsuits in which the same facts are investigated as are the object of this case. As example may be mentioned decisions of this kind, in the matter of the appeals in cassation no. 31.200 about the disappearance of Alfonso Chanfreau Oyarce, no. 33035 about the disappearance of Nicodemus Toro Bravo, no. 2.539 over the disappearance of Mauricio Jorquera Encina, no. 263 over the disappearance of José Herrera Cofré, no. 33.696 about the death of Eulogio Fritz Monsalve, no. 2.538 about the illegal detention of Rodrigo Gonzáles Pérez and no. 972 about the illegal detention of Monica Llanca Iturra.

Let it be registered and passed on. Rol no. 469-98

Pronounced by the ministers señores Guillermo Navas B., Enrique Curry U y José Pérez Z., The Advocates señores Arturo Montes R. and Fernando Castro A. and the Auditor General of the Army, Fernando Torres S. The Advocate señor Montces, although he partook in the viewing of the appeal and agreed with the findings, did not sign because of absence.

Santiago, 19 September 1998.

Complying with the provisions in art. 785 of the CCP, with reference to art. 785 of the CPP the following replacement sentence is pronounced:

Whereas:

Only the first paragraph of the first motivation of the sentence in appeal is reproduced until the words: 'his whereabouts have not been found'. The remaining motives and legal citations are eliminated. In its place comes:

That on 19 July 1974 Pedro Enrique Poblete Córdova has been deprived of his personal freedom, whilst the circumstances in which these acts took place are unknown and neither is the identity of the responsible persons. These happenings must be elucidated by the Military Judge in an accurate and diligent manner, with all means to this end at his disposal. He has to investigate exhaustively indeed and no procedural measure can be taken until he has reached
this goal.

In accordance with the above, and with what is reported by the Prosecutor in his decision (doc. 981) and what is argued in the motivations four and eleven of the cassation judgement:

Is Revoked:

The sentence of 22 April 1997, (doc. 911) and in its place is decided that resolution (doc. 900) Will Not Be Effective. The case is brought back to its summary stage and the judge of the Second Military Court will have to execute the formalities as decreed in doc. 811, 837, 842, 857, 867, 872 and 878 and the ones requested by the injured party in doc. 897, and whatsoever may be necessary to investigate the case exhaustively and dictate, when the moment has come, a just resolution. Agreed by vote against the Auditor General of the Army, Señor Torres, who still had to confirm the judgement for the reasons he gives for his minority vote over the cassation sentence.

Let it be registered and passed on.

Issued by the Ministers señores Guillermo Navas B., Enrique Cury U., y José Luis Pérez Z., de Advocates señores Arturo Montes R. and Fernando Castro A. and the Auditor General of the Army señor Fernando Torres. The Advocate señor Montes did not sign, although he partook in the viewing of the appeal and agreed with the findings, because of absence.

Undersigned: Marcela Paz Urruta Cornejo – Alternate Secretary
Conform: Santiago, 15 September 1998

☞ France: Decision of Constitutional Council of 24 December 1998 on ratification of the ICC Statute

Summary of the decision. General summary No. 98-408 DC of 22 January 1999
(Treaty on the Statute of the International Criminal Court)
The question, submitted to the Constitutional Council on 24 December 1998, by the President of the Republic and the Prime Minister, in accordance with Article 54 of the Constitution, on whether, taking into account the obligations undertaken by France, the authorisation to ratify the treaty on the statute of the International Criminal Court signed in Rome on 18 July 1998 should be preceded by an amendment of the Constitution;

The Constitutional Council

In view of the Constitution of 4 October 1958;

In view of the preamble of the Constitution of 27 October 1946;

In view of the amended Ruling No. 58-1067 of 7 November 1958 on the Organic Law concerning the Constitutional Council, in particular, its Articles 18 sub 2, 19 and 20;

In view of the Decree of 2 December 1910 on the promulgation of the Convention concerning the Laws of War on Land, signed in The Hague 18 October 1907 and the additional regulations concerning the laws and customs of war on land;

In view of the Decree of 22 August 1928 which promulgates the Protocol concerning the Prohibition of the Use in War of Asphyxiating, Poisonous or Other Gases, and of Bacteriological Methods of Warfare, signed in Geneva, 17 June 1925;

In view of the Decree No. 45-2267 of 6 October 1945 on the promulgation of the agreement between the provisional Government of the French Republic and the Governments of the United States, the United Kingdom of Great Britain and Northern Ireland, and of the Union of Soviet Socialist Republics concerning the prosecution and the punishment of major war criminals of the European powers of the Axis, signed in London, 8 August 1945, together forming the Statute of the International Military Tribunal;

In view of the Decree No. 46-35 of 4 January 1946 on the promulgation of the Charter of the United Nations including the Statute of the International Court of Justice, signed in San Francisco on 26 June 1945;

In view of the Decree No. 50-1449 of 24 November 1950 on the publication of the Convention on the Prevention and Punishment of the Crime of Genocide approved by the General Assembly of the United Nations on 9 December 1948;

In view of the Decree No. 52-253 of 28 February 1952 on the publication of the Convention regarding the Treatment of Prisoners of War, of the Convention relating to the Protection of Civilians in Time of War, of the Convention for the Amelioration of the Condition of the Wounded and Sick and the Shipwrecked Members of Armed Forces at Sea, of the Convention for the Amelioration of the Condition of the Wounded and Sick in Armed Forces in the Field, signed in Geneva on 12 August 1949;

In view of the Act No. 64-1326 of 26 December 1964 aiming at establishing the imprescriptibility of crimes against humanity;

In view of the Act No. 83-1130 of 23 December 1983 authorising the accession of the French Republic to the Additional Protocol to the Conventions of Geneva on 12 August 1949 relating to the Protection of the Victims of non- International Armed

Conflicts (Protocol II), passed in Geneva, 8 June 1977, together: Decree No. 84-727 of 17 July 1984 on the publication of the Protocol;

In view of Act No. 87-1134 of 31 December 1987 which authorises the ratification of a convention on the banning or limitation of the use of certain conventional arms that can be considered as producing excessive traumatic effects or as striking without discrimination (together Protocols I and II), concluded in Geneva on 10 October 1980, together: Decree No. 88-1020 of 2 November 1988 on the publication of this Convention;

In view of the Act No. 90-548 of 2 July 1990 authorising the ratification of the Convention on the Rights of the Child, signed in New York 26 January 1990, together: Decree No. 90-917 of 8 October 1990 on the publication of this Convention;

In view of the Act No. 95-1 of 2 January 1995 on the adaptation of the French legislation to the provisions of Resolution 827 of the Security Council of the United Nations instituting an international tribunal in order to judge the persons presumed responsible of serious violations of international humanitarian law committed on the territory of the former Yugoslavia since 1991;

In view of the Act No. 96-432 of 22 May 1996 on the adaptation of the French legislation to the provisions of Resolution 955 of the Security Council of the United Nations instituting an international tribunal in order to judge the persons presumed responsible for acts of genocide or other serious violations of international humanitarian law committed in 1994 on Rwandan territory and, while concerning Rwandan citizens, on the territory of neighbouring states;

Having heard the rapporteur;

On the Contents of the International Obligation as Submitted to the Constitutional Council:

Considering that the treaty signed in Rome 18 July 1998 holds the creation of the International Criminal Court and lays down its Statute;

that the treaty specifies that this Court, of permanent nature and endowed with international legal personality, can exercise its competence regarding the most serious crimes, committed by persons that affect the whole of the international community and who, following the terms of the preamble of the Treaty, are likely to threaten 'peace, security and the well-being of the world';

that the treaty points out that the Court, which can exercise its responsibilities and powers on the territory of member states, 'is complementary to the national criminal jurisdictions';

that it stipulates that the Court 'is tied to the United Nations by an agreement that needs to be approved by the assembly of states taking part in the present statute, then concluded by the President of the Court in its name';

that it rests with the Assembly of the member states to adopt, with a majority of two-thirds of its members, the regulation on procedure and proof concerning the court;

Considering that the Court, which will have its seat in The Hague, in the Netherlands, 'Host State', is made up of, in particular, a preliminary section, a section of first instance and a section of appeal;

that the judges, numbering at least eighteen, are elected by the Assembly of member states, for a term of office of nine years;

that the section of appeals is made up of a president and four judges, the section of first instance and the preliminary section though are made up of at least six judges;

that the judiciary duties are carried out in every section by chambers;

that the judges carry out their duties in all independence and are not reeligible;

that they adopt, with an absolute majority, the regulation necessary for the daily functioning of the Court;

Considering that the other organs of the Court are the office of the prosecutor and the office of the Registrar of the Court;

that the office of the prosecutor, made up of a prosecutor, who is in charge, and of assistant prosecutors, 'acts independently as a separate organ at the heart of the Court';

that the prosecutors are elected by the Assembly of member states and are in office for nine years;

that they are not reeligible;

that finally, the office of the clerk, managed by a Registrar, is responsible for the non-judiciary aspects of the administration and the service of the Court;

Considering that the member state or the Security Council acting by virtue of chapter VII of the United Nations can refer to the prosecutor a situation in which crimes coming under the competence of the Court seem to have been committed;

that in addition, the prosecutor can set up an inquiry regarding information concerning the same crimes if the Preliminary Chamber, after examination of the supporting facts that he has collected, grants him permission;

Considering that the Preliminary Chamber, after the opening of an inquiry, is the only one competent to take, on request of the prosecutor, restrictive or custodial measures such as the issue of an arrest warrant or the summons to appear;

that the above-mentioned Chamber has the general power of monitoring the inquiries and prosecutions carried out by the prosecutor;

that this power is exercised in particular in matters of proof, concerning the collecting, the examining or the verifying of certain elements of proof for the trial on the request of the prosecutor or on the request of the prosecuted person;

that, within a reasonable period of time after the handing over of the person to the Court, the Preliminary Chamber should if possible confirm the charges on which the prosecutor intends to base himself on in order to request for referral to Court;

that the Court will hold to this end a hearing, in the presence of the prosecutor and of the person concerned, during which the Court will make sure that 'there exists sufficient proof that gives serious reasons to believe that the person has committed each of the crimes that are attributed to him';

that if such proof is not available, the Court can either not confirm the above-mentioned charges or require from the prosecutor an alteration of the charges or additional investigation;

Considering that the trial will not begin in the Chamber of First Instance until after the confirmation of the charges;

that in case of a guilty verdict, the Chamber of First Instance decides on the punishment to be administered;

that appeal against the decision as pronounced can be made in the Appeals Chamber which has the same powers as the Chamber of First Instance;

that the Appeals Chamber can revoke or alter the decision or the conviction or order a new trial before a different Chamber of First Instance;

Considering that the prison sentences pronounced by the Court are executed in a state designated by the Court on the list of states that have made known that they are willing to receive the convicted prisoners;

that, if no state has been designated, the punishment is executed 'in a penitentiary institution provided by the hosting state';

that the Court supervises the execution of the prison sentences;

On the Applicable Norms of Reference:

Considering that the French people have, by the preamble of the Constitution of 1958, solemnly proclaimed 'their commitment to human rights and to the principles of national sovereignty such as have been defined by the Declaration of 1789, confirmed and completed by the preamble of the Constitution of 1946';

that it emerges, furthermore, from the preamble of the Constitution of 1946 that the protection of the dignity of the human being against any form of slavery and degradation is a principle of constitutional value;

Considering that, in its Article 3, the Declaration of the human and civil rights states that 'the principle of all sovereignty rests essentially with the nation';

that Article 3 of the Constitution of 1958 stipulates, in its first paragraph, that 'the national sovereignty belongs to the people who exercise it through their representatives and by way of referendum';

Considering that the preamble of the Constitution of 1946 proclaims, in its fourteenth paragraph, that the French Republic 'complies with rules of international public law' and, in its fifteenth paragraph, that 'under condition of reciprocity, France agrees to the limitations on sovereignty necessary to the organisation and to the protection of peace';

Considering that, in its Article 53, the Constitution of 1958 sanctions, just as Article 27 of the Constitution of 1946 did, the existence of 'treaties or agreements relating to the international organisation';

that in virtue of Article 55 of the Constitution of 1958: 'The treaties or agreements properly ratified or passed have, from the moment of publication, an authority superior to the authority of laws, on condition of, for each agreement or treaty, its application by the other party';

Considering that the result from these texts of constitutional value is that the respect for the national sovereignty does not represent an obstacle, on the foundation of the aforementioned regulations of the preamble of the Constitution of 1946, for France to conclude international obligations in order to promote peace and security of the world and to ensure respect for the general principles of international public law;

that the obligations subscribed to this purpose can in particular provide for the creation of a permanent international jurisdiction aimed at protecting the fundamental rights belonging to every human being, while sanctioning the most serious infringements that will be brought to court, and competent to judge the persons responsible for crimes of such seriousness that they affect the international community as a whole;

that regarding this purpose, the obligations arising from such commitments imposes itself on each of the member states independent of the conditions of their execution by other member states;

that in such a way, the condition of reciprocity mentioned in Article 55 of the Constitution will not apply;

Considering, however, that in case these commitments include a clause conflicting with the Constitution, they implicate the rights and liberties constitutionally guaranteed or undermine the essential conditions for the exercise of national sovereignty, the authorisation to ratify them calls for a constitutional amendment;

Considering that it is, with regard to these principles, for the Constitutional Council to carry out the examination of the treaty on the International Criminal Court signed in Rome, July 18th 1998;

On the Respect of the Regulations of the Constitution Relating to the Criminal Responsibility of the Holders of Certain Official Capacities:

Considering that under the provisions of paragraph 1 of Article 27 of the Statute: 'This Statute shall apply equally to all persons without any distinction based on official capacity. In particular, official capacity as a Head of State or Government, a member of a Government or parliament, an elected representative or a government official shall in no case exempt a person from criminal responsibility under this Statute, nor shall it, in and of itself, constitute a ground for reduction of sentence.' And that to paragraph 2 of Article 27 has been added that 'Immunities or special procedural rules, which may attach to the official capacity of a person, whether under national or international law, shall not bar the Court from exercising its jurisdiction over such a person;'

Considering that it follows from Article 68 of the Constitution 'that the President of the Republic enjoys immunity for acts fulfilled during the exercising of his position and apart from high treason';

that moreover, during his stay in office, his criminal responsibility can only be implicated before the High Court of Justice, according to the conditions set by the same article;

that pursuant to Article 68-1 of the Constitution, the members of Government can be judged for crimes and offences committed while exercising their positions only by the Court of justice of the Republic;

that finally, the members of Parliament, by virtue of the first paragraph of Article 26 of the Constitution, enjoy an immunity based on the opinions or votes expressed during the exercise of their position, and, by application of the second paragraph of the same article, can be the object, in criminal or correctional matters, apart from the case of *in flagrante delicto* or of definitive conviction, of an arrest or of any other measure deprivatory or restrictive to liberty only with the authorisation of the office of the assembly to which they belong;

Considering that it follows from that that Article 27 of the Statute is contrary to the special regulations on responsibility as instituted by the Articles 26, 28 and 68-1 of the Constitution;

On the Respect for the Constitutional Principles Applicable to Criminal Law and to Criminal Procedure

Considering that in accordance with the provisions of Article 5, the International Criminal Court is competent regarding crimes of genocide, crimes against humanity, war crimes and the crime of aggression;

that the Court will, however, only be able to exercise its competence regarding the crime of aggression when it has been defined by a new treaty on the amendment of the Statute, in accordance with the Articles 121 and 123;

Considering that Article 6 lists the acts that, 'committed with the intention to destroy, in whole or in part, a national, ethnic, racial or religious group', can be considered under the criminal qualification of the 'crime of genocide';

that Article 7 though, specifies the acts that, 'committed as part of a widespread or systematic attack directed against any civilian population, with knowledge of the attack', can be criminally qualified as 'crimes against humanity';

that finally, Article 8 indicates that the Court has competence with regard to 'war crimes' and draws up the list;

that on this list appear in particular the crimes that 'fit into a plan or policy or when they are part of a series of similar crimes committed on a large scale';

Considering that under the provisions of Article 29 of the Statute: 'The crimes that come within the competence of the Court are imprescriptible';

that no rule, nor principle of constitutional value, forbids the imprescriptibility of the most serious crimes that affect the international community as a whole;

Considering that Article 66 maintains the presumption of innocence of which every person benefits until his guilt has been established before court;

that it rests with the prosecutor to prove the accused guilty;

that in accordance with Article 67, the accused benefits from the guarantee of 'not finding oneself imposed with the reversal of the burden of proof nor with responsibility of refutation';

that consequently the requirements that are a result of Article 9 of the Declaration of human rights and civil rights are respected;

Considering that it results from Article 22 of the Statute that a person is only criminally responsible if his behaviour constitutes, the moment the behaviour occurs, a crime that falls within the competence of the Court;

that the definition of crime is of strict interpretation and can not be stretched by analogous interpretation;

that Article 25 defines the cases of individual criminal responsibility susceptible to conviction;

that in accordance with Article 30, no one is criminally responsible when there is no intention and knowledge joining the material element of the crime;

that, in addition, Articles 31 and 33 list the grounds for exemption of criminal responsibility that can be accepted;

that in this way, the statute determines exactly the field of application of the incriminations as exemptions of criminal responsibility and defines the crimes, in their materiel element as well as in their moral element in clear and precise enough terms to allow for the determination of the actors of the infractions and to avoid arbitrariness;

that motivation by its nature also avoids arbitrariness, required by Article 74 of the Statute, of the decision as passed by the Chamber of First Instance, as well as the motivation of the ruling of the Chamber of Appeal as provided for by Article 83;

that these stipulations respect the principle of legality of offences and punishments that follow from the Articles 7 and 8 of the Declaration of human and civil rights;

Considering that the result of paragraph 1 of Article 11 is that the Court is only competent with regard to crimes committed after the coming into force of the Statute;

that Article 24 lays down the principle of 'non-retroactivity *ratione personae*' and the principle of direct application of the most favourable law;

that in this way the principle of non-retroactivity of the harshest criminal law, which results from Article 8 of the Declaration of the Rights of Man and of the Citizen, has been fulfilled;

Considering that pursuant to the regulations of Article 89 of the Statute, the Court can ask the State on whose territory the person is likely to be found, whichever his nationality, for the arrest and handing over, and seek for this purpose the co-operation of that State;

that when the Court presents such a request, it is exercising its competence such as specified by Articles 5 to 13 of the statute, concerning the situations that have been referred to the prosecutor or for which situations the prosecutor has opened an inquiry on his own initiative;

that the request for arrest and the handing over aims at either a person who has already been considered guilty by the Court, or at a person who is the object of an arrest warrant issued by the Preliminary Chamber and of whom, under the provisions of Article 58, there are 'good reasons to believe' that the person 'has committed a crime that comes under the competence of the Court' while his arrest is justified by one of the grounds set out in Article 58(1)(b);

that in view of the purpose of the handing over and of the guarantees of the procedure implemented by the Court, no principle or rule of constitutional value has been infringed;

Considering that by applying the dispositions of Article 59, one has proceeded, in accordance with the legislation of the state that receives the request, to the provisional arrest or to the arrest and handing over;

that the arrested person is referred without further delay to the judicial authorities of the state which check, in accordance with its legislation, in particular, on the legality of the arrest and of the respect of the rights of the person concerned;

that the competent judiciary authorities can decide on the release of the person;

that the respect of the rights of defense from the very first procedure before the Court and during the trial itself is assured;

that particularly, according to Article 55, the person interrogated by the prosecutor, or by the national judiciary authorities can be assisted at any moment by the counsel for the defense of his own choice or appointed;

that only the Preliminary Chamber of the Court can issue the necessary mandates in particular the arrest warrants;

that the person handed over to the Court can ask for his provisional release while waiting to be judged;

that the result of the provisions of Article 60 are that the Preliminary Chamber of the Court re-examines periodically its decision to release or to keep in detention;

that the Court ensures that the detention before the trial will not be extended in an excessive way due to an unjustifiable delay which would be attributable to the prosecutor;

that the Division of First Instance, pursuant to Article 64, 'sees to it that the trial is led in an fair and swift way, while fully respecting the rights of the accused';

that the trial is public, with the restriction of the right of the Chamber of First Instance to decide for a closed hearing due to special circumstances;

that the sentence is delivered in public;

that the constitutional requirements relating to the rights of the defense and to the existence of a fair and just trial, that ensures the balance of the rights of the parties, are fulfilled;

Considering that Article 23 states that a person who has been convicted by the Court can only be punished in accordance with the provisions of the Statute;

that the punishments that can be pronounced against a person declared guilty of a crime are set by Article 77;

that in the case of a guilty verdict, the punishment is decided on while taking into account, in accordance with the regulations of Articles 76 and 78, the conclusions and relevant elements of proof as presented at the trial, the gravity of the crime and the personal situation of the condemned;

that these rules do not incur any criticism of unconstitutionality and are in particular in accordance with the principles of the need and of the legality of punishments;

Considering that the judges that make up the Court exercise their duty in total independence, the Articles 40 and 48 of the Statute provides for that purpose for the necessary incompatibilities and immunities;

that, in addition, the judges that are assigned to the section of appeals cannot sit in other section;

that Articles 41 and 42 of the Statute set the procedure according to which discharging and the challenging of a juror as well as of the prosecutor can take place;

that finally, Article 46 provides for a procedure according to which a member of the Court can be relieved from his duties in the case of grave mistakes or grave breaches of duty;

that in this way the requirements of impartiality and independence of the Court have been met;

Considering that, following the provisions of Articles 81 to 83 of the Statute, one may appeal against certain decisions of the Preliminary Chamber and of decisions pronounced by the Court in the formation of Chamber of First Instance;

that a procedure of review of a decision on the guilt or the punishment is also instituted by Article 84;

that Article 85 institutes in addition a procedure of indemnification of persons that are victim of an illegal arrest or detention, as well as persons that have been subjected to punishment due to a conviction that has later been revoked;

that in the case of a grave and obvious judicial error, an indemnification can also be given;

that Article 68 of the Statute requires the Court to take all measures likely to ensure the security and the respect of the private lives of the victims and the witnesses, in particular by infringing upon the principle of open debate concerning the hearing of vulnerable persons;

that Article 75 specifies that the Court establishes 'principles applicable to forms of compensation to be given to the victims';

that, on this basis, the Court will be able to determine, in its decisions, the extent of the damage and harm suffered by the victims, and to pronounce against a convicted person, a ruling giving the compensation that should be granted;

that the indemnity granted will be paid by a fund created for the benefit of the victims by the Assembly of member states;

that the whole of these rules is in accordance with the Constitution;

On the Respect of the Essential Conditions of the Exercise of National Sovereignty

On the complementarity between the international criminal court and the national jurisdictions:

Considering that the regulations of the tenth paragraph of the preamble and of the first Article of the Statute stipulate that the Court 'is complementary to the national criminal jurisdictions';

that this complementarity implies, as results from the regulations of Articles 17 and 20 of the Statute, that a case is judged inadmissible by the Court either when it 'has been investigated by a State which has jurisdiction over it' or when after the inquiry 'the State has decided not to prosecute the person concerned', or, finally, when the person has already been tried for conduct which is the subject of the complaint';

that, in addition, it follows from Article 18 that the prosecutor notifies the state concerned that an inquiry will be opened or is opened and that, for its part, the state can inform the Court that it opens or has opened an inquiry for the acts in accordance with the information that has been notified to him;

that on its request, the state sees itself entrusted with the care for the inquiry, unless the Preliminary Chamber authorises the prosecutor to conduct it;

Considering meanwhile that, notwithstanding the principle of complementarity, paragraph 1 of Article 17 allows the Court to have jurisdiction over a case in case of lack of willingness of the state to pursue prosecutions to the end or when the lack of willingness of the state leads it to decide not to prosecute;

that paragraph 2 of Article 17 specifies the criteria that are laid down for the Court to determine if there is a lack of willingness of a state; that such a lack of willingness can only be upheld if the procedure has been started 'for the purpose of shielding the person concerned from criminal responsibility', or if 'there has been an unjustified delay in the proceedings which in the circumstances is inconsistent with an intent to bring the person concerned to justice', or finally when 'the proceedings were not or are not being conducted independently or impartially, and they were or are being conducted in a manner which, in the circumstances, is inconsistent with an intent to bring the person concerned to justice';

that, furthermore, under the provisions of Article 20 of the Statute, in a case where the person concerned has already been judged by another jurisdiction for behaviour aimed at by Article 5, the Court will also be able to judge this person if the procedure before the national jurisdiction 'had as its purpose the shielding of the person concerned from his criminal responsibility' or 'has not been ... led in an independent and impartial way ... but in a way that, under the circumstances, contradicted with the intention to bring the person concerned to justice';

Considering, in addition, that the Court will judge a case admissible when the competent state is not capable of pursuing an inquiry to the end or when the decision not to prosecute is the result of this same incapability;

that, according to paragraph 3 of Article 17, this incapability corresponds to the hypothetical case that 'the State is unable to obtain the accused or the necessary evidence and testimony or otherwise unable to carry out its proceedings';

Considering, on the one hand, that the stipulations of the Treaty that bring restrictions to the principle of complementarity of the Court with regard to the national criminal jurisdictions, in the case where the member state deliberately backs out of its obligations arising from the Convention, result from the rule '*pacta sunt servanda*', in accordance with which any treaty in force ties the parties and has to be executed by them in good faith;

that these regulations establish restrictively and objectively the hypothetical cases in which the International Criminal Court will be able to declare itself competent;

that, consequently, they do not disregard the essential conditions for the exercise of national sovereignty;

Considering, on the other hand, that the stipulations that equally allow the Court to consider itself competent in the hypothetical case of collapse or of the unavailability of the judicial apparatus are not in disregard of the essential conditions for the exercise of the national sovereignty;

Considering, on the other hand, that it follows from the Statute that the International Criminal Court could legitimately be referred to due to the sole fact of application of an amnesty law or of internal rules in matters of prescription;

that in a similar case, France, apart from lack of willingness or of unavailability of the state, could be made to arrest and to bring to Court a person because of facts covered, under French law, by amnesty or prescription;

that, under these circumstances, the essential conditions of the exercise of the national sovereignty would be undermined;

Concerning International Co-operation, Judicial Assistance and the Powers of the Prosecutor:

Considering that Article 54 of the Statute specifies the duties and the powers of the prosecutor in matters of inquiry;

he has to, in order to lead these, ask the co-operation of the states;

he can also hold an inquiry on the territory of a state;

that in such a hypothetical case, he has to comply either with the stipulations of chapter IX relating to international co-operation and the judicial assistance, or with the stipulations of sub-paragraph 4 of paragraph 3 of Article 57;

Considering that the result of the aforementioned chapter IX is that the Court is authorised to put requests for co-operation and assistance to the member states;

that the states grant these requests in accordance with the procedures provided by their national legislation, in particular concerning the identification and the interrogation of persons, the gathering of pieces of evidence, the executions of searches and of seizures;

that as emerges from Article 93, if the execution of a particular measure of assistance is prohibited in the requested state by virtue of a fundamental juridical principle of general application in that state, the latter is not held to lend the requested assistance in the way sought by the Court, but has to begin consultations with the Court;

that in accordance with the same Article; a state can reject totally or partially a request for assistance of the Court if the object is the disclosure of pieces of evidence or the submission of documents that affect national security, of which the protection is ensured by Article 72;

that the Articles 94 and 95 of the statute provide for procedures of respite of execution of the requests for assistance as expressed to the states;

that the whole of these stipulations guarantee a respect of the essential conditions for the exercise of national sovereignty;

Considering that paragraph d of Article 57 only allows the prosecutor, authorised by the Preliminary Chamber, to take certain measures of inquiry on the territory of a state, without ensuring the co-operation of the state, in the case where no authority or competent element of the national judicial apparatus is available to act on the request for co-operation;

that, therefore, these stipulations are not able to undermine the essential conditions of the exercise of national sovereignty;

Considering, on the other hand, that in accordance with paragraph 4 of Article 99 of the Statute, the prosecutor can, apart from even the case where the national judicial apparatus is unavailable, carry out certain acts of inquiry out of the presence of the authorities of the required state and on the territory of the latter;

he may, in particular, collect statements of witnesses and inspect 'a public site or other public place';

that in the absence of special circumstances, and even if these measures rule out any force, the power assigned to the prosecutor to carry out these acts out of the presence of the competent French judicial authorities is by nature likely to undermine the essential conditions for the exercise of the national sovereignty;

Concerning the Execution of Punishments Pronounced by the International Criminal Court:

Considering that in accordance with the provisions of Article 103 of the Statute, the State that declares itself prepared to receive persons convicted by the International Criminal Court can add conditions to their acceptance, which have to be approved by the Court;

that these conditions can be 'of a nature as to change considerably the conditions or the period of the detention';

Considering that it follows from these stipulations that France, in declaring itself prepared to receive the convicted, will be able to subordinate its agreement to conditions, in particular, on the application of the national legislation relating to the execution of custodial sentence;

France could in addition refer to the possibility of granting the convicted persons an exemption from execution from punishments, total or partial, which follow from the exercise of the right of pardon;

that, therefore, the stipulations of Part X of the Statute, relating to the execution of punishments, do not undermine the essential conditions to the exercise of the national sovereignty, nor does it undermine Article 17 of the Constitution;

Considering that none of the other stipulations of the treaty submitted to the Constitutional Council in accordance with Article 54 of the Constitution is conflicting with it;

Considering that, for grounds set out above, the authorisation to ratify the treaty on the Statute of the International Criminal Court requires an amendment of the Constitution;

Decides:

First Article. – The authorisation to ratify the treaty on the Statute of the International Criminal Court requires an amendment of the Constitution.

Second Article. – The present decision will be notified to the President of the Republic, as well as to the Prime Minister, and will be published in the *Journal Officiel* of the French Republic.

As deliberated by the Constitutional Council during its session of 22 January 1999, where were seated: M.M. Roland Dumas, President, George Abadie, Michel Ameller, Jean-Claude Colliard, Yves Guena, Mme Noëlle Lenoir, M. Pierre Mazeaud et Mme Simone Veil.

☛ Spain: Decision of National Criminal Court on whether Spain has jurisdiction over General Augusto Pinochet Ugarte

Administration of Justice.
National Court Criminal Division: Plenary Session (All Judges Sitting)

Appeal Record 173/98 Division One. Summary Proceedings 1/98
Central Trial Court Number Six

Decision
Criminal Division. Plenary Session

Presiding Judge:
Executive President Siro Francisco García Pèrez
Judges:
Don Francisco Castro Meije; Don Carlos Cezóu González; Don Jorge Campos Martínez; Dona Angela Murillo Bordallo; Don Juan José López Ortega; Don Carlos Ollero Butler; Don Manuela Fernández Prado; Don José Ricardo de Prada Solaesa; Antonio Díaz Delgado; Luis Martínez de Salinas Alonso

Madrid, 5 November 1998

Matters of Fact

One. Central Trial Court number Six issued the following decision on 15 September 1998 proceedings number 1/98:
I Order As Follows
    One. This Court is competent to continue conducting the proceedings.
    Two. An International Commission Rogatory is to be issued, addressed to the judicial authorities of Santiago, Chile, requesting them to confirm as soon as possible whether there are any proceedings pending against Augusto Pinochet Ugarte, and if so, how many proceedings and which are the crimes of which he is accused'.

Two. The Justice Department [Ministerio Fiscal] lodged an interlocutory appeal against this decision, which was dismissed by a further decision issued by the Court on 1 October 1998, against which the Justice Department lodged a further appeal, and the latter was admitted to sole effect.

Three. The pertinent evidence and record were transferred to Division One of this Court, and after the first stage of the proceedings had been conducted, under article 197 of the Organic Law of the Judiciary, the Court issued an order dated 22nd October of this year, ordering that all the Judges of the Court were to hear the case for consideration and issuing a decision, and also that there would be a public hearing, and it established the date and time when it was to be held.

Four. The hearing took place on 29 October, with the Justice Department represented by Ignacio Pelez as appellant, and solicitor Juan E. Garcés Ramón, as counsel for Josefina Llidó Mengual, María Alsina and the Association of Relatives of Disappeared Prisoners, as the appellees.

The appeal was considered and a vote taken on the morning of the following day, 30 October of this year.

At about 2 p.m., a unanimous vote was taken on the decision and informed accordingly to the parties, and the result of the vote was made public.

Five. The justice in charge of submitting a proposed decision to the other members was Judge Carlos Cezôn González.

Arguments of Law

One. Grounds for the appeal.
The grounds for the appeal lodged by the Justice Department against the decision issued by Central Trial Court Number Six, which has confirmed that Spain is competent to continue conducting the summary proceedings, are as follows:

One. It is denied that the events which are the object of the summary proceedings constitute the crime of genocide.

Two. Article 6 of the Convention for the Prevention and punishment of the Crime of Genocide establishes competence to judge the crime of genocide by the courts of the country where the crime was committed.

Three. The legal definition of the events as terrorism is also challenged.

Four. It is claimed that there has been erroneous interpretation of article 5 of the Convention on Torture dated 10 December 1984.

Five. Existence of a lawsuit pending judicial decision and *res judicata.*

Two. True scope of the provision contained in Article 6 of the Convention for the Prevention and Punishment of the Crime of Genocide.

The second grounds for the appeal lodged by the Justice Department will be analysed first by transcribing what the judges sitting in plenary session stated in their decision issued yesterday in the appeal appearing in Record 84/98 of Division Three (lodged against the decision issued by Trial Court number Five, declaring that Spain is competent to judge the events which are the object of summary proceedings 19/97 being conducted at that court on genocide and terrorism, relating to events which took place in Argentina between 1976 and 1983).

The Convention for the Prevention and Punishment of the Crime of Genocide is dated 9 December 1948. Spain adhered to it on 13 September 1968 with reservations regarding the entirety of Article (9) on the jurisdiction of the International Court of Justice in matters involving disputes between the contracting parties relating to the interpretation, application or execution of the Convention, including those relating to the responsibility of a State in matters of genocide or any of the other acts listed in Article (3). The

Convention became valid for Spain on 12 December 1968. The Convention recalls that the General Assembly of the United Nations stated in its Resolution 96(1) dated 11 December 1946 that genocide is a crime under international law which is contrary to the spirit and the aims of the United Nations and is condemned by the civilised world (Preamble) and it establishes that the contracting parties undertake to prevent and punish genocide committed either in times of peace or of war (Art. 1), whether the responsible parties be rulers, officials or private persons (Art. 4), that the contracting parties undertake to enact the legislation necessary to ensure the application of the provisions of the Convention and particularly to establish effective criminal penalties to punish persons guilty of genocide or any of the other acts listed in Article 3 (Art. 5) and that any contracting party may resort to the competent agencies of the United Nations so that the latter may take, in accordance with United Nations Charter, the measures they deem appropriate to prevent and punish acts of genocide or any of the other listed in Article 3 (Article 8).

Article 6 establishes that: 'Persons charged with genocide or any of the acts enumerated in article III shall be tried by a competent tribunal of the State in the territory of which the act was committed, or by such international penal tribunal as may have jurisdiction with respect to those Contracting Parties which have accepted its jurisdiction.'

For the appellants (only the Justice Department in this appeal), the above provision (which forms part of our internal legislation, in accordance with Article 96 of the Spanish Constitution and Art. 1(5) of the Civil Code) would exclude, for the crime of genocide, the jurisdiction of Spain if the crime was not committed on national territory.

The judges sitting in Plenary Session did not concur with this opinion. Article 6 of the Convention does not preclude the existence of judicial agencies with jurisdictions other than those in the territory where the crime was committed or that of an international tribunal. Article 6 of the Convention establishes an international criminal tribunal and imposes on the States, which are parties to it, the duty to ensure that genocide be judged compulsorily by the judicial agencies of the State in which the crimes were committed. However, it would be contrary to the spirit of the Convention, which seeks to compromise between the contracting parties by resorting to their respective laws governing crime, with prosecution for genocide as a crime under international law, thus avoiding the commission with impunity of such a serious crime, to consider that this article or the Convention limit the exercise of jurisdiction, excluding any jurisdiction other than the one envisaged by the legal provision. The fact that the contracting parties have not agreed on universal prosecution for the crime by each of their national jurisdictions does not preclude the establishment, by a State which is a party to the Convention, of that type of jurisdiction for a crime which involves the whole world and affects the international community and, indeed, all of humanity directly, as stated in the Convention itself. Under no circumstances are we to understand that the above Article 6 prevents signatory States from exercising the right to prosecute established in their internal legislation. It would be unthinkable that, as a result for applying the Convention for the Prevention and Punishment of the Crime of Genocide, Spain, for example, could not punish a Spanish national responsible for genocide who had committed the crime outside Spain and was currently in our country, provided the requirement specified in Article 23(2) of the Organic Law of the Judiciary was met. Neither do the terms of Article 6 of the Convention of 1948 constitute an authorisation to exclude jurisdiction for the punishment of genocide of a State which is a party, such as Spain, whose law establishes extraterritoriality with regard to prosecution for such crime in paragraph four of Article 23 of the Organic Law of the Judiciary, and this is not incompatible with the Convention in any way.

It must be admitted, as a result of the priority of international treaties over internal legislation (Art. 96 of the Spanish Constitution and 27 of the Vienna Convention on Treaty Law of 1969), that Article 6 of the Convention for the Prevention and Punishment of the Crime of Genocide imposes accessory action by jurisdictions other than those envisaged in the legal provision, and thus the jurisdiction of a State should abstain from exercising jurisdiction regarding events constituting genocide which are the object of prosecution by the courts of the country in which they took place or by an international criminal court.

Three. Applicability at this time of Article 23(4) of the Organic Law of the Judiciary, as the current law on procedure.

Article 23(4) of the Organic Law of the Judiciary states that Spain is competent to hear cases involving certain acts by Spaniards or foreigners outside national territory which can be defined, according to Spanish criminal law, as one of the crimes listed in it. It is not applied retroactively when the proclaimed jurisdiction is exercised while the provision is valid, as it is in this case, irrespective of when the events being dealt with took place. The said Article 23(4) of the Organic Law of the Judiciary is not a provision for punishment, but rather a procedural one. It does not define or punish any action or omission and merely proclaims Spanish jurisdiction for prosecuting crimes which are defined and punished by other laws. The procedural provision in question does not establish sanctions and does not restrict individual rights, and consequently its application for the purpose of criminal prosecution for acts which took place before it became valid is not contrary to Article 9(3) of the Spanish Constitution. The legal consequence, which restricts rights, arising from the commission of a crime of genocide -the punishment – is the result of the legal provision punishing genocide and not of the procedural law which assigns jurisdiction to Spain to punish the crime. The principle of legality (Art. 25 of the Spanish Constitution) establishes that acts must constitute a crime – in accordance with Spanish law, according to Article 23(4) above mentioned – at the time they take place and that the sentence which may be handed down be determined by a law in force before the crime took place, but it does not require that the jurisdiction and procedural provision be prior to the triable action. Jurisdiction is a promise of the prosecution, not of the crime.

Consequently, it is not necessary to resort, in order to establish Spain's competence to prosecute for a crime of genocide committed abroad by nationals or foreigners during the years 1976 to 1983 up to the time the Organic Law on the Judiciary came into force, to the provisions of Article 336 of the Provisional Law on the Organisation of the Judiciary dated 15 September 1870, revoked by the Organic Law of the Judiciary of 1985, which assigned jurisdiction to the Spanish courts to judge Spanish or foreign nationals who had committed the crime of genocide outside Spanish territory since the date when this crime was included in the Criminal Code current at the time by Law 47/71 dated 15th November, under the heading of crimes against the external security of the State, and the grounds that extraterritorial prosecution for the other crimes against the external security of the State was covered by the principle of protection have no legal relevance.

This paragraph is a transcription of paragraph three of the Arguments of Law relied on by the decision issued by the judges sitting in plenary session yesterday on the above mentioned appeal appearing in Record 84/98 of Division Three, and only one reference has been adjusted in view of the case examined in this decision.

Four. Matters of Fact alleged in the summary proceedings.

In order to issue a decision on the appeal, it will be necessary to determine whether the matters of fact alleged in the summary proceedings can be defined, according to Spanish criminal law, as crimes of genocide or terrorism. This does not require any opinion on the consistency or rationality of the evidence for the allegations. The appeal does not challenge the extent of incrimination on the consistency of the matters of fact, which may be qualified as genocide or terrorism for the attribution of the challenged jurisdiction. The parties to the appeal have not denied that the alleged events consist of deaths, illegal arrests and torture for reasons of ideological cleansing or understanding of national identity and values, attributed to the rulers and members of the Armed Forces or security forces, and also with the participation of organised groups, all of whom acted clandestinely in these events which took place in Chile during the military regime which took power in Chile on 11 September 1973.

Five. Whether the alleged events can be qualified as genocide according to Spanish criminal law.

The first part of this appeal will now be considered, and the above-mentioned decision issued yesterday will be referred to.

Article 23(4) of our Organic Law of the Judiciary establishes that Spain is competent to deal with acts of Spanish or foreign nationals which take place outside Spain and which can be defined, according to Spanish criminal law, as one of the crimes listed in this legal provision, starting with genocide (letter listed in this legal provision, starting with genocide (letter a) and continuing with terrorism (letter b) and including, lastly, only other crime which 'according to international treaties or conventions, is to be judged in Spain' (letter g).

Genocide is a crime consisting of the total or partial extermination of a human race or group, by killing or neutralising its members. This is understood on a social level, without any need for a typical formula. It is a concept, which is felt by the international community, that is, by individuals, states and international organisations. Genocide has been experienced throughout history by many groups, and technology placed at the service of the accurate retrieval of past events enabled humanity to appreciate the specific horrors of the persecution and holocaust suffered by the Jewish people during the Second World War after its conclusion. Consequently, genocide is a reality, which is known, understood and felt by society. In 1946, the General Assembly of the United Nations (Resolution number 96) accepted the recommendation of the VI Commission and accepted that genocide is a crime against the Law of People, and the parties responsible, whether they be private persons, functionaries or official representatives of the State, must be punished for it.

The feature, which characterises genocide, according to the above Resolution 96, is the extermination of a group for racial, religious, political or other reasons, being an act, which affects the conscience of society. Without distinction, it constitutes a crime against humanity to take action leading to the extermination of a human group, whatever the features may be by which the group is distinguished. The Statute of the Court of Nuremberg mentions, along the same lines, 'crimes against humanity, namely murder, extermination, enslavement, deportation and other inhuman acts against any civilian population before or during the war, or persecution for political, racial or religious reasons ...' (Art. 6).

In 1948, the Convention for the Prevention and Punishment of the Crime of Genocide was signed. We have already referred to it in paragraph Two of these Arguments of Law. The Convention states that genocide is a crime under international law, which is contrary to the spirit and the aims of the United Nations and is condemned by the civilised world. The Preambles states that during all periods of history, genocide has resulted in great loss of life, and it states that to free humanity from such an odious scourge, international co-operation is required.

Article 1 of the Convention states as follows: 'The contracting parties confirm that genocide, whether it be committed in times of peace or of war, is a crime under international law, and they undertake to prevent and punish it.'

Article 2 contains the definition of genocide as 'any of the acts mentioned below, committed with the intention of destroying either totally or partially, a national, ethnic, racial or religious group, as such.'

And these acts committed with the aim of exterminating a group are, according to Article 2 of the Genocide Convention to which we have referred, the killing of members of the group, the infliction of serious injury on the physical or mental integrity of those members of the group, the intentional subjection of the group to conditions of existence which will lead to their total or partial physical destruction, measures aimed at preventing births in the group and the abduction by force of children from the group to remove them to another group.

These are horrendous actions, which justify the words 'odious scourge' used in the Preamble to the Convention. The description of behaviours is associated with the social concept – which is understood and felt – of genocide, which we have referred to. The required intention to destroy the group totally or partially is an aspect of the actions affecting a group.

In 1968, Spain adhered to the Convention, and in 1971, by virtue of Law 44/71 dated 15 November it included the crime of genocide in the then current Criminal Code – Article 137 *bis* – as a crime against the rights of people, defined as follow: 'Those who, with the intention of totally or partially destroying a national ethnic, social or religious group, commit any of the following acts ...'. And the Spanish Criminal Code current at the time went on to mention specific acts of genocide (deaths, injuries, subjection to conditions of existence endangering the life of or seriously affecting health of people, the enforced removal of people, and others).

It must be pointed out that the word 'social' (contrary to the definition given in the 1948 Convention) responds to what we have called the social idea or interpretation of genocide, a concept which is understood by society without any need for a typical formula. The idea of genocide remains incomplete if the features of the group enduring the horrors and the exterminating action are limited. Moreover, the lack of a comma between the words 'national' and 'ethnic' cannot give rise to any conclusions about limitations in our internal legislation, up to the time of the Criminal Code of 1995, of the type of genocide with regard to its international concept.

In 1983, when a partial and urgent reform of the Criminal Code took place, the word 'social' was replaced by 'racial' in the said Article 137 *bis*, although a comma between 'national' and 'ethnic' would remain absent, and in 1995, when the penultimate reform of the revoked Code took place, the justification of terrorism would be punished.

The new Criminal Code includes genocide among crimes against the international community in its Article 607 and defines it according to the 1948 Convention as 'the aim totally or partially to destroy a national, ethnic, racial or religious group'.

These are the first paragraphs of Argument of Law number Five of the decision issued by the Plenary Session yesterday, which has been frequently referred to.

With regard to the event which took place in Chile alleged in the summary proceedings to which this appeal relates, the Justice Department maintains that the matters of fact alleged in the summary proceedings cannot constitute genocide, since the persecution which took place in Chile during the military regime from 11 September 1973 onwards was not carried out against any national, ethnic, racial or religious group. The alleged plural and multi-personal action, in the terms in which it is mentioned in the summary proceedings, was against a group of Chilean nationals or persons resident in Chile who could be distinguished by certain features, and who undoubtedly were the object of a distinction made by the parties responsible for their persecution and harassment, and such acts of persecution and harassment consisted of deaths and illegal arrests, and in many cases the fate of the arrested parties is still unknown. They were abducted without notice from their homes and suddenly and for ever expelled from society, thus giving rise to the uncertain concept of the 'disappeared', subjected to torture and imprisonment in clandestine or improvised detention centres, with no observance of the rights assigned to arrested persons by any legislation, and imprisoned or sentenced in penitentiary centres without their relatives being informed as to their whereabouts. The events alleged in the summary proceedings undeniably constitute the intention to exterminate a group of the Chilean population, without excluding similar residents. It was an act of persecution and harassment intended to destroy a certain sector of the population, which was a very varied group, but one, which could be distinguished by certain features. The group which was persecuted and harassed consisted of citizen who did not respond to the type pre-established by the promoters of repression as that appropriate for the new order which was sought to be imposed in the country. The group consisted of citizens who opposed the military regime imposed on 11 September, who did not fit in with the understanding of national values. The repression did not seek to change the attitude of the group, but rather to destroy the group by means of arrests, torture, disappearances, deaths and harassment of the members of a group which was clearly defined, that is, identifiable, by the parties responsible for repression. It was not a random and indiscriminate action. According to the report drawn up by the National Commission for Truth and Reconciliation set up by the democratic government in Chile in 1990, between 11 September 1973 and 10 March 1990, the number of deaths in the country for which State agents were responsible amounted to 1,068, and the number of persons who disappeared to 957.

We can now return to the arguments of law contained in the decision issued yesterday.

These alleged events constitute the crime of genocide. We know why the term 'political' or the words 'or others' do not appear in the 1948 Convention, whose Article 2 lists the features of the groups which are the object of the destruction characteristic of genocide. But silence does not signify inevitable exclusion. Whatever the intentions were of the people who worded the text, the Convention acquired validity by virtue of the subsequent signing and adhesion to the treaty by members of the United Nations who shared the view that genocide was an odious scourge which they must undertake to prevent and punish. Article 137 *bis* of the revoked Spanish Criminal Code and Article 607 of the current Criminal Code, which took into account the world concern that gave rise to the 1948 Convention, cannot exclude from their definitions events such as those alleged in these proceedings. The need felt by the countries which were parties to the 1948 Convention to punish genocide and to prevent it being committed with impunity, as it was considered a horrendous crime under international law, requires that the phrase 'national group' mean not 'a group of persons who form part of the same nation', but simply a national human group, a human group distinguished by certain characteristics and which forms part of a greater group. The limited interpretation of this type of genocide which the appellants seek to make would prevent the definition as genocide of acts as odious as the systematic elimination by the people in power of a group of AIDS sufferers, as a group with a particular characteristic, or of the elderly, also as a group with a particular feature, or of foreigners residing in a country, who in spite of being from different nations may be considered to be a national group in relation to the country in which they live and where they are distinguished precisely by not being nationals in that state. This social concept of genocide, which is felt and understood by the community and which gives rise to its rejection of and horror at the crime, would not allow for exclusions such as the above-mentioned. The prevention and punishment of genocide, that is, as an international crime and an evil which directly affects the international community, according to the intentions of the 1948 Convention which can be inferred from the text, cannot exclude certain national groups distinguished by particular features, who are discriminated against with regard to others. Neither the 1948 Convention nor our Criminal Code nor the revoked criminal code expressly rule out this necessary inclusion.

In these terms, the events alleged in these terms, the matters of fact alleged in the summary proceeding constitute genocide, and consequently Article 23(4) of the Organic Law of the Judiciary is applicable to the case. At the time of the events and in the country in which they took place, efforts were made to destroy a national group with certain features, namely those who could not be included in the national reorganisation plan or those who, according to the persecutors, did not fit in. The victims included foreigners and in particular a large number of Spaniards. All the actual or potential Chilean or foreign victims formed part of a group with certain features in the country and which it was endeavoured to exterminate.

Six. Definition of the alleged events as terrorism.
Again reference will be made to the Arguments of Law of the decision issued by the plenary session on the appeal appearing in record number 84/98 of Division Three. They constitute a reply to the third grounds of this appeal.

The definition of the alleged events as terrorism does not contribute anything new to the resolution of the case, since the alleged events have already been considered liable to constitute the crime of genocide and are the same events, which are being considered, in the framework of legal subsumption. Terrorism is also a crime for which international prosecution is envisaged, as defined in Article 23(4) of our Organic Law of the Judiciary, and it has already been mentioned (in paragraph Two of these Arguments of Law) that the provision, which is a current procedural one, is applicable irrespective of the time when the crimes were committed. However, the court must state whether the matters of fact alleged in the summary proceedings, which are liable to be defined as constituting the crime of genocide, can also be qualified as terrorism. The Court considers that the events cannot be excluded from the definition of terrorism simply because of our law requiring the existence of the intention to subvert the constitutional order. The subversive tendency relates to the legal or social order of the country in which the crime of terrorism is committed or which is directly affected by it as the target of the attack, and this necessary transfer of an event does not preclude the liability to be defined as terrorism according to Spanish criminal law – Article 23(4) of the Organic Law of the Judiciary. Moreover, we find in the deaths, injuries, coercion and illegal arrests which are the object of the proceedings the particular feature that they were carried out by persons forming part of an armed gang, irrespective of the institutional functions discharged by them, since it must be taken into account that the said deaths, injuries, coercion and illegal arrests were carried out clandestinely and not in the course of the regular discharge of official functions, although under the cover of the latter. The association to carry out illegal acts of destruction of a group of persons distinguished by certain features was a secret one and developed parallel to the institutional organisation of which the authors formed part, but it cannot be confused with the latter. Furthermore, the following elements also existed: a structure (a stable organisation), a result (the production of insecurity, anxiety or fear in a group or encouragement of such fear among the general population) and a teleological element (understood as the rejection of the legal order current in the country at the time), which are characteristic of armed action.

Antonio Quintano Ripollés wrote the following in the 1950s: 'One form of terrorism has been the regrettable proliferation in our time, so favourable to all sorts of State monopolies, of terrorism from above, that is, practised by the State openly through its official or unofficial agencies. It is clear that this goes beyond internal criminal law proper, although it might be covered by international criminal law as regards the so-called crimes against humanity or genocide. It is without doubt the vilest aspect of terrorism, as it eliminates all risks and takes advantage of authority to commit its crimes under the cover of official duty and even of patriotism.'

Seven. Crimes of torture. The fourth grounds of the appeal.
Once again, the text of the decision issued yesterday will be referred to.

The alleged torture forms part of the greater crime of genocide or terrorism. Therefore, it would be useless to consider whether the crime of torture is, according to our law, a crime for which universal prosecution is envisaged according to Article 23(4) of the Organic Law of the Judiciary, in relation to Article 5 of the Convention of 10 December 1984 against Torture and Other Cruel, Inhuman or Degrading Treatment or Punishment. If Spain is competent to prosecute for genocide abroad, the investigation and trial must necessarily extend to crimes of torture which are an aspect of genocide, and not only in the case of the Spanish victims as might result from Article 5(1)(c) of the said Convention, which is not a duty imposed on the signatory state. Spain would have its own jurisdiction deriving from an international treaty in the case of Paragraph 5(2) of the said Convention, but as we have already mentioned, this matter is legally irrelevant for the purposes of the appeal and the summary proceedings.

Eight. Res judicata and existence of a lawsuit pending legal decision.

The Justice Department alleged that there was a lawsuit pending legal decision and *res judicata* in its petition to conclude the summary proceedings dated 20 March of this year (page 5.531 of the record), and repeated this in the interlocutory appeal lodged prior to this appeal, on which a decision was issued, and also during the hearing held on 29th October. The reasons invoked were that in Chile the events being judged in these proceedings had already been the object of a trial and the existence of criminal proceedings dealing with the same events being conducted at the Court of Appeal at Santiago, Chile, instituted as a result of two actions for crimes of multiple homicide and kidnappings instituted against the former president of Chile, Augusto Pinochet Ugarte.

Thus, it is being alleged that the court is incompetent because it does not meet the requirement established in paragraph two of Article 23 of the Organic Law of the Judiciary ('if the criminal has not been acquitted, pardoned or sentenced abroad, or, in the latter case, if he has not served his sentence').

The Justice Department has expressly quoted the cases involving the disappearance of Antonio Llidó Mengual (a Spanish priest arrested by security agents in Santiago in October 1974 and imprisoned in a detention centre, there being no information on his fate since then), the disappearance of Michelle Pena (arrested in Santiago by agents of the DINA in June, 1975 and taken to a detention centre, there being no information since then on her fate or on that of the child she was expecting, as she was pregnant when she was arrested) and the death of Carmelo Soria Espinoza, a Spaniard who held dual Spanish and Chilean nationality and who was arrested in Santiago on 15 July 1976 by agents of the DINA and found dead the next day), as crimes on which Chilean justice has already ruled.

In all three cases, the courts of Chile dismissed the prosecution by virtue of the application of Decree-Law 2.191 of 1978 issued by the Government Council of the Republic, pardoning the parties responsible for crimes (with certain express exceptions) committed during the currency of the stage of siege, namely between 11 September 1973 and 10 March 1978, provided they were not being tried or had not been sentenced. The court decisions appear on pages 5743 et seq. and 5752, 5753 and 5756 et seq. of the summary proceedings.

It also appears in the summary proceedings, on pages 5.783 et seq. that the proceedings conducted as a result of the death of Spanish priest Juan Alsina Hurtos (who was arrested on 19 September 1973 by a military patrol of the Yungay Regiment of San Felipe and executed by the parties who arrested him at the Bulnes bridge over the river Mapocho on the same day) were dismissed with regard to the two persons accused by virtue of the same Decree-Law.

The crimes to which reference has been made are to be deemed not to have been prejudged. Irrespective of whether Decree-Law 2.191 of 1978 can be considered to be contrary to international *ius cogens,* it cannot be considered to be a true pardon according to Spanish legislation applicable to these proceedings, but rather a provision which abolishes punishment for reason of political convenience, and consequently it is not applicable to the case of an accused party acquitted or pardoned abroad (Art.

23(2)(c) of the Organic Law of the Judiciary), but rather in the case of behaviour which is not punishable, by virtue of a subsequent legal provision abolishing punishment, in the country where the crime is committed (Art. 23(2)(a) of the said Law), and this is not valid in any event in cases of extraterritoriality of Spanish jurisdiction by virtue of the principles of universal protection and prosecution, in view of the provisions of the above mentioned Article 23(5) of the Organic Law of the Judiciary.

The four cases mentioned above (among many other, similar ones) cannot be deemed to have been tried or dismissed in Chile, and they justify the validity of the jurisdiction, which is being challenged.

Nine. Article 2(1) of the Charter of the United Nations is not a legal provision which can invalidate, in this case, Article 23(4) of the Organic Law of the Judiciary. Final considerations.

To conclude, Spanish courts are competent to judge the events which are the object of these proceedings.

Article 2(1) of the Charter of the United Nations ('The Organisation is based on the principle of sovereign equality of all its Members') is not a legal provision which invalidates the proclamation of jurisdiction made in Article 23(4) and which has been quoted frequently in this decision.

When the Spanish courts apply the said legal provision, they are not interfering in the sovereignty of the state where the crime was committed, but rather they are exercising Spanish sovereignty with regard to international crimes.

Spain is competent to judge the events by virtue of the principle of universal prosecution for certain crimes – a category of international law – established by our internal legislation. It also has a legitimate interest in the exercise of such jurisdiction because more than fifty Spanish nationals were killed or disappeared in Chile, victims of the repression reported in the proceedings.

Therefore,

The Judges in Plenary Session at the Criminal Division of the National Court Agree to Dismiss the Appeal and to Confirm Spanish Jurisdiction to Judge the Events which are the Object of the Proceedings

This decision is unappealable.
The decision is to be notified to the Justice Department and to the appellees.
This is the order of the Judges listed above.

Madrid, 5 November 1998

☞ **Spain: Order of Judge Garzón of indictment against General Pinochet. 10 December 1998**

Proceedings: Summary 19/97 Terrorism and Genocide 'Condor Operation'
Central Court of Instruction Number Five. National Court. Madrid.

Order[3]

In Madrid on tenth of December one thousand nine hundred and ninety-eight

Background

One. On 16 October 1998, criminal charges were filed against Augusto Pinochet and others for the offences of genocide, terrorism and torture, as part of Investigation 19/97 Item III relating to the so-called 'Condor Plan'.

Two. On the same date, an arrest warrant and an international arrest order were issued against Augusto Pinochet for the aforementioned offences.

Three. On 18 October 1998, the arrest warrant and the international arrest warrant was extended.

Four. On 3 November 1998, it was decided to propose to the Government the extradition of Augusto Pinochet Ugarte, who was detained for this purpose in London (England). The request was duly submitted and is currently being considered.

Five. On 4 and 5 November, a plenary session of the Criminal Division of the Spanish National Court unanimously held in two judgements both in relation to proceedings 19/97 before this Court and 1/98 before Central Court number 6 which are investigating the events in Argentina and Chile between 1976 and 1983 and between 1973 and 1990 respectively, which presumably constitute offences of genocide, terrorism and torture, that the Spanish Courts have jurisdiction to investigate and hear same.

Six. By judgement of 20 October 1998, Central Court number 6 waived its jurisdiction over Investigation 1/98 in favour of this Court which by a judgement of 20 October 1998 was incorporated into Investigation 19/97 Item III, giving rise to a joinder of proceedings, which decision was confirmed by the Plenary Session of the Criminal Division of the National Court in a judgement dated 23 November 1998.

Facts

[...]

Legal Reasoning

One. The procedural issues in connection with the competence and jurisdiction of the Courts of Spain for the investigation, knowledge and issue of formal conclusions as to the facts of the case have been resolved in the official findings dated 25 March 1998, 11 June 1998 and 15 September 1998, but above all in the Resolution of the Plenary Session of the Criminal Division dated 4 and 5 November 1998. Likewise the issues concerning privilege and the lack of immunity of Augusto Pinochet Ugarte were addressed and resolved in the Ruling of 3 November 1998, on the basis of which extradition is proposed, substantiated by the Decision of the House of Lords in England, issued on 25 November 1998.

Therefore, in respect of these issues, one need only ratify the arguments presented:

At this point, to satisfy the requirements of Article 384 of the Criminal Procedures Law – edict on the procedures for the trial of the accused – one needs to establish the legal/penal classification of this crime, for merely provisional purposes, of the facts

---

3. This is an excerpt of the indictment of Augusto Ugarte Pinochet. The original is 366 pages long, largely taken up with listing over 3,000 victims.

summarised in this Resolution, and assign a judgement as to imputability, likewise of a provisional nature, on the essence of the events where evidence of criminal liability is concentrated.

Two. The facts as related could constitute:

1. The crime of genocide according to Article 607, Paragraphs 1, 1st, 2nd, 3rd, 4th and 5th of the Penal Code.

The Legal Precept states:
'Those persons who, with the intention of partially or totally destroying a national group, perform any one of the following actions will be punished:
　　1. By a prison sentence of fifteen to twenty years if they kill any member of such group.
　　2. By a prison sentence of fifteen to twenty years if they sexually assault any member of such group or inflict injuries as described in Article 149.
　　3. By a prison sentence of eight to fifteen years if they subject the group or any member of the group to living conditions that endanger their life or seriously threaten their health or produce any of the injuries described in Article 150.
　　4. The same punishment will be applied to those persons who force members of the group to move from one place to another, apply any measures designed to impede their normal way of life or reproduction, or forcibly transfer individuals from one group to another.
　　5. By a prison sentence of four to eight years if they cause any injury other than those described in s. 2 and 3 of this paragraph.'
　　'Genocide comprises the ultimate crime, the most serious violation of the rights of mankind that can possibly be committed' (translator's note: this and subsequent such translations are non-official). These are the words used in the so-called 'M. B. Whitaker Report' which addresses the Study of Prevention and Repression of the Crime of Genocide in the context of Resolution 1983/83 of the Social – Economic Council of the United Nations dated 27 May 1983 revised edition dated 2 July 1985, E/CN. 4/ Sub.2/1985/6 and comprises an essential document for the appraisal of the crimes under discussion.
　　The duty of the international community should be to detect it, pursue it, and punish it as appropriate, without allowing the political pressures of any government or regime to open the doors to immunity, because if this is allowed, it would expedite the performance of new criminal actions that humanity rejects and repudiates. In the same sense one needs to emphasise that the right to live is the first of human rights and all other rights are tributaries of the same. The right to conserve life is not only an issue which concerns the government of the individual or the group in question but also a concern of the international community, particularly when this community is the holder of the right that is being violated.
　　Resolution 96 (I) of the United Nations General Assembly, affirms that the pursuit and punishment of the crime of genocide is a matter of national interest and, it should be added, of national and international obligation, for that reason it is a crime which is 'condemned by the civilised world' and a legal commitment exists whereby it must be pursued both in times of peace and times of war.

It is a norm, which is imperative, or *ius cogens*, according to the International Court of Justice (consultative opinion on the reservations to the Convention on the Prevention and Punishment of Genocide of 9 December 1948, of 15, 23 and 28 May 1951). As a *ius cogens* norm it must be, and is, accepted pacifically by the international community which can only be affected by a subsequent modification, through mechanisms specifically foreseen in Article 53 of the Vienna Convention on the Law of Treaties of May 23, 1969.

What is more, and given its character (*ius cogens*), which is rooted in Common International Law, the norm is wider than that which is contained in the 1948 Convention, and therefore starting from the basic minimum, that the former contains the principles collected in the latter, they are obligatory for all States even outside the linkage which is derived from the Convention itself and are applicable in accordance with the principle of universal jurisdiction and require co-operation which is, again, universal for all and in the face of all (*erga omnes*).

The difficulties that will arise to impede the achievement of the foregoing will be great and even harder to overcome when the body that threatens death, or is the executor or accomplice of murder, is the State itself, especially if one bears in mind the obstructive behaviour of the Government in question in relation to the action by the United Nations foreseen in the Convention on the Prevention and Punishment of the Crime of Genocide dated 9 December 1948, which Spain subscribed to on 13 September 1968, with express and total reservation as to Article 9, referring to the Jurisdiction of the International Tribunal of Justice for the interpretation, application, and execution of the Convention. Accepting the commitment, whenever a legitimate interest is involved – represented in this case by the existence of victims who are Spaniards and descendants of Spaniards – as is reflected in Article 23.4 of the Spanish Organic Law on Judicial Power, to pursue the crime of genocide, as is the case in a similar sense, with Article 6 of the German STGB and the Israeli Law 5710/50.

The crime of genocide is defined in the Convention of 9 December 1948, and where Spain is concerned, is included in our Internal Laws of Jurisdiction, as a result of our adhesion to the Convention, through the Law 44/1971 of 15 November, which adds Article 137 *bis*, within Chapter III, as one of the crimes against the Rights of the People under Title I (Crimes against the Foreign Security of the State) within Book II of the Penal Code.

Since then, this crime has not disappeared from our Penal Code. It is currently regulated, as mentioned earlier, by Article 607, Chapter II (The Crime of Genocide) Major Heading XXIV (Crimes against the International Community) Book II of the Penal Code. From the point of view of classification, the most relevant differentiation in this case between the crime as defined in 1971 and current legislation is the substitution of the expression 'national ethnic group' by 'national, ethnic . . . group' and 'social group' by 'racial group'. The first difficulty that may arise is whether the Spanish legislator, on eliminating the orthographic comma between 'national' and 'ethnic' which now exists, meant to restrict the scope of application of the precept, or, on the contrary, allows an interpretation in accordance with the Convention. This domestic legislation remained in force for almost five years after the inception of the Spanish Constitution of 1978, in which Article 10.2 makes express reference to the interpretation of International Treaties and Agreements in respect of fundamental rights. Therefore, the interpretation according to the Constitution and the 1948 Convention of the expression 'national ethnic groups' existing in Article 137 *bis*, in force until 1983, obliges one to insert a comma between 'national' and 'ethnic', exactly as has happened in the modification referred to, and, therefore, not to restrict the national groups object of genocide to those of a purely ethnic nature. This argument is valid even though the events which are the subject of this investigation took place before the inception of the current Spanish Constitution, because in virtually all cases one is faced with abduction, a crime of permanent consummation, and convert, in turn, genocide into a crime of permanent consummation, and because the crime of genocide continues to be committed as long as the actions designed to partially eliminate a group subsist, which happened in Chile many years after our Constitution came into force.

The problems which may arise from the specific wording of the provisions of Section 137 *bis* of the Penal Code may be avoided by the use of the approach based on Article 10.2 of the Constitution, instead of that relating to international legislation on treaties and specifically the Vienna Convention on the Law of Treaties. While it is true that this international legislation refers to the fact that the provisions of domestic law cannot be relied upon to breach a Treaty, it is nonetheless also true that Article 5 of the Convention on the Crime of Genocide does not provide for the direct and immediate effectiveness of same, but rather imposes on the parties the commitment to adopt the necessary measures to ensure the application of the Convention and to provide effective criminal sanctions for guilty persons. There is therefore an express reference to the effectiveness of domestic legislation implementing the Convention as stated in the Preamble to the 1971 Law, which incorporates the crime of genocide into the Spanish Penal Code.

In summary, therefore, the national group approach must overcome an initial problem, the possible non-alignment of Spanish legislation as to the crime of genocide when the atrocities were committed by the Chilean exterminators, since they did not affect a 'national ethnic group'. This problem may be overcome by reverting to the Constitution, which declares as unconstitutional the limitation of national groups to those of an ethnic nature, by interpretation of internal legislation on fundamental rights in accordance with the 1948 Convention as required by Article 10.2 of the Constitution. But, what is more, the hypothesis of genocide is also applicable in relation to an ethnic group (the Mapuches).

Three. The second problem posed by the national group argument in classifying the behaviour of the Chilean exterminators is the concept itself. However, as will be seen later, this concept is viable. 'National group' may mean 'a group belonging to a nation', i.e., 'the group of a nation' in the territorial sense, although in international legislation and practice the expression means above all 'a group of common national origin'- (Cf. Cherif Bassiouni, *International Criminal Law*, Crimes, 1986, p. 291). This expression is thus used, e.g., in Paragraph 1 of Article 1 of the International Convention on the Elimination of All Forms of Racial Discrimination, 21 December 1965, which, in defining the concept of 'racial discrimination', refers to all distinctions, exclusions, restrictions or preferences based, among other things, on reasons of race, national origin or ethnic origin. In the discussions during the drafting process of the 1948 Convention, it was intended to specify this as a group of a single nationality or citizenship, from the same ethnic origin, or as a reference to national minorities and even those belonging to different nationalities within a State or nation. The Convention chose the expression 'national group', this being considered inclusive of these cases which are, in reality, restrictive. In this sense it can be said that within the concept of genocide, the idea of 'national' is used to identify permanent groups of people with a common origin. Apart from this, in the crime of genocide, the group to be totally or partially destroyed serves to determine the specific, subjective element, cause or intention sought with its destruction. Genocidal conduct is not only carried out with the intention of destroying a group, but also because they belong to a nation, ethnic group, race or religion. Obviously this idea does not exclude the genocide of national groups, the destruction of groups with a common origin, but differentiated within the same nation, this being understood to mean the territorial scope or group of inhabitants ruled by the same government. It is obvious that such groups within their own national identity exist within the nation. Generally in these cases the cohesion of these groups is ethnic – which would explain the restrictive Spanish legislation prior to 1983 – racial or religious but other differentiating elements are not excluded by this idea, e.g., territorial, historic or linguistic factors. There is no doubt that the total or partial destruction of the Scots, Catalans, Basques or Corsicans for the mere fact of their being such would be genocide of national, but not necessarily ethnic, groups, regardless of whether the reason were their language, tradition, territorial ambitions or ideology, as the decisive factor is that the reason for the destruction of the group would be, precisely, the fact that they belonged to such a national group united by some permanent, common, differentiating feature.

In the same way, the definition of national group does not exclude those cases where the victims are part of the same group as the transgressors, i.e., the cases of 'self-genocide' such as occurred with the mass killings in Kampuchea.

In the 'Whitaker Report' mentioned above, it is emphasised that 'genocide does not necessarily mean the destruction of an entire group (...) The term used in Article 2 of the Convention seems to indicate quite a high number in relation to the total strength of the group or also an important part of that group, such as its leaders'. '(...) The group of victims may, in fact, be either a minority or a majority in a country; (...) the definition does not exclude the case where the victims belong to the same group as that to which the perpetrator of the crime belongs. The United Nations Rapporteur on the mass killings carried out by the Khmer Rouge in Kampuchea qualifies this massacre as 'self-genocide', an expression which implies the mass destruction in the interior of the group itself of an important number of that group; as Pieter Drost said (*The Crime of State II*, Genocide. Leyden, A.W. Sythoff, 1959), 'The most serious form of the crime of genocide is the deliberate destruction of the physical – or psychological – life of human beings taken individually, because of their belonging to any collective human group as such.'

The document concludes, that 'in order to be qualified as genocide, the crimes committed against a certain number of individuals must be aimed at their collective group or at them as members or links in that collective group'.

Among the crimes against humanity, which is not the same as genocide, the Charter of the Nuremberg International Military Court included 'persecution for political, racial or religious reasons in the carrying out of, or in connection with, any crime under the jurisdiction of this Court'.

However, although it is recognised in international literature that historically the destruction of national, ethnic, racial or religious groups has clearly been politically motivated, and in spite of the precedent of the Charter of Nuremberg, it is clearly deduced from analysis of the proceedings and studies of the 1948 Convention that the Sixth Commission responsible for drafting it, after prolonged debate, deliberately excluded political groups as the object of the crime of genocide, mainly because of the opposition of the Soviet Union. This does not mean that the destruction of groups for political reasons was left outside the scope of genocide. It is much more accurate to say that it means such political reasons must be centred on a national, ethnic, racial or religious group for its total or partial destruction to constitute genocide. Without this extra identification, the destruction of ideological or political groups was considered to be outside the scope of the crime of genocide by the 1948 Convention.

This exclusion has been contested repeatedly by the most expert scientific opinions, especially because, as Professor José Manuel Gómez Benítez says ('Genocide and the Immunity of Heads of State') 'Reality, above all, has imposed a different way of interpreting the Convention. Exterminations of groups of people for political reasons have been so obvious and atrocious that it has become increasingly unjustifiable to maintain that they do not fit within the legal definition of genocide because they do not coincide with any of the groups referred to in the text of the Convention.'

'It could be added that the concept of genocide is a living concept and should necessarily include those cases which really give it meaning in the light of events that have occurred since the Convention came into force. One of the cases which most clearly supports this interpretation, which should not be understood as by extension but rather as an integral of the true range that should be assigned to the term national group, is the self-genocide in Kampuchea referred to above, in respect of which it has been internationally recognised, especially by the United States in 1994, that between 17 April 1975 and 7 March 1979, what occurred in Democratic Kampuchea (Cambodia) was truly genocide of national groups for political reasons, although it came to affect not only the same Khmer group as the exterminators, but also the very members of the Khmer Rouge who differed ideologically from the controlling group. It is widely recognised that the first groups to be eliminated belonged to police forces, soldiers of the defeated army and high-ranking civil servants of previous regimes, sometimes together with their families. Later came ethnic minorities and immediately afterwards, in the context of the ideological ambition to eliminate the capitalist classes of all those Cambodians whom the leaders of the Khmer Rouge under the command of Pol Pot considered as suspect of individualistic activities or in favour of the concept of private property; at this point the massacres started to include as victims members of the Khmer Rouge squads and Khmer peasants. All of this without counting thousands of individual executions, tortures, and deportations.' (J. M. Gómez Benítez, Ibid.).

In addition, it must not be forgotten that the Congress of the USA itself passed the Cambodian Genocide Justice Act, which sought to place those responsible for that genocide before the courts.

Four. The foregoing reasoning has been developed to express that, on the one hand, the concept of 'national group' argued for here is not, in essence, identical with that of 'political group' but that, on the other hand, it does not exclude 'political groups' in the formulation of this concept.

Legal Doctrine, when referring to the Nazi genocide, establishes that it was the result, not of an international war, but of a calculated policy of collective killing undertaken by a State that entailed the 'systematic and structured eradication of innocent people by the bureaucratic apparatus of that State'. (Irving Horowitz, *Taking Lives: Genocide and State Power.* New Brunswick Transaction Books, 1980). Something very similar may be said of the genocide being judged herein. In Chile, as in Argentina, the military Commanders, Augusto Pinochet and the rest of the members of the governing military Junta, imposed, in September 1973, through a coup d'État, a regime of terror based on the calculated systematic and violent elimination, by the State, of thousands of people over several years, under the disguise of a war against subversion; the aim was to eradicate the very structure of the national group, through killing, imprisoning, and causing to disappear the persons who exercised some form of leadership or of an ideological initiative in each one of the sectors as described above under the heading of 'Facts'; i.e., it was a question of a preordained action governed by principles much deeper than those of mere political disagreement, but included ideological, religious and ethnic aspects overlapping with same and with the leitmotif of fighting against and eradicating 'the Communist/Marxist conspiracy which is threatening Western civilisation'.

When the motivation behind the victims' persecution is ethnic (Gypsies, Jews, indigenous natives) the aggressor is not moved by purely racial motives, abstracted from any other ideological component, but rather builds up sentiments which give rise to criminal actions on an essentially political base, to the extent that a premise of this type, – be it fascist, communist, capitalist or any other – rests on a specific rational conception, which thereafter determines the action. That is to say the political-ideological motive is the essential driving force for the conduct.

In this case nobody doubts that the partial or total destruction of a group identified as such, attacked by an aggressor thus motivated, constitutes a crime of genocide.

And so one should not have any doubt when it comes to qualifying the opposite assumption in the same way. This means that when the action comprises an attack on the very members of the national group (an essentially political concept) and is undertaken for motives that are essentially political, though they may be joined to others of a racial or religious or ideological nature, which are manifested in concrete actions in the form of a more intense aggression, sadism, violence, torture and ill-treatment when the victim in question is a native, a Jew, a non-conforming Catholic or simply an intellectual who disagrees with the party line of the aggressor group, or a non-theist, those individuals are assimilated to 'Communists and Marxists'.

Not to accept this interpretation is to be blind to the living concept of genocide, which cannot stagnate, bound by an interpretation contrary to the true nature of events, and unaltered, anchored to doctrines established by the immediate precedent of the Second World War, but today has evolved, in rhythm with the way atrocities against humanity have progressively been refined and developed and 'conditioned by' the new situations, different to those advanced by the Convention of 9 December 1948.

This interpretation, which fits in with the appraisals expounded above in respect of self-genocide, is also compatible with Article 25 of the Spanish Constitution and with the definition contained in the Convention governing the Prevention and Punishment of Genocide and with Article 15.2 of the International Covenant for Civil and Political Rights of 19 December 1966 in accordance with which none of that which is provided for in this article would be incompatible with 'the trial nor the sentence of a person for acts or omissions which at the moment of their execution were criminal in accordance with general principles of law, recognised by the International Community', and Article 607 of the Spanish Penal Code and integrates the present reality of this type of crime and, above all, is clearly applicable to the case of genocide in Chile that is being evaluated in these proceedings.

In conclusion, if the political motivation cannot be eliminated when this genocidal act is carried out for ethnic or religious reasons, it is even more the case that the categorisation as genocide cannot be ignored when the criminal action is based on political motivations and the object of the aggression is exactly the same group of persons (national group to whom the aggressor also belongs, being the sector which is dominant through the use of force) and the instruments are the same – deaths, kidnapping followed by disappearance, tortures, sexual aggressions or forced displacements – and for the same purpose of eliminating ideological discrepancy and political opposition, and in any case is evident on the basis of either supposition. Therefore, the political parties as basic elements of co-existence and integration in democracy (Art. 6 in relation to Art. 1 of the Spanish Constitution) are an integral part of the national group in which their constitutional function is developed, and, therefore, all aggression to them and, specially, to the leadership which they provide, attacks the very identity of the group. In an identical sense one may speak of the other ideological sectors which make up the concept of national group, for which purpose one need not exclusively refer to aspects which are based on the territorial location of the group, but also on those which give it a real and specific cultural, professional, social, and political identity.

The following may be cited as norms and resolutions or scientific doctrines, which support the interpretation hereby sustained:

1. Resolution 96 (I) already referred to of the United Nations General Assembly of December 11, 1946, the destruction of racial, religious or political groups is genocide.
2. The Consultative Opinion already referred to, on Reservations to the Convention on Genocide of 1948, International Tribunal of Justice 1951.
3. Article 5 (h) of the Statute of the International Tribunal for Ex-Yugoslavia sanctions persecution for political, racial, and religious motives.
4. M. B. Whitaker Report, on the Question of the Prevention and Repression of the Crime of Genocide. Resolution 1983/83 of the Social and Economic Council of the United Nations of May 27, 1983, revised edition dated July 2, 1985, E/CN-4/Sub2/1985/6.
5. *The Crimes of State*, 11th Genocide. Leyden, A.W. Sythoff, 1950, by Pieter Drost.
6. The crime of political genocide, remedying the black stain of the Convention against Genocide. Author Beth Van Schaack, in 'The Yale Law Journal' n° 106, 1997.

Five. Indeed, the elimination of people undertaken by the accused and the other members of the Governing Military Junta should not be considered in part as a series of unconnected events with no common link; nor as a multiplicity of isolated actions that happened to take place at the same time; in fact one is looking at a planned and co-ordinated campaign, with the smallest detail catered for, waged against part of a Chilean national group to which all belong. This is revealed by the selection of persons which they seek to eliminate, the methods of arrest and disappearance used, the existence of centres specifically destined for use as concentration camps, the practice of torture under 'scientific control', clandestine burials, and conspiracy with the military of foreign countries to act outside the Chilean borders against Chilean citizens, the training of Special Forces, the creation of clandestine organisations which obey secret orders such as the DINA or CNI.

This whole set of circumstances, together with the absolute nature of the Junta's power makes sense if it is aimed at an objective far beyond mere reprisals against the political opposition, which, according to the means employed and the ends aimed at, could also constitute in itself a terrorist activity. This means that what one hopes to achieve is the ideological, political and religious regeneration of the group through the violent elimination of those 'elements' (citizens) who are considered 'expendable' or who impede the project of a New Order, or, the same thing, all those who oppose, or present a danger – albeit fictitious – to, the group which has triumphed and oppresses the other.

The reality of these affirmations is evident from the narrative of facts contained in this document, and from the indications (testimonies) that will be expressed later on and which are based on them.

The Resolution of the Inter-American Human Rights Commission dated 15 October 1996 states: 'The Military Government that led the country from 11 September 1973 until 11 March 1990 carried out a systematic policy of repression which resulted in the disappearance of thousands of victims, summary executions, illegal killings and torture … That government had used practically all known methods for the physical elimination of dissidents.'

The objective of the destruction of a significant sector of the national group structures in its diverse sectors, as shown in the list, which is not exhaustive, contained in 'Facts', is revealed in the selective elimination with criminal intent against the leadership of such sectors, organised on an institutional basis, against more than 50 percent of the population of the Chilean Nation, victim of the self-genocide or intra-genocide by the then-Head of State, leaders of the Executive, Legislative and Judicial Powers, municipal authorities, universities, churches, trades unions, political parties, professional and cultural associations, the foundations on which the nation was based. In this fashion the destruction of this group was achieved, in benefit of the dominant group, headed by the military structure, for which the accused, Augusto Pinochet Ugarte, is jointly liable.

In addition, the mechanics of the operation and the choice of coercive measures used by the alleged perpetrators, once accepted the existence of the national group, were specifically aimed at ending the life of the victims or subjecting them to physical and mental injury, or forcing them to move from their homes against their will or to seek exile in numerous cases or attacked their sexual freedom in a systematic fashion. This behaviour appears logical and makes sense if it forms part of a plan of purification of the group itself once the elements, which threaten its unity, have been eliminated. That is to say the leaders who give it cohesion.

Six. As pointed out earlier in this document, the criminal acts as described also have other sides and permit different applications, equally acceptable and described herein. Indeed, one examines herein the conduct of Augusto Pinochet and of the other jointly responsible persons who acted under his orders with the aim of systematically eliminating the dissident or person deemed to be dissident because of that person's ideological convictions or simply belonging to an ideological group.

During the discussions of what groups would be classified as the object of genocide in the drafting of the 1948 Convention, the majority of the participants maintained that ideological or political groups should be treated the same way as religious groups, since both upheld a common idea (ideology) that united their members.

The events as investigated could be subsumed, in addition to the partial destruction of a national group, as the destruction of a group for religious reasons, understanding this conduct as equivalent to the destruction of a religious group.

One of the 'leitmotifs' behind which the repressive military action stood, was the preservation of what they called the Western and Christian morality, in contrast to Marxism and internationalism, in other words, Atheism. Likewise, the objective was the elimination of those persons opposed to the official religious stance of the governing Junta, such as occurred with the group 'Christians for Socialism'.

In the preceding pages the equivalency between the destruction of a group for reasons of religion and the destruction of religious groups has been expounded; in this sense one must point out that the idea, as to doctrine, is consolidated, that the terms religion or belief also include believers in God, atheists, and agnostics, according to the Footnote to Article 1 of the Draft of the International Convention for the Elimination of All Forms of Intolerance and Discrimination based on Religion or Beliefs, approved by the Committee of the General Assembly of the United Nations in 1967, reproduced in all legal doctrine.

Historically this procedure was applied to the mass deportation of Tibetan children to Chinese centres of Marxist education to prevent them receiving any religious education (Cf., 'Le Tibet et La République Populaire de China' in the *Revue de Droit Penal et Criminologie*, February 1961, p. 541; also *The Tibetan Question and the Authority of Law*, International Commission of Jurists, Geneva 1959; both quoted by Javier Saenz de Pipaûn y Mengs in *International Political Delinquency with special reference to the crime of genocide*, Institute of Criminology of the Complutense University of Madrid, 1973, p. 152.). Although it is true that in that instance, the group in question was clearly a national group in the traditional sense of the expression, with a clear Buddhist religious identity, it is no less true that the acts were considered genocide in that they constituted the destruction of a group for ideological, religious reasons. There is a great degree of parallelism between this oriental Marxist style, ideological religious purge and what was attempted, but in reverse, by Augusto Pinochet in 1973. Meaning, that it was a question of combating everything that went against the official religious ideology of the dominant group represented by the Ruling Military Junta.

Thus this action is aimed at a group held together by their common atheist or agnostic ideology, which, by definition, does not accept Christian doctrine and beliefs. Therefore, one may assert that in Chile, as happened in Argentina, although with differing aspects, even more clearly between March 1976 and December 1983, in a reversed image of what the Chinese Marxists intended, the intention was to destroy, according to the criteria of the perpetrators of genocide, those who did not profess a determined religious ideology (atheists or agnostics) or did not adhere to the faith in the way that the oppressors wished. This would explain, in the case of Chile, the existence of Churches that fought against the actions of the military commanders and the persecution of these religious dissidents – Christians for Socialism – and non religious groups (Marxists or otherwise).

The destruction of a group because of their atheism or their common non-acceptance of the official religious ideology of the perpetrators of genocide, is also, according to this, the destruction of a religious group, insofar as the group to be destroyed also behaves technically as the object of identification of the motivation or subjective element of the genocidal behaviour. It appears, indeed, that genocidal behaviour may be defined both positively, according to the identity of the group to be destroyed, (e.g., Moslems), and negatively, with greater genocidal scope (e.g. all non-Christians, all atheists, all Christians of certain types, etc.). This idea holds, therefore, that it is genocide of a religious group when the destruction takes place in a systematic and organised manner, totally or partially, of a group because of their atheist or non-Christian convictions, i.e., in order to impose a determined Christian ideology on the former and the latter if they do not conform, eliminating them if this objective is not fulfilled, or simply because of their convictions

In addition, Fact Eighteen describes a supposed crime of genocide for ethnic reasons. In fact, the Araucanian tribe of Mapuches has its own ethnic identity with its own culture, religion, language and customs, different from the modern configuration of society. This difference has been legally recognised as part of the native culture and, therefore, enjoys the right, recognised by national and international organisations, to its own existence which cannot be attacked in any of its aspects and which if it is attacked in some of the ways foreseen in the Convention against Genocide and Article 607 of the Penal Code, gives rise to the generally reproachable conduct which is here being prosecuted.

The aggression against the Mapuche people is not fortuitous nor can its significance be diluted by inclusion in any of the previous groups referred to (self-genocide or genocide for ideological motives); rather it has its own identity and, as is stressed in Amnesty International's Report and the report by the Inter-Church Committee for Human Rights in Latin America, entitled 'People of the Land', and as we will have occasion to note throughout this cause, the aggression was carried out more intensively, because of the relationship to this ethnic group, with the intention of destroying their form of life, eliminating distribution of lands and properties, and obliging some of its members to disperse or simply eliminating them.

In addition, the conditions of detention, the humiliations, and tortures were also intensified by reason of the fact that they belonged to an ethnic or religious (Jewish) group.

Seven. The facts as presented may likewise be considered crimes of terrorism, developed through numerous acts of executions, beatings, abductions, arson and bombings according to Articles, 515, 516 – 2nd, and 571 of the Penal Code.

The requirements that the penal text impose in this case do concur, as is revealed by the dynamics of the crime as described:

1. It seems clear that the teleological element required by the Spanish Penal Code – subverting the constitutional order or causing serious breaches of the peace – should not be understood as merely Spanish constitutional and public order as this would prevent the prosecution of any terrorist offence committed outside Spain, in open conflict with the universal vocation proclaimed by Article 23.4 of the Organic Law on Judicial Power (L.O.P.J.). On the contrary it must refer to a constitutional order equivalent to that of Spain, i.e., any that requires that 'the State be social, and democratic by law, upholding freedom, justice, equality, a political pluralism as the supreme values of its legal system, as proclaimed in Article 1 of the Spanish Constitution. That is, precisely, the kind of constitutional order that was illegally and illegitimately overthrown by the Junta of the Chiefs of the Armed Forces, later the Governing Junta, headed by Mr. Pinochet Ugarte

through the coup d'État on 11 September 1973. Therefore, it may be affirmed that such criminal action considered by itself constitutes the first attack on public peace and constitutional order in Chile and means that the teleological element exists to its full extent. It should be borne in mind that the Chilean Constitution remained in force until 1980 and expressly forbade acts such as those committed by the aforementioned.

2. As regards the specification of the crime committed, there is no doubt whatsoever that the whole catalogue of crimes referred to in the Penal Code as constituting crimes of terrorism (arson, murder, infliction of physical injuries, torture, illegal arrest, disappearances etc.) was covered.

3. Finally, as regards the objective element of whether or not a terrorist or armed gang existed, it could be said that one may invoke Article 577 of the current Penal Code (formerly Article 174 *bis* (b) of the old Penal Code that has now been repealed) which presupposes the non-existence of a terrorist organisation or armed gang and thus the matter is resolved. However, it must be stressed that there was clearly a previously conceived plan by the Military Governing Junta of Chile headed by Augusto Pinochet to conspire against, and thereafter systematically carry out, through organisations specifically created for this purpose – the DINA, the CNI and others mentioned in the Facts – a whole series of attacks against political opponents which were motivated by the same objective, namely, that of attacking the group of persons who were ideologically opposed, not only within Chile, but also abroad, using for this purpose explosives, military weapons and Italian terrorist organisations – Avanguardia Nazionale – or the intelligence services of other countries – such as Argentina, Paraguay or Uruguay – which together with Chile formed part of the 'Condor Plan' constituting an authentic terrorist organisation operating outside any legal standards including those dictated by the Governing Junta itself.

The difficulties which arise in relation to the apparent contradiction in terms when referring to State terrorism are resolved by proceeding on the basis that the dictatorship is characterised by the inoperativeness of the principle of legality so that the very organs of the State act outside such legality, although formally it exists. The truth is that in the case under consideration, as we have seen, a whole series of institutional bodies and structures were created outside the scope of formal legality, but by those in charge of the State and, in particular, by those managing the State, in order to carry out murders, abductions, torture, forced disappearances of persons etc., so as to eliminate political dissidence and end any ideological dispute in any sector.

The fact that terrorism is included in Article 23.4 of the Organic Law on Judicial Power as an offence capable of being prosecuted universally, must be understood to refer not so much to terrorism, whether national or international, which occurs in Spain, because this is already covered by domestic legislation, but rather to cases in which Spain as a member of the international community has an interest in prosecuting, but the prosecution of the offence must unavoidably be carried out in accordance with Spanish law.

Spain's interest, as a member of that Community, does not lie in the fact that there is a Spanish victim or victims but rather in the fact that terrorism forms part of the concept of crimes against humanity and the countries share a common interest in prosecuting it since it constitutes a clear case of international criminal responsibility, where terrorism is of this kind and, in particular, is used as a method of political and ideological repression and is carried out using the structures of the State or the State itself through its representatives. In this respect it is important to cite the resolution of the United Nations General Assembly in which it urges the adoption of all measures necessary to combat and eliminate all terrorist acts no matter where or by whom they have been committed (Doc. A/50/186 of the General Assembly of 22 December 1995).

Moreover, it is true to say that the principle of extraterritorial jurisdiction in the area of terrorism cannot under any circumstances be invoked for the purpose of protecting the Spanish State, but rather for the purpose set forth in the previous paragraph.

The fact that terrorism is deemed to be an international crime means that it is not governed by the requirement of double incrimination and, therefore, can still be prosecuted if it was not prosecuted in the country in which the events occurred at the time they occurred, because what is important is the principle of universal prosecution imposed by the principles of supranational intervention and extraterritorial jurisdiction, in reliance on Article 23.4 of the Organic Law on Judicial Power read in conjunction with Article 15.2 of the International Covenant on Civil and Political Rights signed in New York on 19 December 1966.

As a result of the foregoing, it must be concluded that the reference in the Organic Law on Judicial Power to terrorism 'according to Spanish criminal law' means that both the Spanish institutional order and the institutional order of other countries are protected when attacked by any such offences against persons and human rights. In other words, international legal interests, not merely domestic interests, are protected.

In the instant case it can be seen how as soon as the Governing Junta began to operate, its leaders, headed by Augusto Pinochet, arranged all the means necessary and gave the appropriate instructions so that the widespread repression would be clandestine, co-ordinated and organised both within and outside the country; they did not hesitate to seek assistance from other terrorist organisations or from other services equally conversant with terrorist activity.

Eight. The actions may also constitute the crime of torture under Articles 173 and 174 of the Penal Code. The crime of torture was introduced into Spanish criminal law, although not identified as such, by Organic Law 31/78 of July, in Article 204 *bis* of the Penal Code under the heading of Crimes against Internal State Security; it is currently included under a separate heading in Articles 571 and 574 of the Penal Code. In this respect when considering torture as a universally prosecutable crime, one should bear in mind Article 7 of the International Covenant on Civil and Political Rights of 16 December 1966, ratified by Spain on 27 April 1977 which forbids torture, inhuman and degrading treatment. Article 5.1.c of the Convention against Torture and other Cruel, Inhuman and Degrading Treatment and Punishments approved on 10 December 1984 in New York and ratified by Spain on 21 October 1987, states as follows: 'All signatory States shall take the necessary measures to establish their jurisdiction over the crimes referred to in Article 4 … when the victim is a national of that State and the State considers it appropriate.' Article 3 of the Four Geneva Conventions of 12 July 1949 ratified by Spain, which refers to the basic rules applicable to any armed conflict, including non-international or domestic conflicts, forbids torture and inhuman treatment at any time and in any place. The same principle is expressed in Article 6 (c) of the Statute of the Nuremberg Tribunal and Article 5(e) of the Statute of the Tribunal for ex-Yugoslavia created in 1995.

Moreover, Article 23.4(g) of the Organic Law on Judicial Power of 1 July 1985 provides that the Spanish Courts are competent to hear cases regarding acts committed by Spaniards or foreigners outside the national territory capable of being classified as an offence and which, in accordance with international treaties and conventions, should be prosecuted by Spain.

Finally, Article 15 of the International Covenant on Civil and Political Rights of 19 December 1966, having established the principle of legality, states as follows: 'Nothing in this Article shall prejudice the trial and punishment of any person for any act or omission which, at the time when it was committed, was criminal according to the general principles of law recognised by the community of nations.'

Therefore, the mandate is contained in international legislation, the offence has been specified in the Penal Code since 1978 and the procedural rules are to be found in the Organic Law on Judicial Power, applicable on the basis of the aforementioned international conventions and the principle of legal procedure '*tempus regit actum*'. In any event, given the difficulty that could be raised by article 9.3 of the Spanish Constitution, the acts constituting torture must necessarily be investigated – since they were classified as an offence in July 1978 and, in any event as one of the instruments by which the crime of genocide alleged to have been committed by the accused was carried out (Art. 607 of the Penal Code read in conjunction with Article 135 *bis* of the consolidated text of the Penal Code of 1973) and the crime of terrorism itself to the extent that they may give rise to serious injuries and even death.

Nine. Having classified the facts for the purposes of criminal law and made some additional comments concerning jurisdiction in line with the order of a Plenary Session of the National Court Criminal Division of 5 November 1998, the content of which is assumed and deemed to be incorporated herein as well as the order proposing the extradition of Pinochet Ugarte dated 3 November 1998, it is advisable to address, if only briefly, certain aspects relating to the ongoing nature of some of the alleged offences charged herein and the fact that some of the victims, specifically Orlando Letelier and the Spanish citizen Carmelo Soria, were specifically protected persons and the consequence of the obligation to investigate.

Both had the status of an internationally protected person at the time of his execution and death at the hands of the DINA which was ultimately following the orders of Augusto Pinochet Ugarte and, therefore, the Convention on the Prevention and Punishment of Crimes against Internationally Protected Persons, approved by resolution of the General Assembly of 14 December 1973 (Spanish Official Journal (BOE) of 7 February 1986) applies to the case.

On the date of the attack on Orlando Letelier, as recognised in the judgement itself, he enjoyed such status.

On the date of the abduction, torture and murder of Carmelo Soria Espinoza, at the hands of agents of the Chilean State on 14 July 1976, he was an international functionary of the United Nations, appointed by the Secretary General and therefore enjoyed all the privileges and immunities conferred by the Convention signed by the CEPAL (Economic Commission for Latin America) and the Chilean Government on 29 October 1974. He was also protected by the provisions of the United Nations Charter and the United Nations Convention on prerogatives and immunities and, very specifically, by the first-mentioned Convention.

All these aspects are proven in proceedings. [...]

The Convention on the Prevention and Punishment of Crimes against Internationally Protected Persons provides as follows: An "Internationally Protected Person" means:

Article 1. (b) any representative or official of a State, or and official or other agent of an international or an organisation of an intergovernmental character, who at the time when and in the place where a crime is committed against him . . . is entitled, pursuant to international law to special protection from any attack on his person, freedom or dignity, as well as the members of his family who form part of his household.'

Article 2.1 includes the offences, which must be considered as such for the purposes of the application of the Convention, when performed intentionally:
'a) murder, kidnapping or other attack upon the person or liberty of an internationally protected person'.

Article 3 provides that:
'Each State shall take such measures as may be necessary to establish its jurisdiction over the crimes set forth in Article 2 in the following cases:

a) Where the crime is committed in the territory of that State or on board a ship or aircraft registered in that State.

3. This Convention shall not exclude any criminal jurisdiction exercised in accordance with national law',

Article 7 provides:
'The States Party in whose territory the alleged offender is present, shall, if it does not extradite him, submit, without exception whatsoever and without unjustified delay, the case to its competent authorities for the purpose of prosecution through proceedings in accordance with the law of that State';
Finally, Article 8.4 provides:

'Each of these crimes shall be treated, for the purposes of extradition between States Parties, as if it had been committed not only in the place in which it occurred but also in the territories of the States required to establish their jurisdiction in accordance with paragraph 1 of Article 3.'

This means that in the light of the impossibility of pursuing the prosecution against Augusto Pinochet 'as the alleged offender' for the acts committed in Chile, due to the application of the self-amnesty law, despite the fact that there are sufficient and indeed extensive evidence to establish a *prima facie* case that he committed and participated in the aforementioned crimes (Art. 1.2 of the Convention), he must be tried either in the country where he is at present or in Spain, which demands his extradition for these acts as constituting crimes of genocide, terrorism and torture. Therefore, from this perspective under no circumstances can the extradition be denied without incurring the obligation to try him in England or before the Courts of Justice in Chile after the adoption of the relevant legal measures including the appropriate constitutional amendment. Otherwise there would simply be a concealment of the very situation of impunity and immunity which Mr. Pinochet Ugarte enjoys in Chile and which the House of Lords, within whose jurisdiction he is present, has rejected at the request of the Spanish Courts (see section 22(2) (d) of the English Extradition Act, 1989 which adopts this approach).

Ten. In accordance with the provisions of Article 384 of the current Criminal Procedure Law and despite not having the testimony of the accused Mr. Pinochet Ugarte, which has been sought by letters rogatory, there is sufficient rational indicia of criminal responsibility against him and, therefore, it is necessary to order that he be indicted so that he may be informed of the specific acts of which he is accused and for which he will be tried in due course. Therefore, having addressed the legal concepts, in accordance with the arguments contained in the foregoing reasoning, one should mention, if only briefly, the alleged participation of the accused Mr. Pinochet Ugarte and, secondly, provide a list, which is not claimed to be exhaustive, since the investigation is still in progress, of the indicia of criminal conduct which have been considered to date and on which this order is based.

The indicia obtained are of two classes, – it is necessary to emphasise the difficulty involved in obtaining information and proof due to the lack of co-operation on the part of the Chilean authorities, which has only been offset by the efforts of the victims and international bodies as well as other countries which have responded to requests for judicial assistance, – direct, in other words, those which show a specific albeit presumed relationship between the act described and the legal consequence of same and the participation in that act of the person or persons who are mentioned in the description of the facts; and indirect, in other words, indicia which without specifically referring to the situation to which they apply, reaffirm or support other direct indicia or strengthen the description of events or render it coherent, or explain why the events occurred in a certain sequence rather than in a different sequence, or, in short, help one to under-stand a specific situation by endowing it with a logical meaning, allowing one to avoid absurd interpretations and focus on the reality of the act committed, taking into account personal circumstances and the circumstances of time and place existing.

Eleven. As regards the subjective elements of the aforementioned crimes, – genocide, terrorism and torture – it seems clear that they are clearly intentional unlawful acts which respectively entail the following:

a) direct deceit to destroy the human group in its various manifestations,

b) the intention to attack constitutional stability, public order or the international community by means constituting a crime against humanity, and

c) in this same context to degrade the person as a member of the human race and the international community by attacking such valuable rights as life, physical integrity or freedom.

Finally, the subjective element means that the conduct, although affecting each of the subjects individually, forms part of an overall plan devised in advance to achieve the objectives proposed, a) the partial disappearance of the national group through the selective elimination of persons belonging to the national group itself for ideological, (political), ethnic and religious reasons, intensifying the repression in the latter cases, and in all cases imposing forced removal, exile, massive expulsions from jobs, or sexual aggression and multiple forms of abuse; b) the development of a criminal terrorist effort, organised and co-ordinated within and outside the country (Condor Plan), for the elimination of political opponents or of persons who, according to the persons in charge, potentially pose a risk; and c) the performance of systematic torture in all cases.

In the proceedings there are indicia of an agreement between the military personnel in charge, headed by Augusto Pinochet Ugarte, to bring the Chilean constitutional system to an end and assassinate the President elected in accordance with the constitution and commence a whole system of selective but massive repression as described and for this purpose they provided all the institutions and subordinate persons within the hierarchy with all the means which were not formally legal as well as the illegal means necessary and the impunity required – there is no exercise of '*ius puniendi*' by the State, its institutions not only inciting but also co-ordinating the campaign of terror – to undertake the task entrusted. Thus, a system of summary executions without trial was established, with mass burials in unidentified places, clandestine detention centres which operated as concentration camps, a 'scientific' system of torture was designed, and organisations like the DINA and the CNI were established to carry out paramilitary activity. In order to carry out such action within and outside the country, a system of international terrorist co-ordination was designed to obtain support and assistance from other countries or other terrorist organisations in order to eliminate or unlawfully hand over prisoners who were subsequently executed (Condor Plan).

At the head of this organisational chart of terror was allegedly Augusto Pinochet Ugarte, who although not participating in the material execution of the acts did conceive the plan and finance it with public funds from the State itself, whose power he usurped and exercised together with other high-ranking officers of the Governing Junta from 11 September 1973 onwards.

The alleged participation of Augusto Pinochet as instigator in the prior action giving rise to the criminal acts (illegal arrests, murders, disappearances, torture) is clear; a) is direct and authority is exercised over certain persons. As Head of the Governing Junta and President of the Republic he had the power to bring the situation to an end immediately, but instead he incited and encouraged it by giving the relevant orders to his subordinates, sometimes even directly exercising absolute control over the execution of an act from the position of sole Head of the DINA; b) is for the purpose of the commission of certain offences such as those listed to which should be added the misappropriation of public resources by using public funds for illegal or criminal purposes, or offences against property arising from the violent seizure of the property of the victims; c) against clearly defined persons who comprise those listed in this order and all those who have not been identified but who have a real identity and importance and who were victims of the criminal action described; d) is also effective and is the cause of the perpetrator's decision to commit the act, who receives the order from the higher-ranking military officers, the latter in turn receiving orders from the members of the Governing Junta; e) is open, clear and undisguised as shown by the course of events and the absence of criminal sanctions or even the slightest administrative sanctions; f) is intentional, since one cannot seriously say there was ignorance, error or negligence, but rather awareness and the will to directly execute acts; and g) is followed by the execution of the crime agreed, an aspect which at this stage does not need to be stated more explicitly.

Augusto Pinochet, in his role as Director of the criminal plan provisionally established, as already mentioned, performed a series of necessary, irreplaceable and essential acts, without which there would have been no commission, persistence in, and continuance of, the criminal conduct, which was carried out in accordance with the previously agreed plan under which each of the participants played their respective roles which they had assumed and in which they could hardly be replaced according to 'the theory of scarce resources'. In fact, the members of the Governing Junta, the high-ranking officers involved, in particular, those of the intelligence services or those who fulfilled orders of their immediate superiors, can hardly escape being considered co-perpetrators. However, undoubtedly this description cannot be avoided in the case of Augusto Pinochet Ugarte (Arts. 27 and 28 of the Penal Code).

Twelve. The list of indicia which have been mainly taken into account in drawing up this order is as follows:
[List of 107 indicia]

Thirteen. Since in the light of the indicia and reasoning set forth, the acts and alleged crimes described are attributable to Augusto Pinochet Ugarte, he must be indicted in accordance with Article 384 of the Criminal Procedure Law. Furthermore, having regard to the fact that extradition proceedings against him are currently pending, it is necessary to maintain the defendant in provisional custody given the risk that he might evade justice; this is a definite risk in the light of the declarations formally made by representatives of the Chilean Government – Minister for Foreign Affairs – in our own country. Therefore, the measure becomes necessary under Articles 503, 504 and 539 of the Criminal Procedure Law without prejudice to what may be appropriate once he has been made available to the Spanish Courts and has complied with the requirement to appear before the Court imposed by Article 504 *bis* 2 of the Criminal Procedure Law.

Fourteen. In accordance with the provisions of Article 589 et seq. of the Criminal Procedure Law, any civil liability which may ultimately be established must be secured, but this can only be done when such liability is duly quantified. At present it is sufficient to issue a provisional declaration of such liability and ratify the attachment of the defendant's property and accounts imposed by the order of 19 October 1998.

Whereas having regard to the aforementioned articles and any other relevant articles of general application

I. Order

1. The Indictment of Augusto Ugarte Pinochet for the acts and alleged crimes established in this order, who will hereinafter be notified as a party to the proceedings once he is made available to this Court.
2. Notify him of the writ and take his declaration.
3. The ratification of the unconditional, provisional detention of the defendant in custody and the international warrant of arrest based on the facts contained in this order.
4. A provisional declaration, without prejudice to any declaration ultimately made, of the defendant's civil liability, and ratification of the attachment ordered on 19 October 1998.
5. That a certificate of the defendant's convictions and of any summons issued and charges pending against him be furnished (hoja histôrico-penal).
6. That an attested copy of this order be sent to the English Judicial Authorities through diplomatic channels, without prejudice to the right to send said order by fax, when translated.

Notify this order to the Public Prosecutor's Office and all other parties in the proceedings.

The Hon. Mr. Baltasar Garzôn Real, Judge of the Fifth Central Magistrates' Court of the National Court sitting in Madrid, so resolves, orders and signs. I certify.
Execution. What has been decided is hereupon fulfilled. I certify.

7. 1 NATIONAL POLICY STATEMENTS

☞ USA: Department of Defense Law of War Program

Directive, 9 December 1998
G-C, DoD
Subject: DoD Law of War Program
References:
(a) DoD Directive 5100.77, 'DoD Law of War Program', 10 July 1979 (hereby cancelled)
(b) DoD Directive 2310.1, 'DoD Program for Enemy Prisoners of War (EPOW) and other Detainees (Short Title: DoD Enemy POW Detainee Program)', 18 August 1994
(c) DoD Directive 5000.1 'Defense Acquisition', 15 March 1996
(d) Hague Convention No. IV, 'Respecting the Laws and Customs of War on Land', 18 October 1907
(e) through (1), see enclosure 1

1. Reissuance and Purpose
This Directive:
1.1. Reissues reference (a) to update policy and responsibilities in the Department of Defense for a program to ensure DoD compliance with the law of war obligations of the United States.
1.2. Expands the responsibilities of the Secretary of the Army as the DoD Executive Agent for the investigation and reporting of reportable incidents.
1.3. Establishes the DoD Law of War Working Group.

2. Applicability and Scope
2.1. This Directive applies to the Office of the Secretary of Defense, the Military Departments, the Chairman of the Joint Chiefs of Staff, the Combatant Commands, the Defense Agencies, and the DoD Field Activities (hereafter referred to collectively as the DoD Components).
2.2. In implementation of this Directive, reference (b) addresses the DoD program for care and treatment of enemy prisoners of war (EPW), retained persons, and detainees. A reportable incident (as defined in subsection 3.2., below) involving possible, suspected, or alleged violations of the protections afforded EPWs, retained persons, or detainees is included in the scope of this Directive.
2.3. In further implementation of this Directive, that part of the law of war relating to legal reviews of the development, acquisition, and procurement of weapons and weapon systems for the DoD Components is addressed in DoD Directive 5000. 1 (reference (c)) and in related guidance pertaining to Special Access Programs.

3. Definitions

3.1. Law of War. That part of international law that regulates the conduct of armed hostilities. It is often called the law of armed conflict. The law of war encompasses all international law for the conduct of hostilities binding on the United States or its individual citizens, including treaties and international agreements to which the United States is a party, and applicable customary international law.

3.2. Reportable Incident. A possible, suspected, or alleged violation of the law of war.

4. Policy

It is DoD policy to ensure that:

4.1. The law of war obligations of the United States are observed and enforced by the DoD Components.

4.2. An effective program to prevent violations of the law of war is implemented by the DoD Components.

4.3. All reportable incidents committed by or against US or enemy persons are promptly reported, thoroughly investigated, and, where appropriate, remedied by corrective action.

4.4. All reportable incidents committed by or against allied persons, or by or against other persons during a conflict to which the US is not a party, are reported through command channels for ultimate transmission to appropriate US Agencies, allied governments, or other appropriate authorities. Once it has been determined that US persons are not involved in a reportable incident, an additional US investigation shall be continued only at the direction of the appropriate Combatant Commander. On-scene commanders shall ensure that measures are taken to preserve evidence of reportable incidents pending turnover to US, allied, or other appropriate authorities.

5. Responsibilities

5.1. The General Council of the Department of Defense shall:

5.1.1. Provide overall legal guidance in the Department of Defense on the Law of War Program, to include review of policies developed under or relating to the program, co-ordination of special legislative proposals and other legal matters with other Federal Departments and Agencies, and resolution of disagreements on questions of law.

5.1.2. Establish a DoD Law of War Working Group consisting of representatives from the General Counsel of the Department of Defense (GC, DoD), the Legal Counsel to the Chairman of the Joint Chiefs of Staff, the International and Operational Law Division of the Office of the Judge Advocate General of each Military Department, and the Operational Law Branch of the Office of the Staff Judge Advocate to the Commandant of the Marine Corps. The DoD Law of War Working Group shall develop and co-ordinate law of war initiatives and issues, manage other law of war matters as they arise, and provide advice to the General Counsel on legal matters covered by this Directive.

5.1.3. Co-ordinate and monitor the Military Departments' plans and policies for training and education in the law of war.

5.2. The Under Secretary of Defense for Policy shall:

5.2.1. Exercise primary staff responsibility for the DoD Law of War Program.

5.2.2. Ensure that the Assistant Secretary of Defense (International Security Affairs) shall provide overall development, co-ordination, approval, and promulgation of major DoD policies and plans, including final co-ordination of such proposed policies and plans with DoD Components and other Federal Departments and Agencies as necessary, and final co-ordination of DoD positions on international negotiations on the law of war and U.S. signature or ratification of law of war treaties.

5.3. The Heads of the DoD Components shall:

5.3.1. Ensure that the members of their Components comply with the law of war during all armed conflicts, however such conflicts are characterized, and with the principles and spirit of the law of war during all other operations.

5.3.2. Institute and implement effective programs to prevent violations of the law of war, including law of war training and dissemination, as required by references (d) through (h).

5.3.3. Ensure that qualified legal advisers are immediately available at all levels of command to provide advice about law of war compliance during planning and execution of exercises and operations; and institute and implement programs to comply with the reporting requirements established in section 6., below.

5.4. The Assistant Secretary of public affairs shall monitor the public affairs aspects of the DoD Law Of War Program and provide public affairs guidance, as appropriate, to the DoD Components.

5.5. The Secretaries of the Military Departments shall develop internal policies and procedures consistent with this Directive in support of the DoD Law of War Program to:

5.5.1. Provide directives, publications, instructions, and training so that the principles and rules of the law of war will be known to members of their respective Departments, the extent of such knowledge to be commensurate with each individual's duties and responsibilities.

5.5.2. Ensure that programs are implemented in their respective Military Departments to prevent violations of the law of war, emphasizing any types of violations that have been reported under this Directive.

5.5.3. Provide for the prompt reporting and investigation of reportable incidents committed by or against members of their respective Military Departments, or persons accompanying them, in accordance with directives issued under paragraph 5.8.4., below.

5.5.4. Where appropriate, provide for disposition, under the Uniform Code of Military Justice (reference (i)), of cases involving alleged violations of the law of war by members of their respective Military Departments who are subject to court-martial jurisdiction.

5.5.5. Provide for the central correction of reports and investigations of reportable incidents alleged to have been committed by or against members of their respective Military Departments, or persons accompanying them.

5.5.6. Ensure that all reports of reportable incidents are forwarded to the Secretary of the Army in his or her capacity as the DoD Executive Agent under subsection 5.6., below.

5.6. The Secretary of the Army, as the Executive Agent for the Secretary of Defense for reportable incidents, shall act for the Secretary of Defense in developing and co-ordinating plans and policies for, and in supervising the execution of, the investigation of reportable incidents and, subject to DoD 8910.1-M (reference (j)), the collection, recording, and reporting of information concerning reportable incidents. This authority is separate from and subject to the responsibilities assigned the Combatant Commanders in subsections 4.4., above, and 5.8., below, and the responsibilities assigned the Secretaries of the Military Departments in subsection 5.5.1., above.

5.7. The Chairman of the Joint Chiefs of Staff shall:

5.7.1. Provide appropriate guidance to the Commanders of the Combatant Commands, consistent with 10 USC 163 (a)(2) (reference (k)), conforming with the policies and procedures in this Directive. This guidance will include direction on the collection and investigation of reports of enemy violations of the law of war.

5.7.2. Designate a primary point of contact in his organization to administer activities under this Directive.

5.7.3. Issue and review appropriate plans, policies, directives, and rules of engagement, as necessary, ensuring their consistency with the law of war obligations of the United States.

5.7.4. Ensure that plans, policies, directives, and rules of engagement issued by the Commanders of the Combatant Commands are Consistent with this Directive, and the law of war.

5.8. The Commanders of the Combatant Commands shall:

5.8.1. Institute effective programs within their respective commands to prevent violations of the law of war and ensure that their commands' plans, policies, directives, and rules of engagement are subject to periodic review and evaluation, particularly in light of any violations reported.

5.8.2. Implement guidance from the Chairman of the Joint Chiefs of Staff for the collection and investigation of reports of enemy violations of the law of war.

5.8.3. Designate the command legal adviser to supervise the administration of those aspects of this program dealing with possible, suspected or alleged enemy violations of the law of war.

5.8.4. Issue directives to ensure that reportable incidents involving US or enemy persons are reported promptly to appropriate authorities, are thoroughly investigated, and the results of such investigations are promptly forwarded to the applicable Military Department or other appropriate authorities.

5.8.5. Determine the extent and manner in which a reportable incident not involving US or enemy persons will be investigated by US forces and ensure that such incidents are reported promptly to appropriate US Agencies, allied governments, or other appropriate authorities.

5.8.6. Ensure all plans, policies, directives, and rules of engagement issued by the command and its subordinate commands and components are reviewed by legal advisers to ensure their consistency with this Directive and the law of war.

5.8.7. Ensure that law of war training and dissemination programs of subordinate commands and components are consistent with this Directive and the law of war obligations of the United States.

5.9. The Assistant Secretary of Defense for Command, Control, Communications and Intelligence shall ensure that the Director, Defense Intelligence Agency, shall provide information from the intelligence community to the Secretary of the Army and to the Commanders of the Combatant Commands, consistent with their respective obligations under subsections 5.6. and 5.8., above, concerning reportable incidents perpetrated against captured or detained US persons, or committed by or against US allies, or committed by or against other persons during a conflict to which the United States is not a party.

6. Information Requests

6.1. Reports of Incidents. All military and civilian personnel assigned to or accompanying a DoD Component shall report reportable incidents through their chain of command. Such reports also may also be made through other channels, such as the military police, a judge advocate, or an Inspector General. Reports that are made to officials other than those specified in this subsection shall, nonetheless, be accepted and immediately forwarded through the recipient's chain of command.

6.2. Initial Report. The commander of any unit that obtains information about a reportable incident shall immediately report the incident through command channels to higher authority. The initial report shall be made through the most expeditious means available.

6.3. Higher authorities receiving an initial report shall:

6.3.1. Request a formal investigation by the cognizant military investigation authority.

6.3.2. Submit a report of any reportable incident, by the most expeditious means available, through command channels, to the responsible Combatant Commander. Normally, an OPREP-3 report, established in Joint Pub 1-03.6, Joint Reporting System, Event/Incident Reports (E/IR), will be required. Copies of the E/IR shall be provided to the DoD Component officials designated by the Heads of the DoD Components concerned.

6.3.3. Submit a report, in accordance with DoD Instruction 5240.4 (reference (1)), concerning any criminal case, regardless of the allegation, that has received, is expected to receive, or which, if disclosed, could reasonably be expected to receive, significant media interest.

6.4. The Combatant Commander shall report, by the most expeditious means available, all reportable incidents to the Chairman of the Joint Chiefs of Staff, the Secretary of Defense, and the Secretary of the Army in his role as the Executive Agent under subsection 5.6., above.

6.5. DoD Notifications. Notifications of a reportable incident shall be forwarded to the Chairman of the Joint Chiefs of Staff; the GC, DoD; the Assistant Secretary of Defense for Public Affairs; and the Director General of the Department of Defense, who will inform their counterparts in any Military Service or Department concerned.

6.6. Information Requirements. The Event/Incident Reports referred to in this Directive and further described in reference (1) are exempt from licensing in accordance with paragraph 5.4.2. of DoD 8910.1-M (reference (j)).

7. Effective Date and Implementation

This Directive is effective immediately. Forward two copies of implementing documents to the General Counsel of the Department of Defense and the Under Secretary of Defense for Policy within 120 days.

Enclosures – 1

E1. References, continued

E1.ENCLOSURE I

REFERENCES, continued

(e) Geneva Convention for the Amelioration of the Condition of the Wounded and Sick in Armed Forces in the Field, 12 August 1949

(f) Geneva Convention for Amelioration of the Condition of the Wounded, Sick and Shipwrecked Members of the Armed Forces at Sea, 12 August 1949

(g) Geneva Convention Relative to the Treatment of Prisoners of War, 12 August 1949

(h) Geneva Convention Relative to the Protection of Civilian Persons in Time of War, 12 August 1949

(i) Sections 801-940 of title 10, United States Code, 'Uniform Code of Military Justice'

(j) DoD 8910.1-.m 'DoD Procedures for Management of Information Requirements,' June 1998, authorized by DoD Directive 8910.1, 11 June 1993

(k) Section 163(a)(2) of title 10, United States Code

(l) DoD Instruction 5240.4, 'Reporting of Counterintelligence and Criminal Violations,' 22 September 1992

7.21   NATIONAL LEGISLATION TO IMPLEMENT IHL TREATIES

☞ Belgium: 10 February 1999 – Act relating to the repression of serious violations of international humanitarian law[4]

Albert II, King of the Belgians,

To all, present and to come, I salute you.

The Chambers have adopted and We sanction the following:

Article 1

The present Act regulates the matter referred to in Article 78 of the Constitution.

Article 2

The heading of the Act of 16 June 1993 relating to the punishment of grave breaches of the International Conventions of Geneva of 12 August 1949 and to the Protocols I and II of 8 June 1977, additional to these Conventions is replaced by the following heading:

'Act relating to the punishment of grave breaches of international humanitarian Law'.

Article 3

To the first Article of the same Act the following amendments are made:

A. A 1st Paragraph is inserted, written as follows:

'1st paragraph. The crime of genocide, such as defined hereafter, constitutes a crime of international law and is punished in accordance with the provisions of the present Act, whether committed in times of peace or in times of war. In accordance with the Convention for the prevention and the punishment of the crime of genocide of December 1948, and without prejudice to the criminal provisions applicable to the breaches committed by negligence, the crime of genocide is included in any of the acts hereafter, committed with the intention to destroy, as a whole or part of, a national, ethnical, racial or religious group such as:

1. Murder of members of the group;

2. Grave assault to the physical or mental integrity of members of the group;

---

4. Editor's Note: The 1993 Law which the 1999 Law amends is reprinted directly below. Although it falls outside the period of coverage of volume 2, it was felt that for clarity and convenience, and because of its importance, it would be useful to make an exception and include it here.

3. Intentional subjection of the group to living conditions which lead to its total or partial physical destruction;

4. Measures aiming at impeding births within the group;

5. The forced transfer of children to another group.'

B. A 2nd Paragraph is inserted, written as follows:

'2nd paragraph. The crime against humanity, such as defined hereafter, constitutes a crime of international law and is punished in accordance with the provisions of the present Act, whether committed in times of peace or in times of war. In accordance with the Statute of the International Criminal Court, crime against humanity is included in any of the acts hereafter, committed within the framework of a general or systematic attack launched against a civilian population and with full knowledge of this attack:

1. murder;

2. extermination;

3. subjection to slavery;

4. deportation or forced transfer of the population;

5. imprisonment or other forms of grave deprivation of physical liberty in breach of fundamental provisions of international law;

6. torture;

7. rape, sexual slavery, forced prostitution, forced pregnancies, forced sterilisation and all other forms of sexual violence of comparable gravity;

8. persecution of any group or of any identifiable community for motives of political, racial, national, ethnical, cultural, religious or sexist nature or according to other criteria universally recognised as inadmissible in international law, connected to all acts aimed at in the present Act.'

C. The present text of the 1st Article becomes the 3rd Paragraph.

Article 4

The 2nd Article of the same Act is replaced by what follows:

'2nd Article. The breaches listed in the 1st and 2nd Paragraphs of the 1st Article and in the Nrs. 1, 2 and 11 to 15 of the 3rd Paragraph of the 1st Article are punished by life sentence.

The breaches listed in Nrs. 3 and 10 of the 3rd Paragraph of the same Article are punished by imprisonment of twenty to thirty years. The breaches are punished by life sentence if they have resulted in the death of one or more persons.

The breaches listed in Nr. 8 of the 3rd Paragraph of the same Article is punished by imprisonment of fifteen to twenty years. The same breach as well as the one referred to in Nr. 16 of the 3rd Paragraph of the same Article are punished by imprisonment of twenty to thirty years if they have resulted in either a seemingly incurable illness, a permanent disability to work, the complete loss of the use of an organ, or a serious mutilation. They are punished by life sentence if they have resulted in the death of one or more persons. The breaches listed in the Nrs. 4 to 7 and 17 of the 3rd Paragraph of the same Article are punished by imprisonment of ten to fifteen years. In the case of aggravating circumstances provided for in the preceding paragraph, they are punished, in accordance with the case, by sentences provided for in that paragraph.

The breaches listed in Nrs. 18 to 20 of the 3rd Paragraph of the same Article are punished by imprisonment of ten to fifteen years, with reservation of the application of the strictest criminal provisions that punish the grave assaults on the dignity of a person.

The breach provided for in Nr. 9 of the 3rd Paragraph of the same Article is punished by imprisonment of ten to fifteen years. It is punished by imprisonment of fifteen to twenty years when it has led to serious consequences to the public health.'

Article 5
To the 5th Article of the same Act the following amendments are made:
A. In the first Paragraph, the words 'of the 3rd Paragraph' are inserted after the words 'Nrs. 9, 12, and 13';
B. In the 2nd Paragraph, the words: 'of the crime of genocide or of a crime against humanity, such as defined by the present Act, or' are inserted after the words 'to lead to perpetration';
C. The Article is completed by the 3rd Paragraph, written as follows:
'3rd Paragraph. The immunity granted to the official position of a person does not prevent the application of the present Act.'

Let us promulgate the present Act, let us order that the Act be affixed with the seal of the State and published by the *Moniteur Belge*.

Done in Brussels, 10 February 1999.
Albert
For the King:
The Minister of Justice T. van Parys

☛ **Belgium: Act of 16 June 1993 on the punishment of serious violations of the international Conventions of Geneva of 12 August 1949 and to the Protocols I and II of 8 June 1977, additional to these Conventions (M. B. 5 August 1993)**

First chapter. Serious violations
Article 1
They are crimes of international law and are punished in accordance with the provisions of the present Act, the serious violations referred to hereafter, that infringe upon the rights, by action or omission, of the persons and the goods protected by the Conventions signed in Geneva on August 12th 1949 and passed by the Act of September 3rd 1952 and by the Protocols I and II, additional to these Conventions, adopted in Geneva June 8th 1977 and passed by the Act of April 1986, without prejudice to the criminal regulations applicable to the other violations to the Conventions referred to by the present Act and without prejudice to the criminal regulations applicable to the violations committed by negligence:
1. intentional homicide;
2. torture or other inhuman treatments including biological experiments;
3. the fact of intentionally causing great suffering or serious harm to the physical integrity and the health;
4. the fact of forcing into serving in the armed forces of the enemy or of the adverse party a prisoner of war, a civilian protected by the Convention relating to civilians in times of war or a person protected in that same respect by the Protocols I and II additional to the international Conventions of Geneva of August 12th 1949;

5. the fact of depriving a prisoner of war, a civilian protected by the Convention on the protection of civilians in times of war or a person protected in that same respect, by the Protocols I and II additional to the international Conventions of Geneva of 12 August 1949, of his right of being judged properly and impartially under the prescriptions of these provisions;

6. the deportation, the transfer or the unlawful displacement, the unlawful detention of a civilian protected by the Convention on the protection of civilians in times of war or a person protected in those same respects by the Protocols I and II additional to the international Conventions of Geneva of 12 August 1949;

7. the taking of hostages;

8. the destruction and the appropriation of goods, not justified by military necessity such as permitted under international law and executed on a large scale in an unlawful and arbitrary manner;

9. the acts and omission, not legally justified, that are likely to damage the health and the physical and mental integrity of persons protected by one of the Conventions relating to the protection of the wounded and sick and the shipwrecked, in particular any medical act that will not be justified by the state of the health of these persons or that will not be in accordance with the generally recognised rules of the medical profession;

10. unless they are justified under the conditions provided for under nr. 9, the acts that consist in inflicting to the persons referred to in nr. 9, even with their consent, physical mutilations, medical or scientific experiences or the removing of tissue or organs for transplantations, unless it concerns donations of blood for transfusions or donations of skin destined for grafts, to the extent that these donations are voluntary, consented and destined for the purpose of treatment;

11. the fact of submitting a civilian population or civilians to an attack;

12. the fact of launching an indiscriminate attack against the civilian population or goods of civilian origin, while knowing that this attack will cause loss of human lives, injuries to civilians or damages to goods of civilian origin, that would seem excessive compared to the actual and immediate expected military advantage, without prejudice to the criminality of the attack of which the harmful effects, even if proportionate to the expected military advantage, would be incompatible with the principles of international law, such as have resulted from established customs, the principles of humanity and the demands of the public conscience;

13. the fact of launching an attack against works or installations that contain dangerous forces, while knowing that this attack will cause the loss of human lives, injuries to civilians or damages to goods of civilian origin, that would be excessive compared to the expected actual and military advantage, without prejudice to the criminality of the attack of which the harmful effects even if proportionate to the expected military advantage would be incompatible with the principles of international law, such as have resulted from established customs, the principles of humanity and the demands of the public conscience;

14. the fact of submitting to an attack undefended localities or demilitarised zones;

15. the fact of submitting a person to an attack while knowing he is out of combat;

16. the fact of perfidiously using the distinctive sign of the Red Cross or of the Red Crescent or of other signs of protectors recognised by the Conventions and the Protocols I and II additional to these Conventions;

17. the transfer into occupied territory of a part of the civilian population by the occupying force, in the case of an international armed conflict, or by the occupying authority in the case of a non-international armed conflict;

18. the fact of delaying without any justification the repatriation of prisoners of war or of civilians;

19. the fact of applying the practices of *apartheid* or other inhuman or degrading practices based on racial discrimination and causing outrages against the personal dignity;

20. the fact of directing attacks against historical monuments, works of clearly recognised art or cultural sites which represent the cultural or spiritual heritage of a people and to whom a special protection has been granted in accordance with a specific agreement while no proof exists of violation by the adverse party of the ban on the use of these goods for support of the military effort, and while these goods are not located in the near proximity of military objectives.

The facts referred to under nrs. 11, 12, 13, 14, 15, and 16 are considered as serious violations under the present Article if they lead to death or cause a serious assault on the physical integrity or on the health of one or more persons.

2. The violations listed in the nrs. 1, 2 and 11 to 15 of the first article are punished by the highest possible sentence provided for in criminal matters by the Military Criminal Code.

The violations listed in the nrs. 3 and 10 of the same Article are punished with life sentence of forced labour. They are punished by the highest possible sentence provided for in criminal matters by the Military Criminal Code if they have resulted in the death of one or more persons.

The violation referred to in nr. 8 of the same Article is punished by forced labour of fifteen to twenty years. This violation as well as the one referred to in nr. 16 of the same Article are punished by forced labour for life if they have resulted in either a seemingly incurable illness or in a permanent disability to work, or in the loss of complete use of an organ or a serious mutilation. They are punished by the highest possible sentence provided for in criminal matters by the Military Criminal Code if they have resulted in the death of one or more persons.

The violations listed in nrs. 4 to 7 and 17 of the same Article are punished by a term of forced labour. In the case of aggravating circumstances provided for in the previous paragraph, they will be punished, in accordance with the case, with sentences set in that paragraph.

The violations listed in the nrs. 18 to 20 of the same Article are punished with forced labour of ten to fifteen years, with the reservation of the application of more severe criminal provisions punishing grave assaults on the dignity of a person.

The violation provided for in nr. 9 of the same Article is punished by forced labour of ten to fifteen years. The violation is punished with forced labour of fifteen to twenty years if it has resulted in serious consequences to the public health.

3. Those who manufacture, keep or transport an instrument, device or any object, erect a building or transform an existing building, while knowing that the instrument, device, object, building or transformation is destined to commit one of the violations provided for in the first Article or to facilitate the perpetration, are punished with a

sentence provided for the violation of which they have allowed or facilitated the perpetration.

4. To be punished with a sentence provided for the committed violation:

— the order, even when not followed by any effect, to commit one of the violations provided for by Article 1;

— the proposal or offer to commit such an offence and the acceptance of such a proposition or offer;

— the provocation to commit such an offence, even when not followed by effect;

— the complicity, in accordance with Article 66 and 67 of the Criminal Code, in such an offence, even when not followed by any effect;

— the omission to act, within the limits of their possibilities of action, on the part of those that had knowledge of the orders issued for the execution of such an violation or of facts by which the execution begins, and could have prevented the commission or could have put an end to it;

— the attempt, in accordance with Articles 51 to 53 of the Criminal Code, to commit such a violation.

5. 1. No interest, no necessity of political, military or national nature, can justify, even as reprisals, the violations provided for by Articles 1, 3 and 4 without prejudice to the exceptions mentioned in Nrs. 9, 12 and 13 of the first Article.

2. The fact that the accused has acted on the order of his government or of a superior does not relieve him of his responsibility if, in the existing circumstances, the order could obviously lead to the perpetration of a serious violation of the Conventions of Geneva of August 12th 1949 and to their first additional Protocol of June 8th 1977.

6. Without prejudice to the Articles 4 and 8 of the present Act, all provisions of the first book of the Criminal Code, with the exception of Article 70, are applicable to the offences provided for by the present Act.

Chapter II. On the competence, the procedure and the execution of the sentences

7. The Belgian jurisdictions are competent to judge the violations laid down by the present Act, irrespective of the place where these have been committed.

As regards violations committed in a foreign country by a Belgian against a foreigner, the complaint of the foreigner or of his family or the official opinion of the authority of the country where the violation has been committed, is not required.

8. Article 21 of the Preliminary Title of the Criminal Procedures Code and Article 91 of the Criminal Code relating to the prescription of public action and sentences are not applicable to the violations laid down in the first Article by the present Act.

9.1 With reservation of Articles 99 to 108 of the Convention of Geneva relating to the Treatment of Prisoners of War of August 12th 1949, of Article 75 of the Additional Protocol I and of Article 6 of the additional Protocol II of June 8th 1977, the violations provided for by the present Act fall, when Belgium is at war, within the competence of the military jurisdiction.

2. When a violation that falls within the competence of the regular jurisdiction, is related to a violation that comes by virtue of nr. 1 of the present Article under the competence of the military jurisdiction, each of these violations is judged by the military jurisdiction.

3. When a violation laid down in the present Act falls within the competence of the military jurisdiction, the public action is put into effect either by the summons of the accused by the Public Prosecutor before the jurisdiction of judgement or by a complaint

of any person that claims being wronged by the violation and who will institute a civil action before the President of the Judiciary Commission on the bench of the Council of War under the conditions as laid down in Article 66 of the Code of Criminal Procedure.

In this last case, the decision not to prosecute can only be taken by the Council of War made up of only one civilian member assisted by the clerk of the court or by the Military Court made up of only its president and of two of its military members who have the rank of major, assisted by a clerk of the court, without prejudice to the application of Articles 111 to 113, 140 and 147 of the Code of Military Criminal Procedure. This decision will only be pronounced, having heard the claims of the Public Prosecutor, under the conditions laid down in Article 128 of the Code of Criminal Procedure or when the public action is not admissible; it will include conviction of the plaintiff to the expenses stated by the State and by the accused. The procedure of referral to the discipline of the corps laid down in Article 24(1) of the Code of Military Criminal Procedure, is never applicable to the violations provided for by the present Act.

☛ Ireland: Geneva Conventions (Amendment) Act, 1998, Number 35 of 1998

[...]
Geneva Conventions (Amendment) Act, 1998

An Act to enable effect to be given to the Protocols Additional to the Geneva Conventions of 1949 adopted at Geneva on 8 June 1977 and for that purpose to amend the Geneva Conventions Act, 1962, the Red Cross Acts 1938-1954, and section 1 of the Prisoners of War and Enemy Aliens Act, 1956, and to Provide for Connected Matters, [13th July, 1998]

Be it enacted by the Oireachtas as follows:
(Definition)
1. In this Act 'the Principal Act' means the Geneva Conventions Act, 1962.

(Amendment of section 2 of Principal Act)
2. The Principal Act is hereby amended by the substitution for section 2 of the following section:
2. In this Act:
'court' does not include a court-martial;
'International Fact-Finding Commission' means the International Fact-Finding Commission established under Article 90 of Protocol I;
'the Minister' means the Minister for Foreign Affairs;
'protected internee' means a person protected by the Convention set out in the Fourth Schedule to this Act and Protocol 1 and interned in the State;
'protected prisoner of war' means a person protected by the Convention set out in the Third Schedule to this Act (including a person protected as a prisoner of war under Protocol I) or a person entitled under Protocol 1 to the same protection as a prisoner of war;
'the protecting power', in relation to a protected prisoner of war or a protected internee, means the power or organisation which is carrying out, in the interests of the power of which he or she is a national, or of whose forces he or she is, or was at any material time, a member, the duties assigned to protecting powers under the Convention

set out in the Third Schedule to this Act, the Convention set out in the Fourth Schedule to this Act or Protocol I;

'Protocol I' means the Protocol, additional to the Geneva Conventions of 12 August 1949, and relating to the Protection of Victims of International Armed Conflicts (Protocol I) adopted at Geneva on 8 June 1977, the text of which is set out in the Fifth Schedule to this Act;

'Protocol II' means the Protocol, additional to the Geneva Conventions of 12 August 1949, and relating to the Protection of Victims of Non International Armed Conflicts (Protocol II) adopted at Geneva on 8 June 1977, the text of which is set out in the Sixth Schedule to this Act;

'the Scheduled Conventions' means the Conventions set out in the Schedules to this Act.'

(Amendment of section 3 of Principal Act)

3. – Section 3 (which relates to grave breaches of the Scheduled Conventions) of the Principal Act is hereby amended by the substitution for subsection (1) (as amended by section 10 of the Criminal Justice Act, 1964), of the following subsections:

'(l) Any person, whatever his or her nationality, who, whether in or outside the State, commits or aids, abets or procures the commission by any other person of a grave breach of any of the Scheduled Conventions or Protocol I shall be guilty of an offence and on conviction on indictment –

(a) in the case of a grave breach involving the wilful killing of a person protected by the Convention or Protocol in question, shall be liable to imprisonment for life or any less term,

(b) in the case of any other grave breach, shall be liable to imprisonment for a term not exceeding 14 years.

(1A) Any person, whatever his or her nationality, who, whether in or outside the State, fails to act, when under a duty to do so, to prevent the commission by another person of a grave breach of any of the Scheduled Conventions or Protocol I shall be guilty of an offence and on conviction on indictment shall be liable to imprisonment for a term not exceeding 10 years.

(1B) For the purposes of this section –

(a) a grave breach of any of the Scheduled Conventions is anything referred to as a grave breach of the Convention in the relevant Article, that is to say-

(i) in the case of the Convention set out in the First Schedule to this Act, Article 50,

(ii) in the case of the Convention set out in the Second Schedule to this Act, Article 51,

(iii) in the case of the Convention set out in the Third Schedule to this Act, Article 130,

(iv) in the case of the Convention set out in the Fourth S.3 Schedule to this Act, Article 147, and

(b) a grave breach of Protocol 1 is anything referred to as a grave breach of the Protocol in paragraph 4 of Article 11, or paragraph 2, 3 or 4 of Article 85, of the Protocol.

(Amendment of section 4 of Principal Act)

4. – (l) Section 4 (which relates to minor breaches of the Scheduled Conventions) of the Principal Act is hereby amended by –

(a) in subsection (1), the insertion after 'scheduled Conventions' of 'or of Protocol I or Protocol II',

(b) the insertion after subsection (1) of the following subsection:

'(1A) Any person, whatever his or her nationality, who, in the State, fails to act, when under a duty to do so, to prevent the commission by another person of a minor breach of any of the Scheduled Conventions or Protocol 1 or Protocol II shall be guilty of an offence.'

(c) in subsection (2), the insertion after 'scheduled Conventions' of 'or of Protocol I or Protocol II',

(d) the insertion after subsection (2) of the following subsection:

'(2A) Any citizen of Ireland who, outside the State, fails to act, when under a duty to do so, to prevent the commission by another person of a minor breach of any of the Scheduled Conventions or Protocol 1 or Protocol II shall be guilty of an offence.'

(e) in paragraph (a) of subsection (3), the substitution for 'six' of '12' and for 'fifty pounds' of '£1,500',

(f) in paragraph (b) of subsection (3), the substitution for 'three hundred pounds' of '£15,000', and

(g) the substitution for subsection (4) of the following:

'(4) In this section 'minor breach' means –

(a) contravention of a provision of any of the Scheduled Conventions or of Protocol I which is not any such grave breach of that Convention or that Protocol as is mentioned in the relevant Article thereof referred to in section 3 of this Act, or

(b) a contravention of Protocol II.'

(2) Notwithstanding section 10 (4) of the Petty Sessions (Ireland) Act, 1851, summary proceedings for an offence under section 4 of the Principal Act may be instituted within two years from the date of the offence.

(Substitution of section 5 of Principal Act)

5. – The Principal Act is hereby amended by the substitution for section 5 of the following section:

'5. If, in any proceedings under this Act in respect of any breach of any of the Scheduled Conventions or of Protocol I or Protocol II, a question arises under Article 2 or 3 of any of the Scheduled Conventions or Article 1 or 3 of Protocol I or Article 1 of Protocol II (which relate to the circumstances in which the Conventions and Protocols apply), that question shall be determined by the Minister and a certificate purporting to set out any such determination and to be signed by or on behalf of the Minister shall be received in evidence and be deemed to be so signed, without further proof, unless the contrary is shown.'

(Judicial notice of report of International Fact Finding Commission)

6. – The Principal Act is hereby amended by the insertion after section 5 of the following section:

'5A. In any proceedings under this Act, judicial report of notice shall be taken of a report of the International Fact-Finding Commission, submitted under paragraph 5 of Article 90 of Protocol I.'

(Additional Schedules to Principal Act)

7. – The Principal Act is hereby amended by the insertion after the Fourth Schedule thereto of the Schedules set out in the Schedule to this Act as the Fifth and Sixth Schedules to the Principal Act.

(Certification by order of any reservation or declaration to Protocol I or Protocol II)
8. – (1) If the ratification by the State of Protocol I or Protocol II is subject to any reservation or accompanied by a declaration –
(a) the Minister may by order certify that such a reservation or declaration has been made and the terms in which it was made, and
(b) the Protocol shall for the purposes of this Act be construed subject to and in accordance with any reservation or declaration so certified –
(2) If such a reservation or declaration is withdrawn (in whole or in part) the Minister may by order certify that fact and revoke or amend any order made under subsection (1) of this section containing the terms of that reservation or declaration.

(Restriction of use of civil defence international distinctive sign and other distinctive signals)
9. – (1) It shall not be lawful for any person –
(a) other than a person involved in civil defence, to use or display the sign of an equilateral blue triangle on, and completely surrounded by, an orange ground, being the international distinctive sign of civil defence,
(b) other than a person involved in the protection of works and installations containing dangerous forces (within the meaning of Article 56 of Protocol I), to use or display the sign consisting of a group of three bright orange circles of equal size, placed on the same axis, the distance between each circle being one radius, being the international special sign for works and installations containing dangerous forces, as provided for in paragraph 7 of that Article, or
(c) other than a person attached to a medical unit or transport, to use any of the distinctive signals specified in Articles 8 and 9 of Chapter III of Annex 1 to Protocol I, being the signals of identification for medical units and transports.
(2) It shall not be lawful for any person to use for the purpose of trade or business or any other purpose whatsoever, without the consent of the Minister for Defence –
(a) any design so nearly resembling the sign referred to in subsection (1)(a) of this section as to be capable of being mistaken for that sign,
(b) any design so nearly resembling the sign referred to in subsection (1)(b) of this section as to be capable of being mistaken for that sign, or
(c) any signal so nearly resembling any of the signals referred to in subsection (1)(c) of this section as to be capable of being mistaken for one of those signals.
(3) The restriction effected by subsection (1)(a) or (b) or (2) (a) or (b) of this section does not apply where a sign is used pursuant to a right acquired through the use of that sign prior to the commencement of this Act.
(4) The Minister for Defence may make regulations to supervise the display of the international distinctive sign of civil defence or of the international special sign for works and installations containing dangerous forces.
(5) A person who contravenes this section or regulations made under subsection (4) of this section shall be guilty of an offence and shall be liable on summary conviction to a fine not exceeding £1,500.

(6) On conviction for an offence under this section the Court may order the forfeiture of any sign used in the commission of the offence or anything on which the sign is displayed.

(7) Where any sign is forfeited under this section such sign shall be disposed of in accordance with the directions of the Minister for Defence and any moneys arising from any such disposition shall be paid into or disposed of for the benefit of the Exchequer in such manner as the Minister for Finance may direct.

(8) Where an offence under this section is committed by a body corporate and is proved to have been so committed with the consent or connivance of or to be attributable to any neglect on the part of any person, being a director, manager, secretary or other officer of the body corporate, or a person who was purporting to act in such capacity, that person shall, as well as the body corporate, be guilty of an offence and shall be liable to be proceeded against and punished as if he or she were guilty of the first-mentioned offence.

(9) In a prosecution for an offence under this section it shall be presumed, until the contrary is shown, that the Minister for Defence did not consent to the use for the purpose of trade or business or any other purpose whatsoever of the sign, design or signal in question.

(Regulations)
10. – (1) The Minister for Defence may, without prejudice to his or her power under section 4 (as amended by section 8 of the Red Cross Act, 1954) of the Red Cross Act, 1938, make regulations, in accordance with the provisions of any of the Scheduled Conventions, Protocol I or Protocol II, as the case may be, as he or she considers necessary for any or all of the following:
(a) prescribing the form of flags, emblems, signs, signals, designations, designs, wordings, uniforms or insignia for use for the purposes of giving effect to any of the Scheduled Conventions, Protocol I or Protocol II and regulating their use,
(b) prescribing the form of identity cards for use for the purposes of giving effect to any of the Scheduled Conventions or Chapter I or V of Annex I to Protocol I and regulating their use,
(c) prohibiting, restricting or directing the use of such flags, emblems, signs, signals, uniforms or insignia as specified in the regulations, for the purposes of giving effect to Article 38 or 39 of Protocol I or Article 12 of Protocol II.

(2) A person who contravenes or fails to comply with any regulation made under this section shall be guilty of an offence and shall be liable on summary conviction to a fine not exceeding £1,500.

(3) Every regulation made by the Minister for Defence under this section or section 9(4) of this Act shall be laid before each House of the Oireachtas as soon as may be after it is made and, if a resolution annulling the regulation is passed by either such House within the next 21 days on which that House has sat after the regulation is laid before it, the regulation shall be annulled accordingly but without prejudice to the validity of anything previously done thereunder.

(4) Every regulation made under this section may contain such incidental, supplementary and consequential provisions as appear to the Minister for Defence to be necessary.

(Identity cards for journalists)

11. – (1) The Minister may, on behalf of the Government, issue, for the purposes of Article 79 of Protocol I, an identity card, similar to the model in Annex II to Protocol I, to a journalist, referred to in that Article, whom the Minister considers to be engaged or likely to be engaged as such in dangerous professional missions in areas of armed conflict.

(2) An identity card issued under this section to a journalist may be issued to the Journalist subject to such terms or conditions as the Minister decides.

(3) The Minister may, from time to time, specify in regulations a fee to be paid by a person for the issue of an identity card under this section.

(Information cards for evacuated children)

12. – The Minister may establish a card in respect of a child evacuated under Article 78 of Protocol I, containing a photograph of the child and the information required under paragraph 3 of that Article, which shall be sent to the Central Tracing Agency of the International Committee of the Red Cross.

(Amendment of Red Cross Acts, 1938 to 1954)

13. – (l) Section 6 (1) of the Red Cross Act, 1938, is hereby amended by the substitution for 'ten pounds' of '£1,500'.

(2) The Red Cross Act, 1954, is hereby amended –

(a) in section 3, after the definition of 'the Civilians Convention' by the insertion of the following definitions:

'"Protocol I" means the Protocol, additional to the Geneva Conventions of 12 August 1949, and relating to the Protection of Victims of International Armed Conflicts (Protocol I) adopted at Geneva on 8 June 1977;

"Protocol II" means the Protocol, additional to the Geneva Conventions of 12 August 1949, and relating to the Protection of Victims of Non-International Armed Conflicts (Protocol II) adopted at Geneva on 8 June 1977';

(b) in section 4(2)(a)(i), after 'Wounded and Sick Convention' by the insertion of 'Part II of Protocol 1 and Part III of Protocol II',

(c) in section 4(2)(a)(ii), after 'Maritime Convention' by the insertion of ', Part II of Protocol I and Part III of Protocol II',

(d) in section 4(2)(b), after 'Prisoners of War Convention' by the insertion of 'and Part III of Protocol III,

(e) in section 4(2)(c), by the insertion after 'Civilians Convention' of ', Part IV of Protocol I and Part IV of Protocol II

(f) in section 7(l) –

(i) by the deletion in paragraph (b) after 'Convention,' of 'and',

(ii) by the substitution in paragraph (c) for 'Convention.' of 'Convention, and', and

(iii) by the insertion after paragraph (c) of the following paragraph:

'(d) the authorisations or assignments referred to in Articles 8 and 61 of Protocol 1, or the facilities referred to in Article 81 of Protocol I',

and

(g) in section 7(2), by the substitution for 'or commission' of, 'commission, assignment or facility'.

(Amendment of Prisoners of War and Enemy Aliens Act, 1956.)

14. – Section 1 of the Prisoners of War and Enemy Aliens Act, 1956, is hereby amended
–

(a) in subsection (1), by the insertion after the definition of 'the Civilians Convention' of the following definition:

'"Protocol I" means the Protocol, additional to the Geneva Conventions of 12 August 1949, and relating to the Protection of Victims of International Armed Conflicts (Protocol I) adopted at Geneva on 8 June 1977;',

and

(b) by the substitution for subsection (2) of the following subsections:

'(2) Any reference in this Act to prisoners of war is, primarily, to –

(a) persons who, in relation to the State and a war or armed conflict in which the State is a participant, are prisoners of war within the meaning of Paragraph A of Article 4 of the Prisoners of War Convention or paragraph 1 of Article 44 of Protocol I or who are entitled under paragraph 4 of the said Article to protections equivalent in all respects to those accorded to prisoners of war or armed conflict by the said Convention and Protocol, and

(b) persons who, in relation to the State and a war in which the State is not a participant, are, by reference to subparagraph (2) of Paragraph B of Article 4 of the Prisoners of War Convention, to be treated as prisoners of war under that Convention, but any such reference shall also be construed as including a reference to the persons who in relation to the State and a war or armed conflict in which the State is a participant, having –

(i) committed a belligerent act, are, pursuant to Article 5 of the Prisoners of War Convention, to enjoy the status of prisoners of war under that Convention, or

(ii) taken part in hostilities, are, pursuant to Article 45 of Protocol I, to be presumed to be prisoners of war, until such time as their status has been determined by a competent tribunal.

(2A) Any reference in this Act to prisoners of war includes a reference to mercenaries (within the meaning of Article 47 of Protocol I) who as such have fallen into the power of, or been received on the territory of, the State.'

(Restriction of application of section 12 of Extradition Act, 1965 (military offences))

15. – The restriction on granting extradition contained in section 12 of the Extradition Act, 1965, does not apply in the case of an offence involving a grave or minor breach of any of the Scheduled Conventions or Protocol I or a minor breach of Protocol II.

(Contributions to International Fact-Finding Commission

16. – There may be paid by the Minister to the International Fact-Finding Commission, out of moneys provided by the Oireachtas, contributions, towards the administrative expenses of the Commission, of such amounts as the Minister, with the consent of the Minister for Finance, may sanction.

(Expenses)

17. – The expenses incurred by the Minister or the Minister for Defence in the administration of this Act or anything relating thereto shall, to such extent as may be sanctioned by the Minister for Finance, be paid out of moneys provided by the Oireachtas.

(Short Title, collective citation, construction and commencement)

18.– (l) This Act may be cited as the Geneva Conventions (Amendment) Act, 1998.

(2) The Principal Act and this Act (other than sections 13 and 14) may be cited together as the Geneva Conventions Acts, 1962 and 1998, and shall be construed together as one.

(3) The Red Cross Acts, 1938 to 1954, and section 13 of this Act may be cited together as the Red Cross Acts, 1938 to 1998.

(4) The Prisoners of War and Enemy Aliens Act, 1956, and section 14 of this Act may be cited together as the Prisoners of War and Enemy Aliens Acts, 1956 and 1998.

(5) This Act shall come into operation on such day as the Minister may appoint by order.

☞ Kazakhstan: Penal Code of Kazakhstan (extracts), 16 July 1997[5]

General part
Section 1 – Penal Law

Article 1. – The penal legislation of the Republic of Kazakhstan

1. The penal legislation of the Republic of Kazakhstan is constituted exclusively of the present penal legislation of the Republic of Kazakhstan. Other Acts that make provisions for the penal responsibility, are only applicable after their introduction in the present Code.

2. The present Code is based on the Constitution of the Republic of Kazakhstan as well as on the principles and norms universally recognised in international law.

Article 2. – The foundation for the penal responsibility

The only foundation of the penal responsibility consists in the committing of an offence or of an act that is incriminated by the present Code. Nobody can incur once again penal responsibility for the same offence.

Article 4. – The application of the Penal Law and the time aspect

The incrimination and the punishabililty of a fact are determined by the Act that is in force when the fact is committed. The moment of the commission of the offence is the one of the committing of a socially dangerous act (or an omission) regardless of the moment when the consequences occur.

Article 5. – The retroactivity of the Penal Law

An Act that lifts the incrimination or the punishability of an act and that moderates the responsibility or the punishment or that improves in any other way the situation of a person that has committed the offence, is retroactive, i.e., its reach is extended to the persons that have committed the acts incriminated before the entering into force of this Act for which these persons serve a sentence or have completed it but have been convicted.

2. In the case where a new Act moderates the incrimination of an act for which the

---

5. Document and translation from the Russian by the Advisory Service of the International Committee of the Red Cross, Geneva.

author serves a sentence, the administered sentence has to be reduced to the limits of the sanction provided for by the new Act.

3. An Act that incriminates an act and reinforces the responsibility or the punishment or aggravates in another way the situation of a person that has committed this act, is not retroactive.

Article 6. – The application of the penal law to persons that have committed offences on the territory of the Republic of Kazakhstan.

1. The present Code provides for the responsibility of a person that has committed an offence on the territory of the Republic of Kazakhstan.

2. The offence committed on the territory of the Republic of Kazakhstan is an act that has begun, continued or ceased on the territory of the Republic of Kazakhstan. The present Code is equally applicable to violations committed on the Continental Shelf and in the Exclusive Economic Zone of the Republic of Kazakhstan.

3. A person that has committed an offence on board of a ship or of an aircraft assigned to a (air)port in the Republic of Kazakhstan and that finds itself in maritime or air space outside of the territory of the Republic of Kazakhstan incurs penal responsibility according to the present Code if this question is not regulated by an international treaty of the Republic of Kazakhstan. The present Code also provides for the penal responsibility of a person who has committed an offence on board of a military vessel or of a military aircraft of the Republic of Kazakhstan wherever they are.

4. The issue of penal responsibility that rests with the representatives of the foreign states and with other citizens enjoying immunity who are the authors of the offences committed on the territory of the Republic of Kazakhstan, is regulated in accordance with the rules of international law.

Article 7. – The application of the penal law to persons that have committed violations outside the territory of the Republic of Kazakhstan

1.The present Code provides for the penal responsibility of the citizens of the Republic of Kazakhstan who have committed offences outside the territory of the Republic of Kazakhstan if these offences are incriminated by the state on whose territory they have been committed and if these persons have not been judged by another state. If the persons have been judged, the punishment can not exceed the upper threshold of the punishment as provided by the law of the state on whose territory the offence has been committed. The same provision applies to stateless persons.

2. The sentence and other penal consequences, that are the consequence of an offence committed on the territory of another state, are of no legal penal significance regarding the answer to the question of penal responsibility that rests with that person for an offence committed on the territory of the Republic of Kazakhstan except for the opposite case provided for by an international treaty of the Republic of Kazakhstan or if the offence, committed on the territory of another state, does not affect the interests of the Republic of Kazakhstan.

3. The present Code provides for the penal responsibility for offences committed on the territory of a foreign state by the personnel of military units of the Republic of Kazakhstan situated outside its territory except for the opposite case provided for by an international treaty of the Republic of Kazakhstan.

4. The present Code provides for the penal responsibility of the offences committed by foreigners outside the Republic of Kazakhstan in the case where these offences are directed against the interests of the Republic of Kazakhstan or in the cases provided for by an international treaty of the Republic of Kazakhstan if these persons have not been judged in another state and prosecuted on the territory of the Republic of Kazakhstan.

Article 8. – The extradition of persons that have committed offences

1. The citizens of the Republic of Kazakhstan who have committed offences on the territory of another State are not extradited to that State except in the opposite case provided for by international treaties.

2. Foreigners and stateless persons that have committed offences outside the territory of the Republic of Kazakhstan and that are on its territory can be extradited to a foreign state in order to be judged or to fulfill a punishment in accordance with an international treaty of the Republic of Kazakhstan.

Section II – Offence

Article 34. – Extreme necessity

1. Not considered as an offence is damage to the interests, protected by the present Code, in the case of extreme necessity or the damage done to eliminate a danger that represents an immediate threat to life, to health, to the rights and legal interests of the society or of the State if that danger could not be eliminated by any other means and the limits of extreme necessity are not exceeded.

2. An act exceeding the limits of extreme necessity is damage that, in an explicit way, does not correspond to the nature and to the degree of danger and to the circumstances in which the danger was eliminated, when the interests protected by the law suffer a damage equal or superior to the one that has been prevented. Such an act can only incur responsibility if the damage caused was intentional.

Article 37. – The execution of an order or of an instruction

1. Not considered as an offence is damage to the interests protected by the present Code done by a person who carries out a compulsory order or instruction. The penal responsibility for such damage falls to the person that has issued the illegal order or instruction.

2. The person that has intentionally committed an offence while carrying out a manifestly illegal order or instruction incurs penal responsibility in general. Not carrying out of a manifestly illegal order or instruction rules out penal responsibility.

Section V – Exemption from Penal Responsibility and Punishment

Article 69. – The exemption from penal responsibility in relation to the expiry of the prescription

6. The prescription does not apply to crimes against peace or the security of humanity.

Article 75. – The exemption from fulfilment of the punishment in relation to the expiry of the prescription of the sentence

4. It is up to the Tribunal to decide on the application of the prescription of persons that are sentenced to death or to life imprisonment. If the tribunal does not find it possible to apply prescription, then the sentencing to death is replaced by life imprisonment and the latter is replaced by imprisonment for a period of 25 years. The prescription does not apply to crimes against peace and the security of humanity.

Special Part
Chapter 4 – Crimes Against Peace and the Security of Humanity

Article 156. – The planning, the preparation, the starting or the waging of a war of aggression

1. The planning, the preparation or the starting of a war of aggression are punishable by imprisonment for a period of 7 to 12 years.

2. The waging of a war of aggression is punishable by imprisonment for a period of 10 to 20 years or by death penalty or by life imprisonment.

Article 157. – Propaganda in favour of a war of aggression and public appeals for a war of aggression

1. Propaganda in favour of a war of aggression and public appeals for a war of aggression are punishable by fine of a sum equivalent to 3000 monthly indexes of reference at the most, or of a sum equivalent to the salary or to other income of the sentenced person obtained during a period of 3 to 9 months or by imprisonment for a period of up to 3 years.

2. The same acts committed using the media or by a high ranking civil servant are punishable by a fine of a sum equivalent to 5000 monthly indexes of reference or of a sum equivalent to a salary or to other income of the sentenced person received during a period of 6 to 12 months or by imprisonment for a duration of 2 to 5 years. This person will be deprived of the right to occupy certain positions or to carry out certain activities during a period of up to 3 years.

Article 158. – The production or the proliferation of arms of mass destruction
The production, the acquisition or the distribution of biological and chemical arms or other arms of mass destruction that are banned by an international treaty of the Republic of Kazakhstan are punishable by imprisonment for a period of 5 to 10 years.

Article 159. – The use of forbidden means and methods of waging a war

1. The inhuman treatment of prisoners of war or of the civilian population, the deportation of the civilian population, the pillage of national goods in occupied territories, the use in an armed conflict of means and methods forbidden by an international treaty of the Republic of Kazakhstan are punishable by imprisonment for a maximum period of 12 years.

2. The use of arms of mass destruction banned by an international treaty of the Republic of Kazakhstan is punishable by imprisonment for a period of 10 to 20 years or by death penalty or life sentence.

Article 160. – Genocide

Genocide or intentional acts aiming to destroy entirely or partially a national, ethnical, racial or religious group by the murdering of members of the group, grave violation to the physical integrity of members of the group, measures to impede births within the group, forced transfers of children, forced displacement or the creating of other living conditions that bring about the physical destruction of members of the group are punishable by imprisonment for a period of 10 to 20 years or by death penalty or by life sentence.

Article 161. – Ecocide

The massive destruction of the fauna and flora, the pollution of the atmosphere, of agrarian resources and of water as well as the committing of other acts that have caused or are likely to cause an environmental disaster are punishable by imprisonment for a period of 10 to 15 years.

Article 162. – Mercenaries

1. The recruitment, training, financing of a mercenary or any provisioning to the mercenary or bringing a mercenary into action in an armed conflict or hostilities are punishable by imprisonment for a period of 4 to 8 years.

2. The same acts committed by a person who in that way abuses his official powers or a minor are punishable by imprisonment for a period of 7 to 15 years and – optionally – of seizure of his goods.

3. The participation of a mercenary in an armed conflict or in hostilities is punishable by imprisonment for a period of 3 to 7 years.

4. The acts provided for paragraph 3 of the present Article that have led to the death of people or other grave consequences are punishable by imprisonment for a period of 10 to 20 years together with a seizure of the goods or by death sentence together with seizure of goods or by life sentence together with seizure of goods.

Note: Any person is considered a mercenary who acts with a view to get a payment or any other personal benefit and who does not belong to a party in the conflict, does not live permanently in his territory and who is not dispatched by another state to fulfil his official duties.

Article 163. – The Attacks against persons or organisations that enjoy international protection

1. Attacks directed against representatives of a foreign state or against employees of international organisations that enjoy an international protection or against members of their families that live with them as well as against the premises used for working purposes or residences or means of transport that benefit from an international protection as well as the abduction of these persons or forced deprivation of their liberty if these acts are committed in order to cause a war or to deteriorate international relations are punishable by imprisonment for a period of 3 to 8 years and – optionally – by seizure of goods.

2. The same acts committed on several occasions either with the use of arms or as a result of a previous agreement or which has led to grave violation to the physical integrity or that has led to the non-intentional death of a person are punishable by imprisonment for a period of 10 to 15 years and – optionally – by the confiscation of goods.

Article 164. – The incitement to social, ethnical, racial or religious hatred

1. Intentional acts aimed at inciting to social, ethnical, racial or religious hatred or aimed at offending the national dignity or the religious sentiments of citizens as well as the propaganda on the exclusivity, the superiority or the inferiority of the citizens for religious, social, ethnical or racial reasons when these acts are committed in public or while using the media are punishable by a fine of a sum equivalent to 100 monthly indexes of reference or to a salary or to another income received during a period of one month or by detention of a period of up to 6 months or to do works for a period of a maximum of 2 years.

2. The same acts committed by a group of persons on several occasions either linked to violence or to the threat of resorting to violence, or by one person that abuses his official powers or by an official of a social association are punishable by a fine of a sum equivalent to 100 to 300 monthly indexes of reference or by a sum equivalent to a salary or to another income of the sentenced person received during a period of 1 to 3 months or by imprisonment for a period of a maximum of 4 years or for a deprivation of liberty for the same period and – optionally – by a deprivation of the right to occupy certain positions or to carry out certain activities during a period of up to 3 years.

3. The acts provided for in paragraphs 1 and 2 of the present article having led to serious consequences are punishable by imprisonment for a period of 3 to 10 years and – optionally – by the deprivation of the right to occupy certain positions or to exercise certain activities during a maximum period of 3 years.

Chapter 16 – Military Offences

Article 366. – The notion of military offence

Acknowledged as military offences are the offences provided for by the present chapter that are committed in breach of terms established for the fulfilment of military service by military personnel enlisted as conscripts or under the terms of a contract in the armed forces of the Republic of Kazakhstan, other military troops and units of the Republic of Kazakhstan or by citizens who are reserves during the period of exercise.

Article 367. – Disobedience or other non-execution of an order

1. Disobedience or a formal refusal to execute an order of a superior or any other intentional non-execution of an order of a superior given in due form that has seriously damaged the interests of the service is punishable by restrictive measures for a period of at least 2 years or by an arrest for a period of up to 6 months or by the obligation to serve in a disciplinary unit for a period of up to 2 years.

2. The same acts committed by a group of persons, a group of persons as a result of a prior agreement or an organised group as well as acts that have led to serious consequences are punishable by imprisonment for a period of up to 5 years.

3. The acts provided for by paragraphs 1 and 2 of the present article and committed in times of war or during hostilities are punishable by imprisonment for a period of 5 to 20 years, if there are aggravating circumstances then they are punishable by death penalty or life sentence.

4. The failure to carry out an order because of negligence that has led to serious consequences is punishable by restrictive measures for a period of up to 12 months or

by an arrest of a period of 3 to 6 months or by the obligation to serve in a disciplinary unit for a period of up to 12 months.

5. The act provided for in paragraph 4 of the present article and committed in times of war or during hostilities is punishable by imprisonment for a period of 3 to 10 years.

Article 385. – Marauding

Theft of objects belonging to the dead and to the wounded, committed on the battleground is punishable by imprisonment of a period of 3 to 10 years.

☛ **Yemen: Act No. (21) of the Year 1998 Concerning the Military Violations and Punishments**[6]

[ACT OF 25 JULY 1998]
Title I – General Provisions
Chapter II – Field of Application

Article 3. Subject to the present Act are:
(...) f- Prisoners of war.
Article 5. Any person, subject to the provisions of the present Act, who might have committed an act outside the Republic of Yemen, as the principal author or co-author of the violations provided for by this Act, will be punished pursuant to these provisions, even if the violation is not punished by the law of the country where it has taken place.

When the act is punishable, this will not prevent a second trial before the military tribunals and one has to take into account the period of time of the punishment done by the aforementioned person.

Title III – The Military Violations and Punishments
Chapter III – War Crimes

Article 20. Any person will be punished with imprisonment for a maximum period of five years or with a punishment that corresponds to the results of the violation, who abandons his duties in a zone of military operations and robs a prisoner, a dead or a wounded person and will be held to give back what he has robbed or its equivalent.

Article 21. Any person, subject to the provisions of the present Act, will be punished with imprisonment for a maximum period of ten years or with a sanction corresponding to the results of the violation, who has committed, in wartime, any one of the acts that endanger persons and goods protected under the international Conventions to which the Yemeni Republic is/will be a party and the following acts are considered, in particular, as war crimes punished in accordance with the present Act:
1. The fact of killing prisoners of war or civilians, and this sanction will not exempt the punishable person from the penal action if the victim [of death] was inviolable;

---

6. Document and translation from the Arabic by the Advisory Service of the International Committee of the Red Cross, Geneva.

2. Torture or bad treatment of prisoners or the fact of intentionally inflicting tremendous suffering or submitting them to any scientific experiments;

3. The fact of intentionally inflicting serious damage to the physical and mental integrity and to the health of the military or civil prisoners or to force them to serve in the armed forces;

4. The unlawful detention of civilians or the fact of taking them as hostage or using them as a human shield during military operations;

5. The deceitful use of the distinctive sign of the Yemeni Red Crescent or of any of the other international signs of protection that are in accordance with international conventions;

6. The launching of an attack against the civilian population and non-combat persons and the plundering and looting of goods, while deciding to restitute the goods or insure them in the case of destruction;

7. The launching of an attack against public and private civilian installations.

8. The launching of an unjustified attack against demilitarised zones.

Article 22. As regards the violations provided for in the present chapter, the right of public action is imprescriptible.

Article 23. In the case of the commission of any of the violations provided for in the present chapter, the commander and the subordinate will be responsible for the violation and they will not be exonerated from the provided punishment unless the acts have been committed against their will, or without their knowledge or if it was impossible for them to avoid it.

7.22   NATIONAL LEGISLATION TO IMPLEMENT OBLIGATIONS *VIS-À-VIS* THE INTERNATIONAL COURT AND TRIBUNALS

☛ **Greece: Law 2665 of 15/17 December 1998. Implementation of Resolutions 827/25.5.1993 and 955/6.11.1995 of the United Nations Security Council whereby two International Criminal Tribunals were instituted for the prosecution of breaches of International Humanitarian Law in the territory of the former Yugoslavia and Rwanda (GG A 279)[7]**

Article One – Definitions
1.   By virtue of article 25 of the Charter of the United Nations, as ratified by Necessity Law 585/1945 (GA 242), are hereby implemented resolutions 827/25.5.1993 and 955/6.11.1995 of the United Nations Security Council whereby two International Criminal Tribunals were instituted for the prosecution of serious breaches of International Humanitarian Law in the territory of the former Yugoslavia and Rwanda, respectively, in application of Chapter VII of the Charter.

7. Document and translation by Dr Maria Gavouneli, Hellenic Institute of International and Foreign Law, Greece.

2. 'International Tribunal' means the International Criminal Tribunal referred to in resolutions 827/1993 and 955/1994 and 'statute' means the one referred to in the annexes to those resolutions.

3.   The text of resolutions 827/1993 and 955/1994 in its original English and in translation into the Greek language as follows: [...]

Article Two – Scope of application
The provisions of the present Law apply to all persons prosecuted for the crimes referred to in articles 2-5 of the Statute of the International Tribunal for the former Yugoslavia and in articles 2-4 of the Statute of the International Tribunal for Rwanda.

Article Three – Extension of the scope of application of Greek criminal laws
The Greek criminal laws shall also apply to the crimes provided for in articles 2-5 of the Statute of the International Tribunal for the former Yugoslavia and in articles 2-4 of the Statute of the International Tribunal for Rwanda, irrespective of the place where they were committed.
In this case the victim is entitled to participate in the trial as a civil claimant according to the provisions of the Code of Criminal Procedure.

Article Four – *Non bis in idem*
No person shall be tried before the Greek courts for an act for which he has already been tried by the International Tribunal. If criminal proceedings are already under way, the court or the judicial council shall declare the case inadmissible.

Article Five – Primacy of the International Tribunal
1. If the International Tribunal or the Prosecutor request the surrender of a person, against whom criminal charges have already been brought by the competent Greek authorities, such criminal charge is declared inadmissible and the case is referred to the International Tribunal for trial, provided:
a) the person is charged by the International Tribunal with the same act he was charged with in Greece; and
b) the International Tribunal has territorial and temporal jurisdiction, according to article 8 of the Statute of the International Tribunal for the former Yugoslavia and article 7 of the Statute of the International Tribunal for Rwanda.
2. The Athens Three-Member Court of Appeal shall decide on the identification of the person and the act as well as on the territorial and temporal jurisdiction of the International Tribunal. Against such a decision an appeal is allowed before *Areios Pagos*, pursuant to the provisions of article 451 of the Code of Criminal Procedure.

Article Six
The request for the surrender of a person already charged by the Greek authorities shall be transmitted by the Minister of Justice to the Public Prosecutor at the Athens Court of Appeal. The Public Prosecutor shall refer it to the Three-Member Judicial Council which shall decide in public whether the prerequisites of article five are fulfilled.
The defendant shall be summoned fifteen days in advance to express his views in person or through counsel.
Against the decision of the Judicial Council an appeal is allowed before *Areios Pagos*.

As to the rest the provisions of the Code of Criminal Procedure apply.

Article Seven
The request by the International Tribunal for the surrender of a defendant shall be addressed to the Minister of Justice, who shall refer it to the Public Prosecutor at the Athens Court of Appeal.

In case the International Tribunal or the Prosecutor requests enquiries to be made, the conduct of such enquiries shall be entrusted by the Public Prosecutor at the Athens Court of Appeal to a special Appellate *Juge d'instruction* appointed by the Court of Appeal Directorate.

The Appellate *Juge d'instruction* may travel, with the permission of the Public Prosecutor at *Areios Pagos*, beyond the territorial limits of the Court of Appeal in order to conduct such enquiries, or the Public Prosecutor may delegate such conduct to the ordinary *Juge d'instruction* of the competent Court of First Instance.

Such enquiries shall be conducted in accordance with Greek law.

Article Eight
The request for the surrender of a defendant or the conduct of enquiries shall be supported at least by the following:
1. Information verifying the identity of the defendant, such as a detailed description, photograph, fingerprints or any other appropriate means of identification;
2. The warrant of arrest, a concise statement of the act and all documents that may be deemed necessary to establish a probable cause for referring the defendant to court for trial;
3. A certified copy of the indictment or the judgement of conviction as well as testimonial evidence.

Article Nine
The Public Prosecutor at the Athens Court of Appeal shall issue an arrest warrant immediately upon receipt of the request.
If the person arrested questions his identification, he may petition the Judicial Council of the Court of Appeal within two working days from his arrest. The Three-Member Judicial Council of the Court of Appeal shall be convened in public within fifteen (15) days at the latest from the date of the petition and shall decide within ten (10) days.

The defendant shall be summoned before the Judicial Council of the Court of Appeal three days in advance.

Article Ten
1. The Judicial Council of the Court of Appeal, having examined the person arrested, if present, and having heard the Public Prosecutor and the person arrested or his counsel, shall adjudicate with reasons on the request for the surrender and shall decide:
a) whether the person arrested is the same person as the person whose surrender is requested,
b) whether the supporting documentation required by the present law for such surrender exist,

c) whether the charges brought against the person arrested or, if a judgement of conviction exists, whether the crime for which he was convicted are among those for which surrender is allowed according to the present law.

2. The Judicial Council of the Court of Appeal shall further examine whether, on the basis of the supporting official evidentiary documents, there is reasonable basis for the charges against the person arrested and shall decide whether this would allow for his arrest and referral to trial in Greece should the crime have been committed on Greek territory. The Judicial Council of the Court of Appeal may also compile, through one of its members, all useful evidentiary material, postponing its final decision for a maximum period of fifteen (15) days. The provision of article 449 paragraph 2 of the Code of Criminal Procedure applies in this respect.

3. The person whose surrender is requested and the Public Prosecutor may appeal against the final decision of the Judicial Council of the Court of Appeal before the competent criminal section of *Areios Pagos* within three (3) days from the date the decision shall be issued.

A report on the appeal shall be compiled by the Registrar of the Court of Appeal.

4. *Areios Pagos* shall adjudicate in council within ten (10) days in application by analogy of articles 448 and 450 of the Code of Criminal Procedure.

The defendant shall be summoned to appear in person or through his representative at least three (3) days in advance in care of the Public Prosecutor at *Areios Pagos*.

5. If *Areios Pagos* orders the surrender, the decision shall be executed within one (1) month at the latest from the date it was issued. In such a case the Public Prosecutor at the Court of Appeal shall submit the decision along with the relevant file to the Minister of Justice, who shall be entrusted with its execution.

6. If a final decision on the surrender is not issued within three (3) months from the date of the arrest, the person arrested shall be deemed free.

Article Eleven – Summons of witnesses and experts

A summons for witnesses and experts shall be transmitted by the International Tribunal to the Ministry of Justice and served to the addressee by the Public Prosecutor of the place where the addressee lives.

Witnesses and experts thus summoned who absent themselves without a valid reason may be compelled to appear before the International Tribunal by force, if so requested, and handed over to the Dutch authorities.

The provisions of articles 224-228 of the Criminal Code apply also to the corresponding acts committed before the establishment of the International Tribunal.

Article Twelve – Communication of information to the Tribunal

The competent Greek authorities shall communicate to the International Tribunal the criminal records as well as any other relevant information requested for the purposes of a criminal case under the same terms and conditions as such data shall be communicated to the Greek judicial authorities.

Article Thirteen

1. Should the International Tribunal in application of article 27 of the Statute of the International Tribunal for the former Yugoslavia and article 26 of the Statute of the International Tribunal for Rwanda, designate Greece as the place where the sentence

is to be served, the Minister of Justice upon receipt of the relevant notification shall transmit the case file to the Public Prosecutor at the Court of Appeal who shall present it to the Three-Member Court of Appeal with a view to have the decision recognised and the sentence converted.

2. The decision of the International Tribunal shall not be recognised for the purposes of paragraph 1 if

a) it may not as yet be executed,

b) the act is not criminal according to Greek law, or

c) there is *res iudicata* on the basis of the Greek judgement of conviction.

3. The Court of Appeal shall recognise the decision of the International Tribunal and shall convert a liberty depriving sentence

a) to incarceration for the same period of time, if it does not exceed five (5) years or

b) to temporary imprisonment for the same period or for life, if it refers to a longer sentence.

4. The sentence shall be temporary imprisonment may not exceed in any case a period of twenty-five (25) years.

5. The sentence shall be carried out according to the provisions of Greek legislation.

Article Fourteenth – Pardon or commutation of sentences

If the Minister of Justice considers that there are reasons to grant a pardon or commute the sentence of a person serving sentence in Greece, according to article 13 of the present law, the Minister may notify the International Tribunal submitting at the same time the relevant file.

Article Fifteenth

The present law comes into force from the date of its publication in the Government Gazette.

9.21 PEACEKEEPING

☞ United Nations: Secretary-General's Bulletin: Observance by United Nations Forces of International Humanitarian Law, August 1999

United Nations ST/sGB/1999/13

Secretariat 6 August 1999. Secretary-General's Bulletin

Observance by United Nations of International Humanitarian Law

The Secretary-General, for the purpose of setting out fundamental principles and rules of international humanitarian law applicable to United Nations forces conducting operations under United Nations command and control, promulgates the following:

Section 1

Field of application

1.1 The fundamental principles and rules of international humanitarian law set out in the present bulletin are applicable to United Nations forces when in situations of armed conflict they are actively engaged therein as combatants, to the extent and for the duration of their engagement. They are accordingly applicable in enforcement actions, or in peacekeeping operations when the use of force is permitted in self-defence.

1.2 The promulgation of this bulletin does not affect the protected status of members of peacekeeping operations under the 1994 Convention on the Safety of United Nations and Associated Personnel or their status as non-combatants, as long as they are entitled to the protection given to civilians under the international law of armed conflict.

Section 2
Application of national law

The present provisions do not constitute an exhaustive list of principles and rules of international humanitarian law binding upon military personnel, and do not prejudice the application thereof, nor do they replace the national laws by which military personnel remain bound throughout the operation.

Section 3
Status-of-forces agreement

In the status-of-forces agreement concluded between the United Nations and a State in whose territory a United Nations force is deployed, the United Nations undertakes to ensure that the force shall conduct its operations with full respect for the principles and rules of the general conventions applicable to the conduct of military personnel. The United Nations also undertakes to ensure that members of the military personnel of the force are fully acquainted with the principles and rules of those international instruments. The obligation to respect the said principles and rules is applicable to United Nations forces even in the absence of a status-of-forces agreement.

Section 4
Violations of international humanitarian law

In case of violations of international humanitarian law, members of the military personnel of a United Nations force are subject to prosecution in their national courts.

Section 5
Protection of the civilian population

5.1 The United Nations force shall make a clear distinction at all times between civilians and combatants and between civilian objects and military objectives. Military operations shall be directed only against combatants and military objectives. Attacks on civilians or civilian objects are prohibited.

5.2 Civilians shall enjoy the protection afforded by this section, unless and for such time as they take a direct part in hostilities.

5.3 The United Nations force shall take all feasible precautions to avoid, and in any event to minimize, incidental loss of civilian life, injury to civilians or damage to civilian property.

5.4 In its area of operation, the United Nations force shall avoid, to the extent feasible, locating military objectives within or near densely populated areas, and take all necessary precautions to protect the civilian population, individual civilians and civilian objects against the dangers resulting from military operations. Military installations and equipment of peacekeeping operations, as such, shall not be considered military objectives.

5.5 The United Nations force is prohibited from launching operations of a nature likely to strike military objectives and civilians in an indiscriminate manner, as well as operations that may be expected to cause incidental loss of life among the civilian population or damage to civilian objects that would be excessive in relation to the concrete and direct military advantage anticipated.

5.6 The United Nations force shall not engage in reprisals against civilians or civilian objects.

Section 6
Means and methods of combat

6.1 The right of the United Nations force to choose methods and means of combat is not unlimited.

6.2 The United Nations force shall respect the rules prohibiting or restricting the use of certain weapons and methods of combat under the relevant instruments of international humanitarian law. These include, in particular, the prohibition on the use of asphyxiating, poisonous or other gases and biological methods of warfare; bullets which explode, expand or flatten easily in the human body; and certain explosive projectiles. The use of certain conventional weapons, such as non-detectable fragments, anti-personnel mines, booby traps and incendiary weapons, is prohibited.

6.3 The United Nations force is prohibited from employing methods of warfare which may cause superfluous injury or unnecessary suffering, or which are intended, or may be expected to cause, widespread, long-term and severe damage to the natural environment.

6.4 The United Nations force is prohibited from using weapons or methods of combat of a nature that may cause unnecessary suffering.

6.5 It is forbidden to order that there shall be no survivors.

6.6 The United Nations force is prohibited from attacking monuments of art, architecture or history, archaeological sites, works of art, places of worship and museums and libraries, which constitute the cultural or spiritual heritage of peoples. In its area of operation, the United Nations force shall not use such cultural property or their immediate surroundings for purposes which might expose them to destruction or damage. Theft, pillage, misappropriation and any act of vandalism directed against cultural property is strictly prohibited.

6.7 The United Nations force is prohibited from attacking, destroying, removing or rendering useless objects indispensable to the survival of the civilian population, such as foodstuff, crops, livestock and drinking-water installations and supplies.

6.8 The United Nations force shall not make installations containing dangerous forces, namely dams, dikes and nuclear electrical generating stations, the object of military operations if such operations may cause the release of dangerous forces and consequent severe losses among the civilian population.

6.9 The United Nations force shall not engage in reprisals against objects and installations protected under this section.

Section 7
Treatment of civilians and persons *hors de combat*

7.1 Persons not, or no longer, taking part in military operations, including civilians, members of armed forces who have laid down their weapons and persons placed hors de combat by reason of sickness, wounds or detention, shall, in all circumstances, be treated humanely and without any adverse distinction based on race, sex, religious convictions or any other ground. They shall be accorded full respect for their person, honour and religious and other convictions.

7.2 The following acts against any of the persons mentioned in section 7.1 are prohibited at any time and in any place: violence to life or physical integrity; murder as well as cruel treatment such as torture, mutilation or any form of corporal punishment; collective punishment; reprisals; the taking of hostages; rape; enforced prostitution; any form of sexual assault and humiliation and degrading treatment; enslavement; pillage.

7.3 Women shall be especially protected against any attack, in particular against rape, enforced prostitution or any other form of indecent assault.

7.4 Children shall be the object of special respect and shall be protected against any form of indecent assault.

Section 8
Treatment of detained persons

The United Nations force shall treat with humanity and respect for their dignity detained members of the armed forces and other persons who no longer take part in military operations by reason of detention. Without prejudice to their legal status, they shall be treated in accordance with the relevant provisions of the Third Geneva Convention of 1949, as may be applicable to them mutatis mutandis. In particular:

(a) Their capture and detention shall be notified without delay to the party on which they depend and to the Central Tracing Agency of the International Committee of the Red Cross (ICRC), in particular in order to inform their families;

(b) They shall be held in secure and safe premises which provide all possible safeguards of hygiene and health, and shall not be detained in areas exposed to the dangers of the combat zone;

(c) They shall be entitled to receive food and clothing, hygiene and medical attention;

(d) They shall under no circumstances be subjected to any form of torture or ill-treatment;

(e) Women whose liberty has been restricted shall be held in quarters separated from men's quarters, and shall be under the immediate supervision of women;

(f) In cases where children who have not attained the age of sixteen years take a direct part in hostilities and are arrested, detained or interned by the United Nations force, they shall continue to benefit from special protection. In particular, they shall be held in quarters separate from the quarters of adults, except when accommodated with their families;

(g) ICRC's right to visit prisoners and detained persons shall be respected and guaranteed.

Section 9
Protection of the wounded, the sick, and medical and relief personnel

9.1 Members of the armed forces and other persons in the power of the United Nations force who are wounded or sick shall be respected and protected in all circumstances. They shall be treated humanely and receive the medical care and attention required by their condition, without adverse distinction. Only urgent medical reasons will authorize priority in the order of treatment to be administered.

9.2 Whenever circumstances permit, a suspension of fire shall be arranged, or other local arrangements made, to permit the search for and identification of the wounded, the sick and the dead left on the battlefield and allow for their collection, removal, exchange and transport.

9.3 The United Nations force shall not attack medical establishments or mobile medical units. These shall at all times be respected and protected, unless they are used, outside their humanitarian functions, to attack or otherwise commit harmful acts against the United Nations force.

9.4 The United Nations force shall in all circumstances respect and protect medical personnel exclusively engaged in the search for, transport or treatment of the wounded or sick, as well as religious personnel.

9.5 The United Nations force shall respect and protect transports of wounded and sick or medical equipment in the same way as mobile medical units.

9.6 The United Nations force shall not engage in reprisals against the wounded, the sick or the personnel, establishments and equipment protected under this section.

9.7 The United Nations force shall in all circumstances respect the Red Cross and Red Crescent emblems. These emblems may not be employed except to indicate or to protect medical units and medical establishments, personnel and material. Any misuse of the Red Cross or Red Crescent emblems is prohibited.

9.8 The United Nations force shall respect the right of the families to know about the fate of their sick, wounded and deceased relatives. To this end, the force shall facilitate the work of the ICRC Central Tracing Agency.

9.9 The United Nations force shall facilitate the work of relief operations, which are humanitarian and impartial in character and conducted without any adverse distinction, and shall respect personnel, vehicles and premises involved in such operations.

Section 10
Entry into force
The present bulletin shall enter into force on 12 August 1999

(Signed) Kofi A. Annan
Secretary-General

BIBLIOGRAPHY

BIBLIOGRAPHY 1998-1999[1]

0.   INTERNATIONAL HUMANITARIAN LAW GENERALLY

Books

- Bouchet-Saulnier, Françoise, *Dictionnaire pratique du droit humanitaire* (Paris, La Decouverte & Syros 1998) 420 pp.
- Coolen, G. L., *Humanitair Oorlogsrecht* (Deventer, W.E.J. Tjeenk Willink Publ. 1998) 211 pp.
- David, Eric, *Principes de Droit des Conflits Armés*, 2nd edn. (Brussels, Bruylant 1999) 860 pp.
- Deyra, Michel, *Droit international humanitaire* (Paris, Gualino 1998) 151 pp.
- Gardam, Judith, ed., *Humanitarian Law* (Aldershot, Dartmouth Press/Ashgate Publishing Ltd. 1999) 570 pp.
- Green, L.C., *Essays on the Modern Laws of War,* 2nd edn. (Ardsley NY, Transnational Publishers 1999) 604 pp.
- Meron, Theodor, *Bloody Constraint: War and Chivalry in Shakespeare* (New York/Oxford, Oxford University Press 1998) 246 pp.
- Meyer, Michael A. and Hilaire McCoubrey, eds., *Reflections on Law and Armed Conflict: The Selected Works on the Laws of War by the late Professor G.I.A.D. Draper, OBE* (The Hague, Kluwer Law International 1998) 288 pp.
- Schmitt, Michael N. and Leslie C. Green, eds., *The Law of Armed Conflict: into the next millennium* (Newport, RI, Naval War College 1998) – LXXII, 535 pp.
- 1 *Yearbook of International Humanitarian Law* (The Hague, T.M.C. Asser Press 1998) 696 pp.

Articles

- Alesky, Pamela D., 'Yugoslavia and international humanitarian law', 35 *International Politics* (1998) pp. 1-30

1. The bibliography was compiled by Jann K. Kleffner and Avril McDonald. Thanks to members of the Board of Editors of the *YIHL* for their input. Editor's Note: The bibliography is arranged according to the classification scheme used in the Documents section (see pp. 433-436). We have tried to be as inclusive as possible, but inevitably there will be some omissions, for which we apologise. We invite authors and publishers to inform the *YIHL* about their publications, for inclusion in future bibliographies. The bibliography in volume 3 will include publications from 1999 and 2000. Where page numbers or other identifying information is not provided, it was not available at press-time. Titles may be cited more than once because they come under different headings.
Publishers are invited to send publications for review.

- Bugnion, François, 'Le droit international humanitaire à l'épreuve des conflits de notre temps', 81 *IRRC* No. 835 (1999) pp. 487-498
- Grossrieder, Paul, 'Un avenir pour le droit international humanitaire et ses principes', 81 *IRRC* No. 833 (1999) pp. 11-18
- McDonald, Avril, 'The Year in Review', 1 *YIHL* (1998) pp. 113-160
- McDonald, Avril, 'Introduction to International Humanitarian Law and the Qualification of Armed Conflicts', in Peter J. van Krieken, ed., *Refugee Law in Context: The Exclusion Clause* (The Hague, T.M.C. Asser Press 1999) pp. 79-104
- McDonald, Gabrielle Kirk, 'The changing nature of the laws of war', 156 *MLR* (1998) pp. 30-51
- Nahum, Fasil, 'The challenges for humanitarian law and action at the threshold of the twenty-first century: An African perspective', 81 *IRRC* No. 833 (1999) pp. 45-54
- Orend, Brian, 'Kant on international law and armed conflict', 11 *Can. JL & Jur.* (1998) pp. 329-381
- Roberts, Adam ,'The role of humanitarian issues in international politics in the 1990s', 81 *IRRC* No. 833 (1999) pp. 19-44
- Schmitt, Michael N., 'Bellum Americanum: the U.S. view of twenty-first century war and its possible implications for the law of armed conflict', 19 *Mich. JIL* (1998) pp. 1051-1090

1.   SOURCES AND GENERAL PRINCIPLES

1.12   Hague Law

Articles

- Durand, André, 'Le Comité international de la Croix Rouge à l'époque de la première Conférence de La Haye (1899)', 81 *IRRC* No. 834 (1999) pp. 353-364

1.13   Geneva Law

Articles

- Fenrick, William, 'The application of the Geneva Conventions by the International Criminal Tribunal for the Former Yugoslavia', 81 *IRRC* No. 834 (1999) pp. 317-330
- Forsythe, David, '1949 and 1999: Making the Geneva Conventions relevant after the Cold War', 81 *IRRC* No. 834 (1999) pp. 265-276
- Harovel, Véronique, 'Les projets genevois de révision de la Convention de Genève du 22 août 1864 (1868-1898)', 81 *IRRC* No. 834 (1999) pp. 365-386
- Holleufer, Gibert, 'Peut-on celebrer le 50ᵉ anniversaire des Conventions de Genève?', 81 *IRRC* No. 833 (1999) pp. 135-148
- Rey-Schyrr, Catherine, 'Conventions de Genève de 1949: une percée décisive, première partie', 81 *IRRC* No. 834 (1999) pp. 209-239
- Rey-Schyrr, Catherine, 'Conventions de Genève de 1949: une percée décisive, seconde partie', 81 *IRRC* No. 835 (1999) pp. 499-529

- Sandoz, Yves, 'Le demi-siècle des Conventions de Genève', 81 *IRRC* No. 834 (1999) pp. 241-264

1.22   Superfluous Injury and Unnecessary Suffering

Articles
- Clark, Roger S., 'Methods of warfare that cause unnecessary suffering or are inherently indiscriminate: a memorial tribute to Howard Berman', 28 *Calif. Western ILJ* (1998) pp. 379-389

1.25   Military Necessity

Articles
- Carnahan, Burrus, 'Lincoln, Lieber and the Laws of War: The origins and limits of the principle of military necessity', 92 *AJIL* (1998) pp. 213-231
- Hladik, Jan, 'The 1954 Hague Convention for the Protection of Cultural Property in the Event of Armed Conflict and the Notion of Military Necessity: the Review of the Convention and the Adoption of the Second Protocol thereto (26 March 1999)', 81 *IRRC* No. 835 (1999) pp. 621-635

2.   **CONFLICTS, ARMED FORCES AND COMBATANTS**

2.11   International Armed Conflicts

Articles and Reports
- Boister, Neil and Richard Burchill, 'The international legal definition of the South African armed conflict in the South African courts: war of national liberation, civil war, or war at all?', 45 *NILR* (1998) pp. 348-362
- Frerks, R., ed., 'Proceedings of Seminar on Intrastate Conflict and Options for Policy'. Held at the Ministry of Foreign Affairs, The Hague, 16-17 November 1998 (The Hague, Clingendael 1999) 76 pp.
- Meron, Theodor, 'Classification of armed conflict in the Former Yugoslavia', 92 *AJIL* (1998) pp. 236-242
- Rosensweig, Laurie, 'The laws of war in Shakespeare: international vs. internal armed conflict', 30 *NY Univ. JIL & Pol.* (1998) pp. 251-290

2.12   Non-International Armed Conflicts

Books
- Baker, P.H. and A.E. Weller, *An Analytical Model of Internal Conflict and State Collapse: Manual for Practitioner* (Washington, DC, The Fund for Peace 1998) 58 pp.
- Grado, Valentina, *Guerre civili e terzi stati* (Padoue, CEDAM 1998) 416 pp.

Articles
- Domestici-Met, Marie-Jose, 'Cent ans après La Haye, cinquante ans Genève: le droit international humanitaire au temps de la guerre civile', 81 *RICR (IRRC)* No. 834 (1999) pp. 277-301
- Hadden, Tom and Colin Harvey, 'The law of internal crisis and conflict', 81 *IRRC* No. 833 (1999) pp. 119-134
- Kalshoven, Frits, 'A Colombian view on Protocol II', 1 *YIHL* (1998) pp. 262-267
- Symposium on Method in International Law, 93 *AJIL* (1999) pp. 291-423 [presenting 7 methodological approaches to the responsibility of individuals for human rights abuses in internal armed conflict]:
    - Abbott, Kenneth, W., 'International relations theory, international law, and the regime governing atrocities in internal conflicts', pp. 361-379
    - Charlesworth, Hilary, 'Feminist methods in international law', pp. 379-394
    - Dunoff, Jeffrey L. and Joel P. Trachtman, 'The law and economics of humanitarian law violations in internal armed conflict', pp. 394-409
    - Koskenniemi, Martti, 'Letter to the editors of the symposium', pp. 351-361
    - O'Connell, Mary Ellen, 'New International Legal Process', pp. 334-351
    - Simma, Bruno and Andreas L. Paulus, 'The responsibility of individuals for human rights abuses in internal conflicts: a positivist view', pp. 302-316
    - Slaughter, Anne-Marie and Steven R. Ratner, 'The Method is the Message', pp. 410-423
    - Wiesser, Siegfried and Andrew R. Willard, 'Policy-oriented jurisprudence and human rights abues in internal armed conflict: toward a world public order of human dignity', pp. 316-334
- Weyembergh, A., 'La notion de conflit armé, le droit international humanitaire et les forces des Nations Unies en Somalie (A propos de l'arrêt de la Cour militaire du 17 décembre 1997)', 79 *RDPC* (1999) pp. 177-201

2.21 Armed Forces and Combatant Status

Articles
- Avar, Vural, 'The Turkish armed forces in 2000 and beyond', *Nato's Sixteen Nations and Partners for Peace*, vol. special suppl. (1998) pp. 15-23
- de Rover, Cees, 'Police and security forces, a new interest for human rights and humanitarian law', 81 *IRRC* No. 835 (1999) pp. 637-647
- Tomitaro, Yoneda, 'Re-examination of the role of armed forces in space and discipline of international space law: meta-international law approach', 11 *Korean Journal of Air and Space Law* (1999) pp. 405-414

2.22   Non-State Actors

Books
- Reno, W.S.K., *Warlord Politics and African States* (Boulder, Col., Lynne Rienner 1998) 257 pp.

Articles and Reports
- Beard, Jack, 'Countering the threat posed by non-state actors in the proliferation of weapons of mass destruction', 92 *Proceedings of the ... annual meeting* (1998) pp. 173-177
- Dahmane, Farid Wahid, 'Les mesures prises par le Conseil de Sécurité contre les entités non-étatiques: une tentative de cerner l'application du chapitre VII aux crises internes', 11 *African Jl & CL* (1999) pp. 227-244
- Kooijmans, P.H., 'The Security Council and non-state entities as parties to conflicts', in Karel Wellens, ed., *International Law: theory and practice: essays in honour of Eric Suy* (The Hague, Nijhoff 1998) pp. 333-346

2.231   Mercenaries

Books
- Musah, Abdel-Fatau and J. 'Kayode Fayemi, eds., *Mercenaries – An African Security Dilemma* (London, Pluto Press 2000) 334 pp.

Articles
- McCormack, Tim, 'The Sandline affair: Papua New Guinea resorts to mercenarism to end the Bougainville conflict', 1 *YIHL* (1998) pp. 292-300

3.   **PROTECTED PERSONS**

3.12   Prisoners of War

Articles
- Ampferl, Monika, 'La recherche des Allemands prisonniers ou portés disparus au cours de la Seconde Guerre mondiale', 81 *RICR (IRRC)* No. 834 (1999) pp. 387-402
- Brown, Gary D., 'Prisoner of war parole: ancient concept, modern utility', 156 *MLR* (1998) pp. 200-223

3.131   Civilians Generally

Books
- Longman, Timothy Paul, *Proxy targets: civilians in the war in Burundi* (New York, Human Rights Watch 1998) 125 pp.
- Sandvik-Nylund, Monika, *Caught in Conflicts: Civilian Victims, Humanitarian Assistance and International Law* (Turko/Åbo, Institute for Human Rights/Åbo Akademi University 1998) 153 pp.

Articles
- Peter, Chris Maina, 'Protecting the innocent: civilians in the Middle of Armed Conflict', 53 ZöR (1998) pp. 45-67
- Tribunsky, A.V., 'Protection of civilians during armed conflicts', 4 *Moscow JIL* (1998) pp. 42-48

3.132   Women and Children

Books

- Pol, P., *We have to Sit Down: Women, War and Peace in Southern Sudan* (Utrecht, Pax Christi Netherlands 1998) 112 pp.
- Dombrowski, Nicole Ann, ed., *Women and War in the Twentieth Century: Enlisted With or Without Consent* (New York, Garland Publishing 1999) 377 pp.

Articles and Reports

- Askin, Kelly Dawn, 'Sexual violence in decisions and indictments of the Yugoslav and Rwandan Tribunals: current status', 93 *AJIL* (1999) pp. 97-123
- Charlesworth, Hilary, 'Feminist methods in international law', 93 *AJIL* (1999) pp. 379-394
- Gardam, Judith, 'Women, human rights, and international humanitarian law', 38 *IRRC* No. 324 (1998) pp. 421-432
- *In the Firing Line: War and Children's Rights* (London, Amnesty International 1999) 118 pp.
- McDonald, Avril, 'Prosecuting IHL violations against women: a note on the relevant provisions of the ICC Statute', 14 *Nemesis* (1998) pp. 132-142
- McDonald, Avril, 'Prosecuting sex crimes at the *ad hoc* Tribunals: the decisions in the cases of *Akayesu, Čelebići* and *Furundžija*', 15 *Nemesis* (1999) pp. 72-82
- The International Committee of the Red Cross, 'The involvement of children in armed conflict', 38 *IRRC* No. 322 (1998) pp. 105-125

4.   METHODS, MEANS AND TYPES OF WARFARE

4.111   Existing Weapons

Articles

- Coupland, Robin M. and Peter Herby, 'Review of the legality of weapons: a new approach', 81 *IRRC* No. 835 (1999) pp. 583-592

4.1111   Conventional Weapons
            [see also below: 10. Arms Control and Disarmament]

Articles

- Zöckler, Markus C., 'Commentary on Protocol IV on Blinding Laser Weapons', 1 *YIHL* (1998) pp. 333-340

4.1112   Weapons of Mass Destruction
            [see generally below: 10. Arms Control and Disarmament]

4.11121   Nuclear Weapons

Books
- Sayed, Abdulhay, *Quand le Droit Est Face à son Néant: Le Droit à l'Épreuve de l'Emploi de l'Arme Nucléaire* (Bruxelles, Bruylant 1998) 200 pp.

Articles
- Kristjansdottir, Edda, 'The legality of the threat or use of nuclear weapons under current international law: the arguments behind the World Court's Advisory Opinion', 30 *NY Univ. JIL & Pol.* (1998) pp. 291-368
- Vachon, Christyne J., 'Sovereignty versus globalization: the International Court of Justice's Advisory Opinion on the Threat or Use of Nuclear Weapons', 26 *Denver JIL & Pol.* (1998) pp. 691-724
- Verhaegen, J., 'Une question cruciale de droit international humanitaire (A propos de l'avis consultatif du 8 juillet 1996 de la Cour Internationale de Justice)', 79 *RDPC* (1999) pp. 202-207
- Verwey, Wil, 'The International Court of Justice and the legality of nuclear weapons: some observations', in Karel Wellens, ed., *International Law: Theory and Practice: essays in honour of Eric Suy* (The Hague, Nijhoff 1998) pp. 751-763
- Warner, Daniel, 'The Nuclear Weapons Decision by the International Court of Justice: locating the raison behind the raison d'état', 27 *Millenium* (1998) pp. 299-324
- Zegveld, Liesbeth (reporter), 'The ICJ Advisory Opinion on the Legality of Nuclear Weapons', in *Contemporary International Law Issues: New Forms, New Applications*. Proceedings of the Fourth Hague Joint Conference held in the Hague, the Netherlands 2-5 July 1997 of the American Society of International Law and the Nederlandse Vereniging voor Internationaal Recht (The Hague, T.M.C. Asser Institute 1998) pp. 76-89

[see also: Selected bibliography on the ICJ Nuclear Weapons Cases in 7 *Transn. L & Contemp. Probs.* (1997) pp. 487-493]

4.11122   Chemical and Biological Weapons

Books
- Tabassi, Lisa Woollomes, ed., *OPCW: The Legal Texts* (The Hague, T.M.C. Asser Press 1999) 579 pp.

Articles
[see also below: 10. Arms Control and Disarmament]
- Meselson, M., J. Robinson, J. Crawford, J. Dugard and P. Heymann, 'A Draft Convention to Prohibit Biological and Chemical Weapons Under International Criminal Law', *The CBW Conventions Bulletin*, No. 42 (1998). *Quarterly Journal of the Harvard Sussex Program on CBW Armaments and Arms Limitation*

4.142   Cultural Property and Places of Worship

Articles

- Blum, Yehuda Z., 'Restitution of Jewish cultural property looted in World War II: to whom?', 11 *Leiden JIL* (1998) pp. 257-264
- Henckaerts, Jean-Marie, 'New rules for the protection of cultural property in armed conflict', 81 *IRRC* No. 835 (1999)
- Hladik, Jan, 'The review process of the 1954 Hague Convention for the Protection of Cultural Property in the Event of Armed Conflict and its impact on international humanitarian law', 1 *YIHL* (1998) pp. 313-322
- Hladik, Jan, 'The 1954 Hague Convention for the Protection of Cultural Property in the Event of Armed Conflict and the notion of military necessity', 81 *IRRC* No. 835 (1999) pp. 621-635
- O'Keefe, Roger, 'The meaning of 'cultural property' under the 1954 Hague Convention', 46 *NILR* (1999) pp. 26-56

4.144   The Natural Environment

Articles

- Parsons, Rymn James, 'The fight to save the planet: U.S. Armed Forces, "Greenkeeping", and enforcement of the law pertaining to environmental protection during armed conflict', 10 *Georgetown Int. Environ. LR* (1998) pp. 441-500
- Schmitt, Michael N., 'War and the environment: fault lines in the prescriptive landscape', 37 *AV* (1999) pp. 25-67

4.146   Civil Defence

Articles

- Jeannet, Stephane, 'Civil defence 1977-1997: from law to practice', 38 *IRRC* No. 325 (1998) pp. 715-723

4.16   Humanitarian Assistance Operations

Books

- Moore, Jonathan, ed., (under the auspices of the ICRC), *Hard Choices: Moral dilemmas in humanitarian intervention* (Lanham, Rowman and Littleman 1998)

Articles

- Chua, Adrian T.L. and Rohan J. Hardcastle, 'Humanitarian assistance: towards a right of access to victims of natural disasters', 38 *IRRC* No. 325 (1998) pp. 589-609
- Herby, Peter, 'Arms transfers, humanitarian assistance and international humanitarian law', 38 *IRRC* No. 325 (1998) pp. 685-691. In French: 'Transferts d'armes, assistance humanitaire et droit international humanitaire', 80 *RICR* No. 832 (1998) pp. 741-749
- Munro, Alan, 'Humanitarianism and conflict in a post-Cold War world', 81 *IRRC* No. 835 (1999) pp. 463-476
- Rottensteiner, Christa, 'The denial of humanitarian assistance as a crime under international law', 81 *IRRC* No. 835 (1999) pp. 555-582

4.21   Land Warfare

Articles
- Doty, Grant R., 'The United States and the development of the laws of land warfare', 156 *MLR* (1998) pp. 224-255

4.22   Air and Missile Warfare

- Gomez, Javier Guisandez, 'The law of air warfare', 38 *IRRC* No. 323 (1998) pp. 347-363

4.23   Naval Warfare

Books
- Busuttil, James J., *Naval Weapons Systems and the Contemporary Law of War* (Oxford, Oxford University Press 1998) 270 pp.
- Politakis, George P., *Modern Aspects of the Laws of Naval Warfare and Maritime Neutrality* (London, Kegan Paul 1999) 678 pp.

5.   TERMINATION OF ARMED CONFLICTS

5.1   Ceasefire, Armistices and Peace Agreements

Articles
- Ardalan, Sabrineh and Paul R. Williams, 'The Northern Ireland Peace Agreement: evolving the principle of self-determination', 12 *Leiden JIL* (1999) pp. 155-171
- Canal-Forgues, Eric, 'La surveillance de l'application de l'arrangement du 26 avril 1996 (Israel-Liban): une tentative originale de mise en oeuvre de l'obligation de respect du droit international humanitaire', 102 *RGDIP* (1998) pp. 723-746
- Gilbert, Geoff, 'The Northern Ireland Peace Agreement, minority rights and self-determination', 47 *ICLQ* (1998) pp. 943-950
- 'The general framework agreement for peace in Bosnia and Herzegovina', in Gisvold, Gregory and Michael O'Flaherty, eds., *Post-War Protection of Human Rights in Bosnia and Herzegovina* (The Hague, Nijhoff 1998) pp. 272-308
- Ni Aolain, Fionnuala, 'The fractured soul of the Dayton Peace Agreement: a legal analysis', 19 *Mich. JIL* (1998) pp. 957-1004
- *Northern Ireland Peace Agreement*: United Kingdom of Great Britain and Northern Ireland – Government of Ireland – Alliance Party – Progressive Unionist Party – Sinn Fein – Social Democratic Labour Party – Ulster Unionist Party – Women's Coalition: Agreement reached in the multi-party negotiations (Belfast, 10 April 1998) 37 *ILM* (1998) pp. 751-779

5.3   Amnesties, Truth and Reconciliation Commissions

Books and Reports
- *Truth & Reconciliation Commission of South Africa Report*, 5 vols. (London, Macmillan 1998) [includes searchable CD-ROM]

– *Final Report: The Truth and Reconciliation Commission [South Africa]: Summary and Guide* (The Hague, Embassy of South Africa 1998) 56 pp.
– Wink, W., *Healing a Nation's Wounds: Reconciliation on the Road to Democracy* (Life and Peace Institute 1997) 80 pp.
– Witte-Rang, M.E., *A Way Out of Conflict: A Report on Reconciliation Activities in Projects of Partners of Dutch Church-Related NGOs and the Dutch Government* (Utrecht, OIKOS 1998) 52 pp.

Articles
– Bradley, Evelyn, 'In search for justice: a Truth and Reconciliation Commission for Rwanda', 7 *JIL & Prac.* (1998) pp. 129-158
– Dugard, John, 'Reconciliation and justice: the South African experience', 8 *Transn. L & Contemp. Probs.* (1998) pp. 277-311
– Ellian, Afshin, 'Reconciliation and criminal law during the political transition', 7 *Tilburg For. LR* (1998) pp. 27-34
– Klosterman, Theresa, 'The feasibility and propriety of a Truth Commission in Cambodia: Too little? Too late?', 15 *Arizona JI & CL* (1998) pp. 833-869
– Gibson, Lauren and Naomi Roht-Arriaza, 'The developing jurisprudence of amnesty', 20 *HRQ* (1998) pp. 843-885
– Gisvold, Gregory, 'A Truth Commission for Bosnia and Herzegovina? Anticipating the Debate', in O'Flaherty, Michael and Gregory Gisvold, eds., *Post-war protection of human rights in Bosnia and Herzegovina* (The Hague, Nijhoff 1998) pp. 241-261
– King, Julie C. and Paul Lansing, 'South Africa's Truth and Reconciliation Commission: the conflict between individual justice and national healing in the post-apartheid age', 15 *Ariz. JI & CL* (1998) pp. 753-789
– Klug, Heinz, 'Amnesty, amnesia and remembrance: international obligations and the need to prevent the repetition of gross violations of human rights', 92 *Proceedings of the ... annual meeting* (1998) pp. 316-320
– Minow, Martha, 'Between vengeance and forgiveness: South Africa's Truth and Reconciliation Commission', 14 *Negotiation Journal* (1998) pp. 319-355
– Parlevliet, Michelle, 'Considering truth: Dealing with a legacy of gross human rights violations', 16 *NQHR* (1998) pp. 141-174
– Roht-Arriaza, Naomi, 'Truth Commissions and amnesties in Latin America: The second generation', 92 *Proceedings of the ... annual meeting* (1998) pp. 313-316
– Schlunck, Angelika, 'Truth and Reconciliation Commissions', 4 *ILSA JI & CL* (1998) pp. 415-422

5.4   Reparations/Compensation

Articles
– Cotler, Irwin, 'Nuremberg 50 years later: The restitution of Jewish Property and Norwegian Justice', 67 *Nordic JIL* (1998) pp. 275-287
– Wassgren, Hans, 'The UN Compensation Commission: Lessons of legitimacy, state responsibility, and war reparations', 11 *Leiden JIL* (1998) pp. 473-492

6. INTERNATIONAL CRIMINAL LAW (GENERAL)

Books
- Bassiouni, M. Cherif., ed., *International Criminal Law*, 2nd edn. (Irvington-on-Hudson, NY, Transnational Publishers 1998) 3 vols.
- La Rosa, Anne-Marie, *Dictionnaire de droit international pénal: termes choisis* (Paris, PUF 1998) 118 pp.
- van der Beken, Tom, *Forumkeuze in het internationaal strafrecht: verdeling van misdrijven met aanknopingspunten in meerdere staten* (Antwerp, Maklu 1999) 486 pp.

Articles and Reports
- Cassese, Antonio, 'On the current trends towards criminal prosecutions and punishment of international humanitarian law', 9 *EJIL* (1998) pp. 1-17
- Cassese, Antonio, 'Reflections on International Criminal Justice', *MLR* (1998) pp. 1-10
- Cosnard, Michel, 'Quelques observations sur les décisions de la Chambre des Lords du 25 novembre 1998 et du 24 mars 1999 dans l'affaire Pinochet', 103 *RGDIP* (1999) pp. 309-328
- Dominice, Christian, 'Quelques observations sur l'immunité de jurisdiction pénale de l'ancien chef d'Etat', 103 *RGDIP* (1999) pp. 297-308
- Dupuy, Pierre-Marie, 'Crimes et immunités, ou dans quelle mesure la nature des premiers empêche l'exercise des secondes', 103 *RGDIP* (1999) pp. 289-296
- Fox, Hazel, 'The first Pinochet case: Immunity of a former Head of State', 48 *ICLQ* (1998) pp. 207-216
- Greppi, Edoardo, 'The evolution of individual criminal responsibility under international law', 81 *IRRC* No. 835 (1999) pp. 531-553
- Haag, Inger (reporter), 'Toward transnational norms of criminal procedure: emerging issues of defendants' rights', in *Contemporary International Law Issues: New Forms, New Applications*, pp. 1-20, *supra* 4.11121
- 'In re. Pinochet' [collection of short articles on various criminal proceedings concerning General Pinochet], 93 *AJIL* (1999) pp. 690-711
- Joyner, Christopher C. and M. Cherif Bassiouni, eds., *Reining in Impunity for International Crimes and Serious Violations of Fundamental Human Rights: Proceedings of the Siracusa Conference 17-21 September 1998* (Ramonville St. Ange, Éditions érès (Nouvelle études pénales/Association internationale de droit penal) (1998)
- Klabbers, Jan, 'The General, the Lords, and the Possible End of State Immunity', 68 *Nordic JIL* (1999) pp. 85-95
- Symposium on Method in International Law, 93 *AJIL* (1999) pp. 291-423 (presenting 7 methodological approaches to the responsibility of individuals for human rights abuses in internal armed conflict), *supra* 2.11
- Meron, Theodor, 'Is international law moving towards criminalization?', 9 *EJIL* (1998) pp. 18-31
- Néel, Lison, 'Échecs et compromis de la justice pénale internationale' (Note), *Études Internationales* (1998) pp. 85-106
- Piotrowicz, Ryszard, 'Crime and punishment, or the establishment of a true international court of justice', 72 *Australian LJ* (1998) pp. 844-850

- Ratner, Steven R., 'The schizophrenias of international criminal law', 33 *Texas ILJ* (1998) pp. 237-256
- Stroh, Dagmar Patricia (reporter), 'Transnational crimes: national and international jurisdiction', *Contemporary International Law Issues: New Forms, New Applications*, pp. 37-56, *supra* 4.11121
- Tomuschat, Christian, 'Das Strafgesetzbuch der Verbrechen gegen den Frieden und die Sicherheit der Menschheit: Code of Crimes against the Peace and Security of Mankind, Entwurf der International Law Commission', 25 *Europäische Grundrechte Zeitschrift* (1998) pp. 1-7
- Varadarajan, Latha, 'From Tokyo to The Hague: a reassessment of Radhabinodh Pal's Dissenting Opinion at the Tokyo Trials on its golden jubilee', 38 *Indian JIL* (1998) pp. 233-247

6.1   The Crimes (general)

Articles
- Nowak, Manfred, 'Disappearances in Bosnia and Herzegovina', in Michael O'Flaherty and Gregory Gisvold, eds., *Post-war protection of human rights in Bosnia and Herzegovina* (The Hague, Nijhoff 1998) pp. 107-121
- Rottensteiner, Christa, 'The denial of humanitarian assistance as a crime under international law', 81 *IRRC* No. 835 (1999) pp. 555-582
- Salzman, Todd A., 'Rape camps as a means of ethnic cleansing: religious, cultural, and ethical responses to rape victims in the Former Yugoslavia', 20 *HRQ* (1998) pp. 348-378
- Swaak-Goldman, Olivia Q., 'The Crime of persecution in international criminal law', 11 *Leiden JIL* (1998) pp. 145-154
- Viseur-Sellers, Patricia, 'Emerging jurisprudence on crimes of sexual violence', 13 *Amer. Univ. ILR* (1998) pp. 1523-1531

6.11   War Crimes

Books
- Cooper, Belinda, ed., *War Crimes: The Legacy of Nuremberg* (New York, TV Books 1999) 350 pp.
- Gutman, Roy, David Rieff and Kenneth Anderson, eds., *Crimes of War: What the Public Should Know* (New York, Norton 1999) 399 pp.
- Meron, Theodor, *War Crimes Law Comes of Age: Essays* (Oxford, Oxford University Press 1998) 310 pp.

Articles
- Drumbl, Mark A., 'Waging war against the world: the need to move from war crimes to environmental crimes', 22 *Fordham ILJ* (1998) pp. 122-153
- Fenrick, William F., 'Should crimes against humanity replace war crimes?', 37 *Columbia JTL* (1999) pp. 767-785
- Graditzky, Thomas, 'La responsabilité pénale individuelle pour violation du droit international humanitaire applicable en situation de conflit armé non international',

80 *RICR* No. 829 (1998) pp. 29-57. [In English: 'Individual criminal responsibility for violations of international humanitarian law committed in non-international armed conflicts', 38 *IRRC* No. 322 (1998) pp. 29-56

- Kaemmerer, Joern Axel, 'Kriegsrepressalie oder Kriegsverbrechen? Zur rechtlichen Beurteilung der Massenexekutionen von Zivilisten durch die deutsche Besatzungsmacht im Zweiten Weltkrieg', 37 *AV* (1999) pp. 283-317
- Marchisio, Sergio, 'The Priebke Case before the Italian Military Tribunals: a reaffirmation of the principle of non-applicability of statutory limitations to war crimes and crimes against humanity', 1 *YIHL* (1998) pp. 344-353
- Wallach, E., 'The procedural and evidentiary rules of the post-world war II war crimes trials: did they provide an outline for international legal procedure?', 37 *Columbia JTL* (1999) pp. 851-883
- Watson, Peter, 'Crimes of war: a personal account of the horrors revealed by an investigation of a Nazi war criminal', 4 *ILSA JI & CL* (1998) pp. 683-696
- Zeileissen, Ch., 'War crimes under the jurisdiction of the Tribunal on the Former Yugoslavia', 3 *Aust. Rev. Int. & Eur. L* (1998) pp. 47-100
- Ziegler, Andreas R., 'In Re G', 92 *AJIL* (1998) pp. 78-82

6.12   Genocide

Books

- Adelman, Suhrke, *The Path of Genocide – The Rwanda Crisis from Uganda to Zaire* (New Brunswick NJ, Transaction Publishers 1999) 287 pp.
- Burr, M., *Quantifying Genocide in Southern Sudan and the Nuba Mountains, 1983-1998*, (US Committee for Refugees, 1998) 76 pp.
- Jonassohn, Kurt, *Genocide and Gross Human Rights Violations* (New Brunswick NJ, Transaction Publishers 1998) 338 pp.
- Klinghoffer, A.J., *The International Dimension of Genocide in Rwanda* (Basingstoke, Macmillan 1998) 219 pp.
- Nyankanzi, Edward L., *Genocide: Rwanda & Burundi* (Rochester, VT, Schenkman Books 1998) 200 pp.

Articles

- Cissé, Catherine, 'The end of a culture of impunity in Rwanda? Prosecution of genocide and war crimes before Rwandan Courts and the International Criminal Tribunal for Rwanda', 1 *YIHL* (1998) pp. 161-188
- Dadrian, Vahakn N., 'The historical and legal interconnection between the Armenian genocide and the Jewish Holocaust: from impunity to retributive justice', 23 *Yale JIL* (1998) pp. 503-559
- De Weese, Geoffrey S., 'The failure of the International Court of Justice to effectively enforce the Genocide Convention', 26 *Denver JIL & Pol.* (1998) pp. 625-654
- Hillgruber, Christian, 'Die Jurisdiktionsgewalt des IGH nach Art IX Genozidkonvention und ihre Grenzen: zum Zwischenurteil des IGH im 'Case concerning application of the Convention on the Prevention and Punishment of the Crime of Genocide' (*Bosnia-Herzegovina* v. *Yugoslavia*) vom 11. Juli 1996, 53 *ZöR* (1998) pp. 363-382

– Knowles, Catherine S., 'Life and human dignity, the birthright of all human beings: an analysis of the Iraqi genocide of the Kurds and effective enforcement of human rights', 45 *NLR* (1998) pp. 152-216
– Lippman, Matthew, 'The Convention on the Prevention and Punishment of the Crime of Genocide: fifty years later', 15 *Arizona JI & CL* (1998) pp. 415-514
– Maison, Raffaelle, 'Le crime de génocide dans les premiers jugements du Tribunal penal international pour le Rwanda', 103 *RGDIP* (1999) pp. 129-145
– Nygren Krug, Helena, 'Genocide in Rwanda: lessons learned and future challenges to the UN human rights system', 67 *Nordic JIL* (1998) pp. 165-213
– Ratner, Steven R., 'The Genocide Convention after fifty years', 92 *Proceedings of the ... annual meeting* (1998) pp. 1-3
– Steven, Lee A., 'Genocide and the duty to extradite or prosecute: why the United States is in breach of its international obligations', 39 *Virg. JIL* (1999) pp. 425-466
– Sychold, Martin M., 'Ratification of the Genocide Convention : the legal effets in light of reservations and objections', 8 SZIER/RSDIE (1998) pp. 533-552
– Yacoubian, George S., 'The efficacy of international criminal justice: evaluating the aftermath of the Rwandan genocide', 161 *World Affairs* (1999) pp. 186-192

6.13   Crimes Against Humanity

Books

– Bassiouni, M. Cherif, *Crimes against humanity in international criminal law*, 2nd edn. (The Hague, Kluwer Law International 1999) 610 pp.

Articles

– de Hemptinne, Jerome, 'La définition du crime contre l'humanité par le tribunal pénal international pour l'ex-Yougoslavie', 9 *Revue trimestrielle des droits de l'homme* (1998) pp. 763-779
– Fenrick, William F., 'Should crimes against humanity replace war crimes?', 37 *Columbia JTL* (1999) pp. 767-785
– Grynfogel, Catherine, 'Les limites de la complicite de crime contre l'humanite', *RSCDPC* (1998) pp. 523-533
– Hwang, Phyllis, 'Defining crimes against humanity in the Rome Statute of the International Criminal Court', 22 *Fordham ILJ* (1998) pp. 457-504
– Maier, Julio B.J., 'Derecho penal internacional. Crimenes contra la humanidad. Extraterritorialidad de la ley penal aplicable y competencia de juzgamiento', Vol. I-II *Revista Juridica de Buenos Aires* (1998) pp. 3-18
– Moshan, Brook Sari, 'Women, war, and words: the gender component in the Permanent International Criminal Court's definition of crimes against humanity', 22 *Fordham ILJ* (1998) pp. 154-184
– Robinson, Darryl, 'Defining "Crimes Against Humanity" at the Rome Conference', 93 *AJIL* (1999) pp. 43-57
– Starita, M., 'La questione della prescrittibilità dei crimini contro l'umanità: in margine al caso Priebke', 81 *RDI* (1998) pp. 86-109
– van Schaack, Beth, 'The definition of crimes against humanity: resolving the incoherence', 37 *Columbia JTL* (1999) pp. 787-850

6.14   Aggression

Articles
- Ricman, Gregg, 'Sanctions and Iranian aggression', 92 *Proceedings of the ... annual meeting* (1998) pp. 71-74

6.2   Defences

Books
- Nill-Theobald, Christiane, *"Defences" bei Kriegsverbrechen am Beispiel Deutschlands und den USA – Zugleich ein Beitrag zu einem Allgemeinen Teil des Völkerstrafrechts*, edition iuscrim, Vol. S 72 (Freiburg, 1998) 465 pp.
- Osiel, Mark, *Obeying Orders – Atrocity, Military Discipline, and the Law of War* (New Brunswick NJ, Transaction Publishers 1999) 398 pp.

Articles
- Bantekas, Ilias, 'The contemporary law of superior responsibility', 93 *AJIL* (1999) pp. 573-595
- Gaeta, Paola, 'La rilevanza dell'ordine superiore nel diritto internazionale penale', 81 *RDI* (1998) pp. 69-85
- Gaeta, Paola, 'The defence of superior orders: the statute of the International Criminal Court versus customary international law', 10 *EJIL* (1999) pp. 172-191
- Jia, Bing Bing, 'The doctrine of command responsibility in international law: with emphasis on liability for failure to punish', 45 *NILR* (1998) pp. 325-347
- Kaemmerer, Joern Axel, 'Kriegsrepressalie oder Kriegsverbrechen? Zur rechtlichen Beurteilung der Massenexekutionen von Zivilisten durch die deutsche Besatzungsmacht im Zweiten Weltkrieg', 37 *AV* (1999) pp. 283-317
- Martines, Francesca, 'The defences of reprisals, superior orders and duress in the Priebke case before the Italian Military Tribunal', 1 *YIHL* (1998) pp. 354-361
- Rowe, Peter, 'Duress as a defence to war crimes after Erdemović: a laboratory for a permanent court?', 1 *YIHL* (1998) pp. 210-228

6.3   Repression of Breaches (general)

Books
- Beigbeder, Yves, *Judging war criminals: the politics of international justice* (New York: St. Martin's Press 1998)
- Bell, Howard, *Prosecuting war crimes and genocide: the twentieth century experience* (University of Kansas Press 1999)
- Bremer, Kathrin, *Nationale Strafverfolgung internationaler Verbrechen gegen das humanitäre Völkerrecht: am Beispiel einer Rechtsvergleichung Deutschlands, der Schweiz, Belgiens und Großbritanniens* (Frankfurt am Main, Lang 1999) 433 pp.
- Freeman Harris, Marshall, *The Report of the Century Foundation/Twentieth Century Fund task force on apprehending indicted war criminals: making justice work* (New York, Century Foundation Press 1998)
- Ikenberry, John G., *Judging War Criminals: The Politics of International Justice* (New York, St. Martin's 1999) 224 pp.

– Pellandini, Cristina, ed., *Répression nationale des violations du droit international humanitaire (systèmes romano-germaniques): rapport de la réunion d'experts, Genève, 23-25 septembre 1997*, (Geneva, ICRC 1998)
– Robertson, Geoffrey, *Crimes against Humanity: The Struggle for Global Justice* (London, Lane/Penguin 1999) 474 pp.

Articles
– Ambos, Kai, 'Völkerrechtliche Bestrafungspflichten bei schweren Menschen-rechtsverletzungen', 37 *AV* (1999) pp. 318-356.
– Cassese, Antonio, 'On the current trends towards criminal prosecution and punish-ment of breaches of international humanitarian law', 9 *EJIL* (1998) pp. 2-17
– Charney, Jonathan, 'Progress in international criminal law?', 93 *AJIL* (1999) pp. 452-464
– Dugard, John, 'Bridging the gap between human rights and humanitarian law: the punishment of offenders', 38 *IRRC* No. 324 (1998) pp. 445-453
– Gutman, Roy W., 'Les violations du droit international humanitaire sous le feu des projecteurs: le rôle des médias', 80 *RICR* No. 832 (1998) pp. 667-675
– Meron, Theodor, 'Is international law moving towards criminalization?', 9 *EJIL* (1998) pp. 18-31
– Morris, Madeline, 'Facilitating accountability: the potential value of international guidelines against impunity', 4 *ILSA & Comp.* (1998) pp. 401-406
– Moynier, Gustave, 'Draft convention for the establishment of an international judicial body suitable for the prevention and punishment of violations of the Geneva Convention (Geneva, 1872)', 38 *IRRC* No. 322 (1998) pp. 72-74
– Moynier, Gustave, 'Projet de convention pour la création d'une institution judiciaire internationale propre à prévenir et à réprimer les infractions à la Convention de Genève (Genève, 1872)' 80 *RICR* No. 829 (1998) pp. 76-78
– Rajagopal, Balakrishnan, 'The Pragmatics of Prosecuting the Khmer Rouge', 1 *YIHL* (1998) pp. 189-204
– Sarooshi, Danesh, 'The Powers of the United Nations International Criminal Tribunals', 2 *MPYBUNL* (1998) pp.141-167
– Schilling, Theodor, 'Ungeschriebene Strafpflichten: eine wertende Bestandsaufnahme des Völker-, Gemeinschafts-, und (deutschen) Verfassungsrechts,' 54 *ZöR* (1999) pp. 357-407

6.31   International Courts (general)

Articles and Proceedings
– Arbour, Louise, 'History and future of the International Criminal Tribunals for the Former Yugoslavia and Rwanda', 13 *Amer. Univ. ILR* (1998) pp. 1498-1504
– Bang-Jensen, Nina, 'Tribunal justice: the challenges, the record, and the prospects', 13 *Amer. Univ. ILR* (1998) pp. 1560-1564
– Binder, David, 'Internationale Gerichtshöfe einst und jetzt: Jan Hus und Milosevic auf der Anklagebank', 53 *Internationale Politik* (1998) pp. 47-51
– Bothe, Michael, 'International humanitarian law and War Crimes Tribunals: recent developments and perspectives', in Karel Wellens, ed., *International law: Theory and Practice: essays in honour of Eric Suy* (The Hague, Nijhoff 1998) pp. 581-595

- 'Essays on the Laws of War and War Crimes Tribunals in honour of Telford Taylor', 37 *Columbia JTL* (1999) pp. 649-1047
- Ferencz, Benjamin B., 'International Criminal Courts: the legacy of Nuremberg?', 10 *Pace ILR* (1998) pp. 203-235
- Gjelten, Tom, 'Tribunal justice: the challenges, the record, and the prospects', 13 *Amer. Univ. ILR* (1998) pp. 1555-1560
- Leigh, Monroe and Mauri Shenk, 'International Criminal Tribunals for the Former Yugoslavia and Rwanda', 32 *The International Lawyer* (1998) pp. 509-513
- Nizich, Ivana, 'Tribunal justice: the challenges, the record, and the prospects', 13 *Amer. Univ. ILR* (1998) pp. 1544-1555
- Sob, Pierre, 'The dynamics of International Criminal Tribunals', 67 *Nordic JIL* (1998) pp. 139-163
- Soofi, Ahmer Bilal, 'Experience of UN War Crimes Tribunal and the need for a permanent International Criminal Court', 51 *Pakistan Horizon* (1998) pp. 37-52
- 'War Crimes Tribunals: the record and the prospects: Conference organized by the American University Washington College of Law and the American Society of International Law, held at the Washington College of Law on 31 March-1April 1998', 13 *Amer. Univ. ILR* (1998) pp. 1383-1584
- Warbrick, Colin, 'International Criminal Courts and fair trial', 3 *Journal of Armed Conflict* (1998) pp. 45-64
- Yacoubian, George S., 'Sanctioning alternatives in international criminal law: recommendations for the International Criminal Tribunals for Rwanda and the Former Yugoslavia', 161 *World Affairs* (1998) pp. 48-54

6.311   Nuremberg and Tokyo

Books
- King, Henry T., 'The meaning of Nuremberg', 30 *Case Western Reserve JIL* (1998) pp. 143-148
- Pritchard, R. John, ed., *The Tokyo Major War Crimes Trial: the records of the International Military Tribunal for the Far East: with an authoritative commentary and comprehensive guide* (Lewiston NY, Edwin Mellen Press 1998)

6.312   International Criminal Tribunal for the Former Yugoslavia

Books
- Klip, André and Göran Sluiter, eds., *Annotated Leading Cases of International Criminal Tribunals: Volume 1: The International Criminal Tribunal for the Former Yugoslavia 1993-1998* (Antwerp, Intersentia Law Publishers 1999) 800 pp.
- Jones, John R.W.D., *The Practice of the International Criminal Tribunals for the Former Yugoslavia and Rwanda* (Irvington-on-Hudson, NY, Transnational Publishers, Inc. 1998) 355 pp.
- Vitucci, Maria Chiara, *Il tribunale ad hoc per la ex Iugoslavia e il consenso degli stati* (Milano, Giuffre 1998) 108 pp.
- *The war crimes trials for the Former Yugoslavia : prospects and problems: May, 28 1996* (Washington DC, Commission on Security and Cooperation in Europe 1996) 111 pp.

Articles

- Affolder, Natasha A., 'Tadić, the anonymous witness and the sources of international procedural law', 19 *Michigan JIL* (1998) pp. 445-495
- Alvarez, Jose E., 'Rush to closure: lessons of the Tadić judgment', 96 *Michigan LR* (1998) pp. 2031-2112
- Akhavan, Payam, 'Justice in The Hague, peace in the former Yugoslavia? A commentary on the United Nations War Crimes Tribunal', 20 *HRQ* (1998) pp. 737-816
- Ambos, Kai and Albin Eser, 'The power of national courts to compel the production of evidence and its limits: an *amicus curiae* brief to the International Criminal Tribunal for the Former Yugoslavia', 6 *Eur. J Crime, Crim. L & Crim. Jus* (1998) pp. 3-20
- Ambos, K., 'Strafverteidigung vor dem UN-Jugoslawiengerichtshof', 51 *Neue juristische Wochenschrift* (1998) pp. 1444-1447
- Ambos, K., 'Zur Stellung von Verteidiger und Beschuldigtem vor dem UN-Jugoslawiengerichtshof', 18 *Neue Zeitschrift für Strafrecht* (1998) pp. 123-126
- Amley, Edward A. and Mark Thieroff, 'Proceeding to justice and accountability in the Balkans: the International Criminal Tribunal for the Former Yugoslavia and Rule 61', 23 *Yale JIL* (1998) pp. 231-274
- Beresford, Stuart, 'The International Criminal Tribunal for the Former Yugoslavia: the first four years', 9 *Otago LR* (1999) pp. 557-578
- Bodley, Anne, 'Weakening the principle of sovereignty in international law: the International Criminal Tribunal for the Former Yugoslavia', 31 *NY Univ. JIL & Pol.* (1999) pp. 417-471
- Ciampi, A., 'Sull'applicazione della teoria dei poteri impliciti da parte del Tribunale penale internazionale per la ex-Iugoslavia', 81 *RDI* (1998) pp. 130-143
- Creta, Vincent M., 'The search for justice in the Former Yugoslavia and beyond: analyzing the rights of the accused under the Statute and the Rules of Procedure and Evidence of the International Criminal Tribunal for the Former Yugoslavia', 20 *Houston JIL* (1998) pp. 381-418
- Fenrick, William J., 'The development of the law of armed conflict through the jurisprudence of the International Criminal Tribunal for the Former Yugoslavia', 3 *Journal of Armed Conflict* (1998) pp. 197-232
- Fenrick, William, J., 'The application of the Geneva Conventions by the International Criminal Tribunal for the Former Yugoslavia', 81 *IRRC* No. 834 (1999) pp. 317-330
- Gaeta, Paola, 'Is NATO authorized or obliged to arrest persons indicted by the International Criminal Tribunal for the Former Yugoslavia?', 9 *EJIL* (1998) pp. 174-181
- Greenwood, Christopher, 'The development of international humanitarian law by the International Criminal Tribunal for the Former Yugoslavia', 2 *MPYBUNL* (1998) pp. 97-140
- Hafner, Gerhard, 'Limits to the procedural powers of the International Tribunal for the Former Yugoslavia', in Karel Wellens, ed., *International law: theory and practice: essays in honour of Eric Suy* (The Hague, Nijhoff 1998) pp. 651-677
- Hampson, Françoise J., 'The International Criminal Tribunal for the former Yugoslavia and the reluctant witness', 47 *ICLQ* (1998) pp. 50-74
- Hogan-Doran, Justin, 'Murder as a crime under international law and the Statute of the International Criminal Tribunal for the Former Yugoslavia: of law, legal language, and a comparative approach to legal meaning', 11 *Leiden JIL* (1998) pp. 165-181

- Linton, Suzannah, 'Reviewing the Case of Drazen Erdemovič: unchartered waters at the International Criminal Tribunal for the Former Yugoslavia', 12 *Leiden JIL* (1999) pp. 251-270
- Malanczuk, Peter, 'A note on the judgement of the Appeals Chamber of the International Criminal Tribunal for the Former Yugoslavia on the issuance of *Subpoenae Duces Tecum* in the *Blaškič* case', 1 *YIHL* (1998) pp. 229-244
- McDonald, Gabrielle Kirk, 'The Prosecutor v. Duško Tadić', 13 *Amer. Univ. ILR* (1998) pp. 1460-1467
- McDonald, Gabrielle Kirk, 'The International Criminal Tribunal for the Former Yugoslavia', 13 *Amer. Univ. ILR* (1998) pp. 1422-1439
- Meron, Theodor, 'The Hague Tribunal: working to clarify international humanitarian law', 13 *Amer. Univ. ILR* (1998) pp. 1511-1518
- Murphy, Sean D., 'Progress and jurisprudence of the International Criminal Tribunal for the Former Yugoslavia', 93 *AJIL* (1999) pp. 57-97
- Nouvel, Yves, 'Précisions sur le pouvoir du Tribunal pour l'Ex-Yougoslavie d'ordonner la production des preuves et la comparution des témoins: l'arrêt de la Chambre d'Appel du 29 octobre 1997 dans l'Affaire Blaskic', 102 *RGDIP* (1998) pp. 157-164
- Oellers-Frahm, Karin, and Britta Specht, 'Die Erdemovich-Rechtsprechung des Jugoslawientribunals: Probleme bei der Entwicklung eines internationalen Strafrechts, dargestellt am Beispiel des Notstands', 58 *ZaöRV* (1998) pp. 389-414
- Petrovic, Drazen, 'The post-Dayton role of the International Criminal Tribunal for the Former Yugoslavia', in O'Flaherty, Michael and Gregory Gisvold, eds., *Post-war protection of human rights in Bosnia and Herzegovina*, (The Hague, Nijhoff 1998) pp. 195-214
- Riad, Fouad, 'Portrait du Tribunal pénal international pour l'ex-Yougoslavie', in *Boutros Boutros-Ghali: Amicorum discipulorumque liber*, Vol. 1 (1998) pp. 661-643
- Scharf, Michael P., 'Trial and error: an assessment of the first judgment of the Yugoslavia War Crimes Tribunal', 30 *NY Univ. JIL and Pol.* (1998) pp. 167-200
- Scharf, Michael P., '*The Prosecutor* v. *Slavko Dokmanovič*: Irregular Rendition and the ICTY', 11 *Leiden JIL* (1998) pp. 369-382
- Schmalenbach, Kirsten, 'Die Auslieferung mutmaßlicher deutscher Kriegsverbrecher an das Jugoslawientribunal', 36 *AV* (1998) pp. 285-304
- Sharp, Walter Gary, 'In search of peace and justice: War criminals at large in the Former Yugoslavia', 32 *The International Lawyer* (1998) pp. 489-498
- Sluiter, Göran, 'Samenwerking tussen Staten en het Joegoslavië Tribunaal na de Blaskic Subpoena beslissing, 91 *Militair Rechtelijk Tijdschrift* (1998) pp. 41-51
- Swaak-Goldman, Olivia, '*Prosecutor* v. *Erdemovič*', 92 *AJIL* (1998) pp. 282-287
- Swaak-Goldman, Olivia, '*Prosecutor* v. *Delalič*', 93 *AJIL* (1999) pp. 514-519
- Tieger, Alan, 'The Prosecutor v. Duško Tadić', 13 *Amer. Univ. ILR* (1998) pp. 1443-1447
- Tolbert, David, 'The International Tribunal for the Former Yugoslavia and the Enforcement of Sentences', 11 *Leiden JIL* (1998) pp. 655-670
- 'Tribunal pénal international pour l'ex-Yougoslavie (Chambre de première instance IIter), 5 mars 1998: plaidoyer de culpabilité, – condition – peine détermination – contrainte – accord de marchandage judiciare', 78 *RDPC* (1998) pp. 8-7-824
- Turns, David, 'The International Criminal Tribunal for the Former Yugoslavia: the *Erdemovič* case', 47 *ICLQ* (1998) pp. 461-474

- Wauters, Jasper M., 'Torture and related crimes: a discussion of the crimes before the International Criminal Tribunal for the Former Yugoslavia', 11 *Leiden JIL* (1998) pp. 155-164
- Wedgwood, Ruth, 'The International Criminal Tribunal and Subpoenas for State Documents', 11 *Leiden JIL* (1998) pp. 635-654
- Wladimiroff, Michail, 'The Prosecutor v. Duško Tadić', 13 *Amer. Univ. ILR* (1998) pp. 1447-1455
- Zic, Kristijan, 'The International Criminal Tribunal for the Former Yugoslavia: applying international law to war criminals,' 16 *Boston Univ. ILJ* (1998) pp. 507-533

6.313   International Criminal Tribunal for Rwanda

Books

- Jones, John R.W.D., *The Practice of the International Criminal Tribunals for the Former Yugoslavia and Rwanda* (Irvington-on-Hudson, NY, Transnational Publishers, Inc. 1998)
- Morris, Virginia and Michael P. Scharf, *The International Criminal Tribunal for Rwanda,* vols. I and II (Irvington-on Hudson, NY, Transnational Publishers, Inc. 1998)

Articles

- Amann, Diane Marie, '*Prosecutor v. Akayesu*', 93 *AJIL* (1999) pp. 195-199
- Calathes, William and Todd Howland, 'The U.N.'s International Criminal Tribunal: is it justice or jingoism for Rwanda? A call for transformation', 39 *Virg. JIL* (1998) pp. 135-167
- Cissé, Catherine, 'The end of a culture of impunity in Rwanda? Prosecution of genocide and war crimes before Rwandan Court and the International Criminal Tribunal for Rwanda', 1 *YIHL* (1998) pp. 161-188
- Eyeni Mbu, Nelson, 'Implementation of humanitarian law by means of repression: the case of the International Criminal Tribunal for Rwanda', 1 *Revue scientifique du droit* (1998) pp. 59-87
- Helfer, Laurence R., '*Prosecutor v. Akayesu*', 93 *AJIL* (1999) pp. 195-205
- Magnarella, Paul J., 'Some milestones and achievements at the International Criminal Tribunal for Rwanda: the 1998 Kambanda and Akayesu cases', 11 *Florida JIL* (1997) pp. 517-538
- Maison, Raffaelle, 'Le crime de génocide dans les premiers jugements du Tribunal pénal international pour le Rwanda', 103 *RGDIP* (1999) pp. 129-145
- Morris, Virginia, 'Prosecutor v. Kanyabashi, Decision on jurisdiction', 92 *AJIL* (1998) pp. 66-70.
- Niang, Mame Mandiaye, 'Le Tribunal pénal international pour le Rwanda. Et si la coutumace était possible!', 103 *RGDIP* (1999) pp. 379-404
- Pillay, Navanethem, 'The Rwanda Tribunal and its relationship to national trials in Rwanda', 13 *Amer. Univ. ILR* (1998) pp. 1473-1480
- Rudasingwa, Theogene, 'The Rwanda Tribunal and its relationship to national trials in Rwanda', 13 *Amer. Univ. ILR* (1998) pp. 1484-1489
- Sluiter, Göran, 'To cooperate or not to cooperate? The case of the failed transfer of Ntakirutimana to the Rwanda Tribunal', 11 *Leiden JIL* (1998) pp. 383-395

- 'The International Tribunal for Rwanda: Rules of procedure and evidence' adopted on 5 July 1995, as amended on 6 June (1997)', 10 *Afr. JI & CL* (1998) pp. 767-800
- 'The International Tribunal for Rwanda: The Prosecutor v. Jean Kambanda', 10 *Afr. JI & CL* (1998) pp. 836-853

6.314   International Criminal Court

Books
- Bassiouni, M. Cherif, ed., *The Statute of the International Criminal Court: A Documentary History* (Irvington-on-Hudson, NY, Transnational Publishers 1998) 824 pp.
- Bassiouni, M. Cherif, ed., *ICC Ratification and National Implementing Legislation; CPI Ratification et Legislation Nationale d'Application; CPI Ratificación y Legislación Nacional de Actuación* (Association Internationale de Droit Pénal, érès 1999)
- Lattanzi, Flavia, *The International Criminal Court: Comments on the Draft Statute* (Naples, Editoriale Scientifica 1998)
- Lee, Roy S., *The International Criminal Court: The Making of the Rome Statute* (The Hague, Kluwer Law International 1999)
- von Hebel, Herman A. M., Johan G. Lammers and Jolien Schukking, eds., *Reflections on the International Criminal Court –Essays in Honour of Adriaan Bos* (The Hague, T.M.C. Asser Press 1999) 211 pp.
- Triffterer, Otto, *Commentary on the ICC Statute* (Baden-Baden, Nomos Verlagsgesellschaft 1999)

Articles and Reports
- Acke, Arianne, 'Het Statuut van Rome voor een internationaal Strafgerechtshof', 7 *Zoeklicht* (1998) pp. 18-20
- Ambos, Kai, 'Der neue Internationale Strafgerichtshof: ein Überblick', 51 *Neue juristische Wochenschrift* (1998) pp. 3743-3746
- Armstead, J. Holmes, 'The International Criminal Court: history, development and status', 38 *Santa Clara LR* (1998) pp. 745-835
- Arsanjani, Mahnoush, 'The Rome Statute of the International Criminal Court', 93 *AJIL* (1999) pp. 22-43
- Baker, Alan, 'The international criminal court: Israel's unique dilemma', 18 *Justice / The International Association of Jewish Lawyers and Jurists* (1998) pp. 19-25
- Bloch, David S. and Elon Weinstein, 'Velvet glove and iron fist: a new paradigm for the permanent War Crimes Court', 22 *Hastings I & CLR* (1998) pp. 1-46
- Boister, Neil, 'The exclusion of Treaty crimes from the jurisdiction of the proposed International Criminal Court: law, pragmatism, politics', 3 *Journal of Armed Conflict* (1998) pp. 27-43
- Boon, Kristen, Gerhard Hafner, Jonathan Huston and Anne Ruebesame, 'A Response to the American view as presented by Ruth Wedgwood', 10 *EJIL* (1999) pp. 108-123
- Brown, Alaistair, 'International Criminal Court', 142 *Sollicitors Journal* (1998) pp. 953-958
- Carrillo-Salcedo, Juan-Antonio, 'La Cour pénale internationale: l'humanité trouve une place dans le droit international', 103 *RGDIP* (1999) pp. 23-28

- Cassese, Antonio, 'The Statute of the International Criminal Court: some preliminary reflections', 10 *EJIL* (1999) pp. 144-171
- Condorelli, Luigi, 'La Cour pénale internationale: un pas de géant (pourvu qu'il soit accompli)', 103 *RGDIP* (1999) pp. 7-22
- Consigli, Jose Alejandro and Gabriel Pablo Valladares, 'Los tribunales internacionales para ex Yugoslavia y Ruanda. Precursores Necesarios de la Corte Penal Internacional', I-II *Revista Juridica de Buenos Aires* (1998) pp. 41-54
- Commentaire in Revue française de Science politique, Presses Universitaires de France, Paris no. 38 1999, pp. 315-328. Décision No. 98-408 DC du 22 janvier 1999 Cour pénale internationale. *Journal officiel* (24 janvier 1999) pp. 1317
- David, Eric, 'The International Criminal Court: what is the point?', in Karel Wellens, ed., *International law: theory and practice: essays in honour of Eric Suy* (The Hague, Nijhoff 1998) pp. 631-650
- Dotinga, Harm (reporter), 'Toward a permanent International Criminal Court: the last stumbling blocks', in *Contemporary International Law Issues: New Forms, New Applications, supra* 4.11121
- Dugard, John, 'Obstacles in the way of an International Criminal Court', 57 *Cambridge LJ* (1998) pp. 329-342
- Erb, Nicole Eva, 'Gender-based crimes under the Draft Statute for the Permanent International Criminal Court', 29 *Colum. HRLR* (1998) pp. 401-435
- Gerber, Steven J., 'Establishment of an International Criminal Court', 4 *ILSA JI & CL* (1998) pp. 423-425
- Gowlland-Debbas, Vera, 'The relationship between the Security Council and the projected International Criminal Court', 3 *Journal of Armed Conflict* (1998) pp. 97-119
- Guariglia, Fabricio, 'Creacion de la Corte Penal Internacional. Algunos aspectos del Estatuto de Roma', I-II *Revista Juridica de Buenos Aires* (1998) pp. 27-40
- Hall, Christopher Keith, 'The third and fourth sessions of the UN Preparatory Committee on the establishment of an International Criminal Court', 92 *AJIL* (1998) pp. 124-133
- Hall, Christopher Keith, 'The first proposal for a permanent international criminal court', 38 *IRRC* No. 322 (1998) pp. 57-74
- Hall, Christopher Keith, 'Première proposition de création d'une cour criminelle internationale permanente', 80 *RICR* No. 829 (1998) pp. 59-78
- Harris, David, 'Progress and problems in establishing an International Criminal Court', 3 *Journal of Armed Conflict* (1998) pp. 1-7
- Hermsdörfer, Willibald, 'Zum Anpassungsbedarf des deutschen Strafrechts an das Statut des Internationalen Strafgerichtshofs', 12 *Humanitäres Völkerrecht* (1999) pp. 22-26
- Hermsdörfer, Willibald, 'Historischer Schritt im Völkerstrafrecht. Das Statut des Internationalen Strafgerichtshofs', 53 *Internationale Politik* (1998) pp. 55-60
- Hermsdörfer, Willibald, 'Zum Statut des Internationalen Strafgerichtshofs: ein Meilenstein im Völkerstrafrecht', 40 *Neue Zeitschrift für Wehrrecht* (1998) pp. 193-200
- 'The International Criminal Court trigger mechanism and the need for an independent prosecutor, July 1997', 1 *International Criminal Court Briefing Series* (1997) 12 pp.
- Jarasch, Frank, 'Errichtung, Organisation und Finanzierung des Internationalen Strafgerichtshofs und die Schlussbestimmungen des Statuts', 12 *Humanitäres Völkerrecht* (1999) pp. 10-21

- Kreß, Claus, 'Die Kristallisation eines allgemeinen Teils des *Völkerstrafrechts*: die allgemeinen Prinzipien des Strafrechts im Statut des Internationalen Strafgerichtshofs', 12 *Humanitäres Völkerrecht* (1999) pp. 4-9
- Kirsch, Philippe and John T. Holmes, 'The Rome Conference on the International Criminal Court: the negotiating process', 93 *AJIL* (1999) pp. 2-12
- La Haye, Eve, 'The Jurisdiction of the International Criminal Court: Controversies over the Preconditions for Exercising its Jurisdiction', 46 *NILR* (1999) pp. 1-25
- Lattanzi, Flavia, 'Compétence de la Cour pénale internationale et consentement des Etats', 103 *RGDIP* (1999) pp. 425-444
- Luchaire, François, 'La Cour pénale internationale et la responsabilité du chef de l'Etat devant le Conseil constitutionnel', *Revue du Droit public et de la Science politique en France et à l'étranger* (1999) pp. 457-479
- MacPherson, Bryan F., 'Building an International Criminal Court for the 21st century', 13 *Connecticut JIL* (1998) pp. 1-60
- Martin, Pierre-Marie, 'La Cour pénale internationale: quel avenir pour une illusion?', 36 *Recueil Dalloz* (1998) pp. 337-340.
- McCoubrey, Hillaire, 'War crimes jurisdiction and a permanent International Criminal Court – advantages and difficulties', 3 *Journal of Armed Conflict* (1998) pp. 9-26
- McDonald, Avril, 'Prosecuting IHL violations against women: a note on the relevant provisions of the ICC Statute', 14 *Nemesis* (1998) pp. 132-142
- Nanda, Ved P., 'The establishment of a permanent International Criminal Court: challenges ahead', 20 *HRQ* (1998) pp. 413-428
- Pejic, Jelena, 'Creating a Permanent International Criminal Court: the obstacles to independence and effectiveness', 29 *Colum. HRLR* (1998) pp. 291-354
- Pellet, Alain, 'Pour la Cour pénale internationale, quand même: Quelques remarques sur sa compétence et sa saisine', 5 *L'Observateur des Nations Unies* (1998) pp. 143-163
- Pfanner, Toni, 'The establishment of a permanent criminal court: ICRC expectations of the Rome Diplomatic Conference', 38 *IRRC* No. 322 (1998) pp. 21-27
- Pfanner, Toni, 'Création d'une cour criminelle internationale permanente: Conférence diplomatique de Rome: résultats escomptés par le CICR', 80 *RICR* No. 829 (1998) pp. 21-28
- Rebagliati, Orlando R., 'La Corte penal internacional,' I-III *Revista Juridica de Buenos Aires* (1998) pp. 27-40
- Report of the twenty-ninth United Nations issues conference: *The UN Security Council and the International Criminal Court: how should they relate?*: Report of the twenty-ninth United Nations issues conference, 20-22 February 1998, convened at Arden House, Harriman, New York. (Muscatine, Iowa, Stanley Foundation 1998) 42 pp.
- Robinson, Darryl, 'Defining "Crimes Against Humanity" at the Rome Conference', 93 *AJIL* (1999) pp. 43-57
- Roggemann, Herwig, 'Der Ständige Internationale Strafgerichtshof und das Statut von Rom 1998', 52 *Neue Justiz* (1998) pp. 505-509
- 'Rome Statute of the International Criminal Court: adopted by the United Nations Diplomatic Conference of Plenipotentiaries on the Establishment of an International Criminal Court on 17 July 1998', 73 *Die Friedenswarte* (1998) pp. 348-414

– 'Rome statute of the International Criminal Court, adopted by the United Nations Diplomatic Conference of Plenipotentiaries on the Establishment of an International Criminal Court on 17 July 1998 United Nations Diplomatic Conference of Plenipotentiaries on the establishment of an International Criminal Court', (1998) pp. 88

– Scheffer, David J., 'The United States and the International Criminal Court', 93 *AJIL* (1999) pp. 12-22

– Schlunck, Angelika, 'Die Umsetzung des internationalen Strafgerichtshofs in das deutsche Recht unter Berücksichtigung der Rechtshilfe', 12 *Humanitäres Völkerrecht* (1999) pp. 27-31

– Shaw, Malcolm, 'The International Criminal Court: some procedural and evidential issues', 3 *Journal of Armed Conflict* (1998) pp. 65-96

– Stahn, Carsten, 'Zwischen Weltfrieden und materieller Gerechtigkeit: die Gerichtsbarkeit des Ständigen Internationalen Strafgerichtshofs', 25 *Europäische Grundrechte Zeitschrift* (1998) pp. 577-591

– Sur, S., 'Vers une Cour pénale internationale: la Convention de Rome entre les O.N.G et le Conseil de Sécurité', 103 *RGDIP* (1999) pp. 29-45

– Tallgren, Immi, 'Completing the "international criminal order" – the rhetoric of international repression and the notion of complementarity in the Draft Statute for an International Criminal Court', 67 *Nordic JIL* (1998) pp. 107-137

– Tomuschat, Christian, 'Das Statut von Rom für den Internationalen Strafgerichtshof', 73 *Die Friedenswarte* (1998) pp. 335-347

– van Troost, Lars, 'Internationale rechtshulp onder het ontwerp-statuut voor een permanent internationaal strafhof', 47 *AA* (1998) pp. 30-34

– Troost, Lars van, 'Een internationaal strafhof: Het Statuut van Rome in vogelvlucht', 47 *Ars Aequi* (1998) pp. 882-887

– Weckel, Philippe, 'La Cour pénale internationale: présentation générale', 104 *RGDIP* (1999) pp. 983-993

– Wedgwood, Ruth, 'The International Criminal Court: An American view', 10 *EJIL* (1999) pp. 93-107

– Wong, Felicity, 'An International Criminal Court', 98 *New Zealand LJ* (1998) pp. 219-220

– Zimmermann, Andreas, 'The creation of a permanent International Criminal Court', 2 *MPYBUNL* (1998) pp.169-237

– Zimmermann, Andreas, 'Die Schaffung eines ständigen Internationales Strafgerichtshofes. Perspektiven und Probleme vor der Staatenkonferenz in Rom', 58 *ZaöRV* (1998) pp. 47-106

– Zwanenburg, Marten, 'The Statute for an International Criminal Court and the United States: peacekeepers under fire?', 10 *EJIL* (1999) pp. 124-143

– Zwanenburg, Marten, 'The Statute for an International Criminal Court and the United States: Peace without Justice?', 12 *Leiden JIL* (1999) pp. 1-7

6.33   National Courts

Articles and Reports

– Boustany, Katia, 'Brocklebank: A questionable decision of the Court Martial Appeal Court of Canada', 1 *YIHL* (1998) pp. 371-374

- Brown, Bartram S., 'Primacy or complementarity: reconciling the jurisdiction of national courts and international criminal tribunals', 23 *Yale JIL* (1998) pp. 383-436
- Consigli, José Alejandro, 'The Priebke Extradition Case before the Argentine Supreme Court', 1 *YIHL* (1998) pp. 341-343
- Cooke, John S., 'Manual for Courts-Martial 20x', 156 *Military LR* (1998) pp. 1-29
- de Gouttes, Regis, 'Un exemple de poursuites de crimes contre l'humanité devant les juridictions nationales: le proces des criminels de l'ancien régime du colonel Menghistu en Ethiopie', *RSCDPC* (1998) pp. 697-702
- Drumbl, Mark A., 'Rule of law amid lawlessness: counseling the accused in Rwanda's domestic genocide trials', 29 *Colum. HRLR* (1998) pp. 545-639
- Enache-Brown, Colleen and Ari Fried, 'Universal crime, Jurisdiction and Duty: the Obligation of *Aut Dedere Aut Judicare* in International Law', 43 *McGill LJ* (1998) pp. 613-633
- Fischer, Horst, 'Some aspects of German state practice concerning IHL', 1 *YIHL* (1998) pp. 380-392
- Grynfogel, C., 'De Touvier à Papon, la complicité de crime contre l'humanité', 78 *RDPC* (1998) pp. 758-779
- Pillay, Navanethem, 'The Rwanda Tribunal and its relationship to national trials in Rwanda', 13 *Amer. Univ. ILR* (1998) pp. 1473-1480
- Pellandini, Cristina, ed., 'Répression nationale des violations du droit international humanitaire (systèmes romano-germaniques): rapport de la réunion d'experts, Genève, 23-25 septembre 1997', (Geneva, ICRC 1998)
- Rudasingwa, Theogene, 'The Rwanda Tribunal and its relationship to national trials in Rwanda', 13 *Amer. Univ. ILR* (1998) pp. 1484-1489
- Schabas, William, 'Mugesera v. Minister of Citizenship and Immigration', 93 *AJIL* (1999) pp. 529-533
- Stern, Brigitte, 'In re. Javor; In re. Munyeshyaka,' 93 *AJIL* (1999) pp. 525-529
- van Elst, R., 'De zaak Darco Knezevic: rechtsmacht over Joegoslavische en andere buitenlandse oorlogsmisdadigers', 73 *Nederlands Juristenblad* (1998) No. 35 pp. 1587-1593
- Ziegler, Andreas R., 'In Re G', 92 *AJIL* (1998) pp. 78-82.

7. **IMPLEMENTATION OF IHL**

Books

- Vite, Sylvain, *Les procedures internationales d'establissement des faits dans la mise en oeuvre du droit international humanitaire* (Bruxelles, Bruylant 1999) 508 pp.

Articles and Reports

- 'Australia: International War Crimes Tribunal Act 1995: International War Crimes Tribunal Consequential Amendments Act 1995', 24 *Commonwealth Law Bulletin* (1998) pp. 426-427
- Doswald-Beck, Louise, 'Implementation of International Humanitarian Law in Future Wars', *Naval War Review* (1999) pp. 24-52
- Dutli, Maria Teresa, 'National implementation measures of international humanitarian law: some practical aspects', 1 *YIHL* (1998) pp. 245-261

- Eyeni Mbu, Nelson, 'Implementation of humanitarian law by means of repression: the case of the International Criminal Tribunal for Rwanda', 1 *Revue scientifique du droit: Law review: Igazeti isobanura amategeko* (1998) pp. 59-87
- Gargiulo, Pietro, 'The Italian Law for the Ban of Anti-Personnel Landmines', 1 *YIHL* (1998) pp. 323-332
- Josipovič, Ivo, 'Implementing legislation for the application of the law on the International Criminal Tribunal for the Former Yugoslavia and criteria for its evaluation', 1 *YIHL* (1998) pp. 35-68
- Moir, Lindsay, 'The implementation and enforcement of the laws of non-international armed conflict', 3 *Journal of Armed Conflict* (1998) pp. 163-195
- Muyot, Alberto T. and Vincent Pepito F. Yambao, 'Steps taken to ensure implementation of international humanitarian law in the Philippines', 81 *IRRC* No. 834 (1999) pp. 303-316
- National Implementation of international humanitarian law – Annual Report of the ICRC Advisory Service (Geneva 1998) 124 pp.
- Sluiter, Göran, 'Obtaining evidence for the International Criminal Tribunal for the Former Yugoslavia: an overview and assessment of domestic implementing legislation', 45 *NILR* (1998) pp. 87-113

7.4   ICRC

Books

- Harquel, Veronique, *Histoire de la Croix-Rouge* (Paris, PUF 1999) (Collection Que sais-je?, 831)
- Moorehead, Caroline, *Henry Dunant's Dream – War, Switzerland and the History of the Red Cross* (London, Harper Collins 1998) 780 pp.

Articles

- Baudendistel, Rainer, 'Force versus law: the International Committee of the Red Cross and chemical warfare in the Italo-Ethiopian war 1935-1936', 38 *IRRC* No. 322 (1998) pp. 81-104. In French: 'La force contre le droit : Le Comité international de la Croix-Rouge et la guerre chimique dans le conflit italo-ethiopien 1935-1936', 80 *RICR* No. 829 (1998) pp. 85-110
- Blondel, Jean-Luc, 'Cooperation between National Societies and the International Committee of the Red Cross: an essential and demanding partnership', 38 *IRRC* No. 323 (1998) pp. 197-204. In French: 'La cooperation entre les Sociétés nationales et le Comité international de la Croix-Rouge: un partenariat nécessaire et exigeant', 80 *RICR* No. 830 (1998) pp. 209-216
- de los Angeles, Maria and Varona Hernandez, 'La cooperation en tant que méthode nécessaire à l'exécution et au développement des activités de la Croix-Rouge cubaine', 80 *RICR* No. 830 (1998) pp. 229-234
- Dogny, Violene, 'La cooperation du Comité international de la Croix-Rouge avec les services de recherches des Sociétés nationales dans les Etats nouvellement indépendants de l'ex-URSS', 80 *RICR* No. 830 (1998) pp. 217-227
- Durand, André, 'Le Comité international de la Croix Rouge à l'époque de la première Conférence de La Haye (1899)', 81 *IRRC* No. 834 (1999) pp. 353-364

– Hanley, Teresa and John Mitchell, 'Cooperation entre la Croix-Rouge britannique et le CICR: délégation d'un projet "eau et assainissement" en Bosnie-Herzegovine', 80 *RICR* No. 830 (1998) pp. 283-286

– Ipsen, Knut, 'Das Rote Kreuz und die *friedenssicherung'*, 12 *Humanitäres Völkerrecht* (1999) pp. 81-83

– Kraehenbuehl, Pierre, 'Cooperation between the International Committee of the Red Cross and National Societies in Bosnia-Herzegovina: broadening the Red Cross response', 38 *IRRC* No. 323 (1998) pp. 249-262. In French: 'Cooperation entre le Comité international de la Croix-Rouge et les Sociétés nationales en Bosnie-Herzegovine: donner une assise plus large a l'action de la Croix-Rouge', 80 *RICR* No. 830 (1998) pp. 267-282

– Lendorff, Andreas and Andreas Lindner, 'Operational cooperation between participating National Societies and the International Committee of the Red Cross', 38 *IRRC* No. 323 (1998) pp. 233-248. In french: 'La cooperation opérationnelle entre les Sociétés nationales participantes et le Comité international de la Croix-Rouge', 80 *RICR* No. 830 (1998) pp. 249-266

– Nwobodo, Ofor, 'Operational cooperation between the International Committee of the Red Cross and the Nigerian Red Cross Society', 38 *IRRC* No. 323 (1998) pp. 221-232. In French: 'Cooperation opérationnelle entre le CICR et la Croix-Rouge du Nigeria', 80 *RICR* No. 830 (1998) pp. 235-248

– Perret, Francoise, 'Activities of the International Committee of the Red Cross in Cuba, 1958-1962', 38 *IRRC* No. 325 (1998) pp. 655-670. In french: 'L'action du Comité international de la Croix-Rouge à Cuba, 1958-1962', 80 *RICR* No. 832 (1998) pp. 707-723

– Rey-Schirr, Catherine, 'Les activités du Comité international de la Croix-Rouge dans le sous-continent indien à la suite de la partition (1947-1949)', 80 *RICR* No. 830 (1998) pp. 287-313

– Rey-Schyrr, Catherine, 'Conventions de Genève de 1949: une percée décisive première partie', 81 *IRRC* No. 834 (1999) pp. 209-239

– Rey-Schyrr, Catherine, 'Conventions de Genève de 1949: une percée décisive seconde partie', 81 *IRRC* No. 835 (1999) pp. 499-529

– Tauxe, Jean-Daniel, 'Faire mieux accepter le Comité international de la Croix-Rouge sur le terrain, 81 *RICR* No. 833 (1999) pp. 55-61

8.   THE LAW OF NEUTRALITY

Articles

– Da Costa Leite, Joaquim, 'Neutrality by agreement: Portugal and the British Alliance in World War II', 14 *Amer. Univ. ILR* (1999) pp. 185-199

– Ramiro Guelar, Diego, 'Argentinean neutrality and the "Black Legend"', 14 *Amer. Univ. ILR* (1999) pp. 201-204

– Guttman, Ego, 'The Concept of neutrality since the adoption and ratification of the Hague Neutrality Convention of 1907', 14 *Amer. Univ. ILR* (1999) pp. 55-60

– Marquina, Antonio, 'The Spanish Neutrality during the Second World War', 14 *Amer. Univ. ILR* (1999) pp. 171-184

– Minear, Larry, 'The theory and practice of neutrality: Some thoughts on the tensions', 81 *IRRC* No. 833 (1999) pp. 63-72

- Petrochilos, Georgios C., 'The relevance of the concepts of war and armed conflict to the law of neutrality', 31 *Vanderbilt J Transnat. L* (1998) pp. 575-616
- Rubin, Seymour J., 'The Washington Accord fifty years later: neutrality, morality, and international law', 14 *Amer. Univ. ILR* (1999) pp. 61-82
- Schindler, Dietrich, 'Neutrality and morality: developments in Switzerland and in the international community', 14 *Amer. Univ. ILR* (1999) pp. 155-170
- Vagts, Detlev F., 'The traditional legal concept of neutrality in a changing environment', 14 *Amer. Univ. ILR* (1999) pp. 83-102
- Wahlbaeck, Krister, 'Neutrality and morality: the Swedish experience', 14 *Amer. Univ. ILR* (1999) pp. 103-121

8.3   Naval Warfare

Books

- Politakis, George P., *Modern Aspects of the Laws of Naval Warfare and Maritime Neutrality* (London, Kegan Paul 1998) 678 pp.

9.   **INTERNATIONAL ORGANISATIONS AND INTERNATIONAL ACTIONS**

9.1   International Organisations

Articles

- Cassese, Antonio, '*Ex iniuria ius oritur*: are we moving towards international legitimation of forcible humanitarian countermeasures in the world community?', 10 *EJIL* (1999) pp. 23-30
- Simma, Bruno, 'NATO, the UN and the Use of Force, Legal Aspects', 10 *EJIL* (1999) pp. 1-22

9.11   United Nations Organisation

Books

- Lailach, Martin, *Die Wahrung des Weltfriedens und der internationalen Sicherheit als Aufgabe des Sicherheitsrates der Vereinten Nationen*, doctoral thesis, Göttingen 1997 (Berlin, Duncker & Humblot 1998) 349 pp.
- Oesterdahl, Inger, *Threat to the Peace: The Interpretation by the Security Council of Article 39 of the UN Charter* (Uppsala, Iustus Foerlag/Uppsala University, Swedish Institute of International Law 1998) 176 pp.

Articles

- Dahmane, Farid Wahid, 'Les mesures prises par le Conseil de Securité contre les entités non-étatiques : une tentative de cerner l'application du chapitre VII aux crises internes', 11 *Afr. JI & CL* (1999) pp. 227-244
- Higgins, Rosalyn, 'Some thoughts on the evolving relationship between the Security Council and NATO', in *Boutros Boutros-Ghali: Amicorum discipulorumque liber*, Vol. 1 (1998) pp. 511-530

- Iovane, Massimo, 'La NATO, le organizzazioni regionali e le competenze del Consiglio di Sicurezza delle Nazioni Unite in tema di mantenimento della pace', 53 *La Comunita Internazionale* (1998) pp. 43-71
- Koeck, Heribert Franz, 'Legalität und Legitimität der Anwendung militärischer Gewalt – Betrachtungen zum Gewaltmonopol der Vereinten Nationen und seinen Grenzen', 54 *ZöR* (1999) pp. 133-160
- Kooijmans, P.H., 'The Security Council and non-state entities as parties to conflicts', in Karel Wellens, ed., *International law: Theory and Practice: essays in honour of Eric Suy* (The Hague, Nijhoff 1998) pp. 333-346
- Lobel, Jules and Michael Ratner, 'Bypassing the Security Council: ambiguous authorizations to use force, cease-fires and the Iraqi inspection regime', 93 *AJIL* (1999) pp. 124-154
- Weyembergh, A., 'La notion de conflit armé , le droit international humanitaire et les forces des Nations Unies en Somalie (A propos de l'arrêt de la Cour militaire du 17 decembre 1997)', 79 *RDPC* (1999) pp. 177-201

9.12   Other

ECOWAS
Reports
- Meeting of Ministers of defence, internal affairs and security, Banjul, 23-24 July 1998, adopted by the meeting of heads of state at Abuj 30-31 October 1998: *ECOWAS mechanism for conflict prevention, management, resolution, peace-keeping and security*, 11 *Afr. Jl & CL* (1999) pp. 148-166

NATO
Articles
- Gaeta, Paola, 'Is NATO authorized or obliged to arrest persons indicted by the International Criminal Tribunal for the Former Yugoslavia?', 9 *EJIL* (1998) pp. 174-181
- Higgins, Rosalyn, 'Some thoughts on the evolving relationship between the Security Council and NATO', in *Boutros Boutros-Ghali: Amicorum discipulorumque liber*, Vol. 1 (1998) pp. 511-530
- Iovane, Massimo, 'La NATO, le organizzazioni regionali e le competenze del Consiglio di Sicurezza delle Nazioni Unite in tema di mantenimento della pace', 53 *La Comunita Internazionale* (1998) pp. 43-71
- Krebs, Ronald R., 'Perverse institutionalism: NATO and the Greco-Turkish conflict', 53 *International Organization* (1999) pp. 343-377
- McGwire, Michael, 'NATO expansion: "a policy error of historic importance"', 24 *Review of International Studies* (1998) pp. 23-42
- Pradetto, August, 'NATO Intervention in Kosovo? Kein Eingreifen ohne UN-mandat', 53 *Internationale Politik* (1998) pp. 41-46
- Rubin, Seymour J., 'The Washington Accord fifty years later: neutrality, morality, and international law', 14 *Amer. Univ. IL Rev.* (1999) pp. 61-82
- Woodliffe, John, 'The evolution of a new NATO for a new Europe', 47 *ICLQ* (1998) pp. 174-192

[see also journals specifically covering NATO: *NATO's Sixteen Nations:Independent Review of Economic, Political and Military Power* and *NATO Review/Revue de l'OTAN*]

OSCE
Articles
[journals specifically covering the OSCE: *Helsinki Monitor* and *OSCE Bulletin*]

WEU
Articles
- Vierucci, Luisa, 'The WEU and peacekeeping', 51 *Studia Diplomatica* (1998) pp. 101-106

9.21   Peacekeeping

Books
- Magyar, K.P. and E. Conteh-Morgan, eds., *Peacekeeping in Africa* (New York, Macmillan 1998) 208 pp.
- Moxon-Browne, Edward, ed., *A future for peacekeeping?* (Basingstoke, Macmillan/New York, St. Martin's Press 1998) 214 pp.
- Nederveen Pieterse, J., *World Orders in the Making: Humanitarian Intervention and Beyond* (New York, Macmillan Press 1998) 276 pp.
- Poulton, Robin-Edward, Jacqueline Seck and Ibrahim ag Youssouf, *Collaboration internationale et construction de la paix en Afrique de l'Ouest: l'exemple du Mali* (New York, Nations Unies 1999) 58 pp.
- Sánchez, Pablo Antonio Fernández, *Operaciones de las Naciones Unidas para el mantenimiento de la paz*, 2 Vols. (Huelva, Universitat de Huelva 1998)
- Schultz, Marcus, *Die Auslandsentsendung von Bundeswehr und Bundesgrenzschutz zum Zwecke der Friedenswahrung und Verteidigung: völker- und verfassungsrechtliche Analyse unter besonderer Berücksichtigung der Entscheidung des Bundesverfassungsgerichtes zum Einsatz deutscher Streitkräfte vom 12. Juli 1994*, doctoral thesis Würzburg, 1997 (Frankfurt am Main, Lang 1998) 557 pp. (Schriften zum Staat- und Völkerrecht, Vol. 77)
- United Nations: *UN peacekeeping: 50 Years: 1948-1998* (New York, United Nations Department of Public Information 1998) 88 pp.
- Whitman, J., *What We Do When We Fail: The Limits of United Nations Peacekeeping* (New York, Macmillan 1998) 196 pp.
- Zandee, Dick, *Building blocks for peace: civil-military interaction in restoring fractured societies* (The Hague, Clingendael 1998) 79 pp.

Articles
- Bourantonis, Dimitris and Georgios Kostakos, 'Innovations in peacekeeping: the case of Albania', 29 *Security Dialogue* (1998) pp. 49-58
- Cox, Katherine E., 'Beyond self-defense: United Nations peacekeeping operations & the use of force', 27 *Denver JIL & Pol.* (1999) pp. 239-273
- Dhia, Abdelaziz Ben, 'Le role du Sécrétaire général des Nations Unies en matière de maintien de la paix et de la sécurité internationales', in *Boutros Boutros-Ghali: Amicorum discipulorumque liber*, Vol. 1 (1998) pp. 227-244

- Diehl, Paul F., Daniel Druckman and James Wall, 'International Peacekeeping and Conflict Resolution: a Taxonomic Analysis with Implications', 42 *Journal of Conflict Resolution* (1998) pp. 33-55
- Dotinga, Harm (reporter), 'The Promise of and Obstacles to Effective Peace-keeping by the CIS, NATO, OSCE, WEU, and UN', in *Contemporary International Law Issues: New Forms, New Applications, supra* 4.1121
- Egeland, Jan, 'Peace-making and the prevention of violence: the role of governments and non-governmental organizations', 81 *IRRC* (1999) pp. 73-84
- Prince El Hassan Bin Talal: 'Peace making under Dr. Boutros-Ghali: a profile of the Jordanian stand-by forces in UN peacekeeping operations', in *Boutros Boutros-Ghali: Amicorum discipulorumque liber,* Vol. 1 (1998) pp. 445-450
- Gaeta, Paola, 'Is NATO authorized or obliged to arrest persons indicted by the international criminal tribunal for the former Yugoslavia?', 9 *EJIL* (1998) pp. 174-181
- Grassi, Stefano, 'L'introduzione delle operazioni di peace-keeping nel Trattato di Amsterdam', 53 *La Comunita Internazionale* (1998) pp. 295-326
- Greco, Ettore, 'New trends in peace-keeping: the experience of Operation Alba', 29 *Security Dialogue* (1998) pp. 201-212
- Guillaume, Gilbert, 'L'introduction et l'exécution dans les ordres juridiques des Etats des résolutions du Conseil de sécurité des Nations-Unies prises en vertu du chapitre VII de la Charte', 50 *RIDC* (1998) pp. 539-549
- Huijssoon, Willem A. and Jürgen Altman, 'Compiled questionnaire answers on the application of ground sensors during peace-keeping operations', in Jürgen Altmann, Horst Fischer and Henny van der Graaf, eds., *Sensors for Peace: Applications, Systems and Legal Requirements for Monitoring in peace operations* (New York, UN 1998) pp. 225-269
- Khanna, Jyoti, Todd Sandler and Hirofumi Shimizu, 'Sharing the financial burden for U.N. and NATO peacekeeping', 42 *Journal of Conflict Resolution* (1998) pp. 176-195
- Liegois, Michel, 'Maintien de la paix et diplomatie coercitive: le cas de la Bosnie', 29 *Etudes Internationales* (1998) pp. 867-887
- Llorens, Jorge Cardona, 'La cooperation entre les Nations Unies et les accords et organismes régionaux pour le réglement pacifique des affaires relatives au maintien de la paix et de la sécurité internationales', in *Boutros Boutros-Ghali: Amicorum discipulorumque liber,* Vol. 1 (1998) pp. 251-289
- Lupi, Natalia, 'Report by the enquiry commission on the behaviour of Italian peace-keeping troops in Somalia', 1 *YIHL* (1998) pp. 375-379
- MacQueen, Norrie, 'Peacekeeping by attrition: the United Nations in Angola', 36 *Journal of Modern African Studies* (1998) pp. 399-422
- Molina, Maria and Robert M. Young, 'IHL and Peace Operations: Sharing Canada's Lessons Learned from Somalia', 1 *YIHL* (1998) pp. 362-370
- Siekmann, Robert C. R., 'The fall of Srebrenica and the attitude of Dutchbat from an international legal perspective', 1 *YIHL* (1998) pp. 301-312
- Suhrke, Astri, 'Facing genocide: the record of the Belgian Battalion in Rwanda', 29 *Security Dialogue* (1998) pp. 37-48
- van Brabant, Koenraad, 'Security and protection in peacekeeping: A critical reading of the Belgian inquiry into events in Rwanda in 1994', 6 *International Peacekeeping* (1999) pp. 143-153

- Vierucci, Luisa, 'The WEU and peacekeeping', 51 *Studia diplomatica* (1998) pp. 101-106
- Weyembergh, A., 'La notion de conflit armé, le droit international humanitaire et les forces des Nations Unies en Somalie (A propos de l'arrêt de la Cour militaire du 17 décembre 1997)', 79 *RDPC* (1999) pp. 177-201
- Zwanenburg, Marten, 'Compromise or Commitment: Human Rights and International Humanitarian Law Obligations for UN Peace Forces', 11 *Leiden JIL* (1998) pp. 229-246

9.23   Fact-Finding and Monitoring

Articles
- Giladi, Rotem M., 'The practice and case law of Israel in matters related to international law: the Israel-Lebanon Monitoring Group: treaties and other instruments recently concluded by the State of Israel', 32 *Israel LR* (1998) pp. 355-392

10.   **ARMS CONTROL AND DISARMAMENT**

[Journals specifically covering arms control and disarmament: Désarmement : revue périodique publiée par les Nations Unies/ Disarmament: a periodic review by the United Nations and Disarmament forum/ Forum du desarmement. – Geneva: United Nations Institute for Disarmament Research, 1998 appears every 3 months. – continuation of UNIDIR Newsletter]

Books
- van der Meulen, J.W. *Troepenvermindering in Central Europe* (The Hague, Atlantische Commissie 1977) 44 pp.

Articles
- Butfoy, Andrew, 'Is arms control approaching a dead-end?', 52 *Austl. Jl Affairs* (1998) pp. 293-307
- Carnahan, Burrus M. and Katherine L. Starr, 'Law and policy in the Amendment of Arms Control Agreements', 20 *Loyola Int. & Comp. LJ* (1998) pp. 615-640
- Carter, Kim S., 'New crimes against peace?: the application of international humanitarian law compliance and enforcement mechanisms to arms control and disarmament treaties,' in Canadian Council on International Law/Conseil canadien de droit international and the Markland Group, ed., *Treaty Compliance: Some Concerns and Remedies* (1998) pp. 1-20
- den Dekker, Guido, 'The law of arms control and sub-regional arms control in the Former Yugoslavia: "hard" law in a "soft" law context', 45 *NILR* (1998) pp. 363-387
- den Dekker, Guido and Ramses A. Wessel, 'Military enforcement of arms control in Iraq', 11 *Leiden JIL* (1998) pp. 497-511
- Ferm, Ragnhild, 'Arms control and disarmament agreements', *SIPRI Yearbook* (1998) pp. 577-597
- Ginifer, Jeremy, 'Protecting displaced persons through disarmament', 40 *Survival London* (1998) pp. 161-176

- Bonnie, D. Jenkin and Theodore M. Hirsch, 'Arms control and disarmament', 32 *International Lawyer* (1998) pp. 427-436
- Matthews, Robert J. and Timothy L.H. McCormack, 'The influence of humanitarian principles in the negotiation of arms control treaties', 81 *IRRC* No. 834 (1999) pp. 331-352
- Quashigah, Kofi, 'The role of Africa in arms control and disarmament', 11 *Afr. Jl & CL* (1999) pp. 67-85
- von Tangen Page, Michael, 'Arms decommissioning and the Northern Ireland Peace Agreement', 29 *Security Dialogue* (1998) pp. 409-420

10.11   Mines

Articles

- Caflisch, Lucius and François Godet, 'De la réglementation a l'interdiction des mines antipersonnel', 8 *SZIER/RSDIE* (1998) pp. 1-50
- Georghiades, Korinna M., 'The Ottawa Convention : meeting the challenge of Anti-Personnel Mines?' 14 *International Relations* (1998) pp. 51-70
- Goose, Stephen D, 'The Ottawa Process and the 1997 Mine Ban Treaty', 1 *YIHL* (1998) pp. 269-291
- Lachowski, Zdzislaw, 'The Ban on anti-personnel mines', *SIPRI Yearbook* (1998) pp. 545-574
- Maslen, Stuart and Peter Herby, 'Interdiction internationale des mines antipersonnel: génèse de négociation du "traité d'Ottawa"', 80 *RICR* No. 832 (1998) pp. 751-774; in English: 'An international ban on anti-personnel mines: history and negotiation of the "Ottawa treaty"', 38 *IRRC* No. 325 (1998) pp. 693-713
- Price, Richard, 'Reversing the gun sights: transnational civil society targets land mines', 52 *International Organization* (1998) pp. 613-644
- Roberts, Shawn, 'No exceptions, no reservations, no loopholes: the campaign for the 1997 Convention on the Prohibition of the Development, Production, Stockpiling, Transfer, and Use of Anti-Personnel Mines and on their Destruction', 9 *Colorado Jl Environ. L & Pol.* (1998) pp. 371-391

10.12   Small Weapons and Others

Books

- Eskidjian, S., *Small Arms, Big Impact: A Challenge to the Churches*. A Report of the Consultation on Microdisarmament organized by the World Council of Churches Programme to Overcome Violence. Rio de Janeiro, May 1998. Background Information, Commission of the Churches on International Affairs (1998) 155 pp.

10.21   Nuclear Weapons

Articles

- Aamodt, Jason B. and Lakshamn D. Guruswamy, 'Nuclear arms control; the environmental dimension', 10 *Colorado Jl Environ. L & Pol.* (1999) pp. 267-318

– Beard, Jack, 'Countering the threat posed by non-state actors in the proliferation of weapons of mass destruction', 92 *Proceedings of the ... annual meeting* (1998) pp. 173-177

– Chellaney, Brahma, 'India's nuclear planning, force structure, doctrine and arms control posture', 53 *Austl. J Int. Affairs* (1999) pp. 57-69

– Keeley, James F., 'Compliance and the Non-proliferation Treaty : developments in safeguards and supply controls', in Canadian Council on International Law/Conseil canadien de droit international and the Markland Group, ed., *Treaty compliance: some Concerns and Remedies* (1998) pp. 21-34

– Kile, Shannon, 'Nuclear arms control', *SIPRI Yearbook* (1998) pp. 403-442

10.22   Chemical and Biological Weapons

Articles

– Dorn, A. Walter and Douglas S. Scott, 'The compliance regime under the Chemical Weapons Convention: a summary and analysis', in *Treaty compliance: some concerns and remedies*, Canadian Council on International Law/Conseil canadien de droit international and the Markland Group, ed. (1998) pp. 87-132

– Feakes, Daniel, 'Building the international regime against chemical and biological weapons', 22 *Atlantisch Perspectief* (1998) pp. 21-26

– Greenlee, Robert F., 'The Fourth Amendment and facilities inspections under the Chemical Weapons Convention', 65 *Univ. Chicago LR* (1998) pp. 943-974

– Hart, John and Jean Pascal Zanders, 'Chemical and biological weapon developments and arms control', *SIPRI Yearbook* (1998) pp. 457-489

– King, Faiza Patel (reporter), 'The Ban on Chemical Weapons and Related Arms Control Issues', in *Contemporary International Law Issues: New Forms, New Applications, supra* 4.11121

– Mathews, Robert J., 'Entry into force of the Chemical Weapons Convention', *SIPRI Yearbook* (1998) pp. 490-500

– Sims, Nicholas A., 'Strengthening compliance systems for disarmament treaties: the biological and chemical weapons conventions', in Canadian Council on International Law/Conseil canadien de droit international and the Markland Group, ed., *Treaty compliance: some concerns and remedies* (1998) pp. 133-144

11.   CONFLICT PREVENTION AND RESOLUTIONS

11.1   Conflict Prevention

Books

– Bonvicini, G., B. Plate and R. von Rummel, eds., *Preventing Violent Conflict: Issues from the Baltic and Caucasus* (Baden-Baden, Nomos Verlagsgesellschaft 1998) 327 pp.

– Clément, Sophia, *Conflict Prevention in the Balkans: Case Studies of Kosovo and the FYR of Macedonia,* Chaillot Papers (Paris, Institute for Security Studies 1998) 78 pp.

- *Conflict Prevention, Post-conflict Reconstruction: Perspectives and Prospects* (Washington, DC, World Bank 1998) 44 pp.
- Danile, D.C.F., B.C. Hayes and C. de Jonge Ouderaat, *Coercive Inducement and the Containment of International Crisis* (Washington DC, USIP Press 1998) 288 pp.
- Reychler, Luc, 'Democratic peacebuilding and conflict prevention', in Karel Wellens, ed., *International Law: Theory and Practice: essays in honour of Eric Suy* (The Hague, Nijhoff 1998) pp. 83-106
- Russbach, Remi, 'Conflits armés, prévention et santé publique', 81 *RICR* No. 833 (1999) pp. 85-102
- Peck, Connie, *Sustainable Peace: The Role of the UN and Regional Organisations in Preventing Conflict* (Lanham, MD, Rowman & Littlefield 1998) 297 pp.
- *Prevention and Management of Violent Conflicts: An International Directory,* 1998 edn., (Utrecht, European Centre for Conflict Prevention 1998)
- *Searching for Peace in Africa: An Overview of Conflict Prevention and Management Activities* (Utrecht, European Centre for Conflict Prevention 1999)
- Stremlau, J. and F.R. Sagasti, *Preventing Deadly Conflict. Does the World Bank have a Role?* (Washington DC, Carnegie Commission on Preventing Deadly Conflict 1998) 100 pp.
- Troebst, S., *Conflict in Kosovo: Failure of Prevention? An Analytical Documentation, 1992-1998* (Flensburg, European Centre for Minority Issues 1998) 107 pp.

Articles and Reports
- Ali, Said Ali, 'The future of development work in the Red Cross and Red Crescent Movement? Between the need for assistance and the requirements of prevention', 81 *IRRC* No. 835 (1999) pp. 477-485
- Findlay, Trevor, 'Armed Conflict Prevention, Management and Resolution', *SIPRI Yearbook* (1998) pp. 31-74
- Lippold, Achim, 'Die Vereinten Nationen und die Zukunft der präventiven Diplomatie: Ein Beitrag zur aktuellen Debatte über die Umsetzung der Agenda für den Frieden', 11 *Humanitäres Völkerrecht* (1998) pp. 24-32
- Meeting of Ministers of defence, internal affairs and security Banjul, 23-24 July 1998, adopted by the meeting of heads of state at Abuj 30-31 October 1998, ECOWAS mechanism for conflict prevention, management, resolution, peace-keeping and security , 11 *African Jl & CL* (1999) pp. 148-166
- Report on the Seminar on 'Preventive Diplomacy and Peacebuilding in Southern Africa (Stadtschlaining 1998) 48 pp.

11.2 Conflict Resolution

Books
- Coppieters, B., G. Nodia and Y. Anchabadze, *Georgians and Adkhazians: The Search for a Peace Settlement (*Köln, BIOST 1998) 178 pp.
- Hopmann, P.T., *The Negotiation Process and the Resolution of International Conflicts* (Columbia, University of South Carolina Press 1998) 365 pp.
- Joseph, R., ed., *State, Conflict and Democracy in Africa* (Boulder CO, Lynne Rienner 1998) 600 pp.

- Juhn, T., *Negotiating Peace in El Salvador: Civil-Military Relations and the Conspiracy to End the War* (New York, Macmillan 1998) 250 pp.
- Ma'oz, Moshe and Avraham Sela, eds., *The PLO and Israel: From Armed Conflict to Political Solution 1964-1994* (Basingstoke, Macmillan 1998) 310 pp.
- Maynard, Kimberly, *Healing Communities in Conflict: International Assistance in Complex Emergencies* (New York, Colombia University Press 1999) 280 pp.

Articles and Reports
- Egeland, Jan, 'Peace-making and the prevention of violence: The role of governments and non-governmental organizations', 81 *RICR* No. 833 (1999) pp. 73-84
- Findlay, Trevor, 'Armed Conflict Prevention, Management and Resolution', *SIPRI Yearbook* (1998) pp. 31-74
- Meeting of Ministers of defence, internal affairs and security Banjul, 23-24 July 1998, adopted by the meeting of heads of state at Abuj 30-31 October 1998 'ECOWAS mechanism for conflict prevention, management, resolution, peace-keeping and security', 11 *African JI & CL* (1999) pp. 148-166
- Diehl, Paul F., Daniel Druckman and James Wall, 'International Peacekeeping and Conflict Resolution: a Taxonomic Analysis with Implications', 42 *Journal of Conflict Resolution* (1998) pp. 33-55
- Sabet, Amr G.E., 'The Peace Process and the politics of conflict resolution', 27 *Journal of Palestine Studies* (1998) pp. 5-19

11.3   The Peace Movement

Books
- Brown, M.E., O.R. Coté, S.M. Lynn-Jones and S.E. Miller, *Theories of War and Peace* (Cambridge, MA, MIT Press 1998) 566 pp.
- Galtung, J. and C.G. Jacobsen, *Practicing Peace by Peaceful Means* (Transcend 1999)
- Galtung, J., *Practicing Conflict Transformation,* United Nations (Transcend 1998) 150 pp.
- Lepgold, J. and T.G. Weiss, eds., *Collective Conflict Management and Changing World Politics* (New York, State University of New York Press 1998) 245 pp.
- Kacowics, A.M., *Zones of Peace in the Third World: South America and West Africa in Comparative Perspective* (New York, New York State University Press 1998) 267 pp.
- Kegley, C.W., Jr., and G.A. Raymond, *How Nations Make Peace* (New York, Macmillan 1999) 256 pp.
- Kozhemiakin, A.V., *Expanding the Zone of Peace? Democratization and International Security* (New York, Macmillan 1998) 200 pp.
- Montgomery, T.S., ed., *Peacemaking and Democratization in the Western Hemisphere* (North South Centre Press, Lynne Rienner 1998) 360 pp.
- *A Peace of Timbuktu: Democratic Governance, Development and African Peacemaking* (New York, United Nations Publications 1998) 392 pp.
- *People Building Peace: 35 Inspiring Stories from Around the World* (Utrecht, European Centre for Conflict Prevention 1999)
- Zandee, D., *Building Blocks for Peace: Civil-Military Interaction in Restoring Fractured Societies* (The Hague, Clingendael 1998) 79 pp.

Articles and Reports
- Meeting of Ministers of defence, internal affairs and security Banjul, 23-24 July 1998, adopted by the meeting of heads of state at Abuj 30-31 October 1998 'ECOWAS mechanism for conflict prevention, management, resolution, peace-keeping and security', 11 *Afr. Jl & CL* (1999) pp. 48-166

TABLE OF CASES *

INTERNATIONAL

---

* The table of cases was compiled by Mrs. B.M. Hall, Elie, UK.

REGIONAL

NATIONAL

INDEX

The index contains references to all matters of substance dealt with in the text of the articles. Detailed references to cases dealt with will be found in the accompanying Table of Cases. Multilateral agreements are indexed under *Agreements, multilateral, classified by subject.* The section on Correspondents' Reports is also indexed but for information on the practice of individual states regarding the principal instruments of international humanitarian law referred to, the reader should consult the index under the states concerned. The index does contain, however, references to other material from this section, such as municipal legislation which is not purely concerned with the subject matter of the listed instruments: for example, references will be found to subjects such as amnesty, extradition, war crimes tribunals. Footnotes containing substantive material are also indexed, as are references to the work of scholars the first time such work is listed.

The index was compiled by Mrs. B.M. Hall, Elie, UK.

Abbreviations frequently used

ICC	International Criminal Court
ICTR	International Criminal Tribunal for Rwanda
ICTY	International Criminal Tribunal for the Former Yugoslavia
IHL	International Humanitarian Law
ILC	International Law Commission
UN	United Nations Organisation

YEARBOOK OF INTERNATIONAL HUMANITARIAN LAW

Volume 1 - 1998

contains articles focusing on the following areas:

- IHL and UN Military operations (Christopher Greenwood)
- National Legislation to cooperate with the ICTY (Ivo Josipović)
- The relationship between IHL and human rights law (Raul Vinuesa)
- The year in review (Avril McDonald)
- Prosecution of genocide before the ICTR and Rwandan courts (Catherine Cissé)
- Prosecuting the Khmer Rouge (Balakrishnan Rajagopal)
- The *Ntakirutimana* case in the USA (Jordan Paust)
- Duress in the *Erdemović* case (Peter Rowe)
- The issuance of *subpoenae duces tecum* in the *Blaškić* case (by Peter Malanczuk)
- Implementation of IHL (Maria Teresa Dutli)
- A Colombian View of Protocol II (Frits Kalshoven)
- The Landmines Treaty (Stephen Goose)
- The 'Sandline Affair' (Tim McCormack)
- The fall of Srebrenica and the role of Dutchbat (Robert Siekmann)
- The Cultural Property Convention review process (Jan Illadik)
- The Italian law to ban antipersonnel mines (Pietro Gargiulo)
- Protocol IV on blinding laser weapons (Markus Zöckler)
- The *Priekbe* case (with contributions by Jose Alejandro Consigli, Sergio Marchisio and Francesca Martines)
- Canadian and Italian forces in Somalia (with contributions by Robert Young and Maria Molina, Katia Boustany and Natalia Lupi)
- German state practice regarding IHL (Horst Fischer)

Correspondents' Reports: a guide to state practice regarding International Humanitarian Law

Documentation

ISBN 90-6704-107-6
700 pages, hardbound
Price NLG 295.00 / USD 177.00 / GBP 103.25

Distributed for T.M.C. ASSER PRESS by Kluwer Law International.